ENCYCLOPEDIA OF
GOVERNMENT AND POLITICS

ENCYCLOPEDIA OF GOVERNMENT AND POLITICS

Volume I

EDITED BY

Mary Hawkesworth
and
Maurice Kogan

LONDON AND NEW YORK

First published in 1992
by Routledge
11 New Fetter Lane, London EC4P 4EE

Simultaneously published in the USA and Canada
by Routledge
a division of Routledge, Chapman and Hall, Inc.
29 West 35th Street, New York, NY 10001

Typeset in 10/12½pt Ehrhardt Linotronic 300 by Intype, London
Printed in England by Clays Ltd, St Ives plc

This paper is manufactured in accordance with the proposed ANSI/NISO Z 39.48–199X and
ANSI Z 39.48–1984

British Library Cataloguing in Publication Data
Encyclopedia of government and politics.
1. Political science
I. Hawkesworth, Mary *1952–*   II. Kogan, Maurice *1930–*
320

Library of Congress Cataloging-in-Publication Data
Encyclopedia of government and politics/edited by Mary Hawkesworth and Maurice Kogan.
p.   cm.
Includes bibliographical references and index.
ISBN 0–415–03092–7 (set)
1. Political science—Encyclopedias. I. Hawkesworth, M. E.,
1952–   . II. Kogan, Maurice.
JA61.C66   1992
320′.03—dc20
91–30399
CIP

ISBN 0–415–07224–7 (Volume 1)
ISBN 0–415–07225–5 (Volume 2)
ISBN 0–415–03092–7 (set)

In memory of Victor A. Olorunsola, Dean of the College of Arts and Sciences, University of Louisville, Kentucky.

PUBLISHING STAFF

EDITORIAL
Jonathan Price, Shan Millie

SUBEDITORIAL
Emma Waghorn, Kerry Munro, Alex Clark

INDEX
Peter Rea

PRODUCTION
Nigel Marsh

PROMOTION
Judith Watts, Jane Gardner

CONTENTS

Part IX International relations

Part X Major issues in contemporary world politics

NOTES ON CONTRIBUTORS

Jeffrey Anderson is an Assistant Professor of Political Science at Brown University, Providence, Rhode Island. His current research focuses on West German economic policy-making in the context of the tensions and opportunities of European integration and unification with East Germany. He has published articles in many journals including *West European Politics, Governance* and the *Journal of Public Policy* and is the author of a book on regional political economy entitled *The Territorial Imperative* (Cambridge University Press, 1992).

Peter R. Baehr is Professor of Human Rights at the University of Leiden and Utrecht and was formerly Professor of International Relations at the University of Amsterdam. He was Executive Secretary of the Scientific Council for Government Policy in the Hague, and was Chair of the Dutch Advisory Committee on Human Rights and Foreign Policy. Publications include, as co-editor, *Policy Analysis and Innovation* (1981) and *Mensenrechten: Bestandeel van het Buitenlands Beleid* (1989).

J. F. P. Blondel is Professor of Political Science at the European University Institute, Florence. He was formerly Professor of Government at the University of Essex. He was Visiting Professor at Carleton University, Canada and, more recently, Visiting Scholar at the Russell Sage Foundation, New York. Publications include *Comparative Legislatures* (Prentice-Hall, 1973), *World Leaders* (Sage, 1980), *The Organization of Governments* (Sage, 1982), *Political Leadership* (Sage, 1987) and *Comparative Government* (Philip Allan, 1990).

Tom Bottomore has taught at the London School of Economics and was Professor and Head of Department of Political Science, Sociology and Anthropology at Simon Fraser University, Vancouver, from 1965 to 1968. Until 1985 he was Professor of Sociology at the University of Sussex, and has been President of the International Sociological Association and of the British Sociological Association. Publications include *Political Sociology* (Pluto Press, 1979, 2nd edition, 1992), *Theories of Modern Capitalism* (Allen & Unwin, 1985), *Sociology: A Guide to Problems and Literature* (Allen & Unwin, 3rd edition, 1987) and *Elites and Society* (Routledge, 2nd edition, 1992). His current research interests are concentrated on economic sociology.

Mike Bowker is currently lecturing in International Relations at the University of East Anglia. He has also taught at Surrey and Essex Universities as well as at Queen's, Belfast. He has published a number of articles on East–West relations and is co-author, with Phil Williams, of *Superpower Detente: A Reappraisal* (Sage, 1988), and co-editor of

From Cold War to Collapse: Theory and World Politics in the 1980s (Cambridge University Press, 1992).

G. R. Boynton is Professor of Political Science at the University of Iowa. His publications include *Mathematical Thinking About Politics* (1980), *Representatives and Represented* (1975) and *Legislative Systems in Developing Countries* (Duke University Press, 1975). His primary research interests include analytical political theory and the comparative study of legislatures.

Naomi Caiden is currently Professor and Chair of the Department of Public Administration, California State University, San Bernardino. She was Chair of the Section on International and Comparative Administration of the American Society for Public Administration (1988–9), and received a National Distinguished Service Award in recognition of outstanding academic contributions from the American Association for Budget and Program Analysis. Publications include *Planning and Budgeting in Poor Countries*, with Aaron Wildavsky, (Transaction Publishing, 1980). Her current research is in public administration and budgeting.

Ronald H. Chilcote is Professor of Political Science and Economics at the University of California, Riverside. He is founder and currently Managing Editor of the journal *Latin American Perspectives*, and his many publications include *Power and the Ruling Classes in Northeast Brazil* (Cambridge University Press, 1990) and *The Portuguese Revolution of 25 April 1974* (University of Coimbra, 1987). His research has focused on Portuguese-speaking Africa, Brazil and Portugal.

Lori Fisler Damrosch is Professor of Law at Columbia University, where she is also a member of the Faculty of International Affairs. She has served as counsel for the United States before the International Court of Justice and other international tribunals. She is the editor of *The International Court of Justice at a Crossroads* (Transnational, 1987) and *Law and Force in the New International Order* (Westview Press, 1991) and has published many articles on international law and the foreign relations law of the United States. Her current research interests include the settlement of international disputes and approaches to international law in the countries formerly in the Soviet bloc.

David Denver is Senior Lecturer in Politics at Lancaster University. His publications include *Elections and Voting Behaviour in Britain* (Philip Allan, 1989) and, as co-editor with I. Crewe, *Electoral Change in Western Democracies* (Croom Helm, 1988).

Barend A. de Vries works for the World Bank, and is Adjunct Professor at Georgetown University, Washington, DC. He has worked for the International Monetary Fund, and has taught Economics at the Johns Hopkins and George Washington Universities. He has published numerous articles and papers on international economics and development issues, including *The Export Experience of Developing Countries* (1967) and *Remaking the World Bank* (Seven Locks Press, 1987). He is currently studying the economics underlying the statements on peace and justice made by the Catholic and various Protestant churches.

Paul F. Diehl is Associate Professor of Political Science and a faculty member of the

Program in Arms Control, Disarmament and International Security at the University of Illinois at Urbana-Champaign. He has published many articles on international conflict, arms control and peace-keeping, and is the co-author of *Territorial Changes and International Conflict*, and editor of *The Politics of International Organization*.

Mattei Dogan is Scientific Director at the Centre National de la Recherche Scientifique, Paris, and also Professor at the University of California, Los Angeles. He is Chair of the Research Committee on Political Elites of the International Political Science Association. His publications include, as editor, *Comparing Pluralist Democracies: Strains on Legitimacy* (Westview Press, 1988).

R. Bruce Douglass is an Associate Professor in the Department of Government, Georgetown University, Washington, DC, and is co-director of a project examining Liberalism and Catholicism, sponsored jointly by the Department of Government at Georgetown and the Woodstock Theological Center. His publications include *Liberalism and the Good* (Routledge, 1990) as co-editor. Current research includes a study on the fate of individualism in Marx's politics.

Richard Ellis is Assistant Professor of Political Science at Willamette University, Salem, Oregon. He is co-author, with Aaron Wildavsky, of *Dilemmas of Presidential Leadership: From Washington Through Lincoln* (Transaction Publishers, 1989) and, with Michael Thompson and Aaron Wildavsky, of *Cultural Theory* (Westview Press, 1990), and is author of *American Political Cultures* (Oxford University Press, forthcoming 1993).

Tom Farer is Professor and Director of the Joint-Degree Program on Law and International Relations at the American University, Washington, DC. He has taught at Columbia, Harvard, Johns Hopkins, Princeton, Rutgers and Tulane Universities, and is former President of the Inter-American Committee on Human Rights and the University of New Mexico. His publications include *Warclouds on the Horn of Africa*, *Toward a Humanitarian Diplomacy*, *US Ends and Means in Central America* and *The Grand Strategy of the United States in Latin America*.

Adele K. Ferdows is Professor of Political Science at the University of Louisville and a nationally recognized expert on Iran and women in Islam. She has contributed many articles to *Women and the Islamic Revolution* (Westview Press, 1983), *The Iranian Revolution and the Islamic Republic* (Syracuse University Press, 1986) and *Women and the Family in Iran* (E. J. Brill, 1986). She spent the 1988–9 academic year doing research in Iran.

Elizabeth G. Ferris is presently serving as Study and Interpretation Secretary for Refugees of the World Council of Churches (WCC) in Geneva, Switzerland. She is researching global refugee issues and is responsible for WCC's programmatic work with refugees in Latin America and North America. She taught Political Science at Lafayette College, Miami University (Ohio) and Pembroke State University, and served as a Fulbright Professor at the National Autonomous University of Mexico. Her publications include *Refugees in World Politics* (Praeger, 1985) and *The Central American Refugees* (Praeger, 1987).

Lawrence Freedman is Professor in the Department of War Studies at King's College, University of London. His publications include *The Evolution of Nuclear Strategy*, (2nd edition, Macmillan, 1989).

Jack A. Goldstone is Professor of Sociology and Director of the Center for Comparative Research in History, Society and Culture at the University of California, Davis. He is the author of *Revolution and Rebellion in the Early Modern World* (University of California Press, 1991) and co-editor of *Revolutions of the Late Twentieth Century* (Westview Press, 1991).

Guy Goodwin-Gill is Professor of Law at Carleton University, Ottowa, and is Editor-in-chief of the *International Journal of Refugee Law*. He is the author of *International Law and the Movement of Persons Between States* (Clarendon Press, 1978).

Adam Graycar is Chief Executive Officer of South Australia's Ministry of Higher Education. He was appointed in 1985 by the Government of South Australia as Australia's first Commissioner for the Ageing. He was also Foundation Director of the Social Welfare Research Centre, University of New South Wales. He has taught Social Administration at Flinders University, South Australia, and has held visiting posts at Brandeis University, University of California, Berkeley, Yale University and the Centre for Environmental Studies in London.

Fred I. Greenstein is Professor of Politics at Princeton University, and has published numerous books and articles on personality and politics, children and politics, American political parties and the American Presidency. His publications include *Children and Politics* (Yale University Press, 1965), *Personality and Politics: Problems of Evidence, Inference and Conceptualization* (Markham, 1969), *The Hidden-Hand Presidency: Eisenhower as Leader* (Basic Books, 1982) and *How Presidents Test Reality: Decisions on Vietnam, 1954 and 1965* (Russell Sage, 1989).

Stephany Griffith-Jones is a Fellow at the Institute of Development Studies, Sussex University. She has worked in the Central Bank of Chile and has acted as consultant to several international organizations, including the World Bank, the European Economic Community, the United Nations Children's Fund and the United Nations Conference on Trade and Development. She has written widely on international debt and international finance.

Pascale Gruson is Chargie de Recherches at the Centre National de la Recherche Scientifique and is active in the Centre d'Etude des Mouvements Sociaux, Ecole des Hautes Etudes en Sciences Sociales, Paris. Her current research is concerned mainly with French higher education in the comparative context of Western higher education systems as a whole.

Philip Gummett is Senior Lecturer in Government and Technology Policy, and Chair of the Board of Studies in Science and Technology Policy at the University of Manchester. His publications include *Scientists in Whitehall* (Manchester University Press, 1980) and, as co-editor with J. Reppy, *The Relations Between Defence and Civil*

Technologies (Kluwer, 1988). His current interests lie primarily in developments within the defence sector and their impact on industrial and national technology bases.

P. Edward Haley is Professor of International Relations at Claremont McKenna College and Claremont Graduate School, Claremont, California and is Senior Research Associate at the Keck Center for International Strategic Studies. He has served as Dean of the School of International Studies, University of the Pacific, and as Director of the Keck Center for International Strategic Studies. He has also served on the staffs of members of the US Senate and House of Representatives. His publications include *Nuclear Strategy, Arms Control and the Future* (Westview Press, 1988), *Qaddafi and the United States since 1969* (Praeger, 1984) and *Congress and the Fall of South Vietnam and Cambodia* (Associated University Presses 1981).

Grant Harman is Professor of Educational Administration and Chair of the Academic Senate at the University of New England. His previous posts were at the Australian National University and the University of Melbourne. His current interests are in higher education policy and comparative studies.

Albert Harris teaches at Humboldt State University, California. He has conducted public policy research for the Battelle Institute, Seattle and for the University of Washington. As a member of the faculty at the University of Louisville, Kentucky, he conducted research on the international political economy. His publications include *US Trade Problems in Steel* (Praeger, 1983) and *Negotiation and Coercion* (Kendall-Hunt, 1991). His current research interests are international negotiation and bargaining.

Mary Hawkesworth is Professor of Political Science at the University of Louisville, Kentucky. Her publications include *Beyond Oppression: Feminist Theory and Political Strategy* (Continuum Press, 1990), and *Theoretical Issues in Policy Analysis* (State University of New York Press, 1988). Her current research interests are contemporary political philosophy, feminist theory and social theory.

Ferrel Heady is Professor Emeritus of Public Administration and Political Science at the University of New Mexico, Albuquerque. He has served as Academic Vice-President and President of the University of New Mexico. He was Professor of Political Science at the University of Michigan, Ann Arbor, and was President of the American Society for Public Administration. His publications include *Public Administration: A Comparative Perspective* (4th edition, Marcel Dekker, 1991).

Barry Hindess is Professor of Political Science in the Research School of the Social Sciences, Australian National University. His publications include *Freedom, Equality and the Market* (Tavistock, 1988), *Choice, Rationality and Social Theory* (Unwin Hyman, 1988) and *Political Choice and Social Structure* (Edward Elgar, 1989).

Leslie Holmes is currently Professor and Head of the Department of Political Science at the University of Melbourne. He has taught at the Universities of Essex, Kent and Aberystwyth, and has been on the Executive Committee of both the British National Association for Soviet and East European Studies and the Political Studies Association of the UK. He is on the editorial board of the journals *The Australian Journal of Slavonic and East European Studies* and *Politics*. His publications include *The Policy of Process in Communist States* (Sage, 1981) and *Politics in the Communist World* (Oxford University Press, 1986). His current research interests are change in the Soviet Union and Eastern Europe and the establishment of Special Economic Zones in the Soviet Union.

Ole R. Holsti is Professor of Political Science at Duke University, Durham, North Carolina, and has taught at Stanford University, the University of California, Davis, and the University of British Columbia. He has won many awards, including the Nevitt Sanford Award for Distinguished Contributions to Political Psychology in 1988. He was President of the International Studies Association from 1979 to 1980, and served on the council of the American Political Sciences Association as well as on the Advisory Board of the University Press of America. He has written numerous articles and his publications include *American Leadership in World Affairs: The Breakdown of Consensus* (Allen & Unwin, 1984) and, as co-editor, *Change in the International System* (Westview Press, 1980).

Kenneth R. Hoover is Professor and Chair of the Department of Political Science at Western Washington University. He has been Senior Fellow at the Center for Twentieth Century Studies, University of Wisconsin-Milwaukee and Professor and Chair of the Department of Political Science at the University of Wisconsin-Parkside. His publications include *The Elements of Social Scientific Thinking* (5th edition, St Martin's Press, 1992) and, with Raymond Plant, *Conservative Capitalism in Great Britain and the United States: A Critical Appraisal* (Routledge, 1989). His current research interests are contemporary ideologies, the Mondragon co-operatives and methodology.

Jeffrey C. Isaac is Associate Professor of Political Science at Indiana University, Bloomington. His publications include *Power and Marxist Theory: A Realist View* (Cornell University Press, 1987) and articles in such journals as *Polity*, *Political Theory*, *History of Political Thought* and *Praxis International*. He has just completed a book on the political writings of Hannah Arendt and Albert Camus.

Rita Mae Kelly is a Professor of Justice Studies, Political Science and Women's Studies at Arizona State University, Tempe. She was President of the Policy Studies Organization (1988–9) and of the Western Political Science Association (1988–9), and was the editor of *Women and Politics* from 1986 to 1991. Her publications include *Advances in Policy Studies since 1950* (Transaction Press, 1982), *Comparable Worth, Pay Equity and Public Policy* (Greenwood Press, 1988), *Women and the Arizona Political Process* (University Press of America, 1988), *Productivity in the Public Sector* (St. Martin's Press, 1988), *Gender, Bureaucracy and Democracy* (Greenwood Press, 1989) and *The Gendered Economy* (Transaction Press, 1991). She is currently working on projects concerning women and politics and feminism and policy studies.

Robert O. Keohane is Stanfield Professor of International Peace and Chair of the Department of Government, Harvard University. He received the second annual Grawemeyer Award for Ideas Improving World Order for *After Hegemony: Cooperation and Discord in the World Political Economy* (Princeton University Press, 1984). He is co-author, with J. S. Nye, of *Power and Interdependence: World Politics in Transition* (Little, Brown & Co., 1977) and also wrote *International Institutions and State Power: Essays in International Relations Theory* (Westview Press, 1989).

Samuel S. Kim is Lecturer in Public and International Affairs at the Woodrow Wilson School of Public and International Affairs, Princeton University. His publications include *China, the United Nations, and World Order* (Princeton University Press, 1979), *The Quest for a Just World Order* (Westview Press, 1984), and as co-editor, *The United Nations and a Just World Order* (Westview Press, 1991) and *China's Quest for National Identity* (Cornell University Press, 1992). His current research includes several projects on East Asian international relations and world order issues.

Peter Knoepfel is Professor of Comparative Public Administration and Public Policies at the Institute for Advanced Studies in Public Administration, Lausanne. He is a member of the Committee of the Swiss Association of Political Sciences and President of the Swiss Commission of Observation of the Environment. His research interests concern comparative environmental policies in air pollution and agriculturally induced water pollution.

Maurice Kogan is Professor of Government and Social Administration and Joint Director of the Centre for the Evaluation of Public Policy and Practice at Brunel University. He is the author or joint author of several works on educational, health, higher education, social services and science policy and on the struggle for power in the British Labour Party.

David Kowalewski is Associate Professor of Political Science at Alfred University, Alfred, New York. His publications include *Transnational Corporations and Caribbean Inequalities* (Praeger, 1982). His articles on international organizations have appeared in journals including *Comparative Political Studies* and the *Journal of Political and Military Sociology*. He is currently researching the political economy of Asia.

Joseph LaPalombara is the Arnold Wolfers Professor of Political Science at Yale University, where he also directs the Institution for Social and Policy Studies. His publications include *Political Parties and Political Development*, as co-editor with M. Weiner (Princeton University Press, 1966), as co-author, *Crises and Sequences in Political Development* (Princeton University Press, 1971), *Politics within Nations* (Prentice-Hall, 1974) and *Democracy Italian Style* (Yale University Press, 1987).

J. A. Laponce is Professor of Political Science at the University of British Columbia; he also co-chairs the Research Committee on Political Geography of the International Political Science Association. He is President of the Academy of Humanities and Social Services of the Royal Society of Canada and is co-editor of the *International Political Science Review*. He has contributed articles to numerous journals, and his publications include *People vs Politics* (Toronto University Press, 1970), *Languages and Their Territories* (Toronto University Press, 1987) and *Left and Right* (Toronto University Press, 1981).

Rosalind Levačič is a lecturer in economics at the Open University. Her particular interests are the economics and finance of education. Her publications include *Macro-economics: An Introduction to Keynesian-Neoclassical Controversies*, with A. Rebmann (Macmillan, 1982), *Economic Policy Making* (Harvester Wheatsheaf, 1987) and, as editor, *Financial Management in Education* (Open University Press, 1989).

Joni Lovenduski is Reader in Politics at Loughborough University. In 1986 she became Convenor of the Standing Group on Women and Politics of the European Consortium for Political Research. Her publications include *Women and European Politics* (Harvester Wheatsheaf, 1986) and, as co-editor, *The New Politics of Abortion* (Sage, 1986) and, with J. Hills, *The Politics of the Second Electorate: Women and Public Participation* (Routledge & Kegan Paul, 1981).

Robin W. Lovin is Associate Professor of Ethics and Society at the Divinity School of the University of Chicago, where he has been a member of the faculty since 1978. He previously taught at Emory University, Atlanta, Georgia. His publications include *Christian Faith and Public Choices* (1984) and *Religion and American Public Life* (Paulist Press, 1986).

Denis McQuail is Professor of Mass Communication at the University of Amsterdam, and previously taught in the Sociology Department of Southampton University. He has served as Academic Adviser to the British Royal Commission on the Press and to the Scientific Council for Government Policy in the Netherlands. In 1989 he was Senior Research Fellow at the Gannett Center for Media Studies, Columbia University. His publications include *Mass Communication Theory* (Sage, 1983 and 1987) and, as co-editor, *New Media Politics* (Euromedia Research Group, 1986) and *Electronic Media and Politics in Western Europe: A Handbook* (Euromedia Research Group, 1986). He has been editor of the *European Journal of Communication* since 1985. His current research concerns new electronic media policy-making.

Edward McWhinney is a member of the Institut de Droit International and the Académie Internationale de Droit Comparé and was a member of the Permanent Court of Arbitration from 1985 to 1991. He has taught at Yale and held chairs in leading US and Canadian universities. He is currently Professor of International Law and Relations at Simon Fraser University, Vancouver. He has been a Visiting Professor at many world centres including the Max-Planck-Institut, the Meiji University, Tokyo, the University of Paris I (Sorbonne), the Collège de France and the Hague Academy of International Law. He has been a consultant and adviser to the United Nations and to various national governments, and was a Special Adviser to the Canadian Delegation to the UN General Assembly 1981–3.

James M. Malloy is Professor of Political Science and Research Professor at the University Center for International Studies, University of Pittsburgh. His publications include, as co-editor with M. A. Seligson, *Authoritarians and Democrats: Regime Transition in Latin America* (University of Pittsburgh Press, 1987). He is presently working on issues of regime transition, economic adjustment and the role of private sector interest groups in Latin America.

Talukder Maniruzzaman is Professor of Political Science at the University of Dhaka.

He was Professor and Head of the Department of Political Science at the University of Rajshahi, Bangladesh, and has won several scholarships and fellowships, including the Nuffield Foundation Fellowship at the University of London and a fellowship at the Woodrow Wilson International Center for Scholars, Washington DC. He has contributed to several edited volumes and encyclopedias, including the section on Bangladesh in *The Cambridge Encyclopaedia of India, Pakistan, Bangladesh, Sri Lanka, Nepal, Bhutan and Maldives* (Cambridge University Press, 1989). His current research concerns the impact of arms transfers on developing states.

Martin N. Marger is Associate Professor of Sociology at Michigan State University. He taught previously at Waynesburg College and Northern Kentucky University. His publications include *Elites and Masses* (2nd edition, Wadsworth, 1989) and *Race and Ethnic Relations: American and Global Perspectives* (2nd edition, Wadsworth, 1991). His current research interests focus on the processes of economic and social adaptation among immigrants.

Geoffrey Marshall is a Fellow of Queen's College, Oxford and an Oxford University lecturer in politics, where he has been teaching since 1957. He has been Assistant Editor of *Public Law* since 1960. His publications include *Parliamentary Sovereignty* (Oxford University Press, 1957), *Police and Government* (Methuen, 1965), *Constitutional Theory* (Oxford University Press, 1971), *Constitutional Conventions* (Oxford University Press, 1984) and, as editor, *Ministerial Responsibility* (Oxford University Press, 1989).

T. David Mason is Associate Professor of Political Science at Mississippi State University, where he also holds partial appointments with the university's Social Science Research Center and the Center for International Security and Strategic Studies. His research on civil violence has appeared in many anthologies and journals, including *Western Political Quarterly, Asian Affairs* and *Studies in Comparative International Development*. He is co-editor of *US–Japan Trade Friction: Its Impact on Security Cooperation in the Pacific Basin* (Macmillan, 1991).

Sonia Mazey is Lecturer in Politics in the Government Department of Brunel University. She has published several articles on French politics and European Community policy making. She is co-editor of *Mitterrand's France* (Croom Helm, 1987) and co-author of *The European Community: Developments and Issues* (McGraw-Hill, forthcoming).

Toivo Miljan is a Professor in the Department of Political Science at Wilfrid Laurier University, and has been Adjunct Professor of Political Science at the Swedish School of Business and Economics, Helsinki, since 1988. He is the Co-director of the Centre of Foreign Policy and Federalism. His publications include *Food and Agriculture in Global Perspective* (Pergamon Press, 1980) and, as editor, *The Political Economy of North–South Relations* (Broadview Press, 1987). His recent work has concentrated on the Soviet Union and the Baltic States.

William L. Miller holds the Edward Caird Chair of Politics at the University of Glasgow. He has directed ESRC-funded Election Survey studies of the Scottish electorate in 1974 and 1979, and of the British electorate in 1987. His publications – as author or co-author – include *Electoral Dynamics* (Macmillan, 1977), *Elections and Voting* (Macmillan, 1987), *Irrelevant Elections: The Quality of Local Democracy in Britain* (Oxford University Press, 1988), *How Voters Change* (Oxford University Press, 1990) and *Media and Voters* (Oxford University Press, 1991). He is currently researching public attitudes to political rights in Britain and in Eastern Europe.

Helen Milner is an Associate Professor in the Department of Political Science at Columbia University. Her publications include *Resisting Protectionism: Global Industries and the Politics of International Trade* (Princeton University Press, 1988) and a co-edited work, *East–West Trade and the Atlantic Alliance* (Westview Press, 1990). Her current research interests concern trade policy in the industrialized countries and the domestic politics of international economic co-operation.

George Modelski is Professor of Political Science at the University of Washington. He was a member of the Institute of Advanced Studies, Australian National University from 1957 to 1967. His publications include *A Theory of Foreign Policy* (Praeger, 1962), *Principles of World Politics* (Free Press, 1972), *Long Cycles in World Politics* (Macmillan, 1987) and, as co-editor, *Documenting Global Leadership* (Macmillan, 1989).

Craig N. Murphy is Associate Professor of Political Science at Wellesley College, Massachusetts. His publications include *The Emergence of the New International Economic Order Ideology* (Westview Press, 1984) and as co-author with E. Augelli, *America's Quest for Supremacy and the Third World* (Pinter, 1988). He is working on a political history of international organization and industrial change.

John D. Nagle is Professor of Political Science at the Maxwell School of Syracuse University, New York. He held a Fulbright Senior Research Fellowship in Germany in 1974–5, and a research position with the Library of the Bundestag in 1976. His publications include *The National Democratic Party of Germany* (University of California Press, 1970), *System and Succession: The Social Bases of Political Elite Recruitment* (University of Texas Press, 1977), which was supported by the American Philosophical Association and the Conference Group on German Politics, and *Introduction to Comparative Politics: Political System Performance in Three Worlds* (3rd edition, Nelson-Hall Publishers, 1992).

Kai Nielsen is Professor and Head of the Department of Philosophy at the University of Calgary. He is a past President of the Canadian Philosophical Association, and is a member of the Royal Society of Canada. His publications include *Equality and Liberty: A Defense of Radical Egalitarianism* (Rowman & Allenheld, 1985) and *Marxism and the Moral Point of View* (Westview Press, 1989).

Robert C. Oberst is Associate Professor of Political Science at Nebraska Wesleyan University. He has published extensively in scholarly journals about Sri Lanka and is a co-author of *Politics and Government in South Asia*.

Øyvind Østerud is Professor of International Conflict Studies in the Department of

Political Science, University of Oslo. He was a Visiting Scholar at the London School of Economics in 1983 and at the Australian National University, 1987–8. His publications include *Agrarian Structure and Peasant Politics* (1978) and, as editor, *Studies of War and Peace* (Norwegian and Oxford University Press, 1986). His current research interests include sovereign statehood and nationality conflicts, decolonization and the politics of the Third World, and superpower rivalry and regional conflicts.

Michael Pacione is Reader and Head of the Department of Geography at the University of Strathclyde, Glasgow. He has held academic positions at Queen's, Belfast, and was Visiting Professor at the University of Guelph, Ontario. He has published over sixty papers in an international range of academic journals, and is editor of twelve books in the field of human geography, including *Problems and Planning in Third World Cities* (Croom Helm, 1981) and *Progress in Political Geography* (Croom Helm, 1985). He is the author of *Rural Geography* (Harper & Row, 1984) and *Urban Problems: An Applied Urban Analysis* (Routledge, 1990). His current research is focused on the quality of life in modern societies, and the impact of public policy and planning on metropolitan and rural change.

Dennis Palumbo is Regents' Professor of Justice Studies and Political Science at Arizona State University. He has taught undergraduate courses and has been principal and co-principal investigator on several large research grants from the National Institute of Justice, National Institute of Health and the National Traffic and Highway Safety Administration. He has evaluated several programmes in Arizona and, most recently, prepared a report for the Arizona State Legislature on Home Arrest in Arizona. He has authored, co-authored and edited numerous books and articles on criminal justice, policy analysis and programme evaluation, and was founding editor and co-editor of the *Policy Studies Review*.

Michael Parenti has taught at a number of colleges and universities, including the University of Vermont and the State University of New York at Stony Brook and at Albany. He was a Guest Professor of Political Science at Howard University (1987–8), Guest Professor at the University of Canterbury, New Zealand and a Distinguished Residence Professor at California State University-Northridge. His publications include *Democracy for the Few* (5th edition, St Martin's Press), *The Sword and the Dollar: Imperialism, Revolution and the Arms Race* (St Martin's Press, 1989) and *Makebelieve Media* (forthcoming).

Stanley G. Payne is Hilldale-Jaime Vicens Vives Professor of History at the University of Wisconsin-Madison. He is the author of *Fascism: Comparison and Definition* (University of Wisconsin Press, 1980) and of numerous works on Spanish and Portuguese history, including *Falange: A History of Spanish Fascism* (1961) and *The Franco Regime 1936–1975* (University of Wisconsin Press, 1987).

George Philip is Reader in Comparative and Latin American Politics at the London School of Economics and Political Science. He is the author of *Oil and Politics in Latin America* (Cambridge University Press, 1982), *The Military in Latin American Politics* (Croom Helm, 1985) and *The Presidency in Mexican Politics* (Macmillan, 1992).

Adamantia Pollis is Professor of Political Science in the Graduate Faculty at the New School for Social Research, New York. She has been Visiting Professor at the University of the Aegean and has also taught at City University of New York (Queens College), Columbia University and Essex University. She has written extensively on various aspects of human rights and the politics of Greece, Turkey and Cyprus. Her publications include, as editor, *The Contemporary Mediterranean World* (Praeger, 1983), and as co-editor with Peter Schwab, *Toward a Human Rights Framework* (Praeger, 1982), and *Human Rights: Cultural and Ideological Perspectives* (Praeger, 1979).

G. Bingham Powell is Professor of Political Science at the University of Rochester, New York, where he was Chair of the Department 1986–9. He is co-author of *Comparative Politics: System, Process and Policy* (1978) and author of *Contemporary Democracies: Participation, Stability and Violence* (Harvard University Press, 1982), which in 1983 won the American Political Science Association's Woodrow Wilson Prize for the best book in Political Science in the previous year. His current research is focused on conditions for citizen influence in contemporary democracies.

David C. Rapoport has taught Political Theory at the University of California at Los Angeles since 1961. His many publications include *Assassination and Terrorism* (CBC, 1971), *The Morality of Terrorism*, as co-editor (2nd edition, 1988) and *Inside Terrorist Organizations*, as editor (Columbia University Press, 1989). He is the co-editor of the *Journal of Terrorism and Political Violence* and is presently a Harry Frank Guggenheim Fellow working on a study of religion and violence.

Bernard Reich is Professor of Political Science and International Affairs and Chair of the Department of Political Science at George Washington University, Washington, DC. He has lived in the Middle East on Fulbright and National Science Foundation Fellowships and has visited there often for research and conferences. He is the author, editor or co-editor of more than fifty books, book chapters or articles on the Middle East.

Stanley A. Renshon is a member of the Political Science Faculty of the City University of New York (Herbert Lehman College and the Graduate School and University Center). He is the author of *Psychological Needs and Political Behaviour: A Theory of Personality and Political Efficacy* (Free Press, 1974), is editor of the *Handbook of Political Socialization: Theory and Research* (Free Press, 1977) and has published numerous articles on political psychology and behaviour. He was appointed editor of the journal *Political Psychology* in 1989.

R. A. W. Rhodes is Professor of Politics and Head of Department at the University of York. He has taught at the Universities of Birmingham, Strathclyde and Essex. His publications include *The National World of Local Government* (Allen & Unwin, 1986) and *Beyond Westminster and Whitehall* (Unwin Hyman, 1988). He is the editor of *Public Administration* (the journal of the Royal Institute of Public Administration). His current research focuses on policy networks in British government, British contributions to administrative theory and the implementation of Thatcherite policies.

Shamit Saggar is a lecturer in politics at the University of London (Queen Mary and

Westfield College) and has also taught at the Universities of Essex and Liverpool. He is also a research associate in the Public Policy Research Unit of the college. He has been the recipient of the Stein Rokkan postgraduate fellowship (1988) and the Sir Robert Menzies fellowship in Australian Studies (1991). Dr Saggar has been a commentator for the BBC on ethnic minority voting patterns. He has undertaken commissioned research on behalf of the Commission for Racial Equality (Britain) and the National Institute for Research Advancement (Japan). His publications include *Race and Public Policy: A Study of Local Politics and Government* (Avebury, 1991) and *Race and Politics in Britain* (Philip Allan, 1992). He is also working on a comparative study of race and public policy in advanced industrial states.

E. S. Savas is Chair and Professor of the Department of Management, School of Business and Public Administration of the City University of New York and also founder and Director of the Privatization Research Organization at the university. He was formerly Manager of Urban Systems for IBM, and has been an adviser and consultant to the Federal Government and to numerous city and state governments in the United States, as well as to the President's Commission on Privatization, the World Bank, the United Nations, UN Development Program, UN Industrial Development Organization, International Labour Office and the US Agency for International Development. His publications include *Privatization: The Key to Better Government* (Chatham House, 1987).

John R. Schmidhauser is Professor of Political Science at the University of Southern California. He has also been a Visiting Professor at Simon Fraser University and the University of Virginia, and has served as a member of the US House of Representatives. He has contributed articles to many international journals and volumes, and his own publications include *Judges and Justices: The Federal Appellate Judiciary* (Little, Brown & Company, 1979), *Constitutional Law in American Politics* (Brooks/Cole Publishing Company, 1985) and *Comparative Judicial Politics* (Butterworth, 1987).

Timothy Shaw is Professor of Political Science and International Development Studies at Dalhousie University in Nova Scotia. He has been a visiting faculty member at the University of Ife (now Obafemi Awolowo University), the Universities of Zambia and Zimbabwe, Makerere University and Carleton University, and was a World University of Canada Associate in Zimbabwe in 1989. He is General Editor of the Macmillan and St Martin's Press Series on International Political Economy and author of *Towards a Political Economy for Africa: The Dialectics of Dependence* (Macmillan, 1985) and *Reformism and Revisionism in Africa's Political Economy in the 1990s: The dialectics of adjustment* (Macmillan, 1992).

Michael Sheehan is Senior Lecturer in International Relations in the Department of Politics and International Relations, University of Aberdeen. His publications include *The Arms Race* (Basil Blackwell, 1983), *Arms Control: Theory and Practice* (Basil Blackwell, 1988), and, as co-author, *A Bibliography of Arms Control Verification* (Aldershot, 1990).

Anthony D. Smith is Professor of Sociology at the University of London at the London School of Economics and Political Science. His publications include *The Ethnic*

Revival in the Modern World (Cambridge University Press, 1981), *State and Nation in the Third World* (Harvester, 1983), *The Ethnic Origins of Nations* (Basil Blackwell, 1986) and *National Identity* (Penguin, 1991). He has also written a Trend Report and many articles on nationalism and ethnicity. His current interests include the relationship between the visual arts and nationalism, myths of ethnic election and the relationship of social class to nations. He is the editor of *Ethnic and Racial Studies*.

Barbara Stallings is Professor of Political Science at the University of Wisconsin-Madison. Her publications include *Banker to the Third World: US Portfolio Investment in Latin America 1900–86* (University of California Press, 1987) and, as co-editor with R. Kaufman, *Debt and Democracy in Latin America* (Westview Press, 1989). She has been working with a group of colleagues on a multi-year project, 'The Politics of Adjustment in the Third World', and is now studying the role of Japan in the Third World.

Leslie Stevenson is Reader in Logic and Metaphysics at the University of St Andrews, where he has taught philosophy since 1968. His publications include *Seven Theories of Human Nature* (2nd edition, Oxford University Press, 1987), *The Metaphysics of Experience* (Oxford University Press, 1982) and, as editor, *The Study of Human Nature* (Oxford University Press, 1981).

Michael Thompson is Director of the Musgrave Institute, London, and Honorary Research Fellow in the Department of Geography, University College London. He is a self-employed anthropologist and works on the development and application of cultural theory. His main interests are consumer behaviour, energy policy, the environmental problems in the Himalayan region, risk perception and technical change.

Johannes Otto Vang is a former staff member at the World Health Organization's Regional Office for Europe in Copenhagen, and is Professor of Technology Assessment at the University of Linköping, Sweden. He remains a consultant for WHO. He has taught at the University of Lund, Sweden, and at the University of Kuwait, and has completed many assignments and consultative commitments in health administration and organization. He has published numerous works on surgery, metabolism, and health-care administration and policy.

John A. Vasquez is Professor of Political Science at Rutgers University, New Jersey. He is co-author, with Richard Mansbach, of *In Search of Theory* (Columbia University Press, 1981), author of *The Power of Power Politics: A Critique* (Frances Pinter, 1983) and editor of *Classics of International Relations* (Prentice-Hall, 1986, 1990) and *Evaluating US Foreign Policy* (Praeger, 1986). He has also co-edited, with Marie Henehan, *The Scientific Study of War: A text-reader* (Lexington Books, 1992) and is currently completing *The War Puzzle* (Cambridge University Press, forthcoming), a book on foreign policy practices and war.

Andrew Vincent is Senior Lecturer in Politics in the School of European Studies, University of Wales, Cardiff. His publications include *Philosophy, Politics and Citizenship*, with Raymond Plant (Basil Blackwell, 1984) and *Theories of the State* (Basil Blackwell,

1987). He has also edited a volume of essays, *The Philosophy of T. H. Green* (Gower, 1986). He has contributed numerous articles to philosophy and politics journals, and is currently completing a project on contemporary political ideologies, to be published by Basil Blackwell.

Paul J. Weber is Distinguished Teaching Professor at the University of Louisville and Chair of the Political Science Department. He has edited *Equal Separation: Understanding the Religion Clauses of the First Amendment* (Greenwood Press, 1990) and is co-author of *Unfounded Fears: The Politics of a Constitutional Convention* (Greenwood Press, 1989) as well as numerous articles on religion and politics.

Aaron Wildavsky is Professor of Political Science and Public Policy and a member of the Survey Research Center at the University of California at Berkeley. He is co-author with Mary Douglas, of *Risk and Culture* (University of California Press, 1982) and, with Michael Thompson and Richard Ellis, of *Cultural Theory* (Westview Press, 1990).

Harmon Zeigler is Phibbs Distinguished Professor at the University of Puget Sound, Tacoma, Washington, and Affiliate Professor at the University of Washington, Seattle. He is the author of *Pluralism, Corporatism and Confucianism* (Temple University Press, 1988) and, with Thomas R. Dye, *The Irony of Democracy* (Brooks Cole, 8th edition, 1989). His most recent work is *The Political Community* (Longman, 1990).

Zoran Zic teaches Soviet and Comparative Politics and International Relations at Rockford College, Illinois. He has worked as a researcher at the Institute of International Politics and Economy, Belgrade, and at the Center for Strategic Studies in Belgrade, where he specialized in foreign relations of the Soviet Union and East European countries, East–West relations and European security issues.

PREFACE

This encyclopedia is the product of over three years of negotiation, planning, persuasion and, in a few cases, coercion. We are grateful to all of our colleague contributors who have worked so well to produce an outstandingly interesting and distinguished account of the main themes and subjects which constitute the study of politics and government.

We both owe debts to our home institutions. The Dean of the College of Arts and Sciences, the Dean of the Graduate School, and the President's Research Initiative of the University of Louisville provided Mary Hawkesworth with both moral and material support, and also agreed to her absence on sabbatical leave at Brunel University at a critical time in the editing of the encyclopedia. The Department of Government at Brunel University provided a supportive and convenient base from which the two editors were able to collaborate during this time.

We owe particular thanks to our commissioning editor, Jonathan Price, who pressed us forward with scholarly and gentle encouragement. Our spouses, Ulla Kogan and Philip Alperson, are used to both of our working ways but deserve our gratitude all the same. The organizing skills of Sally Harris, who has seen so many books to the press from the Department of Government at Brunel University, remain a source of wonder to all who see her at work.

M. H.
M. K.

ENCYCLOPEDIA OF GOVERNMENT AND POLITICS

VOLUME I

PART I

INTRODUCTION

I

THE SCIENCE OF POLITICS AND THE POLITICS OF SCIENCE

MARY HAWKESWORTH

The very idea of an *Encyclopedia of Government and Politics* raises important questions about the relationship between knowledge and politics. Although the concept originates from the Greek *egkuklios paideia* or general education, the notion of an encyclopedia in contemporary parlance invokes a far more ambitious and dangerous project. The transition from ancient to modern conception involves a shift from the classical objective of initiating the student into the modes of analysis and domains of inquiry characteristic of an educated person to the radical eighteenth-century objective of systematizing all human knowledge. Even in ancient times cultivating the intellect was acknowledged to pose a threat to established institutions, for education entails a distancing from tradition and the possibility of a sustained challenge to prevailing conventions and norms. The eighteenth-century experience of the French *encyclopédistes*, however, dramatically reinforced the association between the acquisition of knowledge and the threat to the *status quo*. When the *encyclopédistes'* determination to chart the branches of human knowledge met with the recurrent efforts by church and state to censor and suppress the resulting *Encyclopédie*, the dynamic of liberation/subversion was irrevocably appended to the concept of knowledge. The first major effort to produce an encyclopedia thus proved itself to be a profoundly political affair.

Confronted with the rapid development of scholarly fields, the *encyclopédistes* believed that a general inventory of knowledge was both possible and imperative. Convinced of the solidarity of the sciences, the *encyclopédistes* undertook the careful organization and classification of seemingly diverse material in order to reveal the underlying unity of knowledge. They heralded the discovery of unifying principles in the three faculties of the human mind – reason, intellect, and imagination – as the means not only to explode vulgar errors and weaken propensities toward dogmatism, but also to lay the foundation for

5

change in the general way of thinking. Central to this change was a repudiation of medieval metaphysics and a commitment to empiricism, understood as a reliance upon the senses as the principal sources of knowledge, and upon experience and experiment as the grounds upon which to test knowledge claims. Empiricist techniques were considered the key to liberating the mind from superstition and providing the means for objective knowledge of the natural and social worlds (Diderot *et al.* 1751–65).

The epistemological emphasis upon the human senses had a number of social, political and ethical corollaries. When the senses were accredited as the sole source of evidence, the doctrine of *homo mensuris* – the human being as measure of all things – subtly shifted the focus of human attention to the conditions and rewards in this world and away from those promised in a putative afterlife. This doctrine, brazenly egalitarian, empowered the individual knower by insisting that each individual possessed the capacity to judge truth and falsity without reference to any higher authority. The promotion of individual happiness and the elimination of human misery were validated as legitimate criteria against which to measure existing institutions. Informed by individualist assumptions and inspired by utilitarian objectives, the *encyclopéd-istes'* 'general way of thinking' posed a radical threat to a social order dependent upon hierarchy, religion and deference. Their science sustained standards of evaluation that warranted collective action to transform social relations. Progress was the concomitant of knowledge because science was inherently liberating. It could free the individual from slavish obligations to king and collective precisely because it freed the mind from unsupportable superstitions, supplanting prejudice and dogma with humane standards for assessing the merits of existing institutions, thereby providing both motive and legitimation for action to change any institutions found to be markedly deficient. The threat posed by the *Encyclopédie* was not overlooked by the authorities of the *ancien régime*. In 1751, the Archbishop of Paris issued a *mandement* against the *Encyclopédie*; in 1752 the Royal Council of State issued an order prohibiting further publication of the work. In 1759, the *Parlement de Paris* condemned the project and a decree in *Conseil du Roi* revoked the *Encyclopédie*'s 'privilege', effectively suppressing the work until 1766.

To promote their transformative objectives, the *encyclopédistes* devised a methodology to ensure that their science would be accessible to the literate public. The *Encyclopédie* was designed to be both 'dictionary and treatise of everything the human mind might wish to know' (Diderot *et al.* 1751–65). As dictionary, the seventeen volumes emphasized careful definitions of topics, arranged alphabetically. As treatise, each entry sought to view its topic from every possible angle, 'transcending the general movement of contemporary thought in order to work for future generations'. In delving into the details of the topic, the analyst sought to illuminate the depth and complexity of issues and the means by which apparently disparate dimensions of a problem could be brought into synthesis. In addressing a topic, each author was asked to consider '*genre, differencia specifica*, qualities, causes, uses and the elaboration of method'. On the conviction that knowledge depended upon correct use of language, special effort was made to be as precise as possible in the use of terms and to integrate the exact scientific explanation of phenomena into the accepted language of the day. Excessive recourse to jargon and mystification through the introduction of obfuscating terminology was shunned. Because the *Encyclopédie* incorporated the works of some of the most renowned authors of the day, no effort was made to correct the mistakes of the contributors. Indeed, in later editions, certain controversial essays were published intact, but immediately followed by refutations of central claims and arguments. Such a tolerance for intellectual debate was supported by the *encyclopédistes'* belief that a key element in the 'revolution of the human mind' to which they aspired was a heightened capacity for scepticism and critique (Lough 1968; Wade 1977).

The legacy of the *encyclopédistes* is rich and varied. Their convictions about the unity of the sciences and the progressive nature of scientific inquiry have had a profound influence upon subsequent developments in the social sciences. Their contention that empiricism constituted the sole method for the acquisition of knowledge remained largely unchallenged among social scientists for two centuries. The individualist premises that undergird their work have shaped the intellectual investigations and the political aspirations of subsequent generations. Their appeal to social utility as the principal criterion for assessing social and political institutions has shaped political discourse and research methodologies in both the nineteenth and twentieth centuries. Moreover, their attention to the political consequences of particular modes of knowledge resonates in the recent arguments of critical theorists and post-modernists, who examine the relation between social science and prevailing regimes of power.

This *Encyclopedia of Government and Politics* stands in complex relation to the *Encyclopédie*, incorporating certain of its norms and strategies, while implicitly or explicitly repudiating others. Its format is modelled upon the revised version of the *Encyclopédie méthodique* (1782–1820), organized topically with a specialized focus rather than alphabetically. Leading scholars in the field were commissioned to write articles that would provide both an overview of a designated topic and a critique of alternative methodological approaches to that topic. Avoidance of unnecessarily technical jargon, precision in definition, and clarity in presentation constituted guiding principles. While the *encyclopédistes'* goal to systematize all human knowledge was intentionally abandoned, efforts were made to provide comprehensive coverage of political studies in the late twenti-

7

eth century. Specific inclusions and omissions reflect compromises necessitated by the uneasy coexistence of aspirations to timeliness and to timelessness.

Perhaps the major break with the *Encyclopédie* involves the rejection of commitments to the unity of the sciences, empiricism, and the optimistic equation of 'knowledge' with 'progress'. In contrast to the notion that the fundamental capacities of the human mind fix a simple strategy for the acquisition of knowledge in the natural and the social sciences, this encyclopedia begins with the assumption that research strategies and methodological techniques have far more to do with debates within scholarly disciplines than with fundamental faculties of the human mind. As a consequence, diversity in issues investigated, methodologies adopted, and strategies of analysis and argumentation accredited are expected as the norm, not only with respect to demarcating the natural sciences from the social sciences, but also within the social sciences themselves. Thus it is taken as given that various scholars committed to institutional, statistical, theoretical, structural, functionalist, psychological, semiotic, hermeneutic and genealogical methods will construe the political world differently. To assume unity of knowledge only serves to mask the discrepancies illuminated by various research strategies, pre-emptively precluding consideration of important dimensions of the politics of knowledge.

To conceive of the 'politics of knowledge' in this sense requires a break with empiricism, which posits a simple and direct relation between knower and known. According to empiricist precepts, the senses function as faithful recording mechanisms, placing before the 'mind's eye' exact replicas of that which exists in the external world, without cultural or linguistic mediation. Precisely because observation is understood as exact replication, empiricist strategies for the acquisition of knowledge are said to be 'neutral' and 'value-free'. From the empiricist view, scientific investigations can grasp objective reality, because the subjectivity of individual observers can be controlled through rigid adherence to neutral procedures in the context of systematic experiments and logical deductions.

Empiricist assumptions have been central to the development of the discipline of political science and to the scientific study of politics in the twentieth century (Tanenhaus and Somit 1967; Greenstein and Polsby 1975; Finifter 1983; Seidelman and Harpham 1985). (In this case, as in numerous cases throughout the essay, hundreds of texts could be cited to support this claim. For the sake of brevity, a few well-known examples have been chosen. Except in cases of direct quotation then, references should be taken as representative rather than exhaustive.) A break with empiricism then requires careful justification. Towards that end, the following section will explicate and critique the positivist and Popperian conceptions of science that have profoundly influenced the recent practice of political science. An alternative conception of science will then be advanced and its implications for the understanding of politics and for the structure of this encyclopedia will be explored.

Although such an excursion into the philosophy of science may at first appear far removed from the central concerns of political scientists, a clear understanding of the assumptions about science that inform disciplinary practices is important for a variety of reasons. Not only will a brief review of contending conceptions of science clarify the methodological presuppositions of political scientists, but it will also lay the foundation for challenging the myth of methodological neutrality. In so doing it will identify new areas for investigation concerning the political implications of particular modes of inquiry and thereby foster theoretical self-consciousness about the relation of political science to contemporary politics.

CONTENDING CONCEPTIONS OF SCIENCE

Within the social sciences, empiricist commitments have generated a number of methodological techniques to ensure the objectivity of scientific investigations. Chief among these is the dichotomous division of the world into the realms of the empirical and the non-empirical. The empirical realm, comprising all that can be corroborated by the senses, is circumscribed as the legitimate sphere of scientific investigation. As a residual category, the non-empirical encompasses everything else – religion, philosophy, ethics, aesthetics and evaluative discourse in general, as well as myth, dogma and superstition – which is relegated beyond the sphere of science. Within this frame of reference, social science, operating within the realm of the observable, restricting its focus to descriptions, explanations and predictions that are intersubjectively testable, can achieve objective knowledge. The specific techniques requisite to the achievement of objective knowledge have been variously defined by two conceptions of science which have shaped the practice of political science – positivism and critical rationalism.

On the grounds that only those knowledge claims founded directly upon observable experience can be genuine, positivists adopted the 'verification criterion of meaning' (which stipulates that a contingent proposition is meaningful, if and only if it can be empirically verified) as their core concept (Joergenson 1951; Kraft 1952; Ayer 1959). The verification criterion was deployed to differentiate not only between science and non-science, but between science and 'nonsense'. In the positivist view, any statement which could not be verified by reference to experience constituted nonsense: it was literally meaningless. The implications of the verificationist criterion for a model of science were manifold. All knowledge was believed to be dependent upon observation, thus any claims, whether theological, metaphysical, philosophical, ethical, normative or aesthetic, which were not rooted in empirical observation were rejected as meaningless. The sphere of science was thereby narrowly circumscribed and scientific knowledge was accredited as the only valid knowledge. In addition, induction, a method of knowledge acquisition grounded upon observation of particulars as the foundation for empirical generalizations, was taken to provide the essential logic of science.

The task of science was understood to comprise the inductive discovery of regularities existing in the external world. Scientific research sought to organize in economical fashion those regularities which experience presents in order to facilitate explanation and prediction. To promote this objective, positivists endorsed and employed a technical vocabulary, clearly differentiating facts (empirically verifiable propositions) and hypotheses (empirically verifiable propositions asserting the existence of relationships among observed phenomena) from laws (empirically confirmed propositions asserting an invariable sequence or association among observed phenomena) and theories (interrelated systems of laws possessing explanatory power). Moreover, the positivist logic of scientific inquiry dictated a specific sequence of activities as definitive to 'the scientific method'.

According to this model, the scientific method began with the carefully controlled, neutral observation of empirical events. Sustained observation over time would enable the regularities or patterns of relationships in observed events to be revealed and thereby provide for the formulation of hypotheses. Once formulated, hypotheses were to be subjected to systematic empirical tests. Those hypotheses which received external confirmation through this process of rigorous testing could be elevated to the status of 'scientific laws'. Once identified, scientific laws provided the foundation for scientific explanation, which, according to the precepts of the 'covering law' model, consisted in demonstrating that the event(s) to be explained could have been expected, given certain initial conditions (C_1, C_2, C_3, ...) and the general laws of the field (L_1, L_2, L_3, ...). Within the framework of the positivist conception of science, the discovery of scientific laws also provided the foundation for prediction which consisted in demonstrating that an event would occur given the future occurrence of certain initial conditions and the operation of the general laws of the field. Under the covering law model, then, explanation and prediction have the same logical form, only the time factor differs: explanation pertains to past events; prediction pertains to future events.

Positivists were also committed to the principle of the 'unity of science', i.e. to the belief that the logic of scientific inquiry was the same for all fields. Whether natural phenomena or social phenomena were the objects of study, the method for acquiring valid knowledge and the requirements for explanation and prediction remained the same. Once a science had progressed sufficiently to accumulate a body of scientific laws organized in a coherent system of theories, it could be said to have achieved a stage of 'maturity' which made explanation and prediction possible. Although the logic of mature science remained inductive with respect to the generation of new knowledge, the logic of scientific explanation was deductive. Under the covering law model, causal explanation, the demonstration of the necessary and sufficient conditions of an event, involved the deductive subsumption of particular observations under a general law. In addition, deduction also played a central role in efforts to explain laws and theories: the explanation of a law involved its deductive subsumption under a theory; and explanation of one theory involved its deductive subsumption under wider theories.

The primary postulates of positivism have been subjected to rigorous and devastating critiques (Popper 1959, 1972a, 1972b). Neither the logic of induction nor the verification criterion of meaning can accomplish positivist objectives; neither can guarantee the acquisition of truth. The inductive method is incapable of guaranteeing the validity of scientific knowledge owing to the 'problem of induction' (Hume 1739, 1748). Because empirical events are contingent, i.e. because the future can always be different from the past, generalizations based upon limited observations are necessarily incomplete and, as such, highly fallible. For this reason, inductive generalizations cannot be presumed to be true. Nor can 'confirmation' or 'verification' of such generalizations by reference to additional cases provide proof of their universal validity. For the notion of universal validity invokes all future, as well as all past and present, occurrences of a phenomenon; yet no matter how many confirming instances of a phenomenon can be found in the past or in the present, these can never alter the logical possibility that the future could be different, that the future could disprove an inductively derived empirical generalization. Thus, a demonstration of the truth of an empirical generalization must turn upon the identification of a 'necessary connection' establishing a causal relation among observed phenomena.

Unfortunately, the notion of necessary connection also encounters serious problems. If the notion of necessity invoked is logical necessity, then the empirical nature of science is jeopardized. If, on the other hand, positivism appeals to an empirical demonstration of necessity, it falls foul of the standard established by the verification criterion of meaning, for the 'necessity' required as proof of any causal claim cannot be empirically observed. As Hume pointed out, empirical observation reveals 'constant conjunction' (a 'correlation' in the language of contemporary social science); it does not and cannot reveal necessary connection. As a positivist logic of scientific inquiry, then, induction encounters two serious problems: it is incapable of providing validation for the truth of its generalizations and it is internally inconsistent, for any attempt to demonstrate the validity of a causal claim invokes a conception of necessary connection that violates the verification criterion of meaning.

The positivist conception of the scientific method also rests upon a flawed psychology of perception. In suggesting that the scientific method commences with 'neutral' observation, positivists invoke a conception of 'manifest truth' which attempts to reduce the problem of the validity of knowledge to an appeal to the authority of the source of that knowledge (for example, 'the facts "speak" for themselves'). The belief that the unmediated apprehension of the 'given' by a passive or receptive observer is possible, however, misconstrues both the nature of perception and the nature of the world. The human mind is not passive but active; it does not merely 'receive' an image of the given, but rather imposes order upon the external world through a process of selection, interpretation and imagination. Observation is always linguistically and culturally mediated. It involves the creative imposition of expectations, anticipations and conjectures upon external events.

Scientific observation, too, is necessarily theory-laden. It begins not from 'nothing', nor from the 'neutral' perception of given relations, but rather from immersion in a scientific tradition which provides frames of reference or conceptual schemes that organize reality and shape the problems for further investigation. To grasp the role of theory in structuring scientific observation, however, requires a revised conception of 'theory'. Contrary to the positivist notion that theory is the result of observation, the result of the systematization of a series of inductive generalizations, the result of the cumulation of an interrelated set of scientific laws, theory is logically prior to the observation of any similarities or regularities in the world; indeed, theory is precisely that which makes the identification of regularities possible. Moreover, scientific theories involve risk to an extent that is altogether incompatible with the positivist view of theories as summaries of empirical generalizations. Scientific theories involve risky predictions of things that have never been seen and hence cannot be deduced logically from observation statements. Theories structure scientific observation in a manner altogether incompatible with the positivist requirement of neutral perception, and they involve unobservable propositions that violate the verification criterion of meaning: abstract theoretical entities cannot be verified by reference to empirical observation.

That theoretical propositions violate the verification criterion is not in itself damning, for the verification criterion can be impugned on a number of grounds. As a mechanism for the validation of empirical generalizations, the verification criterion fails because of the problem of induction. As a scientific principle for the demarcation of the 'meaningful' from the 'meaningless', the verification criterion is self-referentially destructive. In repudiating all that is not empirically verifiable as nonsense, the verification criterion repudiates itself, for it is not a statement derived from empirical observation nor is it a tautology. Rigid adherence to the verification criterion then would mandate that it be rejected as metaphysical nonsense. Thus the positivist conflation of that which is not amenable to empirical observation with nonsense simply will not withstand scrutiny. Much (including the verification criterion itself) that cannot be empirically verified can be understood and all that can be understood is meaningful.

As an alternative to the defective positivist conception of science, Karl Popper advanced 'critical rationalism' (1972a, 1972b). On this view, scientific theories are bold conjectures which scientists impose upon the world. Drawing insights from manifold sources in order to solve particular problems, scientific theories involve abstract and unobservable propositions which predict what may happen as well as what may not happen. Thus scientific theories generate predictions that are incompatible with certain possible results of observation, i.e. they 'prohibit' certain occurrences by proclaiming that some things could not happen. As such, scientific theories put the world to the test and demand a reply. Precisely because scientific theories identify a range of conditions that must hold, a series of events that must occur and a set of occurrences that are in principle impossible, they can clash with observation; they are empirically testable. While no number of confirming instances could ever prove a theory to be true due to the problem of induction, one disconfirming instance is sufficient to disprove a theory. If scientific laws are construed as statements of prohibitions, forbidding the occurrence of certain empirical events, then they can be definitively refuted by the occurrence of one such event. Thus, according to Popper, 'falsification' provides a mechanism by which scientists can test their conjectures against reality and learn from their mistakes. Falsification also provides the core of Popper's revised conception of the scientific method.

According to the 'hypothetico-deductive model', the scientist always begins with a problem. To resolve the problem, the scientist generates a theory, a conjecture or hypothesis, which can be tested by deducing its empirical consequences and measuring them against the world. Once the logical implications of a theory have been deduced and converted into predictions concerning empirical events, the task of science is falsification. In putting theories to the test of experience, scientists seek to falsify predictions, for that alone enables them to learn from their mistakes. The rationality of science is embodied in the method of trial and error, a method which allows error to be purged through the elimination of false theories.

In mandating that all scientific theories be tested, in stipulating that the goal of science is the falsification of erroneous views, the criterion of falsifiability provides a means by which to reconcile the fallibility of human knowers with a conception of objective knowledge. The validity of scientific claims does not turn on a demand for an impossible neutrality on the part of individual scientists, on the equally impossible requirement that all prejudice, bias, pre-judgment, expectation or value be purged from the process of observation or on the implausible assumption that the truth is manifest. The adequacy of scientific theories is judged in concrete problem contexts in terms of their ability to solve problems and their ability to withstand increasingly difficult empirical tests. Those theories which withstand multiple intersubjective efforts to falsify them are 'corroborated', identified as 'laws' which with varying degrees of verisimilitude capture the structure of reality, and for that reason are tentatively accepted as 'true'. But in keeping with the critical attitude of science even the strongest corroboration for a theory is not accepted as conclusive proof. For Popperian critical rationalism posits that truth lies beyond human reach. As a regulative ideal which guides scientific activity truth may be approximated, but it can never be established by human authority. Nevertheless, error can be objectively identified. Thus informed by a conception of truth as a regulative ideal and operating in accordance with the requirements of the criterion of falsifiability, science can progress by the incremental correction of errors and the gradual accretion of objective problem-solving knowledge.

Most of the research strategies developed within political science in the twentieth century draw upon either positivist or Popperian conceptions of the scientific method. The legacy of positivism is apparent in behaviouralist definitions of the field which emphasize data collection, hypothesis formulation and testing, and other formal aspects of systematic empirical enterprise, as well as in approaches which stress scientific method, statistical models and quantitative research designs. It surfaces in conceptions of explanation defined in deductive terms and in commitments to the equivalence of explanation and prediction. It emerges in claims that political science must be modelled upon the methods of the natural sciences for those alone are capable of generating valid knowledge. It is unmistakable in the assumption that 'facts' are unproblematic, that they are immediately observable or 'given', and hence their apprehension requires no interpretation. It is embodied in the presumption that confirmation or verification provides a criterion of proof of the validity of empirical claims. And it is conspicuous in the repudiation of values as arbitrary preferences, irrational commitments or meaningless propositions which lie altogether beyond the realm of rational analysis (Storing 1962; Eulau 1963; Kaplan 1964; Meehan 1965; Eulau and Marsh 1969; Welsh 1973).

Popper's insistence upon the centrality of problem solving and incrementalism in scientific activity resonates in the works of those committed to a pluralist approach to political analysis. Popperian assumptions also surface in the recognition that observation and analysis are necessarily theory-laden, as well as in the commitment to intersubjective testing as the appropriate means by which to deflect the influence of individual bias from substantive political analyses. They are manifest in the substitution of testability for verifiability as the appropriate criterion for the demarcation of scientific hypotheses and in the invocation of falsification and the elimination of error as the strategy for the accumulation of political knowledge. They are reflected in the pragmatic notion that the existing political system constitutes the appropriate 'reality' against which to test political hypotheses. They are obvious in the critique of excessive optimism concerning the possibility of securing truth through the deployment of inductive, quantitative techniques, in the less pretentious quest for useful knowledge and in the insistence that truth constitutes a regulative ideal rather than a current possession of political science. They are conspicuous in arguments that the hypothetico-deductive model is applicable to political studies and in appeals for the development of a critical, non-dogmatic attitude among political scientists. Moreover, Popperian assumptions are apparent in a variety of strategies devised to bring reason to bear upon normative issues, while simultaneously accepting that there can be no ultimate rational justification of value precepts. Popperian presuppositions about the fundamental task of social science are also manifest in the pluralists' commitment to a conception of politics premised upon a model of the market that focuses research upon the unintended consequences of the actions of multiple actors rather than upon the particular intentions of political agents (Cook 1985; Lindblom and Cohen 1979; MacRae 1976; Wildavsky 1979).

Popperian critical rationalism provides ample justification for abandoning methodological strategies informed by defective positivist precepts. It does not, however, provide either a satisfactory account of science or a sufficiently sophisticated foundation for political inquiry. Although Popper's critical rationalism is a significant improvement over early positivist conceptions of science, it too suffers from a number of grave defects. The most serious challenge to critical rationalism has been raised by post-positivist presupposition theories of science (Polanyi 1958; Humphreys 1969; Suppe 1977; Brown 1977; Bernstein 1978, 1983; Hesse 1980; Longino 1990; Stockman 1983; Gunnell 1986). Presupposition theories of science concur with Popper's depiction of observation as 'theory-laden'. They agree that 'there is more to seeing than meets the eye' (Humphreys 1969: 61) and that perception involves more than the passive reception of allegedly manifest sense-data. They suggest that perception depends upon a constellation of theoretical presuppositions that structure observation, accrediting particular stimuli as significant and specific configurations as meaningful. According to presupposition theories, observation is not only theory-laden but theory is essential to, indeed, constitutive of all human knowledge.

As a form of human knowledge, science is dependent upon theory in multiple and complex ways. Presupposition theories of science suggest that the notions of perception, meaning, relevance, explanation, knowledge and method, central to the practice of science, are all theoretically constituted concepts. Theoretical presuppositions shape perception and determine what will be taken as a 'fact'; they confer meaning on experience and control the demarcation of significant from trivial events; they afford criteria of relevance according to which facts can be organized, tests envisioned and the acceptability or unacceptability of scientific conclusions assessed; they accredit particular models of explanation and strategies of understanding; and they sustain specific methodological techniques for gathering, classifying, and analysing data. Theoretical presuppositions set the terms of scientific debate and organize the elements of scientific activity. Moreover, they typically do so at a tacit or preconscious level and it is for this reason that they appear to hold such unquestionable authority.

The pervasive role of theoretical assumptions upon the practice of science has profound implications for notions such as empirical 'reality', and the 'autonomy' of facts, which posit that facts are 'given', and that experience is ontologically distinct from the theoretical constructs that are advanced to explain it. The post-empiricist conception of a 'fact' as a theoretically constituted entity calls into question such basic assumptions. It suggests that 'the noun, "experience", the verb, "to experience" and the adjective "empirical" are not univocal terms that can be transferred from one system to another without change of meaning. . . . Experience does not come labelled as "empirical", nor does it come self-certified as such. What we call experience depends upon assumptions hidden beyond scrutiny which define it and which in turn it supports' (Vivas 1960: 76). Recognition that 'facts' can be so designated only in terms of prior theoretical presuppositions implies that any quest for an unmediated reality is necessarily futile. Any attempt to identify an 'unmediated fact' must mistake the conventional for the 'natural', as in cases which define 'brute facts' as 'social facts which are largely the product of well-understood, reliable tools, facts that are not likely to be vitiated by pitfalls . . . in part [because of] the ease and certainty with which [they] can be determined and in part [because of] the incontestability of [their] conceptual base' (Murray 1983: 321). Alternatively, the attempt to conceive a 'fact' that exists prior to any description of it, prior to any theoretical or conceptual mediation, must generate an empty notion of something completely unspecified and unspecifiable, a notion that will be of little use to science (Williams, 1985: 138).

Recognition of the manifold ways in which perceptions of reality are theoretically mediated raises a serious challenge not only to notions of 'brute data' and the 'givenness' of experience, but also to the possibility of falsification as a strategy for testing theories against an independent reality. For falsification to provide an adequate test of a scientific theory, it is necessary that there be a clear distinction between theoretical postulates and independent correspondence rules that link theoretical principles to particular observations. Embodying the idea of theory-independent evidence, neutral correspondence rules are essential to the very possibility of refutation, to the possibility that the world could prove a theory to be wrong. If, however, there is no tenable distinction between theoretical assumptions and correspondence rules, if what is taken to be the 'world', what is understood in terms of 'brute data' is itself theoretically constituted (indeed, constituted by the same theory that is undergoing the test), then no conclusive disproof of a theory is likely. For the independent evidence upon which falsification depends does not exist; the available evidence is preconstituted by the same theoretical presuppositions as the scientific theory under scrutiny (Moon 1975: 146, Brown 1977: 38–48; Stockman 1983: 73–6).

Contrary to Popper's confident conviction that empirical reality could provide an ultimate court of appeal for the judgement of scientific theories and that the critical, non-dogmatic attitude of scientists would ensure that their theories were constantly being put to the test, presupposition theorists emphasize that it is always possible to 'save' a theory from refutation. The existence of one disconfirming instance is not sufficient to falsify a theory because it is always possible to evade falsification on the grounds that future research will demonstrate that a counter-instance is really only an 'apparent' counter-instance. Moreover, the theory-laden character of observation and the theory-constituted character of evidence provide ample grounds upon which to dispute the validity of the evidence and to challenge the design or the findings of specific experiments which claim to falsify respected theories. Furthermore, post-positivist examinations of the history of scientific practice suggest that, contrary to Popper's claim that scientists are quick to discard discredited theories, there is a great deal of evidence that neither the existence of counter-instances nor the persistence of anomalies necessarily lead to the abandonment of scientific theories. Indeed, the overwhelming evidence of scientific practice suggests that scientists cling to long-established views tenaciously, in spite of the existence of telling criticisms, persistent anomalies and unresolved problems (Ricci 1984; Harding 1986). Thus it has been suggested that the 'theory' that scientists themselves are always sceptical, non-dogmatic, critical of received views and quick to repudiate questionable notions has itself been falsified and should be abandoned.

The problem of falsification is exacerbated by the conflation of explanation and prediction in the Popperian account of science. For the belief that a corroborated prediction constitutes proof of the validity of a scientific explanation fails to recognize that an erroneous theory can generate correct predictions (Moon 1975: 146–7; Brown 1977: 51–7). The logical distinction between prediction and explanation thus provides further support for the view that no theory can ever be conclusively falsified. The problem of induction also raises doubts about the possibility of definitive refutations. In calling attention to the possibility that the future could be different from the past and present in unforeseeable ways, the problem of induction arouses the suspicion that a theory falsified today might not 'stay' falsified. The assumption of regularity which sustains Popper's belief that a falsified theory will remain falsified permanently is itself an inductionist presupposition which suggests that the falsifiability principle does not constitute the escape from induction which Popper had hoped (Stockman 1983: 81–2). Thus despite the logical asymmetry between verification and falsification, no falsification can be any stronger or more final than any corroboration (Brown 1977: 75).

Presupposition theorists acknowledge that 'ideally, scientists would like to examine the structure of the world which exists independent of our knowledge – but the nature of perception and the role of presuppositions preclude direct access to it: the only access available is through theory-directed research' (Brown 1977: 108). Recognition that theoretical presuppositions organize and structure research by determining the meanings of observed events, identifying relevant data and significant problems for investigation and indicating both strategies for solving problems and methods by which to test the validity of proposed solutions, raises a serious challenge to the correspondence theory of truth. For it both denies that 'autonomous facts' can serve as the ultimate arbiter of scientific theories and suggests that science is no more capable of achieving the Archimedean point or of escaping human fallibility than is any other human endeavour. Indeed, it demands acknowledgement of science as a human convention rooted in the practical judgements of a community of fallible scientists struggling to resolve theory-generated problems under specific historical conditions. It sustains an image of science that is far less heroic and far more human.

As an alternative to the correspondence theory of truth, presupposition theorists suggest a coherence theory of truth premised upon the recognition that all human knowledge depends upon theoretical presuppositions whose congruence with nature cannot be established conclusively by reason or experience. Theoretical presuppositions, rooted in living traditions, provide the conceptual frameworks through which the world is viewed; they exude a 'natural attitude' which demarcates what is taken as normal, natural, real, reasonable or sane, from what is understood as deviant, unnatural, utopian, impossible, irrational or insane. In contrast to Popper's conception of theories as conscious conjectures which can be systematically elaborated and deductively elucidated, the notion of theoretical presuppositions suggests that theories operate at the tacit level. They structure 'pre-understandings' and 'pre-judgements' in such a way that it is difficult to isolate and illuminate the full range of presuppositions which affect cognition at any given time (Bernstein 1983: 113–67). Moreover, any attempt to elucidate presuppositions must operate within a 'hermeneutic circle'. Any attempt to examine or to challenge certain assumptions or expectations must occur within the frame of reference established by the other presuppositions. Certain presuppositions must remain fixed if others are to be subjected to systematic critique. This does not imply that individuals are 'prisoners' trapped within the framework of theories, expectations, past experiences and language in such a way that critical reflection becomes impossible (ibid.: 84). Critical reflection upon and abandonment of certain theoretical presuppositions is possible within the hermeneutic circle; but the goal of transparency, of the unmediated grasp of things as they are, is not. For no reflective investigation, no matter how critical, can escape the fundamental conditions of human cognition.

A coherence theory of truth accepts that the world is richer than theories devised to grasp it; it accepts that theories are underdetermined by 'facts' and, consequently, that there can always be alternative and competing theoretical explanations of particular events. It does not, however, imply the relativist conclusion that all theoretical interpretations are equal. That there can be no appeal to neutral, theory-independent facts to adjudicate between competing theoretical interpretations does not mean that there is no rational way of making and warranting critical evaluative judgements concerning alternative views. Indeed, presupposition theorists have pointed out that the belief that the absence of independent evidence necessarily entails relativism is itself dependent upon a positivist commitment to the verification criterion of meaning. Only if one starts from the assumption that the sole test for the validity of a proposition lies in its measurement against the empirically 'given' does it follow that, in the absence of the 'given', no rational judgements can be made concerning the validity of particular claims (Bernstein 1983: 92; Brown 1977: 93–4; Stockman 1983: 79–101; Gunnell 1986: 66–8).

Once the 'myth of the given' (Sellars 1963: 164) has been abandoned and once the belief that the absence of one invariant empirical test for the 'truth' of a theory implies the absence of all criteria for evaluative judgement has been repudiated, then it is possible to recognize that there are rational grounds for assessing the merits of alternative theoretical interpretations. To comprehend the nature of such assessments it is necessary to acknowledge that although theoretical presuppositions structure the perception of events, they do not create perceptions out of 'nothing'. Theoretical interpretations are 'world-guided' (Williams 1985: 140). They involve both the pre-understanding brought to an event by an individual perceiver and the stimuli in the external (or internal) world which instigate the process of cognition. Because of this dual source of theoretical interpretations, objects can be characterized in many different ways, 'but it does not follow that a given object can be seen in any way at all or that all descriptions are equal' (Brown 1977: 93). The stimuli that trigger interpretation limit the class of plausible characterizations without dictating one absolute description.

Assessment of alternative theoretical interpretations involves deliberation, a rational activity which requires that imagination and judgement be deployed in the consideration of the range of evidence and arguments that can be advanced in support of various positions. The reasons offered in support of alternative views marshal evidence, organize data, apply various criteria of explanation, address multiple levels of analysis with varying degrees of abstraction and employ divergent strategies of argumentation. This range of reasons offers a rich field for deliberation and assessment. It provides an opportunity for the exercise of judgement and ensures that when scientists reject a theory, they do so because they believe they can demonstrate that the reasons offered in support of that theory are deficient. That the reasons advanced to sustain the rejection of one theory do not constitute absolute proof of the validity of an alternative theory is simply a testament to human fallibility. Admission that the cumulative weight of current evidence and compelling argument cannot protect scientific judgements against future discoveries which may warrant the repudiation of those theories currently accepted is altogether consonant with the recognition of the finitude of human rationality and the contingency of empirical relations.

Presupposition theorists suggest that any account of science which fails to accredit the rationality of the considered judgements that inform the choice between alternative scientific theories must be committed to a defective conception of reason. Although the standards of evidence and the criteria for assessment brought to bear upon theoretical questions cannot be encapsulated in a simple rule or summarized in rigid methodological principles, deliberation involves the exercise of a range of intellectual skills. Conceptions of science that define rationality in terms of one technique, be it logical deduction or empirical verification, are simply too narrow to encompass the multiple forms of rationality manifested in scientific research. The interpretive judgements that are characteristic of every phase of scientific investigations, and that culminate in the rational choice of particular scientific theories on the basis of the cumulative weight of evidence and argument, are too rich and various to be captured by the rules governing inductive or deductive logic. For this reason, *phronesis*, practical reason, manifested in the processes of interpretation and judgement characteristic of all understanding, is advanced by presupposition theorists as an alternative to logic as the paradigmatic form of scientific rationality (Brown 1977: 148–52; Bernstein 1983: 54–78).

Presupposition theorists suggest that a conception of practical reason more accurately depicts the forms of rationality exhibited in scientific research. In contrast to the restrictive view advanced by positivism which reduces the arsenal of reason to the techniques of logic and thereby rejects creativity, deliberative judgement and evaluative assessments as varying forms of irrationality, *phronesis* constitutes a more expansive conception of the powers of the human intellect. Presupposition theorists suggest that a consideration of the various processes of contemplation, conceptualization, representation, remembrance, reflection, speculation, rationalization, inference, deduction and deliberation (to name but a few manifestations of human cognition) reveals that the dimensions of reason are diverse. They also argue that an adequate conception of reason must encompass these diverse cognitive practices. Because the instrumental conception of rationality advanced by positivists is clearly incapable of accounting for these various forms of reason, it must be rejected as defective. Thus presupposition theorists suggest that science must be freed from the parochial beliefs that obscure reason's diverse manifestations and restrict its operation to the rigid adherence to a narrow set of rules. The equation of scientific rationality with an infallible formal logic must be abandoned not only because there is no reason to suppose that there must be some indubitable foundation or some ahistorical, invariant method for scientific inquiry in order to establish the rationality of scientific practices, but also because the belief that science can provide final truths cannot be sustained by the principles of formal logic, the methods of empirical inquiry or the characteristics of fallible human cognition. *Phronesis* constitutes a conception of rationality that can encompass the diverse uses of reason in scientific practices, identify the manifold sources of potential error in theoretical interpretations, and illuminate the criteria of assessment and the standards of evidence and argument operative in the choice between alternative theoretical explanations of events. As a conception of scientific rationality, then, *phronesis* is more comprehensive and has greater explanatory power than the discredited positivist alternative.

Presupposition theorists offer a revised conception of science which emphasizes the conventional nature of scientific practices and the fallible character of scientific explanations and predictions. Confronted with a world richer than any partial perception of it, scientists draw upon the resources of tradition and imagination in an effort to comprehend the world before them. The theories they devise to explain objects and events are structured by a host of presuppositions concerning meaning, relevance, experience, explanation and evaluation. Operating within the limits imposed by fallibility and contingency, scientists employ creative insights, practical reason, formal logic and an arsenal of conventional techniques and methods in their effort to approximate the truth about the world. But their approximations always operate within the parameters set by theoretical presuppositions; their approximations always address an empirical realm which is itself theoretically constituted. The undetermination of theory by data ensures that multiple interpretations of the same phenomena are possible.

When alternative theoretical explanations conflict, the judgement of the scientific community is brought to bear upon the competing interpretations. Exercising practical reason, the scientific community deliberates upon the evidence and arguments sustaining the alternative views. The practical judgement of the practitioners in particular fields of science is exercised in weighing the evidence, replicating experiments, examining computations, investigating the applicability of innovative methods, assessing the potential of new concepts and considering the validity of particular conclusions. Through a process of deliberation and debate, a consensus emerges among researchers within a discipline concerning what will be taken as the valid theory. The choice is sustained by reasons which can be articulated and advanced as proof of the inadequacy of alternative interpretations. The method of scientific deliberation is eminently rational: it provides mechanisms for the identification of charlatans and incompetents, as well as for the recognition of more subtle errors and more sophisticated approximations of truth. But the rationality of the process cannot guarantee the eternal verity of particular conclusions. The exercise of scientific reason is fallible; the judgements of the scientific community are corrigible.

The revised conception of science advanced by presupposition theorists suggests that attempts to divide the world into ontologically distinct categories of 'facts' and 'values', or into dichotomous realms of the 'empirical' and the 'normative', are fundamentally flawed (Hawkesworth 1988). Such attempts fail to grasp the implications of the theoretical constitution of all knowledge and the theoretical mediation of the empirical realm. They fail to come to grips with valuative character of all presuppositions and the consequent valuative component of all empirical propositions. The theoretically mediated world is one in which description, explanation and evaluation are inextricably linked. Any attempt to impose a dichotomous relation upon such inseparable processes constitutes a fallacy of false alternatives which is as distorting as it is logically untenable. For the suggestion that 'pure' facts can be isolated and analysed free of all valuation masks the theoretical constitution of facticity and denies the cognitive processes through which knowledge of the empirical realm is generated. Moreover, the dichotomous schism of the world into 'facts' and 'values' endorses an erroneous and excessively limiting conception of human reason, a conception which fails to comprehend the role of practical rationality in scientific deliberation and which fails to recognize that science is simply one manifestation of the use of practical reason in human life. Informed by flawed assumptions, the positivist conception of reason fails to understand that *phronesis* is operative in philosophical analysis, ethical deliberation, normative argument, political decisions and the practical choices of daily life as well as in scientific analysis. Moreover, in stipulating that reason can operate only in a naïvely simple, 'value-free', empirical realm, the positivist presuppositions that inform the fact/value dichotomy render reason impotent and thereby preclude the possibility that rational solutions might exist for the most pressing problems of the contemporary age.

Although the arguments that have discredited empiricism are well known to philosophers, they have had little impact on the conduct of substantive political studies. This is especially unfortunate because the critique of empiricism has wide-ranging implications for the discipline of political science. The post-empiricist conception of knowledge suggests that divergent theoretical assumptions should have a pervasive influence upon the understanding of the political world, sanctioning contentious definitions of politics and focusing attention upon disparate variables, while simultaneously masking the controversial character of evidence adduced and the contestability of accredited strategies of explanation. Thus the post-positivist conception of science opens new areas of investigation concerning disciplinary presuppositions and practices: What are the most fundamental presuppositions of political science? What limitations have been imposed upon the constitution of knowledge within political science? By what disciplinary mechanisms has facticity been accredited and rendered unproblematic? How adequate are the standards of evidence, modes of analysis, and strategies of explanation privileged by the dominant tradition? Have methodological precepts subtly circumscribed contemporary politics?

Questions such as these focus attention upon the political implications of determinate modes of inquiry. The politics of knowledge emerges as a legitimate focus of analysis, for the analytic techniques developed in particular cognitive traditions may have political consequences that empiricist precepts render invisible. In circumscribing the subject matter appropriate to 'science', restricting the activities acceptable as 'empirical inquiry', establishing the norms for assessing the results of inquiry, identifying the basic principles of practice, and validating the ethos of practitioners, methodological strictures may sustain particular modes of political life. For this reason, the empiricist myth of methodological neutrality must be supplanted by an understanding of methodology as 'mind engaged in the legitimation of its own political activity' (Wolin 1981: 406). Such a revised conception of methodology requires detailed examination of the complex relations among various conceptions of politics, various techniques of political analysis and various forms of polity. The next section briefly considers the stakes involved in such investigations in the context of competing definitions of politics.

POLITICS: CONSTITUTIVE DEFINITIONS

Within the field of political science there is no one definition of politics that holds the allegiance of all political scientists. The lack of a universally agreed-upon definition does not imply that the topic is indefinable, that politics is a simple concept that admits of no further definition and, hence, must be grasped intuitively (Moore 1903). Nor does it imply that political scientists do not know what they are doing. On the contrary, contending definitions reflect important epistemological and methodological disagreements within the discipline. Alternative conceptions of politics construe the political world differently, in part because they derive from different understandings of reason, evidence and explanation, and in part because they are informed by radically different understandings of human possibility. As a consequence, the stakes in these conceptual disputes involve not just disciplinary politics, but also the shape of politics in the contemporary world. To explore these stakes, it is helpful to compare a classical definition of politics with a range of definitions advanced by contemporary political scientists.

In the classical conception advanced by Aristotle (1958) in *The Politics*, the activities of ruling and of politics were not equivalent. While ruling typically involved hierarchical relations of domination and subordination, politics was possible only as a relation among equals. In contrast to endeavours related to subsistence, production and reproduction that occurred in a sphere governed by necessity, politics existed only in a realm of freedom. On Aristotle's view, the participation of equals in collective decision making concerning the content and direction of public life constitutes the essence of politics. If the participation of equal citizens in an interchange of ruling and being ruled comprises the activity of politics, the citizens' achievement of a mode of life characterized by human excellence is its aim. To achieve this end, Aristotle noted that citizens must share a common system of values, they must be united in their perceptions of the just and the unjust. Only under such conditions could citizens escape the mire of conflicting wills and act co-operatively to achieve their common objectives. Thus political life is a testament to human freedom: within the political community, equal citizens identify the values they wish to live by and create rules and institutions to instantiate those values.

When Aristotle dubbed politics the master art, he suggested that politics necessarily involves a form of practical knowledge concerning both what is good for the community and how to attain that good. Political knowledge provides answers to questions such as: How ought people to live? What rules should govern collective life in order to enable citizens to achieve human excellence? What practices and institutions are most conducive to the achievement of the human *telos* – the highest and best form of human existence?

As a person interested in the comparative study of politics, Aristotle knew full well that such questions could be answered at two markedly different levels: at the first level, by citizens within a political community who were actively shaping their collective life; at the second level, by a political observer comparing the responses of various political communities to the same questions. In collecting hundreds of constitutions, Aristotle gained impressive evidence of the extent to which engagement in politics enabled determinate peoples to express their freedom. Reflecting the varying values of particular polities, diverse constitutions embodied alternative conceptions of the good life.

Aristotle did not believe that documenting alternative forms of political organization required a relativist endorsement of differing modes of life as equally beneficial. On the contrary, he was convinced that systematic political inquiry could provide an authoritative and final answer to the question of the highest form of human existence. Operating at the second level, political knowledge could afford definitive answers to the central political questions. Investigation of particular constitutions would make it possible to extract the essence of politics.

Aristotle's conceptions of politics and of political knowledge are intimately connected to a specific research strategy and a particular model of explanation. His strategy requires a preliminary gathering of diverse instances of a phenomenon and particular attention to received views about that phenomenon. Examination of similarities and differences then allows careful classification according to essential properties, which are inherently teleological. Methodologically,

> political inquiry requires a move from partial perspectives to an integral view, from opinions to a grasp of the thing in its wholeness. It proceeds by taking a variety of viewpoints into account, weighing them against each other and seeking the comprehensive view that can withstand criticism. In the course of inquiry, there is a growing awareness of the shape of things as a whole and this awareness gradually reveals the partiality and distortion of the original perspectives.
>
> (Miller 1979: 167)

Comprehension emerges from a sustained engagement with experiences whose meaning initially appears vague or inchoate. Use of this method produces *aletheia*, truth, that which remains when all error is purged.

Aristotle's technique for the acquisition of political knowledge presuppposes that reason can distinguish essence from appearance, actuality from potentiality. His research methodology suggests that the attainment of truth is possible, even if the process is arduous and demanding. His distinction between the activity of politics and the second order activity of political theory also illuminates a critical disjuncture between freedom, power and truth. For it acknowledges that citizens may exercise their freedom, act in good faith and use their power to institutionalize values that fall short of the achievement of the human *telos*. Within politics, freedom and the power of people to realize their shared values may eclipse truth. Political theorists who systematically investigate the nature and purposes of political life may grasp the truth about human possibility. But the possession of truth remains at a great remove from the power to institutionalize its precepts.

In contrast to the Aristotelian conception, twentieth-century definitions of politics have intentionally eschewed any reference to the human *telos*. Informed by empiricist assumptions, political scientists abandoned consideration of what might be in order to concentrate upon description and explanation of what is. Thus, they attempted to devise value-free definitions of politics grounded squarely upon the empirically observable. A brief examination of the definitions most frequently invoked by political scientists suggests, however, that each definition subtly structures the boundaries of the political in a thoroughly value-laden fashion.

For the first half of the twentieth century, the 'institutional definition' of politics dominated the discipline of political science. On this view, politics involves the activities of the official institutions of state (Goodnow 1904; Hyneman 1959). Established by tradition and constitution, existing governmental agencies constitute the focal point of empirical political research. Typically adopting a case-study approach, political scientists examine constitutional provisions to identify the structures of governance and the distribution of powers within those structures in particular nations. Great effort is devoted to the interpretation of specific constitutional provisions and to the historical investigation of the means by which such provisions are subtly expanded and transformed over time. This approach often tends to be heavily oriented towards law, investigating both the legislative process and the role of the courts in interpreting the law. Foreign policy is typically conceived in terms of the history of diplomacy, and domestic policy is understood in relation to the mechanisms by which governments affect the lives of citizens.

While the focus on the official institutions of state has a certain intuitive appeal, the institutional definition of politics can be faulted for sins of omission. If politics is to be understood solely in terms of the state, what can be said of those societies in which no state exists? If the constitution provides a blueprint for the operations of the state, how are states that lack constitutions to be understood? What can be known about states whose constitutions mask the real distribution of power in the nation? If governments are by definition the locus of politics, how are revolutionary movements to be classified? The institutional definition of politics provides neither a neutral nor a comprehensive account of political life. It accredits a particular mode of decision making within the nation-state by stipulative definition. In so doing, it subtly removes important activities from the realm of the political.

Concerns such as these led many scholars to reject the institutional definition of politics as underinclusive. By structuring the focus of political analysis exclusively on the institutions of state governance, this definition fails to encompass the full range of politics. It cannot account for political agents such as political bosses, political parties and pressure groups operating behind the scenes to influence political outcomes. It excludes all modes of political violence, except those perpetrated by states, from the sphere of the political. It thereby delegitimizes revolutionary activity, regardless of precipitating circumstances. And in important respects the institutional definition of politics narrowly construes the range of human freedom, identifying constitutionally designated mechanisms for social transformation as the limit of political possibility. In addition, the institutional definition of politics fails to do justice to international relations, leaving altogether unclear the political status of a realm in which there exists no binding law and no authoritative structures capable of applying sanctions to recalcitrant states.

To avoid the limitations of the institutional definition, many political scientists have argued that politics is better understood as a struggle for power (Mosca 1939; Lasswell 1950; Catlin 1964; Morgenthau 1967). Within this frame of reference, individuals participate in politics in order to pursue their own selfish advantage. The central question for political research then is 'who gets what, when, how' (Lasswell 1950). Such a research focus necessarily expands political inquiry beyond the bounds of governmental agencies, for although the official institutions of state constitute one venue for power struggles, they by no means exhaust the possibilities. Within the struggle-for-power conception, politics is ubiquitous.

In an important sense, the struggle-for-power definition of politics not only expands the sphere of political research beyond the institutions of state, it also extends political analysis beyond the realm of the empirically observable. The exercise of power often eludes direct observation and the effects of power are more easily inferred than empirically documented. Thus it is not surprising that many political researchers working with the conception of politics as power-struggle ground their investigations upon a number of contentious assumptions. Perhaps the most fundamental of these is a conception of the person as a being actuated primarily by the *libido dominandi*, the will to power. Precisely because individuals are taken to be governed by an unquenchable desire for power, politics is said to be essentially a zero-sum game in which competition is unceasing, and domination for the sake of exploitation is the chief objective. But the posited will to power, which constitutes the explanatory key to the inevitable nature of political life, is lodged deep in the human psyche – wholly unavailable for empirical observation. Although proponents of the struggle-for-power definition have claimed simply to be 'political realists', it is important to note the circularity that informs their cynical 'realism'. Politics is defined as a struggle for power 'because' human beings are driven by the *libido dominandi*; but the evidence that people are driven by the *libido dominandi* is inferred from their involvement in politics.

An unacceptable degree of circularity also infects the response of political 'realists' to their critics. Critics have objected that the struggle-for-power definition fails to explain the full range of political phenomena: If politics is merely a competition through which individuals seek to impose their selfish objectives on others, why have values such as equality, freedom and justice played such a large and recurrent role in political life? With its relentless emphasis upon the pursuit of selfish advantage, the struggle-for-power conception of politics seems unable to account for this dimension of politics. Political 'realists', such as Gaetano Mosca, have suggested that appeals to noble principles constitute various forms of propaganda disseminated to mask the oppressive character of political relations and thereby enhance the opportunities for exploitation. According to Mosca (1939), no one wants to confront the naked face of power. Political leaders do not wish to have their selfish objectives unmasked because it will make their achievement more difficult. The masses do not wish to confront their own craven natures. So rulers and followers collude in the propagation of 'political formulae' – noble phrases that accord legitimacy to regimes by masking the ruler's self-interest. Whether the appeal be to 'divine right of kings', 'liberty, fraternity and equality', or 'democracy of the people, by the people and for the people', the function of the political formula is the same: a noble lie that serves as legitimating myth. Thus political realists discount the role of substantive values in politics by unmasking them as additional manifestations of the will to power, a will that is posited and for which no independent evidence is adduced.

Although such a degree of circularity may impugn the logical adequacy of the struggle-for-power conception of politics, it does not mitigate the unsavoury consequences of the widespread dissemination of the definition by political scientists. When 'science' asserts that politics is nothing more than the struggle for power, the moral scope of political action is partially occluded. If people are convinced that politics necessarily involves the pursuit of selfish advantage, then the grounds for evaluating political regimes is severely circumscribed. In an important sense, the distinction between a good ruler (i.e. one who rules in the common interest) and a tyrant (i.e. one who rules in self-interest) ceases to have meaning. For if all politics is by definition a struggle for selfish advantage, then what distinguishes one ruler from another cannot be the divergent ends pursued by each. All that distinguishes a 'noble statesperson' from an 'ignoble oppressor' is the nature of the political formula disseminated. A 'good ruler' is simply an excellent propagandist. What distinguishes regimes is not the values pursued, but the ability of the political leaders to manipulate popular beliefs. Within the frame of cynical 'realism', it makes no sense to denounce the systematic manipulation of images as an abuse of the democratic process, for manipulation is a constant of political life. What cynical science must denounce is the illusory notion that democracy could be anything more.

Pluralists have advanced a third conception of politics that has had an enormous influence upon the discipline of political science. Devised to avoid the shortcomings of both the institutional and the struggle-for-power definitions, pluralists conceive politics as the process of interest accommodation. Unlike the cynical insistence that power is the only value pursued in politics, pluralists argue that individuals engage in politics to maximize a wide range of values. While some political actors may pursue their selfish advantage exclusively, others may seek altruistic ends such as equality, justice, an unpolluted environment, or preservation of endangered species. Without pre-emptively delimiting the range of values that might be pursued, pluralists suggest that politics is an activity through which values and interests are promoted and preserved. In contrast to the institutional definition's focus on the official agencies of government, pluralists emphasize that politics is a process of 'partisan mutual adjustment' (Lindblom 1965), a process of bargaining, negotiating, conciliation and compromise through which individuals seeking markedly different objectives arrive at decisions with which all are willing to live. On this view, politics is a moderating activity, a means of settling differences without recourse to force, a mechanism for deciding policy objectives from a competing array of alternatives (Crick 1962).

The pluralist conception of politics incorporates a number of modernist assumptions about the appropriate relation of the individual to the state. Pervaded by scepticism concerning the power of human reason to operate in the realm of values and the concomitant subjectivist assumption that, in the absence of absolute values, all value judgements must be relative to the individual, pluralists suggest that individuals must be left free to pursue their own subjectively determined ends. The goal of politics must be nothing more than the reconciliation of subjectively defined needs and interests of the individual with the requirements of society as a whole in the most freedom-maximizing fashion. Moreover, presupposing the fundamental equality of individuals, pluralists insist that the state has no business favouring the interests of any individual or group. Thus, in the absence of rational grounds for preferring any individual or value over any other, pluralists identify coalition building as the most freedom-maximizing decision principle. Politics *qua* interest accommodation is fair precisely because the outcome of any negotiating situation is a function of the consensus-garnering skill of the participants. The genius of this procedural conception of politics lies in its identification of solutions capable of winning the assent of a majority of participants in the decision process.

Pluralists have ascribed a number of virtues to their conception of politics. It avoids the excessive rationalism of paternalist conceptions of politics that assume the state knows what is in the best interests of the citizenry. It recognizes the heterogeneity of citizens and protects the rights of all to participate in the political process. It acknowledges the multiple power bases in society (for example, wealth, numbers, monopoly of scarce goods or skills) and accords each a legitimate role in collective decision making. It notes not only that interest groups must be taken into account if politics is to be adequately understood, but also that competing interests exist within the official institutions of state; that those designated to act on behalf of citizens must also be understood to act as factions, whose behaviour may be governed as much by organizational interests, partisanship, and private ambitions as by an enlightened conception of the common good.

Despite such advantages, pluralism, too, has been criticized for failing to provide a comprehensive conception of politics. In defining politics as a mechanism for decision making which constitutes an alternative to force, the interest-accommodation definition relegates war, revolution and terrorism beyond the sphere of politics. In emphasizing bargaining, conciliation and compromise as the core activities of politics, the pluralist conception assumes that all interests are essentially reconcilable. Thus it sheds little light upon some of the most intractable political issues that admit of no compromise (for example, abortion, apartheid or racism or, more generally, 'holy war'). Moreover, in treating all power bases as equal, pluralists tend to ignore the structural advantages afforded by wealth and political office. The notion of equal rights of participation and influence neglects the formidable powers of state and economy in determining political outcomes. In addition, the interest-accommodation definition of politics has been faulted for ethnocentrism. It mistakes certain characteristics of political activity in Western liberal democracies for the nature of politics in all times and places.

Although the pluralist conception fails to achieve a value-neutral, comprehensive definition of politics, it too has a subtle influence upon the practice of politics in the contemporary world. When accredited by social scientists as the essence of politics, the interest-accommodation conception both legitimizes the activities of competing interest groups as the fairest mechanism of policy determination and delegitimizes revolutionary action and political violence as inherently anti-political. Even in less extreme circumstances, the pluralist definition of politics may function as a self-fulfilling prophecy, severely curtailing the options available to a political community by constricting the parameters within which political questions are considered.

The pluralist conception of politics presupposes the validity of the fact–value dichotomy and the emotivist conception of values. As a version of non-cognitivism, emotivism is a meta-ethical theory which asserts that facts and values are ontologically distinct and that evaluative judgements involve questions concerning subjective emotions, sentiments or feelings rather than questions of knowledge or rational deliberation (Hudson 1970). Applied to the political realm, emotivism suggests that moral and political choices are a matter of subjective preference or irrational whim about which there can be no reasoned debate.

Although emotivism has been discredited as an altogether defective account of morality and has been repudiated by philosophers for decades, emotivism continues to be advanced as unproblematic truth by social scientists (MacIntyre 1981; Warwick 1980). And there is a good deal of evidence to suggest that 'to a large degree, people now think, talk and act as if emotivism were true' (MacIntyre 1981: 21). Promulgated in the texts of social science and incorporated in pop culture, emotivist assumptions permeate discussions of the self, freedom and social relations (Bellah et al. 1985). Contemporary conceptions of the self are deeply infused with emotivist and individualist premises: the 'unsituated self' who chooses an identity in isolation and on the basis of arbitrary preferences has become a cultural ideal. Freedom is conceived in terms of the unrestrained pursuit of idiosyncratic preferences in personal, economic, moral and political realms. Moral issues are understood in terms of maximizing one's preferred idiosyncratic values, and moral dilemmas are treated as strategic or technical problems related to zero-sum conditions under which the satisfaction of one preference may obstruct the satisfaction of another preference. Respect for other individuals is equated with recognition of their rights to choose and to pursue their own preferences without interference. Condemnation of the immoral actions of others is supplanted by the non-judgemental response of 'walking away, if you don't like what others are doing' (Bellah et al. 1985: 6). Emotivism coupled with individualism encourages people to find meaning exclusively in the private sphere, thereby intensifying the privatization of the self and heightening doubts that individuals have enough in common to sustain a discussion of their interests or anxieties (Connolly 1981: 145).

Any widespread acceptance of emotivism has important ramifications for political life. At its best, emotivism engenders a relativism which strives 'to take views, outlooks and beliefs which apparently conflict and treat them in such a way that they do not conflict: each of them turns out to be acceptable in its own place' (Williams 1985: 156). The suspension of valuative judgement aims at conflict reduction by conflict avoidance. By walking away from those whose subjective preferences are different, individuals avoid unpleasant confrontations. By accepting that values are ultimately arbitrary and hence altogether beyond rational justification, citizens devise a *modus vivendi* which permits coexistence amidst diversity.

This coexistence is fragile, however, and the promise of conflict avoidance largely illusory. For the underside of emotivism is cynicism, the 'obliteration of any genuine distinction between manipulative and non-manipulative social relations' and the consequent reduction of politics to a contest of wiles and wills ultimately decided by force (MacIntyre 1981: 22, 68). Thus when intractable conflicts arise because avoidance strategies fail, they cannot be resolved through reasoned discourse, for on this view, rational discussion is simply a façade which masks arbitrary manipulation. Thus the options for political life are reduced by definition either to the intense competition of conflicting interests depicted in the pluralist paradigm or to the resort to violence.

The political legacy of emotivism is radical privatization, the destruction of the public realm, 'the disintegration of public deliberation and discourse among members of the political community' (Dallmayr 1981: 2). For widespread acceptance of the central tenets of emotivism renders public discussion undesirable (for it might provoke violence), unnecessary (for the real outcomes of decisions will be dictated by force of will), and irrational (for nothing rational can be said in defence of arbitrary preferences). Privatization produces a world

31

in which individuals are free to act on whim and to realize their arbitrary desires, but it is a world in which collective action is prohibited by a constellation of beliefs which render public deliberation impotent, if not impossible. The pluralist conception of politics is not the sole disseminator of emotivism in contemporary societies, but its confident proclamation of interest accommodation as the only viable mode of politics contributes to a form of public life that is markedly impoverished. That it appeals to scientific expertise to confer the 'legitimacy of fact' upon its narrow construal of political possibility should be the cause of some alarm to members of a discipline committed to value-free inquiry.

To escape problems of ethnocentrism and devise a conception of politics that encompasses the political experiences of diverse cultures and ages, in the 1960s behavioural political scientists suggested a new approach that would be both broadly comparative and thoroughly scientific. Extrapolating from organic and cybernetic analogies, both systems analysis and structural-functionalism conceived politics as a self-regulating system existing within a larger social environment and fulfilling necessary tasks for that social environment (Easton 1971; Almond and Coleman 1960; Mitchell 1958, 1967). On this view, politics involves performance of a number of functions without which society could not exist. The task of political science was to identify these critical political functions, show how they are performed in divergent cultural and social contexts, and ascertain how changes in one part of the political system affect other parts and the system as a whole so as to maintain homeostatic equilibrium. Once political inquiry had generated such a comprehensive understanding of political processes, political scientists could then provide meaningful cross-cultural explanations and predictions. The goal of the systematic cross-cultural study of politics, then, was to generate a scientific understanding of the demands made upon political systems (for example, state building, nation building, participation, redistribution), the nature of the systems' adaptive responses, including the conversion processes which operate to minimize change, and the scope of political development in terms of structural differentiation and cultural secularization which emerge when the system confronts challenges that surpass its existing capabilities.

Despite its wide popularity, this functionalist conception of politics encountered difficulties with its effort to identify the core political functions without which societies could not survive. Although scholars committed to the functionalist approach generally concurred with David Easton that the political system involves 'those actions related to the authoritative allocation of values' (Easton 1971: 143-4); they disagreed about precisely what those actions entailed. Mitchell (1958, 1967) identified four critical political functions: the authoritative specification of system goals; the authoritative mobilization of resources to implement goals; the integration of the system (centre and periphery); and the allocation of values and costs. Easton (1971), as well as Almond and Coleman (1960), offered a more expansive list including interest articulation, interest aggregation, rule making, rule application, rule adjudication, political recruitment, political socialization and political communication.

Critics noted that neither enumeration was sufficiently precise to satisfy expectations raised by the model. Neither delineated clearly between the system and its boundaries; neither specified a critical range of operation beyond which the system could be said to have ceased to function; neither explained the requirements of equilibrium maintenance with sufficient precision to sustain a distinction between functional and dysfunctional processes. In short, critics suggested that terminological vagueness and imprecision sustained the suspicion that the putative political functions were arbitrary rather than 'vital' or indispensable (Landau 1968; Gregor 1968; Stephens 1969).

In contrast to the promise of scientific certainty that accompanied the deployment of the functionalist conception of politics, critics also pointed out that the model generated no testable hypotheses, much less identified 'scientific laws' of political life. In marked contrast to the optimistic claims advanced by its proponents, critics argued that the chief virtue of the functionalist conception was heuristic: it provided an elaborate system of classification that allowed divergent political systems to be described in the same terms of reference. A common vocabulary of analysis enabled comparison of similarities and differences cross-culturally (Dowse 1966; Gregor 1968).

Additional limitations were noted by critics of the functionalist conception of politics. The model's emphasis upon system maintenance and persistence rendered it singularly incapable of charting political change. While traditional modes of political analysis classified revolutions and *coups d'état* as fundamental mechanisms of political transformation, functionalist analyses could depict such events as adaptive strategies by which the 'system' persists. Thus the systems approach blurred important issues pertaining to the character of political regimes and the significant dimensions of regime change (Groth 1970; Rothman 1971).

If functionalist analyses tended to mask political change at one level, at another level they tended to impose an inordinate uniformity upon the scope of political development. Within the functionalist literature, the pattern of development characteristic of a few Western liberal democracies such as the United States and Great Britain was taken as paradigmatic of all political development. Succumbing to a form of 'inputism', political scientists proclaimed that certain modes of economic development rendered certain political developments inevitable. The dissemination of capitalist markets would produce strains upon traditional societies, resulting in increasing demands for political participation, which would eventually culminate in the achievement of liberal democracy. Despite the clear ideological content of this projection and despite critics' cogent repudiation of the scientific pretensions of functionalism, this model of development has been repeatedly hailed by political scientists as a matter of indisputable, empirical fact. What is important to note here is not merely that political scientists operating within this tradition have mistaken the political choices of particular political communities for the universal political destiny of the species or that their beliefs about the value-neutrality of their scientific endeavour have blinded them to the hegemonic aspects of their projections, but also that political scientists have used their leverage as 'experts' to advise developing nations to adopt strategies that produce the world prophesied by political science. However flawed their foundation, scientific assertions have been used to dictate 'rational strategies' for political development, which foreclose options and drastically curtail the freedom of citizens in developing countries.

Where Aristotle advanced a conception of political knowledge that preserved the distinction between the free choices of political agents in particular nations and the truth possessed by political theorists, under the guise of value-free empirical inquiry, contemporary political scientists have used scientifically accredited 'facts' to supplant political choice. Under the rubric of realism, they have recommended action to enhance the stability of regimes by minimizing 'dysfunctional' and 'destabilizing' forces such as citizen participation. Under the precept of scientific prediction, they have promoted capitalist market relations as the substance of an inevitable political development. Although implementation of such policy advice is typically justified as another example of knowledge hastening progress, there are good reasons to challenge such optimism. When the liberation–subversion dynamic surfaces in relation to knowledge accredited by contemporary political science, there is at least as great a likelihood that scientific knowledge will subvert freedom as that it will contribute to undisputed 'progress'.

Behaviourism in political science was committed to the belief that definitions are and must be value-free, that concepts could be operationalized in a thoroughly non-prescriptive manner and that research methodologies are neutral techniques for the collection and organization of data. Behaviourism conceived the political scientist as a passive observer who merely described and explained what exists in the political world. Post-behaviourism challenged the myth of value-neutrality, suggesting that all research is theoretically constituted and value permeated. But, in illuminating the means by which the conviction of value-free research masked the valuative component of political inquiry, post-behaviourism did not question the fundamental separation between events in the political world and their retrospective analysis by political scientists. In recent years, critical theorists and post-modernists have suggested that this notion of critical distance is yet another myth. Emphasizing that every scientific discourse is productive, generating positive effects within its investigative domain, post-modernists caution that political science must also be understood as a productive force which creates a world in its own image, even as it employs conceptions of passivity, neutrality, detachment and objectivity to disguise and conceal its role (Foucault 1973, 1979). Even a cursory examination of the four allegedly value-neutral definitions of politics that have dominated twentieth-century political science suggests that there are good reasons to treat the post-modernists' cautions seriously. For each definition not only construes the political world differently, but also acts subtly to promote specific modes of political life.

IMPLICATIONS: THE STRUCTURE OF THE ENCYCLOPEDIA

If post-empiricist conceptions of knowledge and science, as well as post-modernist cautions concerning the productive effects of disciplinary practices are to be taken seriously, then an encyclopedia produced in the late twentieth century must differ in important respects from its predecessors. The attempt to provide an overview of the main topics investigated within the subfields of the discipline must be matched by a strategy that allows questions concerning the constitutive components of political research to surface. Rather than succumb to myths of value-neutrality, the volume must attempt to illuminate the substantive implications of diverse methodologies. Rather than accredit the notion of an unproblematic scientific objectivity, efforts must be made to explicate and assess the standards that inform disciplinary judgements.

Toward these ends, this encyclopedia has recruited contributors committed to a wide range of methodological approaches. Each author has been asked to provide a concise critical analysis, rather than a descriptive capsule sketch, of the topic under investigation. In particular, authors have been asked to address methodological as well as substantive issues pertaining to the subject, engaging relevant debates concerning the strengths and weaknesses of alternative research strategies and differentiating fruitful from flawed approaches.

This encyclopedia is organized by subfield. Rather than seeking methodological uniformity within each subfield, efforts have been made to recruit scholars who adopt contending approaches to related topics in the hope that the juxtaposition of competing accounts will help illuminate the theoretical presuppositions and the political implications of alternative modes of inquiry. The inclusion of alternative approaches is thus designed to enrich the portrayal of political life, to heighten understanding of the limitations of particular approaches and to increase the analytical sophistication of readers.

Structuring this encyclopedia along these lines involves a number of dangers. In attempting to provide a systematic account of the state of political studies that includes political theory, contemporary ideologies, comparative political institutions, processes and behaviour, political cleavages within the nation-state, theories of policy making, comparative examination of a range of substantive policy areas, as well as international relations and major issues confronting the contemporary world, the encyclopedia faces the formidable danger that it will fail to provide a comprehensive and comprehensible account of such a broad array of topics. In adopting a strategy that challenges the empiricist foundation that sustains the bulk of research in contemporary political science, the volume confronts the possibility of dismissal concomitant to any effort to challenge established traditions and entrenched power, for the behaviourists who continue to dominate the discipline of political science may choose to ignore rather than engage sustained critique. Moreover, in advancing a conception of political science that supplants claims to transcendent truth with recognition of the far more fallible foundations of human cognition, the project risks rejection by those who prefer a more heroic, albeit fictive, depiction of the discipline's authority. Such risks are as unavoidable as they are rife.

The production of this encyclopedia, however, also affords a number of opportunities. It provides an occasion for a systematic stocktaking – for a review of the substantive research findings generated within the discipline, for a reassessment of the role of diverse analytical techniques in shaping those substantive claims, and, more generally, for an examination of the theoretical underpinnings of political inquiry. It invites a re-evaluation of the relations between knowledge and power within disciplinary discourses. It encourages renewed investigation of the extent to which solutions to the problems confronting contemporary politics are constrained by outmoded and unwarranted disciplinary assumptions. In so doing, the encyclopedia will stimulate creative thinking about the world captured in the discourses of political science. The extent to which the encyclopedia contributes to this end will be the ultimate measure of its utility.

REFERENCES

Almond, G. and Coleman, J. (eds) (1960) *The Politics of Developing Areas*, Princeton: Princeton University Press.

Aristotle (1958) *The Politics*, trans. and ed. E. Barker, London: Oxford University Press.

Ayer, A. J. (ed.) (1959) *Logical Positivism*, New York: Free Press.

Bellah, R., Madsen, R., Sullivan, W., Swidler, A. and Tipton, S. (1985) *Habits of the Heart: Individualism and Commitments in American Life*, New York: Harper & Row.

Bernstein, R. (1978) *The Restructuring of Social and Political Theory*, Philadelphia: University of Pennsylvania Press.

——(1983) *Beyond Objectivism and Relativism*, Philadelphia: University of Pennsylvania Press.

Brown, H. (1977) *Perception, Theory and Commitment: The New Philosophy of Science*, Chicago: Precedent Publishing Company.

Catlin, G. (1964) *The Science and Method of Politics*, New York: Archon Press.

Connolly, W. E. (1981) *Appearance and Reality in Politics*, Cambridge: Cambridge University Press.

Cook, T. (1985) 'Postpositivist critical multiplism', in R. Shotland and M . Marks (eds) *Social Science and Social Policy*, Beverly Hills: Sage Publications.

Crick, B. (1962) *In Defence of Politics*, London: Weidenfeld & Nicolson.

Dallmayr, F. (1981) *Beyond Dogma and Despair*, Notre Dame: University of Notre Dame Press.

Diderot, D. *et al.* (1751–65) *Encyclopédie, ou dictionaire raissoné des sciences, des arts et des métiers, par une société de gens de lettres*, 17 vols, Paris: Le Breton, Briasson, David & Durand.

Dowse, R. (1966) 'A functionalist's logic', *World Politics* (July): 607–22.

Easton, D. (1971) *The Political System: An Inquiry into the State of Political Science*, 2nd edn, New York: Knopf.

Encyclopédie méthodique ou bibliothèque universelle de toutes les connaissances humaines, Paris: Panckoucke, 1782–94; Agasse, 1794–1820.

Eulau, H. (1963) *The Behavioral Persuasion in Politics*, New York: Random House.

Eulau, H. and March J. (eds) (1969) *Political Science*, Englewood Cliffs, NJ: Prentice-Hall.

Finifter, A. W. (ed) (1983) *Political Science: The State of the Discipline*, Washington, DC: American Political Science Association.

Foucault, M. (1973) *The Order of Things: An Archaeology of the Human Sciences*, New York: Vintage Books.

——(1979) *Discipline and Punish: The Birth of the Prison*, New York: Vintage Books.

Goodnow, F. (1904) 'The work of the American Political Science Association', *Proceedings of the American Political Science Association* 1: 37.

Greenstein, F. and Polsby, N. (eds) (1975) *Handbook of Political Science*, vols I–VII, Reading, Mass: Addison-Wesley.

Gregor, A. J. (1968) 'Political science and the use of functionalist analysis', *American Political Science Review* (June): 425–39.

Groth, A. J. (1970) 'Structural functionalism and political development: three problems', *Western Political Quarterly* (September): 485–99.

Gunnell, J. (1986) *Between Philosophy and Politics*, Amherst: University of Massachusetts Press.

Harding, S. (1986) *The Science Question in Feminism*, Ithaca: Cornell University Press.

Hawkesworth, M. E. (1988) *Theoretical Issues in Policy Analysis*, Albany, NY: SUNY Press.

Hesse, M. (1980) *Revolutions and Reconstructions in the Philosophy of Science*, Brighton: Harvester Press.

Hudson, W. D. (1970) *Modern Moral Philosophy*, New York: Anchor Books.

Hume, D. (1739) *A Treatise of Human Nature*, ed. L. A. Selby-Bigge, Oxford: Clarendon Press.

——(1748) *An Enquiry Concerning Human Understanding*, e.d. L. A. Selby-Bigge, Oxford: Clarendon Press.

Humphreys, W. (ed.) (1969) *Perception and Discovery*, San Francisco: Freeman, Cooper.

Hyneman, C. (1959) *The Study of Politics*, Urbana: University of Illinois Press.

Joergenson, J. (1951) *The Development of Logical Empiricism*, vol. II, no. 9 of the *International Encyclopedia of Unified Science*, Chicago: University of Chicago Press.

Kaplan, A. (1964) *The Conduct of Inquiry: Methodology for Behavioral Science*, San Francisco: Chandler Publishing.

Kraft, V. (1952) *The Vienna Circle*, New York: Philosophical Library.

Landau, M. (1968) 'On the use of functional analysis in American political science', *Social Research* (Spring): 44–75.

Lasswell, H. (1950) *Politics: Who Gets What, When, How*, New York: P. Smith.

Lindblom, C. (1965) *The Intelligence of Democracy: Decision-Making Through Mutual Adjustment*, New York: Free Press.

Lindblom, C. and Cohen, D. (1979) *Usable Knowledge: Social Science and Social Problem Solving*, New Haven: Yale University Press.

Longino, H. (1990) *Science As Social Knowledge: Values and Objectivity in Scientific Inquiry*, Princeton: Princeton University Press.

Lough, J. (1968) *Essays on the Encyclopedie of Diderot and D'Alembert*, London.

MacIntyre, A. (1981) *After Virtue*, Notre Dame: University of Notre Dame Press.

MacRae, D. (1976) *The Social Function of Social Science*, New Haven: Yale University Press.

Meehan, E. (1965) *The Theory and Method of Political Analysis*, Homewood, Ill.: Dorsey Press.

Miller, E. (1979) 'Metaphor and political knowledge', *American Political Science Review* 73 (1): 155–70.

Mitchell, W. C. (1958) 'The polity and society: a structural functional analysis', *Midwest Journal of Political Science* 2: 403–40.

——(1967) *Sociological Analysis and Politics*, Englewood Cliffs, NJ: Prentice-Hall.

Moon, D. (1975) 'The logic of political inquiry: a synthesis of opposed perspectives', in F. Greenstein and N. Polsby (eds) *Handbook of Political Science*, vol. I, Reading, Mass.: Addison-Wesley.

Moore, G. E. (1903) *Principia Ethica*, London: Cambridge University Press.

Morgenthau, H. (1967) *Politics Among Nations: The Struggle for Power and Peace*, New York: Knopf.

Mosca, G. (1939) *The Ruling Class*, New York: McGraw-Hill.

Murray, T. (1983) 'Partial knowledge', in D. Callahan and B. Jennings (eds) *Ethics, The Social Sciences and Policy Analysis*, New York: Plenum Press.

Polanyi, M. (1958) *Personal Knowledge*, Chicago: University of Chicago Press.

Popper, K. (1959) *The Logic of Scientific Discovery*, New York: Basic Books.

——(1972a) *Conjectures and Refutations: The Growth of Scientific Knowledge*, 4th edn rev., London: Routledge & Kegan Paul.

——(1972b) *Objective Knowledge: An Evolutionary Approach*, Oxford: Clarendon Press.

Ricci, D. (1984) *The Tragedy of Political Science: Politics, Scholarship and Democracy*, New Haven: Yale University Press.

Rothman, S. (1971) 'Functionalism and its critics: an analysis of the writings of Gabriel Almond', *Political Science Reviewer* (Fall): 236–76.

Seidelman, R. and Harpham, E. (1985) *Disenchanted Realists: Political Science and the American Crisis, 1884–1984*, Albany, NY: SUNY Press.

Sellars, W. (1963) *Science, Perception and Reality*, New York: Humanities Press.

Stephens, J. (1969) 'The logic of functional and systems analyses in political science', *Midwest Journal of Political Science* (August): 367–94.

Stockman, N. (1983) *Anti-Positivist Theories of Science: Critical Rationalism, Critical Theory and Scientific Realism*, Dordrecht: D. Reidel.

Storing, H. J. (ed.) (1962) *Essays on the Scientific Study of Politics*, New York: Holt, Rinehart & Winston.

Suppe, F. (ed.) (1977) *The Structure of Scientific Theories*, 2nd edn, Urbana: University of Illinois Press.

Tanenhaus, J. and Somit, A. (1967) *The Development of Political Science: From Burgess to Behavioralism*, Boston: Allyn & Bacon.

Vivas, E. (1960) 'Science and the studies of man', in H. Schoek and J. Wiggans (eds) *Scientism and Values*, Princeton: D. van Nostrand Company.

Wade, I. (1977) *The Structure and Form of the French Enlightenment*, 2 vols, Princeton: Princeton University Press.

Warwick, D. (1980) *The Teaching of Ethics in the Social Sciences*, Hastings-on-Hudson, NY: Institute of Society, Ethics and the Life Sciences.

Welsh, W. (1973) *Studying Politics*, New York: Praeger.

Wildavsky, A. (1979) *Speaking Truth to Power*, Boston: Little, Brown & Co.

Williams, B. (1985) *Ethics and the Limits of Philosophy*, Cambridge, Mass.: Harvard University Press.

Wolin, S. (1981) 'Max Weber: legitimation, method and the politics of theory', *Political Theory* 9 (3): 401–24.

PART II

POLITICAL THEORY: CENTRAL CONCEPTS

2

CONCEPTIONS OF THE STATE

ANDREW VINCENT

The state is one of the most difficult concepts in politics. For some scholars the discipline of politics is wholly concerned with the state; for others politics exists in social contexts outside the sphere of the state. One of the most intractable problems in such debates is that there is little agreement on what is being studied. Is the state a body of governing institutions; a structure of legal rules; a subspecies of society; or a body of values and beliefs about civil existence? These and many other questions plague the study of the state. We will first look at the origin of the word; then at the state's problematic relation to other political concepts; the contending views of its history; finally, the variety of theoretical approaches to it.

The word state derives from the Latin *stare* (to stand) and *status* (a standing or condition). Roman writers, such as Cicero and Ulpian, as well as later medieval lawyers, used such terms as *status civitatis* or *status regni*. This use of *status* referred to the condition of the ruler, the fact of possessing stability, or the elements necessary for stability. Standing or status was usually acquired through family, sex, profession and most importantly property. This is where we also find the subtle linkage with the word 'estate'. The English word 'state' is, in fact, a contraction of the word 'estate'. This is similar to the old French word *estat* and modern French *état*, both of which imply a profession or social status. Groups had different status and thus estate. The term 'estates of the realm' is derived from this. Parallels can be found in other European languages, as in the Spanish *estado*. The highest estate, with property, rank and family, was usually the ruling group or person. The highest estate had potentially the greatest authority and power. Such authority was often seen as the guarantee of order and public welfare. It was thus linked to stability, which derived from the same root term. Those in authority – the highest estate – had insignia, crests and so forth showing their stateliness.

Some argue that we find an awareness of the state in the above usage in the twelfth century or even before (Post 1964; Mitteis 1975). A popular line of interpretation stresses a later, more definite noun usage in which the state is understood as a public power above both ruler and ruled, which constitutes the locus of political and legal authority. It is not simply a matter of standing, stability or stateliness, although this terminology is carried over into the more modern usage, but a definite new form of continuous public power which constitutes a new type of civil existence.

There are two basic positions taken on this latter noun usage of state. Both identify the origin of the state in the sixteenth century; whereas one sees Machiavelli as the prime mover (Cassirer 1946; Meinecke 1957), the other identifies heirs of Italian humanism in France such as Guillaume Budé, Bernard du Haillan and Jean Bodin, as the real formulators of the modern idea (Hexter 1973; Church 1972; Skinner 1978; Dyson 1980).

There appear to be a number of formal characteristics intrinsic to the state. It has a geographically identifiable territory with a body of citizens. It claims authority over all citizens and groups within its boundaries and embodies more comprehensive aims than other associations. The authority of the state is legal in character and is usually seen as the source of law. It is based on procedural rules which have more general recognition in society than other rules. The procedures of states are operated by trained bureaucracies of office holders. The state also embodies the maximal control of resources and force within a territory. Its monopoly is not simply premised on force: most states try to claim legitimacy for such a monopoly, namely, they seek some recognition and acceptance from the population. In consequence, to be a member of a state implies a civil disposition. Further, the state is seen as sovereign, both in an internal sense within its territory, and in an external sense, namely, the state is recognized by other states as an equal member of international society. It should be noted, however, that the idea of the state changes with different senses of sovereignty. Finally, the state is a continuous public power distinct from rulers and ruled.

The state stands in a complex relation to a number of political concepts such as society, community, sovereignty and government. Many of these concepts have senses which coincide with particular views of the state. The state can, for example, be said to create all associations within itself. In this sense nothing is distinct from the state. Society becomes an aspect of the state. On the other hand, if sovereignty is regarded as popular, residing in the people who create the state for limited ends, then the position is reversed and society can be viewed as prior and independent of the state. Similarly, the state can be seen as synonymous with government (many contemporary pluralist writers appear to adopt this view) or separate from government and giving authority to it. These issues present the student of politics with fundamental and intractable problems of interpretation.

Essentially there are three general perspectives on the history of the state.

The first argues that the state dates back to the early Greek *polis* (city-state) of around 500 BC. For Aristotle, political science was the study of the *polis*. There were unquestionably conceptions of territory, citizenship, authority, law and so on entailed in the *polis*; however, there was no conception of separate powers of government, no conception of a separate civil society and no very precise idea of a legal constitution. Furthermore, the life of the *polis* was deeply integrated in religious, artistic, and ethical practices. It was also on such a small scale, compared to modern states, that, overall, it is stretching the imagination to call it a state in any contemporary sense. Empires were also too loose and fragmented structures to call states.

The second perspective dates the state from the early Middle Ages. Roman and canon law had established ideas of transcendent public welfare. Public power and law were associated with the office of the monarch, initially identi-fied with Papal sovereignty. There were also concepts of citizenship and the rule of law in medieval political thought. The problems with this view are, first, etymological – can one argue seriously about a term where it does not exist? The word state does not appear in political parlance until approximately the sixteenth century. Second, the feudal structure of the Middle Ages tended to have a fragmenting effect. Feudal life was made up of a massive subsystem of associations. Many of the larger associations, the nobility, church and guilds, had their own laws and courts. Monarchy was not in a pre-eminently sovereign position. It was often regarded as an elective office and not necessarily heredi-tary. The monarchs also relied heavily on the support of the nobility and other estates to help them rule. Medieval society was criss-crossed with overlapping associations and conflicting loyalties. Monarchs were reliant on the community of the realm and consequently were often regarded as subject to the law, not as its source. Finally, it is difficult to identify clearly defined territorial units with consistently loyal populations in the Middle Ages. The only loyalty that transcended local groups attachments was the Church. All were members of the *respublica christiana*. It was crucial for this vision to break down before the idea of independent political units could grow.

The third perspective dates the emergence of the state from the late Middle Ages and more specifically from the sixteenth century. This view finds support from the etymology. It is a view shared by a number of more recent authorities (as argued above on the origin of the word). However, there is some debate as to which theorists introduced the idea (Machiavelli or Bodin), and when and where the practice of the modern state began. The contending authorities, as discussed earlier (p. 44), focus their attention, respectively, on Renaissance Italy and France under the early absolutist monarchs.

Having examined the main outline of its historical origin we will now turn to the variety of academic approaches to the study of the state and their respective merits. Essentially there are five approaches and these often overlap, necessarily at times. The five are:

1 juristic or legal;
2 historical;
3 sociological/anthropological;
4 political-scientific;
5 philosophical/normative.

The legal approach has the oldest pedigree. It dates back to the use of Roman law vocabulary in the earliest descriptions of the state. Words like power, authority and legitimacy, when used in relation to the state from the sixteenth century, had deep roots in Roman law. The early critiques of feudal rule, initially by Papal lawyers, derived from Roman law sources. These formed the background for notions of authority and law focused on centralized rule. However, the temptation to characterize the state as a hierarchical body of legal rules, linked by some sovereign authority, can be found in many theorists this century (for example, Hans Kelsen 1945). In fact, the intellectual tradition of legal positivism shows a marked preference for this interpretation. Others find this approach too limiting. They contend that there are many more factors that enter into the definition and character of the state than simply a hierarchy of legal rules.

Many historians have written detailed studies of the growth of the state (for example, Strayer 1970; Shennan 1974; Anderson 1974). Some lay more emphasis on the factors which are connected to the rise of the state, as in the growth of Renaissance city states, the Reformation, the breakup of the Holy Roman Empire, the growth of centralized salaried bureaucracies, standing armies, centralized taxation, or dynastic and religious wars. Others lay more emphasis on the history of certain ideas accompanying the events in state growth (Skinner 1978). For the pure historian the practice of the state is much more messy and pragmatic than legal or philosophical theories would lead us to believe. Theory alone is too simple and abbreviated to catch all the diverse interests and pressures which accompanied state growth. The weakness of this historical approach is that the state is not just an empirical entity which can be grasped by examining historical events. Statehood involves, from its earliest manifestations in the European political vocabulary, ideas and theories of civil existence. To neglect such a dimension of the state impoverishes our understanding.

Sociologists and anthropologists have tended to view the state as a way of organizing society, one that is found in certain more developed economies. In other words, 'state societies' are a subspecies of the genus of society (see Lowie 1927; Krader 1968). Another way of putting this is that the state is a subspecies of government. State organization is one form in which humans have organized their social existence. Writers such as Marx, Durkheim, Duguit, Weber and MacIver largely viewed the state in this manner. The state was explained through the broader study of society.

One of the difficulties in summarizing this sociological approach is that it encompasses such a diverse range of views, whether it be Durkheim's positivism, Marxist political economy or Talcott Parsons's functionalism (Poggi 1978; Badie and Birnbaum 1983). On a very general level this approach stresses the economic and social preconditions of states; the types of states and what causes them to appear; and the factors giving rise to the responsiveness and durability of states. Talcott Parsons, for example, saw the state as a unique product of the division of labour in advanced industrial societies (Parsons 1967). Specialized organizations developed in relation to this division of labour and became centred on the state. The state thus implied a level of industrialization. It could therefore be described as a collection of specialized agencies associated with the division of labour in advanced industrialized societies. Its function is to mediate and reduce conflict and tension between the different sectors of society. States come into being when they possess enough resources to be able to dominate the peripheries and reconcile tensions (see Nettl 1968).

Political science has in this century been more inclined to stress the empirical approach, relying on low-level generalizations within explanatory frameworks. The demand of an empirical theory is that it can be rigorously tested. It tends to integrate ideas developed within the disciplines of political sociology, political economy and psychology. It reflects, to some degree, a growing commitment to scientism, specifically with the 1950s behavioural revolution in the work of figures like David Easton (see Easton 1965). Empirical theory was seen as the key to the future advancement of the subject. In comparative politics functionalism and neo-functionalism were imported from sociology. Developmental and modernization theory emerged from the functionalist form of analysis. The state is seen to be a specialized agency which comes about to perform certain functions at an advanced stage of modernization. The history of the state is one of changing economic and social practices which can be measured statistically. Much of the early literature on comparative politics developed along these lines (see Tilly 1975).

Contemporary political science employs a variety of theories to explain the state. The most well known have been: pluralism and neo-pluralism; elite theory; corporatism and neo-corporatism; various forms of Marxism; and forms of political economy, particularly public choice theory. For political scientists, such theories can provide empirical testable insights into the state (Dunleavy and O'Leary 1987).

Empirical pluralist and neo-pluralists view society as constituted by groups and the state as virtually synonymous with government, which is a target or location for pressure or interest group activity. Power is about resources that

47

groups can command in the competitive market. For some, government reflects the dominant coalition on a particular policy (Latham 1965). Other pluralists see government as an impartial umpire or neutral arbiter; this is reflected in Dahl's account of polyarchy (Dahl 1971). Most pluralists incorporate a theory of democracy, viewed as a form of interest articulation and market competition, into their view of the state. Such a notion of democracy is seen as more realistic than the older classical participatory notions of democracy. For pluralists such as Dahl and Schumpeter, democracy is concerned with the competition between groups and the selection of leaders (Schumpeter 1943). The successful group(s), from the electoral process, formulate policy through government functionaries.

If pluralism is society-centred, another approach which has developed during the 1980s contrasts itself to the above in being state-centred (see Nordlinger 1981; Evans *et al.* 1985). The state is seen to be both an important complex actor and relatively autonomous from societal interests. The institutional order and legal structures of the state are taken seriously. State officials and processes are considered independently from societal preferences and choices. In fact, the state is seen as one of the factors which moulds individual choices. Some see this as part of a slow process of bringing the state back into political science. Within political science, however, many would contend that this state-centred approach is in danger of becoming *too* state-centric. The state always acts in some societal interest. From a more traditional normative perspective, it would be argued that the state-centred approach still does not offer a proper account of what the state is or take seriously enough the logic of state autonomy.

Early elite theorists, such as Mosca, Pareto and Michels, argued that all societies are dominated by small minorities, a thesis most cogently encapsulated in Michels' 'iron law of oligarchy' (Michels 1959). Regardless of the type of regime, they asserted the continuity of elites in politics, maintaining that this was an empirical, scientifically verifiable fact. This contrasted sharply with the more traditional pluralist vision of government. More recent elite theories have been dominated by the attempt to integrate elitism and pluralism, giving rise to the term 'democratic elitism' (Bachrach 1967). Elite theory still focuses on the role of elite domination in the state. The empirical studies of elite theorists concentrate on the small groups that influence and structure policy, examining the social background, recruitment and attitudes of such groups. States can thus be categorized according to the nature, unity, and diversity of elites.

Corporatist theories are, at the present moment, in considerable flux. Some corporatists use the term state as a synonym for government; for others it represents the fusion of certain important interests into the structure of government (Schmitter 1974). In this sense corporatism is differentiated from pluralism by the more limited number of groups competing, the nature of the groups and their status in relation to government. In Cawson's classification there are three main forms of corporatism in contemporary political science: (1) a totally new form of economy, different from capitalism and socialism; (2) a form of state within the capitalist society; and (3) a way in which interests are organized and interact with the state (Cawson 1986: 22).

In Marxism the state is related historically to certain class interests, the defence of private property and capital accumulation. The state has developed apace with capitalist economies. Two views, however, have tended to dominate Marxist thinking on the state to the present day. The first sees the state as an oppressive or coercive instrument of the dominant bourgeoisie, holding capitalism in place. This class state will either be crushed or wither away after revolution and be replaced either by the dictatorship of the proletariat or by communism. The second view (most dynamically influenced by the writings of the Italian Marxist Gramsci) is that the state is seen to have relative autonomy from the economic base and acts as a site of conflict between competing class interests. Also, in this second account, state dominance is exerted subtly through ideological hegemony (Miliband 1973; Jessop 1983; Carnoy 1984).

Finally, the economistic approach to the state embeds it ultimately in individual choice. It is rooted in methodological individualism. The state emerges from the logic of self-interested individual choice, a clear example being public choice theory (Buchanan 1975). Collective action, in terms of minimal objectives such as law, order and defence, helps an individual to minimize costs and maximize benefits. It is therefore in the interests of rational self-interested individuals to create a state to achieve these ends (Buchanan and Tullock 1962).

A similar argument can be found, in a different intellectual format, in the libertarian writings of Robert Nozick (1974) and Anthony de Jasay (1985). However, such a theory cannot allow too active and interventionary a state, since it would confer more costs than benefits on individuals. It needs, therefore, constitutional restraints premised on individual choice. Much of the economistic approach to the state tends to be explored by varieties of pro-market liberal and libertarian theory, although many would still claim the roots of their economic arguments in positivistic empirical analysis.

There are two basic weaknesses with such political science approaches. First, they do not deal with normative questions about the state. They explain and describe states, yet do not answer such questions as: 'What is the state or what ought it to be?' Second, all the above approaches are handicapped by the fact that much of the practice of the state is linked intricately with normative values and conceptions of human nature. The scientific and positivistic imperatives of political science implicitly eschew values and demand empirical rigour – which in politics (for some) is a chimera. Further, there are a range of suppressed normative assumptions in the varying 'rigorous' theories which are not articulated. The larger claims of empiricism in political science are questionable as regards a complete understanding of the state.

The final philosophical/normative conception of the state, together with the legal approach, constitutes the main element of classical political theory, specifically from the sixteenth century. Classical theory has an avowed normative task and has been concerned with reflection on issues such as human nature, morality, the family and forms of constitution. There are two preeminent tasks of classical political theory with regard to the state that have continuing relevance: the first is to reflect on the right, best or most just order; the second is concerned with the identity and nature of the state, which is intricately bound up with values and ideas of civil existence. The problem with many empirical theories of the state is that they take the identity and nature of the state as unproblematic. Classical political theory has never taken the state for granted. However, classical political theory sometimes loses touch with the historical and political reality of the state and consequently gives false impressions of its character.

We are so used to perceiving the state as a form of government or set of institutions that it is difficult to think of it in relation to a broader framework of normative assumptions and values. For many philosophical theorists, the state is partly constitutive of political reality. The state forms, in other words, the presupposition of civilized and intellectual life, in which politics is discussed. It embodies a sense of the right social order within which citizens are integrated. Individuals have a rational disposition towards the state which cannot be investigated on any purely empirical level.

As with political science, there is a diversity of philosophical/normative theories of the state (Dyson 1980; Vincent 1987). There are also a number of different classifications of normative accounts of the state. It is, for example, feasible to classify via various ideological traditions (for example, the liberal and socialist states). This classification misses the point that such ideological traditions do not conceive the state very differently, though there may be differences in the extent of state action. A further problem is that certain of the more empirical conceptions of the state, such as pluralism and corporatism, have been developed separately as normative theories. Fascist writers in the 1920s tried to develop a distinctive, normative corporate state theory. Such an effort is questionable, as there is no highly distinctive normative account of the state present in corporatism. There is a stronger case to be made for a normative account of a pluralist state. Marxists also have developed tentative normative theories of the state, although they have always been handicapped by the negative critiques of the state rooted in the premises of Marxist political economy. The present classification of normative theories will be:

1 absolutist;

2 constitutional;

3 ethical;

4 pluralist.

The first important landmark in normative theory was the attempt to see the state as embodied in the absolute sovereign person. This is an idea developed in the works of Bodin, Hobbes and Boussuet and in the attempted practice of monarchs like Louis XIV. It can be found from early in the sixteenth century onwards, particularly in France. At its height, the sovereign person was seen to be legitimated by divine right and owning the kingdom (Rowen 1980). The sovereign's interests were the state's interests. The embodiment of the state in the sovereign illustrates the continuing importance of sovereignty in the history of the state. The impersonal state of the twentieth century finds its root in the personal state of the sixteenth century. The weakness of the absolutist theory was that it was too focused on the monarch. It was in practice an absurdity. It is also doubtful that it ever existed fully in practice. Limitations on royal power existed throughout the absolutist era. It was also often dependent on the character of the monarch and the economic and political circumstances of the kingdom. However, it provided a lasting vocabulary for the discussion of the state.

The constitutional theory encapsulates the longest, most influential, and yet most tangled state idea. Essentially this theory identifies the state with a complex of institutional structures and values which, through historical, legal, moral and philosophical claims, embodies limitation and diversification of authority and a complex hierarchy of rules and norms, which act to institutionalize power and regulate the relations between citizens, laws and political institutions. The deep roots of this theory lie in Roman law and the ideas and practices of medieval Europe. The limitations of the constitutional theory are not imposed on the state but are constitutive of a particular theory of the state. The priority of certain rules within the constitutional theory is premised on their seriousness. All limitation is self-limitation in terms of statehood. By the nineteenth century, constitutionalism had become most closely associated with liberalism and liberal democracy, although its origins are occasionally dated back to theorists like John Locke. Other ideologies, such as conservatism and parliamentary socialism, have also found a comfortable home within the constitutional theory. The forms of limitations employed within constitutional theories have varied enormously, ranging across legal and historical themes such as the ancient constitution doctrine, fundamental and common law, the rule of law doctrine, conventions, written documents, bills of rights; institutional devices such as the mixed and balanced constitution, the doctrine of checks and balances, the separation of powers, or federalism; complex political and moral devices such as representative democracy, the separation between state and society, contractualism, natural and human rights doctrines, consent theories and so forth. It would be no exaggeration to say that the agenda of most contemporary political theory now is rooted in the constitutional state framework.

The weakness of the constitutional theory is its success. Everyone is or wants to be a constitutionalist. This has led paradoxically to its trivialization. Constitutionalism can become a series of formal procedural devices without normative significance. First, political scientists have devoted their energy, through such devices as elite or pluralist theory, to tell us what is really going on in such states. This has only promoted cynicism. Second, there has been considerable internal conflict within liberal democratic constitutionalism on the reach of government. Some, for example, have been keen to limit the role of the state in the sphere of the economy, others to deny such limitations and to argue for a strong developmental role for the state. This latter argument has given rise to a debate between minimal state and developmental state theories (Marquand 1988).

A third powerful normative theory has roots in the more total life of the Greek *polis*. It developed in the context of the German idealist tradition against the crucial backdrop of the French revolution (Hegel 1967). The ethical state is seen to be the result of a long historical development from the Greeks. It is not an accidental phenomenon, but rather develops out of the inner nature of humans as rational creatures. The state and citizens are seen to have a common rational substance. The state is the *modus operandi* of citizens and institutions. It is still rooted in the notion of constitutionalism, but with the crucial difference that it is directed at the maximal ethical self-development and positive freedom of its citizens. It is thus the unity of a cognitive disposition with the purposes of institutional structures and rules. The state embodies the rational customs and laws which rule individual behaviour. The state is thus neither simply a system of laws and constitutional order nor a body of particular institutions; rather, it represents a rational ethical order implicit in the consciousness of individual citizens. The weaknesses of this theory are its apparent archaism and inappropriateness to the contemporary world. The idea of an ethical state (with an overarching ethical code or general will) strikes most students of politics as suspect and worryingly autocratic, at least in potential. However it has undeniably had some role to play in reassessments of the state at the beginning of this century (Vincent and Plant 1984).

The normative pluralist theory perceived the state, in the broadest sense, to be a synthesis of living semi-independent groups (see Gierke 1934; Maitland 1911; Figgis 1914; Hsiao 1927; Nicholls 1975). Groups are integrated not absorbed. Narrowly focused, pluralism centres on the government (as in political science pluralism). The state is the summation of group life. It represents all groups in totality. In representing the whole it is distinct from all other groups. The state, as the representation of the total system of groups, prevents injustices being committed by individuals or groups, secures basic rights and regulates group behaviour. The pluralist state is not sovereign, partly because it is constituted by groups whose independence is recognized within the idea of the state. Groups possess real legal personality and only plural group life can defend liberty. The weakness of such a theory of the state is that pluralists never precisely resolve the relation of the government to groups – namely – which has dominance? There was also a certain naïvety about the groups themselves. Groups can often be oppressive and restrictive on liberty. Also, how can any consensus really be formed in such a society when it is peopled by such diverse interests? Normative pluralists fail to answer these questions satisfactorily.

The manner in which we study the state can vary enormously. A balanced picture can only be acquired if we remember that it is not just a historical and sociological phenomenon but also a tissue of values and normative aspirations about civil existence.

REFERENCES

Anderson, P. (1974) *Lineages of the Absolutist State*, London: New Left Books.

Bachrach, P. (1967) *The Theory of Democratic Elitism*, London: University of London Press.

Badie, B. and Birnbaum, P. (1983) *The Sociology of the State*, Chicago: Chicago University Press.

Buchanan, J. (1975) *The Limits of Liberty: Between Anarchy and Leviathan*, Chicago: Chicago University Press.

Buchanan, J. and Tullock, G. (1962) *The Calculus of Consent*, Ann Arbor: University of Michigan Press.

Carnoy, M. (1984) *The State and Political Theory*, Princeton: Princeton University Press.

Cassirer, E. (1946) *The Myth of the State*, New Haven: Yale University Press.

Cawson, A. (1986) *Corporatism and Political Theory*, Oxford: Basil Blackwell.

Church, W. F. (1972) *Richelieu and Reasons of State*, Princton: Princeton University Press.

Dahl, R. (1971) *Polyarchy: Participation and Opposition*, New Haven: Yale University Press.

Dunleavy, P. and O'Leary, B. (1987) *Theories of the State: The Politics of Liberal Democracy*, London: Macmillan.

Dyson, K. H. F. (1980) *The State Tradition in Western Europe: A Study of an Idea and Institution*, Oxford: Martin Robertson.

Easton, D. (1965) *A Systems Analysis of Political Life*, New York: John Wiley.

Evans, P. B., Rueschmeyer, D. and Skocpol, T. (eds) (1985) *Bringing the State Back In*, Cambridge: Cambridge University Press.

Figgis, J. N. (1914) *Churches in the Modern State*, London: Longmans Green & Co.

Gierke, O. von (1934) *Natural Law and the Theory of Society*, Cambridge: Cambridge University Press.

Hegel, G. W. F. (1967) *The Philosophy of Right*, Oxford: Oxford University Press.

Hexter, J. H. (1973) *The Vision of Politics on the Eve of the Reformation: More, Machiavelli and Seyssel*, London: Allen Lane.

Hsiao, K. C. (1927) *Political Pluralism: A Study in Contemporary Political Theory*, London: Kegan Paul.

Jasay, A. de (1985) *The State*, Oxford: Basil Blackwell.

Jessop, B. (1983) *The Capitalist State*, Oxford: Martin Robertson.

Kelsen, H. (1945) *The General Theory of Law and State*, New York: Russell & Russell.

Krader, L. (1968) *The Formation of the State*, Englewood Cliffs, NJ: Prentice-Hall.

Latham, E. (1965) *The Group Basis to Politics*, New York: Cornell University Press.

Lowie, R. H. (1927) *The Origins of the State*, New York: Harcourt Brace.

Maitland, F. W. (1911) 'Moral and legal personality', Appendix C in D. Nicholls *The Pluralist State*, London: Macmillan.

Marquand, D. (1988) *The Unprincipled Society: New Demands and Old Politics*, London: Jonathan Cape.

Meinecke, F. (1957) *Machiavellianism: The Doctrine of Raison d'État and its Place in Modern History*, London: Routledge & Kegan Paul.

Michels, R. (1959) *Political Parties*, New York: Dover.

Miliband, R. (1973) *The State in Capitalist Society*, London: Quartet Books.

Mitteis, H. (1975) *The State in the Middle Ages: A Comparative Constitutional History of Feudal Europe*, Amsterdam: North Holland.

Nettl, J. P. (1968) 'The state as a conceptual variable', *World Politics* 20: 559–92.

Nicholls, D. (1975) *The Pluralist State*, London: Macmillan.

Nordlinger, E. A. (1981) *On the Autonomy of the Democratic State*, Cambridge, Mass.: Harvard University Press.

Nozick, R. (1974) *Anarchy, State and Utopia*, New York: Basic Books.

Parsons, T. (1967) *Sociological Theory and Modern Society*, New York: Free Press.

Poggi, G. (1978) *The Development of the Modern State*, London: Hutchinson.

Post, G. (1964) *Studies in Medieval Legal Thought: Public Law and the State 1100–1322*, Princeton: Princeton University Press.

Rowen, H. (1980) *The King's State: Proprietary Dynasticism in Early Modern France*, New Jersey: Rutgers University Press.

Schmitter, P. C. (1974) 'Still the century of corporatism?', *Review of Politics* 36: 85–131.

Schumpeter, J. (1943) *Capitalism, Socialism and Democracy*, London: Allen & Unwyn.

Shennan, J. H. (1974) *The Origins of the Modern European State 1450–1725*, London: Hutchinson.

Skinner, Q. (1978) *The Foundations of Modern Political Thought*, vols 1 and 2, Cambridge: Cambridge University Press.

Strayer, J. R. (1970) *On the Medieval Origins of the Modern State*, Princeton: Princeton University Press.

Tilly, C. (ed.) (1975) *The Formation of National States in Western Europe*, Princeton: Princeton University Press.

Vincent, A. W. (1987) *Theories of the State*, Oxford: Basil Blackwell.

Vincent, A. W. and Plant, R. (1984) *Philosophy, Politics and Citizenship*, Oxford: Basil Blackwell.

FURTHER READING

Badie, B. and Birnbaum, P. (1983) *The Sociology of the State*, Chicago: Chicago University Press.

Black, A. (1988) *State, Community and Human Desire*, Hemel Hempstead: Harvester Wheatsheaf.

Bosanquet, B. (1899) *The Philosophical Theory of the State*, London: Macmillan.

Carnoy, M. (1984) *The State and Political Theory*, Princeton: Princeton University Press.

Cheyette, F. L. (1982) 'The invention of the state', in B. K. Lackner and K. R. Philp (eds) *Essays in Medieval Civilization: The Walter Prescott Webb Memorial Lectures*, Austin: University of Texas.

D'Entreves, A. P. (1967) *The Notion of the State*, Oxford: Clarendon Press.

Dyson, K. H. F. (1980) *The State Tradition in Western Europe: A Study of an Idea and Institution*, Oxford: Martin Robertson.

Evans, P. B., Rueschmeyer, D. and Skocpol, T. (eds) (1985) *Bringing the State Back In*, Cambridge: Cambridge University Press.

Jordon, B. (1985) *The State: Authority and Autonomy*, Oxford: Basil Blackwell.

Lubasz, H. (ed.) (1964) *The Development of the Modern State*, New York: Macmillan.

MacIver, R. M. (1926) *The Modern State*, Oxford: Oxford University Press.

McLellan, G., Held, D. and Hall, S. (eds) (1984) *The Idea of the Modern State*, Milton Keynes: Open University Press.

Nicholls, D. (1975) *The Pluralist State*, London: Macmillan.

O'Connor, J. (1973) *The Fiscal Crisis of the State*, New York: St Martin's Press.

Tilley, C. (ed.) (1975) *The Formation of National States in Western Europe*, Princeton: Princeton University Press.

Tivey, L. (ed.) (1981) *The Nation State: The Formation of Modern Politics*, Oxford: Martin Robertson.

Vincent, A. (1987) *Theories of the State*, Oxford: Basil Blackwell.

Weber, M. (1948) 'Politics as a vocation', in H. H. Gerth and C. Wright Mills (eds) *From Max Weber*, London: Routledge & Kegan Paul.

3

CONCEPTIONS OF POWER

JEFFREY ISAAC

The concept of power is at the heart of political enquiry. Indeed, it is probably the central concept of both descriptive and normative analysis. When we talk about elections, group conflicts and state policies, we seek to explain events and processes in the political world by fixing responsibility upon institutions and agents. We are thus talking about power. When we ask about the constitution of the good or just society, we are constrasting present conditions with some projected alternative set of arrangements that might better enable people to conduct their lives. Here too we are talking about power. It would seem impossible to engage in political discourse without raising, whether implicitly or explicitly, questions about the distribution of power in society.

It is at least partly for this reason that social and political theorists have spent so much time arguing about the concept of power – what it means, what it denotes, how it might figure in appropriately scientific analysis or how it might be ill-suited to such analysis, and, finally, why scholars and citizens should care about any of the above. Indeed, it is a striking fact that while most political theorists would agree that power is a focal concept, they would probably agree upon little else. This has led to some awkward situations where theorists speak to each other using the same terms but meaning radically different things. Such problems of translation have never reached a point of incommensurability, and it is probably fair to say that most political theorists operate with some basic core conception of power. The core is the notion, articulated in different ways, that the concept of power refers to the abilities of social agents to affect the world in some way or other.

The word 'power' derives from the Latin *potere*, meaning 'to be able'. It is generally used to designate a property, capacity, or wherewithal to effect things. The concept has clear affinities with the concept of domination. The latter means some sort of mastery or control; derived from the Latin *dominium*, it was originally used to designate the mastery of the patriarch over his household or domain (Tuck 1979: 5–13). While the concept of power has often been interpreted as a synonym for domination, the latter connotes an asymmetry about which the former is agnostic. The concept of power also has close connections with the concept of authority. But the latter has a normative dimension, suggesting a kind of consent or authorization, about which the former is similarly agnostic. The grammars of these concepts, and their inter-relationships, are interesting and important (Pitkin 1972; Morriss 1980), but I will here concentrate upon the core notion of power as capacity to act, a genus of which the concepts of domination and authority can be seen as species.

Such a core, however, is itself quite nebulous, and it certainly admits of many different interpretations. As a consequence, a good deal of substantive inquiry and debate has been muddled by seemingly interminable and often rarified conceptual argument. A cynical commentator would chalk up much of this disagreement to the endless methodological fixations of political theor-ists, who sustain subdisciplines, journals and careers by furthering meta-theoretical argument *ad infinitum* (Shapiro 1989). Such cynicism would not be unwarranted, but I think that there is more to it than this. If it is true that it is impossible to carry out political analysis without implicating the concept of power, it is also true that it is impossible to talk about power without implicating a broader set of philosophical, indeed metaphysical, questions about the nature of human agency, the character of social life and the appropriate way to study them. These broader questions are, as the history of modern social science attests, deeply contentious, and it should thus be of no surprise that this controversy has extended to the concept of power as well.

In an essay such as this it would be impossible to provide a detailed and nuanced account of such controversy. I will thus present its rough outlines. There are, I would suggest, four main models of power in modern political analysis:

1 a voluntarist model rooted in the traditions of social contract theory and methodological individualism;
2 a hermeneutic or communicative model rooted largely in German phenom-enology;
3 a structuralist model rooted in the work of Marx and Durkheim;
4 a post-modernist model, developed in different ways in the writing of Michel Foucault and certain contemporary feminists.

Each of these models offers not only a definition and elaboration of the concept of power, but a conception of humans, social institutions, and methods of analysis as well. Before outlining these models, I should make three things clear. First, I will treat models as no more than rough categories or general 'ideal types'. I in no way intend to suggest a kind of substantive consensus among theorists typical of each model who, despite certain similarities, often share many differences on all sorts of matters. Second, while each of these models is sufficiently distinct and autonomous to be discussed separately, it is not the case, the views of methodological ideologists notwithstanding, that these models are in all respects mutually exclusive. This is, of course, a complicated question, but I will suggest that each model in fact presents some important insights, and that theorists of power should probably think in more synthetic terms than they are accustomed to. Third, what I will discuss below are different models of the concept of power, not different theories of its distribution in particular forms of society. The discussion, in other words, will be largely meta-theoretical. Many political theorists, including participants in conceptual debates about power, have mistakenly believed that there is a one-to-one correspondence between meta-theory and theory, so that, for instance, a subscriber to Robert Dahl's arguments about the behavioural study of power is necessarily a pluralist, and vice versa. As I have argued elsewhere (Isaac 1987), this is not the case.

THE VOLUNTARIST MODEL

In referring to this model as a voluntarist one, I wish to call attention to the fact that from this view power is thought of almost exclusively in terms of the intentions and strategies of its subjects. This view is common to all of the participants in the so-called 'three faces of power' debate, and it is shared by most 'rational choice' theorists as well. Such a view is rooted in the tradition of methodological individualism, for which all claims about social life are reducible to claims about individuals (Bhaskar 1979), and it is therefore no coincidence that it can be traced back to the writing of Thomas Hobbes. Such a view, however, is capable of being extended from individual to collective subjects, so long as these are thought of as unitary aggregations of individual wills, and are treated as strategic actors seeking to maximize some kind of utility or value.

The classic statement of the voluntarist model is Robert Dahl's *International Encyclopedia of the Social Sciences* essay (Dahl 1968). For Dahl power is a capacity to get others to do what they would not otherwise do, to set things in motion and 'change the order of events'. As he writes: 'Power terms in modern social science refer to subsets of relations among social units such that the behavior of one or more units (the response units, R) depend in some circumstances on the behavior of other units (the controlling units, C)' (ibid.: 407.) As Dahl's language of stimulus and response suggests, this notion of power rests upon a Newtonian analogy. We are all naturally at rest or at constant velocity, until our movements are altered by an external force. Power is such a force. For Dahl the concept of power is thus a causal concept. But Dahl, a behaviouralist, insists that his conception of causality is strictly Humean. As he writes elsewhere: 'The only meaning that is strictly causal in the notion of power is one of regular sequence: that is, a regular sequence such that whenever A does something, what follows, or what probably follows, is an action by B' (Dahl 1965: 94).

As I have argued elsewhere (Isaac 1987), this view fails to distinguish between the successful exercise and the possession of power, conceiving of power exclusively in terms of the contingent success of agents in securing their purposes. It is also empiricist in its view of causality and scientific explanation, both of which, for Dahl, are conceived in Humean terms. In this sense, appearances to the contrary, it is a view shared by Dahl's most vocal and well-known critics, Bachrach and Baratz (1970) and Lukes (1974). For all these theorists power is a behavioural relation of actual cause and effect, exhausted in the interaction between parties. While these theorists in different ways allow the importance of collective rules and resources, all also insist that these are to be sharply distinguished from, and have no necessary connection to, power. Lukes, frequently taken to be a 'radical' critic of Dahl, attests to this when he avers that all three faces of power 'can be seen as alternative interpretations and applications of one and the same underlying concept of power' (Lukes 1974: 27). For this concept power is the ability to advance one's interests in conflict with others.

This concept can be traced back to the writings of some of the 'founders' of modern political theory. Thus Thomas Hobbes defines power, in terms of the purposes of individuals, as the 'present means, to obtain some future Good' (Hobbes 1968: 63). Both Hobbes and Locke hold that 'Power and Cause are the same thing', conceiving such causation in mechanistic, Newtonian terms (quoted in Ball 1988: 83). As Locke writes:

> A body at rest affords us no idea of any active power to move; and when it is set in motion itself, that motion is rather a passion than an action in it. For when the ball obeys the motion of the billiard-stick, it is not any action of the ball, but bare passion. Also when by impulse it sets another ball in motion that lay in its way, it only communicates the motion it had received from another, and loses in itself so much as the other received: which gives us [an] idea of an active power of moving.
>
> (Locke 1961: 194–5)

It was David Hume who canonized this view, insisting that 'the idea of power is relative as much as that of cause; and both have reference to an effect, or some other event constantly conjoined with the former' (Hume 1962: 77). In this view power is nothing more than empirical causation. The formulations of Hobbes and Hume are important because they make explicit what is only implicit in many more contemporary formulations: that such a view of power presupposes an atomistic view of social relations, a Humean conception of causality, and an empiricist or 'covering law' model of scientific explanation.

Hume is quite clear that any claims about underlying causes or pre-existing powers are invalid: 'the distinction . . . betwixt power and the exercise of it is . . . without foundation' (quoted in Ball 1988: 85).

A certain reading of these texts became the basis for the behavioural revolution in power research. Many of the behaviouralists also drew upon the work of Max Weber, who defined power as 'the probability that one actor in a social relationship will . . . carry out his own will' (Weber 1968: 53) against the resistance of others. This conception, quite influential, joins the Humean conception of causality and atomistic ontology with a phenomenological emphasis upon intentionality. The writings of Laswell and Kaplan (1950), March (1953), Simon (1953) and Dahl (1957) all treat power as a relation of empirical causation, whereby one agent prevails over another in a conflict of some sort or other. Subsequent critics, such as Nagel (1975), while they introduce sophisticated methodological arguments, clearly continue in this genre. As Nagel writes, aptly summarizing the behavioural view despite many disagreements: 'the causal version of power has achieved widespread acceptance' (Nagel 1975: 11).

This view is also shared by many rational choice theorists. While most of these theorists reject many of the more positivistic epistemological premises of behaviouralism, they share the behavioural view that social life is to be understood in terms of the contingent interactions between individuals and groups. They also share the typically behavioural aversion toward theoretical abstraction and the postulation of hidden causes and underlying structures. Unlike many behaviouralists, rational choice theorists are particularly interested in the motives, incentives and co-ordination problems involved in strategic bargaining. This interest can also be traced back to Hobbes's notions of reputation and anticipated reaction (Hampton 1986; Gauthier 1969) and Weber's concern with strategic action, but its more rigorously formalistic orientation is of more recent vintage.

Peter Blau's *Exchange and Power in Social Life* (Blau 1964) was an early effort to apply the concepts of microeconomics – self-interest, maximization, marginal cost and marginal benefit – to the conceptualization of power. For Blau power is an exchange relation between parties where an imbalance in the services exchanged (what Blau calls a 'payments deficit') is compensated for by the subordination of one party to the other. While other rational choice theorists depart from Blau on many issues, they share his interest in what Brian Barry calls 'an economic analysis' of power (Barry 1976). Barry agrees with the behaviouralists that power is a way of gaining compliance on the part of others, but, taking this concern with strategic action one step further, he writes that power is 'the possession of the means of securing compliance by the manipulation of rewards or punishments' in order to modify the behaviour of others (ibid.: 90). In this view power necessarily involves considerations of marginal cost and benefit on the part of the agents involved. Such a focus opens up many interesting game-theory questions regarding the strategic leverage of numerical minorities, the effects of procedural rules upon strategic bargaining, and the consequences of boundary conditions upon co-ordination problems affecting group bargaining (Shapley and Shubik 1954; Harsanyi 1962; Olson 1965; Shepsle and Weingast 1987).

The voluntarist model derives much of its attractiveness from its scientific pretensions. Indeed, what holds it together as much as its atomistic social assumptions is its commitment to a covering law model of scientific explanation, and its claim to be able to offer predictive and thus 'falsifiable' generalizations. To this extent the powerful barrage of criticisms of empiricist philosophy of science that have been articulated in the past twenty years cannot but serve to weaken its appeal (Isaac 1987). But the model has been confronted by other criticisms as well. Some have claimed that while the model rigorously conceptualizes problems surrounding the exercise of power, it is unable to offer theoretical explanations of how and why agents are able to exercise power as they do. Others have raised questions about the blindness of the model to questions of ideology and to the way agents' preferences and practical horizons are constituted by pre-existing normative and cultural forms that are not the *ex nihilo* creations of any maximizing individual or group. Each of these criticisms is given voice in different ways by the hermeneutic model.

THE HERMENEUTIC MODEL

Hermeneutics is the study of meaning (Palmer 1969). The hermeneutic model of power holds that power is constituted by the shared meanings of given social communities. This approach shares with rational choice theory the idea that beliefs are the central ingredients of power relations, and that considerations of rationality necessarily come into play in social life. It differs, however, in rejecting the idea that instrumental rationality or cost–benefit thinking is a universal attribute of human beings (Wilson 1970). By contrast, hermeneutics is concerned with the varying symbolic and normative constructs that shape the practical rationalities of situated social agents. This involves an ontological belief that humans are by nature linguistic beings and that it is thus in language that the character of a society, including its forms of power, is to be found. It also involves the epistemological belief that some form of hermeneutic understanding, rather than scientific empirical generalization, is the appropriate method of studying social power.

The hermeneutic approach has acquired an increasing prominence in contemporary social theory (Bernstein 1974, 1983). Charles Taylor, for example, has argued that the first principle of any social explanation must be the uniquely linguistic and conceptual character of human social life. As he writes:

The point is that the objects of public experience – rite, festival, election, etc. – are not like the facts of nature. For they are not entirely separable from the experience they give rise to. They are partly constituted by the ideas and representations which underly them. A given social practice, like voting in the ecclesia, or in a modern election, is what it is because of a set of commonly understood ideas and meanings, by which the depositing of stones in an urn, or the marking of bits of paper, counts as the making of a social decision. These ideas about what is going on are essential to define the institution.

(Taylor 1979: 34)

An appreciation of this can be traced throughout the 'canon' of Western political philosophy – Aristotle, Machiavelli, Montesquieu, Tocqueville. None of these writers treated power as simply an empirical compliance relation, and all of them sought to account for the norms, mores and 'spirit of the laws' that constituted forms of social power.

Hegel's section on 'Lordship and Bondage' in *The Phenomenology of Mind* (Hegel 1967) is undoubtedly an important ancestor of contemporary hermeneutic thinking about power. Hegel's basic point is that even relationships of extreme domination, which would appear to be entirely anomic, are sustained by the need for some kind of mutual recognition on the part of its agents. Hegel's emphasis on the centrality of consciousness and reciprocity represented a departure from the more atomistic conceptions found in Hobbes and Hume and in the English tradition more generally. This emphasis can be found in the writing of a good many nineteenth-century German social theorists, including Ranke, Dilthey, Simmel and Weber (Manicas 1987).

More recent theorists have built upon this approach. Thus Peter Winch insists that the exercise of power presupposes a normative context giving meaning to behavioural interactions, a context that the voluntaristic approach is unable to countenance:

An event's character as an act of obedience is intrinsic to it in a way which is not true of an event's character as a clap of thunder, and this is in general true of human acts as opposed to natural events. . . . There existed electrical storms and thunder long before there were human beings to form concepts of them. . . . But it does not make much sense to suppose that human beings might have been issuing commands and obeying them before they came to form the concept of command and obedience. For their performance of such acts is itself the chief manifestation of their possession of those concepts. An act of obedience itself contains, as an essential element, a recognition of what went before it as an order.

(Winch 1970: 9–10)

A command thus presumes some mode of mutual understanding, and obedience some 'uptake' of the appropriate command. While Hannah Arendt's view is both more idiosyncratic and more normative, she too insists that power cannot be understood on the voluntarist, Newtonian model: 'Power corresponds to the human ability not just to act but to act in concert. Power is never the property of the individual; it belongs to a group and remains in existence only so long as the group keeps together' (Arendt 1972: 143). According to Arendt, humans are uniquely communicative beings, and it is through their shared meanings and relationships that their capacities to act are sustained.

This view is also advanced, in a different way, by Talcott Parsons. Parsons sought to develop a comprehensive theory of 'the social system', synthesizing the insights of both the voluntaristic and phenomenological traditions. He thus emphasized the importance of both strategic interaction and the 'internaliz-ation' of social norms. According to Parsons, power is

> a generalized capacity to secure the performance of binding obligations by units in a system of collective organization when the obligations are legitimized with reference to their bearing on collective goals and where in case of recalcitrance there is a presumption of enforcement by the negative situational sanctions – whatever the actual agency of that enforcement.

> (Parsons 1969: 361)

What binds these various formulations together is their emphasis upon norms. For all of the proponents of the hermeneutic model, power is embedded in a system of values which constitute the very identities, as well as the possibilities for action, of social agents. While this model has much to recommend it, a number of critics have argued that its emphasis on language blinds it to the more 'material' dimensions of power, which may be real even if they are not recognized as such by social agents (Mills 1959; Gellner 1970; Habermas 1983).

THE STRUCTURAL MODEL

The structural model shares with the hermeneutic model an aversion to meth-odological individualism and an appreciation of the importance of norms. However, it avoids an exclusively normative treatment of power, contending that power has a structural objectivity that is missed by both voluntaristic and hermeneutic approaches. The structural model can be traced back to Marx's analysis of the capitalist mode of production in *Capital* (Marx 1967) and to Durkheim's *Rules of Sociological Method* (Durkheim 1966). Both theorists insist upon the pre-given reality of structural forms that both enable and constrain human conduct. These forms may have a normative dimension, but they are not reducible to the beliefs that social agents have about them. As Durkheim writes:

> When I fulfill my obligations . . . when I execute my contracts, I perform duties which are defined, externally to myself and my acts, in law and in custom. . . .

> The system of signs I use to express my thought, the system of currency I employ
> to pay my debts, the instruments of credit I utilize in my commercial relations . . .
> function independently of my own use of them.
>
> (Durkheim 1966: 56)

According to the structural model, power can be defined as the capacities to
act possessed by social agents in virtue of the enduring relations in which they
participate (Isaac 1987: 80). It does not arise *ex nihilo* in behavioural interaction,
nor is it a purely normative or symbolic reality. Rather, it has a 'materiality',
deriving from its attachment to structural rules, resources, positions and
relationships. As I have argued elsewhere (ibid.), such a view is presupposed
by a good deal of neo-Marxist analysis of class and feminist analysis of gender.

The structural model involves a relational social ontology (Bhaskar 1979).
Against voluntarism it maintains that society is not reducible to the properties
of individuals, and that in fact it consists of relatively enduring relations in
which individuals participate. Indeed, following Marx, the model holds that
'the individual is the social being . . . which can individuate itself only in the
midst of society' (Isaac 1987: 111–12). Such a view does not reify social
structures. Rather, such structures are viewed, in the words of Anthony Giddens, as the media and outcomes of human agency. As he puts it, there is a
'duality of structure' (Giddens 1976). Social structures do not exist separate
from the activities they govern and human agents' conceptions of these activities, but they are also material conditions of such activities. There would be
no language, for example, without speakers speaking; and yet language is at
the same time the medium without which speech would be impossible. Language thus has structural properties upon which agents draw. In this respect
it is more generally paradigmatic of social structures, which provide capacities
to their participants. In this view, for example, to be a capitalist is to have
power. But this power does not arise from the contingent interactions of
capitalists and workers, nor is it exhausted by the beliefs and normative commitments of capitalists and workers. Rather, it is a property of the structure of
capitalism, one which agents draw upon and exercise in their conduct in order
to achieve their specific objectives. The structural view shares much with the
hermeneutic view, yet it remains committed to the project of scientific explanation and to the view that it is the task of science to hypothesize about
underlying structures. In this latter belief it departs most decisively from the
voluntaristic model, substituting typically realist conceptions of science for
empiricist ones (Ball 1975; Bhaskar 1975; Isaac 1987).

The structural view has attained an increasing prominence in social and
political science. It is contested, of course, especially by adherents to a more
voluntaristic model. But it also faces a challenge from less conventional, 'post-
modernist' writers. These tend to argue that the structural model remains
wedded to certain typically 'modernist' beliefs in the unity of the subject and

the privileged status of scientific discourse. Some of these criticisms, especially the latter one, echo the Frankfurt school's critique of instrumental reason and modern social science (Benhabib 1986). But critical theory's understanding of power is actually quite close to the structural view identified here. In common with structuralists, critical theorists tend to think of power as embedded in structured relationships and seek to deploy some kind of critical social science to identify such structures (Fay 1987).

THE POST-MODERNIST MODEL

Post-modernists, along with hermeneutic and structural theorists, reject individualism and voluntarism, and believe that language and symbols are central to power. They claim, however, that scientific discourse possesses no distinctively epistemic validity. Instead they insist that structural conceptions of power, like hermeneutic ones, unjustifiably privilege certain conceptions of knowledge and certain conceptions of human agency. As Jane Flax writes:

> Postmodern discourses are all 'deconstructive' in that they seek to distance us from and make us skeptical about beliefs concerning truth, knowledge, power, the self, and language that are often taken for granted within and serve as legitimation for contemporary Western culture.

> (Flax 1987: 624)

This is a view shared by many feminists (Ferguson 1987). Thus Nancy Hartsock argues that a reconceptualization of power requires 'a relocation of theory onto the epistemological terrain defined by women's lives', and that such a development would 'stress those aspects of power related to energy, capacity, and potential' rather than those connected with compliance and domination (Hartsock 1983: 151, 210). Similarly Allison Jaggar insists that there is a distinctively feminist 'epistemological standpoint' from which a more 'positive' conception of power might be articulated and justified (Jaggar 1983). What is distinctive about these theorists is their claim that conceptions of power are gender-specific and grounded not simply in philosophical differences but in radically different kinds of experience. The feminist view of power highlights certain kinds of relations – typically those involving mutuality – over others, and, like Arendt's view (pp. 62–3), it is quite explicitly normative, purporting not simply to identify but to valorize realms of experience and human possibility previously hidden by more accepted, masculinist models of power.

This is a major point of contact between feminists and the work of Michel Foucault, which, in his words, seeks to advance the 'insurrection of subjugated knowledges' that have been 'disqualified' and 'buried' by received and more accepted discourses (Foucault 1977: 81–2). Like them, Foucault claims that his genealogical analyses of power are 'anti-sciences'. His conception of power has many affinities with the structural model. He quite explicitly rejects a voluntaristic model, which views power as that 'which prohibits, which refuses, and which has a whole range of negative effects: exclusion, rejection, denial, obstruction, obfuscation, etc.' (ibid.: 183–4). As with the structural model, he views power as constituted by certain structures or 'discourses', and considers power to have a 'positive' as well as a 'negative' dimension. In other words, Foucault believes that social agents are constituted and enabled by the relations of power in which they participate, and that whatever 'resistances' power engenders they are themselves constrained by the structures in which they emerge. Foucault's writings on power have spawned an enormous critical literature. What is most important here is that, despite his affinities with the structural model, certain of Foucault's philosophical commitments decisively separate him from this model. First, he rejects any 'global' or 'totalizing' approaches to the study of social power, insisting that such discourses are 'totalitarian'. He thus favours the local analysis of 'micro-power', holding that only such knowledge can avoid becoming entrapped in modern forms of power and domination. Second, in so far as Foucault endorses a 'struggle against the coercion of a theoretical, unitary, formal and scientific discourse' (ibid.: 85), he seems to insist that even his 'local knowledges' are anti-epistemological in any sense. Third, identifying the concept of the human subject with modern forms of domination, Foucault, while talking of 'resistances', has little to say about the duality of structure and agency, and less about the way in which agents can and do transform the conditions under which they live. Finally, drawing upon Nietzsche, he seems to ontologize domination in some form or other. Rejecting the problems of freedom and justice, he maintains that 'right should be viewed . . . not in terms of a legitimacy to be established, but in terms of the methods of subjugation that it instigates' (ibid.: 96). In all these respects Foucault's conception of power is profoundly deconstructive. And, if it is clear that he wishes to offer some alternative, his formulations seem to defy any systematic theoretical or normative approach to social life (Taylor 1984).

It is worth noting, as a number of commentators have done, that there is a deep tension between the feminist approach to power, which valorizes feminine experience and orients itself toward some more or less genuine emancipation, and the radical anarchism, if not nihilism, of Foucault. Thus the post-modernist model constitutes substantive unity less than any other model does. Rather, what defines it above all else is a kind of suspicion of existing theoretical approaches and the claims of epistemological privilege that they support.

CONCLUSION

Each of the four models of power I have outlined has a point, and each fixes on some crucial dimension of social life. Each of the first three models underscores an important theme – the centrality of strategic agency, shared norms, and structured relationships to the conceptualization of power. And the fourth, post-modernist, model also offers an important insight into the fractured and problematic character of social life, insisting that power is complex, ambiguous, and located in a multiplicity of social spaces, and that traditional conceptions and methods remain insensitive to much of this.

In my view the structural alternative offers the best possibility of a creative synthesis of these insights. While it retains a commitment to certain standards of scientific explanation and criticism, it also allows for the insights provided by the alternative models. It acknowledges the importance of human agency and the self-understandings of agents. And, through Giddens's notion of the duality of structure and agency (p. 64), it is capable of incorporating both the voluntarist insight into the importance of strategic manoeuvering and the contingency of outcomes and the Foucauldian insight into the constitutive, positive character of power, which enables as well as constrains.

In this context this can be only a suggestion, one which will undoubtedly engender critical responses. It is probably fair to say that no single model of power states everything that needs to be said about the subject, and that what is needed above all else is for these models to critically engage each other. Controversy about the concept of power would seem endemic to social theory. The best that we can hope for is that such remains wedded to real substantive theoretical and practical problems, and that it remains self-critical and continually open to contestation and revision.

REFERENCES

Arendt, H. (1972) 'On violence', in *Crises of the Republic*, New York: Harcourt Brace Jovanovich.

Bachrach, P. and Baratz, M. (1970) *Power and Poverty*, New York: Oxford University Press.

Ball, T. (1975) 'Power, causation, and explanation,' *Polity* 2: 189–214.

——(1988) 'The changing face of power,' ch. 4 in *Transforming Political Discourse*, Oxford: Basil Blackwell.

Barry, B. (1976) *Power and Political Theory: Some European Perspectives*, London: Wiley.

Benhabib, S. (1986) *Critique, Norm, and Utopia*, New York: Columbia University Press.

Bernstein, R. (1974) *Praxis and Action*, Philadelphia: University of Pennsylvania Press.

——(1983) *Beyond Objectivism and Relativism*, Philadelphia: University of Pennsylvania Press.

Bhaskar, R. (1975) *A Realist Theory of Science*, Brighton: Harvester Press.

——(1979) *The Possibility of Naturalism*, Atlantic Highlands, NJ: Humanities Press.

Blau, P. (1964) *Exchange and Power in Social Life*, New York: John Wiley and Sons.

Dahl, R. (1957) 'The concept of power', *Behavioural Science* 2: 201–15.

——(1965) 'Cause and effect in the study of politics', in D. Lerner (ed.) *Cause and Effect*, New York: Free Press.

———(1968) 'Power', *International Encyclopedia of the Social Sciences*, New York: Free Press.

Durkheim, E. (1966) *Rules of Sociological Method*, New York: Free Press.

Fay, B. (1987) *Critical Social Science*, Ithaca, NY: Cornell University Press.

Ferguson, K. (1987) 'Male-ordered politics', in T. Ball (ed.) *Idioms of Inquiry*, Albany, NY: SUNY Press.

Flax, J. (1987) 'Postmodernism and gender relations in feminist theory,' *Signs* 12: 621–43.

Foucault, M. (1977) *Power/Knowledge*, New York: Pantheon.

Gauthier, D. (1969) *The Logic of Leviathan*, Oxford: Clarendon Press.

Gellner, E. (1970) 'Concepts and society', in B. Wilson (ed.) *Rationality*, Oxford: Basil Blackwell.

Giddens, A. (1976) *New Rules of Sociological Method*, New York: Basic Books.

Habermas, J. (1983) 'Hannah Arendt on the concept of power', in *Philosophical-Political Profiles*, Cambridge, Mass.: MIT Press.

Hampton, J. (1986) *Hobbes and the Social Contract Tradition*, Cambridge: Cambridge University Press.

Harsanyi, J. (1962) Measurement of social power, opportunity costs, and the theory of two-person bargaining games', *Behavioural Science* 7: 67–80.

Hartstock, N. (1983) *Money, Sex and Power*, New York: Longman.

Hegel, G. W. F. (1967). *The Phenomenology of Mind*, New York: Harper.

Hobbes, T. (1968) *Leviathan*, ed. C. B. Macpherson Middlesex: Penguin.

Hume, D. (1962) *Enquiry Concerning Human Understanding*, Oxford: Clarendon Press.

Isaac, J. (1987) *Power and Marxist Theory: A Realist View*, Ithaca, NY: Cornell University Press.

Jaggar, A. (1983) *Feminist Politics and Human Nature*, Totowa: Rowman & Allanheld.

Laswell, H. and Kaplan A. (1950) *Power and Society*, New Haven: Yale University Press.

Locke, J. (1961) *An Essay Concerning Human Understanding*, vol. 1, London: J. M. Dent & Sons.

Lukes, S. (1974) *Power: A Radical View*, London: Macmillan.

Manicas, P. (1987) *A History and Philosophy of the Social Sciences*, Oxford: Basil Blackwell.

March, J. (1953) 'An introduction to the theory and measurement of influence', *American Political Science Review* 49: 431–51.

Marx, K. (1967) *Capital*, vol. 1, New York: International Publishers.

Mills, C. W. (1959) *The Sociological Imagination*, Oxford: Oxford University Press.

Morriss, P. (1980) 'The essentially uncontestable concepts of power', in M. Freeman and D. Robertson (eds.) *The Frontiers of Political theory*, New York: St Martin's Press.

Nagel, J. (1975) *The Descriptive Analysis of Power*, New Haven: Yale University Press.

Olson, M. (1965) *The Logic of Collective Action*, Cambridge, Mass.: Harvard University Press.

Palmer, R. (1969) *Hermeneutics*, Evanston: Northwestern University Press.

Parsons, T. (1969) 'On the concept of power', in *Politics and Social Structure*, New York: Free Press.

Pitkin, H. (1972) *Wittgenstein and Justice*, Berkeley: University of California Press.

Shapley, L. and Shubik, M. (1954) 'A method for evaluating the distribution of power in a committee system', *American Political Science Review* 48: 787–92.

Shapiro, I. (1989) 'Gross concepts in political argument', *Political Theory* 17: 51–76.

Shepsle, K. and Weingast, B. (1987) 'The institutional foundations of committee power', *American Political Science Review* 81: 80–104.

Simon, H. (1953) 'Notes on the observation and measurement of power,' *Journal of Politics* 15: 500–16.

Taylor, C. (1979) *Hegel and Modern Society*, Cambridge: Cambridge University Press.

——(1984) 'Foucault on truth and freedom,' *Political Theory* 12: 152–83.

Tuck, R. (1979) *Natural Rights Theories*, Cambridge: Cambridge University Press.

Weber, M. (1968) *Economy and Society*, Berkeley: University of California Press.

Wilson, B. (ed.) (1970) *Rationality*, Oxford: Basil Blackwell.

Winch, P. (1970) 'The idea of a social science', in B. Wilson (ed.) *Rationality*, Oxford: Basil Blackwell.

FURTHER READING

Bachrach, P. and Baratz M. (1970) *Power and Poverty*, New York: Oxford University Press.

Barrett, M. (1980) *Womens' Oppression Today*, London: Verso.

Barry, B. (1976) *Power and Political Theory: Some European Perspectives*, London: Wiley.

Bell, R., Edwards, D. V. and Harrison R., (eds.) (1969) *Political Power: A Reader in Theory and Research*, New York: Free Press.

Dahl, R. (1961) *Who Governs?*, New Haven: Yale University Press.

Foucault, M. (1977) *Power/Knowledge*, New York: Pantheon.

Giddens, A. (1979) *Central Problems in Social Theory*, Berkeley: University of California Press.

Isaac, J. (1987) *Power and Marxist Theory: A Realist View*, Ithaca, NY: Cornell University Press.

Lukes, S. (1974) *Power: A Radical View*, London: Macmillan.

Niebuhr, R. (1932) *Moral Man and Immoral Society*, New York: Charles Scribner's Sons.

Polsby, N. (1980) *Community Power and Political Theory*, New Haven: Yale University Press.

Poulantzas, N. (1973) *Political Power and Social Classes*, London: New Left Books.

4

CONCEPTIONS OF LAW

GEOFFREY MARSHALL

Law can be described in short as an ordering and regulation of human behaviour. However, this fails to distinguish it from other modes of ordering and regulation that derive, for example, from morality, religion or social convention. The exact relationships between these different forms of ordering and whether they can or cannot be clearly distinguished has perhaps been the major source of disagreement among legal theorists.

Two kinds of dispute about law have been involved: first as to its source, and second as to its elements and structure. If, as those theorists commonly described as natural lawyers believe, all law stemmed from divine law or some law of right reason immanent in the nature of things, then all human law must depend in part for its validity on compliance with that higher law. If, on the other hand, law may proceed independently from or be 'posited' by a human legislator or legislators, then it may be considered valid independently of its correspondence with divine or natural law or with justice, morality or reason. This, in brief, was the view adopted by 'legal positivists'.

In addition to disagreeing about the source and authority of law, legal philosophers have also held different theories about the way in which the elements of the legal system should be characterized. Legal philosophers, such as Thomas Hobbes, Jeremy Bentham and John Austin, depicted the operation of laws as the issue by a legislator (whether divine or human) of commands or imperatives that emphasized their collective will. On the other hand, some twentieth-century critics, such as Hans Kelsen and H. L. A. Hart, have pictured legal systems in terms of presumptive norms and rules.

Many jurists, particularly in the United States and Europe, have devoted themselves not to formal analyses of the legal system as a whole but to studies of the judicial process or to the interplay of social and economic forces that affect legal institutions and legal decision making. The so-called realist or instrumentalist school in the United States included John Chipman Gray, Jerome Frank and Karl Llewellyn. In Scandinavia, realist and sceptical theories of law emerged in the work of Axel Hägerström, Karl Olivecrona and Alf Ross (Olivecrona 1939; Ross 1958). Within analytic legal philosophy the dispute between positivist and anti-positivist theories has continued. One modern form of non-positivist theory is seen in the writings of Ronald Dworkin (1977, 1986). It should also be added that there exists a self-denominated 'critical legal studies' movement, originating in the United States, that sees all formal legal structures as manipulated by dominant social interests, and the making of law by judges and legislators as exercises in the deployment of political power. If this conception of law is correct, the great majority of legal philosophers since Aristotle have been wasting their time.

THE CONCEPT OF LAW

In the English-speaking world a major part of the debate about the general character of law in the last thirty years has focused upon issues raised in H. L. A. Hart's work *The Concept of Law* (Hart 1961). The main purpose of Hart's book was to mount an attack on the imperative theory of law exemplified in the work of John Austin, who in 1832 in *The Province of Jurisprudence Determined* (Austin 1954) had portrayed law as consisting essentially of commands or coercive orders backed by force emanating from a sovereign legislator whom subjects were habitually accustomed to obey. Hart attacked this 'gunman theory' by arguing that the idea of orders habitually obeyed fails to capture both the variety of types and purposes of law and the idea that laws are obligatory or binding in ways that habits and practices are not. Whilst criminal laws might be analogous to commands, civil laws and rules of procedure cannot easily be so pictured. The role of legal rules is not only to command, but also to enable and to permit private arrangements (for example contracts, marriages and wills). They have a multiplicity of purposes. Besides punishing offenders, laws may distribute benefits, regulate organizations, educate law students, excite the envy of foreigners, support conventional morality and so forth. The key to the understanding of a legal system, Hart proposes, is to be found in the idea of a rule rather than in that of command. Conforming to rules differs from habitual conduct in that it involves the idea of obligation and a critical attitude to deviation by those who are subject to the rules. In any one legal system some primary rules determine duties, obligations, rights and powers. Other secondary rules will determine procedures for law making, define institutions and provide for legal change. A legal system is simply, Hart suggests, a combination of these two sorts of rules. Each system will be distinguished by a rule of recognition – a special secondary rule which lays down the standard or conditions under which valid laws may be made in the particular system. In the United Kingdom the rule of recognition will identify the Queen and both Houses of Parliament as the source of authorized law making and of change in existing laws. In the United States the notional rule of recognition will identify the constituent people of the United States acting through the procedures laid down in the Federal Constitution as the ultimate source of valid law.

The idea of such a standard-setting or pedigree rule is not dissimilar to that set out in the work of the Austrian jurist Hans Kelsen (1961, 1970, 1991). Kelsen's theory, like Hart's, is positivist in that it separates questions of morality and moral obligation from those of legal validity and legal obligation. In both systems law is valid and legally binding because it is properly made in terms of a rule which complies with criteria set out in the ultimate rule or norm of the system. In Kelsen's theory the validity of each law depends upon its ultimate derivation from a basic norm or 'Grundnorm' and upon the system of norms being efficacious and subject to general obedience. The validity of the Grundnorm itself must be presupposed. Hart criticizes this idea as based on a misunderstanding. The basic rule of recognition in a legal system may be viewed – as may the other rules – from two viewpoints: one internal, the other external. From the internal viewpoint of those who use and work the system, the basic or pedigree rule is an operative rule of law. But as the standard of validity it cannot itself in the same sense be valid or invalid. Neither can the legal system as a whole. Validity is a relational term that determines the status of a lower rule in terms of a higher rule or standard. The existence and character of the ultimate standard or rule of recognition is a matter of social fact. From the viewpoint of an external observer it is simply the standard adopted in a particular society to regulate and identify its laws. Legal validity and legality is always in this sense relative to a particular set of legal rules. There is no legal validity floating in the air. The question of whether a legal rule is valid can only be raised when the rules in question are identified. An act may be lawful in terms of English law but not in terms of French law or international law or the law of the European Community. It is a matter of social fact which set of rules a particular community observes.

Several aspects of Hart's concept of law have met with criticism. Three issues have been:

1 the relation between law, justice and morality;
2 the idea of law as composed of rules; and
3 the application of rules in the judicial process.

LAW, MORALITY AND LEGAL POSITIVISM

Legal positivists have often been criticized for neglecting the connections between law and morality. Critics have pointed out the essential role played by such ideas as reasonableness, due process, and fairness in the common law and in the constitutional law of most developed states. These facts are not inconsistent with Hart's variety of positivism (Hart 1961), nor indeed with the views of earlier positivists such as Bentham and Austin (Bentham 1970, Austin 1954). All accepted that there are many connections between law and morality. The development of positive law, for example, is influenced by prevalent moral notions. Morality, again, may be the source of legal criticism or the inspiration for reform of the law. Third, a legal system may consciously make compliance with morality a criterion of validity for some of its laws (as does the United States, or Canada or Germany). The positivist claim would be, however, that this last possibility is a contingent fact about those particular legal systems and not a necessary feature of all systems.

In *The Concept of Law* Hart concedes that legal systems must in practice take account of certain basic features of human existence (Hart 1961). The facts of human vulnerability and limited human altruism imply that legal rules, to be effective and lasting, must make provision for certain minimum needs such as the protection of life and security, without which other rules would be pointless and short-lived. Thus there is a minimum content to human laws which is not accidental, but is not a logical requirement for the validity of laws. This is, in Hart's view, the 'core of good sense' in the natural law theorist's belief that law cannot be expounded in purely formal terms. Theorists such as the American jurist Lon Fuller, with whom Hart had a much-discussed debate in 1956 (see Hart 1983), have argued that there are certain requirements that are inseparable from the enterprise of regulating human conduct by rules (Fuller 1964). Rules in their nature must be general, prospective not retrospective, be impartially applied, deal with like cases in a similar way and so on. Hart's reply was that these requirements did not in themselves rule out the possibility that particular laws might none the less be evil or iniquitous. For him the indisputable core of positivism is that law and morality can be separated, at least in the sense that the formal validity of a law is never conclusive as to its moral quality or as to the question of whether it deserves the citizen's obedience.

There is perhaps not a great distance between Hart and Fuller on this point. It can properly be said that if we are discussing modern civilized, and particularly liberal, systems of law, they generally do, by constitutional provisions, make the validity of laws turn not only on formal authoritative enactment but on compliance with basic substantive moral requirements. The difference seems to come only to this: that the natural lawyer wants to say that whether formally specified in the positive rules of a constitution or not, every system must be presumed to incorporate a requirement that provisions violating basic ideas of justice should be treated as invalid and be declared to be so by courts in every system. To a certain degree this view seems to be accepted in the jurisprudence of the Federal Constitutional Court in Germany. The positivist thesis which, by implication, is adopted by courts in most jurisdictions, however, is that only those substantive criteria of validity specified in the positive law of the constitution will be judicially applied. If this permits the enactment of particular unjust laws the problem raised is a moral and political one for citizens and politicians and not a judicial issue for courts of law. For a Hartian positivist, law and morality are always separable in this sense. Judges and lawyers must consider and use moral ideas in many areas of the law but only where the positive law itself imports and requires their use.

LAW AS RULES

The view that law can be understood as a combination of different kinds of rules whose validity is specified by a rule of recognition has been contested by Professor Ronald Dworkin (1977, 1986) on the grounds, first, that law does not consist solely of rules and, second, that in modern developed legal systems there is no single rule of recognition that can act as a test for the validity of particular laws. The theory set out in *The Concept of Law* (Hart 1961) can perhaps be defended against these criticisms. It is not clear that the distinction between rules and principles is a fundamental one. In one sense it is part of a useful analysis of the rule concept. Rules in Dworkin's analysis are seen as fairly precise prescriptions that are said to be applicable in all-or-nothing fashion (Dworkin 1977: 22) whereas principles state aims or goals that may intersect and may have differing weights in accordance with which they may be balanced. Principles, in fact, appear to be rule-like statements that incorporate general or vague terms. But the primary thrust of Hart's *Concept of Law* was directed against the Austinian notion of law as command. Both rules and principles, whether or not they differ otherwise than in degree, may be contrasted with imperative commands and it may be that Hart's theory would not be fatally weakened if it were to concede that a legal system contained a combination of rules and principles.

The status of the most general rule or standard – the pedigree, basic norm or recognition rule – enters the argument at this point. A possible criticism of the rule of recognition is that there may be more difficulty in actually stating it accurately for any particular society than appears from Hart's discussion. In stating fully the basic norm of the United Kingdom legal system, for example, a long and complex proposition would need to be elaborated. Reference would perhaps need to be made to the rules and authority of common law as well as to the authority of Parliament to make statutes. Common law may be superseded by statute but it does not derive from statute and is a separate source of law. In stating or describing the ultimate sources of legal validity we might also wonder what degree of detail needs to be incorporated. Law may be made by Parliament. But do we need to specify Parliament's configuration or membership or the procedure by which it operates? And what is the force of the criticism that such a rule, whether long or short, cannot function as a test for the validity of laws? A simple answer would be that it is not intended to have that function in the sense of enabling a court or observer to decide whether a particular action or disputed rule is or is not lawful, or is a valid rule of the system. To know that it would be necessary to know a great many other things besides the rule of recognition – for example what powers, duties and obligations had been created by laws validly made under it; who had been authorized to act and in accordance with what principles; what subsidiary or delegated powers had been created; what interpretative rules had evolved or been laid down and so forth. The basic norm of a system of rules obviously could never be used as a measuring rod or test of validity in that sense – any more than knowing who had authority to make and change the rules of a game would be sufficient to allow one to act as umpire in relation to the legitimacy of particular actions in the game. That is not the function of such an identifying rule. Its job is rather to act as a signpost or identification of the ultimate source of appeal or authority as to what is legitimate or illegitimate in the system.

THE JUDICIAL APPLICATION OF RULES

Professor Dworkin's criticisms of the positivist rule model of law have been debated at length (see Raz 1979; Cohen 1984; Gavison 1987). A final element in the debate is whether the accusation that positivism is tied to a particular view of adjudication can be fairly maintained. It might certainly seem to follow from the Dworkin rules/principles distinction that if a legal system consisted solely of rules, precise answers to all legal questions would be available. But if the rule/principles distinction is rejected the idea that a legal system consists of rules does not commit its author to the view that all rules are fixed, definite or certain. Hart's discussion of adjudication (which is not a central concern of *The Concept of Law*) does not suggest a belief that rule-interpretation is a matter of mechanical application. It suggests that most legal rules or concepts have a core of meaning in which that application is uncontroversial and a penumbral area in which it is uncertain. But the Hartian model ought not to be tied to any particular thesis about the way in which uncertainty in the application of legal rules should be judicially resolved. The positivist thesis about the exclusion of morality as a necessary constituent in legal validity need not be committed to any particular theory of adjudication. Many critics of legal positivism, however, treat it as if it were synonymous with or entailed a mechanistic, inflexible or conservative view of the judicial process. A positivist model could, on the contrary, accommodate and provide for interpretative rules or codes that instructed judges to apply any theory of interpretation whatsoever, including the Dworkinian recipe that would have judges in

75

difficult, uncertain or hard cases apply principles that would make the best sense of the system's general purposes, whatever the judges took those to be. Perhaps, though, a positivist would prefer to specify those purposes in the system's basic constitutional norms.

In the Hart–Dworkin debate there is perhaps something characteristic of the differences between European and American approaches to the idea of law. European theorists have, from the time of Hobbes, attempted to describe the elements and structure of legal systems as a whole. The interconnections of legal theory with political philosophy, theories of the state and political obligation may have had some influence on this tradition. By contrast, American jurisprudence has concerned itself overwhelmingly, and it might even seem obsessively, with what might appear to be merely one element in a system of law, namely the judicial process. The character and overwhelming political importance of courts and adjudication in the United States may provide a partial explanation. In the writings of the American realist school and in Dworkinian anti-positivism there is almost no mention to be found of any general model of the legal system. In Professor Dworkin's *Law's Empire* (Dworkin 1986) the question 'What is Law?' becomes explicitly the question 'What is the nature of the process by which it is ascertained what the law is in a particular case?' We shall find out what law is when we know how judges should decide cases. That approach may have some value, since courts and adjudicators are to some degree assuming an increasing importance in European legal systems. Nevertheless, not all questions about law are about its application, or even its application in hard cases. There are basic questions for legislators and citizens as well as for judges that involve reflection about legal structures and about the idea and role of law in society.

THE USES AND LIMITS OF LAW

The concept of law and its relation to morality and to political obligation are not matters that concern only legal philosophers. There are times and places when individual citizens have to decide whether they are bound by, or owe allegiance to, law. Sometimes, though rarely, this question relates to the legal system in general. If Lithuania declares itself to be an independent sovereign state, or if Quebec were to secede from Canada unilaterally, as Rhodesia in 1965 rejected its existing legal subordination to the United Kingdom, the citizens of those territories need to decide what their legal and moral obligations are. Courts, also, need to apply some theory about the nature of law and the foundations of a legal system to decide cases testing the actions of the new governmental claimants to the exercise of lawful authority. In the Rhodesian case, and in other Commonwealth territories where *coups d'état* or revolutions have taken place, judges have invoked and debated theories of law –

in particular Kelsen's thesis (p. 72) that the validity of laws in a system is dependent on the effective or generally efficacious operation of the system as a whole.

In liberal societies citizens also believe that there are limits to their obligation to obey particular laws. Both natural law doctrines and legal positivism permit and indeed require disobedience to law in appropriate circumstances, though adherents of natural law would in those circumstances base their rejection of obligation on the view that particular laws that clearly violate the requirements of justice cannot be valid laws, whilst legal positivists would in the same circumstances hold that legally valid and legally binding laws were not morally obligatory, since violation of basic rights was a reason for holding legal obligation to be overridden by moral obligation. Natural lawyers perhaps do not need the concept of civil disobedience (in the sense of disobeying unjust but valid laws) since they can always claim to be exercising their legal right to disregard non-existent legal obligations, where requirements of justice are ignored by lawmakers. A Dworkinian citizen of Law's Empire also might not feel bound to treat the decisions of legislators and even of the highest appeal court as a conclusive final adjudication of what was and was not law. This may make a difference to the tactics of civil disobedience since the stage at which participants switch to or reject unlawful behaviour has often been thought important.

For the legislator and voter an understanding of the character and roles of law is an essential ingredient in decision making. In liberal societies it is believed that there are moral limits to the use of law to coerce or restrain individual action. Should law coerce individuals to prevent self-inflicted harm? Is there an area of private action (decisions involving procreation, marriage, sexual behaviour for example) which law should not penetrate? How far should law be used to restrict the freedom of communication or artistic creativity or to compel racial harmony. What law is and what it can and cannot effectively do are closely connected questions. Some modern legal theorists have attempted to generalize and analyse the technique element or functional uses of law bringing out the range of purposes beyond the coercive or penal functions. There is, for example, a grievance-remedial function; an administrative-regulatory function; a public benefit-conferring function; and a facilitation of private arrangements function (Summers and Howard 1965).

Law, perhaps it should be added, has an educative function. The study of organized society begins with it. Political, social and commercial activity is carried on within a framework whose boundaries are set by the legal and constitutional rules. Political science begins with law though it does not end with it. It is none the less not an isolated science that can stand on its own. The greatest legal scholars have always known this. Mr Justice Oliver Wendell Holmes put it this way: 'If your subject is law, the roads are plain to anthropology, the science of man, to political economy, the theory of legislation, ethics and thus by several paths to your final view of life' (Holmes 1920). Perhaps he exaggerated. But not very greatly.

REFERENCES

Austin, J. (1954) 'The Province of Jurisprudence Determined' (1832), in *Of Laws in General*, ed. H. L. A. Hart, London: Weidenfeld & Nicolson.

Bentham, J. (1970) *Collected Works*, London: Athlone Press.

Cohen, M. (ed.) (1984) *Ronald Dworkin and Contemporary Jurisprudence*, London: Duckworth.

Dworkin, R. (1977) *Taking Rights Seriously*, London: Duckworth.

——(1986) *Law's Empire*, London: Collins.

Fuller, L. L. (1964) *The Morality of Law*, New Haven and London: Yale University Press.

Gavison, R. (ed.) (1987) *Issues in Contemporary Legal Philosophy: The Influence of H. L. A. Hart*, Oxford: Clarendon Press.

Hart, H. L. A. (1983) *Essays in Jurisprudence and Philosophy*, Oxford: Clarendon Press.

——(1961) *The Concept of Law*, Oxford: Clarendon Press.

Holmes, O. W. (1920) *Collected Legal Papers*, New York: Harcourt Brace & Howe.

——(1970) *The Pure Theory of Law* (1932), Berkeley: University of California Press.

Kelsen, H. (1961) *General Theory of Law and State* (1945), New York: Russell & Russell.

——(1991) *General Theory of Norms*, Oxford: Clarendon Press.

Olivecrona, K. (1939) *Laws as Fact*, 2nd edn, London: Stevens.

Raz, J. (1979) *The Authority of Law*, Oxford: Clarendon Press.

Ross, A. (1958) *On Law and Justice*, London: Stevens.

Summers, R. S. and Howard, C. G. (1965) *Law, Its Nature, Functions and Limits*, 2nd edn, Englewood Cliffs, NJ: Prentice-Hall.

FURTHER READING

Allen, C. K. (1958) *Law in the Making*, 6th edn, Oxford: Clarendon Press.

Ewald, W. (1988) 'Unger's philosophy: a critical legal study', 97 *Yale Law Journal* 665.

Finnis, J. M. (1980) *Natural Law and Natural Rights*, Oxford: Clarendon Press.

Greenawalt, K. (1987) *Conflicts of Law and Morality*, Oxford: Clarendon Press.

Hacker, P. M. S. and Raz, J. (1972) *Law, Morality and Society*, Oxford: Clarendon Press.

Harris, J. W. (1979) *Law and Legal Science*, Oxford: Clarendon Press.

——(1980) *Legal Philosophy*, London: Butterworth.

MacCormick, N. (1981) *H. L. A. Hart*, London: Edward Arnold.

Morison, W. L. (1982) *John Austin*, London: Edward Arnold.

Pennock, J. R. and Chapman, J. W. 'The limits of law', *Nomos* 15.

——(1982) *Instrumentalism and American Legal Theory*, Ithaca, NY: Cornell University Press.

——(1984) *Lon L. Fuller*, Stanford: Stanford University Press.

Summers, R. S. and Atiyah, P. S. (1987) *Form and Substance in Anglo-American Law*, Oxford: Clarendon Press.

Unger, R. (1983) 'The critical legal studies movement', 96 *Harvard Law Review* 561.

5

CONCEPTIONS OF JUSTICE

KAI NIELSEN

In thinking about justice, and about morality more generally, the traditions of Aristotle and Locke have had a powerful influence. Both have been adapted to contemporary life in constitutional democracies. 'Sanitized' is perhaps a better description, particularly in the case of Aristotle. It would appear at first sight that Aristotle and Locke conflict but I think this is a superficial observation. Locke is indeed a severe individualist, while Aristotle stresses the social nature of the human animal: how an individual is, in her/his very identity, in her/his very humanity, a part of a greater whole. The very structure of our choices, the beings that we are, the very 'I' that is part of a 'we', are inescapably the expressions of a distinctive social ethos. And this, of course, includes the values and norms we have, our very most primitive conceptions of what is right, just and desirable. Locke, by contrast, sees individuals as independent. He views them as people capable of living in a state of nature, independent, tolerant of differences, seeking knowledge and concerned to protect their autonomy or self-ownership. A Lockean ethic will be concerned most fundamentally with the protection of individual rights. This individualist stress need not conflict with Aristotle's, or for that matter Hegel's, stress on the deep and irreversible way we are social animals through and through: how our very identity is formed by our society. Individualists, with a Lockean orientation, need not ignore their own past and how they are formed by a particular ethos with its distinctive structure of norms. We are socialized in distinctive ways that are inescapable and are a condition for our being human. But we need not be prisoners of our socialization. We are all distinctive sorts of human beings formed by a particular ethos, but within limits. Sometimes, when we are a certain sort of person and fortunately situated, we can change our ethos, moving it in different directions in part as a function of our thoughts, desires, will and actions. And almost always we can by our distinctive reactions situate ourselves in patterns of our own choosing or partly of our own choosing, though set, and inescapably, in the distinctive social context in which we find ourselves. These thoughts do not, of course, come from nowhere. They are not simply the creation of the person who thinks them. But they also are not unaffected by the individual. They are their own and they reflect who they distinctively are. People – or at least a not inconsiderable number of people – think of what kind of world they want and they have the ability to reflect carefully on what kind of world they have, including what distinctive kind of social creatures they and their fellows are, and they sometimes can, under propitious circumstances, forge a world a little more to their own liking, including to their own reflective and knowledgeable liking. There need be no conflict between a Lockean individualism and an Aristotelian stress on our social formation.

Where we may find conflict between Aristotle and Locke is over what is just and over how justice is to be understood. Aristotle's conception of a proper social order, a best regime, is that of a hierarchical world in which magnificent and magnanimous aristocrats rule and in which slaves do everything else. Human flourishing, so important for Aristotle, seems to be very much for the rulers alone. Locke was no egalitarian, but in the state of nature all human beings are free and their natural rights function to preserve and extend their autonomy: their self-ownership. The autonomy and self-ownership we are talking about is something that is to be sought for all human beings capable of autonomy and self-ownership. The moral import of the structure of rights is to protect the autonomy and self-ownership of all.

Classes and strata there will be, but it is Locke's conception that these divisions will not cut so deep as to undermine self-ownership and the natural rights of all human beings. People may have their stations and their duties but they are all, as creatures of God, free and stand with respect to self-ownership and the rights of humans in a condition of equality. A just social order cannot, as in an Aristotelian conception of social justice, allow a society of slaves or serfs where for some people resources external to them are properly subject entirely to communal control such that they, having no control, or very little control, of the means of life, have their autonomy undermined. *Such* class divisions are not morally tolerable for Locke. But this does not mean that no class divisions are tolerable. Locke took what we now call a class-structured society to be normal and proper.

It is true that Locke has no definite conception of human flourishing such as we have in Aristotle, but whatever human flourishing comes to, for Locke it cannot be a condition where human autonomy is undermined. Aristotle's conception of justice was unabashedly aristocratic. However, as I remarked initially, Aristotle can readily be sanitized (MacIntyre 1988; Shklar 1986: 13–33). His aristocratic conceptions could be dropped without at all touching his thoroughly social conception of human nature and its importance for a proper understanding of ethics and politics.

Marx, with clear indebtedness to Aristotle's stress on our sociality, came to stress against the ideology of the rising bourgeois order with its individualism and atomistic conception of human nature, that persons, as social creatures, could, under propitious circumstances, enhance the communal character of their lives (Miller 1981; Kain 1988; Gilbert 1990: 263–91). Moreover, a social order could, and would, come into being which would replace the extensively self-oriented individualism of the bourgeois world, with its stratification into hostile groupings, with a more egalitarian social order which would, in a way the more stratified society could not, enhance both the human flourishing and autonomy of all human beings (Marx 1962; see also Nielsen 1989a: 61–97).

The individualistic social order of which Locke's thought was an expression, as well as the aristocratic, hierarchical social order which Aristotle and the Medievals rationalized, would, as Marx saw it, gradually be replaced by this more egalitarian order. In the formation of this order the re-educative effects of public ownership and democracy, arising in a world of greater material abundance and productive power, will slowly erode the possessive individualism of the previous bourgeois order. Such individualism would gradually disappear and there would come to be a genuine social harmony in which we would acknowledge with a clarity of self-understanding both our communal natures and our self-ownership. Community and self-ownership would be linked.

Given the history of Marxism and (even more importantly) the history of actually existing socialisms claiming to be Marxist, there has been both within and without such societies considerable scepticism about the harmonious linkage of community and autonomy. What was hoped for was that deprivatized citizens would emerge under conditions of a very thoroughgoing equality of condition. They would be persons with both a firm sense of their individuality and their self-ownership, on the one hand, and of there being a 'we' on the other. This 'we' would not be an ethnocentric 'we' but a 'we' which included the whole of humanity. There would be in such socialized individuals not only a sense of distinct communities but a sense of the human community as well. However, what emerged in actually existing socialisms were authoritarian societies, thoroughly stratified, where privileges and power went to a small elite and where there was not only little autonomy but little equality as well. (Though it should also be said that in some respects these societies are more egalitarian than capitalist societies.) It should also be kept in mind that while there was much talk of community, there was in reality little in the way of community. It should be said of these societies what Marx said of medieval societies: that they were *gesellschaften* parading as *gemeinschaften*. They are hardly examples of where autonomy and community became uncoupled for there was little of either in such societies.

What combination of community, autonomy and equality will a thoroughly just society have and what will these things come to in a just society? Fairness seems at least to require some kind of equality but what kind and how extensive is it to be? (Rawls 1971; Hare 1978; Barry 1989). Will it, as many conservatives believe, only be equality of opportunity? (Bell 1979; Frankel 1971). If so, what is that to come to? Or will it, as social democrats and people on the left believe, also require equality of condition? (Barry 1989; Nielsen 1985; Cohen 1989a, 1989b). And again, if so, how is that to be understood and how extensive is it to be? If we try to stick with a conception of equality of opportunity linked with meritocratic conceptions of justice, can we actually achieve or even reasonably approximate equality of opportunity? If people come to the starting gate in the struggle of life in various conditions of advantage and disadvantage, can there be anything like a fair start at the running gate in that struggle even if no one is constrained there by laws or regulations or discrimination? If everyone, advantaged and disadvantaged, were free to run, would we then actually have a condition of fair equality of opportunity? It is doubtful, to put it minimally, that we would (Nielsen 1985: 104–87). Moreover, should equality of opportunity be construed simply as, or construed at all as, everyone being able to engage, without constraint, in a competitive struggle for who is to come out on top? That is a very narrow construal of equality of opportunity. To have fair equality of opportunity it would seem at least to require equal life chances for all and that would seem at least to require something like equality of condition. But, again, how is the latter to be achieved?

We cannot have equality of opportunity without equality of condition, or equality of condition without equality of opportunity. They require each other (Nielsen 1985: 104–87). An equality of opportunity that merely allows people an unencumbered start at the gate is a mockery of the very idea of equality of opportunity. In trying to determine what fair equality of opportunity is, equality of condition is the central thing to focus on for without it there is hardly anything like equal life chances. But how are we to construe equality of condition? Given our (in part) differing needs and preferences, it can hardly be simple equality where everyone in every respect is treated exactly the same, has exactly the same stock of means and the like (Walzer 1983: 14–16, 202–3). Not everyone needs a pacemaker or wants a surfboard or a course in Latin. The thing to aim at is, as far as it is possible, the equal meeting of the needs (*partly* various as they are) of everyone. This, even under conditions of abundance or (if you will) moderate scarcity, is not possible. However, under such conditions (say Switzerland was the world), it is something to be approximated. Where we cannot meet the needs of everyone, we must, as a second best, and with that equal meeting of needs as a heuristic, develop fair procedures for the unequal meeting of needs. For example, those most in need come first, or we should give priority in the meeting of certain needs to those who in turn are the more fruitful in satisfying the needs of others (violinist A gets the good violin rather than violinist B because A's playing satisfies the needs of more people). Here we need to develop ways of ascertaining what our needs are and to develop meta-procedures (perhaps *à la* Habermas or Gauthier) for ascertaining when those particular procedures for the unequal meeting of needs are fair (Habermas 1983; Gauthier 1985, 1986). It is here that the stress on procedures given by Habermas is so central.

Simple equality will not do as a criterion of justice. We plainly need then a more nuanced conception of equality of condition, for without something approximating equality of condition we cannot achieve equality of opportunity, and without equality of opportunity human beings will not have equal life chances, and without an attempt to achieve that (or at least the attempt to approximate it as much as possible), people will not stand to each other in positions of moral equality (Nagel 1979: 106–27). We cannot in such a circumstance have a society of equals (Dworkin 1985: 181–204). Yet across the modern political spectrum there is a very well-entrenched belief in moral equality. This belief is that the life of everyone matters and matters equally and that politically speaking we should have a society of equals. But it appears at least to be the case that if there is no building of a world in which equality of condition can be approximated then there can be no moral equality. Libertarians and other conservatives reject equality of condition as a foolish and perhaps a dangerous bit of utopianism. Yet they are usually believers in moral equality and they want a democratic society of equals. It looks as though, given the soundness of the above argument, they should follow their conservative predecessors from a more aristocratic age and reject moral equality given their dismissal of any belief in equality of condition. Yet conservatives who are also libertarians usually take moral equality very seriously indeed (Nozick 1974). And, as Ronald Dworkin has pointed out, there is a sense in which contemporary conservatives as much as liberals and left wingers believe in a society of equals (Dworkin 1985). It looks at least as if such conservatives do not have their beliefs in reflective equilibrium. It looks, that is, as if they do not have a consistent and coherent pattern of beliefs. Without something approximating equality of condition there can be no moral equality.

However, there are standard difficulties for the egalitarian as well, for if we seek to establish within society something approximating equality of condition, (a) can we do this without a uniformity of ethos that would undermine autonomy and individuality, and (b) would it not require state intervention in the lives of people that would also be destructive of autonomy? Can we, beyond the most minimal and, as we have seen, inadequate conception of equality of opportunity, have both equality and autonomy? Libertarians and other theoreticians of the right have thought that we cannot (Nozick 1974; Hayek 1960; Narveson 1988). A free society, they believe, cannot aim at an egalitarian conception of distributive justice any more than it can aim at an aristocratic conception of justice where in a 'genuine community' people will have their assigned stations and duties. Caste is destructive of justice but so is equality of condition. Societies of both types are paternalistic and at least in effect, if not in intention, authoritarian.

Social justice, or, as with Fredrich Hayek and Robert Nozick, its alleged impossibility, has been at the centre of contemporary discussions of justice. John Rawls, Brian Barry, Thomas Scanlon, Kai Nielsen and Ronald Dworkin have been at the forefront of contemporary discussions of distributive justice and a defence of some egalitarian conception of social justice (Scanlon 1982). It is not that they deny the reality and importance of questions of individual justice (how individuals should treat one another to be fair to each other or what entitlements they should have), but, they argue, that pride of place should be given to questions of social justice: to the articulation of a correct conceptualization of how social institutions are to be arranged and to what must be done to create and sustain just institutions (Rawls 1978). Once those questions are reasonably answered – once we know what just social institutions should be like and how that is to be achieved – then it is easier to settle questions of individual justice. If we could come to understand what a just society would be like we could better understand what our individual responsibilities should be to each other and what we could rightly expect and require of each other.

The Lockean tradition, as against the liberal social democratic tradition of Rawls and Barry and the (broadly speaking) Aristotelian tradition of Alasdair MacIntyre and Charles Taylor, has, by contrast, stressed instead questions of individual justice and most particularly questions of the rights of individuals (Locke 1970; Nozick 1974).[1] Justice from this perspective consists principally in protecting the inalienable rights of individuals: that is, with respect to all individuals, protecting their turf from boundary crossings that are illegitimate. Individuals are seen by this Lockean tradition to be self-sufficient. The principal aim of justice, and the very concept of a well-ordered society, should be to protect their self-ownership (Nozick 1974).

The Aristotelian tradition, by contrast, conceptualizes a just society, including its conception of a well-ordered society, in terms of some comprehensive theory of the good for human beings (MacIntyre 1988; Taylor 1985; Sandel 1982). As well, and again by contrast, the liberal social democratic tradition of Rawls, Barry and Scanlon, though it eschews in its conceptualization of a just society any comprehensive theory of the good, works with a minimal or thin theory of the good. In Rawls's case it comes principally to giving an account of the primary social and natural goods which any person would have to have assured to be able to realize any rational life plan they might have or any comprehensive conception of the good they might have that would similarly respect others.

For both Aristotelians and liberal social democrats, the determining of what rights we have requires a conception of the good. But only the former require a full-blown theory of the good for human beings. Both think against the Lockeans that an account of justice that approaches adequacy cannot just rely on some doctrine of inalienable rights that are recognized on reflection or in intuition to be self-evident. What rights we have and their importance in our lives is determined by conceptions of the good, for social democrats minimal ones, for communitarians a comprehensive theory of the good (Barber 1988: 54–90).

For theories mainly concerned with justice as a property of basic social institutions there are still two quite different stresses. One stress, as with Rawls or Barry, is that the function of justice is to provide a reasonable basis of agreement among people who seek to take due account of *the interests of all*; the other stress, as discussed by David Gauthier and Jan Narveson, sees the function of justice as the construction of social devices which enable people who are essentially egoists to get along better with one another (Gauthier 1986; Narveson 1988).[2] The first conceives of justice as *impartiality*, the second of justice as *mutual advantage*. Both accounts in their most powerful contemporary formulations are constructivist accounts, not relying on moral realist beliefs of either an intuitionist or naturalist variety in which moral truths are discovered as some antecedent reality not dependent on human construction. Constructivist accounts, as with Gauthier, reject such meta-ethical claims or, as with Rawls, do not rely on such claims (meta-ethical claims rejecting other sorts of meta-ethical claims) but proceed in a contract-arian manner by selecting criteria for the correct principles of justice or for just social practices by ascertaining what people, bent on achieving a consensus concerning what to regard as principles of justice and just social practices, would agree on in some suitable hypothetical situation or what they actually would agree on when reasoning under certain constraints and in conditions of undistorted discourse (Habermas 1983; Rawls 1980, 1985).[3] Both accounts are contractarian and both constructivist. What Gauthier rejects, Rawls, more prudently, sets aside as unnecessary for the articulation of a theory of justice.

Historically speaking, the tradition conceiving of justice as impartiality has a broadly Kantian source and that of conceiving of justice as mutual advantage has a Hobbesian source. Brian Barry and Will Kymlicka have recently argued powerfully that these two traditions are in conflict, a conflict of such a sort that they cannot be reconciled (Barry 1989; Kymlicka 1989, 1990). They further claim that in much contemporary theorizing about justice, including most importantly that of John Rawls, these two at least arguably incompatible traditions stand in conflict. We cannot, they maintain, have it both ways, as Rawls in effect argues. The correct move, Barry and Kymlicka assert, is to reject the Hobbesian mutual advantage tradition. The way to go is to accept and clarify the tradition stressing that justice is the impartial consideration of the interests of everyone. That, they argue, is the account to be elucidated and developed.

Influential formulations of both accounts, as seen paradigmatically in the work of Rawls and Gauthier, share the belief, a belief also held by Habermas, that 'justice is what everyone could in principle reach a rational agreement on' (Barry 1989: 7). This, of course, is standardly taken as being partially definitive of social contract theories. The justice as impartiality view and the mutual advantage view have, of course, a different conception of why people are trying to reach agreement. Indeed, when we see what these conceptions are with their differing rationales, we will recognize that they are deeply different theories. The mutual advantage view says that the motive for justice is the pursuit of individual advantage. People in societies such as ours, and more generally in societies in what Hume and Rawls regard as the circumstances of justice (circumstances of limited material resources and conflicting interests or goals), pursue justice, they claim, for mutual advantage. In the circumstances of justice, which are the actual conditions of human life or at least for most human life, people can expect to advance their interests most efficiently through co-operating with other members of society rather than living with them in conditions of conflict. On such a view, rational people will agree on certain constraints – say the ones Gauthier specifies – as the minimum price that has to be paid in order to obtain the co-operation of others.

By contrast the motive for behaving justly on the justice as impartiality view is not reducible to even a sophisticated and indirect self-interest. Rather, the correct motive for behaving justly, on that view, is the belief that what happens to other people matters in and of itself. This being so people should not look at things from their own point of view *alone* but should seek to find a basis for agreement that is acceptable from all points of view (Kymlicka 1990). People, as Rawls puts it in a Kantian vein, are all self-originating sources of valid claims. We accept their claims because we think their interests are as important as our own and indeed that their interests are all equally important. We do not just, or perhaps even at all, take their interests into account because we are trying to promote our own interests. For the impartiality approach, at least on some of its formulations, justice would be the content of an agreement that would be reached under conditions that do not allow for bargaining power to be translated into advantage. By contrast, on the mutual advantage theory, justice can obtain even when people make agreements that are obtained by bargaining under conditions where the bargainers stand in differential power relations and have differential bargaining power. Indeed, where people are so differentially situated any agreement they come to for mutual advantage must reflect that fact. Such an approach is inescapable if appeal to self-interest is the motive for behaving justly. As Barry puts it in characterizing that position, 'If the terms of agreement failed to reflect differential bargaining power, those whose power was disproportionate to their share under the agreement would have an incentive to seek to upset it' (Barry 1989: 9). They would have no sufficient reason for sticking with the agreement. By contrast, the impartiality approach uncouples justice from bargaining power, since it does not require that everyone find it in their advantage to be just. They can have good reasons for being just even when being just is neither in their short-run nor their long-run advantage.

Given this difference in orientation, the kind of agreements for the impartialist that could count as just agreements do not allow bargaining power to be translated into advantage. Indeed, they specifically prohibit it. Both Barry and Kymlicka argue that the mutual advantage approach does not even count as a theory of *justice*. While the mutual advantage approach may generate some basic principles of social co-operation, these will not yield just agreements, since they allow as 'just agreements' agreements obtained under differential power situations. The resulting system of co-operation, with its resulting system of rights and duties, lacks one of the basic properties of a moral system, namely, the property of giving equal weight to the interests of all the parties to the agreement. So while it articulates a system of social co-operation, it is not a moral theory and it is not a theory of justice.

On the mutual advantage account some persons can fall outside the system of rights altogether. Unlike the Kantian impartiality approach, it holds that those without bargaining power will fall beyond the pale of morality. Not every individual will have an inherent moral status. Some, on such an account, can be treated as a means only. This would be true of young children and of the severely retarded and it would be true of future generations (if they are to be spoken of as persons at all). All these people lack bargaining power for they have no way of retaliating against those people who harm them or fail to take into consideration their well-being.

Those are the extreme cases, but sometimes at least the powerful in our class-divided and stratified societies can treat the weak without moral concern: they can exploit them and push them against the wall. Where the dominant class is very secure, as for a time it sometimes is, it can rationally proceed in this way knowing that the dominated class has no effective means of fighting back. If indeed some gain an irresistible, effectively unchallengeable power, then they have with such power, on Hobbes's account, as well as for contemporary Hobbesians, something which 'justifieth all actions really and properly in whomsoever it is found' (quoted in Riley 1982: 39). But in a world so ordered the constraints of justice would have no place. We could have perhaps (given the circumstances) a rational system of co-operation and co-ordination. But we would not have a morality. There is no reasoning here in accordance with the moral point of view. Where the strong can and do enslave or exploit the weak to the advantage of the strong we have something which is paradigmatically unjust. Barry puts the point thus:

> This gives us the defining characteristic of the second approach, namely, that justice should be the content of an agreement that would be reached by rational people under conditions that do not allow for bargaining power to be translated into advantage.
>
> (Barry 1989: 10)

Mutual advantage theory perhaps provides a good analysis of what genuinely rational, purely self-interested people would do. If we are going to engage in amoral *realpolitik* this is perhaps how we should proceed but it does not provide us with anything that even looks like a method of moral justification. A cluster of practices which could be correctly characterized as just practices could not be a set of practices which would sustain or even allow those with greater bargaining power to turn it into such an advantageous outcome that the weak would be killed, die of starvation or live in intolerable conditions of life when that could be avoided. Such practices are paradigmatically unjust practices. If they are not unjust then nothing is.

A mutual advantage theorist might respond that her/his theory could never allow those things to obtain, for, no matter how severe the power differentials, such things (as a matter of fact) would never be to the mutual advantage of the parties (neither the weak nor the strong). But that is clearly a rather chancy empirical claim.[4] Faced, under severe and relatively secure power differentials, with the possibility of starvation, the weak might rationally settle for subsistence wages. Faced with a very marginal subsistence living, families might find it to their advantage (including the children's advantage) to opt for child labour under harsh conditions. With one's back against the wall, one might even find it to one's advantage to sell oneself into slavery or to agree to play a kind of Russian roulette where one might be killed. It is itself a rather chancy empirical claim to say that none of these things would be to the advantage of people in positions of power because the likelihood of the weak sticking with such harshly driven bargains would be too slim. That this would be so in all realistic conditions is far from evident. We can hardly be very confident that positions of power might not be so secure that it would be to the advantage of the powerful to drive such hard bargains. But whatever is in fact the case here about mutual advantage, we can know, impartiality theorists claim, that such bargains are unjust. Thus even if they do turn out to be mutually advantageous, they remain morally unacceptable. To respond 'Well, maybe they won't be mutually advantageous' is not to meet the challenge to mutual advantage theory.

Let us now consider impartiality theories. They take several forms, but whether or not they require the postulation of an original position or a state of nature, such theories view moral reasoning not as a form of bargaining but as a deliberation or debate between agents who share a commitment to impartiality, to the giving of equal weight to the interests and needs of all. Put differently, they are people who are deliberating about which principles should be acceptable to all points of view. That, as Barry has it, is the basic idea of impartiality. Impartiality theorists such as Rawls, Hare, Sumner, Baier, Nielsen, Barry, Scanlon and Dworkin disagree over which principles of social justice are to be adopted, but they all in some sense are egalitarians and argue (*pace* Hayek) that justice as impartiality requires (where possible) the elimination of morally arbitrary inequalities, namely those inequalities arising from differences in social circumstances or natural talents. How fundamentally such an approach differs from the mutual advantage approach can be seen from the fact that an underlying rationale for appealing to impartial agreement is that it substitutes a moral equality for a physical or intellectual inequality. As Kymlicka well puts it, the two views are, morally speaking, a world apart: 'From the point of view of everyday morality, mutual advantage is an alternative to justice, not an alternative account of justice' (Kymlicka 1990: 103).

Appealing here to everyday morality, and not to something more abstract such as the moral point of view, begs the question with mutual advantage theorists, for they are willing to jettison much of everyday morality for a streamlined morality they regard (correctly or incorrectly) as more rational. There are on Hobbesian accounts no natural duties to others, no real moral difference between right and wrong which all persons must respect. There is, as well, no natural moral equality underlying our physical inequality. To the liberal appeal to moral equality (the life of everyone matters and matters equally) the Hobbesian can ask (as James Buchanan does), 'Why care about moral equality?' (Buchanan 1975: 54; see also Gauthier 1986).

Hobbesians, to continue the mutual advantage theorist's counter to impartiality theory, will respond to impartialists that they do not push questions of justification to a deep enough level. They do not realize that a person only has a reason to do something if the action the person contemplates doing satisfies some desires of that person, so that if something's being just is to count as a good reason for doing it, justice must be shown to be in the interest of the agent (Barry 1989: 363). Keeping this in mind we frame the Hobbesian question of why people possessing unequal power should refrain from using it in their own interests.

To this the impartialist can in turn respond in good Kantian fashion that morality needs no external justification. Morality itself provides a sufficient and original source of determination within us that is no more and no less artificial than the Hobbesian self-interested motivation. People can be motivated to act morally simply by coming to appreciate the moral reasons for doing so.

Hobbesians with their instrumentalist conception of rationality will find this impartialist acceptance here artificial and perhaps evasive. But they in turn must face Barry's claim that to equate rationality with the efficient pursuit of self-interest is a view which rests on pure assertion. Rational egoism is not an inconsistent view. There is no showing that to be consistent one must be an impartialist. But there is no good reason to believe that the very meaning of 'rational' is such that if one is rational one must be an egoist. The acceptance of the formal criterion of universalizability together with a recognition that others are fundamentally like us in having needs and goals and indeed in having, generally speaking, some of the same needs and goals, gives us powerful reasons for accepting the claims of an impartial morality (Barry 1989: 273, 285).[5] A person is not being inconsistent if she/he does not care about the needs and goals of others; she/he does not violate the criterion of universalizability, but, as Barry put it, 'the virtually unanimous concurrence of the human race in caring about the defensibility of actions in a way that does not simply appeal to power' (Barry 1989) suggests that this appeal to impartiality and to moral equality are very deeply embedded, considered convictions to some extent held across cultures and over time. To say that such persons act irrationally, if so acting is not in their individual self-interest, or even act in a way that is less than optimally rational, is to utilize what is in effect an arbitrary *persuasive* definition of what it is to be rational.

All constructivist contractualist theories of justice, and of morality more generally, whether mutual advantage theories or impartiality theories, construe justice as those principles and that set of practices on which everyone at least in principle could reach agreement. Barry as much as Rawls construes justice as impartiality in terms of agreement. But there are those who are justice as impartiality theorists but who reject construing justice in terms of agreement (Kymlicka 1989, 1990). Barry gives us a sense of what the stress on agreement would come to:

> [T]he function of justice is to provide a rational basis for agreement among people who do not simply look at things from the point of view of their own interests but seek to take due account of the interests of all. Justice, on this conception, is what can be justified to everyone. . . . It is inherent in this conception that there is a distinctively moral motive, namely, the desire to behave in accordance with principles that can be defended to oneself and others in an impartial way.
>
> (Barry 1989: 272)

Following Scanlon, Barry takes the underlying moral motive to be 'the desire to be able to justify one's actions to others on grounds they could not reasonably reject' (ibid.: 284). Conceptions of this sort are widely held, but Kymlicka among others thinks that they are fundamentally mistaken (Kymlicka 1990: 110–12). Perhaps such a conception would work if we were only considering moral relations between competent adults. But there are as well moral relations between us and children and the mentally disabled. It is senseless to talk about impartial agreement with infants or giving the mentally disabled grounds they could not reasonably reject. Considerations of justice are very stringent between them and us but there is no room for talk of justice coming to what they and we could come to an agreement about.

> If someone is incapable of being a party to an agreement with us, that certainly does not mean we lack any moral motive for attending to his or her interests. The emphasis on agreement within impartiality seems to create some of the same problems that the emphasis on bargaining power creates within mutual advantage theories: some people will fall beyond the pale of morality, including those who are most in need of moral protection.
>
> (Kymlicka 1990: 110)

It is a mistake to claim, as Scanlon does, that morality 'only applies to a being if the notion of justification to a being of that kind makes sense' (Scanlon 1982: 113–14).

Scanlon maintains in defence of his thesis that the fact that a being can feel pain shows that that being has a centre of consciousness and, because of this, that the notion of justification to such a being makes sense. It is because of this, Scanlon claims, that pain is so often taken as a relevant criterion for moral status. But it is false that if a being can feel pain justification can be addressed to that being and that we can in principle at least attain agreement with her/him. Agreement requires the being not just to be able to feel pain and to be a centre of consciousness, but comprehension as well, and while infants and the severely mentally disabled can feel pain they cannot comprehend things so that they could enter into agreements with us, so the notion of justification would not make sense to them. Yet surely they have moral status. That we cannot address justification to a baby does not mean the baby lacks moral status. We give moral status to an infant not because we can address justification to it or to its moral trustee. We give moral status to it because it can suffer or flourish, because the lives of such beings 'can go better or worse, and because we think their well-being is of intrinsic importance' (Kymlicka 1990: 111). Some beings we can address justification to and some we cannot; what 'makes them all moral beings is the fact that they have a good, and their well-being matters intrinsically' (ibid.: 111). But to so argue is to break with the contractarian tradition, including its impartialist versions. But it would seem at least morally arbitrary not to do so.

Kymlicka argues that we should construe justice as impartiality not in the manner of the contractualist as based on some kind of agreement, but that we should simply take impartiality as a criterion that, with or without agreement, gives all interests equal weight. Our moral motivation is not in reaching agreement but in responding to legitimate interests. We simply come to recognize, if we are moral beings, that others have legitimate claims to have their interests taken into account. The thing is to try to find or articulate principles of justice that give equal weight to everyone's interests. Agreement, Kymlicka claims, drops out.

We have clear obligations to those who are powerless to defend, represent or even recognize their own interests. In this vein, and abstracting a little, our clearest obligations are, Kymlicka claims, not to try to reach agreement but to take people's interests into account and to give equal weight to the interests of all human beings. This is the clear claim of justice as impartiality. Our principles of justice are justified when they do that. If they do not give such equal weight to the interests of all, whether we agree about these principles or not, this agreement does not justify them. This commits us to the substantively egalitarian view that the interests of all human beings matter and matter equally. Where that is not our guiding conception we do not, at least on modern conceptions of justice, have justice. Agreement is, of course, of vital epistemological and political import. But at the foundational level, as Kymlicka has it, it does not apply; that is to say, it does not apply where we are saying what justice is and what the foundations of a just society are (Kymlicka 1990: 113). 'At the deepest level,' Kymlicka continues, 'justice is about equal consideration of our legitimate interests, and the many virtues of agreement are assessed by reference to that underlying idea, not vice versa' (ibid.: 112).

There is plainly something right about Kymlicka's argument here, but there may be something wrong as well which gives morals by agreement another inning. What justice as impartiality substantively comes to is giving the interests of all equal weight such that everyone's interests matter and everyone's interests matter equally. Proper names are not relevant in determining whose interest has pride of place when they conflict and both interests cannot be satisfied. Still, in such a situation we must depart from simple equality, and it is there that the careful articulation of principles of social justice such as we find in Rawls, Scanlon and Barry becomes vital. But in making such a differential weighting, such as to proceed by benefiting the worst off maximally in ways that are compatible with retaining autonomy and fair equality of opportunity for all, we should start from a position where we give equal consideration to the interests of all and where we start by giving an initial equal weighting to all interests. It is only when we recognize that not all interests can be satisfied equally that we look for impartial and fair ways of departing from simple equality. But that does not gainsay the point that justice is about the equal consideration of our legitimate interests. This obtains whether or not there is anything that everyone competent to make such judgements and bent on being reasonable would agree on. So far things seem at least to cut against contractarians.

However, let us now ask: how do we know that is so? How do we know that this is what justice is and that this is what justice requires such that we must act in this way if we would be just and that for there to be just social institutions our social practices must be so structured? It is here that agreement may come in by the back door.

Kymlicka writes as if we could just intuit or directly recognize that this is so, that we could just see that these claims are true. But if there are any accounts that are by now widely recognized to be non-starters, it is intuitionism and natural law theories where we in some mysterious way must just have direct access to the truth – indeed, even on some accounts, the certain truth – of certain moral propositions.

How then does Kymlicka know, and how can we know, that his fundamental substantive moral claims, claims not subject to agreement, are true or justified? Perhaps they are (though Kymlicka does not claim that for them) *conceptual* claims such that we can know that they are true by having a grasp of the concept of justice, where to have a grasp of the concept of justice is to know how to use 'justice' or cognate terms correctly. Perhaps the following conceptual chain holds: to be just is to be fair, to be fair is to be impartial, and to be impartial is to give equal consideration to the interests of all human beings. If this is so we could know the truth of Kymlicka's claims by coming to have a good understanding of the use of 'justice'. But that may not give us a way of meeting mutual advantage theories at all. Gauthier, for example, understands perfectly well the ordinary use of 'just' and 'justice' and what it commits us to, if we would stick with it, but he will for his theoretical purposes modify that use until it is compatible with a set of principles that are rationally sustainable and that rational people will agree to be rationally sustainable when these people are reasoning carefully. We cannot go very far in sustaining substantive claims and substantive principles of justice through being clear about the use of 'just' and allied terms. Such considerations may undermine certain absurd claims, but they leave many competitors for what is just in the field.

It may, that is, give us something like the first word but it will not carry us very far beyond that. But then how does Kymlicka know that his substantive claims about justice are justified? He leaves this mysterious. Rawls, Daniels and Nielsen explicitly, and others implicitly, have in such contexts appealed to considered judgements or convictions in wide reflective equilibrium (Rawls 1971: 19–21, 48–51, 577–87; 1975; Daniels 1979; Nielsen 1987, 1988b). It has been mistakenly thought that this is a thinly disguised form of intuitionism with all its difficulties plus even more evident worries about ethnocentrism. However, these charges are mistaken, given the kind of coherentism involved in the appeal to considered judgements in wide reflective equilibrium. It starts from our firmest considered convictions of a rather specific sort, such as to enslave people is wrong, racial prejudice is evil, religious intolerance is unacceptable, and it tries to have a consistent cluster of such beliefs. But it also seeks to show how such specific considered convictions can be derived from and are explainable by more general moral principles, some of which themselves may be considered judgements. 'The interests of all human beings are of equal importance' is one such principle which is also such an abstract considered judgement. We seek by a reciprocal adjusting of many elements, sometimes modifying or abandoning a specific considered judgement or some-times modifying or even abandoning a more general principle or sometimes by coming to articulate a new one with a powerful rationalizing power, until we get what we can recognize to be a consistent and coherent cluster of beliefs. We do this by sometimes trimming, sometimes expanding, our cluster of considered judgements and principles, but always adjusting this *mélange* of convictions and beliefs. We do this until we have something which we have good reasons to believe forms a consistent and coherent cluster. So far we have nothing more than what is given by ethical intuitionism, though there need be, and indeed should be, no claim to a bizarre epistemic status or a truth capturing power for the moral beliefs and principles. Indeed we can, following Rawls, avoid making any claim about the epistemic status of our principles of justice or our various moral claims.

Where wide reflective equilibrium clearly goes beyond ethical intuitionism, which is a narrow reflective equilibrium, is in its stress that other things besides specific moral beliefs and moral principles must be appealed to in gaining the coherent web of belief and conviction that would constitute a wide reflective equilibrium. The consistent set we seek is not only of specific moral convictions and more general principles, but of whole theories of morality, conceptions of the function of morality in society, factual beliefs about the structure of society and about human nature, beliefs about social change (including beliefs about how societies will develop or can be made to develop) as well as specific historical and sociological beliefs about what our situation is. The equilibrium we seek is one in which all these elements are put into a coherent whole. In narrow reflective equilibrium a specific considered conviction might be abandoned because it conflicted with many equally weighty specific considered convictions or a more general moral principle. But in wide reflective equilib-rium they might be rejected as well because they were incompatible with some well-established empirical facts about society or human beings or our particular situation or because they made demands which, given what we know about the world, could not be realized or were beliefs which had moral alternatives which made much more sense in the light of some carefully elaborated social or moral theories or theories about the function of morality in society. There are here a considerable range of considerations, including empirical consider-ations, that are relevant to our decisions about what to do or how to live. We start with specific considered convictions but they are correctable by a whole range of empirical and theoretical convictions as well as by moral principles or moral theories, though sometimes in the case of moral principles and theories it will go the other way and the principles or theories will be correctable by the specific considered judgements. This yields a critical morality that lacks the dogmatism and what in effect, though not in intention, is the conventionalism and subjectivism of moral intuitionism. Moreover, that critical morality also functions as a guard against ethnocentrism. Some of the specific judgements we start with may be ethnocentric but by the time we have got them into wide reflective equilibrium the ethnocentrism will be winnowed out.

So if Kymlicka would avail himself of such a procedure he at least arguably would have a method of reason for his fundamental claims of justice and he need not just assert them, somehow taking them to be natural laws or basic intuitions recoverable on reflection. The method of wide reflective equilibrium could, of course, be used, as well, to argue against an account like Kymlicka's. Its advantage, whichever way it is used, is that we do not need to just assert or to rely on intuition with it but can appeal to a method that is very like the method used in science and in other domains.

However, in doing this he would be implicitly appealing to some agreement, to some consensus, for it is *our* considered convictions that we seek to get into wide reflective equilibrium. This means we are in effect appealing to convictions of a specific people, a specific community with its traditions situated in a determinate cultural space and time. We rely on a consensus in such a community though the shared considered convictions need not be, and typically will not be, only the shared convictions – the considered judgements – of that community. They might in some instances be quite pan-human. But for them to be *our* considered judgements they must rest on a consensus in our community and this, of course, implies an agreement. Thus (*pace* Kymlicka) agreement enters in at a very fundamental level. To show that his impartiality account of justice is justified, he must show that its principles and claims can, relying on considered judgements, be placed in wide reflective equilibrium. But this need not mean that it appeals to the agreement of everyone to whom it is addressed.

Some of the philosophers appealing to wide reflective equilibrium, and in doing so relying very fundamentally on considered convictions (Rawls most prominently), are also constructivists and contractarians and take the method of wide reflective equilibrium and their contractarianism to form a coherent whole. For Rawls, for example, in deciding on how thick the veil of ignorance is to be or how the original position is to be characterized, we at crucial junctures rely on considered convictions as we do in deciding on what it is reasonable to accept. But in turn, in deciding on whether we have for a time achieved a reflective equilibrium, we would need a conception of justice which would be acceptable to the parties under certain idealized conditions. So again, at a very fundamental justificatory level, agreement is appealed to. It is not that the substantive principles and claims of social justice are not what Kymlicka says they are or that justice is what we can agree on in certain idealized situations but that, if we are to show that Kymlicka's or anyone else's substantive claims of justice are justified, we must show that there is such agreement.

We should note in this context that justice is like truth. Truth is not what researchers investigating under ideal conditions and over a considerable time would agree is the case. But that may be the best test for truth. Similarly justice is not what would be agreed to in the original position but that may be the best test for what is just. We have carefully to distinguish what truth and justice mean and what they are from how we ascertain what is true or just.

I want now to consider a way, a rather weak way I am afraid, in which the impartiality approach to justice and the mutual advantage approach *might* be shown to be compatible. The impartiality approaches show us what justice is, how we have to be in order to be just persons of moral principle, what just institutions would look like, and what principles of justice people, reasoning carefully from the moral point of view, would find to be most justified and why. We are asking for moral reasons here which only *per accidens* may sometimes also be reasons of self-interest. Assuming there is something called the moral point of view (one property of which is the impartial consideration of the interests of all), people of moral principle will reason in accordance with it. They will hope and reasonably expect that most of the time their interests will not be hurt by doing so, but they will not think they are justified in doing so only when doing so answers to their own interests or at least does not go against their interests. Their motive for pursuing justice is not the pursuit of individual advantage. What happens to other people matters in and of itself. But we can still ask, and they can ask, '*Why be just?*' Can we give reasons of a broadly prudential sort which will show why a purely self-interested person, if thoroughly rational and clear about the non-moral facts, will do, though out of self-interest, what a just person will do?[6] Kant distinguished between a person of good morals (something an egoist could be) and a morally good person (someone genuinely committed to the moral point of view). Can we show that rational, purely self-interested people, if they were also persons of good morals, would, if they were thoroughly rational, do what just people do, or even do roughly what just people do, though not, of course, for the same reasons? We should recognize in pressing that question that 'Why ought we to be just?', 'Why be fair?', 'Why ought we to do what is right?' or 'Why should we be moral?' are questions that we could not ask from a moral point of view. To ask them is like asking 'Why ought we do what we ought to do?' (Nielsen 1989c).

However, as the extended discussion of 'Why be moral?' has brought out, we can ask: 'Why take the moral point of view at all?' (Baier 1958; Frankena

1980; Nielsen 1989c; Gauthier 1988). From the moral point of view, moral reasons by definition override non-moral reasons, but why take that point of view at all? From the point of view of individual self-interest, from class interests or from the point of view of a group of constrained maximizers bent on co-operation for mutual advantage, moral reasons are not the overriding reasons or at most they are only contingently overriding (Wood 1985, 1984). From the moral point of view they are necessarily overriding but not from these points of view. But why take the moral point of view? Justice, fairness and morality requires it. But so what?

Hobbesian theory can be taken as a powerful attempt to show that we have very strong prudential reasons for being, as the world is and will continue to be, persons of good morals. We have in terms of long-term self-interest the best of reasons to support the continued existence of moral constraints, including just practices. (We could not – logically could not – have moral institutions, at least where the circumstances of justice obtain, that did not include just social practices.) Rational persons, the claim goes, will not be morally good, but they will be of good morals.

The impartialist arguments, such as we have seen Barry and Kymlicka articulating, show, I believe, that Hobbesians (pure mutual advantage theorists) cannot get justice out of purely self-interested reasoning, including constrained maximization, which in the end is itself purely self-interested reasoning.[7] Indeed, it is true, as some modern Hobbesians have powerfully argued, that people can expect to advance their interests most effectively by co-operating and in doing this by agreeing to accept certain constraints on their direct individual utility maximization. By moderating their demands and by cooperating with others they will, as the world goes, in the long run do better. David Gauthier makes a powerful case for that (Gauthier 1986).[8] But these forms of co-operation will not give us morality, will not give us a system of justice, where the interests of all count equally, where what happens to other people matters in and of itself, where the reasons for action must not just be acceptable from the point of view of the agent doing the reasoning but from all points of view. For a social practice to be just it must not only answer to the interests of some individual or some class or elite but it must also answer to the interests of all. But, as we have seen, there can be all kinds of situations (class differentials, caste systems, hierarchical strata, adults and children, the mentally competent and the mentally disabled, developed cultures and non-literate ones) where there are differential power structures and where, by pursuing mutual advantage intelligently in certain circumstances, the powerful would exploit the weak and not for all of that be acting unintelligently. It could, as we have seen, very well in such circumstances be in the mutual advantage of everyone involved. Justice cannot allow differential bargaining power to be translated into advantage: that is, it cannot allow exploitation. People in such circumstances, given their weakness, have reason to co-operate with the strong for otherwise they will be still worse off. And in societies as we know them these circumstances are not infrequent. So, given the differential power situation and the determination of the powerful to do the best they can for themselves, the weak have prudential reasons to co-operate even though they are exploited. But they are not being treated justly; the resulting system of co-operation, though rational, is not moral. Indeed such treatment of people is immoral. We do not reach morality from Hobbesian premises and thus we do not reach justice. The impartialist does not ask why be just but shows what justice is; the Hobbesian asks why be just and tries to show that we should be just because justice pays. What has been shown is that it is not true that justice *always* pays. Some form of social co-operation always pays, but the form of social co-operation people engage in may be very different fran justice. The Habermasian has not shown that the enlightened egoist or the intelligent and informed constrained maximizer must, to be thoroughly rational, be just. But the Hobbesian has not shown that we can get justice out of enlightened egoism.

To this the Hobbesian might reply that a good bit of morality is irrational. The moral point of view requires the equal consideration of interests but it is irrational for an individual or a group to do so when it is not in their interests. What is rational to do is determined by the interests of the individual who is doing the acting. Where parts of morality do not so answer to individual interests they should, the Hobbesian can claim, be jettisoned and what is kept as a system of social co-operation, though considerably less than morality as it has been traditionally conceived, is the rational critical core of morality.

This purely instrumentalist conception of rationality, as we saw Barry arguing, is pure assertion. That it is just this that rationality comes to is not established through an examination of the use of 'rationality'. To give equal weight to the interests of all is not irrational. To say it is a rational thing to do is no more or no less rooted in the use of 'rational' than is the claim that to be rational is always to give self-interested reasons pride of place.

We can appeal to theoretical considerations to support such an instrumentalist conception of rationality, but there are other conceptions of rationality answering to different theoretical purposes. Given Hobbesian purposes we can use that Hobbesian conception of rationality, but, given Habermasian or Aristotelian purposes or the purposes of impartialism, we can use instead these quite different conceptions of rationality. There seem to be no good reasons external to these particular purposes to accept one of these purposes rather than another; and to say that the Hobbesian ones are the really rational ones is plainly question begging. Moreover, the Hobbesian conception is subject to *reductio* arguments. *If* it fits the interests of one class to enslave another class and work them to the edge of starvation, that would, on such a Hobbesian account, not only be what reason *permits;* it would be what reason *requires,* but a theory of rationality that had that implication would not only be morally repugnant, it would be groundless and thoroughly implausible.[9]

NOTES

1 Nozick (as do many other libertarians) takes himself to be a genuine descendant of Locke. This has been impressively challenged by Virginia Held (1976) and Shadia Drury (1979).
2 Gauthier's position is the canonical one here. Narveson's far cruder politically committed work seeks to follow Gauthier. It is a question worth pursuing to ask how much, if any, of Herzog's trenchant critique of Narveson rubs off on Gauthier.
3 The latter claim is Habermas's and, unlike Rawls, he is not loath to make meta-ethical claims. However Rawls, with his method of avoidance, does resolutely set aside meta-ethical claims.
4 This is reminiscent of utilitarian arguments to ward off *reductio* arguments against utilitarianism.
5 To say that something is universalizable is to say that, if X is good for Y or is something Y ought to do, it is something that is good for anyone else or something anyone else ought to do if that someone is relevantly like Y and is relevantly similarly situated. 'Relevantly' here needs to be cashed in contextually. See Nielsen (1989b).
6 I am inclined to think 'non-moral facts' is pleonastic but that belief is contentious.
7 Gauthier remarks 'my discussion assumes rational, utility-maximizing individuals who are not mistaken about the nature of morality or, more generally, who recognize that *the sole rationale* for constraint must ultimately be a utility-maximizing one' (Gauthier 1988:182).
8 The work of Will Kymlicka has deeply influenced me in the writing of this essay. His influence, my criticisms to him to the contrary notwithstanding, is particularly evident in the last third of this essay.
9 This contention about rationality is elaborated and defended in Nielsen (1991).

BIBLIOGRAPHY

Aristotle (1975) *The Nicomachean Ethics*, Cambridge, Mass.: Harvard University Press.
——(1977) *Politics*, Cambridge, Mass.: Harvard University Press.
Baier, K. (1958) *The Moral Point of View*, Ithaca, NY: Cornell University Press.
Barber, B. (1988) *The Conquest of Politics*, Princeton: Princeton University Press.
Barry, B. (1989) *Theories of Justice*, Berkeley: University of California Press.
Bell, D. (1979) 'On meritocracy and justice' in D. L. Schaefer (ed.) *The New Egalitarianism*, Port Washington, NY: Kennikat Press.
Buchanan, J. (1975) *The Limits of Liberty: Between Anarchy and Leviathan*, Chicago: University of Chicago Press.
Cohen, G. A. (1989a) 'Are freedom and equality compatible?', in J. Elster and K. O. Moene (eds.) *Alternatives to Capitalism*, Cambridge: Cambridge University Press.
——(1989b) 'On the currency of egalitarian justice', *Ethics* 99 (4): 906–44.
Daniels, N. (1979) 'Wide reflective equilibrium and theory acceptance in ethics', *Journal of Philosophy* 76: 256–82.

Drury, S. (1979) 'Robert Nozick and the right to property', in A. Parel and T. Flanagan (eds) *Theories of Property*, Waterloo, Ontario: Wilfred Laurier University Press.

Dworkin, R. (1985) *A Matter of Principle*, Cambridge, Mass.: Harvard University Press.

Elster, J. (1984) 'Exploitation, freedom and justice', in J. R. Pennock (ed.) *Marxism, Nomos* vol. 26, New York: New York University Press.

Frankel, C. (1971) 'Equality of opportunity', *Ethics* 81 (3): 191–211.

Frankena, W. (1980) *Thinking about Morality*, Ann Arbor: University of Michigan Press.

Gauthier, D. (ed.) (1970) *Morality and Rational Self-Interest*, Englewood Cliffs, NJ: Prentice-Hall.

——(1985) 'Justice as social choice', in D. Copp and D. Zimmerman (eds) *Morality, Reason and Truth*, Totowa, NJ: Rowman & Allenheld.

——(1986) *Morals by Agreement*, Oxford: Clarendon Press.

——(1988) 'Morality, rational choice and semantic representation', *Social Philosophy and Policy* 5 (2): 182.

Gilbert, A. (1990) *Democratic Individuality*, Cambridge: Cambridge University Press.

Habermas, J. (1983) *Moralbewußtsein und kommunikatives Handeln*, Frankfurt am Main: Suhrkamp Verlag; pub. in English (1990) as *Moral Consciousness and Communicative Action*, trans. C. Lenhardt *et al.* Cambridge, Mass.: MIT Press.

Hampshire, S. (1989) *Innocence and Experience*, Cambridge, Mass.: Harvard University Press.

Hardin, R. (1988) *Morality within the Limits of Reason*, Chicago: University of Chicago Press.

Hare, R. M. (1978) 'Justice and equality', in J. Arthur and W. Shaw (eds) *Justice and Economic Distribution*, Englewood Cliffs, NJ: Prentice-Hall.

Hayek, F. (1960) *The Constitution of Liberty*, London: Routledge; Chicago: University of Chicago Press.

——(1973) *Law, Legislation and Liberty*, 3 vols, Chicago: University of Chicago Press.

Held, V. (1976) 'John Locke on Robert Nozick', *Social Research* 43: 169–95.

Heller, A. (1987) *Beyond Justice*, Oxford: Basil Blackwell.

Herzog, D. (1990) 'Gimme that old-time religion', *Critical Theory* 4 (1, 2): 74–85.

Kain, P. J. (1988) *Marx and Ethics*, Oxford: Clarendon Press.

Kymlicka, W. (1989) *Liberalism, Community and Culture*, Oxford: Clarendon Press.

——(1990) 'Two theories of justice', *Inquiry* 33 (1): 81–98.

Levine, A. (1984) *Arguing for Socialism*, London: Routledge & Kegan Paul.

Locke, J. (1970) *Two Treatises of Government*, ed. P. Laslett, Cambridge: Cambridge University Press.

MacIntyre, A. (1988) *Whose Justice? Which Rationality?*, Notre Dame: University of Notre Dame Press.

Marx, K. (1962) *Critique of the Gotha Programme*, ed. C. P. Dutt, New York: International Publishers.

Miller, R. (1981) 'Marx and Aristotle: a kind of consequentialism', in K. Nielsen and S. Patten (eds) *Marx and Morality*, Guelph: Canadian Association for Publishing in Philosophy.

Nagel, T. (1979) *Mortal Questions*, New York: Cambridge University Press.

Narveson, J. (1988) *The Libertarian Idea*, Philadelphia: Temple University Press.

Nielsen, K. (1985) *Equality and Liberty: A Defense of Radical Egalitarianism*, Totowa, NJ: Rowman & Allenheld.

—(1987) 'Searching for an emancipatory perspective: wide reflective equilibrium and the hermeneutical circle', in E. Simpson (ed.) *Anti-foundationalism and Practical Reasoning*, Edmonton: Academic Printing and Publishing.

—(1988a) 'Radically egalitarian justice', in A. F. Bayefsky (ed.) *Legal Theory Meets Legal Practice*, Edmonton: Academic Printing and Publishing.

—(1988b) 'In defense of wide reflective equilibrium', in D. Odegard (ed.) *Ethics and Justification*, Edmonton: Academic Printing and Publishing.

—(1989a) *Marxism and the Moral Point of View*, Boulder, Colo.: Westview Press.

—(1989b) 'Justice, equality and needs', *Dalhousie Review* 69 (2): 211–27.

—(1989c) *Why be Moral?*, Buffalo, NY: Prometheus Books.

—(1991) 'Can there be justified philosophical beliefs?', *Iyyun* 12: 69–94.

Nozick, R. (1974) *Anarchy, State and Utopia*, New York: Basic Books.

Okin, S. M. (1989) *Justice, Gender and the Family*, New York: Basic Books.

Peffer, R. (1990) *Marxism, Morality and Social Justice*, Princeton: Princeton University Press.

Pogge, T. W. (1989) *Realizing Rawls*, Ithaca, NY: Cornell University Press.

Rawls, J. (1971) *A Theory of Justice*, Cambridge, Mass.: Harvard University Press.

—(1975) 'The independence of moral theory', *Proceedings and Addresses of the American Philosophical Association* 47: 7–10.

—(1978) 'The basic structure of the subject', in A. Goldman and J. Kim (eds) *Values and Morals*, Dordrecht: Reidel.

—(1980) 'Kantian constructivism in moral theory', *Journal of Philosophy* 77: 515–72.

—(1985) 'Justice as fairness: political not metaphysical', *Philosophy and Public Affairs* 14 (3): 223–51.

Reiman, J. (1990) *Justice and Modern Moral Philosophy*, New Haven: Yale University Press.

Riley, P. (1982) *Will and Political Legitimacy: A Critical Exposition of Social Contract Theories in Hobbes, Locke, Rousseau and Hegel*, Cambridge, Mass.: Harvard University Press.

Roemer, J. (1988) *Free to Lose*, Cambridge, Mass.: Harvard University Press.

Sandel, M. (1982) *Liberalism and the Limits of Justice*, Cambridge: Cambridge University Press.

Scanlon, T. (1982) 'Contractualism and utilitarianism', in A. Sen and B. Williams (eds) *Utilitarianism and Beyond*, Cambridge: Cambridge University Press.

Schofield, M. and Sorabji, R. (eds.) (1977) *Articles on Aristotle: 3 – Ethics and Politics*, London: Duckworth.

Shklar, J. (1986) 'Injustice, injury and inequality', in F. Lucash (ed.) *Justice and Equality Here and Now*, Ithaca, NY: Cornell University Press.

Sumner, W. (1987) *The Moral Foundation of Rights*, Oxford: Oxford University Press.

Taylor, C. (1985) *Philosophical Papers*, vol. II, Cambridge: Cambridge University Press.

Tully, J. (1982) *A Discourse on Property: John Locke and his Adversaries*, Cambridge: Cambridge University Press.

Walzer, M. (1983) *Spheres of Justice*, Oxford: Basil Blackwell.

Wood, A. W. (1984) 'Justice and class interests', *Philosophica* 3 (1): 9–32.

—(1985) 'Marx's immoralism', in B. Chavance (ed.) *Marx en Perspective*, Paris: Éditions de l'École des Haute Études en Sciences Sociales.

6

CONCEPTIONS OF HUMAN NATURE

LESLIE STEVENSON

Theories of human nature attempt to identify and explain the fundamental features of the human species; and many theorists go on to offer prescriptions as to how human life ought to be conducted, both at the level of individual behaviour, and the level of social and political policy. There has been intense disagreement about a number of basic issues: whether humans are essentially different from other animals; whether they differ importantly from each other (individually, or in races or other groups); whether human nature is constant, or historically and culturally variable; whether human nature is basically good and in need only of appropriate sustenance, or in important respects defective and requiring transformation. There has, as a result, been much argument about the role of government and politics in sustaining or changing human life.

The multiple ambiguity of the term 'nature', as used in this whole debate, should be noted straightaway. In asking how far human nature can be changed, we usually mean human dispositions and behaviour as we know them, in the society we presently live in. But some influential thinkers – notably Hobbes, Locke and Rousseau – have used the phrase 'human nature' (or its equivalents) to express their conception of how human beings would behave if there were no society, no state, government or politics, and presumably little or no education or culture. Sometimes the conception is expressed historically, in a claim about how things were before the beginning of government. The contrast has been variously expressed as between the given and the artificial, the natural and the conventional, the biological and the social, the original and the present day.

Another important ambiguity is about whether the supposed natural state of humanity is to be preferred or avoided. In contemporary discourse what is 'natural' is often assumed to be good (as in natural yoghurt, natural colours, natural lifestyles); certainly what is described as 'unnatural' is thereby condemned as bad. Hobbes famously presented the pre-social 'state of nature' as 'nasty, brutish and short', and saw the social contract as the only rational way of escape from it. Both he and Locke use the state of nature as a device to illuminate the advantages of political society, and to justify certain relationships of authority. But Rousseau, writing about a century later (against the prevailing optimistic mood of the Enlightenment), argued that society had introduced all sorts of unjust inequalities. In his early work the state of nature serves as a critique of many of the crucial features of existing society, and it is easy to see how (in the era of the French revolution) his conceptions could be used to support attempts at radical reform. Rousseau has probably been influential in fostering the idea that what is 'natural' must therefore be best, but it is a highly contentious assumption.

This essay will provide a brief overview of some of the most politically influential conceptions of human nature, noting how normative views can be concealed within apparently factual theories, and comparing them on the issue of constancy versus changeability. Some theorists have held that human nature *could* be substantially altered, given sufficiently radical changes in political or economic structures, or in social practices such as infant-rearing, education, or religious observance. We can call those who offer such remedies 'social engineers', in that they hold that human behaviour could be substantially changed for the better, and human beings made happier, if only their recommended social set-up could be instituted. But other theories, whether biological, social or theological, imply that there are strict limits to how far human nature can be affected by variations in social conditions. The debate here has wide ramifications – into political and social theory, sociology, psychology, biology, philosophy and theology. It is not, however, a lining-up behind simple 'yes' or 'no' answers as to whether human nature can be changed, for we cannot do justice to the different views by trying to divide them neatly into 'constantists' and 'variabilists'. There is, rather, a great variety of views about how far, and under what conditions, human nature might be changed, and how much it must remain the same. So we may as well review our selected theories in historical order.

PLATO

More than two thousand years ago, the Greek philosopher Plato set out a very influential description of an ideal society in his lengthy dialogue, *The Republic*. His discussion ranges very widely, from psychology, metaphysics and moral philosophy to education, art and the status of women. Plato's theory of individual human nature is that in each person there are three mental factors at work – Reason (rationality), Appetite (bodily desires), and Spirit (which is something like courage, pride or personality). These elements each have their proper part to play, but they can sometimes conflict, and what is needed for human flourishing is a harmonious combination of them, with Reason in firm overall control. Different people will have different factors more strongly represented, so there is no natural equality between individuals.

Neither does Plato think there should be social or political equality – thus opposing the democratic tendency of the Athens of his time. For he argues that the best way for society to be organized is for those with the most developed Reason to have authority and power, since they know what is best – it should not be a matter for mere counting of opinions or preferences amongst everyone. In fact, he proposes a strict threefold class division in society, affecting lifelong duties and status, paralleling his tripartite theory of the human mind or soul. There is to be a class of Rulers or Guardians (carefully selected and trained), a class of Auxiliaries which comprises all state-functionaries including soldiers, police and civil servants, and a class of Workers in all trades, agricultural or urban. Plato thinks that society can be stable and harmonious only if each class of people is restricted to their own special function. The trained elite has a duty to rule, even if they would prefer to spend their time in philosophical thought (and they are not to be permitted either families or private property), whereas the Auxiliaries and Workers have no business in ruling, not even in voting for prospective rulers, for they lack all relevant knowledge. For Plato the well-being of the society does not consist in the well-being of its individual members. There is a certain totalitarian air about his ideal republic, revealed also in his recommendations of strict censorship of the arts, to prevent any destabilizing ideas gaining currency.

An elaborate, deeply argued philosophical vision – the theory of Forms as perfect, eternal, unchanging objects of knowledge grasped by the Reasoning element within the human soul – lies behind Plato's conception of knowledge. He implies that what we would now call questions of value, about what is best for individuals and for societies, can be as much matters of knowledge as propositions in mathematics or science. The obvious difficulty for this idea is the widespread, and apparently irresolvable, disagreement that exists (then, and now) about most questions of value. If there are facts about such matters, facts which are knowable by human beings, why the persistent disputes? Plato realizes that there is considerable difficulty in attaining the relevant 'expertise', and he prescribes a detailed programme of education (restricted to those capable of benefiting from it) by which the future Guardians, the 'philosopher-kings', are to be trained. But he can offer no guarantee that even the best-educated elite will always govern in the interest of society as a whole, rather than in their own interest, and he offers no mechanism for changing rulers, or for resolving disputes between them.

Plato's conception is thus a remarkably unpolitical one. He did not say how in real-life politics his prescriptions can be put into practice or be maintained – it is as if he hoped that their intrinsic rationality would persuade people to accept them. (His attempts to apply his theory, when given the chance to educate prospective rulers of Sicily, were notoriously unsuccessful.) His is a timeless, transcendent, other-worldly kind of theory, with no allowance for human dispositions such as family ties which do not fit into his ideal state, no provision for failures to fulfil the social functions he allots, and no recognition of variations between people and societies at different times or places.

HOBBES

Writing about the time of the English civil war in the mid-seventeenth century, Hobbes, in his *Leviathan*, presents pre-social human life as extremely insecure, because of the constant danger of fighting over vital resources. He bases his description of individual human nature on a strictly materialist conception – which he thinks is required by the new methods of physical science – of humans as consisting of nothing more than matter in motion. In Hobbes's view, each individual is purely self-interested, seeking the satisfaction of his or her present desires, and the acquisition of means for future satisfaction: 'I put for a general inclination of all mankind, a perpetual and restless desire of power after power, that ceaseth only in death.' There is no co-operation (except when it serves individuals' self-interests), just a constant competition between individuals of approximately equal strength and intelligence. So even when in possession of house, crops, animals, etc., there will always be fear that these will be forcibly taken by someone else; and this gives each person reason to make pre-emptive strikes against others, extending power in order to increase security. People even come to value power over others for its own sake, and to enjoy 'reputation' (Hobbes shrewdly observes that reputation of power *is* power, since it influences how people act). So without any 'common power to keep them all in awe', people live in a state of war with every individual against everyone else, not always actually fighting, but in constant fear of it. In this condition there is little incentive for any longer-term projects like agriculture, industry or science. There can be no applicable notions of justice, rights, property or law; there is only the fact of physical possession until dispossessed by superior force.

Agreements between individuals are of no use in remedying the state of nature, for when it is in someone's self-interest to break such an agreement, what reason do they have to keep it? 'Covenants, without the swords, are but words, and of no strength to secure a man at all.' In Hobbes's view, this gives each person an overwhelming good reason to accept a social contract by which all subject themselves to the supreme power and authority of a 'sovereign'. 'The only way to erect such a common power, as may be able to defend them from the invasion of foreigners, and the injuries of one another . . . is to confer all their power and strength upon one man, or one assembly of men.' Thus is created a 'commonwealth' (the 'leviathan' of the title of Hobbes's famous book), or what we would now call a state, with a government. Note that this need not be thought of as a historical event: the main point is to show why everyone has good reason to accept the authority of the state (provided that there *is* a single source of power that is effectively unchallenged). The implication of the argument is that any state authority is better than none, and that those that are in actual control deserve allegiance because of that fact alone.

Hobbes's account of the authority he thinks the sovereign (or sovereign body) must have is remarkably authoritarian. Those who are subjects of a monarch have no rights, without his permission, to 'cast off monarchy', that is, to cancel the contract and become a member of another state or of none. And because the contract is between individuals themselves, not between individuals and sovereign, Hobbes says there can be no such thing as breach of contract by the sovereign; he may commit 'iniquity', but not 'injustice'. Further, the sovereign has the right to judge which opinions are dangerous to the state, and may censor publication of them. The sovereign is to make laws and administer them; to conduct foreign policy and decide on war and peace; to appoint all government officials; and distribute reward or punishment as he or she pleases. Hobbes makes no provision against misuses of power: he seems so afraid of the horror of the 'state of nature', as he sees it, that he is prepared to risk despotism to avoid it.

LOCKE

Just a few decades later – about the time of the 'Glorious Revolution' of 1688 in England, by which the power of the monarchy was limited – Locke, in his second *Treatise on Government*, paints a less dark picture of the 'state of nature', and presents the introduction of government more as a matter of convenience than dire necessity. To an extent, he admits (like Aristotle) that human nature is already social, that we are so made that 'it is not good for us to be alone', being naturally disposed to live not merely in families, but as members of wider groupings. However, he still uses very freely the idiom of a pre-social, or at least pre-governmental, state of nature.

Locke conceives of people in this condition as being both free and equal, in that nobody has more power or authority than any other, but he differs from Hobbes in holding that this can be a state of 'peace, goodwill, mutual assistance and preservation'. Another difference from Hobbes's state of nature is that Locke posits a fundamental notion of property, with the distinctive rights of use and disposal, as a corollary of human existence, even in the pre-social state. Whatever someone 'mixes his labour with' for personal use, for example plucking a wild fruit, cultivating crops, or digging ore from the ground, becomes private property: 'as much as anyone can make use of to any advantage of life before it spoils, so much he may by his labour fix a property in'. Clearly, Locke is optimistically assuming that there is no scarcity of vital necessities in the 'state of nature' (he refers to the contemporaneous settlement of almost uninhabited regions of America). Hobbesian competition for resources is surely probable as soon as human population outstrips the capacity of the environment to sustain it, but Locke can claim that human beings are not *inevitably* aggressive towards each other, and that in conditions of economic sufficiency they will not be. According to Locke, there is a 'law of nature' which applies even in this pre-social condition, since rational beings are able to realize that 'no one ought to harm another in his life, health, liberty, or possessions' (he tries to back this up with a pious appeal to the wise intentions of the divine Creator). But he is not so naïve as to suppose that everyone will readily obey this law, and so he maintains that in the pre-social state everyone has a right to punish transgressions of the law of nature, and the injured party has a particular right to take reparations from the offender.

This is the point in Locke's argument where government comes in. Recognizing that it is dangerous to let individuals be judges in their own cases, since they will easily be led into punishment beyond what is justified, he says that civil government is 'a proper remedy for the inconveniences of the state of Nature'. But having learnt from his experience of the Stuart kings, he notes that absolute monarchs can abuse their power. And, in a crucial criticism of Hobbes, he argues that far from being a remedy for the state of nature, absolute sovereignty is no escape from it at all, since individual and sovereign are really in a state of nature with respect to each other as long as there is no legal check on the power of the latter over the former. Locke is thus a foremost theorist of how the legitimacy of government must depend on the consent of the governed, and of how all power needs to be subject to restraint; his ideas strongly influenced the Constitution of the United States of America.

Hobbes and Locke differ in their conceptions of pre-social human nature, and so (it seems) they diverge over what political arrangements they recommend. Or is it really the other way round – that because they have different political views (Hobbes favouring absolute authority, and Locke wanting checks on state power), they think up different theories of human nature to try to justify these views? There is no serious attempt by these writers to find out the facts about the pre-history of humankind, or about how people would behave if there were no state power. It looks very much as if what are presented as factual, even scientific, descriptions of human nature already conceal within themselves the normative preconceptions of their authors – a possibility to which we must be alive in other theories.

ROUSSEAU

In his *Discourse on Inequality*, Rousseau seems to make more of an effort than Hobbes or Locke to paint a historically realistic picture of the stages by which present society must have evolved from the primeval human condition. He refers to some of the zoological reports of exotic creatures and anthropological evidence about primitive cultures which were then circulating in Europe. He speculates about how human language might have evolved out of instinctual cries. He accuses Hobbes of reading back into the state of nature motives like pride which can only exist in society, and he claims (also against Hobbes) that humans have an innate repugnance against seeing a fellow creature suffer, which moderates the competition between individuals. Rousseau's description of 'the noble savage' represents humans as 'wandering in the forests, without work, without speech, without a home, without war, and without relationships', and this 'without any need of his fellow men and without any desire to hurt them'. There was no inequality between individuals, except relatively small differences in strength, intelligence, etc. There was neither education nor historical progress; each generation lived as its ancestors had done.

Rousseau goes on to speculate about our evolution since then. He treats the notion of property, rather than political power, as most distinctive of civil society. He suggests that the true golden age was at the stage when people had come to form families living together in houses, with some degree of interfamilial socialization into communities, property rights recognized for the immediate necessities of life, and offences against these punished – very much Locke's state of nature, in fact. This for Rousseau was 'the true youth of the world', and he interprets all so-called progress since then as really steps towards 'the decrepitude of the species'. He blames the division of labour, especially in agriculture and metallurgy, for starting the rot, making it necessary for many people to work under the direction of others, allowing some to amass huge property, and thus making possible all the manifold forms of exploitation and economic and social inequality of which he was so painfully conscious. His analysis in this work is a tragic one – that the economic progress due to human cleverness has also developed wickedness, and brought out the worst in human nature. But one suspects that his revulsion from certain features of the society he knew leads him to idealize his speculative 'golden age'.

In that work Rousseau did not offer much in the way of a recommendation for how to cure or alleviate the unhappy condition which he diagnosed in society, there being no realistic possibility of a return to the past. But in his later work, especially *The Social Contract*, he took a more positive view, arguing that human nature does after all find its most complete fulfilment in civil society, at least at its best. Like Hobbes and Locke, Rousseau uses the device of a 'social contract' to explain the allegiance owed to political authority. People in the state of nature are supposed to reach a critical stage where they realize that their very survival is at risk, and to find it each to their advantage to enter into an agreement with everyone else. But in Rousseau's version the power is granted not to a Hobbesian absolute sovereign, nor even to an elected government, but rather to the community as a whole, which becomes a moral entity in itself. And this involves his distinctive, but rather mysterious notion of the 'general will', which is always for the good of the whole, and yet cannot be identified with the actually expressed will of the citizens, even if all of them should vote in an assembly. But at this point a theory of human nature as it is ceases to play a role in Rousseau's thought: the 'general will' has to be what people *ought* to want, not what they actually want. Such a notion makes it all too easy for those in power to claim that they know better than the people what would be good for them.

MARX

Karl Marx, writing in the nineteenth century when ideas of historical evolution were all the rage, presents a wide-sweeping theory of the development of human societies through various stages, characterized primarily by the nature of their economic production – from the ancient cultures, through the feudalism of the Middle Ages, into the capitalist mode of production, to be superseded (he predicted) by a revolutionary change to the communist mode. According to Marx's conception of human nature, humans are essentially social beings, who do not merely find their means of subsistence in the world but have to work to produce them – for example, growing crops, domesticating other animals, building shelters and making tools. From this emerges Marx's claim that the specific characteristics of a determinate population depend on the kind of society they are members of, which depends in turn on the existing mode of production of the necessities of life.

Marx presents this 'materialist theory of history' as an objective, scientific analysis of the laws governing human societies. He was not, however, merely a dispassionate academic theoretician, he was keenly aware of what he saw as the grave injustices of the capitalist society of his day. He not only predicted, but longed for, the transition to communism, in which he believed that a system of common ownership of the means of production would allow, for the first time in history, the free development of the potential of all human beings. Although, according to Marxist theory, the revolution could not happen until the economic development of a society made the time ripe, as that time approached there would be opportunity for those with an accurate understanding of the situation to prepare the way by organization and propaganda, and when the chance came, to seize the initiative and bring about the revolutionary transfer of power to the communist party, as Lenin did in 1917. It is only in this sense that Marx can be said to be a social engineer. As to how things were to proceed after the revolution, he was optimistic but very vague; he foresaw the need for a 'dictatorship of the proletariat' for a transitional period, but after then he thought that the state could 'wither away'.

Experience (at least until very recently) has shown quite the reverse happening: the dictatorship of the communist party (the self-appointed representatives of the proletariat) strengthened to totalitarian terror, social engineering was undertaken on a huge scale, and state power extended into almost every feature of life. The Marxist analysis of human nature tends to ignore the persistence of certain kinds of human behaviour even through fundamental economic and political changes – the enjoyment of power and privilege by individuals and ruling groups, the rivalries engendered by nationalist and ethnic feeling, and the desire of many to engage in economic enterprise for themselves.

SOCIAL DARWINISM

In stark contrast to the Marxian conception of human nature, 'Social Darwinism' (which underlies the pronouncements of the more ideological defenders of the 'free market economy') offers an account that enshrines competition as both inescapable and desirable in human life. Darwin himself cannot be held responsible for this view – his theory of evolution by natural selection is an explanation of the origin of the diversity of all living species, not itself a theory of human society. However, since the time of Herbert Spencer in England and W. G. Sumner in the USA (see Jones 1980, Rose 1984), political and social theorists who favour the least possible control by the state over economic activity (the doctrine of '*laissez faire*') have often appealed to certain Darwinian ideas to try to justify their prescriptions. (They can count as social engineers only in the Pickwickian sense that in countries where there has been a tradition of state-managed economy and social services they will want to change these institutions, and so this programme can constitute a revolution of sorts.)

Their creed can be seen as implicit in the phrase 'survival of the fittest' (the words are Spencer's, not Darwin's). This is to be read not merely in the factual, Darwinian sense that only those individuals best fitted to the prevailing environment will survive (or at least, live long enough to leave progeny), but in the normative sense that it is a good thing that this should be so, and that the less fit should not survive, or not survive so well or so long. It is a political ethic that makes a virtue out of competition; and it obviously suits the successful capitalist very well, for it seems to justify ruthless elimination of rivals, to bless economic success with virtue on top of material reward, and to discourage any attempt at redistribution of resources through taxation or any other compulsory measure.

But it does not amount to much of a theory of human nature, for all it does is to point to competitive tendencies in economic activity as one aspect of human behaviour, to claim that these can work to the benefit of everyone, and then to jump to the sweeping conclusion that individual economic freedom is the only thing that is important. It leaves out of consideration all co-operation between people, indeed it seems to treat individuals or families as isolated units without acknowledging membership in larger social groups which have profound effects on individuals' identities, obligations and rights.

SKINNERIAN BEHAVIOURISM

A conception of human nature supporting large-scale social engineering has been extrapolated from the behaviourist psychology of the American psychologist B. F. Skinner, whose theories have had some limited success in explaining and modifying the behaviour of various species of animal under laboratory conditions. In this case the claim for applicability to the problems of human society has been made by Skinner himself, but just what he proposes remains rather vague (Skinner 1953). He believes inherited factors play a fairly small role in determining behaviour, and like Marx he strongly emphasizes the plasticity of human behaviour to social influences (which Skinner will label 'conditioning'). But unlike Marx he suggests that regardless of the historical and economic background, knowledgeable behavioural scientists can intervene to create whatever kind of people are wanted, simply by arranging the conditioning influences accordingly. He thus proposes that social scientists 'design a culture' to optimize individual and social benefits, dispensing with troublesome notions of individual freedom and responsibility as 'unscientific'. On this view, human beings are merely creatures whose behaviour is determined by conditioning influences from their past and present social environment.

Clearly, this leaves very much open just what sort of people and society we should be trying to create; on this point Skinner is much less explicit than Plato, and his view seems to amount to no more than the offer of a behavioural technology (which many would argue has little application to human beings, since there are species-specific limits to conditioning) towards ends or goals which remain unspecified – and could in practice turn out to be those of the commercial advertiser, the religious evangelist, the ruling party's propagandists, or whoever else is able to get access to the main means of conditioning people (such as television).

SOCIO-BIOLOGY

Let us turn from the modern social engineers, the optimists about the transformation of human behaviour through social change, to those who emphasize the fixity of human nature. Prominent recently have been those who take a firmly biological view of human beings as one species amongst others, and claim that the important determinants of our behaviour are innate, bred into us by our evolution and coded in the molecules of our genes.

Let us briefly mention Freud as an interesting intermediate case here. He was a pioneer of the biological approach to human nature, putting forward a theory of instincts, while also emphasizing the importance for character-formation of the early years of strong attachment to parents. He claims to detect the unconscious, instinctual influences behind human behaviour, often dismissing as mere 'rationalizations' the reasons explicity offered. But in practical therapy, Freud appears as more of a rationalist – the aim of his distinctive 'psycho-analytic' treatment being to bring into consciousness, for free rational decision, the features which had been repressed into the unconscious mind. Freud sometimes suggested the applicability of his theories to social questions. But nothing in the way of a social programme or political creed can be ascribed to him, only the general thought that there has to be a compromise between society and individuals. Civilization requires the giving up of some instinctual satisfaction – but if it is to exist at all, allowance must be made in our social arrangements for the innate, unchangeable nature of humankind.

This biological theme has been taken up by others who have studied human beings as one kind of animal amongst others – ethologists such as Konrad Lorenz and, more recently, self-styled 'socio-biologists' such as Edward O. Wilson. Lorenz offers a controversial diagnosis of human aggressive tendencies, on the basis of his theory of intraspecific aggression in a variety of animal species. He explains it as being due to a built-in 'drive' released by distinctive stimuli such as the presence of another male of the same species, and inhibited by certain other signs such as a characteristic posture of submission. Lorenz transferred this theory straight over to human beings, modifying it to take account of the distinctively intercommunal nature of human carnage – which he attributed to the selective pressures of an alleged evolutionary past in which the competition for survival was more between tribes rather than individuals. If there is really such an innate tendency to communal aggression (as the bloody history of ethnic, nationalist and religious conflict suggests), then no social changes can eliminate it. The best that Lorenz can recommend is harmless redirection of it into sports, plus control by rational self-knowledge and a sense of humour.

Wilson and others offer a wider-ranging analysis of innate factors in human nature. There is less talk these days of 'instincts', as used by Freud and Lorenz, and more of a large number of genetically based predispositions which interact in subtle ways, depending on the environment, in the production of behaviour. But the emphasis is still very much on innate tendencies, seen as the result of a long history of natural selection, whose detailed expression may depend on culture and individual conditioning, but which will certainly express themselves somehow or other. Yet much of what the socio-biologists say about human nature is bound to be controversial, for two reasons – because it is so difficult to separate the contributions of heredity, and because of the normative involvements which surround the topic of human behaviour. We cannot make tight connections between particular genes and identifiable kinds of social behaviour, nor is it to be expected that the science of human genetics will bring us to that stage, for there must surely remain some part for culture to play.

For example, the whole area of human sexual roles is hotly debated. Socio-biologists may point to the selective pressure on males (of all species) to spread their genes around as widely as possible, in contrast to that on females to select their partners cautiously for genetic fitness, but they also have to acknow-ledge that pair-bonding is a (fairly) typical feature of human behaviour, unlike the other primates. So they may try to explain both our monogamy and our frequent departures from it in terms of an evolutionary history which grafted pair-bonding (supposedly required by the hunting way of life, with its male absences from home) onto a pre-existing primate pattern of dominant male plus harem. They may try to explain traditional human sexual division of labour by our ancestors' system of males going hunting in groups (involving distinctive male-to-male bonding) while women looked after the young. But feminists, such as Alison Jaggar, resist any attempt to justify the continuation of traditional sexual roles on supposedly biological grounds; they argue that whatever may have been the case in the distant past, it is now very much a matter of culture, and is therefore challengeable and changeable.

If human nature is, at least in part, a matter of genes, then is it open to us to improve it by genetic engineering, intervening to control the very genes of future generations? This could in theory be done (somewhat slowly) by selective breeding, as the eugenics movement advocated earlier in this century (see Rose 1984) – after all, we have in this way been able to alter the characteristics of animals and plants. But perhaps when we gain knowledge of our genes themselves – the way in which they are encoded in the DNA structures of the whole human genome – it might also be done more quickly, if we find techniques to manipulate these genes at will. In both cases a distinction needs to be made between negative and positive programmes, the former aiming only to prevent the birth of physically or mentally handicapped infants, the latter trying to produce the 'best' sorts of human being. This positive selection is much more ambitious and much more controversial: which features are we to select for? Who is to decide about this: prospective parents, the state, or who? How could human reproduction be controlled in the massive way envisaged? How could anybody have the *right* thus to interfere with other people having children? What we have here are not so much theories of human nature, but the possible means to mould it in one direction or another. Whether to use such means at all, and if so how, are questions of value.

There seems to be no escape from the conclusion that in so far as we can ascertain facts about what human nature is (and has been), this does not settle questions of value about what it ought to be. Disputed questions of philosophy and value are involved as soon as anyone tries to apply the scientific method to human nature. For there are those (philosophers, existentialists, Marxists, theologians) who in their different ways maintain that we transcend our biology – by our rationality, our consciousness, our freewill, our social development, or even our relationship to a divine Reality.

BIBLIOGRAPHY

Aristotle (*c* 300 BC) *The Politics* London: Penguin, 1951.

Freud, S. (1915–17) *Introductory Lectures on Psycho-analysis*, London: Penguin, 1973.

Hobbes, T. (1651) *Leviathan*. London: Penguin, 1968).

Jaggar, A. (1983) *Feminist Politics and Human Nature*, Brighton: Harvester.

Jones, G. (1980) *Social Darwinism and English Thought: The Interaction between Biological and Social Theory*, Brighton: Harvester.

Locke, J. (1690) *Two Treatises on Government*, London: Dent, 1924.

Lorenz, K. (1966) *On Aggression*, London: Methuen.

Marx, K. (*c.* 1843–75) *Selected Readings in Sociology and Social Philosophy*, eds T. Bottomore and M. Rubel, London: Penguin, 1963.

Plato (*c.* 380 BC) *The Republic*, London: Penguin, 1955.

Rose, S., Lewontin, R. C. and Kamin, L. J. (1984) *Not in Our Genes: Biology, Ideology and Human Nature*, London: Penguin.

Rousseau, J.-J. (1755) *Discourse on Inequality*, London: Penguin, 1984.

—— (1762) *The Social Contract*, London: Penguin, 1968.

Skinner, B. F. (1953) *Science and Human Behaviour*, New York: Macmillan.

Wilson E. O. (1975) *On Human Nature*, Cambridge, Mass.: Harvard University Press.

7

CONCEPTIONS OF LEGITIMACY

MATTEI DOGAN

Why do people voluntarily follow and obey their rulers? Why do people accept and maintain authorities and institutions? In authoritarian regimes people obey involuntarily, by fear. But, as Xenophon already knew, the power of tyrants is not based uniquely on material force and constraints. Even the most tyrannic rulers try to justify their reign. The key concept to the understanding of this effort of justification is legitimacy, because only legitimacy can transform brutal power into recognized authority.

Legitimacy has always been in the mind of political thinkers. Plato's idea of justice bears on the problem of legitimacy, as well as Aristotle's distinction between monarchy, aristocracy and democracy. In his analysis of the nature of government, Locke displaced the source of legitimacy, replacing the divine right of kings by the consent of the people. No discussion of the concept of power could be complete without reference to legitimacy. For contemporary political systems in which participation of the people is a criterion of political worth, legitimacy is a fundamental concept.

DEFINITIONS OF LEGITIMACY

The concept of legitimacy and its definition have changed significantly since the emergence of democratic governments. As Schaar points out, current definitions of legitimacy dissolve legitimacy into belief or opinion (Schaar 1981). If people hold the belief that existing institutions are appropriate or morally proper, then those institutions are legitimate. Such a reference to beliefs becomes even clearer when we consider the widely accepted definition formulated by Lipset: 'the capacity of the system to engender and maintain the belief that the existing political institutions are the most appropriate ones for the society' (Lipset 1959: 77). It is also clear in Merkl's definition: 'a nation united by a consensus on political values ... a solemnly and widely accepted legal and constitutional order of democratic character ... and an elective government responsive to the expressed needs of the people' (Merkl 1988: 21).

Juan Linz proposes as a 'minimalist' definition 'the belief that in spite of shortcomings and failures, the political institutions are better than any other that might be established, and therefore can demand obedience' (Linz 1988: 65). The concept of 'diffuse regime support' developed by David Easton is another way to define legitimacy (Easton 1965).

The best-known definition of legitimacy today was formulated by Max Weber, who distinguished three types of legitimacy: traditional, charismatic and legal-rational (Weber 1978). This typology has been meaningfully applied in many historical studies: 'Since Weber, we have been busy putting the phenomenon into one or another of his three boxes and charting the progress by which charismatic authority becomes routinized into traditional authority, which . . . gives way in turn to rational legal authority' (Schaar 1981: 15). Legitimacy is particularly important in democracies since a democracy's survival is ultimately dependent on the support of at least a majority of its citizens; it holds that at least a majority must deem it legitimate. Hence, without the granting of legitimacy by the people, a democracy would lose its authority. On the other hand, legitimacy in this sense of public belief and support is considerably less important in non-democratic regimes. In dictatorships, while the granting of support or legitimacy by the people may be an asset, it is not of ultimate importance since authority is based on force.

Authoritarian regimes may lack legitimacy but they still feel a need to acquire it. The subtitle of Michael Hudson's book on Arab politics is very significant: *The Search for Legitimacy* (Hudson 1977). He clearly explains this need:

> The central problem of government in the Arab World today is political legitimacy. The shortage of this indispensable political resource largely accounts for the volatile nature of Arab politics and the autocratic, unstable character of all the present Arab governments . . . . Whether in power or in the opposition, Arab politicians must operate in a political environment in which the legitimacy of rulers, regimes and the institutions is sporadic and, at best, scarce. Under these conditions seemingly irrational behavior, such as assassinations, coups d'etat and official repression, may in fact derive from . . . the low legitimacy accorded to political processes and institutions.
>
> (Hudson 1977: 2)

THE OBSOLESCENCE OF CLASSICAL TYPOLOGIES OF LEGITIMACY

In the Weberian typology, the concepts of legitimacy and democracy are not related. Historically, traditional legitimacy and charismatic legitimacy are only found in authoritarian regimes. They never appear in truly democratic regimes. The implication is that some authoritarian regimes can be legitimate. Among the contemporary countries with legal-rational authority some are legitimate, particularly the pluralist democracies, but most are not, particularly the authoritarian regimes.

Today it is more difficult than in the past to make clear-cut classifications of authority, because the legitimacy of a regime can be based on more than one type of authority. The democracy of the United States is not based exclusively on its short, sacred Constitution. It has developed progressively, generating new practices which were soon formalized and routinized. How much rationality and how much tradition is there in the contemporary Indian democracy?

Even Max Weber has implicitly accepted this idea of mixed legitimacy. He discussed the dynamics of the process of legitimation and delegitimation (Weber 1978). The ideal types that he constructed are antagonistic only in theory. In reality, all traditional systems have some features of legality: the Chinese emperors or the Russians tsars both respected some rules of the game.

The Weberian typology is no longer helpful in the study of contemporary political regimes, because only a few countries maintain a traditional authority (for example Morocco or Saudi Arabia), and the charismatic phenomenon, so frequent between 1917 and 1980, is extremely rare today – Khomeini being the most recent example. Charismatic leadership has been replaced by a personalization of power, nourished in many cases by a cult of personality. It would be a serious mistake to confuse such an engineered idolatry with genuine charismatic leadership.

Among the 160 independent nations of the world in 1990, we can distinguish about forty pluralist democracies endowed with a legal-rational legitimacy. Even monarchies such as Britain, Spain, Belgium, Sweden, Norway, The Netherlands or Japan have a legal-rational rulership – the Crown being only a symbol. These forty countries enjoy a democratic legitimacy.

This simple account shows that two of the three Weberian types of legitimacy are almost empty, and the third one includes only one-quarter of nations. Three-quarters of all countries have authoritarian regimes deprived of true legitimacy, and consequently are not covered by the Weberian typology. In order to adapt this typology to the contemporary world, it would be necessary to add a fourth 'box' for the quasi-legitimacy type, and a fifth one for the totally illegitimate regime. There is, obviously, wide diversity among authoritarian regimes. The question here is, using Easton's terminology, how much diffuse support they enjoy.

OPERATIONALIZING THE CONCEPT OF LEGITIMACY

Scholars and politicians have the tendency to adopt the dichotomy: legitimate versus illegitimate. Since the reality is much more varied, legitimacy must come in degrees. Ranking regimes on an imaginary axis from a minimum to a maximum degree of legitimacy is a promising way for the comparative analysis of political systems. Many scholars have felt the need of such scaling: 'Legitimacy runs the scale from complete acclaim to complete rejection . . . ranging all the way from support, consent, compliance through decline, erosion and loss. In case of conscious rejection we may speak of illegitimacy' (Hertz 1978: 320).

As Juan Linz stresses, 'no political regime is legitimate for 100 per cent of the population, nor in all its commands, nor forever, and probably very few are totally illegitimate based only on coercion' (Linz 1988: 66). Legitimacy never reaches unanimity, nor do groups and individuals ever recognize equally the authority of the political power. There are apathetic popular strata and rebellious subcultures, pacifist dissidents and armed terrorists, and between these extremes many who are only partially convinced by the pretensions of legitimacy claimed by the rulers. The support of the majority is generally considered as a test of legitimacy, but as David Easton observed, it is also necessary to consider the substance and intensity of the popular support (Easton 1965).

Easton argues that the 'ratio of deviance to conformity as measured by violation of laws, the prevalence of violence, the size of dissidence movements or the amount of money spent for security would provide indices of support' (Easton 1965: 163). But it is difficult in empirical research to measure 'violations of laws' or 'dissident movements'.

Thus we should not assume that in a given country legitimacy exists simply because it is not contested. In the poorest countries the problem of illegitimacy is not present in the mind of the majority of the people. In these countries tyrants are often perceived as a fatality. Where violence is absent, legitimacy is not necessarily present. The concept of legitimacy is not adequate for, perhaps, one out of every five Third World countries.

Absence of revolt, however, does not imply adhesion to the regime. Revolt is possible only in certain historical circumstances, when a regime starts a process of liberalization. In a totalitarian regime attempts to revolt can be suicidal. The Chinese communist establishment, by repressing the demonstrations in the Tienanmen Square in June 1989, wanted to stop the incipient liberalization movement.

The number of *coups d'état* is the most visible measure of illegitimacy: look for instance at *coups* in Africa in the last three decades, and earlier in Latin America. This criterion has been adopted by a number of scholars.

Can the legitimacy of a political system be judged in terms of subjective adherence of the people? Obviously, confidence is a subjective phenomenon, even if it is analysed objectively. In countries that do not allow freedom of speech, for example, it is difficult to measure by survey the adherence to the regime.

The main problem with any study of legitimacy is the difficulty in measuring it accurately. Opinion polls attempting to measure a state's legitimacy often measure things related to legitimacy without measuring legitimacy directly. For example, support of leaders and policies, or feelings of patriotism or willingness to fight for the country's defence, are all easily measured by such polls and may be related to a state's legitimacy, but none are real measures of legitimacy itself. Support of a leader and his/her policies does not always include the granting of legitimacy to the larger systems of the state, and lack of support for a specific leader or policy does not always imply a lack of overall legitimacy.

In spite of all these difficulties it is possible to consider legitimacy as an evaluable trait of political systems, and to state if a particular country is more or less legitimate than another. Legitimacy is a concept that can be empirically tested. Only the empirical approach can avoid the tautological circle which too often traps the discussion of legitimacy.

Theoretically, the lower the degree of legitimacy, the higher should be the amount of coercion. Therefore, in order to operationalize the concept of legitimacy it is advisable to take into consideration some indicators of coercion, such as the absence of political rights and of civil liberties. These indicators are based on evaluation of freedom of expression, of association, of demonstration, the degree of military intervention in the political arena, fair elections, freedom of religious institutions, independent judiciary, free competition among parties, absence of government terror, and so on. Raymond Gastil in his *Freedom in the World* (Gastil 1980–9), has attempted, in collaboration with many experts, to rank countries according to these criteria. Such a ranking is an acceptable substitute for scaling legitimacy more directly.

A high level of corruption is one of the best symptoms of delegitimation. The fall of political regimes is often accompanied by a generalized corruption – the most notable historical examples being the fall of the Chinese imperial dynasty, of the reign of the Iranian Shah, and of the Soviet *nomenklatura*. Numerous testimonies and dozens of books denounce institutionalized corruption, at all levels of public administration, in most African countries. The judiciary often represents a regime's last bastion against corruption. When they are also contaminated there is no more hope for the ordinary citizen. Then we can predict a crisis of legitimacy, brought about in reality by a *coup d'état*, revolt or revolution.

Paradoxically, scandals are not symptoms of delegitimation, because they can occur only where there is some freedom of speech. On the contrary, we may be certain that a regime where scandals occur is not totally illegitimate.

In some exceptional cases, the scandal may appear as an irrefutable test of the democratic functioning of the regime. The Dreyfus affair, the Watergate affair and the Irangate affair are superb monuments honouring the French and American democracies. Few countries in the world have a democracy sufficiently well-rooted as to be able to correct a political error against the will of the army or to oblige the president to resign – they probably number not more than thirty, with Italy being one of them: President Leone, involved in a corruption scandal, was obliged to resign in 1976.

LEGITIMACY AND TRUST

The distinction between legitimacy and trust appears in the possible replies to a very simple question: 'Should a police officer be obeyed?' The reply 'The officer should be obeyed because his/her order is right,' implies legitimacy *and* trust; 'This particular police officer is wrong, and an appeal to a higher authority should be made, but for the moment he/she should be obeyed because he/she represents authority' indicates legitimacy without trust. The police as an institution can be perceived as legitimate even if a particular police officer may not be trusted. If too many police officers are corrupt or unnecessarily brutal the legitimacy of the police, as an institution, is contested. The mistrust of police officers can be tested empirically, as can the loss of confidence in the police as an institution. If many other institutions are mistrusted (the army, the political parties, the civil service), the regime itself could become illegitimate.

While the concept of legitimacy refers to the whole political system and to its permanent nature, the concept of trust is limited to the rulers who occupy the power in a transitory way:

> Political trust can be thought of as a basic evolutive or affective orientation toward the government.... The dimension of trust runs from high trust to high distrust or political cynicism. Cynicism thus refers to the degree of negative affect toward government and is a statement of the belief that the government is not functioning and producing outputs in accord with individual expectations.
>
> (Miller 1974: 952)

This distinction between the legitimacy of the regime and confidence in particular institutions or office-holders is appropriate for pluralist democracies. Obviously no political system, not even a democratic one, is perfect. No institution can escape criticism from some segment of society. Unanimity is a ridiculous pretension of totalitarian regimes.

Survey research done in some twenty pluralist democracies during the last two decades has revealed a gap of confidence in major institutions. The ubiquity of this loss of confidence in almost all advanced democracies raises important questions concerning the theory of democracy. Is the decline of public confidence in institutions a manifestation of a deeper loss of legitimacy or only a ritualistic cynicism? S. M. Lipset and W. Schneider, after having analysed a large amount of American survey data (Lipset and Schneider 1983), ask frankly: 'Is there a legitimacy crisis?' An identical question should be asked of all West European democracies (except Ireland) as well as of Japan, Canada and Australia. The diagnosis reached by Lipset and Schneider is that:

> People lose faith in leaders much more easily than they lose confidence in the system. All the indicators that we have examined show that the public has been growing increasingly critical of the performance of major institutions. There has been no significant decline in the legitimacy ascribed to the underlying political and economic systems.
>
> (Lipset and Schneider 1983: 378–9)

Their conclusion is 'that the decline of confidence has both real and superficial aspects. It is real because the American public is intensely dissatisfied with the performance of their institutions. It is also to some extent superficial because Americans have not yet reached the point of rejecting those institutions' (ibid.: 384). Yet in the early 1970s Jack Citrin argued that we should not confuse a crisis of confidence with a crisis of legitimacy (Citrin 1974).

An examination of the results of surveys conducted in 1981 by the European Value Systems Study Group and repeated in twelve countries in 1990 leads us to similar conclusions. At the question 'How much confidence do you have in each of the following institutions?' the majority of Europeans replied that they had 'a great deal' or 'quite a lot' of confidence in the police, the armed forces, the judiciary, the educational system and the church. The proportion is lower for the parliament (43 per cent), the civil service (39 per cent), the press (32 per cent), and labour unions (32 per cent). The astonishingly low confidence in the parliament is a serious strain on legitimacy, particularly in Italy, although even in Britain only 40 per cent of the respondents replied positively (Harding et al. 1986: 78, 95).

A significant part of the population may manifest a low confidence in specific institutions, but only a small minority replied that 'on the whole [they] are unsatisfied or not at all satisfied with the way democracy is functioning in [their] country', and only a fringe minority declared themselves in favour of 'radical or revolutionary change' of the system. The vast majority has faith in the democratic system.

LEGITIMACY AND EFFECTIVENESS

The relationship between legitimacy and the effectiveness of a political system is of crucial importance because the presence or absence of one can, in the long run, lead to the growth or loss of the other. Lipset was probably the first to analyse specifically the relationship between legitimacy and effectiveness, arguing that the stability of a regime depends on the relationship between these two concepts. He defines effectiveness as the actual performance of the government or the 'extent to which the system satisfies the basic functions of government' (Lipset 1959: 77). When faced with a crisis of effectiveness, such as an economic depression, the stability of the regime depends to a large extent on the degree of legitimacy that it enjoys.

This is illustrated in the Lipset matrix (Figure 1), showing the dynamics of legitimacy and effectiveness. If a regime finds itself in box A, with both a high degree of legitimacy and effectiveness, in a moment of crisis it should move to box B, showing a loss of effectiveness but the maintenance of legitimacy. Once the crisis has passed it should then move back to its original position in box A (Lipset 1959: 81).

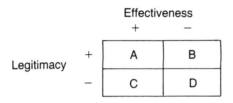

Figure 1   The Lipset matrix

This idea that legitimacy, once obtained, can be preserved is also argued by others. For example, Eckstein (1966) stresses that legitimacy produces a reservoir of support guaranteeing the co-operation of the citizens even in the case of quite unpleasant policies. Legitimacy creates a reservoir of goodwill on which the authorities can draw in difficult times and increases considerably the willingness of the people to tolerate shortcomings of effectiveness. By contrast, if a regime finds itself in box C, with a high degree of effectiveness but a relatively low degree of legitimacy, a crisis in effectiveness would move the regime from box C to box D. The regime would then be likely to break down.

The relationship between these two concepts can be further understood through an analysis of historical examples. During the Great Depression of the 1930s a major crisis in effectiveness seriously affected European as well as American economies. We can contrast the effects of the Depression on the United States and Britain, which had a high level of legitimacy, with the effects on Germany and Austria, where legitimacy was low. In the two first countries, the crisis of effectiveness did not encourage anti-democratic movements and did not bring the regime's legitimacy into question. The people required a change in leadership, not of the regime. In Germany and Austria, however, the crisis of effectiveness led to the collapse of the democratic regime. As has been shown by Kaltefleiter, the unemployment rate and the vote for the National Socialist Party were intimately related (Kaltefleiter 1968).

Movement from box C to box A is also possible since long-term effectiveness can give a regime the chance to build its legitimacy. The rulers in Singapore, South Korea and Taiwan have gained enough legitimacy by their economic success to enable them finally to organize free elections. But the most famous examples are Japan and the Federal Republic of Germany, where democracy was born, or implemented, during a military occupation in a climate of suspicion and scepticism. Their economic miracles raised these two regimes from total absence of legitimacy and from deep national humiliation to the forefront of the most legitimate pluralist democracies.

The same period has seen the collapse of a colossus, not because of a military defeat, but because of a complete failure in effectiveness. The Soviet Union not only had a revolutionary ideology for decades but also had the technological capacity to penetrate and control society in an enormous and relatively rich land. The speed of the breakdown of the communist system in the Soviet Union and in its Eastern European satellites since 1989 demonstrates how the economic ineffectiveness of a regime can ruin its legitimacy. This has culminated in the irony of the defeated ex-enemy, now enjoying a highly legitimate and effective regime, sending aid to a great military power devoid of legitimacy and effectiveness.

ACTORS IN THE PROCESS OF LEGITIMATION

The role of intellectuals in the legitimation process has attracted the attention of many authors. When the intellectual elites are confident in the regime, an optimistic future for the regime could be predicted. But when, on the contrary, the intellectuals are those that oppose the regime, that regime's legitimacy seems more fragile. In China, in the spring of 1989, it was the most educated segment of the society who protested. The students represented less than one per thousand of the Chinese society, but they succeeded in shedding light on the illegitimacy of the regime.

In a comparative analysis of the common factors in the revolutionary movements in Puritan England, in the United States at the time of Washington, in France in 1789 and in Russia in 1917, Crane Brinton (1965) stresses the importance of the intellectual ferment, which subsequently led to the spread of the new ideas to a large part of the population, engendering a crisis of legitimacy.

Other social strata have attracted attention, such as the working class in the Marxist analysis. The clergy have also played an important historic role, as in the Protestant countries in the past, and with the Liberation theology in some

Latin American countries more recently. In the last three decades, the army has been the most visible actor of delegitimation in dozens of developing countries. Today many of the world's authoritarian regimes, particularly in Africa and Asia, are led not by civilians but by military officers.

In summary, the strains on legitimacy and the loss of trust can be explained in part by the difficulty to govern, to steer society. There are two opposite kinds of ingovernability: either the government is overloaded with demands from a very complex society, is doing too much as in the advanced democracies called welfare states, or is not doing enough because the state is economically too weak and lacks the resources required to affect society (except for the 'oil-exporting' countries).

In advanced democracies the loss of confidence in institutions or rulers and the consequent political criticism come from the fact that the rulers have to take decisions under the direct and permanent scrutiny of the public. In a legitimate regime people have the right to criticize. In the authoritarian regimes of developing countries the rulers face different kinds of problems. Their weakness comes not from excessive demands, but from the meagre resources at their disposal.

Power, legitimacy, trust and effectiveness do not have identical meanings in London and Jakarta, or in Washington and Cairo. The ambition to encapsulate these concepts in definitions of universal validity may be a sin of Western cultural ethnocentrism.

REFERENCES

Brinton, C. (1965) *The Anatomy of Revolution*, rev. and expanded edn, New York: Vintage Books.

Citrin, J. (1974) 'The political relevance of trust in government', *American Political Science Review* 68: 973–8.

Easton, D. (1965) *A Systems Analysis of Political Life*, New York: John Wiley.

Eckstein, H. (1966) *Division and Cohesion in a Democracy: A Study of Norway*, Princeton: Princeton University Press.

Gastil, R. D. (1980–9) *Freedom in the World, Political Rights and Civil Liberties*, 6 vols, New York: Freedom House.

Harding, S., Philips, D. and Fogarty, M. (1986) *Contrasting Values in Western Europe*, London: Macmillan.

Hertz, J. (1978) 'Legitimacy, can we retrieve it?', *Comparative Politics* 10: (3): 317–43.

Hudson, M. C. (1977) *Arab Politics. The Search for Legitimacy*, New Haven: Yale University Press.

Kaltefleiter, W. (1968) *Wirtschaft und Politik in Deutschland*, Cologne: Westdeutscher Verlag.

Linz, J. (1988) 'Legitimacy of democracy and the socioeconomic system', in M. Dogan (ed.) *Comparing Pluralist Democracies: Strains on Legitimacy*, Boulder: Westview Press.

Lipset, S. M. (1959) *Political Man, The Social Basis of Politics*, New York: Doubleday.

Lipset, S. M. and Schneider, W. (1983) *The Confidence Gap, Business, Labor and Government in the Public Mind*, Baltimore: Johns Hopkins University Press.

Merkl, P. H. (1988) 'Comparing legitimacy and values among advanced countries', in M. Dogan (ed.) *Comparing Pluralist Democracies: Strains on Legitimacy*, Boulder: Westview Press.

Miller, A. H. (1974) 'Political issues and trust in government 1964–1970', *American Political Science Review* 68 (3): 951–72.

Schaar, J. H. (1981) *Legitimacy in the Modern State*, New Brunswick: Transaction Books.

FURTHER READING

Dogan, M. (ed.) (1988) *Comparing Pluralist Democracies: Strains on Legitimacy*, Boulder: Westview Press.

Habermas, J. (1973) *Legitimation Crisis*, Boston: Beacon Books.

Sternberger, D. (1968) 'Legitimacy', *International Encyclopaedia of Social Sciences*, New York: Macmillan Free Press.

Weber, M. (1978) *Economy and Society*, eds G. Roth and C. Wittich, vol I, Berkeley: University of California Press, particularly the sections on 'The types of legitimate domination', 'Domination and legitimacy', 'Charisma and its transformation'.

PART III

CONTEMPORARY IDEOLOGIES

8

LIBERALISM

R. BRUCE DOUGLASS

Liberalism presents itself today as a coherent body of theory and practice with a well-defined place in the affairs of our time. Its proponents see themselves, typically, as an extension of a long-standing tradition of moral and political reflection that is the source of what has turned out to be the authoritative interpretation of the meaning and significance of the political experience of the West in the modern era. At a time when most of the plausibility has evaporated from the competitors with which it used to do battle, it is cast as a survivor that has stood the test of time and come away vindicated, in the main, by the course that events have taken.

This was not always so. In fact, for much of what is now commonly character-ized, retrospectively, as the history of liberalism, the course of events would in no way have supported such a conclusion. Indeed, for much of the period in question, there scarcely was any such thing, at least not in the minds of those who lived through it. John Locke, for example, whose articulation of the political aspirations of the Whigs in their struggle with the Stuart monarchy in seventeenth-century England is now conventionally treated as a major contri-bution to the founding of the liberal tradition, hardly thought of himself as such. Nor is there much evidence to suggest that Kant, Locke's counterpart on the Continent a century later, was much different in this regard. Even though Kant can be appropriately looked upon as the source of some of the most influential ideas with which liberalism has come to be associated, he did not intend them as such. He, too, was a voice for a developing current of thought (and practice) well before it crystallized into anything like the full-blown partisan doctrine with pretensions of universal validity that it has sub-sequently become.

Nor, once such crystallization did in fact begin to take place, would it have been thinkable to construe the resulting body of ideas as anything other than one point of view among others. For by the time it made sense for those who found themselves thinking in such terms to begin identifying themselves as liberals, it made just as good sense for others to define their politics in very different (and competing) terms. Even as, with the political coming of age of the rising 'middle' class, the process of emancipating individuals to live their lives as they chose, which was at the heart of what the liberal project was about, came into its own as a historical force, it was still manifestly very much in competititon with other alternative visions that challenged root and branch most of what it entailed. Precisely because, in fact, it was so clearly identified with the sweeping change that accompanied the economic revolution that the entrepreneurial class pioneered, it met with active opposition from more than one quarter, and it could not help but be seen, in turn, as the reflection of a distinctly partisan response to the events in question.

Even its identification with change, moreover, had its limits. In the heyday of its ascendency it was not uncommon for adherents to speak as though what it represented was synonymous with all that was progressive. The success that liberals enjoyed in putting their stamp on English society in the middle years of the Victorian era in particular inspired such confidence. But even then it was not difficult to see that there were events in the making that liberals were not at all likely to embrace and, indeed, that they would be predisposed actively to resist. It was no accident, for example, that once the case for the expansion of the franchise to include the middle class had been successfully made, the initiative in advocating further democratization tended to fall to others (most notably, representatives of the working class), and liberals were inclined to greet that prospect with ambivalence at best.

So, too, with the laying of the foundations of the welfare state. Even as the conditions that industrialization brought virtually required the assumption of some degree of collective responsibility for the provision of social welfare (public health and sanitation, for example), the liberal presumption was against it. In particular it was against the assumption of any sort of role by those exercising public power to determine social outcomes. Thus the lead in the creation of social insurance and modern social services was taken by others, and it made sense, especially at a time when working-class parties were coming into their own as a political force, to think of what was emerging in this respect, too, as the fruit of currents of thought and practice other than those that found expression in liberalism (Flora and Heidenheimer 1981).

Moreover, the more momentum the movement in this direction gained, the more uncertain the liberal prospect tended to become. Even as imaginative adaptations to the emerging new realities were undertaken by a whole series of 'new' liberals (Freeden 1978), they themselves had to wonder whether they were not holding on to a fossil that had essentially done its work and was on its way to being superseded. The precipitous decline in electoral fortunes that even the more resourceful liberal parties (most notably, the British Liberal Party) tended to suffer when confronted with any sort of sustained competition from working-class parties could easily be read as a portent of things to come. The longer this went on, the harder it became to think that it represented anything other than an irreversible trend.

This was the case even more after the onset of war in 1914 and the several decades of ongoing social and political upheaval that it set in motion, particularly as the experiments in constitutional government that followed the war succumbed to crisis in one country after another and movements espousing militantly illiberal sentiments came to the fore. The impression that the world that was in the making was one in which liberal thinking simply no longer fitted was powerfully reinforced.

In fact, with the coming of the depression in the 1930s, it was not at all uncommon for liberals themselves to hold liberal ideas responsible for the vulnerabilities that were being exposed, and to wonder, in turn, whether effective protection could be found without turning sharply in another direction. The pull of events was almost inexorably in the direction of the 'end of *laissez-faire*', as Keynes aptly characterized what was taking place (Keynes 1926). As it became evident that the continuing influence of liberal thinking was in large measure responsible for the societies in question finding it difficult to make the necessary adaptations, questions were inevitably raised about the continuing viability of liberalism even as a guide to the making of economic policy.

Nor did the Allied victory in the Second World War altogether relieve the uncertainty. For, as the process of reconstruction got underway, liberals themselves could scarcely help but wonder whether the old problems would not reappear. The likely economic prospect was for a long, protracted period of rebuilding that was destined to be fraught with uncertainty, particularly in view of the devastation caused to the European heartland, and there was no guarantee that the course events had taken after the previous war would not be repeated. Nor was the political prospect much different. For all of the widespread desire to reconstitute democratic government on a more secure basis in the countries where it had failed to take root successfully, it could not be taken for granted that the old sources of instability would not reassert themselves. The success of the democratic recovery was anything but assured, especially in view of the popular following that the communists enjoyed in a number of countries.

At the same time, however, as the apprehensions that these conditions inspired were making themselves felt, the ground was being prepared for a very different mood to emerge in its stead. It soon became evident that the prolonged austerity that had been anticipated was not going to materialize. Indeed, within scarcely a decade it was clear that an economic 'miracle' was in the making. One fear after another dissolved as the effects of the resulting affluence began to be felt, and it did not take long before the appropriate conclusions began to be drawn. Liberals in particular began to speak with an optimism and assurance that had not been heard in decades.

It was not just, of course, the mere fact of affluence *per se* that was responsible for the recovery of nerve that liberals experienced in the post-war era. The sheer magnitude of the growth experienced by much of western Europe in particular was impressive by any standard and could not help but catch the imagination of the people who were expecting much less. However, it was the fact that the growth was as sustained as it was that really made the difference in altering the tenor of liberal thinking. There was scarcely any historical precedent for the continuous, ongoing expansion of output, consumption, investment and employment that took place, and it could not escape attention that the governments of the societies in question had devoted themselves to the active management of economic life in ways that had shown themselves to be conducive to this result. A 'new' capitalism was in the making (Shonfeld 1965), born of a difficult learning experience that had taught invaluable lessons about the pursuit of stable prosperity, and the longer the growth persisted, the more of an inclination there was to assume that the economic problems of the past had been effectively solved.

Every bit as impressive, too, was the fact that the prosperity that was being achieved was not being purchased at the price of deprivation for the majority of the population. Quite the contrary. The benefits of prosperity were spread widely. High levels of employment and steadily expanding consumer demand were treated as essential to economic progress. As Galbraith in particular emphasized (Galbraith 1958), what was distinctive about the threshold that was being crossed was that affluence for the many was coming to be an economic as well as a political necessity. If production was going to be maintained at the desired level, consumption had to be cultivated as a way of life.

Social policy underwent a comparable development, too, as the welfare state truly came into its own as a guarantor of entitlements. Under the impact of the common hardships (and resulting mobilizations) imposed by both the depression and the war, the prejudice against collective provision had faded, and in its place emerged a belief in ensuring each citizen freedom from 'want' as a matter of right. Nor was it just the avoidance of poverty that was intended. The state was to see to it that no one was denied access to basic goods and services, from 'cradle to grave', as a famous liberal apologist for the English version of this development was to characterize its purpose (Beveridge 1942). As tax revenues multiplied and the idea of equality of opportunity caught on, there was an increasing tendency to think in terms of guaranteeing a certain quality of life as well.

There was no mistaking, either, the contribution that liberals and their ideas, from Beveridge to Keynes, had made to these developments. They were hardly alone, and the collaboration of socialists in particular was no less important in setting events on the course they were taking (Crosland 1956). But the active endorsement and even sponsorship of the emerging mix of public and private arrangements that the drift toward planning in post-war liberalism represented went a long way toward explaining the appeal it enjoyed. Much of the thinking that went into the policies in question reflected the prior development of liberal thought and practice over the previous half-century, and the fact that liberals were increasingly inclined to take credit for these policies, and assume their necessity, contributed greatly to the perception that they constituted the foundation of an emerging agreement about how to govern industrial democracies that was on its way to eclipsing any and all of its competitors.

Yet for all the support they received from other quarters, it is not difficult to see why these measures appealed to liberals. An ideological convergence of sorts was indeed in the making, but it was clearly on terms that liberals above all had reason to endorse. Economic planning, social services, social insurance and the rest of what went into the making of the emerging 'public household' to use Daniel Bell's apt term (Bell 1976), were undeniably steps in a collective direction, but by design they were almost always implemented in a way that fell well short of anything like a serious challenge to the liberal presumption in favour of private economic power. The resulting economies might reasonably be characterized as 'mixed', but there could be no question about their essentially capitalist character.

Nor could there be much doubt about the concessions made by the other parties involved. From the socialists' increasingly frank disavowal of nationalization to the Christian Democrats' renunciation of the confessional state, the pattern, in one country after another, was for the adherents of competing currents of thoughts that were at all serious contenders for power to abandon, in effect, much of what historically had put them at odds with liberalism. In the name of one or another kind of *aggorniamento*, they gave up, for all practical purposes, a good part of what previously had given them their identity, and in the process they did away, too, in large measure, with the rationale for any sort of principled opposition to what liberalism represented. Indeed, the accommodation that they made tended to be such that what remained often had the appearance of being little more than a series of variations on liberal themes.

This was especially so with respect to the value placed on civil and political liberties. After the trauma of totalitarianism, their worth tended to be appreciated more widely – and deeply – than ever before, and the more evident it became that their realization could be reconciled with both political stability and economic progress, the harder it became to discover any sort of principled opposition to what they represented. Aside from the occasional cavil from one or another radical critic about 'repressive tolerance', the days were over when their proponents had to contend with suggestions that they were instruments of one or another partisan purpose. In their place emerged a climate of opinion in which, if anything, they were taken for granted as the necessary point of departure for any politics that were to stand a chance of achieving legitimacy.

A premium on toleration was also part of the same climate. With the social and cultural conditions that gave rise to the old ideological combat fading, and the aspiration to the all-out victory they fostered discredited by events, toleration took on an appeal that it had not had since the religious wars occasioned by the Reformation. With groups from Catholics to Communists going out of their way to declare their allegiance to respecting diversity, pluralism came to acquire such significance that, in fact, it began to take on the status of one of the principal defining features of the societies in question. Their 'openness' in this sense became one of the major qualities on which they prided themselves, and the more experience they had with it, the more self-conscious its practice tended to become.

It could therefore only be a matter of time before the trend this represented found theoretical expression. For a brief period it was inhibited by the inclination of many liberals to go along with the suggestion that what was taking place was the transcendence of ideology (Bell 1960–1), and to refrain from giving any elaborate philosophical expression to the ideas that were really at stake. This was particularly the case when the very possibility of moral and political philosophy was called into question by the influence that positivism enjoyed. But once Rawls showed that it was possible – and necessary – to join anew the philosophical issues at stake (Rawls 1971), it quickly became evident that a different construction was needed on what was underway. For as the renaissance of liberal theory that followed showed, liberals themselves clearly were not about to concede that the tradition they represented was finished. Just the opposite. With Rawls leading the way, the view that permeated their writings was that after years of struggle against one competitor after another, liberalism was finally on its way to claiming its rightful place as *the* public philosophy of the West.

Nor, for all the effort that has been put into making the result out to be a common ground capable of accommodating the legitimate interests of other contenders (Rawls 1987), has there ever been much question about the partisan character of what was intended. In fact, the more fully the logic of the turn that liberal reasoning has taken in this latest mutation has come to be revealed, the more obvious its partisan edge has tended to be. For the interpretation that is put on the experience(s) in question is, for all of the talk about neutrality, in no sense a neutral one, and it is not in the least neutral in its practical implications either. As the recurring (albeit highly selective) invocation of Kantian premises reveals, one rather specific way of understanding what has taken place is presupposed, and it is accompanied, predictably, by a preference for a particular way of conceiving of its promise as well.

What in particular is thrown anew into sharp relief in this relation is the distinctiveness of the priority – and meaning – that liberals are inclined to attach to liberty. For it is by no means just as one good among others that it figures in what they have to say. Building on the special significance that personal autonomy has come to acquire as a result of the events of the last century, they would have it understood to be the fundamental good, the realization of which is above all what the recent experience of the West has been about. More than anything else, they insist, the opportunity for individuals to be self-determining – to function, as Rawls puts it, as moral agents, choosing one's own conception of the good and living life accordingly – is what the societies in question have learned is important in the conduct of public affairs, and their achievement, in turn, has been to show how this can be successfully pursued as a way of life.

Nothing has contributed more to this result, moreover, in the account that tends to be favoured by the current generation of liberal theorists, than the growing awareness of the limits of the human capacity to prescribe how life ought to be lived. In marked contrast to the days when liberal arguments were distinguished by the boldness with which they affirmed the power of reason, they now tend to be predicated on an equally dedicated epistemological modesty (Spragens 1981), and it is to the increasingly widespread acceptance of the sense of restraint this entails that they are inclined to attribute the success that the 'liberal' democracies have come to enjoy. There is no way, virtually every liberal thinker of consequence now asserts matter-of-factly, that we can know with any sort of objective certainty what 'God's will' or the 'laws of history' dictate, and it is because this 'fact' is increasingly taken for granted by the peoples in question that they have come to be able to live as they do. Through long (and sometimes bitter) experience they have learned the futility of assigning a public role to what are essentially private visions, and in the process they have come to appreciate, too, the impropriety of doing so as well. Indeed, more: the experience they have had with toleration has taught them, increasingly, to look upon it as the only appropriate response to the challenge posed by the heterogeneity of the good that human beings are prepared to seek.

What they have also learned, it is said, is the value of the resulting diversity. It is not just that they have become accustomed to accommodating beliefs and values different from their own, but that they have also come to appreciate the promise such a practice holds. For the more consistently and deliberately it is pursued, the more evident it becomes that the effect, almost inescapably, is to enlarge steadily the opportunities for individuality to flourish. Instead of their lives conforming to one or another pre-existent pattern, people are virtually invited to experiment and innovate in keeping with their own distinctive tastes and inclinations, with the result that life takes on an increasingly varied and fluid character. So the richness of the variety of which human beings are capable is experienced as never before, and the way is open for it to be explored as an end in itself.

To make the case for embracing this possibility as a matter of principle is, in turn, above all what liberalism has come to stand for (Ackerman 1980; Dworkin 1977–8), and it is clear from virtually everything about the way this is done that it is assumed that the fact that such an opportunity now presents itself to the societies in question represents an historical accomplishment of the first magnitude. For even as they speak in increasingly historicist terms and make a point of avoiding any sort of explicit metaphysical commitments (Rawls 1985), there is no mistaking the presumption that pervades the arguments advanced by Rawls and those who have followed his lead that the way of life to which they seek to give expression amounts to more – much more – than just one more chapter in history's ongoing succession of different ways of ordering human relations. Indeed, just the opposite. If anything, the tendency now, as the Cold War fades and ideas championed by liberals are embraced as symbols of liberation in one popular insurgency after another, is to revive with a vengeance the old liberal conceit that what the liberal vision represents is the definitive conclusion of the quest for the good society, beyond which further progress is neither necessary nor possible (Fukuyama 1989).

Precisely, however, because of the increasingly historicist character of so much of the reasoning to which liberals are now given, this is a claim that is much more easily made than defended. Indeed, philosophically its defence becomes positively anomalous. All along, to be sure, there has been something of an anomaly about the doctrinaire universalism of a creed so firmly committed to making a virtue of toleration. But in the days when liberals were capable of backing up the claims that they made in this regard with bold generalizations about human nature whose merits they were prepared to argue, what they said at least had the appearance of epistemological consistency. Now, however, as any sort of owning up to metaphysical commitments (much less arguing their merits) is dismissed as obsolete (Rorty 1989) and liberal theorists are reduced to appealing to nothing more than (their version of) the considered experience of the West, even that appearance of consistency is gone, and all that remains is a presumption in favour of treating the experience in question as authoritative.

That such a presumption can be taken for granted so matter-of-factly in serious theoretical arguments is a tribute, of course, to the confidence liberals now have that history can be counted on to vindicate what they espouse. But it is also, no less, a reflection of the silences to which they have been reduced. For even as they feed on the good fortune that ideas deriving from their tradition now enjoy, it can scarcely be ignored that they do so as much out of necessity as choice. At a time when they have all but abandoned any pretence of an objective warrant for the practices they favour (Rorty 1989), they are hardly in a position to enter seriously into arguments about their merits in principle. Aside from stipulating what they themselves (as self-conscious Westerners) prize, 'history' is all they have to go on.

As long as the returns that it brings continue to be congenial, this may, of course, as a practical matter suffice. There is nothing, after all, like the confirmation of events to make critical questions seem beside the point. But equally there is nothing like a reversal of fortune to give them fresh relevance, and to expose, in turn, the vacuity of answers that are grounded in nothing but convention. For what is 'self-evident' when things are going smoothly can all too easily turn out to be anything but when they are not.

If the confidence that liberals now tend to have that a corner has been turned and what is in the making is a world in which, for all practical purposes, the triumph of their way of thinking can be treated as an accomplished fact, then this is an eventuality which, presumably, will never need to be confronted. History will indeed settle the issue, and in a manner that makes further argument permanently irrelevant. But if the talk that we are now hearing about the 'end of history' itself turns out to be just one more ideological illusion, just the opposite could occur. This is especially likely if the economic stability and vitality that support the way of life that liberals now take for granted proves to be something less than permanent. In particular, in the event that growth stalls (and/or is seriously challenged), questions that are now being swept under the rug can almost certainly be expected to come surging back into the forefront of public life, and in a form that liberals could well find themselves less prepared than ever to confront. Precisely because they have become so accustomed to taking for granted things that do not deserve at all to be taken for granted, they could well be hard put, in fact, even to make sense of what they are up against. This is the shadow lurking in the background as the reigning public philosophy of the West celebrates the moment of its greatest triumph.

REFERENCES

Ackerman, B. (1980) *Social Justice in the Liberal State*, New Haven and London: Yale University Press.

Bell, D. (1960–1) *The End of Ideology*, New York: Free Press/London: Macmillan.

——(1976) *The Cultural Contradictions of Capitalism*, New York: Basic Books.

Beveridge, W. (1942) *Social Insurance and Allied Services* (Report of the Inter-Departmental Committee on Social Insurance and Allied Services), London: Macmillan.

Crosland, C. A. R. (1956) *The Future of Socialism*, London: Jonathan Cape.

Dworkin, R. (1977–8) *Taking Rights Seriously*, Cambridge: Harvard University Press.

Flora, P. and Heidenheimer, A. (eds) (1981) *The Development of the Welfare State in Europe and North America*, New Brunswick and London: Transaction Books.

Freeden, M. (1978) *The New Liberalism*, Oxford: Clarendon.

Fukuyama, F. (1989) 'The end of history?', *National Interest* 16: 3–18.

Galbraith, J. (1958) *The Affluent Society*, Boston: Houghton-Mifflin.

Keynes, J. (1926) *The End of Laissez-Faire*, London: L. and Virginia Woolf.

Rawls, J. (1971) *A Theory of Justice*, Cambridge: Harvard University Press.

——(1985) 'Justice as fairness: political not metaphysical', *Philosophy and Public Affairs* 14: 223–51.

——(1987) 'The idea of an overlapping consensus', *Oxford Journal of Legal Studies* 7: 1–25.

Rorty, R. (1989) *Contingency, Irony and Solidarity*, Cambridge: Cambridge University Press.

Shonfeld, A. (1965) *Modern Capitalism*, London/Oxford/New York: Oxford University Press.

Spragens, T., Jr (1981) *The Irony of Liberal Reason*, Chicago: University of Chicago Press.

FURTHER READING

Bentham, J. (1948) *A Fragment on Government* and *The Introduction to the Principles of Morals and Legislation*, ed. W. Harrison, Oxford: Oxford University Press.

Dewey, J. (1935) *Liberalism and Social Action*, New York: G. P. Putnam's Sons.

Halevy, E. (1955) *The Growth of Philosophical Radicalism*, Boston: Beacon.

Hamilton, A., Madison, J., and Jay, J. (1961) *The Federalist* ed. J. Cooke, Middletown, Conn.: Wesleyan University Press.

Hartz, L. (1955) *The Liberal Tradition in America*, New York: Harcourt, Brace and World.

Hobhouse, L. (1964) *Liberalism*, Oxford: Oxford University Press.

Kant, I. (1970) *Kant's Political Writings*, ed. H. Reiss, Cambridge: Cambridge University Press.

Keynes, J. M. (1931) *Essays in Persuasion*, New York: Macmillan.

Locke, J. (1952) *A Letter on Toleration*, ed. A. C. Fraser, Oxford: Oxford University Press.

——(1960) *Two Treatises of Government*, ed. P. Laslett, Cambridge: Cambridge University Press.

Mill, J. (1937) *An Essay on Government*, ed. E. Barker, Cambridge: Cambridge University Press.

Mill, J. S. (1962) *On Liberty*, London: Everyman's Library.

Popper, K. (1966) *The Open Society and Its Enemies*, 2 vols, Princeton: Princeton University Press.

Rawls, J. (1971) *A Theory of Justice*, Cambridge University Press.

Ruggiero, G. de. (1927) *The History of European Liberalism*, Oxford: Oxford University Press.

Smith, A. (1976) *The Wealth of Nations*, ed. W. B. Todd, Oxford: Clarendon Press.

9

CONSERVATISM

KENNETH R. HOOVER

The revival of conservatism as a powerful political force has been the distinguishing feature of contemporary politics. As a philosophical orientation, as an ideology, and as a political movement, conservatism has come to set the terms for policy debates in the major nations of the West.

An understanding of the separate strands within conservatism requires a broad analysis of historical definitions as well as a sense of contemporary political forces. What began in the eighteenth century as an orientation against change and the advent of egalitarianism has become, in the latter part of the twentieth century, an ideologically based movement to rationalize a reordering of society, politics and the economy. The movement contains divergent tendencies. As an approach to understanding this phenomenon, we shall begin by characterizing contemporary conservatism and shall then turn to its historical roots to discover the origins of the differences that threaten the viability of conservatism today.

CONTEMPORARY CONSERVATISM

The common theme of political conservatism is an acceptance of inequality. What characterizes conservatives of all kinds is a sense that the differences between people are more important than the similarities. It is in these differences that conservatives locate the keys to the problems of social order, on the one hand, and productivity, on the other. Whereas classical liberals thought that people should be regarded as equals for all civic purposes, conservatives have been more impressed with the need to treat individuals differently depending on a variety of moral and economic criteria (Joseph and Sumption 1979).

Having accepted the fact of human inequality, however, conservatives are not at all agreed on what to do about it. There are two major divisions in conservative thought that may be labelled 'traditionalist' and 'individualist'

(Dolbeare and Dolbeare 1976; Nash 1979). Individualist conservatives argue that, since there is such a manifest difference in individual abilities and talents, society will best be served by the maximum of individual freedom. If people are left free to pursue their own talents and interests without governmental interference, they will learn to be responsible for their own behaviour, and they will be encouraged, especially in a free-market society, to develop abilities that involve the production for goods and services that are in demand by the society. By contrast, traditionalist conservatives generally argue that, given the limitations of human nature and the inequality that results from those limitations, the key problem is how to organize the institutions that will constrain individual behaviour and guide it so that a measure of order and social cohesion can be achieved.

For individualist conservatives, the question of initiative and enterprise is paramount in establishing differences between people; for traditionalists, it is a matter of character and innate ability. Both provide somewhat similar rationales for inequality, but there are important differences that have profound political consequences. Initiative and enterprise are qualities that individualist conservatives imagine to be a matter of volition, and within reach of all people. Character and innate ability, on the other hand, are shaped by heredity, breeding and the civilizing power of institutions – and they are bound to be tested in a world that is made disorderly by the weaknesses of human nature. The political consequence is that individualist conservatism leads to the market-place as the premier institutional form, whereas traditional conservatism points toward entities such as the family, the church and the corporation.

Freedom as a political value is perceived quite differently by individualists and traditionalists. The former adopt the classical liberal position on the centrality of individual liberty, while rejecting most of the community-regarding limits liberals have placed upon it (Friedman 1962). Individualist conservatives would reject what Locke said about restraints on accumulation, Mill on qualitative judgements of utility, or Green on rationality as a guide to true freedom. Libertarianism is the version of freedom congenial to the individualist conservative position, and the logic of material self-interest is its calculus (Buchanan and Tullock 1962; Downs 1965).

Traditional conservatives have a more complicated view of freedom. Their argument is that real freedom is only possible within the proper structure. Without limits, licence is the result, not liberty. Institutional limits create spaces within which choice may be prudently exercised, and such freedom as is beneficial to humans may be exercised responsibly.

The market is the chosen social device of individualist conservatives because it rewards effort, rational choice (in terms of perceived material self-interest) and entrepreneurial skill. Traditionalists have always been chary of the market *per se*, although they have justified the institution of private property as a vital adjunct of other institutional bases for the society: the family, the bourgeois state, the church, and the corporation (Wills 1979). It is the propensity of the market-place to disrupt settled patterns of institutional life that worries traditional conservatives.

These two tendencies have opposed each other on issues such as the desirability of minimum social provision for the disadvantaged. Traditional conservatives believe that levels of society should be dealt with responsibly. Individualist conservatives regard redistributive activities as coercion. Such governmental programmes are regarded simply as interferences with the process of free volition and individual choice that should be allowed to determine the 'true' distribution of rewards according to effort.

Education, abortion and the environment are other issues that divide the two tendencies. Traditional conservatives see the provision of support for education as a critical means of transmitting the moral code and cultural patrimony of Western civilization. Education helps to establish the hierarchies of ability even while it reproduces the values of civilization itself. For individualists, the educational system should resemble a market-place where people can pay for what they would like. Vouchers for educational services provide a means of using this principle while retaining public taxation as a financial basis for the system. The diversification of schooling systems, coupled with a decentralization of control in the hands of parents, places policy making where individualist conservatives think it should be.

Abortion poses a direct opposition between the use of government power to enforce a moral code and the assertion that individuals should be able to choose their own approach to reproduction. Environmental issues create similar difficulties within conservatism. Traditionalists favour conservation through public control where necessary; individualists are likely to support freedom of action or market incentives that reward preservation.

The movement containing these contradictory tendencies may be called conservative capitalism (Hoover and Plant 1989). It is a movement that contains a considerable internal tension between an institutionalist approach and a regard for the sanctity of individual free choice. The latter is a product of capitalist doctrine as it has come to be conceptualized in the West; the former reflects historic commitments to customary practices.

Conservative capitalism thus marks a period of politics that is distinct from the liberal capitalism characterized by the pre-Thatcherite social democratic consensus in Britain, and the general agreement on reform liberal principles that characterized American politics from the New Deal until the fall of the Carter presidency in 1980. In the concluding section of this essay, the future of this coalition will be explored, but first a brief historical survey will provide necessary background.

THE EUROPEAN ROOTS OF CONSERVATISM

In the classical scholarship on conservatism, the defining theme is the orientation toward change. According to the *Oxford English Dictionary*, conservatism first appears as a political term in 1835 in Matthew Arnold's letters, and its meaning has to do with preserving traditional social and political forms. Shortly thereafter, in Disraeli's *Coningsby* (Disraeli 1844), conservatism is described as a sceptical attitude towards secular doctrines of salvation.

Resistance to change had, besides its obvious advantages as a ploy for the preservation of the position of the elite, a philosophical basis in two rather different traditions: the doctrines of natural law, on the one hand, and epistemological scepticism on the other. The former proposed a constancy to human affairs that could be used to deny the possibility of innovation, while the latter undermined the basis upon which proposals for change could be grounded.

The belief in a natural order is as old as philosophy, and the political form given to this belief in the Middle Ages embraces a version of hierarchy that is congenial to those who accept divisions of society on the basis of class or of religious commitment. Just as an acorn grows into an oak tree, there is a natural order in society that, when brought to full maturity through the appropriate institutions, will lead to as much order and justice as human beings are capable of.

While scepticism can be used to undermine custom and tradition, it also has its conservative uses. David Hume (1711–76) opened the way to a devastating critique of the institutional inventions of classical liberalism by alternately exposing the evident rudeness of political arrangements, and deriding the pretensions of theorists who would dignify power with formulas based on consent. Deprived of rationalist certainty, liberalism remains only a speculative system from which a few observations on justice may be derived for the benefit of evolving institutions of law and order (Hayek 1960; Oakeshott 1962).

Natural law is the philosophical well-spring of traditional conservatism, while scepticism remains the touchstone of individualist conservatism. There is no necessary opposition between them, as sceptics of human inventions can blend with pessimists who place justice outside the bounds of human achievement. Yet there is a version of scepticism that erodes the basis of traditional society, as well as the pretensions of the new liberal order. This is the spirit in which Adam Smith approaches political economy (Hirschman 1977), and through his analysis the basis was laid for new variations of liberalism as well as conservatism.

Smith presented classical liberalism with the market-place as the economic analogue of democracy. Here was the opening to mass participation in economic affairs on the basis of labour, if not capital itself. The enemy of the

market was misguided government policy – a government of the privileged –
that found through its mercantilist policies a doctrine that justified a powerful
state and the enrichment of political allies simultaneously. In the spirit of 1776,
Smith was the ally of the masses.

Yet there was a conservative moral strain to Smith's thought as well. He
was preoccupied with the problem of moral behaviour. In *The Theory of Moral
Sentiments* (Smith 1759) he seeks to explain how fair and impartial government
could play a critical role in limiting the kind of self-serving attitude regarding
the appropriation of property that is all too natural, and all too destructive of
personal discipline and productive behaviour.

The extension of this institutional analysis in *An Inquiry into the Nature and
Causes of the Wealth of Nations* (Smith 1776) demonstrates that the market, by
harnessing the power of vanity through the price system, will yield a measure
of self-discipline in the interest of obtaining the best possible return on
investment whether of labour or capital. For Smith, the main problem was the
conversion of destructive behaviour into socially useful energy (Hirschman
1977). At that, he held out no hope of perfection or even of significant
improvement, only the avoidance of harm – and the increase of economic
productivity.

The specifically political intent of conservatism has to do with a resistance
to the use of government to further, most significantly, equality. The resistance
is predicated, in the writings of Edmund Burke (1729–97), the premier articu-
lator of traditional conservatism as a philosophical orientation, upon a distrust
of rationalist abstractions, a positive valuation of custom and tradition, and a
fundamental acceptance of human differences as the basis of civil order (Burke
1976). This conservative orientation did not uniformly require a disavowal of
change, for Burke could accept the American colonial revolt as an assertion
of traditional English rights by disenfranchised citizens. At the same time, he
rejected the French revolution as a murderous exercise in the imposition of
the abstractions, *liberté, egalité, fraternité*. Burkean conservatism amounted to a
faith in a plurality of authoritative institutions that operate to produce an
'organic society' characterized by moderation, discipline and a recourse to
spiritual solace in the face of the vicissitudes of life (Burke 1976; Kirk 1962;
Nisbet 1986).

Simultaneously, in late eighteenth-century Germany, conservatism acquired
a range of meanings clustering around the defence of the status quo, reform
and reaction (Epstein 1966: 4–16). The defining criterion for the orientation
to change had to do with how best to maintain differentiations of status,
authority and rank that fit with conservative conceptions of human nature. For
some the best course involved simple resistance to innovation, for others a
careful moderation of the forces of change, and for the least practical, the
revival of the past.

For both English and German conservatives, nationalism provided a palpable political form for these philosophical yearnings. While the state was viewed with some suspicion, the nation offered, at least in the abstract, the hierarchies of meaning and authority that accommodate a conservative political analysis. The state, as distinct from the nation, may be the vehicle of progressives, liberal reformers or radicals. The nation, while founded in a revolt against medieval imperialism, by the late eighteenth century came to represent the qualitative and spiritual principle that could be opposed to the quantitative and rationalist axioms of classical liberalism and its radical offspring. The fateful alliance of conservatism and nationalism was born of this union of doctrine and politics.

French conservatives such as Joseph de Maistre (1753–1821) mingled nationalism with Christianity to produce a reactionary form of conservatism that took aim at all of the inventions of classical liberalism and radicalism: the social contract was a fiction, the possibility of improving on 'the state of nature' a dangerous illusion, and democracy itself a reproach to divine law. While this sort of recourse to the *ancien régime* limited the appeal of conservatism, the link made between nationalism and Christianity gave a populist opening to conservatism which reappears in contemporary conservative movements.

If an ideology may be defined as a world view that contains a programme of political action, then conservatism became an ideology when it took the form of a partisan credo during the political contests of the nineteenth century. The traditional conservative world view has roots in stoicism and medieval Christian pessimism about human nature. It centres on the need for hierarchy, the consequences of human limitations, and the inescapable role of spiritual faith. What gave conservatism a modern political presence was the evolution of the Tory party in the hands of Disraeli, Alexander Hamilton's creation of a Federalist party in the United States, and the ferment of rightist partisanship on the Continent. In each arena, conservatism became an active ideological force.

While there is resistance to characterizing conservatism as anything more than a set of orientations to change (Rossiter 1982; Huntington 1957), the development of a political programme can be clearly identified. Disraeli countered the utilitarianism of his age with prescriptions for the maintenance of distinctions and the celebration of customary arrangements that went well beyond caution to resolute affirmation. The struggles over the Reform Bills and the alliance with Victorianism defined a distinctively Tory political programme.

The alliance of conservatism, nationalism and imperialism brought Britain to the apogee of its power and influence in world affairs by the turn of the century. The foundations of this power within the conservative class system and the economic relations that flowed from imperialism were shaken to the core by the social and physical devastation of the First and Second World

Wars. Churchill's evocation of Britain's 'finest hour', testimony as it was to the power of nationalist symbolism, also marked the beginning of the end of traditional conservatism in British society. The Conservatives lost power decisively for the first time at the end of the Second World War, and the initiative shifted to the left with the installation of a Labour government in 1945.

While the socialists commanded the rhetorical heights in the ensuing four decades, no small part of the institutional innovations of the social democratic consensus involved a regard for conservative institutional preferences. The distribution of services may have been democratized, but the institutions of the British welfare state retained a substantial measure of hierarchy within and autonomy without. This made more palatable the accommodation that the Conservative Party was led to make through the 1950s, 1960s and 1970s up until the advent of the first Thatcher government.

The result was an entitlement-driven bureaucracy that found itself by the 1970s increasingly isolated and declining in public esteem (Niskanen 1973; Brittan 1983). In an economic environment characterized by rising expectations, shrinking resources and the increasing power of the means of collective action through union control of the Labour Party, the British welfare state came to its great crisis. That the Conservatives could not capitalize on this crisis sooner was partly due to their complicity in it, and to the discredited traditionalism that underpinned their doctrinal approach. It was the development of Margaret Thatcher's distinctive combination of social traditionalism and individualist conservative economic policy that supplied a resolute conservative capitalist programme with which to confront a divided left. It was the unpopularity of such doctrinally driven measures as the poll tax that dismantled this combination and led to the downfall of Thatcher as prime minister.

NORTH AMERICAN CONSERVATISM

The story of the demise of traditional conservative orthodoxy is different in the American context, though the result was remarkably similar. In the newly independent colonies, Alexander Hamilton brought together a formidable group of notables intent on creating a strong national political and commercial system that could confront the rising power of democrats and debtors. His conceptual framework relied on the notion of an elite so composed as to balance contending forces: between those who, in the pursuit of fame, must cultivate public regard, and those who seek dominion and are led to exploit the forces of production (Dolbeare 1984). He envisioned an elite characterized by *noblesse oblige* who would command the apparatus of a powerful federal union in extending the benefits of the new society across the continent.

Hamilton's project foundered in the battle with the democratizing forces led by Thomas Jefferson, and suffered a major institutional blow when Andrew

Jackson vetoed the rechartering of the Bank of the United States in 1832. It is ironic that Jackson undid this conservative institution in the name of *laissez faire* which was to become, 150 years later, the doctrinal basis for a renovated conservatism.

Conservatism as a political credo in the United States suffered its second major blow in the defeat of the South in the Civil War. While many conservative citizens were for the Union, the intellectual basis of the confederate cause comprised a full programme of conservative principles from the reverence for traditional institutions through to the stratification of the population on the grounds of race, gender and class. The victory of the Union abetted the spread of democratic radicalism, and its extension to movements for full civil rights for minorities and women.

While conservative institutionalism was the declining cause of nineteenth-century American politics, conservatism as a firm defence of the limited basis of the constitutional contract remained in place until the New Deal. Though considerably weakened by the democratization of the political process arising from populist, progressive and socialist initiatives, the policy constraints of constitutional conservatism were not truly broken until the Supreme Court acquiesced in the policy innovations of the Roosevelt administration in the late 1930s.

From that point forward, traditional conservatism went slowly into the political night, kept alive only by its opposition to communism during the Cold War. It took the admixture of a new individualist interpretation, and a complex crisis within liberal capitalism, to revive the label and bring conservatism to the forefront of public attention in presidential campaigns, beginning with Barry Goldwater's unsuccessful candidacy in 1964 and culminating in Ronald Reagan's victory in 1980 (Piven and Cloward 1982). Reagan's triumph was even more clearly a case of coalition building between traditionalists and individualists, though contests over policies and priorities were usually decided in favour of the latter. His victory was abetted by the revisionist sociology of intellectuals who renounced the left in favour of a new conservatism that promised a stronger defence of individual freedom than the reformist left had delivered (Steinfels 1979; Kristol 1983).

The Canadian pattern diverges from the British and American in that the 'Red Tory' tradition was an assertive force in shaping institutions of political economy (Taylor 1982). The idea that governmentally based national and provincial economic institutions in banking, transportation, communications and mineral extraction should lead the way in forming a distinctive identity for Canadian culture was the work of traditionalist conservatives with a penchant for institutional innovation. The objective of these efforts was not at variance with the desires of populists and even liberals for much of Canada's history, though there was plenty of room for partisanship in the allocation of influence and control within this institutional framework.

The introduction of *laissez faire* terminology into the Canadian conservative lexicon was inhibited by the persistence of classical liberalism in the opposing party and the delicacy of devolutionist politics in a fragile federation. It was once more the economic burden of the welfare state in the readjustments following the oil embargo and the divisions on the left between establishment liberals and Western populists that created an opening for a new kind of conservatism.

The Mulroney government represented a departure for Canadian conservatism. Free trade and a minimalist role for the state were its hallmarks. The Free Trade Agreement tests the cultural and economic solidarity of Canada in a manner that will directly confront the residual traditionalism and nationalism of conservatives. The programme runs the risk of jeopardizing the future of Canada as a sovereign entity, though, by the axioms of modern economics, there is little choice but to do so if there are to be gains in the gross national product comparable to other industrialized nations. Whether such gains will materialize given the disparities of economic power between Canada and its principle trading partner may well determine the future of conservative political fortunes. Whether conservatism can survive a loss of cultural cohesion and national identity in the name of economic ambition is being tested by the Canadian experience.

CONTINENTAL-EUROPEAN CONSERVATISM

In continental-European politics, the strengths of traditionalist conservatism were also the sources of its weaknesses, though an amelioration of the extremes through the development of Christian democratic parties preserved conservatism as a powerful rival to the left in much of Europe. The appeals of nationalism and of its combination with Christian religious identifications led to a complicity, dating from the late nineteenth century, between chauvinist attitudes and aristocratic forms. Charles Maurras (1868–1952) brought to fruition the anti-semitic pro-fascist potential of this alliance in France during the Second World War and was condemned for it by a court of law when the Vichy regime fell. Houston Stewart Chamberlain (1855–1927) provided a link between British, German and Austrian Aryan nationalism of the kind that nurtured Adolf Hitler. Hitler rapidly outstripped any real link between Nazism and a recognizable conservatism. Anti-semitism became a genocidal fixation that no Christian could justify, plebiscitary rule a substitute for traditional authority, and Hitler's fantasies of Aryan supremacy an excuse for the wholesale destruction of human life. While fascism itself can be intellectually separated from conservatism, the early complicity of some conservative intellectuals, literati and politicians in its rise to power contributed to the decline in the credibility of conservative parties.

Only in Franco's Spain, however, did the union of religion, nationalism and social conservatism reach its institutional peak and survive for an extended period of time. While there is an intellectual basis for a moderate version of Spanish conservatism in the writings of José Ortega y Gasset (1883–1955), the Franco regime went far beyond Ortega's admonitions concerning the masses to institutionalize a repressive hierarchy. The reactionary nature of the combination was fully revealed in the systematic violation of human rights, and in the refusal to consider elementary programmes of social justice of the kind that helped to modernize the rest of Europe in the post-war period. Franco, *El Caudillo*, became an icon of modern conservative politics, and his likeness could be seen all too often in the regimes of Latin America.

The use of police state tactics by governments claiming to be conservative gave the increasingly educated masses a reason to reject the right and, for those with a commitment to solving the world's injustices, grounds to embrace the left. The links between the conservative peasant parties of eastern and central Europe and proto-fascist attitudes of anti-Semitism provided a pretext for the Russian annexation of Latvia, Lithuania, and Estonia at the outset of the Second World War, and the subjugation of eastern Europe in the post-war period. While there were many powerful factors at work in these situations, it is apparent that conservative excesses contributed to the extremes of political confrontation that set the stage for both the Second World War and the Cold War.

In the post-war period, however, a more benign face of conservatism appeared and reclaimed a legitimate place in the politics of the Western democracies. Konrad Adenauer in the Federal Republic of Germany and Charles de Gaulle in France provided models of conservative rule that, especially in the former case, made good the claim that conservatism and democracy can co-exist. In their stout resistance to communism, Continental conservatives, and to a lesser extent American conservatives, were able to raise the credibility of the right whenever it ebbed away from an accommodationist left (Diggins 1975). By emphasizing the themes of cultural solidarity, traditional social values and Christian moral commitment, Adenauer and de Gaulle restored a measure of confidence to the European right.

While Continental conservatives could not respond effectively to the distributive demands of an increasingly potent labour movement, or the social innovations of an affluent middle class, they did succeed in holding together the core of a national identity in an increasingly secular and materialistic culture. If distributive equity remains the lesser theme of contemporary European politics, and the fruits of anti-communism are gathered by the right, the basis for an enduring conservative presence may have been laid. However, there are new sources of tension affecting all of the conservative movements of the West, and these may well determine its survival.

CONSERVATIVE CAPITALISM: LINES OF CLEAVAGE

The contest between the individualist and communitarian elements in conservative capitalism has been made evident in the struggles over income security, education, the devolution of central political authority, and many other issues. What has become increasingly apparent is that there are cross-cutting splits that divide each tendency along lines of class attitude, if not of class itself.

Within traditionalist conservatism, there is a split between establishment conservatives based in the customary institutions of Western society, and moralist conservatives who base their politics in evangelical churches, single-cause organizations and patriotic associations. Both favour the use of governmental authority to shape individual behaviour by limiting certain freedoms. There is, however, a considerable difference of degree and of moral purpose separating these points of view.

While establishment conservatives are supporters of a moderate accommodation with the welfare state as a matter of sustaining social stability, moralist conservatives are more inclined to think of government provision as a means of fostering dependency and personal laxity. Where establishment conservatives find government programmes of population control acceptable, moralists wish to use government policy to restrict abortion, constrain sexual freedom and censor pornography. Establishment conservatives are inclined to restrain licence in individual behaviour, while moralists tend toward the imposition of discipline as a means of moral improvement.

Moralist politics in the United States were a prominent factor in securing Republican control of the US Senate from 1980–6, and in the presidential candidacy of evangelist Pat Robertson in 1988. The selection of Senator Dan Quayle as Vice-President was predicated in part on developing a coalition between the establishment politics of George Bush and the moralist appeal of the Senator from Indiana.

On the individualist side of conservative capitalism, there is a similar division between populist conservatives and corporate conservatives. Populism has a long history in American politics of both left and right. On the right, populism has been associated with nativism and nationalism. In its new incarnation, the populism of the right is concerned with threats to individual freedom arising from government regulation as well as the collusion of the major financial and commercial concerns in an elite politics that threatens small business people, independent entrepreneurs, farmers, non-union workers, and those who believe in the pure theory of the free market. Populist conservatives tend to be wary of major corporations, and especially multinationals.

Those conservatives who are based in the corporate-banking sector and whose interests are tied to the largest units of production also claim allegiance to the free market. Their orientation is to economic development as a solution for social problems, but there is also a willingness to make government an active agent in promoting economic freedom and protecting capitalist interests against internal regulation and external encroachment. By co-operating at the elite level, corporate conservatives see the government as a useful asset in the struggle to maintain the mobility and independence of capital.

Populist conservatives would quite willingly divorce the government from its role in monetary regulation, for example, while corporate conservatives see monetary regulation as a principal means of influencing economic policy in a manner favourable to their interests. The appeal of populism has historically been to the smaller commercial interests, while major corporations have operated with a substantial level of security and continuity. Recent policy changes that have made corporate take-overs easier have sharpened the division between corporate conservatives and populists. The latter find the prospect of genuine competition at the major corporate level to be refreshing, while the targets of take-over efforts seek ways of avoiding the logic of a speculative market.

These internal tensions in conservative capitalism are not yet as consequential as the splits within the left that have permitted conservatives to acquire power in most parts of the Western world. They may, however, have prevented the consolidation of that power. President Reagan's conservative agenda was stymied fairly effectively by Congressional opposition from 1983 on, some of which came from moderate Republican resistance to the violation of customary understandings concerning income security policy, among other issues. Prime Minister Thatcher faced several rebellions from traditionalists in her own party prior to being unseated by a challenge based in that faction. It has been generally apparent that moralist conservatism has been honoured more as a recruiting device than as a source of serious policy initiatives by regimes on both sides of the Atlantic.

It is in the nature of politicians to build coalitions, and the most likely result of these splits is that the challenge of conservative politics will lie more in maintaining coalitions among rival tendencies than in mobilizing any sector in its pure form. At the same time, reform liberals in the United States may be seen to have adopted some of the moralist conservative policies by advocating strong anti-drug initiatives, prosecuting pornographers, or endorsing the death penalty as a way of outflanking the political appeal of the conservative movement.

There is also the possibility of using the contradictory elements of conservative capitalism as mutual reinforcing explanations. Declines in productivity can be attributed to indolence among poor people, rather than to the debilitating effects of corporate warfare. The plight of the poor can be attributed to bad personal choices in a free market, rather than to the perpetuation of inequities in the distribution of life chances. These opportunities for rationalization within the broader ambit of conservative capitalism may override the effects of inconsistent policies on the loyalties of those who vote conservative.

There are several alternatives to the classification scheme suggested in this essay that centre on distinctions between what is new and what is old in conservatism, neo-conservatism (Kristol 1983), the New Right for example (King 1987). The problem with these labels is that there is little agreement as to what it is that is new, possibly because neither the traditionalist nor the individualist stream represent new thinking. Some see the New Right as a combination of moralist and populist conservatism as against the coalition of establishment and corporate conservatism that characterized conservative parties prior to the mid-1970s. This classification captures the sense in which electoral victories have been based on a coalition that has never before had such success. Others see the New Right as a name for individualist conservatism as against traditional conservatism. What is presented as new here is the arrival in the conservative camp of advocates for a minimalist version of classical liberalism. The problem with either variant is that attention is directed away from both the historical basis and the enduring power of the larger conservative frame of reference. There is also the implication that this is a united movement, when in fact it is not. Indeed, some pre-eminent thinkers cited frequently by conservatives, such as Friedrich Hayek, disavow the conservative label entirely (Hayek 1960: 397–411). To refer to conservative capitalism is to suggest the hybrid nature of the movement and to retain the critical conceptual references to its historical roots.

Looking to the future, a shift in emphasis from issues such as anti-communism and economic development to the environment and the issues associated with the politics of human development suggests a long-term threat to the survival of conservative capitalism. The issue of the environment brings the corporate base of conservative politics into a direct confrontation with increasingly large majorities of public opinion. Issues associated with parental care, health benefits and the improvement of educational opportunity may breach the wall of separation conservatives have laboured to build between the market and government.

The record of conservatives in promising sustained economic growth, a reduction in crime and the gradual elimination of social problems has not, on the whole, been persuasive. Western countries have witnessed economic expansion based, in the case of the United States, on personal, corporate and government debt. In Britain, the sale of nationalized assets and the revenue from oil rights has sustained an uneasy compromise between the old welfare state and the new market freedom; however, there may be a limit to the financial underpinnings for such gains as have been made.

The United States has witnessed a major increase in imprisonment and the re-introduction of the death penalty – neither of which seem to have made the streets safer. Agitation on moral issues continues to intensify in the face of continued family breakdown, particularly among the poor. Both countries have experienced a widening of income and wealth inequality even in the face of sustained economic expansion.

Consequently, conservative capitalism has succeeded in reshaping the agenda of Western politics, though it has not yet developed a substructure of the same durability as that of the New Deal in the United States, or the postwar expansion of social services in Britain. While traditional conservatives may be able to address the increasingly significant issues of the environment and human development, the individualist tendency has few solutions to offer. Take away the threat of communism and conservative capitalism as a political movement is in danger of losing its way among its own internal divisions.

REFERENCES

Brittan, S. (1983) *The Role and Limits of Government: Essays in Political Economy*, London: Smith.

Buchanan, J. and Tullock, G. (1962) *The Calculus of Consent: Logical Foundations of Constitutional Democracy*, Ann Arbor: University of Michigan Press.

Burke, E. (1976) *Reflections on the Revolution in France*, ed. C. C. O'Brien, London: Penguin.

Diggins, J. (1975) *Up From Communism*, New York: Harper & Row.

Disraeli, B. (1844) *Coningsby*, London: Penguin.

Dolbeare, K. (1984) *American Political Thought*, Chatham, NJ: Chatham House.

Dolbeare, K. and Dolbeare, P. (1976) *American Ideologies: The Competing Political Beliefs of the 1970s*, 3rd edn, Chicago: Rand McNally.

Downs, A. (1965) *An Economic Theory of Democracy*, New York: Harper & Row.

Epstein, K. (1966) *The Genesis of German Conservatism*, Princeton: Princeton University Press.

Friedman, M. (1962) *Capitalism and Freedom*, Chicago: University of Chicago Press.

Hayek, F. (1960) *The Constitution of Liberty*, London: Routledge; Chicago: University of Chicago Press.

Hirschman, A. (1977) *The Passions and the Interests: Arguments for Capitalism Before Its Triumph*, Princeton: Princeton University Press.

Hoover, K. and Plant, R. (1989) *Conservative Capitalism in Great Britain and the United States: A Critical Appraisal*, London and New York: Routledge.

Huntington, S. (1957) 'Conservatism as an ideology', *American Political Science Review* 51: 454–73.

Joseph, K. and Sumption, J. (1979) *Equality*, London: John Murray.

King, D. (1987) *The New Right: Politics, Markets, and Citizenship*, London: Macmillan.

Kirk, R. (1962) *A Program for Conservatives*, Chicago: Regnery.

Kristol, I. (1983) *Reflections of a Neoconservative: Looking Back, Looking Ahead*, New York: Basic Books.

Nash, G. (1979) *The Conservative Intellectual Movement in America: Since 1945*, New York: Basic Books.

Nisbet, R. (1986) *Conservatism*, Minneapolis: University of Minnesota Press.

Niskanen, W. (1973) *Bureaucracy – Servant or Master?: Lessons from America*, London: Hobart Publications.

Oakeshott, M. (1962) *Rationalism in Politics*, London: Methuen.

Piven, F. F. and Cloward, R. (1982) *The New Class War*, New York: Pantheon.

Rossiter, C. (1982) *Conservatism in America: The Thankless Persuasion*, New York: Viking.

Smith, A. (1759) *The Theory of Moral Sentiments*, Indianapolis: Liberty Press, 1969.

——(1776) *An Enquiry into the Nature and Causes of the Wealth of Nations*, ed. by R. H. Campbell and A. S. Skinner, Oxford: Oxford University Press.

Steinfels, P. (1979) *The Neoconservatives*, New York: Simon and Schuster.

Taylor, C. (1982) *Radical Tories: The Conservative Tradition in Canada*, Toronto: House of Anansi Press.

Wills, G. (1979) *Confessions of a Conservative*, London: Penguin.

FURTHER READING

Anderson, M. (1978) *Welfare*, Palo Alto, Calif.: Hoover Institution Press.

Behrens, R. (1980) *The Conservative Party from Heath to Thatcher: Policies and Politics 1974–1979*, London: Saxon House.

Blumenthal, S. (1988) *The Rise of the Counter-establishment*, New York: Harper & Row.

Dolbeare, K. and Dolbeare, P. (1976) *American Ideologies: The Competing Political Beliefs of the 1970s*, 3rd edn, Chicago: Rand McNally.

Gamble, A. (1981) *Britain in Decline: Economic Policy, Political Strategy and the British State*, Boston: Beacon Press.

Gottfried, P. and Fleming, T. (1988) *The Conservative Movement*, Boston: Twayne.

Hall, P. (1986) *Governing the Economy: The Politics of State Intervention in Britain and France*, New York: Oxford University.

Hayek, F. (1976) *Law, Legislation and Liberty*, London: Routledge & Kegan Paul.

Hoover, K. (1987) 'The rise of conservative capitalism: ideological tensions within the Reagan and Thatcher governments', *Comparative Studies in Society and History* 29 (2): 245–68.

King, D. (1988) 'New right ideology, welfare state form, and citizenship', *Comparative Studies in Society and History* 30 (4): 792–803.

Kirk, R. (1986) *The Conservative Mind: From Burke to Eliot*, 7th edn, Chicago: Regnery.

Krieger, J. (1986) *Reagan, Thatcher, and the Politics of Decline*, New York: Oxford University Press.

Lawson, N. (1980) *The New Conservatism*, London: Centre for Policy Studies.

Machan, T. and Johnson, M. (1983) *Rights and Regulation: Ethical, Political, and Economic Issues*, New York: Ballinger.

Moynihan, D. (1988) *Came the Revolution: Argument in the Reagan Era*, New York: Harcourt Brace Jovanovich.

Murray, C. (1984) *Losing Ground*, New York: Basic Books.

Nisbet, R. (1962) *The Quest for Community*, New York: Oxford University Press.

Novak, M. (1982) *The Spirit of Democratic Capitalism*, New York: Simon and Schuster.

O'Sullivan, N. (1976) *Conservatism*, New York: St Martin's Press.

Palmer, J. and Sawhill, I. (1986) *Perspectives on the Reagan Years*, Philadelphia: Urban Institute.

Phillips, K. (1982) *Post-Conservative America: People, Politics, and Ideology in a Time of Crisis*, New York: Vintage.

Reichley, A. (1981) *Conservatives in an Age of Change: The Nixon and Ford Administrations*, Washington, DC: Brookings Institution.

Ropke, W. (1971) *A Humane Economy*, Chicago: Regnery.

Scruton, R. (1980) *The Meaning of Conservatism*, London: Macmillan.

Shklar, J. (1969) *After Utopia*, Princeton: Princeton University Press.

Sowell, T. (1984) *Civil Rights: Rhetoric or Reality*, New York: William Morrow.

Stockman, D. (1986) *The Triumph of Politics*. New York: Harper & Row.

Thatcher, M. (1976) *Let Our Children Grow Tall*, London: Centre for Policy Studies.

Tocqueville, A. de (1981) *Democracy in America*, New York: Random House.

Vigurie, R. (1983) *The Establishment vs. the People: Is a New Populist Revolt on the Way?*, Chicago: Regnery.

10

MARXISM

TOM BOTTOMORE

Only after Marx's death was his 'critique of political economy' developed as a comprehensive social theory, a world view, and a political doctrine. Engels began the process of codification of Marx's ideas as 'the Marxist world view', which he compared with classical German philosophy (Engels 1888), expounded as 'scientific socialism' (1880), and extended to include a 'dialectic of nature' (1873–83). His works were widely read in the rapidly growing socialist movement, and through these and his correspondence Engels had a profound influence on the first generation of Marxist thinkers. By the end of the nineteenth century Marxism had become established, largely outside the sphere of formal academic institutions, as a distinctive social theory and political doctrine (and to some extent as a comprehensive philosophical system) in which three main elements are distinguishable.

The first element is an analysis of the types of human society and their historical succession, in which a pre-eminent place is assigned to the economic structure or 'mode of production' as a determining or conditioning factor in shaping the whole form of social life. In Marx's own words: 'the mode of production of material life determines the general character of the social, political and spiritual processes of life' (Marx 1859: preface). The mode of production itself comprises two elements, the forces of production (the available technology) and the relations of production (the way in which production is organized, and in particular the nature of the groups in society which either own the instruments of production – the 'masters of the system of production' – or contribute their labour to the productive process – the 'direct producers'). Two of the fundamental ideas of Marxist thought emerged from this analysis: a periodization of history conceived as a progressive movement through the ancient, Asiatic, feudal and modern capitalist modes of production; and a conception of the fundamental role of social classes, defined by their position in the system of production, in constituting and transforming the major types of society.

The second element in Marxism is an explanation of how the change from one type of society to another is brought about. Two processes play a crucial part in such changes: the development of the forces of production and the relations between classes. From one aspect, the main agent of change is the progress of technology, and Marx himself emphasized this in his well-known statement that 'the handmill gives you a society with feudal lords, the steam mill a society with industrial capitalists' (Marx 1847: chapter 2, section 1); but from another aspect it is the struggle between classes over the organization of production as a whole and the general form of social life which produces major transformations. These two processes, however, are related in so far as the evolution of the productive forces is bound up with the rise of a new class, and at the same time makes impossible the continuance of the existing economic and political organization, which has become an obstacle to further development. Thus, in studies of the transition from feudalism to capitalism, which has been a privileged model for the Marxist theory of history, the emergence of modern capitalism is portrayed as the rise of a new class, the bourgeoisie, equipped with a new technology, which by degrees transformed the system of production and established itself as the dominant class. However, differences of emphasis in the description and explanation of historical changes, different degrees of 'determinism' or 'voluntarism', appeared at an early stage in Marxist thought, and have persisted.

The third element in Marxism is the analysis of modern capitalism and its development, to which Marx himself and later Marxists devoted their main efforts. Capitalism is conceived as the final form of class society, in which the opposition and conflict between the two principal classes – bourgeoisie and proletariat – becomes ever clearer and sharper, and the economic contradictions of the capitalist mode of production, manifesting themselves in recurrent crises, steadily grow. At the same time the economic system is increasingly socialized with the rise of cartels and trusts and the development of a close relationship between manufacturing and bank capital, and the strength of the working-class movement as a political force committed to the creation of a new society steadily increases. This analysis of capitalist development, and the growth of mass socialist parties (notably in Germany and Austria), necessarily led to a preoccupation with the conditions in which a transition to socialism would occur, and to the elaboration of Marxism as a political doctrine which provided intellectual guidance to the socialist parties, and which was an important factor in their cohesion as well as an ideological weapon in their struggle against bourgeois dominance.

From the outset, however, there was some diversity of view about the nature and scope of Marxist thought. For Kautsky, whose writings had a pre-eminent place in theoretical discussions throughout the period from the late 1880s to 1914, Marxism was above all a theory of the historical development of human society, a scientific, evolutionist and deterministic theory which had close affinities with Darwinism (as Engels had also affirmed). On the other hand, Plekhanov, the 'father of Russian Marxism', presented Marxism as an all-embracing world view, described as 'dialectical materialism', within which historical materialism was conceived as an application of its general principles to the particular study of social phenomena. During the first decade of the twentieth century the various elements of Marxism were all vigorously developed, but in several different directions and amidst increasing critical debate. In Germany, under Kautsky's influence, Marxism as a scientific theory of historical development and the capitalist economy had a dominant position, although some of its claims had begun to be questioned in the 'revisionist debate' initiated by Bernstein (1899), who contested the ideas of an increasing polarization of society between bourgeoisie and proletariat, and of an eventual economic collapse of capitalism as a result of ever-worsening crises. In Austria, Marxism was also expounded as a social theory, and more specifically as a sociological system, by the group of Austro-Marxists who constituted the first distinct 'school' of Marxist thought (Bottomore and Goode 1978). They were, like Kautsky, positivists, but in a more sophisticated manner, influenced by neo-Kantianism and by Mach; their philosophical views, elaborated principally by Max Adler, were conceived not as a metaphysical system but strictly as a philosophy of science. The Austro-Marxists not only gave a systematic form to Marxist social science but were also innovators in extending this science into new fields in their studies of nationality and nationalism (Bauer 1907), the social functions of law (Renner 1904), and the recent development of capitalism (Hilferding 1910). At the same time they were all active in the rapidly growing socialist movement, so that their work was informed by a continuous close relationship between theory and practice. In Russia, however, where there was no mass socialist movement, Marxism was at first an intellectual movement, shaped largely by Plekhanov's conception of it as a philosophical world view, which Lenin inherited. Out of this matrix developed the idea of bringing a 'socialist consciousness' to the masses from outside, and the construction of a Bolshevik ideology emphasizing the dominant role of a disciplined revolutionary party, which in due course became the ideology of the Soviet state.

MARXISM BETWEEN THE TWO WORLD WARS

The First World War and the Russian Revolution changed profoundly the conditions in which Marxist thought would henceforth develop. The outbreak of war was seen as confirming the theories of imperialism propounded by Hilferding, Bukharin and Lenin, but it also revealed the weakness of the working-class movement in Western Europe in the face of nationalism, and created deep divisions in the German Social Democratic Party which by the end of the war and after the defeat of revolutionary uprisings in 1918–19 had lost its former pre-eminence as the centre of Marxist thought and practice to the Bolsheviks. However, the war itself brought increased state intervention in the economies of the belligerent countries, and it seemed to many Western Marxists, of a more gradualist persuasion, to create new opportunities for a transition to socialism, posing new questions about how that transition would be accomplished and what form a socialist economy would take. It was the revolution in Russia, however, which had the greatest impact on Marxist thought, in several different ways.

First, Soviet Marxists had to grapple in practice with the problems of constructing a socialist society, and during the 1920s there were intense debates about the policies of the transition period, in particular about the pressing need for rapid industrialization of a backward agrarian society as a specific problem which Marxists in the industrially developed countries had never had to confront (Bukharin 1920; Preobrazhensky 1926; Erlich 1960). These preoccupations impressed upon Soviet Marxism one of its distinctive characteristics.

Second, the success of the Bolsheviks in establishing the 'first workers' state', contrasted with the failure of the socialist movement elsewhere in Europe, endowed their version of Marxism (soon to be known as Marxism-Leninism) with a special prestige. Marxism, like the working-class movement itself after the creation of separate communist parties and the foundation of the Third (Communist) International, was sharply divided into two main streams. Soviet Marxism, influenced by the legacy of Plekhanov and Lenin and by the specific socio-economic circumstances of Russia, developed as a comprehensive world view and increasingly, as Stalin consolidated his dictatorship, as a dogmatic state ideology, imposed by the 'vanguard party' and its leaders, which excluded all critical reflection and debate. Marxist thought then became largely identified, in the 1930s, with Soviet Marxism, which was widely disseminated through the Third International and its affiliated parties, acquiring increasing political influence in the prevailing conditions of economic depression and the rise of fascism in the capitalist world.

Outside the Soviet Union, nevertheless, Marxism continued to develop in more diverse, open and critical ways in response to new problems: the apparent stabilization of capitalism in the 1920s; the increasingly bureaucratic and totalitarian character of Soviet society; the economic depression of the 1930s (which failed, however, to engender an effective socialist alternative); the development of the fascist states; and the renewed threat of war. Thus Hilferding (1924) defined the changes in capitalism during and after the war as a development of 'organized capitalism', characterized by an extension of economic planning as a result of the dominance of large corporations and banks, and of greater state involvement in the regulation of economic life. He conceived this continued 'socialization of the economy' as a further stage in the transition to socialism, although later, after the experience of National Socialism in Germany and Stalinism in the Soviet Union, he recognized that the process could well lead, and in these cases had led, to a totalitarian society; in his last work he began a systematic revision of the Marxist theory of the state (Hilferding 1940, 1941). Others, among them Gramsci, Trotsky and Bauer (Beetham 1983), undertook an analysis of the economic and social conditions which had made possible the rise of fascism, and Neumann (1942) published a major study of National Socialist Germany as a regime of 'totalitarian monopoly capitalism', while the psychological bases of the fascist movements also began to be studied (Fromm 1942; Adorno *et al.* 1950).

However, the interpretations of fascism and more generally of the inter-war period as a whole by Western Marxists were diverse, although two main currents of thought can be distinguished. The social democratic Marxists, while recognizing that the fascist regimes had to be opposed by force, remained generally committed to a view of the transition to socialism as a long, evolutionary and relatively peaceful process arising out of the economic development of capitalism itself. Those Marxists who adhered to the new communist parties, however, and notably Korsch (1923), Lukács (1923) and Gramsci (1929–35), rejected the versions of Marxism which presented it as a scientific theory of society, and emphasized the factor of consciousness in the working-class movement; hence the crucial role of revolutionary intellectuals in developing a socialist world view. This was conceived by Lukács as conveying to the working class a true insight into the historical process, or a 'correct class consciousness', but he subsequently disowned the 'revolutionary, utopian messianism' expressed in this book (Lukács 1967) and his later work was primarily devoted to literary criticism and aesthetic theory. Gramsci also conceived the socialist world view as a body of ideas and beliefs elaborated by the intellectuals of a progressive class, which was essential if the class were to establish a social and cultural hegemony, as well as political dominance, and embark successfully on the construction of a new social order.

A similar view of Marxist theory, influenced at the outset by the writings of Korsch and Lukács, was developed by a group of intellectuals associated with the Frankfurt Institute of Social Research (established in 1923), which later flowered luxuriantly into the Frankfurt school of 'critical theory'. Those most closely associated with the Institute in the 1930s – Horkheimer, Marcuse and Adorno – gave to Marxist thought a distinctive academic orientation, disconnected from any direct involvement in political action and increasingly sceptical about the role of the working class as an agent of social transformation in the Western capitalist societies. Their critical studies were directed primarily against bourgeois culture, especially as it manifested itself in philosophy and the social sciences in the form of 'traditional theory', interpreted as the implicit or explicit outlook of the modern natural sciences, expressed in modern philosophy as positivism and empiricism.

By 1939, however, many of these Western Marxist thinkers were either dead or in exile, and the European scene was dominated even more completely by Soviet Marxism. It was only two or three decades later that their ideas began to be influential in a new intellectual renaissance of Marxism.

MARXISM AFTER THE SECOND WORLD WAR

The Second World War and its aftermath created a radically different situation in which Marxist thought could develop. The geographical area in which Soviet Marxism reigned virtually unchallenged was extended by the establishment of Stalinist regimes in the countries of Eastern Europe, though this total dominance was short-lived. Yugoslavia seceded at an early stage from the Soviet bloc, introduced an original economic and social system based upon workers' self-management, and began to develop a distinctive form of Marxist thought, centred upon the *Praxis* group of sociologists and philosophers, which had many affinities and close relations with some forms of Western Marxism (Marković and Cohen 1975: part I). Elsewhere in Eastern Europe, after the death of Stalin, a growing intellectual restlessness and a succession of revolts against the Stalinist system also engendered more dissident forms of Marxist thought, again partly inspired by Western Marxism, and there was increasing contact with Western philosophy and social science.

Outside the Soviet sphere, Marxist thought developed more rapidly than at any time since the first decade of the century. In the immediate post-war period socialist and communist parties were stronger than they had ever been in Western Europe, and Marxist thought was widely diffused, not only in political and cultural movements but also, for the first time, in the academic social sciences, philosophy and the humanities. In some quarters, and notably in the French Communist Party, Marxism retained much of its Stalinist character, but it was strongly contested by a new current of existentialist Marxism inspired by Sartre. Western Marxism as a whole, in its diverse forms, became increasingly critical of the orthodox Soviet version, both as a social theory and as a political doctrine, most trenchantly after the Hungarian revolt in 1956 and the rise of the 'New Left'.

From the late 1950s the pre-war writings of Lukács, Gramsci and the members of the Frankfurt Institute (re-established in Germany in 1951 and gradually assuming the character of a 'school') began to reach a wider audience, but one which was now primarily academic. Except in Italy, where Gramsci's writings played an important part in changing the outlook of the Communist Party, and to a lesser extent in Austria, where Austro-Marxism continued to have some influence in the Socialist Party, Marxist thought spread most rapidly in the universities and in the student movement of the late 1960s. For the first time in Western Europe (and elsewhere) Marxist theory acquired a major place in academic teaching, not only in history, sociology and political science, where it had long had some kind of presence, but in economics and anthropology, philosophy and aesthetics. This efflorescence provoked a new interest in some of Marx's own lesser known writings (unpublished during his lifetime), above all the *Economic and Philosophical Manuscripts* (Marx 1844) which encouraged widespread discussion by philosophers and sociologists of the notion of 'alienation', and the *Grundrisse* (Marx 1857–8) which suggested new conceptions of the process of development of capitalist society.

Many of the ideas newly discovered in these Marxian texts were close to the preoccupations of Lukács, Gramsci and the Frankfurt school, and for a time, under these various influences, Marxist thought in one of its important manifestations became primarily a critique of bourgeois culture as a 'reified' system of thought, constituted, according to the Frankfurt school, by a positivist, scientistic and technological world view. This concern with bourgeois thought-forms, pursued by the following generation of Marxists in this tradition (and notably by Goldmann and Habermas) gave rise to intense methodological debates, concentrating on problems of the theory of knowledge and the philosophy of science (Goldmann 1964; Habermas 1981). Thus Habermas in his earlier writings continued the critique of positivism in the social sciences (Adorno *et al.* 1969; see also Wellmer 1969) and attempted to provide an epistemological foundation for critical theory. Subsequently he developed a theory of communicative action (Habermas 1981) which emphasizes the role of language and communication in social evolution and restates the Frankfurt school view of the domination of modern societies by instrumental or technological rationality (Marcuse 1964), which is contrasted with the function of practical reason in the social 'life-world'. There is an evident continuity with the critical theory of Adorno and Horkheimer in Habermas's preoccupation with cultural phenomena – rationality, legitimation, modernism – but at the same time a partial return to such Marxist themes as class, the economic development of capitalism and the role of the state, which had largely disappeared from critical theory by the late 1960s (Bottomore 1984: 55–85).

The kind of Marxist thought influenced by Lukács, Gramsci, the Frankfurt school, the *Praxis* group, and existentialism can be broadly categorized as 'humanist', in spite of the considerable differences between individual thinkers, in the sense that it was primarily concerned with human consciousness, the interpretation of cultural products and the critique of ideology. But this was not the only type of Western Marxism that flourished in the post-war period. In economics, and to some extent in other social sciences, a more empirical, and in a broad sense positivist, approach prevailed and research was concen-

trated upon such subjects as the post-war development of the capitalist economy, the class structure, and the problems of Third World development in
relation to international capitalism. This orientation of Marxist thought was
strengthened by the introduction of structuralist ideas, already influential in
linguistics and anthropology, through the work of Althusser, who argued that
Marx, after his early 'humanist' period, eliminated the human subject from
social theory and constructed a 'new science' of the levels of human practice
which are inscribed in the structure of a social totality. Marxist theory, in its
mature form, is therefore seen as concerned with the structural analysis of
social totalities (for example, mode of production, social formation), its object
being to disclose the 'deep structure' which underlies and produces the directly
observable phenomena of social life (Althusser 1969, 1970; Godelier 1977:
part I, chapter. 1). Althusser's principal aim was to establish the 'scientificity'
of Marxism, on the basis of a theory of knowledge and science, and the new
conception of theory which he elaborated influenced the social sciences in a
number of different fields: for example, studies of pre-capitalist societies
(Hindess and Hirst 1975; Seddon 1978) and of the class structure in capitalist
societies (Poulantzas 1975). His conception of Marxism as a science, however,
was also strongly criticized, both for its total exclusion of human agency from
the processes of social life, and for an anti-empiricism so complete that it
makes knowledge a purely theoretical, self-contained entity; Althusser's influence waned rapidly in the 1980s. During this period, however, the idea of
Marxism as a 'natural science of society' has been expounded in a more
discriminating way in the realist philosophy of science (Bhaskar 1979, 1991),
which postulates the existence of an underlying structure of social life, possessing 'causal powers', but mediated by human consciousness in the production
of its effects.

PROBLEMS OF MARXISM TODAY

Over the past few decades two major divisions have persisted in Marxist
thought: that between Soviet and Western Marxism, although the former has
by now lost most of its influence and much of its distinctiveness; and more
importantly, that between the broad and partially overlapping categories of
'humanist' and 'scientific' Marxism. At the same time Marxism has become
altogether more varied and diffuse, its boundaries increasingly difficult to
delineate, and more ambiguous in its relation to the social changes of the late
twentieth century. In the present situation Marxism has become to a very great
extent an academic 'subject', a focal point for much intellectual disputation,
while its influence on social and political movements has significantly declined.

In the first respect Marxist thought has become increasingly involved with
more general controversies in the social sciences and the philosophy of science;

and the influence of other theoretical and philosophical views – always present to some extent, as its engagement at various times with positivism, Hegelianism, phenomenology, existentialism and structuralism makes evident – has grown to a point where it can be suggested, for instance, that 'the concept of Marxism as a separate school of thought will in time become blurred and ultimately disappear altogether' (Kolakowski 1969: 204). The alternative, of course, is that Marxism, in the course of its confrontation with alternative theories, will assimilate some of their conceptions and renew itself as one of the most powerful explanatory schemes so far constructed in the social sciences. But the problems that face any regenerated Marxist social theory are formidable: to provide a convincing analysis of the long-term development of capitalist economies, which have been conceptualized in very different ways as 'organized capitalism', 'state monopoly capitalism', or 'corporatism', and most recently in terms of the neo-Marxist approach of 'regulation theory' (Aglietta 1982), and of the reconstruction of socialist economies which aims to achieve some combination of central planning and market relations; to reconsider the role of social classes, and the significance of other social movements, in the recent development of capitalist societies; and to rethink the Marxist theory of the state in relation to the twentieth-century experience of nationalism, totalitarianism and democracy.

Historically, however, Marxism has been a political doctrine just as much as a theory of society, and the two aspects were closely linked at the time when Marxist thought provided the body of ideas which unified and guided mass socialist and communist parties. Today this political function is greatly attenuated. In the West, Marxism now occupies a very small space in the doctrines or political programmes of socialist and social democratic parties; and in recent years, in the region previously dominated by Soviet Marxism, political debate has departed radically from its Marxist framework. The current discussions of democracy and political pluralism owe little to Marxism, and what they reveal above all as a great lacuna in Marxist political thought is the absence of a systematic examination of the idea and practice of democracy, and in particular of what is meant by socialist democracy.

Present-day Marxist thought has a protean character, spreading into, absorbing from and contributing to many other styles of social thought, and it is scarcely to be represented any longer as a highly specific, uniform, and precisely articulated theory of human society and history. But as a very broad and flexible paradigm it continues to exert a major influence on the social sciences and humanistic studies, and in this roundabout way may still have a diffuse effect on political action. As a world view which directly inspires a distinctive political doctrine, however, its influence has undeniably waned, not least because the circumstances and problems of human societies in the late twentieth century differ so radically from those of the time when Marx formulated his major ideas and his early followers elaborated them into a comprehensive scheme of theory and practice.

REFERENCES

Note: Various English-language editions of the works of Marx and Engels exist, all easily accessible and well known. One of the most convenient general sources is Marx, K. and Engels, F., *Collected Works*, London: Lawrence & Wishart; Moscow: Progress, 1975 (reffered to below simply as *Collected Works*).

Adorno, T. W., Frenkel-Brunswick, E., Levinson, D. J. and Sanford, R. N. (1950) *The Authoritarian Personality*, New York: Harper & Row.
——(1969) *The Positivist Dispute in German Sociology*, London: Heinemann, 1976.
Aglietta, M. (1982) *Regulation and Crisis of Capitalism*, New York: Monthly Review Press.
Althusser, L. (1969) *For Marx*, London: Allen Lane.
——(1970) *Reading 'Capital'*, London: New Left Books.
Bauer, O. (1907) *Die Nationalitätenfrage und die Sozialdemokratie*, Vienna: Wiener Volksbuchhandlung.
Beetham, D. (ed.) (1983) *Marxists in Face of Fascism*, Manchester: Manchester University Press.
Bernstein, E. (1899) *Evolutionary Socialism*, New York: Schocken, 1961.
Bhaskar, R. (1979) *The Possibility of Naturalism*, Brighton: Harvester.
——(1991) 'Realism', in T. Bottomore (ed.) *A Dictionary of Marxist Thought*, 2nd edn, Oxford: Basil Blackwell.
Bottomore, T. (ed.) (1991) *A Dictionary of Marxist Thought*, 2nd edn, Oxford: Basil Blackwell.
——(1984) *The Frankfurt School*, Chichester: Ellis Horwood/London: Tavistock.
Bottomore, T. and Goode, P. (eds) (1978) *Austro-Marxism*, Oxford: Oxford University Press.
Bukharin, N. I. (1920) *Economics of the Transformation Period*, New York: Bergman, 1971.
Engels, F. (1873–83) *Dialectics of Nature*, Moscow: Marx-Engels Archiv, 1927.
——(1880) *Socialism: Utopian and Scientific*; English edn. with new introduction, 1892, in *Collected Works*, 1975.
——(1888) *Ludwig Feuerbach and the End of Classical German Philosophy*, in *Collected Works*, 1975.
Erlich, A. (1960) *The Soviet Industrialization Debate, 1924–28*, Cambridge, Mass.: Harvard University Press.
Fromm, E. (1942) *The Fear of Freedom*, London: Routledge & Kegan Paul.
Godelier, M. (1977) *Perspectives in Marxist Anthropology*, Cambridge: Cambridge University Press.
Goldmann, L. (1964) *Towards a Sociology of the Novel*, London: Tavistock, 1975.
Gramsci, A. (1929–35) *Selections from the Prison Notebooks*, London: Lawrence & Wishart, 1971.
Habermas, J. (1981) *The Theory of Communicative Action*, 2 vols, Boston: Beacon Books.

Hilferding, R. (1910) *Finance Capital: A Study of the Latest Phase of Capitalist Development*, London: Routledge & Kegan Paul, 1981.

——(1924) 'Probleme der Zeit', *Die Gesellschaft* 1 (1): 1–17.

——(1940) 'State capitalism or totalitarian state economy?', *Socialist Courier*, New York; repr. (1947) in *Modern Quarterly* I.

——(1941) 'Das historische Problem', Unfinished manuscript first published (1954) in *Zeitschrift für Politik* (New Series), I: 295–324.

Hindess, B. and Hirst, P. Q. (1975) *Pre-capitalist Modes of Production*, London: Routledge.

Kolakowski, L. (1969) *Marxism and Beyond*, London: Pall Mall Press.

Korsch, K. (1923) *Marxism and Philosophy*, London: New Left Books, 1970.

Lukács, G. (1923) *History and Class Consciousness*, London: Merlin Press, 1971.

Lukács, G. (1967) *History and Class Consciousness*, London: Merlin Press, preface.

Marcuse, H. (1964) *One-Dimensional Man*, London: Routledge & Kegan Paul.

Marković, M. and Cohen, R. S. (1975) *Yugoslavia: The Rise and Fall of Humanist Socialism*, Nottingham: Spokesman Books.

Marx, K. (1844) *Economic and Philosophical Manuscripts*, in *Collected Works*, 1975.

——(1847) *The Poverty of Philosophy*, in *Collected Works*, 1975.

——(1857–8) *Grundrisse: Foundations of the Critique of Political Economy (Rough Draft)*, Harmondsworth: Penguin Books in association with *New Left Review*, 1973.

——(1859) *A Contribution to the Critique of Political Economy*, in *Collected Works*, 1975.

Neumann, F. (1942) *Behemoth: The Structure and Practice of National Socialism*, New York: Oxford University Press.

Poulantzas, N. (1975) Classes in Contemporary Capitalism, London: New Left Books.

Preobrazhensky, E. A. (1926) *The New Economics*, Oxford: Oxford University Press, 1965.

Renner, K. (1904) *The Institutions of Private Law and their Social Functions*, London: Routledge & Kegan Paul, 1949.

Seddon, D. (ed.) (1978) *Relations of Production: Marxist Approaches to Economic Anthropology*, London: Frank Cass.

Wellmer, A. (1969) *Critical Theory of Society*, New York: Herder & Herder, 1971.

FURTHER READING

Bottomore, T. (ed.) (1991) *A Dictionary of Marxist Thought*, 2nd edn, Oxford: Basil Blackwell.

——(ed.) (1988) *Interpretations of Marx*, Oxford: Basil Blackwell.

Godelier, M. (1977) *Perspectives in Marxist Anthropology*, Cambridge: Cambridge University Press.

Horvat, B. (1982) *The Political Economy of Socialism: A Marxist Social Theory*, Oxford: Martin Robertson.

Kolakowski, L. (1978) *Main Currents of Marxism*, 3 vols, Oxford: Clarendon Press.

Kühne, K. (1972) *Economics and Marxism*, 2 vols, London: Macmillan, 1979.

Laing, D. (1978) *The Marxist Theory of Art: An Introductory Survey*, Brighton: Harvester.

Lichtheim, G. (1961) *Marxism: An Historical and Critical Study*, London: Routledge & Kegan Paul.

McLellan, D. (1980) *Marxism after Marx*, London: Macmillan.

Mandel, E. (1975) *Late Capitalism*, London: New Left Books.
Miliband, R. (1977) *Marxism and Politics*, Oxford: Oxford University Press.
Williams, R. (1977) *Marxism and Literature*, Oxford: Oxford University Press.

II

FASCISM

STANLEY PAYNE

Fascism has been one of the most controversial political phenomena of the twentieth century, first of all because of the complete absence of any general agreement about the definition of either the term itself or the broader political developments to which it refers. Fascism is frequently employed as a derogatory epithet and applied to widely varying political activities. At one time or another it has been attached by critics to nearly all of the major movements, particularly the more radical ones, whether of the right or left.

Historically, the term originated with the radical nationalist movement of the Fasci Italiani di Combattimento, organized by Benito Mussolini and others in 1919. *Fascio* in Italian means 'bundle' or 'union' and was a common name given to varying types of new political groupings, particularly those of more radical character. The Fasci Italiani di Combattimento were in turn reorganized two years later, in 1921, as the Partito Nazionale Fascista, or Fascist Party for short, converting the original substantive into an adjective. In October 1922 the Fascist leader Mussolini became prime minister of Italy, and in 1925 converted his government into a one-party dictatorship, thus creating the first, and prototypical, 'fascist regime'.

As early as 1923, however, there developed a growing tendency to generalize beyond the Italian example and apply the term fascist or fascism to any form of right-wing authoritarian movement or system. In the broadest sense, therefore, the trend was to identify any form of non-leftist authoritarianism as fascist, while competing left-wing groups, particularly Soviet Stalinists, began to apply the term to leftist rivals. By the 1930s the term fascist had sometimes become little more than a term of denigration applied to political foes, and this categorical but vague connotation has remained to the present day.

Despite the vagueness, a limited consensus has emerged among some of the leading scholars in the study of fascism, who use the term to refer to the concrete historical phenomena of a group of radical nationalist movements which emerged in Europe between the two World Wars, first in the Italian

Fascist and German National Socialist movements and then among their numerous counterparts in other European countries. This consensus is that specific movements bearing the same characteristics did not exist prior to 1919 and have not appeared in significant form in areas outside Europe or in the period after 1945. None the less, disagreement persists among scholars as to whether the various reputedly fascist movements of inter-war Europe can be linked together as a generic and common phenomenon, or whether they so differed among themselves that they can accurately be discussed only as individual phenomena. The weight of opinion now tends to fall on the side of the former argument, viewing fascism not merely as an Italian or German political form but as a more general phenomenon.

A successful definition of fascism as a generic entity must be able to define common unique characteristics of all the fascistic movements in Europe during the 1920s and 1930s while also differentiating them from other political phenomena. Such an understanding must comprehend basic features such as:

1 the typical fascist negations;
2 fascist doctrine and goals; and
3 the relative uniqueness of fascist style and organization.

Fascism postulated a unique new identity and attempted to occupy a new political territory by opposing nearly all the existing political sectors, left, right and centre. Thus it was anti-liberal, anti-communist (and anti-socialist at least in the social democratic sense) and also anti-conservative, though fascists proved willing to undertake temporary alliances with rightist groups, and to that extent diluted their anti-conservatism.

In terms of ideology and political goals, fascist movements represented the most intense and radical form of nationalism known to modern Europe. Their aim was to create new nationalist and authoritarian state systems that were not merely based on traditional principles or models. Fascist groups differed considerably among themselves on economic goals, but had in common the aim of organizing some new kind of regulated, multi-class, integrated national economic structure, which was varyingly called national corporatist, national socialist or national syndicalist. All fascist movements aimed either at national imperial expansion or at least at a radical change in the nation's relationship with other powers to enhance its strength and prestige. Their doctrines rested on a philosophical basis of idealism, vitalism and voluntarism, and normally involved the attempt to create a new form of modern self-determined secular doctrine (although several of the minor fascist movements were remarkably religious in ethos).

Fascist uniqueness was particularly expressed through the movement's style and organization. Great emphasis was placed on the aesthetic structure of meetings, symbols and political choreography, relying especially on romantic and mystical aspects. All fascist movements attempted to achieve mass mobiliz-ation, together with the militarization of political relationships and style, with the goal of a mass party militia. Unlike some other types of radicals, fascists placed strong positive evaluation on the use of violence, and stressed strongly the principle of male dominance. Although they espoused an organic concept of society, they vigorously championed a new elitism and exalted youth above other phases of life. In leadership, fascist movements exhibited a specific tendency toward an authoritarian, charismatic, personal style of command (the *Führerprinzip*, in German National Socialist terminology).

The Italian Fascist movement was first organized in Milan in May 1919 by a small group of military veterans, ex-socialists and former revolutionary syndicalists, and Futurist cultural avant-gardists. At first it failed to attract significant support, adopting at that time an advanced 'leftist' nationalist pro-gramme. Fascism became a mass movement only towards the end of 1920 when it spread into the north Italian countryside, gaining wider backing by its assault on the Socialist Party in rural areas. Fascists at first criticized the Socialists for their internationalism and not for their economics, but the move-ment soon moved to the right on economic issues as well. Fear of socialism made the Fascists seem attractive to conservatives as shock troops, and the Fascists in turn made an appeal to nearly all sectors of society as the only new national movement not bound by the past or by class interests. After the parliamentary system became stalemated, Mussolini led the so-called 'March on Rome' in October 1922 that convinced the King to appoint him as consti-tutional prime minister. The following two years were a time of growing authoritarianism, but also of uncertainty as to what form a Fascist government should take. Only after some hesitation did Mussolini install a direct political dictatorship in January 1925.

The new Fascist regime was then constructed between 1925 and 1929. It adopted the myth of the 'totalitarian state', yet the Mussolini regime was far from a total dictatorship. Its control was limited in large measure to the political sphere. The King, not Mussolini, remained head of state, and many aspects of the Italian Constitution remained in force. Elite sectors of society remained unmolested, the economic system enjoyed considerable freedom, the military remained partially autonomous in administration, censorship in culture was comparatively limited, and a new concordat was signed with the Roman Cath-olic Church. A system of national syndicates, later termed national cor-porations, was organized and administered by the government to regulate economic affairs, but in practice industry and management enjoyed wide auton-omy. Parliament itself was replaced in 1928 with a new 'corporate chamber', composed of representatives chosen not by direct nomination and vote but by government and economic groups. During most of the 1920s the economy prospered, and Italian society seemed to accept the new regime which hailed itself as the alternative to the conventional left and right.

Fascists also proclaimed themselves revolutionaries and empire builders, but Mussolini showed little inclination to carry out a full-scale social or institutional revolution. The Fascist Party itself was reduced to a limited bureaucracy and subordinated to the regular government administration, rather than being placed in complete control of it, as in the Soviet Union. The Fascist regime thus functioned as a limited or semi-pluralist dictatorship rather than as a truly totalitarian system. When the depression of the 1930s brought economic distress, Mussolini did not rely on the new national corporations to rescue the economy so much as on the extension of state administrative agencies. Despite mass propaganda, there was no revolution in the educational system, either.

Mussolini was well aware that he had failed to effect a true revolution, but was none the less increasingly overcome by a kind of megalomania and his own myth of the 'Duce' (leader). He became convinced that Fascism would become great by creating a new African and Mediterranean empire, using the conquest of Ethiopia in 1935 as the beginning of this expansion. He believed that after the construction of a new empire another generation of Fascist dominance in Italy would somehow create a new Fascist culture and the Fascist 'new man'.

Though Italian Fascism created the original terminology, when many commentators speak of 'fascism' they refer primarily to Adolf Hitler's National Socialist movement in Germany, whose character and history were in key respects strikingly different. Whereas Italian Fascism was converted into a major mass movement in scarcely more than two years, the same process in Germany required more than a decade. Hitler's original National Socialist German Worker's Party (NSDAP in German) had to compete with numerous other small radical nationalist and rightist groups. After one brief bid for power in 1923, it had to devote ten years to building up a strong party organization and mass following. Its great opportunity came with the major political and economic crisis provoked by the Depression, which threatened German society with further chaos after the disasters of the First World War and the immediate post-war period.

By 1932 the 'Nazis', as they became known after the pronunciation of the first two syllables of 'National' in German, had become the largest single party in Germany, primarily by promising all manner of things, however contradictory, to diverse sectors of German society. They portrayed themselves as the only strong national force able to bring unity and restore security and prosperity to a divided, languishing country. Adolf Hitler became Chancellor (the equivalent of prime minister) on 30 January 1933, through legal constitutional processes, just as had Mussolini, with a parliamentary majority of Nazis and rightists in support.

Hitler moved to establish a complete political dictatorship within only six months, also becoming legal head of state by taking over the German presidency in mid-1934. A general *Gleichschaltung* or 'co-ordination' of most German institutions was carried out to extend Hitler's control. The German dictatorship became both more efficient and more thoroughgoing than that of Italy, but in Germany the emphasis also lay on government political power rather than on thorough institutional or social revolution. The Nazis proclaimed a new 'people's community' of common interest, with nominal equality of status but with differentiation and subordination of social functions. Most of the country's social and economic structure remained intact and the principle of private property was generally honoured, as in Fascist Italy.

Yet whereas Mussolini had great difficulty creating a fully coherent programme or even defining his own goals, Hitler had certain basic ends in view from the early 1920s onwards. Hitlerian doctrine was grounded in the racial principle of Aryanism or Nordicism, which reduced all values and achievements to racial criteria and the inherent superiority of the Nordic race. In Hitler's thinking, the true Nordic master race could only develop if it were also given 'space', and that meant conquest of *Lebensraum* (space for living) in eastern Europe. Only after a successful war to dominate most of Europe could the true Nazi revolution take place, which in Hitler's view was neither a social or economic revolution, nor even a cultural revolution, but an actual racial and biological revolution to rid the German race of inferior elements and create the new breed of 'supermen'. Economic and political doctrines were secondary to this peculiar ideology grounded in race and war, a kind of international social Darwinism. Thus for Hitler war must precede revolution, for only a successful war could create the conditions for racial revolution.

During the first years of Hitler's regime, in 1933-4, relations with Italy were rather tense. Fascists were well aware of the extremist racial tendencies in Nazi doctrine and of the inferior place of south Europeans in such an ideology. Hitler, however, was the only major European leader to support Italy's conquest of Ethiopia and looked to Mussolini as the only kindred spirit directing one of the larger European countries. His view was that Italy and Germany were natural allies, since Italy was interested in the Mediterranean and Africa, neither of them primary targets of German expansion.

In 1936 Italy and Germany both intervened on the side of the right-wing Spanish Nationalists in the Spanish Civil War. In October of that year they first established the 'Rome-Berlin Axis', a loose understanding aimed at mutual consultation and co-operation. By 1937 Mussolini had fallen under Hitler's spell, his attitude toward Germany fuelled by a combination of fear and envy. Convinced that a militarily powerful Germany would soon dominate Europe, he carried out a partial and superficial 'Nazification' of Italian Fascism in 1938, introducing the goose step and a new doctrine of 'Italian racism'. The latter was a feeble attempt to create a special place for the Italian 'race' in the new racial order, though this belated doctrine defined the Italian race as the product of history and culture, rather than mere biology as in the Nazi scheme.

Mussolini entered the Second World War only in June 1940, shortly before the fall of France. He then endeavoured to launch his own 'parallel war' in Africa and the Balkans to create an autonomous Italian sphere of power. This soon met shattering defeat, and by 1941 Mussolini had become a satellite of Hitler. As the war came directly home to Italy in July 1943, he was overthrown by a coalition of the Italian Crown, the military and dissident Fascists. Rescued by German commandos, Mussolini ruled a new 'Italian Social Republic' in German-occupied northern Italy during 1944–5 in an unsuccessful attempt to rally support for a return to the semi-collectivist doctrines of early radical Fascism.

Hitler's own goals aimed at the domination of nearly all continental Europe, after which Germany could complete the racial revolution and eventually dominate the entire world. After France fell, Hitler turned in 1941 to his principal rival, invading the Soviet Union, declaring a special 'war of racial extermination' for the final conquest of *Lebensraum*.

This also coincided with the most sinister of Nazi policies, the 'Final Solution' for the liquidation of European Jewry. In Hitlerian doctrine, the arch-enemy of the Nordic race, and of all true races, was held to be the Jews, defined as a malevolent 'anti-race' of parasites devoted to racial pollution and the destruction of all true culture. In this paranoid nightmare, Hitler came to believe that the world could only be made safe for the creation of a master race by the total extermination of Jews, a process that had begun as early as 1939–40, but finally took the form of mass extermination camps two years later. By the end of the war and the destruction of Nazism, nearly six million Jews had been liquidated, the greatest single act of deliberate genocide in all human history. (Italian Fascism, by contrast, had not originally discriminated against Jews. The proportion of Jewish members of the Fascist Party in the 1920s was greater than that of Jews in Italian society as a whole, and Fascist officials had publicly lauded Jews. When the first legal measures of discrimination were adopted in 1938 in imitation of Germany, they were unpopular both with the general Italian populace and even with many Fascists themselves.)

German Nazism was by far the most powerful and influential variant of what historical analysts sometimes call 'generic fascism', but fascist-type movements existed in nearly all European countries during the 1930s, as well as in other parts of the world. The great majority of these fascist-type movements were complete failures, for in most countries and under most conditions the extremist doctrines of fascism had little appeal. By the late 1930s, in Europe as a whole, there were considerably more anti-fascists than fascists.

None the less, at least four other fascist movements gained considerable popular support and merit brief attention. For example, the only other fascist-type movement to rival German National Socialism in popular support was the Hungarian Arrow Cross movement. Whereas the Nazis gained 38 per cent of the popular vote in Germany in 1932, the Arrow Cross may have held nearly 35 per cent in the Hungarian elections seven years later. There were proportionately more different fascistic parties and movements in Hungary than in any country in the world, in part because of the trauma of the First World War and because the loss of territory and population was proportionately greater in Hungary than anywhere else. Aggrieved nationalism was, if anything, even keener than in Germany. The Arrow Cross movement of Ferenc Szalasi appealed especially to workers and poor peasants, and espoused a greater degree of social collectivism and economic reorganization than did many other fascistic movements. Szalasi's goal was a 'Greater Danubian Federation' led by Hungary, but he himself did not endorse war and violence to the same extent as Hitler and Mussolini. The Arrow Cross was strongly anti-Semitic, however, and was finally placed in power by Hitler in 1944 after the German military had taken over Hungary. The few fleeting months of Arrow Cross rule that followed prior to the Soviet military conquest did not provide time to create a genuine new system, though radical political and economic changes were imposed.

In Romania, the Legionary, or Iron Guard, movement led by Corneliu Zelea Codreanu became a major force in the late 1930s. Although Romania was one of the victors in the First World War, it was economically backward and politically divided. The Legionary movement was built on the support of university students and eventually developed considerable backing among poor peasants. Iron Guardists were distinct from most fascists in their emphasis on religiosity – Romanian Orthodoxy being strongly endorsed as essential to the life of the nation. Yet the Legionaries did not have a genuine programme; their goal was the '*Omul nou*', the new man, to be created by radical nationalist and religious culture. The existing government and elite were to be swept away in favour of the interests of the common Romanian people, even though it was not clear how these interests were to be articulated and structured. Codreanu and the top Legionary leaders were murdered by the government police in 1938, but the movement was eventually brought into the government in 1940 when General Mihai Antonescu overthrew the monarchy and established a new dictatorship. The Guardists then made a desperate attempt to seize sole authority in January 1941, but were easily defeated by the Romanian army, a blow from which they never recovered.

In Croatia a radical new fascist-type movement, the Ustasi (Insurgents), became influential among young nationalists during the 1930s. After his military conquest of greater Yugoslavia in 1941, Hitler divided the country into zones, making most of Croatia autonomous under the Ustasi leader Ante

Pavelič. The Ustasi regime of 1941–4 was the only other fascist-type regime to rival that of Hitler in sheer gruesomeness. It carried out its own liquidation of native Jewry and then attacked the sizable Serbian population living in southern and eastern Croatia, resulting in possibly 300,000 wanton murders.

The Spanish Nationalist dictatorship of General Francisco Franco that came to power in the Spanish Civil War of 1936–9 also at first contained fascistic features. In 1937 Franco took over the native fascist party, Falange Española (Spanish Phalanx), and made it his official state party, adopting its Twenty-six Point programme (based generally on that of Fascist Italy) as the official ideology of his new state. The Falange enjoyed considerable political influence particularly during 1939–42, when Franco cultivated close relations with Nazi Germany.

The Franco regime, however, was also based on Spanish Catholicism and cultural traditionalism, and carried out a sweeping new right-wing neo-traditionalist revival. Many Catholics and rightists were strongly anti-Falangist, and Franco was careful to limit the influence enjoyed by the new state party. By 1943, when it had become doubtful that Hitler would win the war, Franco initiated a tentative 'defascistization' of his regime. This was rapidly expanded at the end of the war in 1945, when the Falange was drastically downgraded and the regime refurbished as a 'Catholic corporatist' system of 'organic democracy'. Defascistization became, in fact, a continuous and ongoing feature of the regime, which progressively transformed itself in chameleon fashion. An attempt by moderate Falangists to make a comeback was defeated in 1956, and by 1958 the Twenty-six Points had been replaced by nine anodyne 'Principles of the Movement', a series of platitudes about the nation, its unity and familial values. By the time that Franco died in 1975, the quasi-fascist aspects dating from the origins of his regime had long since disappeared.

The dual rightist/fascist character of the early Franco regime presents a striking example of both the potential alliance and disharmonies of fascist groups and the radical right. Although the two sectors had much in common, they were also distinct and marked by significant differences in almost every European country. Radical rightist groups shared some of the fascists' political goals, just as revolutionary leftist movements exhibited some of their stylistic and organizational characteristics. The uniqueness of the fascists compared with the radical right, however, lay in their rejection of the cultural and economic conservatism, and the particular social elitism of the radical right, just as they rejected the internationalism, egalitarianism and materialist socialism of the left. The historical uniqueness of fascism can be better grasped once it is realized that significant political movements sharing all – not merely some – of the common characteristics of fascism existed only in Europe during the years 1915–45.

During the 1930s efforts were made to imitate fascism outside Europe in

China, Japan, southern Asia, South Africa, Latin America and even in the United States. None of these extra-European initiatives gained mass support or enjoyed any political success. The peculiar combination of extreme nationalism together with cultural and social radicalism that made up fascism could grow neither in the soil of non-European democracies nor in more backward and traditionalist societies elsewhere. During its great war effort of 1937–45, imperial Japan adopted only a few of the features of fascism. The legal institutional order of the country was scarcely altered, and comparatively normal parliamentary elections were held in 1942. No single-party system was ever installed in Japan, where leadership was provided by traditional elites and the military.

Fascists claimed to represent all classes of national society, particularly the broad masses. Marxists claimed conversely that they were no more than the tool of the most violent, monopolistic and reactionary sectors of the bourgeoisie. Neither of these extreme interpretations is supported by empirical evidence. In their earliest phase, fascist movements often drew their followers from among former military personnel and small sectors of the radical intelligentsia, in some cases university students. Though some fascist movements enjoyed a degree of backing from the upper bourgeoisie, the broadest sector of fascist support, comparatively speaking, was provided by the lower middle class. Since this was one of the largest strata in European society during the 1920s and 1930s, the same might also have been said for various other political groups. In both Italy and Germany a notable minority of party members were drawn from among urban workers. In Hungary and Romania, primary backing came from university students and poor peasants, and there was also considerable agrarian support in some parts of Italy.

A bewildering variety of theories and interpretations have been advanced since 1923 to explain fascism. One of the most common sets of theories are those of socio-economic causation, primarily of Marxist inspiration, which hold that this phenomenon was the product of specific economic forces or interests, or of specific social groups, such as big business, the bourgeoisie or the petite bourgeoisie. A second set of concepts emphasizes psychocultural motivations, related to certain kinds of personality theories or forms of social psychology. Another approach has been derived from modernization theory, which posits fascism as intimately related to a specific phase in modern development. Theorists of totalitarianism, on the other hand, sometimes include fascism as one major aspect of the broader phenomenon of twentieth-century totalitarianism. The most flexible and effective approaches, however, are historicist in character, employing multi-causal explanations in terms of the major dimensions of European historical development, and especially its key variations in different countries, during the early twentieth century.

An historicist approach would account for fascism by attempting to isolate key historical variables common to those national circumstances in which significant fascist movements arose in various countries. These variables should identify key differences in the areas of national situation, political problems, cultural tendencies, economic difficulties and social structure. The common variable with regard to national circumstance was generally one of status deprivation or severe frustration of nationalist ambitions. In terms of strictly political circumstances, strong fascist movements arose in certain countries when they were just beginning, or had only recently begun, the difficult transition to direct democracy. (Conversely, neither advanced and experienced democracies nor very backward countries not yet introduced to democracy were susceptible.) The key variable of cultural milieu probably had to do with the degree of acceptance of rationalism and materialism, as distinct from idealism and vitalism, the latter currents being much more propitious to fascism. Fascism also developed significantly only in countries experiencing major economic difficulties, but the exact character of those difficulties differed enormously, from highly industrial Germany to very backward Romania. Probably the most common feature of the economic variables involved was a general belief that problems were national in scope yet somehow vaguely international in origin. In terms of social mobilization, differing syndromes may be encountered, but the most common variable concerned widespread discontent among the young and among the lower middle classes generally, though this discontent had to some extent to spread more broadly into the lower classes for fascist movements to develop a strong mass basis. Again, no one or two or even three of the aforementioned variables sufficed to produce a significant fascist movement. Only in those few countries where all five variables were present at approximately the same time were conditions propitious.

That fascism temporarily became a major force in Europe was due above all to the military expansion of Nazi Germany, for the purely political triumphs of fascist movements were very few. Similarly, the complete defeat of Germany and Italy in the Second World War condemned fascism to political destruction, making it impossible for fascist movements to emerge as significant political forces after 1945. Above all, the identification of fascist-type policies not so much with Fascist Italy as with the militarism and mass murder wrought by Nazi Germany fundamentally discredited them for following generations.

Nevertheless, fascism did not completely die in 1945. Efforts to revive fascism have been rather numerous, and literally hundreds of petty neo-fascist grouplets have emerged during the second half of the twentieth century, usually each more insignificant than the next. These groups have been concentrated in western Europe, but are also found in North and South America, as well as in other parts of the world. Neo-fascist parties are usually movements of extreme protest, operating far outside the political mainstream and unable to mobilize support. Extreme racism has been a prime characteristic of such groups in the United States and in some European countries such as France, one recent example being the 'skinhead' white racist movement of the late 1980s. In Germany itself, the only movement that tried to some extent to build on the Nazi heritage failed to mobilize 2 per cent of the vote. The most successful neo-fascist movement, however, has been the 'Italian Social Movement' (MSI), principal Italian successor to the original Fascist Party. The MSI has tried to modernize and revise fascist doctrine in a more moderate and sophisticated direction, and in a few areas of Italy has garnered 6 per cent or more of the vote in local elections.

Does fascism have a future? Worried foes sometimes fear so, but it is doubtful if the specific forms of early twentieth-century European fascism can be successfully revived. Broad cultural, psychological, educational and economic changes have made the re-emergence of something so murderous as Nazism in a large industrial nation almost impossible, just as the late twentieth-century era of international interdependence seems to rule out war among the major European and industrial countries. The prevailing culture of materialism and consumerism militates against extreme positions, and any appeal to mass vitalist and irrationalist politics.

Movements and regimes with most similarities to certain aspects of fascism during the second half of the twentieth century have been much more important in some countries of the Third World than in the West. There nationalist regimes of one-party dictatorship have not been uncommon, and more than a few governments in Afro-Asian countries have preached their own versions of national socialism or national corporatism, also relying on elitism and violence, as well as ideologies of mysticism and idealism, in certain instances. There too the 'cult of personality' and charismatic dictatorship has sometimes been powerful, so that more of the specific features of fascism have assumed prominent roles in Africa and Asia than in the Western world in recent decades. None the less, it is not possible to refer to more than specific features and tendencies, for the nationalist movements and dictatorships of the Third World have also developed unique identities and profiles of their own, and in no case have literally copied or revived European fascist movements and regimes.

When some commentators speculate about the 'return of fascism', they are referring not so much to revival of the specific forms of early twentieth-century European fascism and Nazism as to the emergence of new forms of authoritarianism and dictatorship, which is a rather different question. The 'authoritarianism temptation' in varying forms is present in diverse kinds of extremist politics. While the development of new modern dictatorships in major Western countries is not likely, it cannot be ruled out in all forms. Any new authoritarianism in the 1990s would however, have to develop particular characteristics appropriate for its own times and could never be a literal revival of the past.

FURTHER READING

Cassels, A. (1975) *Fascism*, New York: Thomas Y. Crowell.

Griffin, R. (1990) *The Nature of Fascism*, London: Pinter.

Laqueur, W. (ed.) (1976) *Fascism: A Reader's Guide*, Berkeley and Los Angeles: University of California Press.

Larsen, S. U., Hagtvet, B. and Myklebust, J. (eds) (1980), *Who were the Fascists? Social Roots of European Fascism*, Bergen-Oslo: Universitetsforlaget.

Milza, P. (1985) *Les fascismes*, Paris: Imprimerie Nationale.

Mühlberger, D. (ed.) (1987) *The Social Basis of European Fascist Movements*, London: Croom Helm.

Nolte, E. (1966) *Three Faces of Fascism*, New York: Holt, Rinehart and Winston.

Payne, S. G. (1980) *Fascism: Comparison and Definition*, Madison: University of Wisconin Press.

Rees, P. (1984) *Fascism and Pre-fascism in Europe: A Bibliography of the Extreme Right, 1890–1945*, Brighton: Harvester.

Spielvogel, J. J. (1988) *Hitler and Nazi Germany: A History*, Englewood Cliffs, NJ: Prentice-Hall.

12

FUNDAMENTALISM

ADELE FERDOWS AND PAUL WEBER

In the 1950s and 1960s many social scientists argued that secularization was an inevitable concomitant of modernization. Increasing economic and political development would disseminate secular values, hence the role and impact of religion in society and in politics would subside to negligible levels. The 1970s and 1980s, however, witnessed developments diametrically opposed to those predicted by the modernization theories. Around the world, and particularly in Muslim countries, the power of religion did not diminish but increased substantially instead. Indeed, it can be argued that Westernization and secularization served as a catalyst for the revitalization of religious political movements, mobilizing large numbers of people in support of fundamentalist causes. Thus the contemporary emergence of fundamentalism challenges the central assumptions of the modernization literature and poses important questions for investigation.

One of the most difficult and challenging questions that social scientists confront is how to understand and analyse populist religious fundamentalist movements. In some parts of the world, religious fundamentalism has been the means for progressive social change, improvements in social welfare for the poorest members of society and increased political participation by formerly disenfranchised masses. In other parts of the world, religious fundamentalism has mobilized popular support for conservative causes and for efforts to circumscribe or abolish the rights of certain members of the political community. The same phenomenon then could be said to foster both justice and injustice.

This essay will consider three distinctive forms of religious fundamentalism: Islamic fundamentalism, Christian fundamentalism and Jewish fundamentalism. Although each form of fundamentalism shares a commitment to a hegemonic ideal and manifests a willingness to engage in diverse modes of political action to realize that ideal, the differences among these forms of fundamentalism are more prominent than their commonalities.

ISLAMIC FUNDAMENTALISM

Followers and believers in Islamic fundamentalism not only reject the idea of contradiction between religion and progress or modernization, but claim that religious principles are in fact the most relevant means for development and progress in many Islamic societies.

Islam is regarded as a total and eternal system which is for all times and all places applicable to all peoples. Its major difference from Christianity is that the separation of religion from the state is not even conceivable. Government is part of Islam. The Qur'an is the law and government is established to implement the law. But, it is argued, the implementation of Islamic principles and values does not mean that the conditions of life during Prophet Muhammad's time are to be emulated. In fact, some fundamentalist movements have tried to incorporate more recent values and principles which do not contradict religious precepts in order to strengthen their movements and give them viability in the context of the modern world.

Islamic fundamentalism is a complex phenomenon. On the one hand, historically it has been a means for popular expression of hopes and anxieties, derived from native cultural factors. On the other, it has been the channel for confrontation and struggle in Muslim societies during the post-colonial period. Some Muslim scholars have argued that Islamic fundamentalism has two strands: one positive and another negative. The negative is composed of struggle against secularism and the secularist ideologies of nationalism, capitalism and socialism in the Muslim world. The positive strand is represented by attempts at revitalization and rediscovery of Islam, not only as a total system but also as a complete ideological blueprint for life (Ahmad 1983: 221–8).

Some Muslim thinkers believe that 'fundamentalism' is a peculiar phenomenon born out of the unique conditions in Christian history where effort was made to impose the literalist interpretation of the Bible on all Christians. Christian fundamentalism is seen as more conservative and supportive of the status quo, trying to strengthen the moral and ethical fabric of society. Christian fundamentalists are generally regarded as reactionary and unrealistic by the public while Islamic fundamentalism is highly political and revolutionary, wanting to change every aspect of socio-economic and political life of the people.

Islamic fundamentalism is a phenomenon that has emerged from indigenous and native cultures as a reaction to upheavals facing the Muslim societies and calls for a return to Islam and its fundamental precepts and principles. These precepts are embodied in the culmination of the Qur'anic revelation, the traditions, the utterances and actions of Prophet Muhammad and the first four caliphs (Rashidun), who established the first Islamic community and state which comprise the supreme model for emulation. One well-known Muslim writer has summarized Islamic fundamentalism in this way: 'It is the confirmation of Islamic social morality and the rededication of oneself to the establishment of social justice and equity in society' (Ahmad 1983: 227).

The most important fact about Islam is that there is no distinction between the secular and religious spheres. The Prophet Muhammad himself set up in Medina a governing body of rules and laws. Because of this, Islamic fundamentalism has always remained a latent political force, and a common aspect of the mission of Islamic movements has been their emphasis on Islam, not just as a set of beliefs and rituals, but as a moral and social movement to establish the Islamic order. This has meant a wider participation in Friday public prayer, more media attention to issues of faith and behaviour, Islamic styles of dress, and a heightened sense of religiously inspired social responsibility in general. Hence, Islamic fundamentalism, it is argued, is to be seen as a pragmatic, dynamic and progressive ideology that is well equipped to meet the demands of modern society. The different Islamic fundamentalist movements, despite some local variations and indigenous details, have endorsed similar objectives and exhibited common characteristics. They have demonstrated unwavering commitment to Islam and great capability to face the challenge of modernization creatively (Ahmad 1983: 222).

All Islamic fundamentalist movements seek comprehensive reform, that is, changing all aspects of life, making faith the centre point. They claim that what is needed is not new interpretations of old principles, but a stricter adherence to what had already been revealed to be the true path. The *Shari'a* must serve as the supreme source of law, completely replacing the alien laws imported from the West. The replication and implementation of foreign laws, they insist, is a rejection of God's laws which will lead to the destruction of the foundation of an Islamic society.

Some of the major reasons for the appearance of populist Islamic fundamentalist movements are related to the failure of secular and Western ideologies to resolve the socio-economic and political problems in society. This failure has led to disillusionment, gloom and wariness of the Western ideologies of Marxist materialism and liberal pluralism which had been presented in the guise of theories of modernization only a few decades earlier. With the importation of Western and foreign ideologies of capitalism and socialism by the political rulers and ruling regimes in Muslim societies, the perceived threat of undermining the traditional system of values and social identity was intensified among the masses. This perception of danger forced the population to search for an authentic and indigenous point of reference: an alternative ideology. This ideology was clearly found in Islam. In general, threats to group ethnic identity and social and political integrity from outside lead them to resort to the restoration of traditional values and familiar culture as a defence mechanism against the perceived external threat to the group national integrity and identity.

Many scholars have advanced the view that in most Islamic societies the most important factor in the revitalization and rise of Islamic fundamentalist movements has been the search for identity and security, the discovery of familiar values and beliefs in the midst of swift social, economic and political change. Muslim fundamentalists, therefore, are determined to create lifestyles, social systems, and individual as well as state values that will be able to cope with the tremendous instability and insecurity created by the Westernization of their societies, and to protect and defend their societies from the harmful impact of Western ideologies (Ruthven 1984: 287–352).

It has been asserted that the secularist leaders and rulers in Muslim countries have not only failed in the modernization of their societies but that they have also caused colossal upheavals and confusion, resulting in dependence on the West. This in turn has led to public questioning of the rulers' authenticity and the legitimacy of the political establishment. In addition, political oppression, lack of social justice and economic equity, moral decadence and increasing corruption threatened the eradication of traditional values. It is further argued that this confused state of affairs has contributed to a revival of the political role of religion. Islamic ideology presented a clear vision of the future and the promise to solve all problems, offered solace and a sense of refuge to the followers and believers, assisting them in carrying the heavy burden of life.

The role of the traditional clergy in Islam became vital in this regard due to the fact that historically the Muslim clergy have very often acted as the agents of socialization and political mobilization of the masses. In addition, the clergy have acted as the protectors of the people from the oppressive and unjust authority of rulers and have played the intermediary role between them and the government. The clergy promise to advance the interests of the masses who, in the decades of change, had been largely left out of the domain of modernization culturally, socially, and economically.

History of Islamic Fundamentalism

The roots of Islamic fundamentalist movements are found in the history of Islam, both medieval and modern. The history of Islam has contained an element of fundamentalist reaction from the time of its inception. For example, a group known as the *Kharijites* (exiters), deserted 'Ali, the fourth caliph, accusing him of disobeying the literal meaning of the Qur'an because of his agreement to arbitration over the issue of Mu'awiyya's claim to the caliphate. There is total agreement among all Islamic fundamentalists that the very condensed period of the first sixty years after the rise of Islam (from Prophet Muhammad's prophecy to the death of 'Ali, the last Rashidun caliph) is the foundation of the true and pure Islam.

The twentieth century has witnessed the advent of several Islamic spokesmen and leaders of Islamic thought and ideology whose writings have had immense impact not only on their contemporaries but also for future generations. These writings have occupied the supreme place in forming and shaping a comprehensive Islamic vision and a blueprint for action to confront the threat posed to Islamic ways of life by inroads of Western and modern values and institutions.

One of the most outstanding and important Islamic fundamentalist movements by far has been that of the Ikhwan al-Muslimin in Egypt, founded in 1928 by Hasan al-Banna, a school teacher. The Ikhwan is regarded as one of the most popular and aggressive of Islamic fundamentalist organizations. The influence of the Ikhwan went far beyond Egypt and spread into many neighbouring Arab countries. As a conservative organization, it provided the only channel for the expression of anger, frustration and disillusionment with secularization and Westernization for many millions of Muslims. Throughout the 1970s and 1980s, the Ikhwan remained the only prominent means for the expression of Sunni Islamic political thought in Egypt, Sudan, Syria and Jordan.

A similar organization, Fadayan-i Islam, was founded in the mid-1940s by Navab Safavi in Iran. All the leaders of the group were executed in 1956, after which the organization went underground. It has reappeared following the 1979 revolution under the leadership of Ayatollah Khalkhali (The Executioner Ayatollah) but remains a fringe organization.

Few Islamic thinkers and scholars of the twentieth century can compare with Seyyid Qutb (1906–66), the leader of the Ikhwan in Egypt, in the significant impact upon the revitalization and restoration of Islam and development of Islamic thought and ideology in contemporary Muslim societies. His writings have led to the emergence of several Islamic movements in the Muslim world.

The foundation of Qutb's thought was based on the premise that the Western world (capitalist or Marxist versions) has failed in establishing the promised conscientious and humane societies and that this failure has led the Muslims in search of other acceptable, indigenous alternatives in order to save their societies from the dangers posed by the invasion of alien cultural values. This alternative ideology is found in Islamic culture. Seyyid Qutb's works consist of careful analysis of the 'disease' with which Muslims are afflicted. He found that this disease was nothing but adaptation of foreign ways and alien models and blind imitation of Western ideas in their countries. Some scholars regard Seyyid Qutb as the person who tried to bridge the wide gap between the ultra-conservative, traditional *ulema* and the modern sciences and knowledge by opposing the excessive materialism of the West and secularization of Muslim societies but not opposing modernization and progress in economic and social areas as long as they were not detrimental to the welfare of the society or in conflict with basic Islamic values.

Today, Qutb must rank among the most popular and respected authors in the Islamic world. Indeed he may be the single most widely read writer among Muslims and is highly regarded for the quality of his intellect. His works, originally written in Arabic, have been translated into other languages of both the Islamic and Western worlds (Qutb 1976).

Another example of the Islamic fundamentalist position is that contained in the writings of Allamah Abul Ala al-Mawdudi (1903–79). In fact, no discussion or reporting of Islamic fundamentalist movements would be complete without an examination of the role that Mawdudi's works have played in these movements. Certainly, Mawdudi and the organization he founded, *Jama'at Islami*, which he led, was the most important factor in the establishment of Pakistan during the partition of the Indian subcontinent. In addition to being the founder and leader of the *Jama'at*, he was also its ideologue.

He is described by Wilfred Cantwell-Smith (1957: 234) as 'the most systematic thinker of modern Islam' and is revered in many Muslim countries as one of the foremost exponents and interpreters of fundamentalist Islam.

Until his death, but especially prior to his retirement from the leadership of the *Jama'at* in 1972, Mawdudi was the most controversial, dogmatic and visible fundamentalist leader of his time and his *Jama'at* organization spearheaded the movement for the shift in Pakistan from a Muslim country to an Islamic state.

The foundation of Mawdudi's ideas and assumptions is that Islam is a complete and total ideology which does not need explanation or interpretation except within its own context. For Mawdudi, Islam is perfect and there is no need for its justification. His defence strategy for the preservation of Islamic values and principles is as follows: the Western world is corrupt and morally decadent and must be strenuously opposed. He claims that Islam is a total ideology which has appropriate answers to all human predicaments and social dilemmas. Mawdudi insists, without hesitation, that the *Shari'a* must be supreme and rule over all humankind. Mawdudi was perhaps the most dogmatic and uncompromising of Islamic fundamentalist leaders.

One of the least studied of contemporary Islamic fundamentalist leaders is Ayatollah Ruhollah Khomeini (1902–89). Khomeini's message was lucid and unambiguous. To the classic Islamic call for the struggle against imperialism and secularism, he added the unique and unprecedented corollary that the religious leaders must fully participate in the governance of the Islamic community. He declared that it was not only the right but the responsibility of the religious establishment to rule and control the affairs of the country. This doctrine was at once ultra-conservative and revolutionary. It advocated that all people must participate in politics as a religious duty and that the clerics were bound by religion to govern.

CHRISTIAN FUNDAMENTALISM

Within the Christian context, the term 'fundamentalism' seems to have acquired its current meaning from twelve volumes of essays called *The Fundamentals*, written between 1910 and 1915 by several prominent conservative Protestant scholars (Dixon *et al*. 1910–15). Commissioned and underwritten by two wealthy Californian laymen alarmed by the increasing 'worldliness' of mainline Protestant churches and wanting a forceful statement of the true religion, *The Fundamentals* were a stunning success. Over three million copies were distributed and a movement was launched.

In its historical and current American context the term fundamentalism refers to those primarily Protestant Christians who firmly believe in (a) the literal truth or accuracy of the Bible in all its statements, (b) the need to avoid contemporary seductions in personal conduct (depending on the person and the group to which he or she belongs, this may include such things as abortion, birth control, pornography, divorce, movies, dancing, gambling, drinking of alcoholic beverages and the practice of yoga), and (c) the utter impossibility of achieving eternal salvation by human effort. Salvation is achieved by faith in Jesus Christ which is manifest in a zealous witness to the truth.

While Christian fundamentalism is most prominent in the United States, its influence has spread elsewhere, particularly in Latin America and English-speaking nations. Northern Ireland is home to the Revd Ian Paisley, a fundamentalist leader with American ties who has mixed virulent, anti-Catholicism with conservative Protestant dogma. In England, Festival of Lights, a political movement with some fundamentalist leadership, has worked quietly for two decades to enhance public decency.

Fundamentalism is often confused with other concepts, such as Evangelicalism, of which it is a subset. Evangelicals are biblical literalists who believe it is their primary duty to proclaim the gospel. They may be politically liberal, conservative, radical pacifist or strictly non-political. Fundamentalists are evangelicals who are militantly conservative and who see themselves in a war with secular humanists for cultural dominance in America. There remains a tension within fundamentalist ranks between those who believe the best way to fight is to separate from organized political and social interaction with the larger culture to concentrate on individual conversion and those who believe it necessary to take the battle to the larger political and cultural arena.

Fundamentalism is also sometimes confused with the New Right, a popular American political phenomenon of the 1970s and 1980s. The New Right was a loosely and often tenuously affiliated movement of several major ideologies: Economic Libertarianism, a largely secular movement supporting free enterprise, less government regulation and low taxes; Social Traditionalism, a collection of groups concerned with the breakdown of the traditional family, religion and morality; and Militant Anti-communism, a collection of groups, many with roots in the old right and McCarthyism, who considered the Soviet Union to be a continuing threat and who are concerned with national security and military spending. Perhaps the one thing all three groups have in common is a hatred for liberals, whom they consider the source of many of the world's problems. Fundamentalists are heavily concentrated in the Social Traditionalist stream, although a few theological entrepreneurs such as Hal Lindsey (1970) have attempted to tie in Christian concepts such as millenialism and a final battle between the forces of good and evil at Armageddon with anti-communism and nuclear war.

Contemporary social scientists and journalists have expanded the concept of 'fundamentalist' to encompass any group, no matter what its belief system, which they perceive to be religiously motivated, which proclaims dogmatic adherence to a certain set of religious beliefs and which are socially rigid and led by zealous proselytizers. The expansion of the concept to include non-Christian groups is not without value for there are common threads which run through various religious movements.

The power of contemporary fundamentalist movements has caught most social scientists and Western policy makers by surprise. Exactly why development and so-called modernization had quite the opposite effect from the predicated secularization is a matter of some dispute. Perhaps the most widely held hypothesis, based on a theory of status politics, holds that not only does development proceed with a differential impact, improving the economic lot of elites far more rapidly and dramatically than that of ordinary citizens, but modernization confronts the basic values, traditions and lifestyles of non-elites through conspicuous consumption, the introduction of new materialism, and public displays of heretofore alien symbols, dress, and social activities. Under this hypothesis fundamentalists became politically active in response to perceived threats from the larger environment. The difficulty with this hypothesis is that it is not borne out by available data. What data do show is that fundamentalists in each tradition have moved into the economic middle class, are more urban than rural, are very close to the educational levels of the larger non-fundamentalist majority and tend to be as technologically sophisticated as other citizens. A second hypothesis, which might be called a political entrepreneur theory, posits that fundamentalists were enticed out of their political isolation by other more secular conservative leaders, political entrepreneurs who had considerable organizational skills and who had developed financial resources through mass-mailing techniques. These leaders recognized fundamentalists as social traditionalists who could be mobilized to become active participants in a new conservative majority. Enlisting the fundamentalists gave these entrepreneurs a rich tradition of symbols, rituals and values with which to appeal to 'the silent majority' of Americans, as well as access to local communities and several highly visible and charismatic leaders. A variation of this is the Resource Mobilization Model which posits that fundamentalism, like any social movement among identifiable groups, emerges when three factors are present: opportunities, resources and incentives or motives. These factors were available in Christian, Jewish and Islamic movements.

History of American Christian Fundamentalism

The roots, if not the name of fundamentalism, reach as far back in American history as the two great Awakenings in the 1740–50s and 1830–40s. In each instance a popularized, non-hierarchical and theologically unsophisticated wave of religiosity swept through the Congregational and Episcopal churches through revivalist preaching and, in the rural areas, camp meetings. Separate Baptist and Methodist churches quickly evolved into distinct traditions, gaining adherents not only from among the older mainline churches but from the large numbers of unchurched as well. The message was simple: every person can read and interpret the Bible, immoral acts are to be avoided, salvation comes from faith in Jesus Christ, and spread the Good News. This was broad gauge evangelicalism, and some have argued that in the pre-Civil War period it also represented mainstream America.

The post-Civil War period confronted this righteous, self-assured popular Protestantism with enormous challenges. Immigration, industrialism, Darwinism and socialism, each in a somewhat different way, threatened to overwhelm what was perceived as an emerging Christian culture. Immigration and industrialization brought waves of Catholic and Jewish workers to rapidly expanding cities where drinking, gambling, dancing and other social vices made a mockery of the virtuous life so central to the Protestant ethic. Darwinism confronted the biblical literalism that provided the foundation of evangelical Christianity, and socialism promised a worldly salvation that had no need for faith at all. While mainline churches attempted to incorporate new ideas and adapt to modernization, evangelicals fought back in both public and private arenas. They became, in their own way, extraordinary social reformers, working for prison reform, establishment of private charities for the poor, the ill, the alcoholic; they fought first for public schools and then for Sunday Bible schools, and for laws prohibiting gambling, pornography, prostitution and work on Sunday. Above all they worked for temperance. Although never developing a sophisticated intellectual tradition, they saw Darwinist evolutionary theory as a direct challenge to biblical literalism and fought to keep it out of the public schools. Ironically, despite their social and theological conservatism, evangelicals were among the first to grasp the implications of technological innovations such as the radio and mass fund-raising. For over two decades the *Old Time Gospel Hour* had the largest audience of any radio programme.

Two major crises occurred in the 1920s that radically altered the thrust of evangelicalism/fundamentalism for several decades. In 1925 the widely publicized Scopes trial, in which a young Tennessee teacher was convicted of teaching the theory of evolution, exposed fundamentalist beliefs to widespread ridicule. The late 1920s also saw a major backlash against the prohibition amendment for which fundamentalists had fought so valiantly, and which had proved to be a social disaster. Although the amendment was not officially repealed until 1933, by that time the thoroughly discredited fundamentalists had withdrawn from public debate over social issues to organize and build their own institutions. This retreat was aided in no small measure by the emergence of a doctrine of dispensationalism which held that salvation was an 'other-worldly experience' based on personal victory over sin and on personal witnessing. Fundamentalists, in short, became emphatically nonpolitical. For several groups this 'separation' became a touchstone of true faith.

In the late 1960s fundamentalist preachers, many of whom had developed large church followings and TV ministries, began to speak out on political issues. Pressure began to build as a result of several Supreme Court cases outlawing officially sponsored prayer in the public schools and various legislative enactments which fundamentalists perceived as promoting a general moral permissiveness and undermining the family. Most commentators agree that the 1973 Supreme Court decision in *Roe* v. *Wade* – declaring many restrictive abortion laws to be unconstitutional – was the single most important trigger for political activism. The lobby group, Moral Majority, founded in 1979 by the Revd Jerry Falwell, was the most visible of several groups formed to press for a conservative political social agenda. In 1988 fundamentalist TV minister Pat Robertson mounted a credible, if short-lived, campaign for the Republican nomination for the presidency. By 1989, however, the power, prestige and funding of fundamentalists groups dropped significantly. In large measure their constituency became disillusioned after scandals rocked the TV ministries. In addition, the presidency of George Bush proved to be less receptive than that of Ronald Reagan, and as victories declined so did interest and funds. Moral Majority was disbanded and replaced by a much smaller, less active Liberty Federation. The Revd Jerry Falwell himself drew back to focus his efforts on his church and Liberty University in Lynchburg, Virginia.

Christian fundamentalism has a long tradition; it will not disappear quickly. Political activism among fundamentalists, however, does ebb and flow as the opportunities, resources and incentives dictate. The 1970s and 1980s saw a massive outflow of energy which had a significant influence on the American electorate's shift to a conservative direction. The early 1990s appear to be witnessing a period of withdrawal and regrouping. The Gulf crisis helped accelerate a return to dispensationalism (Iraq is the site of Babylon of biblical times and has great significance in Christian prophecy about the second coming of the Messiah). But while fundamentalism may be in a period of political quiesence, it remains a latent political force among a large minority of American Christians.

JEWISH FUNDAMENTALISM

Jewish fundamentalism has both similarities to and differences from the Christian variety. Unlike the latter its roots lie not in particular biblical or Talmudic texts but in nineteenth-century European Zionism – a movement to create a homeland for Jews in Palestine, the land from which they had been driven by the Romans nearly two thousand years earlier. Jews of the Diaspora lament the destruction of Jerusalem and pray daily for a Messiah who will restore Jewish dominion in the land of Israel. All this, according to Jewish tradition, is to be accomplished by God at the chosen time. Originally something of a radical fringe group of intellectuals, Zionists were condemned by mainstream Jewish leaders for trying to force God's hand through political action. However, the violent outbursts of anti-Semitism across Europe in the 1870s gave credence to the claim that Jews needed a land of their own, and gave Zionism a legitimacy it had lacked earlier.

As the Zionist movement expanded and matured it became clear that there were three groupings or streams of thought. First, religious Zionists who adhered to and believed that a return to Israel was a part of God's overall plan for Jews. Second, labour Zionism which grew out of European socialist roots, and which, while it did not reject religious elements, was far more interested in economic growth and organization. Finally there was a secular, rationalist stream which sought to create a democratic Jewish nation without religious regulations or trappings.

When the state of Israel was formed in 1948 these three streams continued to assure tension and division among the Jewish population. While labour Zionism was the largest stream, it was not strong enough to rule without compromise and creation of coalitions. The second largest grouping, and thus the natural competitor to the Labour Party, were the secularists. As a result the smaller religious parties were the natural coalition choices. Indeed, in order to create a governing coalition in 1948, the Labour Party was forced to enact certain elements of orthodox Jewish law, namely:

1 public observance of all Jewish holidays and the sabbath;
2 respect for the law of kosher in government agencies;
3 public financing for religious schools; and
4 observance of orthodox marriage and divorce laws.

In 1950 these were supplemented by the Law of Return, which stated that every Jew around the world had a right to come to Israel and attain citizenship.

These actions had an enormous impact on later fundamentalism because they established a basis for a religious Jewish identity rather than simply a territorial or ethnic identity. Religiously orthodox Jews, although always a minority in Israel, remained a vibrant, insistent, and often passionate voice in Israeli politics, continuously pushing for greater adherence to the law of the Torah in return for their willingness to become part of any ruling coalition.

The trigger issue which galvanized Jewish fundamentalism was the Six Day War in June 1967. In a stunning victory Israel captured the Sinai peninsula and Gaza Strip from Egypt, the Golan Heights from Syria, and the West Bank, including East Jerusalem, from Jordan. The conquest brought not only large areas of land and a large, hostile Arab population under Israeli control, but posed a religious problem of enormous difficulty to the Israeli government. How much of the land should it keep? Should Jews be allowed to settle in the conquered lands? Out of these questions was born contemporary Jewish fundamentalism.

Many religious Zionists took the Israeli victory as vindication of their belief that they were following God's plan. While others, both within Israel and in the broader international community, believed that Jews were now in a position to trade the captured land (excluding holy sites and some small areas deemed necessary for national security) for guarantees of peace, religious Zionists made retention of the lands a fundamental religious issue on which there could be no compromise and no concessions. They were joined for the first time by militant secular nationalists with whom they formed a contentious, adamant, united front to block any efforts by the government to negotiate.

A primary strategy quickly developed of erecting Jewish settlements in the occupied territories, particularly the West Bank, in order to make return of the land more difficult for the government. In 1974 these efforts led to the formation of Gush Emunim, 'Bloc of the Faithful', a fundamentalist, religio-political movement which both legally and illegally developed new settlements that they defied government to tear down.

A second, more ominous strategy was to harrass and drive out Arabs who refused to sell their land for these settlements. In 1977 a stunning victory of the right-wing Likud Party, led by Menachem Begin, over the Labour Party, resulted in a governing coalition significantly more sympathetic to Gush Emunim goals, and Jewish settlements in the occupied territories quickly expanded. According to one authority, Gush Emunim 'more or less deliberately encouraged the harrassment of Palestinians in the West Bank in order to create tension and increase Israeli reluctance to withdraw from the area' (Tessler 1990: 285). If this was indeed their strategy, they certainly succeeded.

One result was to change the political climate so that a number of new fundamentalist religious parties emerged, including Morasha and Kach, the latter a violence-prone group organized by former American Meir Kahane with the stated objective of expelling all Palestinian Arabs from the conquered land. While these groups remain a small minority in Israel, their emergence has added support for Gush Emunim and the settlement movement. It is now unlikely that any Israeli government could forceably dismantle the settlements or withdraw the military from occupied territory.

A second result of settlement and harrassment by fundamentalist groups was an explosion of protests, commonly called the 'intifada', or uprising, among the over one million Arabs, which all but assured that no peaceful co-existence would be possible in the foreseeable future. A third result was a further erosion of support for Israel around the world, including in the United States and Britain.

Jewish fundamentalism remains a strong, militant force in Israeli politics. Whether their policies will result in a backlash among Israeli citizens and a subsequent decline remains to be seen. It had not happened by late 1991. Only one thing seems certain: whether it is manifested in Islamic, Christian, Jewish or other religious traditions, fundamentalism remains a limited but potent political force and is not likely to disappear in the foreseeable future.

BIBLIOGRAPHY

Ahlstrom, S. E. (1975) *A Religious History of the American People*, vol. 2, Garden City, NY: Doubleday-Image Books.

Ahmad, K. (1983) 'The nature of Islamic resurgence', in J. Esposito (ed.) *Voices of Resurgent Islam*, London: Oxford University Press.

Cantwell-Smith, W. (1957) *Islam in Modern History*, Princeton: Princeton University Press.

Dekmejian, H. R. (1985) *Islam in Revolution: Fundamentalism in the Arab World*, New York: Syracuse University Press.

Dessouki, A. E. H., (ed.) (1982) *Islamic Resurgence in the Arab World*, New York: Praeger.

Dixon, A. C., Meyer, L. and Torrey, R. A. (eds) (1910–15) *The Fundamentals*, 12 vols, Chicago: Testimony Publishing Co.

Fowler, R. B. (1982) *A New Engagement: Evangelical Political Thought, 1966–1976*, Grand Rapids, Mich.: Erdmans.

Hertzke, A. D. (1988) *Representing God in Washington: The Role of Religious Lobbies in the American Polity*, Knoxville: University of Tennessee Press.

Husaini, I. M. (1956) *The Moslem Brethren*, Beirut: Khayat's.

Kliever, L. D. (ed.) (1987) *The Terrible Meek: Religion and Revolution in Cross-Cultural Perspective*, New York: Paragon House Publishers.

Liebman, R. C. and Wuthnow, R. (eds) (1983) *The New Christian Right: Mobilization and Legitimation*, New York: Aldine.

Lindsey, H. (1970) *The Late Great Planet Earth*, Grand Rapids, Mich.: Zondervan Press.

Mawdudi, A. A. (1963) *A Short History of the Revivalist Movement in Islam*, Lahore, Pakistan: Islamic Publications.

Mitchell, R. P. (1969) *The Society of the Muslim Brothers*, London: Oxford University Press.

Neuhaus, R. J. (1984) *The Naked Public Square*, Grand Rapids, Mich.: Erdmans.

Qutb, S. (1976) *Islam, the Misunderstood Religion*, Kuwait: Ministry of Islamic Affairs.

Reichley, A. J. (1985) *Religion in American Public Life*, Washington, DC: Brookings Institution.

Roe v. *Wade* 410 v.s. 113 (1973).

Rubenstein, R. L. (1982) *Spirit Matters: The Worldwide Impact of Religion on Contemporary Politics*, New York: Paragon House Publishers.

Ruthven, M. (1984) *Islam in the World*, London: Oxford University Press.

Sahliyeh, E. (ed.) (1990) *Religious Resurgence and Politics in the Contemporary World*, Albany: State University of New York Press.

Smith, D. E. (1970) *Religion and Political Development*, Boston: Little, Brown & Co.

——(ed.) (1974) *Religion and Political Modernization*, New Haven: Yale University Press.

Tessler, M. (1990) 'Religion and politics in the Jewish state of Israel', in E. Sahliyeh (ed.) *Religious Resurgence and Politics in the Contemporary World*, Albany: State University of New York Press.

PART IV

CONTEMPORARY POLITICAL SYSTEMS

13

LIBERAL DEMOCRACIES

G. BINGHAM POWELL

Liberal democracies are identified by an implicit bargain between the representative governments and their citizens and a specific arrangement which regulates that bargain. The bargain is that the government's legitimacy, its expectation of obedience to its laws, is dependent on its claim to be doing what the
citizens want it to do. The organized arrangement that regulates this bargain
of legitimacy is the competitive political election.

In competitive political elections voters can choose from among alternative
candidates. In practice, at least two organized political parties that have some
chance of winning seem to be needed to make choices meaningful. The people
are allowed basic freedoms of speech, press, assembly and organization so that
they can form and express preferences about political policies. Using these
freedoms, all citizens can participate meaningfully in the competitive elections
which choose the rulers. Such electoral participation means that the people
participate indirectly in the general direction of the public policies of the
society. Participation in policy making by the people is the fundamental meaning of democracy (Cohen 1971: chapter 1).

A number of liberal democracies also make some occasional use of direct
citizen involvement in policy making through the referendum, a popular vote
on a proposed law (Butler and Ranney 1978). However, even in Switzerland,
where the device is used more frequently than elsewhere, most legislation is
made through the representative institutions.

The term 'liberal' in 'liberal democracy' draws attention to two related
features of these political systems. First, their claim to democracy rests on
responsiveness to the wishes of the citizens, not to some vision of citizens'
best interests as defined by the rulers or by some ideological system. Second,
the wishes of a majority are not to override all the political and civil rights of
the minorities. At a minimum these rights include the political freedom to
organize and participate. They may also include rights of due process, privacy
and personal property, although liberal democratic theorists are less unanimous

on the boundaries of these rights. The 'liberal' and the 'democratic' elements in liberal democracy may be in tension if citizen majorities favour policies that curtail political and civil rights. More often the two elements support each other; each is an essential component of liberal democracy.

HISTORICAL AND CONTEMPORARY EXAMPLES OF LIBERAL DEMOCRACY

Liberal democracy is primarily a phenomenon of the twentieth century. In the nineteenth century, only the United States, France and Switzerland had approached universal manhood suffrage by the 1870s; the vote for women came even later. Using quite loose standards of voter eligibility, there were about nine democracies among forty-eight independent nations in 1902. After the First World War internal pressures from social groups and international emulation led to a spread of both representative assemblies (Gerlich 1973: 94–113) and the suffrage (Rokkan 1961: 132–52). By 1929–30 there were perhaps twenty-two democracies among the sixty-five independent nations then in existence. Some of these, most notably Weimar Germany, collapsed in the turmoil of the worldwide economic depression of the early 1930s. Following the victory of the allied powers in the Second World War and the breakup of the European colonial empires, there was a further spread of liberal democratic practices. Many newly independent Third World nations (such as Nigeria, Ghana and Pakistan) began as democracies, but were unable to stabilize their political systems.

The number of liberal democracies has waxed and waned since the 1950s, although gradually increasing with the number of independent states. Some well-established democracies have been overthrown (Chile and Uruguay in 1973, for example), while some authoritarian regimes have been replaced by democracies (for example Spain in 1977). Several states (such as Greece, Turkey and Argentina) have experienced both democratic and authoritarian interludes. Various analyses of the 1960s and 1970s placed the number of stable contemporary democracies between thirty and forty, somewhat less than one-quarter of the world's independent national governments (Dahl 1971; Lijphart 1984; Powell 1982a; Rustow 1967). A careful comparison suggested that as many as 30 per cent of the regimes in 1985 might be classified as liberal democracies, but the stability of some of these seemed doubtful (Coppedge and Reinicke 1988: 101–25). (See also Gastil 1988: 3–86; Anderson 1988: 89–99.)

Most studies of contemporary liberal democracies are dominated by the nations of Western Europe and North America (including Costa Rica and the English-speaking Caribbean), Japan, Australia, New Zealand, India and Venezuela, plus scattered small states. In the late 1980s developments in Latin America, the Pacific rim, and Eastern Europe indicated movement towards features of liberal democracy in all three regions: increasing freedom of information and organization and even semi-competitive elections, in which citizens could vote freely with some constrained degree of choice. In 1989 a spectacular movement towards full liberal democracy took place in the previously tightly controlled regimes of Poland, Hungary, East Germany and Czechoslovakia.

MAJOR VARIANTS OF LIBERAL DEMOCRATIC PROCESSES: CONSTITUTIONS AND PARTY SYSTEMS

The detailed arrangements by which contemporary liberal democracies choose policy makers and make policies are extremely varied and complex. Various analysts focus on different features in constructing 'variants' of liberal democracies: unitary and federal systems, presidential and parliamentary systems, two-party and multi-party systems.

Constitutional organization: decision rules

In stable democracies there is agreement on a 'constitution' (whether a single written document or a set of practices and statutes) that specifies how laws must be made (the 'decision rule') and how the makers are to be chosen. The most fundamental conceptual property of any decision rule is its degree of inclusiveness: what part of the membership must agree before a policy is accepted. In a pure dictatorship, the decision rule would be that one individual (the dictator) decides all the policies. In a majoritarian system, the decision rule is that 50 per cent plus one must agree on a policy before it is accepted. In a completely consensual system, the decision rule is unanimity: everyone must agree to a policy before it can be adopted.

Democratic theorists agree that dictatorships and all decision rules requiring the assent of only a small minority are not compatible with the concept of democracy. Most would agree that complete unanimity is impractical if any policies are to be made. They are divided, however, on whether a simple majority or some more inclusive rule is preferable. Theoretically we expect that the majoritarian form would be more efficient at making policy, but the consensual form would be more protective of the rights of minorities (Buchanan and Tulloch 1962).

Many democracies explicitly require application of a more inclusive decision rule for changing the constitution itself (Lijphart 1984: 187–96). Such rules range from a two-thirds vote in the national legislature to elaborate ratification by regional units, as in the American case of ratification by three-quarters of the states. Others may require more inclusive support for some particular legislation, such as treaty ratification (the United States) or even raising new taxes (Finland).

In addition to explicit requirements for more than majority support for passing legislation, most democracies have institutional arrangements that in effect involve the concurrence of representatives of more than a simple majority of the citizens. Many of the institutional differences in liberal democratic constitutions can be understood as implying an expansion of simple majoritarian decision rules for the representatives.

Lijphart's analysis of majoritarian and consensual elements in twenty-two stable democracies identifies a 'federal-unitary' dimension that includes the number and strength of the legislative chambers, the effective centralization or decentralization of the government, and the arrangements for constitutional change (Lijphart 1984: chapter 13). At the majoritarian extreme are New Zealand and Britain. In these countries there are few restraints on the power (or responsibility) of the central government. At the federal extreme are Germany, the United States and Switzerland, where a variety of different institutions, including a second legislative chamber and regional governments, must be involved in many areas of policy-making. The work of Strom (1984, 1990) suggests that legislative committee systems can also work to give minorities the ability to constrain government policies. Again, the effect is to make policy making in a country such as Norway or Belgium more inclusive than simply majoritarian. In such systems, major policy change must typically engage the consent of representatives of far more than a simple majority of citizens.

The distributions of power between the legislature and the chief executive are another important aspect of the decision rule. In the parliamentary systems of most European nations, the chief executive, the prime minister, is chosen by the legislature and can be removed by it. The executive may dominate the legislature through control of a disciplined majority of legislators, but the two are closely fused. In true presidential systems, such as those of the United States and Venezuela, the legislature and the chief executive are independently elected and have separate resources for shaping decision making. The balance between them will depend on the specific powers of each, as well as interconnections of party control. When party control is divided, these systems will become less majoritarian and require broader coalitions. France and Finland provide cases of mixed 'semi-presidential' regimes (Duverger 1980).

Constitutional organization: election rules

A second critical feature of democratic constitutions specifies the rules by which the representatives who make policy are selected.

As Riker (1982b) has pointed out, it was already suspected in the nineteenth century that the type of electoral election rules known as first-past-the-post would tend to lead to exclusion of smaller parties and creation of majorities. Much later, French sociologist Maurice Duverger (1954) stated the 'law' that such rules tend to create two-party systems. Duverger proposed that the majoritarianism is supported both by 'proximate' or 'mechanical' effects in the aggregation of votes and by 'distal' or psychological effects as voters and politicians anticipate the mechanical effects. Recent research (Rae 1967, 1971; Riker 1982b; Gunther 1989; Lijphart 1990) has discovered evidence of both mechanical and psychological effects, but the former seem to dominate in most cases.

'First-past-the-post' election rules, in which a country is divided into single-representative constituencies and the candidate with the most votes (plurality) wins the district, are widely used today in Britain, the United States, and many nations once under British domination, such as New Zealand, Jamaica, Canada, and so forth. The British general election of 1983 produced an example of the mechanical effects, in which smaller parties with votes evenly distributed across districts do badly, and legislative majorities can be created. The Liberal–Social Democratic Alliance gained 25 per cent of the vote and came in second in more districts than either 'major' party, but gained only a handful of parliamentary seats. On the other hand, the Conservatives gained a solid legislative majority with only about 40 per cent of the popular vote.

The major alternative forms of election rules are the various versions of proportional representation (PR). Favoured by most of the nations of continental Europe, PR provides for multi-member legislative districts, with parties represented in proportion to their voting support in the district. The size and complexity of the districts, the exact rules for distributing 'remainder' votes, and the presence of 'cut-off' rules eliminating parties below a certain size can shape the working of the system (Rae 1967; Groffman and Lijphart 1986; Lijphart 1990). But in a system such as that of the Netherlands or Denmark, the presence of PR allows a large of number of small parties to form, seek, and obtain legislative representation with only a few per cent of the national vote. It is difficult for single parties to gain legislative majorities under PR rules.

Competitive party systems: critical linkage

Competitive party systems shape the critical electoral linkages between citizens and policy makers. Bryce's observation seventy years ago holds true today: no large democracy has been able to do without political parties as the vehicle for organizing and structuring elections (Bryce 1921 (vol. i): 119). Without such organization the ability of citizens to have an impact through elections is extremely limited.

Moreover, parties are a means through which constitutional arrangements shape democratic policy making and, sometimes, a means through which constitutional arrangements can be overcome. Party competition is affected by the historic social and political cleavages of the society (Lipset and Rokkan 1967), the strategies of politicians (Downs 1957; Mueller 1979), and by the values of the society, as well as by the constitutional arrangements. Party systems also have autonomous influence of their own and, usually, substantial ability to sustain themselves over time (Lipset and Rokkan 1967; Inglehart 1984). Lijphart found that the consensual elements other than the unitary-federal ones formed a dimension most closely approximated by the number of effective political parties (Lijphart 1984: chapter 13).

The literature on party systems and party competition is voluminous. (See, for example, discussions in Duverger 1954; Neumann 1956; Downs 1957; Dahl 1966; Lipset and Rokkan 1967; Epstein 1967; Sartori 1976: chapter 6; Powell 1982a: chapter 5; Strom 1985, 1990; Ware 1988.) Two major distinctions dominate much of the analysis. The first of these distinguishes two-party, or at least majority electing, systems from multi-party systems. Theorists and observers who favour clarity of responsibility and the power to implement promises (Schattschneider 1942; Ranney 1962), and/or the pre-election aggregation of citizen preferences (Lipset 1960; Almond and Powell 1966; Epstein 1967) that seem to go with majoritarian government naturally favour two-party systems. Those who favour explicit representation of social and political factions in policy making and elaborately consultative political processes tend to favour multi-party systems (Nordlinger 1972; Lehmbruch 1974; Lijphart 1977, 1984).

A second major distinction between party systems focuses on the degree or type of political conflict that they express. Most party system theorists hold that highly polarized party systems, in which there is a great gap between the espoused policy packages (ideologies) of major parties, or in which 'extremist' parties, who challenge the basic ground rules of the society, gain substantial strength, are dangerous for the continued performance of democracy (Duverger 1954: 419–20). Sartori's influential analysis of polarized pluralism (Sartori 1976: chapter 6) argues that the polarized systems enhance the ideological intensity of policy debate, encourage a pattern of irresponsible 'outbidding' by extremist parties, and discourage turnovers of power that could keep incumbent parties responsible to citizens (see also Powell 1987). Substantial research suggests that polarized or extremist party systems tend to promote instability of party governments, and perhaps mass turmoil as well (Taylor and Herman 1971; Hibbs 1973; Powell 1981, 1986a).

The two distinctions are often associated in argument, as many theorists have explicitly or implicitly linked multi-partism and polarization. It seems to be true that the constitutional arrangements that encourage multi-party legislative representation will also allow extremist party representation if discontent emerges. However, there is less empirical support for the argument that multi-partism as such encourages or exacerbates political conflict (Powell 1981;

1982a: chapter 5; 1987). Some multi-party systems, such as those of Norway and the Netherlands, have continued for long periods without destabilizing political extremism.

Interest group systems

While the 'major variants' of liberal democracy have traditionally been defined by constitutional and party systems, political scientists have also focused considerable attention in the last decade on the ability of certain systems of interest group arrangements to deal more effectively than others with national economic problems. A set of such arrangements called 'democratic corporatism' has included a relatively centralized and comprehensive system of interest groups, continuous political bargaining between groups, political parties and state bureaucracies, and a supportive ideology of national 'social partnership' (Katzenstein 1985: 32). It has been pointed out that the countries having these regularized corporatist relationships (among them Austria, Switzerland and the Scandinavian countries) had better combined inflation/unemployment performance in the difficult years of the mid-1970s and early 1980s than did systems with more competitive interest group and party relationships, such as Britain and the United States (Berger 1981; Schmitter 1981; Cameron 1984; Katzenstein 1985). While research to date has concentrated primarily on labour and industrial relations, investigation of the consequences of various systems of interest group relations in other policy areas and at other times is underway in many countries.

CITIZEN INFLUENCE IN DIFFERENT VARIANTS OF LIBERAL DEMOCRACY

The many details of constitution, party and interest group systems can be simplified theoretically into a single dimension of majoritarianism and consensualism. Where the constitutional arrangements, party and interest group systems work together to elect controlling government majorities, able to make and implement policy without further elaborate bargaining, it should be easy for citizens to assess policy responsibility and hold incumbents accountable. If policy outcomes are unsatisfactory, the incumbents can be ejected and the opposition(s) brought to power. Citizens should frequently get the policies they want without an elaborate process of search and rejection, because incumbents desiring re-election will anticipate citizen's desires (Downs 1957; Pennock 1979: chapter 7).

Such majoritarian governmental systems can also promote mandate processes (Ranney 1962; Birch 1972). If the parties offer alternative policy choices to citizens and keep their promises when elected, citizens can use elections to set the basic policy agenda for the future. Such alternative promises may be an important way for options to be widened and policy change desired by citizens to come into focus. Moreover, the clarity of responsibility in the majoritarian system will make it easy for voters to punish incumbents who fail to keep their promises.

The difficulty for citizen control posed by the majoritarian variants lies primarily in the bluntness of the electoral weapon under conditions of many different political issues. Unless all these issues can align citizens the same way, form a single 'dimension', there will be different possible alliances of citizens on different issues. Citizens in the majority on one issue will be in the minority on another. The tendency of the pure majoritarian variant to 'freeze' into policy all the promises of the party winning office will result in some policies that do not have majority support. (British politics provides various examples of this, such as Labour's nationalization of the steel industry after the 1966 election, or the Conservative government's privatization of utilities after the 1987 election. Both policies were carried out as 'mandates'; both were clearly opposed by citizen majorities.) Situations where the government majorities are created from the operation of the electoral laws on less than a majority of the vote (the most common situation in democracies, as shown by Rae 1967: 74) are even more uncomfortable for the concept of citizen control.

Furthermore, the presence of multiple issue dimensions creates difficulties for simple accountability of incumbents as well. On which issue are they to be held accountable? And what shall the voter do if the opposition promises future policies that are as unpalatable as the incumbent's failures?

The consensual variant of democracy avoids some of these difficulties. An inclusive decision rule and election rules that help bring into power a variety of parties or factions that represent many configurations of voter opinion will open up the possibility of forming different governing coalitions on different issues (King 1981). First, the parties must negotiate parliamentary coalition governments that will have positions corresponding more complexly to the variety of clusters of voter preference, and which may change before the next election. Alternatively a 'minority' government may gather support from different parties outside the government on different issues. Second, the party government will have to negotiate with individuals or parties that have resources from committee positions (Strom 1990), the other legislative house, the regional governments, and so forth. 'Early elimination' of possible majorities (Riker 1982a) will be less frequent.

But the consensual version has the difficulties of its virtues. The complex stages of bargaining make it difficult for voters to see any connection between their choices and government policy. The absence of connection can be frustrating even for those not wedded to a strict mandate model, as Dutch voters emphasized over twenty years ago in their support for the (then) protest party D66. Even more fundamentally, it can be difficult to assess responsibility for policy. American voters facing divided presidential–congressional control, shifting party factions and strong committees in Congress, significant state government authority, and an often intrusive Supreme Court may well find it impossible to know whom to blame for policy failure. Similarly, short-lived coalitions, frequent minority governments, and strong committees can make responsibility equally hard to pin down in Switzerland, Italy or Belgium. It is hard to find a way to express fundamental democratic dissent by throwing out the incumbents when the potential alternative policy makers are also contaminated by power-sharing.

There may be no variant of democracy, or at least none yet identified by political science, that guarantees the most effective single approach to citizen influence. Rather, each of the major variants and their combinations has its own strengths and weaknesses (Powell 1989). The importance of each type of weakness may depend on the number and intensity of the issues that divide (or unite) the citizens, as well as on the qualities that citizens most value. Perhaps it is sufficient at the moment to be aware of the strengths and weaknesses of the different approaches.

CITIZEN PARTICIPATION IN LIBERAL DEMOCRACY

Whatever the possibilities for control created by the different democratic variants, it remains up to the citizens to make use of them. Effective citizen control will require employment of both electoral and non-electoral channels to supplement the blunt, but essential, electoral instruments with forms of participation capable of conveying citizen's desires more clearly and completely (Verba and Nie 1972: 322–7).

Voting participation

It is clear that voting is both the most widely used and most equally used form of citizen participation in liberal democracies (Verba et al. 1978; Barnes Kaase et al. 1979). It is also clear that levels of citizen voting participation differ systematically across the liberal democracies. Voter turn-out in national elections ranges from around 50 per cent of the citizens of voting age in Switzerland and the United States to about 90 per cent in Australia, Austria, Belgium and Italy. Average turn-out in nations without compulsory voting provisions is slightly under 80 per cent (Powell 1982a: 14; 1986b). While turn-out does vary from election to election, usually turn-out within each nation is relatively consistent compared to the striking cross-national differences. Differences in rates of political participation are in part a consequence of differences in the attitudes and characteristics of the citizens (education, interest, confidence, party commitment). Even more important are differences in the institutional context, such as compulsory voting, registration laws, nationally competitive election districts, and, somewhat less certainly, other features of the policy-making and party systems (Powell 1986b; Jackman 1987).

Campaign and communal participation

The importance of institutional setting applies to participation in campaign activity as well as to voting. It is clear that in some countries election activities, such as working for parties and candidates, are dominated by small numbers of dedicated activists or by party members rewarded by patronage. In other countries, especially in the United States, the decentralized but extensive organizations of party and candidates mobilize far more citizens into campaign activity (Barnes, Kaase, *et al.* 1979: 541–2; Verba, *et al.* 1978: 58–9).

None thé less, participation studies (Verba, *et al.* 1978; Barnes and Kaase, *et al.* 1979) suggest that the individual characteristics of citizens, such as education, interest, socio-economic resources and partisanship, are more important in explaining who participates in election campaigns or community activity than in explaining who votes. The combination of a relatively educated and organized citizenry and significantly independent local governments have led, for example, to impressive amounts of communal participation in the United States; it is, however, participation more frequently from the better-off citizens in the society (Verba and Nie 1972). The participatory advantages of citizens with more social and economic resources can be countered in part, but only in part, by deliberate efforts of unions and labour parties to organize and mobilize the disadvantaged. (See Verba *et al.* 1978: 94–142, on the connections between socio-economic resources, organizational systems, and degree and equality of political participation in different democracies.)

Constructing a full picture of the degree, types, and equality of citizen utilization of the possibilities for democratic participation is a still-incomplete task for political science.

Interest groups and citizens in liberal democracies

Groups that endeavour to press the interests and demands of their members on policy makers are found in every kind of political system. The conditions of freedom of organization and communication found in liberal democracies naturally encourage the formation of innumerable interest groups of many kinds. As societies become more complex and organizationally differentiated, and as individual citizens become, on average, better educated and informed, these groups proliferate. Some of these are formed explicitly to articulate political demands; even more are pressed into political service when the groups' interests encounter a potentially political issue. However, for both historical and socio-economic reasons, democracies vary substantially in the density of interest group organization, as well as in the connections between groups and political parties. Citizen participation in voluntary associations seems to be high in the United States and Austria, even higher in Sweden and some other Scandinavian countries (Pestoff 1977: 65; Verba *et al.* 1978: 101).

Some scholars have seen such activity on the part of labour unions, consumer groups, churches, business and professional associations, recreational groups, and so forth as essential to liberal democracy. One line of thought emphasizes conflict mediation. 'Cross-cutting' multiple group affiliations can tie individuals together and encourage taking account of multiple views (Truman 1951; Lipset 1960; Pestoff 1977). Another line of thought focuses on group activity that can mediate between the citizen and the state (Kornhauser 1959), helping citizens to develop and clarify their own desires, interpret them politically and participate in politics beyond the electoral arena (Almond and Verba 1963: 300–22). The group activity can articulate the wants of individual citizens to policy makers with far more clarity and targeted precision than the crude linkage of party and election. They can bring to bear more resources than can the citizen acting alone. Even if organized initially or primarily for some other purpose, their presence can solve many of the problems of organizing and mobilizing faced by discontented, but scattered, individuals (Olsen 1965; Verba *et al.* 1978).

Other democratic theorists have regarded interest groups (pressure groups) suspiciously, stressing that the special demands and advantages of such groups may be contrary to the public interest or the interests of the less well organized, who are also commonly the less educated and well-off members of the society. Schattschneider, for example, wrote of 'the pressure group' as 'a parasite living on the wastage of power exercised by the sovereign majority' (Schattschneider 1942: 190) and later argued that 'the business or upper-class bias of the pressure system shows up everywhere' (ibid. 1960: 30). (See also McConnell 1966.)

In a general sense, of course, competitive elections should help check the tendency of policy makers to respond to the more frequently articulated interests of the better-off and the organized, just as they should check the tendency for policy makers to follow their own desires. In practice, problems of citizen attention, information and competing issues limit the electoral con-straint. Hence the importance of interest group organization for all parts of the citizenry.

CONDITIONS FOR SUSTAINING LIBERAL DEMOCRACY

Liberal democracies exist in societies of many different types and sizes. Given a certain degree of autonomy and the desire for liberal democracy on the part of the citizens, it is possible to introduce and sustain a liberal democracy in any society. Certain conditions of the social setting are, however, much more conducive to liberal democracy and provide better prospects for its survival than others. Moreover, political theorists have long believed that certain variants have greater survival capacity than others.

As a first condition, the international setting will have important effects on the prospects for liberal democracy. In the extreme case, such penetrated societies as the nations of Eastern Europe in the period from 1945 until very recently may not be allowed to develop liberal democracy. The Soviet Union made it very clear in Hungary in 1956 and in Czechoslovakia in 1968 that it would not allow multi-party competition and free elections in those societies, whatever the desires of the citizens. Dramatic changes in the Soviet Union's policies in the late 1980s paved the way for the introduction of democracy in Eastern Europe. Moreover, the financing of internal rebellions by outside governments, or the perception by an internal minority that they might be part of a majority in another state, can fuel internal conflict and weaken a would-be democracy.

Less directly, international conditions can give a strong argument for or against internal proponents of democracy. Pro-democratic forces in Spain and Greece in the 1970s were strengthened by the expectation that liberal democracy would be a prerequisite to full entry to the European Community and its valuable markets. In the broad historical sweep, as Huntington suggests, 'the rise and decline of democracy on a global scale is a function of the rise and decline of the most powerful democratic states' (Huntington 1984: 154).

Second, the level of modernization of the society will affect its prospects for sustaining democracy. The greater wealth and income of economically developed societies make it possible for them to deal with internal conflict, especially economic conflict, in a greater variety of ways. Closely associated, the greater levels of literacy, the more dense communication media, and the more complexly developed patterns of associational life all encourage a citizenry able to deal with democratic participation. The level of modernization is also strongly associated with development of an autonomous, indigenous middle class, which has historically been an important democratizing force. (For reviews of the large literature on these points, see especially Huntington 1968, 1974; Dahl 1971: 62–80; Powell 1982a: 34–41.) Democracy has been sustained in some relatively poor and economically undeveloped societies, such as India, but they are the exception.

Third, the degree of internal social and ethnic fragmentation is likely to affect the prospects for stable and successful liberal democracy (Hibbs 1973: chapter 5; Powell 1982a: 42–7). Nations with divisions of language, ethnicity, race, religion and other demographic characteristics that involve the deep personal identity (and identifiability) of individuals and groups are likely to have a more difficult time in achieving political stability under any system. They often face public policy issues that are particularly difficult to resolve through compromise and partial measures. Situations involving simple divisions of the society into majority and minority ethnic groups can be even more difficult to resolve than multiple groups with no majority.

Moreover, the threat to the identity of individuals and social groups makes for great intensity of feeling and easy development of fear and distrust. Once internal ethnic conflicts are mobilized and fear and grievances accumulated, ethnic conflicts may defy the most imaginative efforts at democratic reconciliation. The long-running conflicts involving Northern Ireland in the UK and the Basques in Spain provide examples. The relative successes of ethnic politics without major deadly conflict in Switzerland, Belgium and Canada show that ethnic homogeneity is not a prerequisite for stable democracy. But it surely makes the task easier.

There seems little doubt that a supportive international environment, socio-economic development and ethnic homogeneity are conditions that make it easier to introduce and sustain liberal democracy. In practice it is also true that the contemporary democracies are found in societies with market-oriented economies. It is difficult to know if this association is the result of the group autonomy encouraged in free markets, or a consequence of incompatibility of general societal command control systems with both liberal democracy and market-oriented economics, but the association is surely present.

Beyond these more or less objective conditions of the social and economic setting for democracy, it is also likely that the cultural traditions and values of a society may can work for or against liberal democracy. As France has demonstrated to the rest of Europe for two hundred years, historical political cleavages and conflicts can haunt a nation's political life and make democratic conflict resolution more difficult. The general association between a Protestant religious heritage and successful democratic development has frequently been noted; particular difficulties for democracy in Islamic nations have been suggested (Huntington 1984). The presence of such citizen attitudes as social trust, subject and participant competence, social co-operativeness (Almond and Verba 1963: 504; Inglehart 1990), and an 'ethos of civic involvement' (Putnam et al. 1983) seem to enhance the stability and performance of liberal democratic systems.

Theorists of the consequences of liberal democratic constitutions and party systems have been seriously divided over the merits of each major variant for sustaining democracy. Under conditions of general citizen agreement on the basic procedures and policies of the society, any of the approaches will probably survive. In his study of twenty-two liberal democracies stable since the Second World War, Lijphart (1984) found examples of both highly majoritarian types (Britain, New Zealand) and highly consensual ones (Switzerland, Belgium). He also found various mixes of centralized, multi-party systems and federalized majority party systems. On the other hand, under conditions of extreme pressure any of them may fail.

Nor is it obvious whether or not intense polarization of citizen opinion is better dealt with through enforced incorporation within two-party, majoritarian politics than through proportional representation and consultation. Supporters of majority government stress its ability to make policy rapidly and decisively, and suggest that this capacity can be critical in times of great stress. At least since the fall of the Weimar Republic, many writers have seen multi-party systems as fatefully unable to deal with major internal crisis (for example, see Bracher 1964; Dahl 1971: 173). A view with often contrary implications is that majoritarian politics is destabilizing in the presence of intense opinion conflicts (Lehmbruch 1974; Lijphart 1977, 1984; Nordlinger 1972). Majoritarianism tends to lead to suppression of minorities and/or too much threat for incumbents to yield power. Societies divided by ethnicity or other sources of intense disagreement must move to non-majoritarian, consultative arrangements. Another suggested element in the situation (Powell 1982a, 1986a) is that multi-party or consensual arrangements may not exacerbate conflict but do tend to move turmoil from the streets (protests and riots) to the constitutional arena (less durable coalitions).

If democratic failure occurs, it may well take different forms in the different democratic variants. Majoritarian systems are more likely to succumb to the temptation of the strong government (of either presidential or parliamentary type) to constrain civic freedom or even competition in the name of stability, or do away with elections entirely in the name of fear or continuity. Consensual systems are more likely to become immobilized, unable to address serious policy issues, lose citizen confidence and open the path to military intervention (see Powell 1982a: 170–4). But there is no magic formula that applies to all cases; rather it is up to the elites in the society to devise ways of overcoming the weaknesses and taking advantages of the strengths that reside in their variant of liberal democracy (Lijphart 1977; Powell 1982a: 218–24). It is the essence of liberal democracy that ordinary citizens must also have the attentiveness and wisdom to support the efforts to sustain democracy and freedom.

LIBERAL DEMOCRACIES AND NON-DEMOCRATIC ALTERNATIVES

As recently as the mid-1970s liberal democracy seemed in retreat. The overthrow of apparently well-established stabilized democracies in Uruguay, Chile, Turkey and the Philippines by military or executive coup; the tragic civil war in Lebanon; the suspension of democratic elections and rights in India and Sri Lanka, suggested that democracy was too fragile to cope with Third World conditions. In the (post-)industrialized West, academics shaken by student revolts, terrorist attacks, 'stagflation', strikes, and declining party identification wrote grimly of the 'ungovernability' of liberal democracies in contemporary societies (for example, see Crozier *et al.* 1975). They despaired over the short-sighted expenditure-driven policies of mass electorates and democratic politicians (for example, see Brittan, 1975).

It seems likely that hard times will come again. Therefore, it seems appropriate to conclude with a few words of comparison between democracies and the non-democratic alternatives. First, the easiest area in which to document superior performance of democracy is in sustaining civil rights and personal freedom from elite abuse. A review of the yearly studies of political rights and civil liberties by Freedom House (Gastil 1978, 1988) makes this association quite clear. Some authoritarian governments permit substantial civil freedom. Some liberal democracies have adopted restrictions on press freedoms and civil rights, or have abused the positions of minorities. But the general intertwining of electoral competition and political rights with civil freedom is obvious.

Moreover, there is some evidence that democracy contributes to the containment of serious violence. This evidence would probably be more compelling if we had better data on violence in authoritarian systems. But Hibbs's very careful analysis of mass political violence on a worldwide scale (Hibbs 1973) found that regimes in which elites were electorally accountable were less likely to use repression against their citizens. He also observed that such elite restraint when confronted with citizen protest and turmoil helped prevent the escalation of serious violence (ibid.: 186–7).

In areas of welfare policy and economic growth, it is more difficult to be sure about the evidence for liberal democracy. Both problems of data and the rather different strategies within each type of regime make comparison a complex task. We would expect from theory, of course, that the liberal democracies would be more likely to develop welfare policies and otherwise respond to consensual policies (if any) preferred by the electorates. It is precisely this expectation that made many scholars of Third World development pessimistic about the ability of liberal democracies to promote the savings needed for long-term growth (for example, see Huntington and Nelson 1976).

Despite both the hopes and fears of policy tendencies in liberal democracies, the best comparisons of welfare policies before 1980 suggest little difference between liberal democracies and other types of regimes in average welfare policies or average growth in either the Third World or in Eastern versus Western Europe (see the review in Powell 1982b: 385–9). More recent studies (Dye and Zeigler 1988), as well as events in Eastern Europe in the late 1980s, seem to favour liberal democracies. At the very least, the 1980s have demonstrated that within each type of political regime many economic patterns are possible. They have also demonstrated that voters in liberal democracies can reject parties proposing endless welfare and tax spirals. Thus there seems reason for measured optimism about the capacity for voters to constrain elite behaviour in modern liberal democracies.

As the decade of the 1990s begins, it is too easy to be optimistic about the performance of liberal democracies compared to non-democratic systems. With the ideology of communism in disarray, Soviet control of its European neighbours apparently released, and central command control systems in economic chaos, the victory of liberal democracy and mixed capitalist economies over their most prominent rival seems at hand. Perhaps a more sober lesson is that no regime offers a perfect solution to governing contemporary society. Churchill's dictum remains the safest:

> Many forms of government have been tried and will be tried in this world of sin and woe. No one pretends that democracy is perfect or all-wise. Indeed, it has been said that democracy is the worst form of government except for all those other forms that have been tried from time to time.
>
> (Churchill 1950: 200)

REFERENCES

Almond, G. and Powell, G. B. (1966) *Comparative Politics: A Developmental Approach*, Boston: Little, Brown & Co.

Almond, G. and Verba, S. (1963) *The Civic Culture: Political Attitudes and Democracy in Five Nations*, Princeton: Princeton University Press.

Anderson, T. D. (1988) 'Civil rights and political liberties in the world: a geographic analysis', in R. D. Gastil (ed.) *Freedom in the World: Political Rights and Civil Liberties 1987–1988*, New York: Freedom House.

Barnes, S. H., Kaase, M. *et al.* (1979) *Political Action: Mass Participation in Five Western Democracies*, Beverley Hills: Sage Publications.

Berger, S. (ed.) (1981) *Organizing Interests in Western Europe*, New York: Cambridge University Press.

Birch, A. H. (1972) *Representation*, London: Macmillan.

Bracher, K. D. (1964) 'The problem of parliamentary democracy in Europe', *Daedalus* 93: 178–98.

Brittan, S. (1975) 'The economic contradictions of democracy', *British Journal of Political Science* 5: 129–59.

Bryce, J. (1921) *Modern Democracies*, 2 vols, New York: Macmillan.

Buchanan, J. and Tullock, G. (1962) *The Calculus of Consent*, Ann Arbor: University of Michigan Press.

Butler, D. and Ranney, A. (1978) *Referendums: A Comparative Study*, Washington, DC: American Enterprise Institute.

Cameron, D. (1984) 'Social democracy, corporatism and labor quiescence: the representation of interests in advanced capitalist society', in J. Goldthorpe (ed.) *Order and Conflict in Contemporary Capitalism*, Oxford: Oxford University Press.

Churchill, W. S. (1950) *Europe Unite: Speeches 1947 and 1948*, ed. R. S. Churchill, Boston: Houghton Mifflin.

Cohen, C. (1971) *Democracy*, New York: Free Press.

Coppedge, M. and Reinicke, W. (1988) 'A scale of polyarchy', in R. D. Gastil (ed.) *Freedom in the World: Political Rights and Civil Liberties 1987–1988*, New York: Freedom House.

Crozier, M., Huntington, S. P. and Watanuki, J. (1975) *The Crisis of Democracy*, New York: New York University Press.

Dahl, R. A. (ed.) (1966) *Political Oppositions in Western Democracies*, New Haven: Yale Univeristy Press.

——(1971) *Polyarchy: Participation and Opposition*, New Haven: Yale University Press.

Downs, A. (1957) *An Economic Theory of Democracy*, New York: Harper & Row.

Duverger, M. (1954) *Political Parties: Their Organization and Activity in the Modern State*, New York: John Wiley.

——(1980) 'A new political system model: semi-presidential government', *European Journal of Political Research* 8: 165–87.

Dye, T. R. and Zeigler, H. (1988) 'Socialism and equality in cross-national perspective', *PS: Political Science and Politics* 21: 45–56.

Epstein, L. D. (1967) *Political Parties in Western Democracies*, New York: Praeger.

Gastil, R. D. (ed.) (1978) *Freedom in the World: Political Rights and Civil Liberties*, New York: Freedom House and G. R. Hall.

——(ed.) (1988) *Freedom in the World: Political Rights and Civil Liberties 1987–88*, New York: Freedom House.

Gerlich, P. (1973) 'The institutionalization of European Parliaments', in A. Kornberg (ed.) *Legislatures in Comparative Perspective*, New York: David McKay.

Groffman, B. and Lijphart, A. (1986) *Electoral Laws and their Political Consequences*, New York: Agathon Press.

Gunther, R. (1989) 'Electoral laws, party systems, and elites: the case of Spain', *American Political Science Review* 83: 835–58.

Hibbs, D. A. (1973) *Mass Political Violence*, New York: John Wiley.

Huntington, S. P. (1968) *Political Order in Changing Societies*, New Haven: Yale University Press.

——(1974) 'Post-industrial politics: how benign will it be?', *Comparative Politics* 6: 163–92.

——(1984) 'Will more countries become democratic?', *Political Science Quarterly* 99: 193–218.

Huntington, S. P. and Nelson, J. (1976) *No Easy Choice: Political Participation in Developing Countries*, Cambridge, Mass.: Harvard University Press.

Inglehart, R. (1984) 'The changing structure of political cleavages in Western society', in R. Dalton, S. Flanagan and P. A. Beck (eds) *Electoral Change in Advanced Industrial Democracies*, Princeton: Princeton University Press.

——(1990) *Culture Shift in Advanced Industrial Society*, Princeton: Princeton University Press.

Jackman, R. (1987) 'Political institutions and voter turnout in the industrial democracies', *American Political Science Review* 81: 405–24.

Katzenstein, P. (1985) *Small States in World Markets*, Ithaca, NY: Cornell University Press.

King, A. (1981) 'What do elections decide?', D. Butler, H. Penniman and A. Ranney (eds) *Democracy at the Polls*, Washington, DC: American Enterprise Institute.

Kornhauser, W. (1959) *The Politics of Mass Society*, Glencoe: Free Press.

Lehmbruch, G. (1974) 'A non-competitive pattern of conflict management in liberal democracies', in K. D. McRae (ed.) *Consociational Democracy*, Toronto: McCelland & Stewart.

Lijphart, A. (1977) *Democracy in Plural Societies*, New Haven: Yale University Press.

——(1984) *Democracies: Patterns of Majoritarian and Consensus Government in Twenty-one Countries*, New Haven: Yale University Press.

——(1990) 'The political consequences of electoral laws 1945–1985', *American Political Science Review* 84: 481–96.

Lipset, S. (1960) *Political Man*, Garden City, NY: Doubleday.

Lipset, S. and Rokkan, S. (1967) *Party Systems and Voter Alignments*, New York: Free Press.

McConnell, G. (1966) *Private Power and American Democracy*, New York: Knopf.

Mueller, D. C. (1979) *Public Choice*, Cambridge: Cambridge University Press.

Neumann, S. (1956) *Modern Political Parties*, Chicago: University of Chicago Press.

Nordlinger, E. (1972) *Conflict and Conflict Management in Divided Societies*, Cambridge, Mass.: Harvard Center for International Studies.

Olson, M. (1965) *The Logic of Collective Action*, Cambridge, Mass.: Harvard University Press.

Pennock, R. (1979) *Democratic Political Theory*, Princeton: Princeton University Press.

Pestoff, V. A. (1977) *Voluntary Associations and Nordic Party Systems*, Stockholm: Liber Tryck.

Powell, G. B., Jr (1981) 'Party systems and political system performance in contemporary democracies', *American Political Science Review* 75: 861–79.

——(1982a) *Contemporary Democracies: Participation, Stability and Violence*, Cambridge, Mass.: Harvard University Press.

——(1982b) 'Social progress and liberal democracy', in G. Almond, M. Chodorow and R. H. Pierce, *Progress and Its Discontents*, Berkeley: University of California Press.

——(1986) 'Extremist parties and political turmoil: two puzzles', *American Journal of Political Science* 30: 357–78.

——(1986b) 'American voter turnout in comparative perspective', *American Political Science Review* 80: 17–44.

——(1987) 'The competitive consequences of polarized pluralism', in J. Holler (ed.) *The Logic of Multiparty Systems*, Dordrecht: Martinus Nijhoff.

——(1989) 'Constitutional design and citizen electoral control', *Journal of Theoretical Politics* 1: 107–30.

Putnam, R., Leonardi, R, Nanetti, R. and Pavoncello, F. (1983) 'Explaining institutional success: the case of Italian regional government', *American Political Science Review* 77: 55–74.

Rae, D. W. (1967) *The Political Consequences of Electoral Laws*, New Haven: Yale University Press.

Ranney, A. (1962) *The Doctrine of Responsible Party Government*, Urbana: University of Illinois Press.

Riker, W. H. (1982a) *Liberalism Against Populism*, San Francisco: W. H. Freeman.

——(1982b.) 'The two-party system and Duverger's law: an essay on the history of political science', *American Political Science Review* 76: 753–66.

Rokkan, S. (1961) 'Mass suffrage, secret voting and political participation', *Archives Européen de sociologie* 2: 132–52.

Rustow, D. A. (1967) *A World of Nations: Problems of Political Modernization*, Washington, DC: Brookings Institution.

Sartori, G. (1976) *Parties and Party Systems*, New York: Cambridge University Press.

Schattschneider, E. E. (1942) *Party Government*, New York: Holt, Rinehart & Winston.

——(1960) *The Semi-Sovereign People*, Hinsdale: Dryden Press.

Schmitter, P. (1981) 'Interest intermediation and regime governability', in S. Berger (ed.) *Organizing Interests in Western Europe*, New York: Cambridge University Press.

Strom, K. (1984) 'Minority governments in parliamentary democracies', *Comparative Political Studies* 17:199–227.

——(1985) 'Party goals and government performance in contemporary democracies', *American Political Science Review* 79: 738–54.

——(1990) *Minority Government and Majority Rule*, New York: Cambridge University Press.

Taylor, M. and Herman, V. (1971) 'Party systems and party governments', *American Political Science Review* 65: 28–37.

Truman, D. (1951) *The Governmental Process*, New York: Knopf.

Verba, S. and Nie, N. H. (1972) *Participation in America*, New York: Harper & Row.

Verba, S., Nie, N. H. and Kim, J. (1978) *Participation and Political Equality: A Seven-Nation Study*, New York: Cambridge University Press.

Ware, A. (1988) *Citizens, Parties and the State*, Princeton: Princeton University Press.

FURTHER READING

Cohen, C. (1971) *Democracy*, New York: Free Press.

Dahl, R. A. (1971) *Polyarchy: Participation and Opposition*, New Haven: Yale University Press.

Downs, A. (1957) *An Economic Theory of Democracy*, New York: Harper & Row.

Gastil, R. D. (ed.) (1988) *Freedom in the World: Political Rights and Civil Liberties 1987–88*, New York: Freedom House.

Huntington, S. P. (1984) 'Will more countries become democratic?', *Political Science Quarterly* 99: 193–218.

Inglehart, R. (1990) *Culture Shift in Advanced Industrial Society*, Princeton: Princeton University Press.

Katzenstein, P. (1985) *Small States in World Markets*, Ithaca, NY: Cornell University Press.

Lijphart, A. (1984) *Democracies: Patterns of Majoritarian and Consensus Government in Twenty-one Countries*, New Haven: Yale University Press.

Olson, M. (1965) *The Logic of Collective Action*, Cambridge, Mass.: Harvard University Press.

Pennock, R. (1979) *Democratic Political Theory*, Princeton: Princeton University Press.

Powell, G. B., Jr (1982) *Contemporary Democracies: Participation, Stability and Violence*, Cambridge, Mass.: Harvard University Press.

——(1982) 'Social progress and liberal democracy', in G. Almond, M. Chodorow and R. H. Pearce (eds) *Progress and Its Discontents*, Berkeley: University of California Press.

Putnam, R., Leonardi, R., Nanetti, R. and Pavoncello, F. (1983) 'Explaining institutional success: the case of Italian regional government', *American Political Science Review* 77: 55–74.

Rae, D. W. (1967) *The Political Consequences of Electoral Laws*, New Haven: Yale University Press.

Riker, W. H. (1982) *Liberalism Against Populism*, San Francisco: W. H. Freeman.

Sartori, G. (1976) *Parties and Party Systems*, New York: Cambridge University Press.

Strom, K. (1990) *Minority Government and Majority Rule*, New York: Cambridge University Press.

Verba, S., Nie, N. H. and Kim, J. (1978) *Participation and Political Equality: A Seven-Nation Study*, New York: Cambridge University Press.

Ware, A. (1988) *Citizens, Parties and the State*, Princeton: Princeton University Press.

14

COMMUNIST AND POST-COMMUNIST SYSTEMS

LESLIE HOLMES

Until the so-called 'East European Revolution' of 1989–90, approximately one-third of the world's population lived in systems claiming to be building communism; such systems can be called communist. Even by late 1990, well in excess of 1.5 billion people lived in communist systems, although most of these systems appeared likely to become 'post-communist' during the 1990s. Most of this essay is concerned with communist states as they were until 1989, although reference will also be made to the 'post-communist' states at appropriate junctures.

Not one of the communist states has ever made the claim that it was already communist – most claiming to be at some stage of socialism – which has led some commentators to argue that the use of the term 'communist' is inappropriate. However, there are two major reasons why the use of the term 'communist' *is* still a better label than any other. First, Marx himself (Marx and Engels 1970: 56–7) argued that the term communism refers to two phenomena – an ideal towards which society moves, and the political movement which abolishes an existing state of affairs so as to create the conditions for the movement towards the ideal. Indeed, he further made it clear that the political movement was closer to what he meant by communism than was the ideal. Second, there are and have been a number of systems in the world that claim or have claimed to be socialist, but which are not organized in the same way as communist states, and which do not claim to be building a Marxist-style communism; examples are Libya, Tanzania, Nicaragua and Burma (Myanmar). In order to avoid confusion with such states, it makes sense to call the latter socialist and the former communist.

There has been a major debate in the field of comparative communism on the question of whether or not self-ascription – which is essentially the criterion used above – is acceptable in determining whether or not a particular country should be classified as 'communist'. Harding (1981: 33) argues that it would be wrong to characterize a regime as communist – or Marxist, as he would prefer to call it – simply in terms of the goals it professes. For him, there have to be the appropriate means and preconditions for their realization. The problem with this argument is that none of the existing communist or even post-communist systems – with the possible, partial exceptions of Czechoslovakia and what was, until October 1990, the German Democratic Republic – had the preconditions necessary for the building of socialism when the communists took power. Harding argues that if a regime does not have the proper level of development, for instance, 'Marxism may well become merely a convenient rhetoric of legitimation for Jacobins, populists, nationalists or tyrants' (ibid.: 33). In fact, there are few if any communist systems which have not been led for at least part of the time by 'Jacobins, populists, nationalists and tyrants', and one wonders which actual regimes could be included using Harding's approach. To be fair to Harding, it seems at times (ibid.: 21) that he wishes to distinguish Marxist from communist regimes. However, on other occasions (ibid.: 23) he does appear to use the term Marxist to apply to *many* of the regimes most observers would choose to call communist, so that the reader is ultimately uncertain as to whether Harding is actually pleading for the use of the term 'Marxist regime' only as an ideal type, or whether he does in fact wish to use it as an alternative label to 'communist'. Let us therefore consider another approach.

One of the most provocative analyses of the issue of what constitutes a communist state is provided by John Kautsky. In a 1973 article, Kautsky argued that none of the variables others have used to identify communist systems is unique to such systems (Kautsky 1973). He argues that the only variable which *does* distinguish them is their symbols, and he feels that symbols are insufficient as a distinguishing criterion. There are two main problems with Kautsky's argument. First, symbols can be important, especially if the actual organization of society is closely related to such symbols. Second, whilst one can certainly isolate each of the variables he identifies – such as a nationalist component in the ideology, an authoritarian political structure, state intervention in the economy, etc. – and find examples of non-communist systems that have a similar approach to these as the communist systems, the particular *mix* of variables is reasonably distinctive in communist states. Thus, whilst Kautsky is unquestionably justified in arguing that we must not treat communist systems as if they are totally different from all other kinds of system (especially non-communist developing countries), he goes too far in arguing that they are indistinguishable from many other systems.

In one of the best-selling introductions to communist systems, the authors argue that there are four defining characteristics of a communist state (White *et al.* 1990: 4–5). First, such states all base themselves upon an official ideology, the core of which is Marxism-Leninism. Second, the economy is largely or almost entirely publicly rather than privately owned, and is organized on the basis of a central plan; they have 'administered' or 'command' economies rather than 'market' economies. Third, they are typically ruled by a single or at least a dominant communist party, within which power is normally highly centralized and organized according to the principle of 'democratic centralism'. Finally, institutions which in the liberal democracies are more or less independent of the political authorities (for example, the press, trade unions and the courts) are in communist states effectively under the direct control of the communist party, exercising its 'leading role.' This seems to be one of the best analyses of the distinguishing features of a communist system; although it will be argued below that the communist states are dynamic and that some of the above features are less pronounced than they once were even in those countries that are not yet 'post-communist', the question then needs to be raised as to whether or not such a dynamism eventually steers these states away from communism. For now, assuming that this fourfold analysis is more or less valid, some of the variables can be examined in more detail.

The term 'Marxism-Leninism' appears to have been first used by the Soviet dictator, Josef Stalin (in power 1929–53). The ideology is a *materialist* one, meaning that its adherents believe that matter – the material world around us – determines the way we think. In this sense, they differ fundamentally from *idealists* – of whom Hegel is a prime example – who believe that ideas are the reality, and that the world around us is merely a reflection of such ideas. Marxism-Leninism is also supposed to be based on a *dialectical* approach to the world; expressed crudely, this states that everything is in a constant state of flux, and that change occurs as a result of the interaction and development of various factors. For Marxist-Leninists, as for Marxists generally, the most important factor is class struggle, which in turn reflects changes in the nature and ownership of the means of production. Marxist-Leninists believe that there are *laws* to such developments and call their ideology 'scientific'. The first Soviet leader, Vladimir Ilyich Lenin, added two particularly important components to this Marxist base. First, he developed the notion of a tightly-knit, centralized and elitist political party. This idea was originally expounded in *What is to be Done?* (Lenin 1902) before the Russian Revolution of October 1917; subsequently, in 1921, he reiterated the need for a tight-knit party, in which factionalism would not be tolerated even *following* a socialist revolution. This constitutes the origins of the Marxist-Leninist emphasis on the monolithic and centralized party. Second, Lenin produced a major analysis of imperialism. Whilst many of his ideas on this have been discredited, a number of revolutionaries in the developing world have been inspired by Lenin's arguments. This is largely because they accepted his view that the world is divided up between imperialist countries and colonies, and because he seemed to show how, largely through a tightly organized and centralized political system, a group of domestic communists would be able to develop their country independently of the imperial powers.

The above analysis of Marxism-Leninism is only a thumb-nail sketch, and the reader is strongly advised to read both the essay on Marxism in this encyclopedia (pp. 155–66) and the sources cited in the bibliography at the end of this essay (especially Harding 1983; McLellan 1979, 1980). At this juncture, it should be pointed out that some communist states have added phrases to 'Marxism-Leninism' to describe their particular ideology. The best-known example is the People's Republic of China (PRC), which at the time of writing still officially described its ideology as 'Marxism-Leninism and Mao Zedong Thought'. The Chinese, more explicitly than many other communists, clearly distinguish between the 'pure' ideology of Marxism-Leninism and the 'practical' ideology of Maoist thought. According to this approach, Marxism-Leninism is primarily a mode of analysis, a general way of interpreting the world – whereas the 'practical' component of the ideology has to apply this general methodology to the concrete situation in a given country at a particular period, and devise policies, and so forth, on the basis of this. One important element that is often to be found in the 'practical' ideology, but which in a real sense contradicts the 'proletarian internationalism' of classical Marxism, is official nationalism. A good example of this can be found in North Korean ideology, which is described as 'Marxism-Leninism and Juche'; Juche is very much a nationalist ideology.

The level and nature of state ownership and central planning of the economy has varied considerably between communist states. At one end of the spectrum are countries in which there has been very little private ownership and a high level of *directive* planning; Albania, North Korea and Cuba are examples. At the other end are countries in which private enterprise has not only been tolerated but has even been encouraged, and in which central planning is/was not only much less comprehensive than in other communist states, but also largely *indicative* (i.e. it tends to be more in the form of reasoned suggestions rather than orders). Examples of this type of economy are Yugoslavia, Hungary until 1989, increasingly the USSR and – at least until mid-1989 – the PRC.

Although all communist states have been ruled by a dominant communist party, there are two common misconceptions that need to be corrected. The first is that all communist systems are clearly one-party states. Whilst the communist party (which may or may not have the word 'communist' in its formal title) *does* typically dominate, a number of communist states for many years formally had a bi- or multi-party system; examples include Bulgaria, the GDR, Poland, the PRC and Vietnam. It must be appreciated, however, that the minor parties do not normally play a very significant role in these countries until the transition to post-communism is underway. Second, in some of the non-European communist states – such as Cuba and Ethiopia – the communist party played little or no role in the early years of communist rule, in some cases simply because it did not exist. In such cases, the country was called communist mainly in terms of the formal commitment of the leaders to Marxist-Leninist ideology and communism as an end goal – although, strictly speaking, some leaders such as Castro did not even commit themselves to these ideas until some time after they had seized power. This is one of the many reasons why analysts sometimes disagree on whether or not to classify a particular system as 'communist'.

As mentioned above, communist parties are structured according to the principle of 'democratic centralism'; indeed, in recent years many other political agencies in communist systems, including much of the state itself, have been formally organized according to this principle. According to Article 19 of the Statute of the Communist Party of the Soviet Union (CPSU) adopted in 1986, democratic centralism within the Party entailed the following:

1 election of all leading Party bodies, from the lowest to the highest;
2 periodical reports of Party bodies to their Party organizations and the higher bodies;
3 strict Party discipline and the subordination of the minority to the majority;
4 the binding nature of the decisions of higher bodies for lower bodies;
5 collective spirit in the work of all organizations and leading Party bodies and the personal responsibility of every Communist for the fulfilment of his/her duties and Party assignments.

It is particularly important to note that the noun in this basic political principle was 'centralism', the modifier 'democratic'; in other words, 'democracy', however defined, was only meant to act as a *control* on a centralized system, not to constitute the basis of the system itself.

The ways in which communist parties exercise their 'leading role' in society, and in particular over other institutions such as the media and trade unions, are several, and it is beyond the scope of this essay to address this issue fully. In many ways, the single most important manifestation of this is the so-called *nomenklatura* system. The way in which this is exercised varies somewhat from country to country, but the basic concept is common. The communist party is organized hierarchically, and at each level a secretary or secretariat will have a list of posts – the *nomenklatura* – at that level. The party must play some role in hiring and/or firing individuals to/from these key posts; in some cases, the party is to be directly involved in this process, in other cases only kept informed. The important point is that the *nomenklatura* includes all the most politically powerful and sensitive posts at a given level, *not* merely party posts. A city-level *nomenklatura* may well include the editorships of the city's newspapers, the directorships of many of the production enterprises, the headships of the city's colleges, etc. Not everyone who is appointed to a *nomenklatura* post will be a member of the party, though in most communist states the majority are.

Using the above criteria, it is possible to identify more than twenty states in four continents that were communist until 1989. Listed alphabetically, they were Afghanistan, Albania, Angola, Benin, Bulgaria, Cambodia (Kampuchea until 1989), China (PRC), Congo, Cuba, Czechoslovakia, East Germany (the GDR), Ethiopia, Hungary, North Korea (DPRK), Laos, Mongolia, Mozambique, Poland, Romania, South Yemen (PDRY), Soviet Union (USSR), Vietnam and Yugoslavia.

However, many of the above countries experienced overt systemic crises in the period 1989–90, so that by mid-1991, only four (China, Cuba, North Korea and Vietnam) would by most criteria still qualify *relatively* clearly as communist. A further thirteen appeared to be at various stages of transition, though not yet clearly 'post-communist' (Afganistan, Albania, Angola, Benin, Cambodia, Congo, Ethiopia, Laos, Mongolia, Mozambique, Romania, USSR, Yugoslavia). Four countries still intact were clearly 'post-communist' (Bulgaria, Czechoslovakia, Hungary, Poland), whilst the remaining two were not only post-communist but had also both united with culturally similar neighbours during 1990 and had thus ceased to exist as sovereign states (GDR, PDRY). In order to understand what brought all this about, it is necessary to analyse the *dynamism* of communist states; what follows must necessarily be presented in a very generalized form, and individual communist states will approximate more or less closely to the pattern outlined.

Communists typically take (as well as lose!) power in crisis situations. The crises most commonly occur either during or in the aftermath of a major international war. In the case of the world's first communist state, Russia (the USSR from 1922 to 1991), the crisis of 1917 was in part a result of the country's poor performance in the First World War. Between 1917 and the mid-1940s, only one other country – Mongolia – came under communist rule (1924); in this particular case, the system was in crisis less because of war than because of domestic factors. But in the aftermath of the Second World War, a spate of new communist states came into being. Thus, between 1945 and 1950, communists came to power in eight East European states as well as in China, North Korea and Vietnam. The circumstances varied in each, but in all of them an old regime had collapsed or was collapsing, and in many of them the Red (Soviet) Army and/or other forms of Soviet involvement assisted indigenous communists to take power. There was only one new communist state in the 1950s (Cuba, 1959), and in one sense even this is questionable, in that Castro did not formally commit himself to Marxism-Leninism until 1961; he came to power not in the aftermath of an international war, but largely as a result of the corruption and widespread unpopularity of the Batista regime. Nor were the 1960s a period of major expansion in the communist world; in the view of many, communists took power in Congo (Brazzaville) in 1968 and in South Yemen in 1969. The second major wave of communist expansion (i.e. after the period 1945–50) took place in the early to mid-1970s. In this case, the major factors leading to crisis were communist success in an international war (in the three Indo-Chinese states of Vietnam, Laos and Cambodia) and the further collapse of various European empires, notably the French and the Portuguese. Thus the ex-French colony of Benin came under communist control in 1972, whilst Angola and Mozambique rapidly came under the control of the MPLA (Popular Movement for the Liberation of Angola) and Frelimo, respectively, following the overthrow of the Caetano regime in Portugal in September 1974 and the subsequent Portuguese abandonment of its centuries-old empire. In the cases of the two other countries that came under communist control in the 1970s – Ethiopia (1974) and Afghanistan (1978) – the crisis that led to the revolutionary change was primarily related to the unpopularity and general decline of legitimacy of the regimes of Emperor Haile Selassie and General Daoud, respectively.

One of the most striking facts to emerge from a comparative analysis of communist accessions to power is that communists do not generally take power in economically highly developed countries or in countries with a strong liberal democratic tradition. In this sense, Marx failed to predict the emergence of the kind of systems we usually call communist. One of the ramifications of the fact that communists usually come to power in developing countries is that the new leaders have generally felt obliged to transform their countries rapidly and fundamentally; they often set about this following their consolidation of power, the duration of which varies considerably from country to country. This desire for rapid transformation can be explained both in terms of their country's need to reach a level of industrialization and general economic development that is, in Marxist terms, appropriate and necessary for the creation of a truly socialist and eventually communist system, and in terms of demonstrating the superiority of the Marxist-Leninist development model over other possible paths – notably capitalism. Given both this commitment to a rapid 'revolution from above' – which typically involves socialization of the means of production and collectivization of agriculture – and the widespread hostility that this frequently engenders, it is common for the transformation to be accompanied by relatively widespread physical terror. Terror has been a salient feature of several communist states, notably the USSR in the 1930s (Stalin's so-called 'Great Terror'), most of Eastern Europe in the late 1940s/early 1950s, Cambodia in the mid- to late 1970s, Afghanistan at the end of the 1970s, and several of the African communist states in the late 1970s and into the 1980s. In some of the Asian communist states, there has tended to be a mixture during the transition phase of overt physical terror and somewhat less draconian 'thought reform'. In the latter, many people who are deemed by the regime to be either openly hostile or else not sufficiently positive in their attitudes towards communism are sent off to 're-education camps'. In most cases, these are essentially prison-camps in which internees are subjected to intensive resocialization techniques (i.e. brainwashing). China, Vietnam, Laos and North Korea have made extensive use of such camps (for further details on terror see Dallin and Breslauer 1970).

It will be fairly obvious from the above that, in the consolidation and rapid transition phases, communist states typically exercise power primarily in the coercive mode. But as time passes, leaders change and the disadvantages of the predominantly coercive mode (for example, it discourages both initiative and accepting responsibility at all levels) become increasingly obvious. Hence communist leaderships normally seek to place less emphasis on coercion and more on legitimation. At least seven modes of legitimation – old traditional, charismatic, teleological (also known as goal-rational), eudaemonic, official nationalist, new traditional, and legal-rational – can be identified, and can to a limited extent be related to different stages of the development of communist states.

In the earliest stages, one of the main tasks of a new communist regime is to discredit its non-communist predecessor, to undermine old traditional legitimation. Many older people, in particular, may still believe in the divine right of monarchs, and hence find it difficult to develop allegiance to the new type of power system.

As part of their attempts to break down old values, and quite possibly at the same time as coercion becomes the dominant form of power, communists may seek to create the impression that their very top leaders are superhuman and have made extraordinary efforts and personal sacrifices to serve the people. This is an attempt to legitimate in terms of leadership charisma, and can be seen in the personality cults communist propagandists have created around leaders such as Lenin (USSR), Mao (PRC) and Ho Chi Minh (Vietnam); in recent times, the most extreme personality cults have been of Kim Il Sung in North Korea and the late Nicolae Ceausescu in Romania.

But charismatic legitimation, like coercive power, typically begins to seem less appropriate and effective as educational standards rise and as the essentially secularizing effects of communist power take effect. Thus communists begin to look for other modes of legitimation. Indeed, it is usually at about this time that the transition from power exercised primarily through coercion towards more legitimation-based power begins to occur. In this period, an emphasis on teleological (or goal-rational) legitimation often becomes evident. At this stage, communists seek authority largely by reference to their all-important role in leading society towards the distant end-goal (or *telos* – hence teleological) of communism (see Rigby 1982). The publication of the CPSU

Programme in 1961 is a good example of this attempt at teleological legitimation.

For a number of reasons – including the cynicism caused by the years of coercion, by new leaders criticizing the faults of their predecessors, and by economic shortages; and doubts about the practicality of achieving many goals within a sufficiently short time-frame that it could act as a stimulus to people – goal-rational or teleological legitimation often fades into the background over time. In its place, typically, is a form of legitimation that is less ambitious and more geared to satisfying the immediate demands of the consumer. Such a form of legitimation is called eudaemonism (here meaning conducive to happiness), since it seeks to satisfy citizens through regime performance. This was very much a feature of many European communist states in the late 1960s and the 1970s, when there was simultaneously an emphasis on realistic socialism (as distinct from the more idealistic socialism implied in teleological legitimation) and the better satisfaction of consumer demands. Many European communist states at that time introduced economic reforms that were designed, *inter alia*, to meet these requirements. China can be seen to have introduced a somewhat similar – if in many ways more radical – plan at the end of the 1970s, whilst Vietnam also moved in this direction in the 1980s.

Unfortunately, the economic reforms are typically far less successful than communist leaderships anticipate, so that legitimation in the eudaemonic mode becomes problematic. There are various responses to this. One is a new emphasis on official nationalism, whereby communist leaders try to gain support for the system by appealing to nationalist feelings in the populace; this attempt may hark back to a glorious pre-communist past (as Ceausescu did in Romania), or it may emphasize contemporary national achievements (for example, the GDR's emphasis on sporting success in the Olympic Games). Such nationalism contains dangers, however; for instance, too much emphasis on the past can undermine the relatively new and radical ideas of communism, whilst official nationalism can trigger unofficial nationalism amongst ethnic minorities.

Another regime response can be called 'new traditionalism'. In this, communist leaderships emphasize the advantages of earlier periods of communism, and either implicitly or explicitly suggest that current difficulties would be reduced if there were to be a return to some of the traditional communist values. Examples of this include Gorbachev's emphasis on the positive aspects of the Lenin era (including Lenin's economic policies from 1921) and, since the middle of 1989, the Chinese leadership's increasingly favourable re-assessment of the Maoist era (1949–76). Once again, there can be problems with this form of legitimation. Contemporary conditions will often be very different from those pertaining in the earlier period, for instance, which means that today's leaders have to be selective in choosing from their predecessors' policies – some of which would be totally inappropriate.

Partially because of the problems of official nationalism and new traditionalism as legitimation modes, many communist leaders either essentially avoid them or else limit their use of them. Instead, there emerged in several communist states in the 1980s an emphasis on legal-rational legitimation. According to some political theorists (see for example Poggi 1978), this form of legitimation is the only one appropriate to the 'modern' state, and there were certainly signs of moves towards modernity in countries such as Hungary, Poland and the USSR, even before 1989. One of the salient features of legal-rationality is an emphasis on the *rule of law* and, as a corollary, the depersonalization of politics and economics. Signs of this development are not only the references in communist politicians' speeches to the rule of law, but also more concrete manifestations, such as the limiting of tenure for political officeholding, granting citizens the right to bring legal charges against officials at any level, genuinely contested elections, and greater tolerance of investigative journalism (for a more detailed comparative analysis of the moves towards legal-rationality see Holmes 1991). In the USSR, these changes have been closely associated with the Soviet leader since March 1985, Mikhail Gorbachev, and are manifest in his emphasis on political and economic restructuring (*perestroika*), greater openness and honesty (*glasnost*) on the part of the authorities, and more political rights for the citizenry (*demokratisatsiya*).

It seems likely that these moves towards legal-rationality have been taken by many communist leaders because other modes of legitimation have not been sufficiently successful. In particular, the relatively recent encouragement of citizens to criticize corrupt, inefficient or arrogant party and state officials can be seen on one level as a method by which the leaders hope to be able to ensure proper implementation of the economic reforms. In the past, the leaders have often adopted policies designed to improve economic performance, only to see their own officials sabotage these policies, since they were perceived as being against those officials' interests. Thus, both Deng (PRC) and Gorbachev – in different ways and to different extents – have used moves towards legal-rationality, including mass involvement in campaigns against corrupt officials, as one way of improving economic performance. The motive for such an approach was probably less a commitment to a genuine rule of law as this is generally understood in the West than to a means of improving such performance. It appears that the leaders' ultimate aim is (or was) to be able to return to a form of eudaemonic legitimation – only this time, based on a real improvement in the economy and thus in living standards.

But developments in the late 1980s suggested that communist leaders cannot control (i.e. limit) the moves towards legal-rationality that they themselves feel compelled to initiate. The moves towards more open politics and privatization (an economic aspect of the general move towards legal-rationality, since it represents a depersonalization and deconcentration of the running of the economy) often encourage citizens to demand and expect more than the communists can and/or are willing to provide. This tension became very visible in the USSR, in China and in several East European states at the end of the 1980s. One response is the move back towards coercion; the Beijing massacre of June 1989 and its aftermath typifies this. But some communist countries – notably most of the East European states – proved incapable of reversing the trend. Many communist leaderships found themselves and their system in a fundamental identity crisis. The more they accepted elements of legal-rationality into the system, the more the 'communist' system began to resemble what for so many years had been portrayed as the arch-enemy, the liberal democratic capitalist system. Even worse, the new hybrid system seemed to incorporate many of the worst aspects of both kinds of system, rather than the best. On the one hand, the communists were now accepting unemployment, inflation and growing inequality. On the other hand, citizens had still not been granted high levels of freedom of speech, freedom of assembly, freedom of travel – or the living standards of the West. In addition to this basic dilemma, the leaderships of many communist states began to lose faith in what they were doing, as the leader of their role-model (i.e. the USSR) acknowledged that his country was in crisis and uncertain of its future direction. It was in this situation of fundamental contradictions, pressure from below, and loss of their principal role-model that many communists realized by 1989–90 that the very dynamism of communist power had brought them to a point at which that power and system had run its course.

At this point, two questions need to be addressed. First, why are some countries further along the path of transition from communism to post-communism than others? Second, what are the salient features of post-communist states?

The answer to the first question is a complex one. Among the many factors to be included in an explanation are political culture, level of economic development, awareness of what is occurring elsewhere in the world, and, it seems, the way in which the communists came to power. Thus there appears to be a reasonably clear pattern whereby countries in which communism was in essence installed by a foreign power move more rapidly to post-communism than countries in which native communists assumed power largely by their own efforts. For example, Poland and Hungary are at a more advanced stage of transition than Yugoslavia or Albania. However, the identity crisis described above also applies to the latter countries, and it is almost certainly only a matter of time before they become 'post-communist' states too.

The second question is also difficult to answer satisfactorily – especially in a relatively short article like this. Most basically, a post-communist state is one which has in the past been ruled by communists, but in which the communists have now lost their politically privileged position. But such a definition tells us relatively little about the new political configurations and values, the economic system, etc. Ideally, it would be desirable to examine these variables in detail; in practice, this is not yet possible, for various reasons. On one level, post-communism is more accurately conceived of as the rejection of something – the coercion, elitism, corruption, mendacity, hypocrisy and incompetence of actual communist systems – than the adoption of a clear set of political, economic and social goals and methods. In this sense, it is easier to agree on what it is not than on what it is. It is true that there appears to be a widespread belief in the various states either at or approaching the post-communist stage that a pluralist political system and a more competitive, largely privatized economic system akin to Western systems is desirable. Under the new arrangements, citizens are to have much greater freedom than they have had to organize themselves without excessive interference from the state; in short, the establishment or revitalization of civil society is a salient feature of early post-communism. Nevertheless, there are also very divergent views within all of these countries on the nature, pace and direction of change that is desirable and/or possible. Even where there is a reasonably high level of consensus on goals, the means for achieving these are in many cases far from clear. Perhaps the best example is the problem of creating a largely privatized, competitive economy – what is often called a 'market' system. Many Poles and Russians, for instance, declare their support for a market system, yet have few concrete ideas on how to create one.

One of the ramifications of this apparent gap between ends and means is that as the euphoria of removing communist governments is replaced by various harsh realities of early post-communism, such as worsening domestic inflation and unemployment in the context of a global recession, a mood of disappointment and even despair may set in. Such despair could in the future be exploited by new, authoritarian, nationalist – and possibly racist – demagogues who, though not communist, may from many perspectives be at least as undesirable as their Marxist-Leninist predecessors. But such a dismal scenario for post-communism is not the only possible one. If the global economy performs well in the 1990s – however improbable this seems at the beginning of the decade – interaction with the rest of the world could secure a brighter future for post-communism.

In the preceding discussion, post-communism has been treated in very general terms, almost as if it is a single phenomenon. Whilst there are many similarities between the various countries at or approaching the stage of post-communism, there are also important differences and potentialities, relating to factors such as level of ethnic homogeneity, availability of natural resources, etc. Partially for this reason, it is quite possible that some post-communist states and societies will perform much better than others. This is another reason why it is not possible to provide a detailed analysis of 'post-communism' – at least at present.

Two final points can be made by way of a conclusion. First, although most communist systems have found themselves in profound identity crises in recent years, some of the values once putatively espoused by communists in power (for example, a commitment to limiting inequalities; state subsidisation of basic foodstuffs, housing, transport, etc; full or near-full employment, etc.) may again become popular in the post-communist era. This said, such values are more likely to be achievable within a social democratic system than a communist one. Second, the fate of the post-communist countries is likely to have implications for those systems that are currently either still communist or in transition. If the post-communist systems are perceived as representing no real improvement on communism, this could provide communists still in power with an opportunity to prolong their rule. However, this would be only a temporary respite. The dynamism of communism in power is such that democratic centralism, the *de facto* one-party state and the centrally planned national economy eventually become outdated and are replaced – suddenly or gradually, violently or peacefully, from below, above or outside, depending on the particular circumstances. Communism is often a relatively effective system for modernizing societies, but it is incompatible with law-based, pluralist modernity or post-modernity.

REFERENCES

Dallin, A. and Breslauer, G. (1970) *Political Terror in Communist Systems*, Stanford: Stanford University Press.

Hammond, T. (ed.) (1975) *The Anatomy of Communist Takeovers*, New Haven: Yale University Press.

Harding, N. (1981) 'What does it mean to call a regime Marxist?', in B. Szajkowski (ed.) *Marxist Governments: A World Survey*, vol. 1, London: Macmillan.

——(1983) *Lenin's Political Thought*, London: Macmillan.

Holmes, L. (1986) *Politics in the Communist World*, Oxford: Oxford University Press.

——(1991) *Crisis, Collapse and Official Corruption in the Communist World*, Cambridge: Polity Press.

Kautsky, J. (1973) 'Comparative communism versus comparative politics', *Studies in Comparative Communism* 6: 135–70.

Lenin, V. I. (1902) *What is to be Done?*, Moscow: Progress Publishers, 1969.

Marx, K. and Engels, F. (1970) *The German Ideology – Part One*, London: Lawrence & Wishart.

McLellan, D. (1979) *Marxism After Marx*, London: Macmillan.

——(1980) *The Thought of Karl Marx*, London: Macmillan.

Poggi, G. (1978) *The Development of the Modern State*, London: Hutchinson.

Rigby, T. H. (1982) 'Introduction: political legitimacy, Weber and communist mono-organisational systems', in T. H. Rigby and F. Feher (eds) *Political Legitimation in Communist States*, London: Macmillan.

White, S., Gardner, J., Schopflin, G. and Saich, T. (1990) *Communist and Postcommunist Political Systems*, London: Macmillan.

FURTHER READING

Brzezinski, Z. (1989) *The Grand Failure*, New York: Charles Scribner's Sons.

Dawisha, K. (1990) *Eastern Europe, Gorbachev and Reform*, Cambridge: Cambridge University Press.

Szajkowski, B. (1981) *Marxist Governments: A World Survey*, 3 vols, London: Macmillan.

Westoby, A. (1983) 'Conceptions of communist states', in D. Held *et al.* (eds) *States and Societies*, London: Martin Robertson.

White, S. and Nelson, D. (eds) (1986) *Communist Politics: A Reader*, London: Macmillan.

15

CONTEMPORARY AUTHORITARIAN REGIMES

JAMES MALLOY

Like many concepts in contemporary political science the concept of authoritarianism is rather controversial. The concept has had a long and rather confusing history in the literature of political inquiry. This confusion and controversy springs from the fact that there is no generally agreed upon definition of the concept to frame our discussions of it and other related concepts, such as democracy and totalitarianism, which are used to classify contemporary political regimes. The whole issue of classifying regimes is confused further because these concepts stand at the interface between would-be scientific accounts of politics and government, and the polemically charged world of actual political practice. These types of concepts therefore not only denote characteristics of regimes but they also connote positive and negative judgements on their normative worth. In general, the concept of an authoritarian regime has in recent times carried a rather negative connotation, although this has not always been the case historically.

The question of normative connotation, in turn, bridges back into the realm of scientific analysis because it speaks to a crucial issue related to all regime forms: namely legitimacy, or the principles upon which political actors attempt to justify the way they organize the process of government in any particular society. The influential political sociologist Max Weber long ago established the view that the key to the long-term stability of any type of regime is the degree to which the populace over which it holds sway comes to believe in the legitimacy of its fundamental principles of organization (Weber 1968). The belief in a regime's legitimacy conveys authority upon specific governments that act in the name of the regime and thereby, in theory at least, increases that government's capacity to maintain order and govern a particular society.

The concepts of regime form and legitimacy bring us immediately to one of the crucial political problems of much of the contemporary world: the problem of governance, or the ability of governments to maintain order and simultaneously resolve the problems that confront a given society. Conceptually that question involves the analysis of the interaction of three distinct dimensions: state, regime and government. Can specific governments channel the power capacities of the state into a form of governance (regime) capable of being sustained over time and throughout changes in governments even when such governments produce policies that solve problems? In the contemporary world, especially among the less developed countries, the bulk of the most crucial problems that confront governments are economic in nature.

Many of the most important questions surrounding the analysis of contemporary authoritarian regimes are linked directly to these conceptual issues of governance and legitimacy. Many analysts explain the emergence of authoritarian regimes as the result of situations in which the legitimacy of other regime forms, such as democracy, is undermined because governments are unable to solve many of the most pressing economic problems confronting a society. The incapacity of governments can set off a crisis of confidence in the existing regime which renders it vulnerable to being overturned by way of insurrection, a *coup d'état* or the like. The new government is often authoritarian in that it seeks to concentrate governmental power in a strong executive which moves to impose solutions to pressing problems by means of force and coercion if necessary. In short 'authoritarianism' is often caused by a severe crisis of governance within a 'democracy'.

In the recent past many strong governments that came about by these means then declared their intentions to create an authoritarian regime within which successive governments would be constituted in an ongoing process of fundamentally reordering and restructuring a society. However, as analysts like Linz (1970) have pointed out, contemporary authoritarian regimes have found it particularly difficult to legitimate themselves because the concept of democracy (however disputed) has today become so pervasive that it has all but monopolized legitimacy throughout the world. Thus authoritarian regimes are immediately perceived as illegitimate, especially in the long term. By this argument contemporary authoritarian regimes are only able to create a transitory sense of legitimacy linked to an immediate crisis at hand; a legitimacy rooted in exceptional circumstances and destined to fade as the crisis either fades or else proves intractable to authoritarian measures as well.

Historically the concept of authoritarianism has a long lineage in which the underlying concept has been linked to numerous other conceptual terms such as autocracy, dictatorship, oligarchy, patrimonialism, sultanism and many others. For much of human history various kinds of authoritarian modes of governance were preponderant throughout the world. In most cases authoritarian regimes were rooted in value systems which conveyed legitimacy on them. For Weber most of these types of regimes fell under a single historical general category which he called traditional authority (Weber 1968).

In the Western world the most important kind of traditional authority, patrimonialism, was linked to the emergence of the modern state. As a regime form patrimonialism was linked to centralizing monarchs who concentrated power in a single personalized central authority from which came law. Over time this top-down system of rule was articulated through sets of civil and military officials who became the core of an administrative apparatus that evolved into the modern bureaucratic and professional military arms of the state.

In the classic patrimonial system, defined by Weber (1968) as a theoretically construed ideal type, politics was dominated by a small political class of notables who contended among themselves for offices in the service of the patrimonial prince; the primary division among them was faction. They were retainers or 'clients' of the patrimonial ruler and they depended upon grace or patronage for their positions. The ruler in turn sought to control the fractious estate of notables by manipulating the flow of patronage or prebends. Some grasp of this traditional regime form of patrimonialism is necessary because many of its central dynamics appear today in what is often called patron–client relations or clientelism. While clientelism is a feature that appears in different guises in many contemporary regimes, it is particularly visible and dominant in contemporary authoritarian governments in the less developed world, which in some respects echo patrimonialism. These 'neo-patrimonial' expressions of authoritarianism, however, are detached from the original traditional legitimating base of patrimonialism, and like other expressions of contemporary authoritarianism they exist in a world where modern democratic values define them as either illegitimate or at best temporary expedients (tutelary regimes) on the way to democracy.

There is another important reason to linger briefly with these traditional modes of authoritarianism or autocracy; they may reveal a core concept of authority which persists, albeit weakly, as a defining and legitimating principle of all expressions of authoritarianism. Articulated originally in organizations like the Roman Catholic Church, this concept links the authority to rule to a body of esoteric and transcendent or sacred knowledge which must be translated into human affairs. This 'authority' to interpret or reveal transcendent esoteric principles pervaded and justified all traditional modes of authority from the golden stool of the ancestors of the Ashanti tribe, through the mandate of heaven of the Chinese, to the doctrine of the divine right of monarchs in the West. Be it in the church, imperial China, or the France of Louis XIV, the image was of a transcendent source of law connected to a central governing authority that defined law and implemented it through a staff of highly trained officials.

This core idea of a central authority that both dictates (gives) and administers law to a society persists into the contemporary world of political regimes in many important ways. We can see traces of it in institutions embedded in otherwise democratic systems – the United States Supreme Court for example. It was clearly evidenced in the plebiscitary connections to the French 'national will' claimed by Charles de Gaulle and more than a little evident in the constitution of the Fifth Republic which de Gaulle 'gave' to the French. More directly we see the persistence of claims to interpret authoritatively secular bodies of knowledge in many 'authoritarian' or 'totalitarian' regimes linked to explicit ideologies, such as Marxism or other expressions of a putative national or collective will, destiny or the like. We also see it in many contemporary authoritarian regimes where strong executives deploy teams of highly trained experts (technocrats) who claim special ability (elitism) to interpret esoteric bodies of knowledge (economics, administration, etc.) that are deemed crucial to promote the economic development and modernization of a country. They often advance the argument that to serve the national good such technically sound principles must be imposed in the face of the selfish particular wills of classes, interest groups, regions or political parties. To this day many political leaders, as well as political analysts, associate central executive authority with a notion of 'general good', while legislative bodies and political parties are often associated with faction and particularist interests. It is not an accident that all authoritarian regimes pivot around a strong executive power.

Hence, while 'liberal democratic' values appear to be carrying the day at the rhetorical level of legitimacy, principles that focus on and justify a central role for strong executives served by a technically sophisticated elite corps of officials are far from absent in the current world scene. What really exists then is an ongoing tension between bottom-up and pluralistic 'democratic' conceptions of regime authority and legitimacy and more top-down monistic conceptions of rule. According to the British political theorist Michael Oakeshott, these notions are linked to two distinct conceptual traditions regarding the organization of the state that have evolved in tense interaction over centuries in the West. One, *universitas*, sees state and society as a singular corporate entity administered by an executive board of fiduciary agents charged with directing the entity to substantive corporate goals or ends; the other, *societas*, sees society as an aggregation or plurality of interests held together in a state by a set of rules or procedures that allow them to pursue their multiple interests in concert. *Universitas* leans toward an executive-centred administrative concept of rule with authoritarian overtones while *societas* leans toward a more legislative-centred concept of democracy in which government articulates (represents) in a rule-bound fashion the multiplicity of interests inherent in society (Oakeshott 1975).

While authoritarian regimes may find it hard to legitimate themselves in the current scene, there is little question that they do hark back to a modernized and technocratic version of *universitas* as a justifying principle; in many situations of chronic economic crisis the argument has its appeal. Moreover, while many countries are currently in transition from authoritarian to democratic regimes they are in fact building systems that embody strong *universitas* components within formally democratic frameworks.

Current conceptualizations of authoritarian regimes in political science were shaped first in the theories of modernization and development that gained dominance in the 1950s and 1960s as a result of the work of a leading core of political scientists linked to the Committee on Comparative Politics of the Social Science Research Council. Using a 'structure function' mode of analysis, this body of theory saw all societies as following a linear path from traditional to modern. In this perspective, 'democracy' was a modern form of government linked to a society reaching a certain level of economic and social development where the necessary social prerequisites (functionally derived) for democracy had been achieved.

In modernization theory democracy was a desirable end state toward which societies could and should aim in their march to development and modernization. The crucial theoretical as well as practical political problems emerged when societies were in transit from traditional modes of state organization to modern modes. In that intermediate phase societies could be diverted into more negative types of regime, usually defined as some species of authoritarianism or totalitarianism. In this body of theory the negative regime types were defined primarily in contrast to the positive regime type – democracy. The negative regime types were also linked to modernization; totalitarianism being viewed as a negative manifestation of modernity and authoritarianism as an expression of traditionalism destined to fade away as societies modernized.

The theory posited a linear movement toward modernity with positive (democratic) and negative (totalitarianism) poles. Authoritarianism became a kind of residual regime category that defined a condition which societies either had to break out of to modernize or lapsed back into when democratic structures were grafted onto more backward societies not yet sufficiently developed to receive and root them. Both democratic and totalitarian regimes were defined in ideal typical terms, while authoritarianism became a category into which fell a variety of regimes that did not fit into either of the two predominant ideal types. Moreover, the different modes of authoritarian governments were not looked at in their own terms but rather as a kind of by-product of the pathology of democracy manifested in various stages of the transition process.

To restate, the critical step in the transit to modernity and its positive expression democracy was the transition phase when societies could either be diverted, at a late stage, into totalitarianism, particularly in the form of communism, or in earlier stages fall back into some species of authoritarianism. Not surprisingly the theory saw what came to be called the 'Third World' of underdeveloped countries as the most likely to lapse into some kind of authoritarian government. Also not surprisingly this theory became the basis of the propensity of governments like that of the United States to develop programmes such as the Alliance For Progress to provide financial and technical aid designed to promote development, modernization and democracy in regions like Latin America. This is an area where the scientific world of political theory and that of political practice clearly overlapped.

An important and somewhat critical variation on the modernization theme came in the work of scholars such as Samuel P. Huntington. In his celebrated *Political Order in Changing Society*, Huntington (1968) argued that rather than produce a stable base for democracy, modernization in fact produced political ferment which, if it went beyond the existing containment capacity of governmental institutions, would produce political decay and the collapse of public order. For Huntington order and security were the primary political values and of necessity preceded any positive regime form. Order and security in turn were dependent on creating governments that could govern and encase that capacity in institutions. In this updated version of Hobbes's *Leviathan*, Huntington, among others, argued that in many underdeveloped societies the military was often the only modern, professionalized and organized national institution available to lead a society through the perilous transition to an institutionalized democracy. In this view, a military-based authoritarian regime could in fact act as a means to create a stable political order that could eventually elaborate the institutional structure necessary to maintain order and governability while containing the disruptive effects of modernization.

This work produced an important shift in the causal train. Modernization often produced decay and disorder creating a primary need to reconstitute governmental capacity, impose order and create institutions. Political decay literally pulled the military into politics where they in fact were one of the few organizations capable of reconstituting a modern state structure (leviathan) that could be eventually democratized. In some crucial ways an institution-building, military-based authoritarian regime could be an agent of controlled modernization and a precursor of modern democracy.

Theoretical concern with authoritarianism was spurred by the proliferation of non-democratic regimes in the underdeveloped world. In places like Africa many of these regimes had a rather personalistic and patrimonial flavour which allowed them to be treated as a regressive feature in the transition phase. A crucial development was the proliferation of military-based authoritarian regimes among the more developed countries of Latin America between 1964 and 1973, and the imposition of an authoritarian regime in Greece from 1967 to 1974. Reacting to these events, social scientists began to look anew at authoritarian Spain and Portugal and to note that behind the democratic façade Mexico was really an authoritarian regime. These regimes lacked the patrimonial flavour of those in Africa and in fact were highly organized and complex regimes that openly proclaimed their intent to spur the economic development and modernization of their respective societies. These claims gained credibility when later observers began to note that rapidly developing Asian countries such as South Korea and Taiwan were being led by strong governments operating within decidedly authoritarian frameworks.

Writing in the midst of these events and processes, Juan Linz in a now classic article (Linz 1970) mounted a strong argument which challenged the bi-polar continuum of democracy and totalitarianism and urged the necessity to recognize a specifically authoritarian regime type. This type was not traditional in form, but distinctively modern. Linz based his concept on the Spanish case and developed a definition which contrasted this regime to many of the recognized features of democracy and totalitarianism.

> Authoritarian regimes are political systems with limited, not responsible, political pluralism: without elaborate and guiding ideology (but with distinctive mentalities); without intensive nor extensive political mobilization (except some points in their development); and in which a leader (or occasionally a small group) exercises power within formally ill-defined limits but actually quite predictable ones.
>
> (Linz 1970: 255)

Linz's influential work helped shape many people's approach to the issue, particularly students of Latin American politics. It was followed by another classic, Guillermo O'Donnell's *Modernization and Bureaucratic-Authoritarianism: Studies in South American Politics* (O'Donnell 1973). Aside from defining a specific type of modern authoritarian regime, the bureaucratic-authoritarian regime, O'Donnell completed the reversal of the relationship between modernization and authoritarian regime forms. Cast in the new framework of dependence theory, the bureaucratic-authoritarian regime was viewed as a necessary product of capitalist development and modernization within relatively developed but dependent societies such as those in the southern cone of South America. Whereas earlier works had related to practical political polemics in a more indirect and implicit manner, O'Donnell's influential work, by linking the phenomena of dependence and capitalism to specific modes of authoritarianism, made a direct link between would-be scientific discourse and the ideologically charged political rhetoric of the day. The discussions that have raged around these issues since highlight the ways in which practical political considerations penetrate and, for good or ill, shape and/or distort theoretical discussions regarding regime forms.

This consequential overlap came out clearly in an article by political scientist Jeanne Kirkpatrick (1979), 'Dictatorship and double standards', in which she differentiated between totalitarian and authoritarian regimes. Relegating the former category exclusively to Marxist-Leninist regimes, Kirkpatrick argued that authoritarian regimes, while repressive, were more benign and capable of reform into capitalist democracy; therefore United States policy in Latin

America, in particular, should reflect those theoretically construed differences. The fire-storm of criticism provoked by this article saw one cartoon retort which noted that the real difference between the two was that while totalitarian regimes arrested, killed and tortured people, authoritarian regimes left many of those functions to the private sector.

The joke was based on a rather important insight into the ongoing totalitarian versus authoritarian conceptual debate; by and large 'totalitarian' was used to refer to regimes linked to command economies (state socialist) while 'authoritarian' referred mainly to regimes linked to economies driven at least in part by markets and private economic interests (capitalist). Using mainly political structural variables to define authoritarianism, Amos Perlmutter sought to go beyond this debate by rejecting the totalitarian category and collapsing those regimes into a very broadened definition of authoritarianism. In Perlmutter's *Modern Authoritarianism: A Comparative Institutional Analysis*, the central category is 'the modern authoritarian model', which he defines as 'an exclusive, centralist political organization populated and dominated by an oligarchic political elite' (Perlmutter 1981: 7).

In contemporary discussion the concept of totalitarianism has in fact faded and we seem to be working now with two very broad categories: democracy and authoritarianism. Not surprisingly the concept of authoritarianism seems more than ever to be a residual category into which are shovelled all regime forms that cannot lay some claim to being democratic; and often the concept of authoritarianism is defined by elaborating traits that are the negatives of positive democratic traits. Perlmutter, for example, goes on immediately to add that 'these regimes are characterized by repression, intolerance, encroachment on the private rights and freedoms of citizens and limited autonomy for nonstatist interest groups' (ibid.: 7).

Given the scope of the category, attention of necessity immediately shifts from the concept of modern authoritarian regime itself to the delineation of sub-types. Unfortunately the list of sub-types expands and contracts depending who is doing the defining and the idiosyncrasies of the particular regime(s) the analyst is examining. At the moment we simply do not have a generally accepted classification scheme of sub-types.

In his broad-brushed approach Perlmutter lays out a scheme of sub-types which can serve as a useful starting point for the analyst seeking an orientation to this conceptual thicket. Focusing on what he calls parallel and auxiliary structures such as police, party, military and professional organizations he stipulates four main types: the Party State; the Police State; the Corporatist State; and the Praetorian State. The latter category is broken down further into the Personal, Oligarchic and Bureaucratic-Authoritarian sub-types. It must be stressed that this and all such schemes remain open to intense criticism and debate. For example, Perlmutter's typology takes one of the most influential concepts regarding modern authoritarianism in Latin America, O'Donnell's bureaucratic-authoritarian regime, and relegates it to the status of a sub-type of a sub-type: a rather debatable move to say the least.

We are obviously not going to settle these conceptual issues here. In broad terms contemporary authoritarian regimes are defined first as negatives of the positive characterization of procedurally bound constitutional democratic regimes. Thus, as Latin American legal theory has it, modern authoritarian regimes are 'regimes of fact' and of 'exception'. Lacking legal, procedural or democratic checks, authoritarian regimes are command systems (usually executive decree) in which governmental power is exercised in an essentially arbitrary and therefore unpredictable pattern. Such regimes usually focus on a strong executive exercising power in conjunction with a cartel of political, military, bureaucratic and other elites (entrepreneurial, labour, professional, etc.) who shape the policies dictated to the larger society. While the prevalence of democratic values seems to check the ability of authoritarian regimes to establish their legitimacy, the persistence of *universitas* concepts of state organization, as well as a perceived need for an authoritative capacity to interpret esoteric but necessary knowledge, does hold out the possibility of some type of legitimation, especially in the face of a severe crisis like war, economic collapse and the like. Structurally such regimes run the gamut from highly personalized neo-patrimonial regimes to highly organized regimes rooted in military, bureaucratic and other institutional bases.

Clearly we are not going to be able to come up with a singular theory of origins for such a complex, varied and global phenomenon. There are some general views available to survey, particularly with regard to the recent experiences of Latin America. In general, we can delineate three types of explanations of origins which, while distinct, often overlap in practice: cultural explanations, broad structural economic explanations, and more specifically political structural and behavioural explanations.

Cultural explanations focus on imputed underlying patterns of institutions and values that predispose a society toward authoritarianism. In its strongest form the view sees authoritarianism as the dominant motif of a society always straining to break out of alien democratic structures artificially grafted onto these societies. This case has been made in its strongest and most convincing form in work on Latin America by authors such as Howard Wiarda (1973). Weaker forms of the argument have some clear merit, especially in regard to the kinds of organizational structures adopted by authoritarian regimes as well as the pre-existence of values that can be used to help construct legitimacy for such a regime. In the strong or deterministic form, however, the argument has numerous problems. One is the fact that culturally the traits highlighted in one regional tradition cannot account for authoritarianism in other regional and cultural contexts. Another follows from a Weberian argument that if all traditional cultures were essentially authoritarian at one point, how is it that today some are modernized forms of authoritarianism, some are neo-patrimonial, while others are democratic? Some other intervening variables must be at work.

A host of broad structural explanations emphasizing socio-economic factors have been advanced to explain the many different types of autocratic, totalitarian and authoritarian regimes that have populated the modern political landscape. Many involve variations on the central thesis of modernization regarding a crisis of transition from traditional to modern society. Authors like Ulam (1960) for example, pointed to the disruptive effects of early capitalist development on traditional societies to explain modern communist revolutions. In the same vein Barrington Moore (1966) stressed the response of pre-existing aristocracies to the commercialization of agriculture as a key to whether countries moved toward democracy, fascism or peasant-based communism. Many of these types of explanations echo the sophisticated analysis of the consequences of modern revolution propounded by Alexis de Tocqueville (1955) in *The Old Regime and The French Revolution*; particularly his insight that modernizing revolutions in traditional autocracies will most likely lead to a greater centralization of power in a Bonapartist-type state. Tocqueville also introduced the theme of the propensity of mass mobilization to lead to the creation of centralized and manipulative control structures.

As far as contemporary authoritarian regimes are concerned, the most systematic and theoretically rich work to date has been that of Guillermo O'Donnell (1973). Although formulated to account for recent authoritarian regimes in the southern cone of South America, O'Donnell's work, with suitable modifications, has broader significance. Cast in the dependence perspective, it reverses the relationship between modernization and regime outcomes; specifically O'Donnell argues that successful modernization in the context of dependent capitalist development produces a highly modernized form of authoritarianism, not democracy. The causal linkage is forged by the political imperatives that spring from the necessity of relatively advanced countries such as Argentina and Brazil to make a transition from easy import-substituting industrialization to a broader and deeper form of capitalist industrialization. The specific imperative is the need to reverse earlier populist policies of co-optive inclusion of working-class groups and now push the same groups back out. This exclusionary imperative demands a government with the will and ability to apply sustained repression of the excluded.

Although rooted in an economic argument, O'Donnell's theory does link into more explicitly political explanations. His work is closely connected to those who see regime formations as shaped by periodic crises produced by the underlying imperative of all societies to resolve an ongoing tension between

238

the need to accumulate capital for investment and the need to build legitimacy for regimes.

My preference is to express that as a tension between political logic and economic logic; a contradiction or trade-off that is particularly severe in less developed countries. Political logic pushes for governments to build support for themselves and the regimes that frame them by, among other things, meeting the concrete bread-and-butter demands of individuals and groups, which often means to increase general levels of consumption. Economic logic however, especially in capital-short countries, demands that an investable surplus be accumulated primarily by restricting consumption. The reality is that any accumulation strategy entails a cost (restrict consumption) that falls unequally on the populace as a whole. Often groups targeted to bear the costs (workers, peasants, popular sectors, middle-class groups) resist, either through political means if available or direct confrontation if not. Thus, periodically countries can become politically immobilized around these issues – open competitive or even semi-competitive democracies are particularly vulnerable – provoking the formation of an authoritarian regime with enough concentrated power to impose the cost allocations inherent in any model of development or stabilization strategy.

Purely political explanations come in a variety of forms. Huntington, again, sees the 'crisis of transition' as a source of the 'political decay' of traditional institutions and thereby a 'praetorian situation' in which social conflict is unmediated by institutions (Huntington 1968). This Hobbesian situation creates an inclination to pull the military into power and create a regime oriented to impose order by force. This explanation is particularly apt for the more underdeveloped countries of Latin America and regions like Africa where the kinds of authoritarian regimes that emerge are highly personalized versions of neo-patrimonialism. A variation on this type of institutional argument would point to moments of crucial transition such as decolonization or economic restructuring as rendering societies particularly vulnerable to a praetorian situation. It is noteworthy that the patterns of highly personalized and factional-ized authoritarianism in contemporary Africa bear marked resemblance to the personal dictatorships of nineteenth-century Latin America, often called the age of the *caudillos* (leaders). In both cases sovereignty, owing to the need to convert the administrative fragments of previous imperial systems into modern nation-states, was the central problem confronting governments. Not unlike Europe in the age of the centralizing monarchs, the problems of state and nation building have called to the fore strong and often charismatic leaders in the less developed world.

One might advance the argument, albeit with some hesitation, that in the developing world extreme praetorian situations tend to produce highly per-sonalized authoritarian regimes of the neo-patrimonial type while issues of economic development and problems of political stalemate in relatively more complex societies produce more organized and technocratically focused types of authoritarian regimes. When these issues are played out in countries with some type of capitalist economy the question of costs of development tend particularly to produce regimes that lean toward the bureaucratic-authoritarian type in contexts as diverse as Argentina, Brazil, Mexico, South Korea and Taiwan. Indeed these cases call into question any facile attempt to state an invariant and positive relationship between capitalism and democracy in the less developed world.

Other types of political explanations focus mainly on issues of why democratic or quasi-democratic regimes 'break down' into authoritarian regimes. In this vein Linz and Stepan have argued for the need to focus on the particular choices made or not made by politically relevant individuals and groups in moments of crisis or severe difficulty (Linz and Stepan 1978). A recent variation on this argument, aimed particularly at Latin America, sees the propensity towards extra-legal changes of government of an authoritarian nature as a product of presidential systems which in that environment have a marked tendency to be stalemated by recalcitrant legislatures. This argument has called for a shift to parliamentary systems as a way out.

In terms of the internal organization and functioning of contemporary authoritarian regimes we again confront a complex and confusing landscape. To simplify matters we might argue that the internal structure and dynamics of authoritarian regimes are shaped by the way they cope with two crucial functions, control and policy making. In broad terms, control in authoritarian regimes is based on a mix of coercion and co-optation. When coercion, either as suppression or mobilization, is preponderant the political salience of the military, police and paramilitary organizations is increased. Coercion can occur as the organized and systematic state terror of the secret police or paramilitary death squads as in Stalin's Soviet Union or Argentina under the military, or the much less-organized, episodic and personalized terror of regimes like El Salvador or Haiti.

Most authoritarian regimes, however, like other regimes, seek to legitimate themselves and control the populace by at least quasi-voluntary means. The main voluntary mechanism is co-optation in which individuals and groups in return for particularized substantive privileges (contract concessions, favourable wages, social security benefits) give to the regime generalized political support and/or acquiescence. The key to co-optation is that the co-opted become dependent on the regime for the flow of particular privileges for which they trade their political rights; the surrender of political rights in turn removes a crucial form of check on governments.

In highly personalized neo-patrimonial regimes co-optation comes in the form of elaborating complex networks of patron–client relations; and therefore the main dynamic of politics is intense factional competition to establish direct personalized ties to the patrimonial centre which is the lodestone of patronage. In this regime form rulers spend an inordinate amount of time seeking to cling to office by manipulating the web of clientelistic factions pivoting around them: factions that penetrate all classes and institutions, including the security forces. In more organized forms of authoritarianism co-optation is often elaborated in corporatist arrangements in which specific recognized groups (trade unions, professional associations, interest groups, etc.) are more or less formally linked into the regime's institutional structure. Often these corporatist arrangements are asymmetric (or what O'Donnell (1977) calls bi-frontal) in that they permit substantial access for some groups (often large national and international business interests) while limiting or blocking the access of others (labour, for example). Where co-optation is preponderant such regimes often take the form of single-party states like Mexico where the ruling party (the Institutional Revolutionary Party or PRI) is the main mechanism of co-optation and control. In practice most contemporary authoritarian regimes, such as Brazil between 1964 and 1983, blend clientelism and corporatist organizations, coercion and co-optation with a resulting mixed pattern of relationships between security organizations, party organizations, official interest organizations and informal factions. These patterns have to be sorted out on a case-by-case basis.

The policy style of personalistic-authoritarian regimes is driven and rather overwhelmed by the dynamics of intra-elite factional politics; intrigue seems to substitute for policy. In more highly organized bureaucratic-authoritarian type regimes the policy process is reflective of the instrumental challenges these regimes set for themselves around the questions of the cost and benefit allocations connected to the process of government-led economic development and/or crisis management. Aside from issues of control the key policy issue to such regimes is 'managing the economy'.

As noted earlier such 'modernizing authoritarian' regimes often seek to legitimize themselves with a *universitas* image of rule in which policy making is monopolized by an apolitical policy elite put in place by a strong executive. Such elites are often highly trained technocrats whose claim to policy dominance is based on their expertise or capacity to interpret and translate into policy packages esoteric technical knowledge such as economic theory. O'Donnell argues that such civilian technocrats form an alliance with military elites which is the crucial structural feature of decision making in the bureaucratic-authoritarian regime (O'Donnell 1977). Policy making itself is often a process in which the executive uses control mechanisms to insulate policy elites from group pressures. Protected from societal pressures the executive-based policy elites, especially economic policy teams, can formulate programmes which are then 'given to society' by executive decree and justified as being in the collective national interest as opposed to those of selfish pressure-groups.

This policy style is both the boon and the bane of contemporary authoritarian regimes. Boon because it allows governments to confront directly stalemate and crisis; bane because, particularly as a crisis recedes, many groups begin to clamour for access to the decision-making process. Indeed many groups, including those who ostensibly benefit from economic policy such as big business, discover that they value ongoing access to the policy process as much as, if not more than, policies designed exclusively by executive-based policy elites, even if they are theoretically in their interest. In short, these bureaucratic-authoritarian regimes often generate from within themselves a 'crisis of representation'. In Latin America at least this issue of representation in the policy process led many key early support groups to break with authoritarian regimes in the mid-1970s and to assume leadership positions in the broad social movements that demanded a return to procedurally defined representative democracy.

The movement toward 'redemocratization' during the 1980s in Latin America, the weakening of authoritarian control in some Asian states and the recent collapse of communist authoritarian regimes have led many to see an all but inevitable global trend toward democracy. This trend is often linked to a parallel drive to adopt more market-centred or 'capitalist' economies, leading many to restate the argument that capitalism and democracy are positively connected. An extreme version of this optimistic forecasting sees an 'end to history' as the world converges on themes of liberal democracy and neo-liberal economics.

There are many reasons to doubt the accuracy of this sanguine view. First, authoritarian regimes continue to exist in places as diverse as China, Africa and the Middle East. Second, the kinds of crisis situations that gave rise to modern authoritarian regimes continue to plague many parts of the globe. One of the major crises involves the need to redefine 'national state' organizations as the forces of regionalism and ethnic and religious-based sub-nationalism push forward to challenge existing state structures.

Just as importantly many countries in the less developed world still confront the myriad problems of fostering economic development. In regions such as Latin America, many countries confront the task of consolidating democratic structures even as they face the results of a decade of severe economic crisis, characterized above all by huge foreign debts. In all of these cases the tension between economic and political logic is more intense than ever, particularly as foreign lenders and organizations like the International Monetary Fund lean on governments to adopt severe austerity programmes which carry with them substantial cost allocations. The costs are particularly high and unevenly distributed within the framework of neo-liberal stabilization and reorganization programmes.

Many have pointed out that these economic issues demand governments that can define, implement and sustain technically sound economic programmes which owing to the issue of costs are often extremely unpopular. To achieve this, governments often have to create a strong executive centre capable of insulating teams of technocratic policy makers from distributive pressures generated by interest groups. Many countries in fact are showing a marked tendency toward detached and authoritarian-like policy styles within formal democratic frameworks. Such styles are maintained either by strong executives managing the economy by decree or by multi-party pacts that convert legislatures into rubber stamps for executive policy packages.

To close we might note that the persistence of complex policy problems, particularly around issues of economic and political logic, will continue to generate the kinds of crisis situations which in the past gave rise to authoritarian regimes. Hence, one possibility might be a cyclical alternation between formal democratic regimes and various kinds of authoritarian 'regimes of exception'. Perhaps even more likely is that the problematic current scene will lead to the appearance of new kinds of regimes that go beyond our current vague categories of 'democratic' and 'authoritarian'. We may see new kinds of hybrid regimes that combine elements of liberal democracy, such as periodic elections, with a strong executive-focused capacity to interpret authoritatively and implement technically sound programmes of economic management. Such hybrids might be based on enduring party pacts or new kinds of civil–military alliances. Be that as it may, it would surely be a mistake to again relegate the concept of authoritarianism to the status of a conceptual museum piece.

REFERENCES

Hobbes, T. (1651) *Leviathan*, ed. and with intro. by C. B. Macpherson, London: Penguin, 1985.

Huntington, S. P. (1968) *Political Order in Changing Society*, New Haven: Yale University Press.

Kirkpatrick, J. (1979) 'Dictatorships and double standards', *Commentary* 68 (2): 34–45.

Linz, J. J. (1970) 'An authoritarian regime: the case of Spain', in E. Allard and S. Rokkan (eds) *Mass Politics: Studies in Political Sociology*, New York: Free Press.

Linz, J. J. and Stepan, A. (1978) *The Breakdown of Democratic Regimes*, Baltimore: Johns Hopkins University Press.

Moore, B. Jr, (1966) *Social Origins of Dictatorship and Democracy: Lord and Peasant in the Making of the Modern World*, Boston: Beacon Press.

Oakeshott, M. (1975) *On Human Conduct*, Oxford: Clarendon Press.

O'Donnell, G. (1973) *Modernization and Bureaucratic-Authoritarianism: Studies in South American Politics*, Berkeley: Institute of International Studies, University of California.

O'Donnell, G. (1977) 'Corporatism and the question of the state', in J. M. Malloy (ed.) *Authoritarianism and Corporatism in Latin America*, Pittsburgh: University of Pittsburgh Press, pp. 47–89.

Perlmutter, A. (1981) *Modern Authoritarianism: A Comparative Institutional Analysis*, New Haven: Yale University Press.

Tocqueville, A. de (1955) *The Old Regime and The French Revolution*, Garden City, NY: Doubleday Anchor Books.

Ulam, A. B. (1960) *The Unfinished Revolution: An Essay on the Sources of Marxism and Communism*, New York: Random House.

Weber, M. (1968) *Economy and Society: An Outline of Interpretive Sociology*, eds G. Roth and C. Wittich, New York: Bedminster Press, vol. 3, p. 1006.

Wiarda, H. J. (1973) 'Toward a framework for the study of political change in the Iberic-Latin tradition: the corporative model', *World Politics* 25 (2): 206–35.

FURTHER READING

General theory

Almond, G. and Coleman, J. S. (eds) (1960) *The Politics of the Developing Areas*, Princeton: Princeton University Press.

Almond, G. and Powell, G. B. (1966) *Comparative Politics: A Developmental Approach*, Boston: Little, Brown & Co.

Finer, S. E. (1962) *The Man on Horseback: The Role of the Military in Politics*, New York: Praeger Press.

Geddes, B. and Zaller, J. (1989) 'Sources of popular support for authoritarian regimes,' *American Journal of Political Science* 33 (2): 319–34.

Huntington, S. P. (1968) *Political Order in Changing Society*, New Haven: Yale University Press.

Huntington, S. P. and Moore, C. H. (eds) (1970) *Authoritarian Politics in Modern Society: The Dynamics of Established One-Party Systems*, New York: Basic Books.

Kirkpatrick, J. (1979) 'Dictatorship and double standards', *Commentary* 68 (5): 34–45.

Linz, J. J. (1970) 'An authoritarian regime: the case of Spain', in E. Allard and S. Rokkan (eds) *Mass Politics: Studies in Political Sociology*, New York: Free Press.

——(1975) 'Totalitarianism and authoritarian regimes', in F. Greenstein and N. Polsby (eds) *Handbook of Political Science*, vol. 3, Reading, Mass.: Addison-Wesley.

——(1978) 'Crisis, breakdown, and reequilibration', in J. J. Linz and A. Stepan (eds) *The Breakdown of Democratic Regimes*, Baltimore: Johns Hopkins University Press.

Moore, B. Jr, (1966) *Social Origins of Dictatorship and Democracy: Lord and Peasant in the Making of the Modern World*, Boston: Beacon Press.

Neumann, F. (1957) *The Democratic and the Authoritarian State*, Glencoe, Ill.: Free Press.

Oakeshott, M. J. (1975) *On Human Conduct*, Oxford: Clarendon Press.

O'Donnell, G. (1973) *Modernization and Bureaucratic-Authoriarianism: Studies in South American Politics*, Berkeley: Institute of International Studies, University of California.

——(1978) 'Reflections on the patterns of change in the bureaucratic-authoritarian state', *Latin American Research Review* 12 (1): 3–38.

O'Donnell, G., Schmitter, P. and Whitehead, L. (1986) *Transitions from Authoritarian Rule*, Baltimore: Johns Hopkins University Press.

Perlmutter, A. (1969) 'The Praetorian State and the Praetorian Army: toward a taxonomy of civil-military relations in developing politics', *Comparative Politics* (2): 382–404.

——(1981) *Modern Authoritarianism: A Comparative Institutional Analysis*, New Haven: Yale University Press.

Remmer, K. L. and Merkx, G. W. (1982) 'Bureaucratic-authoritarianism revisited', *Latin American Research Review* 17 (2): 3–40.

Roth, G. (1968) 'Personal rulership, patrimonialism, and empire-building in the new states', *World Politics* 20 (2): 194–206.

Tocqueville, A. de (1955) *The Old Regime and the French Revolution*, Garden City, NY: Doubleday Anchor Books.

Ulam, A. B. (1960) *The Unfinished Revolution: An Essay on the Sources of Influence of Marxism and Communism*, New York: Random House.

Weber, M. (1968) *Economy and Society: An Outline of Interpretive Sociology*, Berkeley: University of California Press.

Latin America

Booth, J. A. and Seligson, M. A. (1984) 'The political culture of authoritarianism in Mexico: a reexamination', *Latin American Research Review* 19 (1): 106–24.

Cammak, P. (1988) 'The "Brazilianization" of Mexico?', *Government and Opposition* 23 (3): 304–20.

Canak, W. L. (1984) 'The peripheral state debate: state capitalist and Bureaucratic-Authoritarian regimes in Latin America', *Latin American Research Review* 19 (1): 3–36.

Collier, D. (ed.) (1979) *The New Authoritarianism in Latin America*, Princeton: Princeton University Press.

Linz, J. J. (1973) 'The future of an authoritarian situation or the institutionalization of an authoritarian regime: the case of Brazil', in A. Stepan (ed.) *Authoritarian Brazil: Origins, Policies and the Future*, New Haven: Yale University Press.

Linz, J. J. and Stepan, A. (eds) (1978) *The Breakdown of Democratic Regimes: Latin America*, Baltimore: Johns Hopkins University Press.

Lowenthal, A. F. (1974) 'Armies and politics in Latin America', *World Politics* 27 (1): 107–30.

Malloy, J. M. (1977) 'Authoritarianism and corporatism in Latin America: the modal pattern', in J. M. Malloy (ed.) *Authoritarianism and Corporatism in Latin America*, Pittsburgh: University of Pittsburgh.

——(ed.) (1977) *Authoritarianism and Corporatism in Latin America*, Pittsburgh: University of Pittsburgh Press.

Malloy, J. M. and Seligson, M. A. (eds) (1987) *Authoritarians and Democrats: Regime Transition in Latin America*, Pittsburgh: University of Pittsburgh Press.

Migdail, C. J. (1987) 'Mexico's failing political system', *Journal of Interamerican Studies and World Affairs* 29 (3): 107–23.

Remmer, K. L. (1985) 'Redemocratization and the impact of authoritarian rule in Latin America', *Comparative Politics* 17 (3): 253–76.

——(1989) 'Neopatrimonialism: the politics of military rule in Chile, 1973–1987', *Comparative Politics* 21 (2): 149–70.

Reyna, J. L. and Wienert, R. S. (eds) (1977) *Authoritarianism in Mexico*, Philadelphia: Institute for the Study of Human Issues.

Stepan, A. (ed.) (1973) *Authoritarian Brazil: Origins, Policies, and the Future*, New Haven: Yale University Press.

Wiarda, H. J. (1973) 'Toward a framework for the study of political change in the Iberic-Latin tradition: the corporative model', *World Politics* 25 (2): 206–35.

Asia

Baeg, I. H. (1987) 'The rise of bureaucratic-authoritariansm in South Korea', *World Politics* 39 (2): 231–57.

Baxter, C. (1985) 'Democracy and authoritarianism in South Asia', *Journal of International Affairs* 38 (2): 307–19.

King, D. Y. (1981) 'Regime type and performance: authoritarian rule, semi-capitalist development, and rural inequality in Asia', *Comparative Political Studies* 13 (4): 477–504.

Winckler, E. A. (1984) 'Institutionalization and participation on Taiwan: from hard to soft authoritarianism?', *China Quarterly* 99: 481–509.

Africa

Decalo, S. (1985) 'The morphology of radical military rule in Africa', *Journal of Communist Studies* 1 (3,4): 122–44.

Markakis, J. (1985) 'Radical military regimes in the Horn of Africa', *Journal of Communist Studies* 1 (3,4): 14–38.

Markakis, J. and Waller, M. (1985) 'The hammer, the sickle, and the gun', *Journal of Communist Studies* 1 (3,4): 1–13.

Moore, C. H. (1974) 'Authoritarian politics in unincorporated society: the case of Nasser's Egypt', *Comparative Politics* 6 (2): 193–218.

Rothchild, D. and Chazan, N. (1988) *The Precarious Balance: State and Society in Africa*, Boulder: Westview Press.

Scaritt, J. R. (1986) 'The explanation of African politics and society: toward a synthesis of approaches', *Journal of African Studies* 13 (3): 85–93.

Europe

Linz, J. J. (1970) 'An authoritarian regime: the case of Spain', in E. Allard and S. Rokkan (eds) *Mass Politics: Studies in Political Sociology*, New York: Free Press.

16

MILITARY DICTATORSHIPS

TALUKDER MANIRUZZAMAN

Oliver Cromwell is reported to have said, 'Nine citizens out of ten hate me? What does it matter if that tenth alone is armed?' (Fried 1966: 87–8). This short statement by the first and the last military dictator in modern English history sums up much of the substance of military dictatorship. Military dictatorship means the rule by a military officer or a military junta who takes over the state power through a military *coup d'état* and rule without any accountability as long as the officer or the junta can retain the support of the armed forces.

Some scholars working on military rule argue that military governments usually have a large civilian component – bureaucrats, managers, politicians and technocrats. So the dichotomy between military and civilian rules can hardly be sustained. For example, Amos Perlmutter states, 'modern military regimes are not purely military in composition. Instead they are fusionist, that is, they are military–civil regimes' (Perlmutter 1981: 97). Military dictators usually bring civilian technocrats and political renegades into their governing councils, but that does not blur the distinction between military and civilian regimes. The civilian counsellors joining the military government hold office on the sufferance of the military dictator. Moreover, under the military dictatorship it is the military ruler and his advisers from the armed forces who play the predominant role in all 'decisions of decisive consequence'. Thus military dictatorship emerges as a distinct sub-type of authoritarianism. (To avoid excessive repetition we have used the phrases 'military regime', 'military ruler', 'military politician', 'military leadership', 'soldier-ruler' as synonyms for 'military dictatorship'.)

Military dictatorship differs from other forms of authoritarianism in terms of origin or legitimacy or range of governmental penetration into the society or in combinations of all these factors. The present-day military dictatorship is often compared to the absolute monarchies of seventeenth- and eighteenth-century Europe, but the differences between the two types of governments are quite pronounced. First, as force does not automatically create right, any government of military provenance suffers from innate sense of lack of legitimacy. On the other hand, the origin and rule of the European absolute monarchies were clothed in powerful traditional legitimacy. The European monarchs extended the direct control of the central government over the whole, more or less, of culturally homogeneous, state-territories by creating a civil administration, particularly through the apparatus of tax collection (Tilly 1985). Present-day military dictators in the Third World usually resort to repressive measures to manage the problem of national integration of states divided on primordial loyalties. As we shall see later, military leaders only aggravate the problems of nation building after taking over power from the civilian political leaders.

Military dictators also differ from the *caudillos* who flourished in the institutionally decomposed societies of post-independence Latin America. The *caudillos* were not professional soldiers. They were adventurers and warriors utilizing violence for political ends, but they lacked institutionalized armed forces to support their regimes (Rouqui 1987: 39–71).

Military dictators are different from the civilian autocrats in their sources of legitimacy. The civilian dictators in the Third World derive their legitimacy from their leadership in the independence struggle or from the leadership of the single parties founded by them or from some rigged election. They retain their power by maintaining 'a vertical network of personal and patron–client relations' (Jackson and Rosberg 1984: 421–42), a strategy of rulership, as we shall see below (pp. 252–4), also resorted to by military dictators.

Lastly, military dictatorship differs from totalitarian dictatorship on three counts. First, totalitarian dictators claim legitimacy on the basis of their ideologies which, they state, are higher and nobler forms of democracy. Military dictators do not generally espouse elaborate and guiding ideologies, they have only, to use the phrase of Juan Linz, 'distinctive orientations and mentalities' (Linz 1975: 264). Second, unlike military dictators, totalitarian dictators seize power by organizing armed political parties. Once in power, totalitarian dictators establish the supremacy of their parties over all organizations, including the armed forces. Third, while military dictators allow 'a limited, not responsible, pluralism' (ibid.: 264), totalitarian dictators try to control the whole society through the single-party system and widespread use of terror.

The word dictator is derived from the early Roman constitution. This constitution provided for the election of a magistrate as dictator for six months with extraordinary powers to handle some unforeseen crises. This constitutional dictatorship degenerated into military dictatorship when the post-constitutional rulers of the Roman empire used the Praetorian guards as the main base of their power. More recently a few European states – Spain (1920s and 1930s), Portugal (1920s and 1970s) and Greece (late 1960s and mid-1970s) underwent military dictatorships. However, it is in the post-Second

World War states belonging to the Third World that military dictatorship has emerged as 'a distinctly and analytically new phenomenon, restricted to the developing and modernizing world' (Perlmutter 1981: 96). The wide prevalence of military dictatorship in the Third World states can be gauged from the fact that between 1946 and 1984 about 56 per cent of Third World states (excluding the communist states and mini-states with a population below one million) had undergone at least one military *coup d'état*. That 57 per cent of the military coup-affected states in the Third World have been under military rule for half, or more than half, of the last four decades gives us some idea about the depth and intensity of military dictatorship in the *coup*-prone states in the developing areas (Maniruzzaman 1987: 17–18).

GROWTH OF MILITARY DICTATORSHIP

Several schools of thought have evolved to explain military intervention and growth of military dictatorship in developing states. The first school, the organizationalists, focus on the special characteristics that are generally attributed to professional Western military organizations – such as centralized command, hierarchy, discipline and cohesion – to explain military intervention. As Morris Janowitz writes, 'the organizational format designed to carry out the military functions as well as experience in the "management of violence" is at the root of these armies' ability to intervene politically' (Janowitz 1964: 32). However, it is not the organizational strength of the military but rather the military's organizational decay that often creates conditions for various factions within the military to launch sudden and swift raids on the government (Decalo 1976: 14–15).

The organizationalists, whether they speak of the military's organizational strength or decay, place more emphasis on the organizational dynamics within the army than on forces outside the barracks to explain the political behaviour of soldiers. After studying African *coups* since 1967, Clause Welch argues that 'organizational variables are far better predictors of success than are sociopolitical or environmental variables' (see Kelleher 1974: ix).

A second group of scholars places more emphasis on society as a whole to analyse the reasons for military rule. According to S. E. Finer, military intervention results from the 'low or minimal political culture of the society concerned' (Finer 1969: 110–39). Samuel P. Huntington argues that: 'Military explanations do not explain military interventions. The reason for this is simply that military interventions are only one specific manifestation of a broader phenomenon in under-developed societies: the general politicization of social forces and institutions'. (Huntington 1969: 194).

The third group are the sceptical behaviouralists, who stress the internal dynamics of military hierarchies, cliques within the army, corporate interests, personal ambitions, and idiosyncracies of particular military men in explaining the political behaviour of the army (Decalo 1976: 7–22).

Some of the very prominent Latin American scholars, particularly Guillermo O'Donnell, have tried to explain the rise of military ('bureaucratic-authoritarian') dictatorship in Latin America from the 1960s to the mid-1980s in terms of interactions between world economic forces and the indigenous economic trends of relatively more developed countries, such as Argentina, Brazil, Chile and Uruguay. O'Donnell (1978: 19) argues that these bureaucratic-authoritarian regimes arose at 'a particularly diaphanous moment of dependence' of the countries concerned. This 'historical moment' was created by the 'exhaustion' of import-substitution industries as a means of expanding the domestic economy and by the weakening of the international market for Latin American primary exports. The result was economic crisis marked by rising inflation, declining GNP and investment rates, flight of capital, balance of payment deficits, and the like. This crisis in turn activated the popular sector in Latin American countries. This was perceived as a threat by other social classes. Military officers, as we shall discuss later, already indoctrinated in the ideas of 'national security' and afraid of Cuban-style revolution that would mean the end of the army as an institution, stepped in to create bureaucratic-authoritarian regimes in collaboration with civilian technocrats.

Some scholars argue that one of the basic reasons for military intervention in the developing countries is that, unlike the soldiers in the formative phase of the growth of the standing armies in Europe, the soldiers in developing countries face a situation of 'military structural unemployment' (Barros and Coelho 1981: 341–9). The European states developed standing armies between the sixteenth and eighteenth centuries. This was also the period when Europe was a constant theatre of interstate wars. Where are the wars today in the Third World? Our research shows that the median length of wars in Europe during the period 1415–1815 was four years, while the median length of wars during the period 1946–84 was less than two months. Even if we multiply the median length of wars in the Third World countries by nine to make the time span of comparison similar for both areas, the median length of Third World wars comes to one and a half years, about one-third of the length of European wars (Maniruzzaman 1987: 113–15).

While the European armies between 1495 and 1815 were almost continuously engaged in war, the armies in the Third World are only engaged in 'barrack sittings'. Third World armies easily become alienated from society because these organizations, having a monopoly on the instruments of violence, fail to find a meaningful role in society due to the absence or infrequency of war and lack of facilities for proper training. This estrangement from society predisposes them to role expansion. Because of the endemic and 'cumulative crisis' in Third World states, alienated armies easily find opportunities to intervene. As a former chief justice of Pakistan stated sometime after the military take-over in Pakistan in 1958, the valiant armed forces of Pakistan had nothing to do and therefore subjugated their own people (Razzak 1981: 17).

EMPIRICAL STUDIES ON MILITARY INTERVENTION

Present-day social scientists would reject any single master paradigm and argue that no single method of approach can by itself provide a comprehensive understanding of a complex social and political phenomenon (Needler 1978). It is the confluence and interaction of several of the variables discussed above (p. 250) that explains the occurrence of the military *coup d'état* and growth of military dictatorship in any particular country. The crucial question is the relative weight of each variable in the process of interaction.

Statistical tools can be used to understand the particular 'mix' of the variables involved in the process of military take-over of powers of the state.

Of the several empirical studies done on military interventions, two stand out – Jackman's 'The predictability of *coups d'état*: a model with African data' (Jackman 1978) and Londregan and Poole's 'Poverty, the *coup* trap, and the seizure of executive power' (Londregan and Poole 1990). These two studies are well-grounded in theoretical structure and use sophisticated statistical models to explain military *coups d'état*. Jackman's study shows that military *coups d'état* are the function of structural factors (social mobilization, cultural pluralism, party dominance and electoral turn-out) almost in a deterministic pattern, and idiosyncratic factors emphasized by Zolberg (1968: 7) and Decalo (1976: 22) account for only one-fifth of the variance in *coups d'état* (Jackman 1978: 1273).

In their recent study covering 121 countries for the period 1960–82, Londregan and Poole construct a statistical model enabling them to use income level, economic growth rate, past history of *coups*, and interdependence of *coups* and economic growth as independent variables, and the military *coup d'état* as the dependent variable. They find that both high level of income and high level of economic growth as separate factors inhibit *coups d'état*. According to their study, incidence of *coups d'état* is twenty-one times more likely in the poorest countries than among the wealthiest. More interesting is their 'compelling evidence of a "*coup*-trap"; once a country has experienced a coup d'état, it has a much harder time avoiding further *coups*. . . . *Coups* spawn countercoups' (Londregan and Poole 1990: 175, 178).

Although no grand theory has yet emerged, the theoretical and empirical studies discussed above have greatly increased our understanding of the occurrence of the military *coup d'état*. This understanding, however, is not enough. The way that military dictators rule and the policies they pursue condition much of later social, economic and political development of *coup*-affected states. Let us now discuss the methods generally used by military dictators to perpetuate their rule.

STRATEGIES OF RULERSHIP BY MILITARY DICTATORS

The first strategy of rulership by military dictators is to manage their 'constituency', i.e. to keep their hold on the armed forces. In countries with non-professional armies divided on ethnic or religious lines, this strategy often means the establishment of dominance over the whole army by the group led by the military dictator. The establishment of this dominance often requires the use of crude and ruthless violence to suppress the opposition factions within armed forces and to terrorize the civilian population to total submission.

One of the most notorious military dictators in this regard is Mengistu of Ethiopia, who physically liquidated his rivals among the officer corps and used 'red terror' against civil revolutionaries on such a massive scale that even the initial supporters of the military *coup* were not only disenchanted but appalled (Halliday and Molyneux 1983: 122–7). Idi Amin, Bokassa and Mobutu were no less ruthless 'in eliminating and annihilating opposition within the military and outside it' (Perlmutter 1981: 16).

The sub-Saharan military dictators are not the only ones to use violence to keep their hold on the army. In Syria (between 1946 and 1970), officers drawn from two minority communities, the Alawis and the Druze, eliminated officers drawn from the Sunnis (the majority community) through successive *coups* and counter-*coups*. Finally, the Alawis purged the Druze officers through a *coup* in 1970. Hafiz al-Assad, an Alawi, seized power and has ruled Syria to date. Paralleling the Alawis in Syria, Iraqi officers belonging to the Sunni minority community drawn from the small town of Takrit gradually eliminated their opponents, and through the *coup d'état* in 1968 established their absolute control over the armed forces (Maniruzzaman 1987: 32–41).

Developments in the Bangladeshi army followed the common pattern. The army was divided into two groups – those who participated in the liberation war of 1971 and those who had been in West Pakistan and later joined the Bangladeshi army. After several *coups* and counter-*coups* the 'repatriates' from Pakistan established their dominance over the armed forces through the *coup* of 1982 and ruled until 1990 (Maniruzzaman 1989: 216–21).

In countries such as Argentina, Brazil, Pakistan and Peru with professional and disciplined armies, military *coups d'état* become more or less systematic and disciplined operations. This is because unlike the soldier in non-professional armies who is loyal only to himself or at best to his faction, the professional soldier is amenable to the discipline of the army as an institution. Professional armies tend to factionalize at the highest echelon at the time of intervention. The senior officers soon develop a formula for sharing power among themselves and close their differences. Because the power struggle remains limited to upper levels of the hierarchy, discipline among the officers and rank and file remains unaffected.

However, the difference between military dictators coming to power through successive *coups* and counter-*coups* and military dictators seizing power with the help of professional armies is one of degree rather than kind. In Brazil between 1964 and 1985 torture became 'an intrinsic part of the governing process' (Stepan 1971: 262). In Argentina between 1976 and 1983 the military rulers killed between 6,000 and 30,000 Argentines in their 'dirty war' against the leftists (Schumarcher 1984: 1076). In Pakistan, the military government of Zia-ul Huq physically eliminated the nation's first elected prime minister, Zulfiquar Ali Bhutto, on the basis of a judgement given by what has been called 'rigged benches' of the High Court in Lahore and the Supreme Court of Pakistan (Quereshi 1979: 920).

As repression becomes a part of the strategy of rulership, military dictators develop an elaborate network of intelligence services. In his latest work, *Rethinking Military Politics: Brazil and the Southern Cone*, Alfred Stephan (1988) points out how the military intelligence services in Brazil became a formidable threat to the ruling junta itself. As Stephan argues, it was the need for civilian support against the intelligence community that led the Brazilian military to start the process of liberalization which ultimately led to the withdrawal of the military from power. General Zia-ul Huq of Pakistan, to give another example, developed an Inter-Service Intelligence Directorate with 100,000 employees as one of the most influential military and internal security agencies in the Third World for surveillance of politicians as well as officers.

Violence and intelligence surveillance are, however, negative strategies of rulership. A more positive way of keeping the armed forces satisfied is the raising of salaries and other allowances and perquisites of the members of the armed forces. Military rulers almost invariably increase the defence budgets soon after a take-over. Once raised, defence allocations usually remain at high levels in subsequent years. For the decade of the 1960s, the average annual expenditure on defence compared with total state budgets in Asia, sub-Saharan Africa and Latin America was almost double for military governments compared with non-military governments (Kennedy 1974: 163). The rate of growth for defence expenditure in developing countries is surpassing the growth rate in the developed nations (Janowitz 1977: 48). As most of the defence budget in developing countries is spent on buying sophisticated weapons in hard currency from developed countries, such expenditures do not have multiplier effects on national economies.

Another strategy of rulership adopted by military dictators is to depoliticize and control the participation of the masses. To this end, the Latin American military dictators usually resort to the system of corporatism. Under this system the military regimes try 'to eliminate spontaneous interest articulation and establish a limited number of authoritatively recognized groups that interact with the government apparatus in defined and regularized ways' (Malloy 1977: 4). Some military dictators – especially those in the Middle East and sub-Saharan Africa – established one-party systems as the structural mechanism of organizing and controlling participation. In Syria the Ba'ath Party has been subjugated by the army wing of the party since 1966. In Iraq, however, the military and the Ba'ath Party seem to have a symbiotic relationship. The parties created from above by military dictators such as Mobutu in Zaire, Eyadema in Togo and Kerekou in Benin do not seem to have much influence on the policy-making process and are not likely to decide the succession of the present military dictators. These parties are merely appendages of the military regime. Writing in 1966, Aristide R. Zolberg asserted that single parties founded in West Africa are usually paper organizations (Zolberg 1966: 25, 33–34, 128–150). Bienen seems more to the point when he argues that the single-party system is more like US political machines as far as distribution of patronage is concerned (Bienen 1970: 99–127). Indeed, the African one-party system, often headed by the military dictator himself, is part of an overall strategy of ruling through patrimonialism. Mobutu in Zaire provides the most typical example in this regard. In November 1973 Mobutu took over about 2,000 foreign-owned enterprises and distributed these as 'free goods' among the politico-commercial class. Mobutu himself and the members of the polit-buro of the single party, the Popular Revolutionary Movement, partook of this largesse (Young and Turner 1984: 714–49).

MODERNIZATION AND THE ROLE OF MILITARY REGIMES: SOME EMPIRICAL FINDINGS

It seems that in order to make their studies of policy relevant, political scientists in the West, particularly the United States during the 1950s and 1960s, tried to over-estimate the role of the military in the modernization of Third World countries. As armed communist cadres threatened the countries of South-East Asia, Guy Pauker (1959: 325–45) wrote an article in *World Politics* advocating the use of the military to fight and defeat the onward march of the armed communists. Soon a number of respected scholars developed theoretical models depicting the military as a highly modern force, capable of transferring its organizational and technical skills to fields of government and administration (see for example, Pye 1962: 69–89; Halpern 1962: 227–313; Daadler 1962; Johnson 1964).

These theoretical formulations were, to use the facetious phrase of Henry Bienen, 'unencumbered by empirical evidence', but later empirical research on the actual performance of military regimes has largely belied these early theoretical expectations. Indeed, a study by Eric A. Nordlinger (1970: 1131–48), drawing on an analysis of cross-national data from seventy-four non-Western and non-communist countries, found negative and zero-order correlations between the political strength of the military and social and economic modernizations. In another cross-national aggregate study of all independent, non-communist countries with a population greater than one million, covering the period from 1951 to 1970, R. D. McKinlay and A. S. Cohan concluded that 'there is no profound effect on economic performance produced by military regime when MR (Military Regime) and CMR (period of civilian rule in countries that have experienced military regimes) are compared with CR (low income countries who have experienced only civilian rule)' (McKinlay and Cohan 1975: 1–30). Another study based on data covering the period from 1960 to 1970 for seventy-seven independent countries of the Third World reported that, 'In short military intervention in politics of the Third World has no unique effect on social change, regardless of either the level of economic development or geographic region' (Jackman 1976: 1096). In the latest empirical study already quoted above (p. 251), Londregan and Poole conclude:

'Despite the dramatic effect of economic performance on the probability of *coups*, the reverse is not true: a country's past *coup* history has little discernible effect on its economy. We find no evidence that either the recent history of *coups* or the current propensity for a *coup d'état* significantly affect the growth rate'.
(Londregan and Poole 1990: 153).

MILITARY DICTATORSHIP AND THE CIRCLE OF POLITICAL UNDERDEVELOPMENT

The performance of military regimes has been even more disappointing in the sphere of political development than in the sphere of economic development. It is often argued that since most of the new nations are divided on ethnic, religious, linguistic and regional lines, the military alone can bring about the national integration that is a prerequisite for political development.

The performance of military rulers to date does not support this hypothesis. It was the military dictators Ayub Khan and his successor Yahiya Khan who, following a 'policy of blood and iron' in Pakistan, produced the first successful secessionist movement in the Third World. In a similar fashion the process of Nigerian disintegration started after the *coup* of 15 January 1966, when Nzeogwu and his cohorts launched a ruthless attack on prominent military and political figures. The military leadership presided over the civil war in Nigeria for two years with combat deaths running into hundreds of thousands.

Likewise, the Sudanese military rulers have been fighting the guerrillas in the southern part of the country from 1958 up until the present day.

As a matter of fact, in most cases military intervention creates a vicious circle that perpetuates the conditions of political underdevelopment which initially brought about the imposition of military rule. As Huntington has argued (Huntington 1965: 421–7), the key factor in political development is the growth of durable political institutions. The primary resources for developing political institutions in any country are the political skills of its politicians. The political skills needed for developing a viable and self-sustaining political system involve, among others, ideological commitment, the capacity to respond to new challenges, and the arts of administration, negotiation, representation and bargaining. These skills can be acquired only in the hard school of public life. (See Morris-Jones 1957: 49, 57, 71; 1978: 131–43; Weiner 1967: 11–16; Kochanek 1968: xix–xxv.)

Because of their 'military minds' and perspectives, soldier-rulers, from Ayub Khan in Pakistan to Acheampong in Ghana or Castello Branco in Brazil, fail to see the functional aspects of the great game of politics. They severely restrict the free flow of the political process and force would-be politicians into a long period of hibernation. The period of military rule is usually a total waste as far as the development of political skills is concerned. Because about two-thirds of civil and military governments fall victim to military *coups d'état*, the opportunity for people once under a military regime to gain political skills is likely to be continually postponed with the arrival of every new military regime.

Only one-third of the military governments that have existed in the Third World have been succeeded by civilian governments. In some cases of civilian restoration, newly incumbent civilian leaders soon demonstrate their inability to match their official performance with the expectation of the people. This is not unnatural: first, because of general intractability of the problems faced by the developing nations; and second (and more important), because of the lack of political skills in the civilian leaders resulting from the preceding period of military rule. Military officers waiting in the wings then depose the civilian regime in response to even a modest manifestation of public discontent against the civilian government and assert the vindication of their self-fulfilling prophecy of the 'inevitable failure of the self-seeking politicians. Thus the period of waste for political growth begins anew' (Maniruzzaman 1987: 6–7).

ROLE EXPANSION OF THE MILITARY AND DEFENCE VULNERABILITY

As the army begins to 'patrol the society', the frontiers of state remain utterly vulnerable. In the past two decades several armies have been compromised by their political role expansion and suffered humiliating defeats at the hands of other armies encouraged only to excel in professionalism. In the Arab–Israeli War of 1967, the Syrian army's performance suffered immeasurably because of fratricidal feuds among its officers, which resulted in an inability to mount a serious offensive against the Israeli army. The Iraqi army was similarly debilitated by internal political strife (Brown 1967: 269–71).

Egypt's total fiasco in the 1967 war is also attributed to the political role expansion of the Egyptian armed forces. The Egyptian air commanders committed 'monumental neglect of the most elementary rules of protecting aircraft on the ground'. The result was that a large part of the Egyptian air force was completely incapacitated by an Israeli pre-emptive attack on the first day of the war. The Egyptian army disintegrated in less than a week (Brown 1967: 269–71).

Thirteen years of political involvement similarly impaired the fighting edge of the Pakistan armed forces in the 1971 war with India. One could reasonably argue that the Pakistan forces in former East Pakistan, denied all logistic support from West Pakistan because of an Indian blockade, were not in a position to give stiff resistance to the Indians. But the failure of the Pakistani forces to mount a significant challenge to Indian forces on the western front can not be explained by any other terms than inadequate morale and fighting skills of the Pakistanis (Morris-Jones 1972: 188–9).

Another example of how the political role of the armed forces corrodes military vitality is provided by Idi Amin's armed forces in Uganda, which first acted as an instrument of Idi Amin's terror and brutality and then simply disintegrated when faced with poorly equipped Tanzanian troops and a Ugandan exile force in April 1979. More recently an Argentine military spoiled by politics was easily defeated by Great Britain in the Falklands/Malvinas War.

FAILURE OF THE 'NEW PROFESSIONALS'

Nowhere has the claim of superior rule by the military leaders over the politicians been more dramatically and poignantly disproved than in Latin America. Military leaders seized power in Brazil (1964), Argentina (1976), Peru (1968) and Chile (1973) for unlimited periods to effect fundamental transformation in social, economic and political structures. They developed the 'doctrine of national security' to justify their rule (Stepan 1976: 240–60; O'Donnell 1976: 208–13). According to this doctrine, the governments in Latin America were engaged in an internal war with the communist revolutionaries. The days of the 'old professional' soldier who fought conventional wars with external enemies were almost over. The 'new professional soldier', trained in fighting a 'total war' with the internal enemy on military, social, economic and political fronts, was the prime need. Because civilian leaders did not have requisite skills and organizations to fight the new war, it became the manifest destiny of the 'new professional soldiers' to establish control over all aspects of society, bring about rapid socio-economic development, and win the glory of defeating the great threat to Western civilization.

Brazil was the test case for implementation of the doctrine of national security and national development; Brazil had the best soldiers and materials in the whole of Latin America, and the 'new professionals' of Brazil held power for two decades to show their mettle. Yet the economic and political reforms effected by the new professional soldiers proved illusory. The military regimes were bedevilled by the growth of factionalism within the armed forces and conflicts between military governments and military institutions. The result was frequent instability (changes in government personnel, including the president of the nation) and policy incoherence. The strategy of growth followed by the soldier-rulers not only accentuated social and regional cleavages but also led to a debt burden of over US$90 billion by the early 1980s. Popular discontent mounted, and the military governments 'deepened the revolution' by resorting to more and more terror and torture (Maniruzzaman 1987: 11).

The developments in Argentina (1976–83) under the new professionals followed closely the pattern in Brazil (1964–1985). The Argentine economy plunged into deep recession, and foreign debt increased fourfold from US$9.8 billion in 1978 to US$38 billion in 1982. As resistance to government increased, the Argentine military rulers used terror and torture on a scale much larger than those applied by their Brazilian counterparts (Sanders 1983: 2–3).

It was Peru's 'armed intellectuals' who tried to play the most revolutionary role. They nationalized petroleum, fishing and other natural resources, introduced the system of worker participation in industrial plants, decreed new land reforms, enacted new education policy, and organized mass participation in national interest group associations. The 'revolution from above', however, aborted; Peruvians showed an utter disinterest in the soldier-rulers' reforms. The military-sponsored, radical reform measures, on the other hand, dislocated the national economy further (Sanders 1981: 77; Malloy 1982: 4). It was ironic that the Peruvian voters in 1980 forced the ruling army elite to hand power back to the very civilian politician (Fernando Belaúnde) from whom the officers snatched political power in 1968 (Handelman 1981: 132–5).

From the discussion so far certain conclusions emerge. Soldier-politicians seem incapable of furthering major socio-economic development in the countries they rule. The military's performance in the field of political development has been even more dismal. Military regimes accentuate the problems of political development with which the civilian regimes were initially faced, and they deprive the civilian politicians of the opportunity to acquire much-needed political skills, thus perpetuating the chain of political underdevelopment. Finally, role expansion of the military creates both internal and external security vulnerabilities. The study of military withdrawal from politics thus seems imperative.

MILITARY WITHDRAWAL FROM POLITICS

The nature and duration of military withdrawal from politics are, in part, a function of organizational aspects of the armed forces. As we have seen earlier (pp. 252–3), factionalism within non-professional armies creates the syndrome of abrupt intervention–withdrawal–reintervention until one faction comes to dominate the whole army and impose a longer period of military rule.

Military dictators – Ayub Khan (1958–69), Zia-ul Huq (1977–88), military juntas in Brazil (1964–85), Argentina (1966–73) and Peru (1968–80), to mention only a few – who were supported by professional armies usually ruled for longer periods relative to a short duration of rule of the officers leading non-professional armies. Some of the officers coming to power with the support of professional armies withdrew from politics because of sheer exhaustion of ruling the problem-ridden Third World countries (Brazil, Argentina and Peru). Some military dictators are forced to withdraw by spontaneous mass upheavals – for example Bolivia (1946), Sudan (1964), Pakistan (1969), Thailand (1973) and El Salvador (1979). These multi-class upheavals, however, can not install stable civilian governments and usually military juntas resume control (Maniruzzaman 1987: 80–2, 164–5).

One way of preventing the growth of military dictatorship is to create a consensus among the political parties against military rule. This deprives the military juntas of the 'civilian constituency' which according to some scholars is often a prerequisite for a military *coup d'état*. In Venezuela (1958) and Colombia (1957) the leading political parties entered into a political pact for sharing power among themselves for twenty years, eliminating support for army intervention. This coalition of dominant political parties against army rule has enabled these two countries to maintain civilian rule for nearly three decades (Karl 1981; Kline 1979).

The methods of military withdrawal from politics discussed above belong to superstructural architectonic levels and cannot break the cycle of intervention–withdrawal–intervention. Durable and long-term military withdrawal is the function of social revolution: the process of replacing one social class by another as the ruling class, and the cataclysmic social structural transformation wrought in the process. The two archetypical social revolutions – bourgeois and proletarian – consolidated the class rule of bourgeoisie and the proletariat, respectively, and brought the armed forces under the control of the hegemonic classes.

The few cases of long-term withdrawal that have taken place in the Third World states point to the same conclusion. Whether it is a revolution of the

Jeffersonian farmers and the middle classes as in Costa Rica in 1948, or a revolution under a coalition of classes – professional middle class and peasant class – as in Mexico (1911–17), or a socialist revolution led by the scions of upper and middle classes in Cuba (1959) and Nicaragua (1979), or peasant-supported revolution in Venezuela (1958), or reactivated upper classes in Columbia (1957), the cathartic effect is the same – 'politics in command'. Revolution is primarily an intellectual event and only secondarily a military phenomenon. The revolution defines the role of the armed forces in the new society. The fresh political formula with a new scheme of distributing power sanctified by the revolution gives precedence to the role of ideas over arms, to policy over instruments and to politics over guns. In this respect the aftermath of contemporary social revolution is the same as that of the two archetypical social revolutions – bourgeois and proletarian (Maniruzzaman 1987: 212).

CONCLUDING REMARKS

Social revolutions are rare, as are permanent military withdrawals from politics. It seems that Third World states now under military dictatorship will remain so as they approach the year 2000, although the personnel of the military regime may change. The great pro-democratic changes taking place in the East European states are not likely to affect the Third World states much. This is because of differences between the states of Eastern Europe and the Third World in national history and social, economic and political development. Even if there are popular upheavals in some military-ruled states, the armies which have been in power for a long time may not easily surrender power to civilian leadership, as Burma's army has shown recently. Most military dictators will continue to 'pay respect to democracy' by organizing rigged elections and plebiscites.

The developments in some of the Latin American states might be different from those in other regions of the world. The poor economic performance and extremely repressive nature of recent military dictatorships in Argentina, Brazil, Chile, Peru and Uruguay seem to have united all the political parties in those countries against further military intervention. In Argentina, at least, the anti-army feelings have sustained civilian rule since 1983 despite the economic sufferings of the Argentine people. The present democratic 'cycle' in Latin America might be longer than it has been in the past.

A few remarks about the impact of the international political system on the military regimes are in order. As stated earlier (p. 253), military regimes usually increase the defence budget and continue to bring in larger and larger amounts of arms from abroad, which helps the military dictators to lengthen their rule. Moreover, the World Bank and organizations related to it prefer military regimes to civilian regimes in disbursing loans and aid (Petras 1981: 81).

Because of the present relaxation of the Cold War between East and West, the superpowers may be less interested in creating situations of 'proxy wars' and may limit the transfer of arms to Third World states: development in this direction will be conducive to the growth of civilian regimes. Similarly, if the international banks in the West change their strategy of bringing about economic development in the Third World states through authoritarian regimes, the occurrence of military *coups d'état* would decline and civilian regimes could be strengthened. However, the basic structural changes needed for the long-term withdrawal of the military from politics are wrought only through a social revolution from within, and not through a revolution imposed from above or outside. Intrastate social forces rather than interstate politics are the crucial variables in permanent military exit from the political arena.

BIBLIOGRAPHY

Barros, A. S. C. and Coelho, E. C. (1981) 'Military intervention and withdrawal in South America', *International Political Science Review* 2 (3): 341–9.

Bienen, H. (1970) 'One-party systems in Africa', in S. Huntington and C. H. Moore, (eds) *Authoritarian Politics in Modern Society*, New York: Basic Books.

Brown, N. (1967) 'The third Arab–Israel war', *World Today* 23: 269–71.

Daadler, H. (1962) *The Role of the Military in Emerging Countries*, The Hague: Mouton.

Decalo, S. (1976) *Coups and Army Rule in Africa: Studies in Military Style*, New Haven: Yale University Press.

Finer, S. E. (1969) *The Man on Horseback: The Role of the Military in Politics*, London: Pall Mall Press.

Fried, R. C. (1966) *Comparative Political Institutions*, London: Macmillan.

Halliday, F. and Molyneux, M. (1983) *The Ethiopian Revolution*, London: Verso.

Halpern, M. (1962) 'Middle Eastern armies and the new middle class', J. J. Johnson (ed.) in *The Role of Military in Underdeveloped Countries*, Princeton: Princeton University Press.

Handelman, H. (1981) 'Postscript', in H. Handelman and T. Sanders (eds) *Military Government and Movement Toward Democracy in South America*, Bloomington: Indiana University Press.

Huntington, S. P. (1965) 'Political development and political decay', *World Politics* 7 (3): 386–430.

——(1969) *Political Order in Changing Societies*, New Haven: Yale University Press.

Jackman, R. W. (1976) 'Politicians in uniform: military government and social change in the Third World', *American Political Science Review* 70 (4): 1078–97.

——(1978) 'The predictability of *coups d'état*: a model with African data', *American Political Science Review* 72 (4): 1262–75.

Jackson, R. H. and Rosberg, C. G. (1984) 'Personal rule: theory and practice in Africa', *Comparative Politics* 16 (4): 421–42.

Janowitz, M. (1964) *The Military in the Development of New Nations*, Chicago: University of Chicago Press.

———(1977) *Military Institutions and Coercion in Developing Nations*, Chicago: University of Chicago Press.

Johnson, J. J. (1964) *The Military and Society in Latin America*, Stanford: Stanford University Press.

Karl, T. (1981) *Petroleum and Political Pacts: The Transition to Democracy in Venezuela*, Working Paper no. 107, Washington, DC: Woodrow Wilson International Center for Scholars, Latin American Program.

Kelleher, C. McA. (ed.) (1974) *Political-Military Systems: A Comparative Perspective*, Beverly Hills: Sage Publications.

Kennedy, G. (1974) *The Military in the Third World*, London: Duckworth.

Kline, H. F. (1979) 'Colombia: modified two-party and elitist politics', in H. J. Wiarda and H. F. Kline (eds) *Latin American Politics and Development*, Boston: Houghton Mifflin.

Kochanek, S. A. (1968) *The Congress Party of India*, Princeton: Princeton University Press.

Linz, J. (1975) 'Totalitarian and authoritarian regimes', in N. Polsby (ed.) *Handbook of Political Science*, vol. 3, London: Addison-Wesley.

Londregan, J. B. and Poole K. T. (1990) 'Poverty, the *coup* trap, and the seizure of executive power', *World Politics* 42 (2): 151–83.

Lowenthal, A. F. (1974) 'Armies and politics in Latin America', *World Politics* 18 (1): 107–129.

McKinlay, R. D. and Cohan, A. S. (1975) 'A comparative analysis of political and economic performances of military and civil regimes: a cross national aggregate study', *Comparative Politics* 8 (1): 1–30.

Malloy, J. M. (1977) *Authoritarianism and Corporatism in Latin America*, Pittsburg: Pittsburgh University Press.

———(1982) *Peru's Troubled Return to Democratic Government*, Report no. 5, Hanover: Universities Field Staff International.

Maniruzzaman, T. (1987) *Military Withdrawal From Politics: A Comparative Study*, Cambridge, Mass.: Ballinger Publications Company.

———(1989) 'Politics: Bangladesh', in *The Cambridge Encyclopedia of India, Pakistan, Bangladesh, Sri Lanka, Nepal, Bhutan and Maldives*, Cambridge: Cambridge University Press.

Morris-Jones, W. H. (1957) *Parliament in India*, London: Longmans Green.

———(1972) 'Pakistan post-mortem and roots of Bangladesh', *Political Quarterly* 43: 187–200.

———(1978) 'India's political miracle', in *Politics Mainly India*, New Delhi: Longman Orient.

Needler, M. C. (1978) 'The logic of conspiracy: the Latin American military coup as a problem in social sciences', *Studies in Comparative International Development* 13 (3).

Nordlinger, E. A. (1970) 'Soldiers in mufti: impact of military rule upon economic and social change in non-Western states', *American Political Science Review* 64 (4): 1131–48.

O'Donnell, G. (1976) 'Modernization and military coups: theory, comparisons and the Argentine case', in A. Lowenthal (ed.) *Armies and Politics in Latin America*, New York: Holme & Meir.

_____(1978) 'Reflections on patterns of change in the bureaucratic-authoritarian state', the *Latin American Research Review* 13 (1): 3–38.

Pauker, G. J. (1959) 'South-East Asia as a problem area in the next decade', *World Politics* 11 (12): 325–45.

Perlmutter, A. (1981) 'The comparative analysis of military regimes: formations, aspirations and achievements', *World Politics* 33 (1): 96–120.

Petras, J. F. (1981) *Class, State and Power in the Third World With Case Studies*, London: Zed Press.

Pye, L. W. (1962) 'Armies in the process of political modernization', in J. J. Johnson (ed.) *The Role of Military in Underdeveloped Countries*, Princeton: Princeton University Press.

Quereshi, S. A. (1979) 'An analysis of contemporary Pakistan politics: Bhutto versus military', *Asian Survey* 19 (9): 910–20.

Razzak, A. (1981) *Bangladesh: State of the Nation*, Dhaka: Dhaka University Press.

Rouqui, A. (1987) *The Military and the State in Latin America*, Berkeley: University of California Press.

Sanders, T. G. (1981) 'The politics of transition', in H. Handelman and T. G. Sanders (eds) *Military Government and the Movement Toward Democracy in South America*, Bloomington: Indiana University Press.

_____(1983) *Argentina's Return to Democracy: Political Economic Perspectives*, Report no. 29, Hanover: Universities Field Staff International.

Schumarcher, E. (1984) 'Argentina and democracy', *Foreign Affairs* 62 (5): 1070–95.

Stepan, A. (1971) *The Military in Politics: Changing Patterns in Brazil*, Princeton: Princeton University Press.

_____(1976) 'The new professionalism of international warfare and military role expansion', in A. F. Lowenthal (ed.) *Armies and Politics in Latin America*, New York: Holmes & Meir.

_____(1988) *Rethinking Military Politics: Brazil and the Southern Cone*, Princeton: Princeton University Press.

Tilly, C. (1985) 'War and the power of warmakers in Western Europe and elsewhere, 1600–1980', in P. Wallenteen, J. Galtung and C. Portales (eds) *Global Militarization*, Boulder: Westview Press.

Weiner, M. (1967) *Party Building in a New Nation: The Indian National Congress*, Chicago: University of Chicago Press.

Young, C. and Turner, T. (1984) 'The rise and decline of the Zaire state', unpublished manuscript.

Zolberg, A. R. (1966) *Creating Political Order: The Party-States of West Africa*, Chicago: Rand McNally.

_____(1968) 'Military intervention in the new states of Africa', in H. Bienen (ed.) *The Military Intervenes: Case Studies in Political Development*, New York: Russell Sage.

PART V

POLITICAL INSTITUTIONS

17

EXECUTIVES

JEAN BLONDEL

National executives are universal. Every country has an executive, a 'government' in the strict sense of the word, as indeed does every other social organization, from the most simple to the most complex. In all these cases there is always a body, normally relatively small, which has the task of running that organization. Indeed, since the third quarter of the twentieth century, independent governments have come to rule practically the whole of the planet: as a result, the number of national executives has more than doubled since the 1940s. The executive is manifestly a focal point, if not *the* focal point of political life. This remains true even if doubts are sometimes expressed about the ability of executives to affect markedly the course of events, let alone alter drastically the social and economic structure of their country. At least they have, more than any other body, an opportunity to shape society; it is indeed their function to do so.

National governments are at the centre of political life; they are also rather compact bodies, whose views and pronouncements are usually well-publicized. Parties and even legislatures are more amorphous; their 'will' is less clear. Because national governments are relatively small and very visible, it is easier to think of them as groups that have a common goal and indeed act as teams, although they may be disunited and their differences may even come out into the open.

Governments do differ markedly from each other, however. They vary in composition, in internal organization, in selection mechanisms, in duration, in powers – both formal and informal. There are autocratic governments, and governments which emanate from the people or from their representatives; there are egalitarian governments and hierarchical governments; there are governments which seem to last indefinitely and ephemeral governments; finally, there are strong and weak governments.

It is difficult to define governments as their boundaries are somewhat unclear. For instance, they often include under-secretaries or junior ministers

– regarded as members of the government as they are appointed by ministers and leave office at the same time as them – but others also fulfil the same conditions, such as the personal staff of ministers. Thus one may have to take junior ministers into account, as well as the personal staff of leaders, since they may play an important part in decision making. This is the case with many of the advisers of the American president or with the members of the Politburo of the Communist Party of the Soviet Union. While governments may have a clear nucleus, composed of the leaders and at least many ministers, a 'grey zone' whose boundaries are not precise forms, so to speak, the 'tail' of these governments.

It might seem easier to define a national executive by the functions that it fulfils. Yet these, too, are somewhat unclear. Governments are expected to 'run the affairs of the nation', but they do so only up to a point, since they are 'helped' or 'advised' by groups, by parties, by the legislature, and, above all, by the very large bureaucracy that all states have now developed. One can distinguish three functions that governments have to fulfil. First, they have to elaborate policies, and to elaborate policies that are realistic in the sense that they can both be implemented and be politically acceptable (if necessary by using compulsion). An agricultural, industrial or social policy will be elaborated on the basis of the perceived 'needs' of the country as well as on the basis of the impression of what the citizens are prepared to 'live with'. There is thus a function of *conception*. Second, governments have a function of *implementation*, at least in so far as they must find the means by which policies can become reality: they must therefore appoint and supervise a bureaucracy that is able to put the policies in operation. This twofold function can create tensions, as there are profound differences between those who 'dream' and those who 'manage'; this means that members of the government must have a combination of different skills. Yet there is also a third function which may be viewed as intermediate, that of *co-ordination*. An important element of the process of policy elaboration consists in ensuring that the policies do not go against each other and that they, ideally, develop harmoniously. Moreover, policy elaboration entails making choices or at least establishing priorities, both for financial reasons and because of constraints in human resources. As not all can be done at the same time, a timetable has to be drawn up; but such a timetable must take into account the interrelationships between policies and the internal logic of policy development.

Conception, co-ordination and direction of implementation are therefore the three elements of governmental action. These elements are analytically distinct: it is the government's duty to combine them. But this combination inevitably raises problems: depending on circumstances, conception, co-ordination and implementation will be given a different emphasis. It is not surprising that the development of governmental structures in the contemporary world should have been the result of a variety of *ad hoc* experiments which have been more or less successful; not surprisingly, too, the conflict between the three goals or functions of government has been solved only to a rather limited extent.

THE EVOLUTION OF GOVERNMENTAL ARRANGEMENTS

Contemporary governmental arrangements reflect the diversity and increasing complexity of the tasks that are being undertaken by executives. The variations in the structure of these executives are not a new phenomenon: the oligarchical arrangements of the Italian republican cities of the Renaissance were at great variance from those of the absolute monarchies which began to emerge during the sixteenth century, and even more from those of the theocratic and despotic governments which existed in the Muslim world at the same time.

Nineteenth-century developments have endeavoured to 'domesticate' governmental arrangements and give them a less haphazard and more rational character. Two constitutional systems have dominated the European and North American scene for a century. On the one hand, the *cabinet system*, which originated in England and in Sweden, is based on the notion that the head of the government, the prime minister, has to operate in the context of a collegial system, in which a group of ministers fully participates in the decision-making process, while also being in charge of the implementation of the decisions in a particular sector. Cabinet government extended gradually to western European countries. In central and eastern Europe, meanwhile, the remnants of absolutism were gradually undermined, to the extent that the cabinet system seemed likely at one point to replace old absolutist and authoritarian governmental structures everywhere.

In contrast to the cabinet system, the *constitutional presidential system* was first established in the United States and then extended gradually to the whole of Latin America. In this model, the executive is hierarchical and not collective: ministers (often named secretaries in this system) are subordinates of the president and responsible only to him or her. Although this formula is closer to that of the monarchical government than that of the cabinet system, it does imply some demotion for both the head of state (who is elected for a period and often not permitted to be re-elected indefinitely) and for the ministers (as these typically have to be 'confirmed' by the legislature). The formula has proved rather unsuccessful in Latin America, however, as many presidents have been uncomfortable with the limitations to their position, leading to *coups* and the installation of authoritarian and even 'absolute' presidential governments.

At least one of the two constitutional formulas had already encountered difficulties prior to 1914. The problems multiplied after the First World

War, with the emergence of the communist system in Russia; authoritarian governments of the fascist variety in Italy and later throughout much of southern, central and eastern Europe; and, after the Second World War, a large number of absolute presidential systems, civilian and military, in many parts of the Third World. These developments were characterized by the emergence or re-emergence of the role of the strong leader, which constitutional systems had sought to diminish, and the consequential decline of the idea, fostered by cabinet government, of collective or at least collegial government. Yet this period was also characterized by the 'invention' of a new form of executive structure, which was consequential on the development of parties but which had not been brought to its ultimate limits in either of the two constitutional systems: this was the intrusion of parties, and in authoritarian systems usually of the single party, into the machinery of government. This type of arrangement has since been used for decades in communist states and, subsequently, in parts of the Third World. Although many communist states have faced major difficulties since the late 1980s, the single party system remains important in accounting for the structure of government, if only as a transitional system. It also led to the development of dual forms of leadership and of government which have played an important part in the characteristics of executives in the contemporary world.

TYPES OF GOVERNMENTAL STRUCTURES IN THE CONTEMPORARY WORLD

Governments can be classified according to two dimensions (Blondel 1982): on the one hand, they can be more or less collective or more or less hierarchical; on the other, they can be concentrated in one body or be divided into two or more. *Cabinet government* is nominally collective and egalitarian: as decisions have to be taken by the whole body, neither the prime minister nor any group of ministers is formally entitled to involve the whole government. The counterpart of this provision is 'collective responsibility', which stipulates that all the ministers are bound by cabinet decisions; in its most extreme form, the rule suggests that ministers are also bound to speak in favour of all the decisions made by the cabinet.

These principles are markedly eroded in practice in nearly all the countries which operate on the basis of cabinet government, i.e. in Western Europe, many Commonwealth countries (Canada, Australia, New Zealand, India, Malaysia, Singapore, most ex-British Caribbean and Pacific islands), Japan and Israel (Blondel and Müller-Rommel 1988: 13–15). In the first instance, following British practice, collective decision making in many of these countries applies only to members of the cabinet *stricto sensu*: the government can be much larger (especially in Britain, where it comprises, in its widest definition, a hundred members or more), because of the existence of substantial numbers of junior ministers. The latter are bound by the principle of collective responsibility but do not share in the decision-making process. Second, the number and complexity of decisions are such that the cabinet cannot physically, during what are normally short meetings of two to three hours a week, discuss all the issues which have to be decided on. As a result, while the cabinet formally ratifies all the decisions, many of these are *de facto* delegated to individual ministers (when they are within the limits of their department), to groups of ministers sitting in committee (the number of which has increased markedly in many cabinet governments), or to the prime minister and some of the ministers (McKie and Hogwood 1985: 16–35). Cabinet government is at most collegial government and in some cases is even hierarchical.

Cabinet governments do vary, however. Some are truly close to being collective, because of a coalition, for instance, or because of political traditions. The prime minister has to rely on a high degree of interchange with colleagues before decisions are taken. In reality this is not a cabinet government in the strict sense, but a collective executive: the Swiss federal council provides the best example, although there are also cases of collective government in the Low Countries and in Scandinavia. 'Team' cabinets are more common among single-party governments, as found in Commonwealth countries, including Britain. In 'team' cabinets, the ministers have often worked together for a number of years in parliament and have broadly common aims and even a common approach. Much is delegated to individual ministers, to committees, or to the prime minister, but there is a spirit of common understanding. Finally, there are 'prime ministerial' governments, in which ministers are noticeably dependent on the head of the government, perhaps, for example, because he or she has considerable popularity arising from substantial and repeated election victories or from the fact that the head of the government has created the party, the regime, or even the country. Such cases have been frequent in the cabinet governments of the Third World (in the Caribbean or in India, for example); they have also occasionally occurred in Western Europe (in West Germany, France, or even in Britain, for example). The relationship between ministers and prime minister in such cases approaches a hierarchy.

The large majority of the other governmental arrangements are *hierarchical*, in that ministers – and any other members of the government – are wholly dependent on the head of the government and head of state: they are appointed and dismissed at will; their decisions are taken by delegation from the head of the government; they play no formal part in policies that do not affect their department. These arrangements were traditionally those of monarchical systems; the constitutional presidential system did not alter this model. The many authoritarian presidential systems which emerged in the Third World after the Second World War also adopted a similar formula: while about fifty governments are of the cabinet type, as many as eighty countries – mainly in the Americas, Africa and in the Middle East – have authoritarian presidential executives.

There are variations in the extent to which these governments are hierarchical, however. In traditional monarchical regimes, members of some families may be very influential, or, in civilian or military presidential regimes, some individuals may have helped the successful head of government to come to power. Indeed, the president of the USA is freer in this respect than most other constitutional presidents, who are more closely dependent on party support. Moreover, the complexity of issues, especially economic and social, obliges many heads of government not merely to appoint some well-known managers or civil servants, but to pay attention to their views to such an extent that these may exercise influence well beyond their own department. This is why it is difficult to regard the US executive as truly hierarchical: it is more accurately described as atomized. Departments are vast and therefore naturally form self-contained empires. Moreover, any vertical relationships which might exist between departmental heads and the president are undermined by the horizontal relationships existing between each department and Congress, and especially with the committees of Congress relevant to the departments, as these want to ensure that they obtain the appropriations which they feel they need and the laws which they promote. Finally, the links which develop between departments and their clientele (the various interest groups that gravitate around each department) tend to reduce further the strength of the hierarchical ties between departments and president. Admittedly, presidents since Roosevelt in the 1930s have appointed increasingly large personal staffs in order to ensure that presidential policies are carried through (Heclo 1977: 166–8). This has meant, however, that it has become difficult to discover what constitutes the 'real' government of the United States. By becoming gradually a government at two levels, the American government thus resembles in part the dual arrangements which prevail in some countries, and in particular in communist states.

The governments that we have considered so far are concentrated in one body. Indeed, traditional analysis always assumed that governments formed one body. Yet this view is questionable. It is questionable in the context of the modern United States; it is even more questionable in the case of communist states, in which the government has traditionally been closely supervised by the party and in particular by the Politburo, whose First Secretary has been generally regarded as the 'true' leader of the country. Indeed, in the Soviet Union, four distinct bodies have traditionally constituted the government, one of which, the Politburo, has been primarily in charge of policy elaboration and is helped by the Secretariat, while the Presidium of the Council of Ministers has been in charge of co-ordination and the Council of Ministers has dealt with implementation. The links between these bodies are achieved through some of the more important ministers and the prime minister (normally a different person from the First Secretary of the party), who belongs at the same time to the Politburo, to the Presidium and, of course, to the Council of Ministers.

Multi-level governments have thus existed for decades in communist states; comparable systems have developed in some non-communist single-party systems and in a number of military regimes. Supreme Military Councils or Committees of National Salvation have been created to ensure that the regular government (often composed of civil servants) carried out the policies of the military rulers. This formula, which originated in Burma in 1962, was adopted by many African states (for example, Nigeria); it also existed for a period in Portugal after the end of the dictatorship in 1974. These arrangements have had a varying degree of longevity and apparent success; they typically have been less systematically organized than in communist states (Blondel 1982: 78–93, 158–73).

GOVERNMENTAL LEADERSHIP

Executives are fashioned by the role of their leaders. Political leadership is highly visible, much talked about, and complex to assess. The visibility of leadership has been markedly enhanced by the development of the mass media, in particular television, but it has always been prominent: great leaders of the Antiquity, of the Renaissance, and of the modern period were all well known to their contemporaries, despite the fact that they could only be seen and heard by relatively small numbers. Their qualities and defects were probably the subject of many conversations; scholarly work was at any rate devoted to them. Indeed, the studies of historians were primarily concerned with the description of their actions, while the concept of leadership began to be analysed.

Leaders can be judged to be good or bad, heroes or villains; but leaders are also seen as more or less successful, more or less effective. The distinction has been made, in this respect, between *leaders*, in the strong sense of the word, and 'mere' 'power-holders' or, perhaps more accurately, 'office-holders' (Burns 1978: 5). It seems intuitively correct to claim that many rulers – probably the large majority – are not very influential, as they appear to do little to modify the course of events, while only a few are great 'stars' who, at least ostensibly, affect profoundly the destiny of humanity. A further distinction has been made in terms of 'great' leaders who shape their society entirely, who 'transform' its character, and of those who are primarily concerned with the functioning of the society and who make compromises and 'transactions' while accepting the framework within which economic, social and political life takes place (Burns 1978). Such a distinction should not be viewed as a dichotomy, but as two poles of a continuous dimension dealing with the 'extent of change' which leaders wish to bring about (Blondel 1987: 10–26). It is in a somewhat similar context that Max Weber introduced the notion of 'charisma', a concept which has been devalued by comparison with the rather strict conception of Weber, but which has played a major part in the contemporary world. This is particularly because, in new countries, alongside the two other Weberian categories of traditional and bureaucratic-legalistic rule, personal rule has been widespread in order to help maintain regimes, and indeed states lacking basic support (Weber 1968: 214).

The scope of activities of rulers is strongly regulated in the context of two types of rulers only, the prime ministers of parliamentary or cabinet systems and the constitutional presidents. The constitutional monarchs who comprise a third category now usually have a purely symbolic role. The position of prime minister is, ostensibly at least, less prestigious than that of president: it exists normally in conjunction with that of a symbolic monarch (as in Britain, most Scandinavian countries, or the Low Countries) or of a symbolic president (as in West Germany, Italy or India). Although these heads of state have few real powers, they exercise ceremonial functions which give them some authority that is denied to prime ministers; this is indeed the reason why a number of Third World prime ministers, in particular in Black Africa, brought about constitutional changes a few years after independence to allow them to become presidents (as in Kenya, Zambia or the Ivory Coast, for example).

Prime ministers have ostensibly limited power because they exercise it in the context of the cabinet which must concur in all decisions but, as we have already noted (p. 271), there are substantial differences in their influence. The power of presidents is also very varied, although, because they run hierarchical governments, presidents by and large exercise major influence. This is particularly the case in authoritarian presidential systems, which constitute the large majority of cases, since the constitutional presidency, apart from in the United States, has only had limited success. Authoritarian presidents – and in particular military rulers, of whom there are about two dozen at any one time in the contemporary world – either operate without any constitution or devise constitutions designed to suit their ambitions: they are sometimes allowed to be re-elected indefinitely (and sometimes are even appointed for life, as in Malawi and earlier in Tunisia). Authoritarian presidents are allowed to dissolve the legislature, and the government depends entirely on them. The spread of these absolute presidencies has coincided with the attainment of independence by many countries, especially in Africa, while in Asia leaders often remained constrained, to an extent at least, by the limitations imposed on prime ministers. Many authoritarian presidents were the first leaders of their country: they were able to build political institutions and to shape these in the way they wished.

Some were close to being 'charismatic' leaders in the full sense that Weber delineated (Weber 1968: 214–15). In the main they relied on strong popular support, as well as on authoritarian practices; they were the 'fathers' of their countries and often remained in office for two decades or more, thereby forming a disproportionately large number of the longest-serving leaders in the contemporary world. The successors of these first leaders generally found it more difficult to rule in such a 'paternal' and absolute manner: in many cases (in Tunisia and Senegal, for instance) the result has been a more 'domesticated' presidency, albeit still rather authoritarian.

An interesting form of executive leadership is constituted by dual leadership (Blondel 1980: 63–73). Single-leader rule is often considered as the norm, yet there are also many cases where it does not obtain. There are examples of government by council, to which the cabinet system is only partly related; there are 'juntas', in particular among provisional Latin American governments, in which a small number of military officers (often drawn from the three branches of the services) rule the country for a period; but there are, above all, a substantial number of cases of dual leadership.

Dual leadership has existed at various moments in history: for example, Republican Rome was ruled primarily by two consuls. Its modern development arose in the first instance from the desire (or the need) of kings to share a part of their burden with a first or prime minister. This occurred partly as a result of popular pressure, and also occurred in highly authoritarian states, from the early seventeenth century in France with Richelieu to the nineteenth century in Austria with Metternich and in Germany with Bismarck. It results both from legitimacy difficulties (when the king needs to associate a 'commoner' to his power), or as a consequence of administrative necessities.

This is why countries as diverse as France or Finland, on the one hand, and communist states on the other, the kingdoms of Morocco and Jordan at one extreme, and the 'progressive' states of Tanzania, Algeria or Libya at the other, have adopted dual leadership. It exists in both liberal and authoritarian systems, in conservative and 'progressive' systems, and in communist and non-communist systems, although in communist states the distinction between party secretary and prime minister makes the distinction particularly strong as it corresponds to the division between party and state which has traditionally characterized these countries.

Dualist systems are often viewed as transitional, but there are enough cases of dual leadership having lasted for many decades to raise doubts about the 'natural' character of single leadership: between a quarter and a third of the nations of the world are ruled by a system of dual rule and in most of these the system has operated in a stable manner. The two leaders may not be equals, indeed quite the contrary, as the distinction between a leader embodying the national legitimacy and a leader embodying the administrative legitimacy suggests, but the complexity of the modern state is such that it is far from surprising that leadership should often have to be shared in order to be effective.

Thus leaders can play very different parts: it is clear that not all these differences stem from the character of the regime. The role of personal characteristics also appears intuitively to be large, but seems to elude precise measurement and even broader assessment (Bass 1981: 43–96). Studies have begun to assess the impact of personality characteristics on national leadership, though much still remains vague. Intelligence, dominance, self-confidence, achievement, drive, sociability and energy have appeared positively correlated with leadership in a substantial number of studies undertaken by experimental psychologists. Recently, attention has been paid in particular to revolutionary leaders, who have been shown to have a number of traits in common, such as vanity, egotism, narcissism, as well as nationalism, a sense of justice and a sense of mission. They are also characterized by relative deprivation and status inconsistency; it was also found that these leaders had marked verbal and organizational skills (Rejai and Phillips 1983: 37–8). Overall, two factors, drive or energy (labelled 'activity' or 'passivity'), and satisfaction with the job (a 'positive' or a 'negative' approach) appear to be essential, as has been shown in the context of American presidents (Barber 1977: 11–14). Although it is difficult to assess the extent to which, under different conditions, leaders can modify the institutions that they need to exercise their power, and although the part that they play in this respect is often overshadowed by the durable and even ostensibly permanent character of these institutions, it is clear that personal factors account markedly in the development of leadership.

THE IMPACT OF LEADERS AND OF GOVERNMENTS

The career of ministers and leaders is short: it lasts on average only four or five years; very few stay in office for ten years or more. Duration was traditionally longer in communist states than elsewhere, except in traditional monarchies, but the changes that took place in the 1980s markedly reduced it in communist countries as well (Blondel 1985). Such short periods in office make it difficult to measure the realization of governments. First, one needs to distinguish between what 'would' have occurred 'naturally' and what occurred because of what the government decided. Second, it is often not possible to relate particular outcomes precisely to particular governments: for instance because the duration of governments is too short (a year or less); because governments 'slide' into one another, so to speak, as with coalitions and with reshuffles; and because of the 'lag' between policy elaboration and implementation. Thus, not surprisingly, conclusions about the impact of governments have remained rather vague and concerned certain broad characteristics of whole classes of executives more than individual cabinets. It has been possible to establish that social democratic governments have, at least in many respects, an impact on social and economic life, despite the view sometimes expressed that no difference could be detected any longer among governmental parties (Castles 1982). It also seems established that, contrary to what some had claimed, Third World military governments do not perform better economically than civilian governments (McKinlay and Cohan 1975). On the other hand, other generalizations often made about governments have not so far been confirmed; in particular, it has not been proved that the instability of ministerial personnel has the negative consequences for social and economic development that it is often said to have (though it may have a negative impact on the regime's legitimacy).

Nor is it easy to establish fully, for the same reasons, the impact of leaders. 'Great' revolutionaries appear to make a major impact; yet they are helped by the fact that the demand for change in their society is strong and thus provides opportunities that are denied to those who rule a society whose members are satisfied with the *status quo*. Thus the efforts of Lenin or Mao were helped by the turmoil prevailing in Russia and China at the time. The impact of leaders must therefore be assessed not only by examining the policies elaborated and implemented by these leaders, but by examining the demands made by the population and in particular by its most vocal elements. Rulers who administer the system as it is and who do not aim at altering policies may be regarded as having very little impact, even though they may be influential by thwarting a substantial demand for change. Meanwhile, rulers who introduce changes on a relatively narrow front need not necessarily have less impact than those who embark on policies designed to alter their society fundamentally. The role of leadership must therefore be assessed by relating the rulers to the ruled and the characteristics of personalities to the climate among the population. It must also be assessed over time: indeed, it may never be fully determined, as it may be exercised on generations as yet not born. It can also fluctuate, as what has been done by a leader can be undone by his or her successors. For example, Mao's policies have been substantially modified, even overturned by those who have followed him. Thus the impact of the founder of the communist regime in the world's most populated country does not appear as great in the 1990s as it was in the 1970s.

It may seem paradoxical to ask if governments matter when so much emphasis is placed on national executives by the media, organized groups and large sections of the public. This paradox is only one of the many contradictory sentiments that governments appear to create. Perhaps such contradictory views are understandable: governments and their leaders both attract and repel because they are at least ostensibly powerful and give those who belong to them an aura of strength, of *auctoritas*, which fascinates, tantalizes, but also worries and, in the worst cases, frightens those who are the subjects and the spectators of political life. Yet there are also other contradictions and paradoxes of governments, from the great complexity of the tasks to be performed to the often ephemeral character of their members, from the many ways in which they can be organized to the ultimate paradox – namely that, in the end, it is almost impossible to know how much they affect the destinies of humankind.

BIBLIOGRAPHY

Barber, J. D. (1977) *Presidential Character*, Englewood Cliffs, NJ: Prentice-Hall.

Bass, B. M. (1981) *Stogdill's Handbook on Leadership*, New York: Free Press.

Blondel, J. (1980) *World Leaders*, London and Los Angeles: Sage Publications.

——(1982) *The Organization of Governments*, London and Los Angeles: Sage Publications.

——(1985) *Government Ministers in the Contemporary World*, London and Los Angeles: Sage Publications.

——(1987) *Political Leadership*, London and Los Angeles: Sage Publications.

Blondel, J. and Müller-Rommel, F. (eds) (1988) *Cabinets in Western Europe*, London: Macmillan.

Burns, J. McG. (1978) *Leadership*, New York: Harper & Row.

Cammack, P., Pool, D. and Tordoff, W. (1988) *Third World Politics*, London: Macmillan.

Castles, F. C. (ed.) (1982) *The Impact of Parties*, London and Los Angeles: Sage Publications.

Cronin, T. E. (1975) *The State of the Presidency*, Boston: Little, Brown & Co.

Finer, S. E. (1962) *The Man on Horseback*, London: Pall Mall Press.

Headey, B. (1974) *British Cabinet Ministers*, London: Allen & Unwin.

Heclo, H. (1977) *A Government of Strangers*, Washington, DC: Brookings Institution.

Holmes, L. (1986) *Politics in the Communist World*, London: Allen & Unwin.

Hook. S. (1955) *The Hero in History*, Boston: Beacon Press.

Kellerman, B. (ed.) (1984) *Leadership*, Englewood Cliffs, NJ: Prentice-Hall.

McKie, T. T. and Hogwood, B. W. (eds) (1985) *Unlocking the Cabinet*, London and Los Angeles: Sage Publications.

McKinlay, R. D. and Cohan, A. S. (1975) 'A comparative analysis of the political and economic performance of military and civilian regimes: a cross national aggregate study', *Comparative Politics* 8 (1): 1–30.

Neustadt, R. (1960) *Presidential Power*, New York: John Wiley.

Rejai, M. and Phillips, K. (1983) *World Revolutionary Leaders*, London and Los Angeles: Sage Publications.

Rose, R. (1984) *Do Parties Make a Difference?*, London: Macmillan.

Smith, G. (1972) *Politics in Western Europe*, London: Heinemann.

Verney, D. V. (1959) *The Analysis of Political Systems*, London: Routledge & Kegan Paul.

Weber, M. (1968) *Economy and Society*, 3 vols, New York: Bedminister Press.

18

LEGISLATURES

G. R. BOYNTON

It is the century of the legislature. Before and after the Second World War, as colonialism failed and nations grew in number, constitutions incorporating a national legislature replaced extant governing institutions throughout the world. In the late 1980s, the political transformation of Eastern Europe was propelled by the rejuvenation of legislative institutions. Instead of control by the communist party, elections for membership in parliament were held in the first free elections since the Second World War. Legislative institutions have spread throughout the world and their influence appears to be on the rise as the twenty-first century approaches.

The viability of legislatures during this half-century has been mixed, however. In democracies with a longer history, legislatures have maintained or even increased their importance within the governing institutions of the country. In some new democracies legislatures have been stable, important institutions of governing. In many new democracies legislatures have suffered a different fate. In Korea, for example, a thirty-five-year period of Japanese colonial occupation was followed by a national election in 1948 to establish the first National Assembly. The president elected under the new constitution soon turned autocratic and suppressed political opposition. A student revolt in 1960 overturned the Syngman Rhee government, and was followed by free elections for the National Assembly. The new government lasted less than two years before it was overthrown by a military junta. Two years later the military junta held elections and had themselves elected to political office (Kim *et al.* 1984). This pattern of military government punctuated by return to democratic elections (principally elections for the National Assembly) has continued in South Korea, and is prevalent in other new nations as well. Pakistan is another example of punctuated military rule; the army has ruled Pakistan for twenty-four of the nation's forty-three years of independence.

This exceedingly brief excursion into legislative history is designed to make two points. First, legislative stability is as puzzling as is the instability of legislative institutions in some of the newer democracies. Even though stability may seem the natural course of affairs for those of us living in relatively stable systems of governing, we are reminded of the presence of something here by its absence elsewhere. The puzzle is: what is present and absent that yields stability in one case and instability in another? The second point worth noting is that elections and legislatures have become the fall-back position. When the generals or colonels find themselves so divided they cannot rule or when they weary of ruling, as has happened at times in Latin America, it is elections and legislatures to which the country returns. Legislatures rarely control the guns, but they have been remarkably resilient in this half-century (Mezey 1985). The change of the fall-back position is a major change in world history. Around the world, legislatures have been elevated to the position that they have held for roughly two hundred years in Europe.

HOW ELECTIONS MATTER

Some are born to office, some rise through military or civilian bureaucracies, and some are elected to office. Election is a distinctive route into the political elite; it is an avenue that distinguishes legislators from most other members of a nation's political elite. An important question to ask about legislatures is how they differ from other governing institutions of a nation because their members are selected by election.

Who is elected?

Are members of legislatures drawn from segments of society different from those that produce other political elites? This question has been more thoroughly investigated and can be answered more confidently than any other question about legislatures. The answer is no. Most legislators are educated, wealthy men from the higher status sectors of society. Donald Matthews (1985) has drawn together the very large body of research on the social background of legislators and discovered that, in the United States, in Western Europe, in the communist nations, in Latin America, Asia and Africa the results are the same: members of the legislature are drawn from the advantaged classes of society. There are only two variations on this theme. In less developed countries with very small elite populations and large populations of poor, the status gap between legislators and electors is greater than in the more developed countries in which the income distribution is more equal. Only in Scandinavia (Skard 1981) and in some communist nations (Hill 1973) do women approach 50 per cent of the membership of legislatures. *Perestroika* has halved the percentage of women in the Supreme Soviet; before the election of 1989 women held approximately 33 per cent of the seats in the Supreme

Soviet, but in the 1989 election they won only 17 per cent of the seats (Mann et al. 1989).

Legislators are drawn from the very same sectors of society from which other elites are drawn (Matthews 1954; Bell et al. 1961; Putnam 1976). Elections produce a legislature that is quite different in its social experiences from the social experiences of the electorate, but legislators are not, in this respect, distinctive from other political elites. Elections may facilitate circulation of the elite, but it is the elite that is being circulated. The impact of elections must be sought elsewhere.

Legislators and the concerns of constituents

In August 1990, the US military was suddenly mobilized to put a large contingent of troops into Saudi Arabia. A young Michigan couple, planning to be married, was separated when he was transferred to South Carolina in transit to Saudi Arabia. Senator Carl Levin of Michigan, a member of the Armed Services Committee and running for re-election, used his good offices to help the couple arrange to be married at the base where the soldier was temporarily stationed. Senator Levin, the couple and the wedding were featured on television in Michigan and on network news. The story is worth recounting as a reflection on the following statement about legislatures:

> Because in many non-Western cultures the political realm is not as well differentiated from the nonpolitical, Third World legislators have had to deal with requests that their Western counterparts seldom confront. . . . In Thailand, legislators reported that they were asked to act as go-betweens in arranging marriages
>
> (Mezey 1985: 743)

Whether in the United States or in the Third World, elections focus legislators' attention on the concerns of their constituents. If the concern is arranging marriages, legislators become involved when only they have the stature required to provide the assistance.

In Tanzania, legislators said bringing the needs of their constituents to the attention of the government was one of their most important tasks (Hopkins 1970). Members of the Colombian Congress said helping their constituents deal with government offices, identifying regional problems and making them public problems, and working as a broker between their constituency and the government were among their most important tasks as legislators (Hoskin 1971). Chilean legislators invested much effort in assisting constituents with a bulky social security bureaucracy and getting local projects into the budget (Valenzuela and Wilde 1979). Legislators in Kenya, Korea and Turkey said they had been effective in channelling resources to their districts (Kim et al. 1984). The picture does not change for the United States (Olson 1967; Fiorina 1977) or Western Europe (Barker and Rush 1970; Cayrol et al. 1976).

Two themes characterizing constituents' concerns are found in the research. One theme is bureaucratic indifference. Getting the social security bureaucracy to acknowledge and deal with the special circumstances of a constituent is as much a part of the working life of members of the US Congress as it is for the Chilean legislator. The second theme is local economic development. Local development may be an access road or a well in Kenya (Barkan 1979) or it may be a nuclear fuel reprocessing plant in the United States. Whether Kenya or the United States, the best possible site is the concern of planners, but the economic development of the constituency is the concern of the elected legislator.

It is plausible that elections predispose legislators to focus on the concerns of constituents to a greater degree than do other political elites, but an unusual feature of the Korean constitution provides more direct evidence on the point. For a brief period the Korean constitution stipulated that two-thirds of the members of the National Assembly would be elected to their offices and one-third would be appointed. The provision virtually guaranteed that the party of the president would have a substantial majority in the National Assembly. It also made it possible for Kim and Woo (1975) to examine differences in the actions of elected and appointed members of the National Assembly. Elected legislators were substantially more likely to engage in constituency service activities than appointed legislators. Elections matter by focusing legislators' attention on the concerns of constituents.

For whom you speak; to whom you speak

Representation is the Anglo-American way of framing this subject. *The Legislative System* (Wahlke *et al.* 1962), which traced its roots directly back to Edmund Burke, was the influential starting point for two strands of research on the connection between elections and government action. The basic conception is representation as the function by which the views of citizens are mapped into public policy; the views of citizens are represented in the policy-making process. One strand of research based on this conception examined the congruence between constituents' opinions and the voting of legislators. The most straightforward statement of this line of research was 'Congress and the public: how representative is one of the other?' (Backstrom 1977). The theme was most systematically carried through in a set of studies employing sample surveys of the electorate and voting in legislatures (Barnes 1977; Converse and Pierce (1986); Miller and Stokes 1963). The second strand followed Wahlke *et al.* (1962), who did not have access to surveys of citizens, by investigating more fully the representative role orientation of legislators. Since this second research strategy could be employed in countries where survey data were not available, a broader range of countries was included in the research (see for example, Hopkins 1970; Hoskin 1971; Kim 1969; Kim and Woo 1975; Mezey 1972).

The result of the research is an understanding of the weaknesses of this way of framing the relationship between elections and governing. There have been many critiques and attempts at reformulation (Boynton and Kim 1991; Eulau and Karps 1977; Pitkin 1967). Three criticisms are particularly important. First, legislators do not seem to play the role in policy making assumed in the theory; this was one finding of the second strand of research. Second, citizens do not do their part; they do not carry around well-formulated views on the broad range of policy matters governments must handle; this was one finding of the first strand of research. Third, when constituents agree it is easy for legislators to represent agreement. When constituents disagree 'representation' is no assistance in specifying what a legislator will or should do, and constituents disagree more than they agree. What is needed is a reformulation that refocuses the importance of elections and that is more descriptively adequate.

The reformulation can begin by noticing that the arguments of elected officials about what the government should do are always made facing in two directions. They address each other; simultaneously they address the electorate. In addressing each other and the electorate they remember who supported them in the last election and they seek additional supporters in the next election. Instead of representation this formulation focuses on appeal for support. Instead of *acting out* the will of the electorate it is *acting to* create a will in the electorate. Frank Baumgartner (1987) argues for this understanding of policy arguments in the French parliament. By reframing issues, issues framed by the government as technical matters, in terms of equality, French cultural heritage and other important symbols in French politics, opposition parties change the focus of the debate, criticize the government, appeal to their supporters and appeal for new supporters. Boynton (1991) showed that even highly technical argument plays a role in forming views in the arguments about clean air. Shanto Iyengar (1990) showed that the framing and reframing of communication can have a substantial impact on how citizens respond. The important point is not the reframing, however. Reframing is rather rare, but it is a striking example of what elected officials do all the time in appealing to voters from the floor of the chamber. And citizens do respond. Elections are held, and in wealthier societies there are interest group organizations and public opinion polls which fill in between elections. Thus, conversation – the appeal of the official and the response of the electorate and the appeal of the electorate and the response of officials – is a better formulation than representation. Elections are important because they engage politicians in conversation with their constituents (Boynton 1990).

How electoral systems matter

In asking how elections matter the organization of elections has not yet been taken into account. There are substantial differences in electoral systems and the differences have consequences for who the constituents are who receive the attention of legislators and for the conversations between legislators and electorates. Three features of electoral systems are particularly important: the rule for determining a winner; the geographic unit for candidates' election; and control of nominations (Duverger 1963; Rae 1971). The three features are combined in many different ways in the nations of the world, but the most important consequences of the three can be treated independently.

Three criteria are widely used in determining the winner of an election. A candidate may need a majority of the votes cast, or a plurality of the votes cast, or parties may be allocated seats based on the proportion of the vote received in the election. Systems requiring a majority or a plurality of votes result in the parties that receive the largest percentage of the votes nationally receiving a larger percentage of the seats in the legislature than their percentage of votes. Parties that receive smaller percentages of votes in the election receive an even smaller percentage of the seats in the legislature. Allocating seats on the basis of the percentage of votes received in the election, known as proportional representation, is less biased in favour of large parties and against small parties in translating votes into seats. The consequence of the counting procedure is reducing or increasing the number of conversations. Small parties do not survive in majority and plurality systems, and the ensuing conversations are limited to the few that do survive.

At one extreme the country may be divided into geographic units with a single legislator elected from each geographic unit; this requires a majority or plurality rule for determining the winner. The other extreme is using the entire country as the geographic unit for counting votes; this requires some form of proportional allocation of seats based on votes. Who the legislators' constituents are is altered by the geographic unit used for counting votes. Constituents will be geographically contiguous residents in one case. In this case local implies geography. If the nation is the geographic unit used, constituents and local have quite different meanings. For example, constituents might become everyone in the nation who is concerned about the state of the environment, wherever they live.

One cannot be elected without first being nominated. Political parties control nominations in almost every country, but there is great variation in how much control is exercised. It is relatively easy for a party organization to control nominations if the electoral system uses proportional representation because that system requires a national list of candidates. Who gets on the list and the placement on the list become very important for election. Election systems based on smaller geographic units, especially if a primary election is used, minimize the control of nomination by parties. This reduces or increases the number of conversations. When parties exercise tight control the legislator who disagrees with the party is easily replaced in the next election, and the number of conversations is reduced. When parties exercise little control the number of conversations proliferate as individual candidates appeal to different groups in the electorate.

LEGISLATURES AND THE ARGUMENT ABOUT WHAT WE SHOULD DO AS A NATION

Politics is the ongoing argument about what we should do as a nation and how it should be done, where the rules by which we argue may themselves become part of the argument. Legislatures, then, are part of the rules by which we argue. A legislature establishes a privileged status in the argument for a subset of the total population – the legislators. They speak in arenas where others cannot and their arguments are attended to in a way that the arguments of others are not. In becoming legislators they speak and listen where others do not go.

Characterizing legislatures as part of the arrangements by which we conduct arguments may thus seem rather odd. After all, it might be said, legislatures pass laws; legislators should busy themselves passing legislation rather than spending their time arguing. It is certainly true that, with few exceptions, constitutions establishing legislatures stipulate that legislation must be passed by the legislature to become law. In this formal sense legislatures throughout the world pass laws. However, if one expects those laws to be initiated by legislators, to be written by legislators, to be substantially modified during consideration and passage by legislators, or that legislators will fail to pass legislation that is initiated and written elsewhere, the expectation does not match what legislatures do. There is a consensus among legislative scholars that legislatures play only a modest role in initiating and writing legislation (Mezey 1985). Distinctions can be drawn, of course. The US Congress is substantially more influential in formulating policy than are other legislatures. The Costa Rican legislature was found to be more important in the formulation of legislation than the Chilean legislature (Hughes and Mijeski 1973). The German Bundestag is more influential in formulating legislation than the British House of Commons, and both are substantially more influential than the legislature of Kenya (Loewenberg and Patterson 1979). But these distinctions are drawn within a very narrow range. What is needed is a different formulation of the role of legislatures in political life of a country; one that is more descriptively adequate.

The earlier discussion of how elections matter leads to thinking about legislatures as the last election, legislators appealing for support from the floor, and the next election – in other words, the argument about what we should do as a nation and how we should do it. In contrast, thinking about the legislature as a law-writing body de-emphasizes elections and the argument. Then scholars and other observers are surprised when 'politics', the next election, intrudes itself into law writing or not law writing in the legislature (Rockman 1985).

Legislatures and the current state of the argument

An election registers the current state of the argument. All parties argue their position on what the nation should do and how it should be done, which in elections becomes who should do it. The current state of the argument, who is persuaded by whom, is registered when voters go to the polls, and the outcome is embodied in persons in offices. How the offices are arranged, particularly the relationship between the legislature and the executive, is important in how the current state of the argument becomes laws.

In some countries the executive, usually called the president, is selected separately from the election of the legislature, but in other countries the executive, usually called prime minister and cabinet, may, or in some cases, must, be members of the legislature. In a survey of fifty-six legislatures Herman and Mendel (1976) found that fourteen prevented members of the legislature from serving in executive offices, seventeen required some or all of the top executive officers to be drawn from the legislature, and that most did not require the executive to be drawn from the legislature.

Embodying the current state of the argument in persons in office is straightforward in a country with a president and an electoral system that produces few political parties in the legislature. The president is elected and appoints his or her administrative officers – cabinet, heads of ministries, etc. – and the executive is in place. Legislative elections usually produce a majority that organizes the legislature. The majority party in the legislature may or may not be the same as the party of the president, but the current state of the argument is registered in a set of officials to continue the argument. In a country in which the executive comes out of the legislature and with an electoral system that produces many political parties in the legislature there is another step in the argument. A government must be created by forming a coalition in the legislature. Only after a coalition government is established is the current state of the argument fully registered in persons in office. These are two widely used organizations of offices. The United States is a notable presidential system. Many of the European democracies are parliamentary systems with the configuration of offices described. But there are many variations on these themes. In Great Britain, for example, the prime minister and cabinet are drawn from parliament, but the electoral system produces few parties in parliament; thus, there is normally a majority party in parliament and the majority party forms the government without the necessity of forming a coalition.

Research on coalition governments provides evidence for the contention that elections register the current state of the argument by embodying that state in offices. The early research, which traced its roots to Riker's (1962) theory of coalitions, assumed that office seeking was all that was at stake in forming the coalitions. From this perspective, the second step in forming a government would reflect the current (electoral) state of the argument only indirectly – only by establishing the distribution of seats before bargaining over the distribution of the spoils of office. But this conception of coalition formation proved inadequate. The inadequacy of the theory was clearest in failing to account for minority coalitions. If office was the major motivation in forming coalitions, the majority of legislators not in the coalition should have formed a government and split the offices between themselves rather than letting a minority have them. Thirty per cent of the cabinets studied were minority cabinets. There is now general agreement among scholars that forming a coalition government is, at least in part, a continuation of the argument about what the nation should do and how (Browne and Franklin 1986; Budge and Laver 1986; Peterson and De Ridder 1986).

Research on coalition governments also provides evidence that the argument is ongoing, that the argument – within and without the legislature – about what the nation should do does not stop with elections. There is great variation in the length of time coalitions survive; some last only a few months and most last fewer than fifty-two months (Dodd 1976). First, researchers attempted to explain the survival of a coalition based on its characteristics when it was formed. From this perspective, the state of the argument at the time of the election would explain how long a coalition lasted. After the election, governing would be a matter of passing laws representing the state of the argument at election time. This cannot be completely discounted, but it is, at best, a partial explanation. More recently researchers have used post-election events to improve their explanations of coalition durability (Browne et al. 1986; Cioffi-Revilla 1984). Events occur subsequent to the election, the argument continues, and the governing coalition is re-formed registering a new state of the argument.

The research on coalition governments is useful in establishing what happens in all legislatures. The need to form coalitions and the breakdown of coalitions puts in public view the processes going on in all legislatures. Go to any legislature and what you will find is ongoing argument about what the nation should be doing and how it should be done – on the floor, in the corridors, in committees or wherever legislators meet.

The level of detail in the arguments

We can have clean air and a sound economy. That is one level of detail in an argument about the health effects of air pollution and the economy; it is roughly the level of detail found in headlines reporting political campaigns. Saying that vehicles are a major source of pollution that causes health problems for persons with asthma and other lung ailments adds more detail to the arguments about the extent of pollution due to vehicles and how debilitating the pollution is for how many people. More detail can be added by specifying the harmful chemicals emitted by vehicles, how much the chemicals would have to be reduced to reduce health effects to an acceptable level, the determination of an acceptable level, how much emission reduction is provided by current catalytic converters, how far emissions could be further reduced with improved catalytic converters, how much improving catalytic converters will cost, how the chemicals that escape in the sale of petrol contribute to the problem, how the pumps could be redesigned and at what cost, how vehicle petrol tanks could be redesigned to reduce the escape of the harmful chemicals, and so on.

The point is simple. Arguments can be, and are, carried on at all of these levels of detail. Laws can be characterized at all of these levels of detail, but law cannot be written at all of the levels of detail. A law that said 'Henceforth there will be clean air' would not tell anyone, vehicle manufacturers for example, what they must do to conform to the law. Laws are full of details that most citizens and most legislators do not know about and do not know enough to evaluate.

The level of detail in the argument is an idea that can be used to integrate the conception of legislatures as arenas of ongoing argument, the institutional arrangements for formulating legislation, and legislators' attention to the concerns of constituents.

Voters may be convinced it is important to clean the air even if it means some additional cost for vehicles or they may be convinced that the health effects do not warrant the costs to the economy, but it is an extremely rare voter who wants to learn about the chemistry of air quality and its regulation in full detail. The arguments in election campaigns are carried on at a modest level of detail, and votes are cast for the party and candidate who seems most likely to do something.

When a government is formed the argument at one level of detail must be transformed into argument at the much more detailed level of legislation. In most countries this is done by the executive and the experts working for government departments. The executive presents the law to the legislature and the majority party members in the legislature or the majority of members who form a coalition vote yes – most of the time. Legislators, generally, do not have the expertise to evaluate the law in detail. The US Congress is unusual because in the permanent committees members develop enough expertise on a subject to argue about the detail (Boynton 1991; Loewenberg and Patterson 1979). Most of the interaction between Congress and the administration takes place in the committee consideration of the legislation. When legislation moves to the full legislature in the United States, as in other countries, the level of argument returns to the level of detail at which elections are conducted. And the prospects of passage of a bill reported by the committee is as high, 85 to 98 per cent depending on the committee, as in other legislatures (Lewis 1978).

Permanent committees also provide the chairman of the committee considering clean air legislation an opportunity to interject the concerns of the vehicle manufacturers in his Michigan constituency into the legislation. It should be noted, however, that the action of the Michigan congressman is not different in kind from the action of the Kenyan legislator who negotiates special arrangements for his district (Barkan 1979), even though the US Congress is taken to be a strong legislature and the Kenyan legislature a weaker one. Many concerns of constituents are *in the detail*. When that is the case legislators become involved in detail.

CONCLUSION

Politics is the ongoing argument about what we should do as a nation and how we should do it. Elections of legislators matter because elections focus the attention of legislators on their constituents and the arguments that are convincing to constituents. Legislatures are a continuation of the argument at a different level of detail.

The arguments that are elections and the arguments that are legislatures are not idle matters. They are arguments that have major consequences for nations and the individuals and organizations that comprise them. Losing an argument may be exceedingly costly. Vehicle manufacturers in the United States, therefore, are prepared to pay as handsomely as the law allows to assist the member of Congress who takes their concerns seriously in his or her re-election campaigns. In other places guns are used to guarantee winning the argument. Bullets beat votes every time – at least in the short-run. Weapons have been used to win arguments throughout human history. What is unusual about this half-century is the spread of substituting votes for bullets in determining the winners and losers of the argument.

REFERENCES

Backstrom, C. H. (1977) 'Congress and the public: how representative is one of the other?', *American Politics Quarterly* 5: 411–36.

Barkan, J. D. (1979) 'Bringing home the pork: legislative behavior, rural development, and political change in East Africa', in L. D. Musolf and J. Smith (eds) *Legislatures in Development*, Durham, NC: Duke University Press.

Barker, A. and Rush, M. (1970) *The British Member of Parliament and His Information*, Toronto: University of Toronto Press.

Barnes, S. H. (1977) *Representation in Italy*, Chicago: University of Chicago Press.

Baumgartner, F. R. (1987) 'Parliament's capacity to expand political controversy in France', *Legislative Studies Quarterly* 12: 33–54.

Bell, W., Hill, R, J. and Wright, C. R. (1961) *Public Leadership: A Critical Review*, San Francisco: Chandler.

Boynton, G. R. (1990) 'Our conversations about governing', unpublished paper.

——(1991) 'When senators and publics meet at the Environmental Protection Subcommittee', *Discourse and Society* 2: 131–56.

Boynton, G. R. and Kim, C. L. (1991) 'Legislative representation as parallel processing and problem solving', *Journal of Theoretical Politics* 3 (4).

Browne, E. C. and Franklin, M. (1986) 'New directions in coalition research', *Legislative Studies Quarterly* 11: 469–83.

Browne, E. C., Frendreis, J. P. and Gleiber, D. W. (1986) 'The process of cabinet dissolution: an exponential model of duration and stability in Western democracies', *American Journal of Political Science* 30: 628–50.

Budge, I. and Laver, M. (1986) 'Office seeking and policy pursuit in coalition theory', *Legislative Studies Quarterly* 11: 485–506.

Cayrol, R., Paroid, J.-L. and Ysmal, C. (1976) 'French deputies and the political system', *Legislative Studies Quarterly* 1: 67–99.

Cioffi-Revilla, C. (1984) 'The political reliability of Italian governments: an exponential survival model', *American Political Science Review* 78: 318–37.

Converse, P. E. and Pierce, R. (1986) *Political Representation in France*, Cambridge, Mass: Belknap Press.

Dodd, L. C. (1976) *Coalitions in Parliamentary Government*, Princeton: Princeton University Press.

Duverger, M. (1963) *Political Parties*, New York: John Wiley.

Eulau, H. and Karps, P. D. (1977) 'The puzzle of representation: specifying components of responsiveness', *Legislative Studies Quarterly* 2: 233–54.

Fiorina, M. P. (1977) *Congress: Keystone of the Washington Establishment*, New Haven: Yale University Press.

Herman, V. and Mendel, F. (eds) (1976) *Parliaments of the World*, London: Macmillan.

Hill, R. J. (1973) 'Patterns of deputy selection to local soviets', *Soviet Studies* 25: 196–212.

Hopkins, R. (1970) 'The role of the MP in Tanzania', *American Political Science Review* 64: 754–71.

Hoskin, G. W. (1971) 'Dimensions of representation in the Colombian National Legislature' in W. H. Agor (ed.) *Latin American Legislatures: Their Role and Influence*, New York: Praeger.

Hughes, S. W. and Mijeski, K. J. (1973) *Legislative–Executive Policy-Making: The Case of Chile and Costa Rica*, Sage Research Papers in the Social Sciences, Comparative Legislative Studies Series no. 90–007, Beverly Hills: Sage Publications.

Iyengar, S. (1990) 'Framing Responsibility for Political Issues: The Case of Poverty', *Political Behavior* 12: 19–40.

Kim, C. L. and Woo B.-K. (1975) 'Political representation in the Korean National Assembly', in G. R. Boynton and Kim C. L. (eds) *Legislative Systems in Developing Countries*, Durham, NC: Duke University Press.

Kim, C. L., Barkan, J., Turan, I. and Jewell, M. (1984) *The Legislative Connection: The Politics of Representation in Kenya, Korea, and Turkey*, Durham, NC: Duke University Press.

Kim, Y. C. (1969) 'Role orientations and behavior: the case of Japanese prefectural assemblymen in Chiba and Kanagawa', *Western Political Quarterly* 22: 390–410.

Lewis, A. L. (1978) 'Floor success as a measure of committee performance in the House', *Journal of Politics* 40: 460–7.

Loewenberg, G. L. and Patterson, S. C. (1979) *Comparing Legislatures*, Boston: Little, Brown & Co..

Mann, D., Monyak, R. and Teague, E. (1989) *The Supreme Soviet: A Biographical Directory*, Washington, DC: Center for Strategic and International Studies.

Matthews, D. R. (1954) *The Social Background of Political Decision-Makers*, New York: Random House

——(1985) 'Legislative Recruitment and Legislative Careers', in G. Loewenberg, S. C. Patterson and M. E. Jewell (eds) *Handbook of Legislative Research*, Cambridge, Mass.: Harvard University Press.

Mezey, M. L. (1972) 'The functions of a minimal legislature: role perceptions of Thai legislators', *Western Political Quarterly* 25: 686–701.

——(1985) 'The functions of legislatures in the Third World', in G. Loewenberg, S. C. Patterson, M. E. Jewell (eds) *Handbook of Legislative Research*, Cambridge, Mass.: Harvard University Press.

Miller, W. E. and Stokes, D. E. (1963) 'Constituency influence in Congress', *American Political Science Review* 57: 45–56.

Olson, K. G. (1967) 'The service function of the United States Congress', in A. de Grazia (ed.) *Congress: The First Branch of Government*, Garden City, NY: Doubleday.

Peterson, R. L. and De Ridder M. M. (1986) 'Government formation as a policy-making arena', *Legislative Studies Quarterly* 11: 565–81.

Pitkin, H. (1967) *The Concept of Representation*, Berkeley: University of California Press.

Putnam, R. D. (1976) *The Comparative Study of Political Elites*, Englewood Cliffs, NJ: Prentice-Hall.

Rae, D. W. (1971) *The Consequences of Electoral Laws*, New Haven: Yale University Press.

Riker, W. (1962) *The Theory of Political Coalitions*, New Haven: Yale University Press.

Rockman, B. A. (1985) 'Legislative–executive relations and legislative oversight', in G. Loewenberg, S. C. Patterson and M. E. Jewell (eds) *Handbook of Legislative Research*, Cambridge, Mass.: Harvard University Press.

Skard, T. (1981) 'Progress for women: increased female representation in political elites in Norway', in C. F. Epstein and R. L. Coser (eds) *Access to Power: Cross-National Studies of Women and Elites*, London: Allen & Unwin.

Valenzuela, A. and Wilde, A. (1979) 'Presidential politics and the decline of the Chilean Congress', in L. D. Musolf and J. Smith (eds) *Legislatures in Development*, Durham, NC: Duke University Press.

Wahlke, J. C., Eulau, H., Buchanan, W. and Ferguson, L. C. (1962) *The Legislative System*, New York: John Wiley.

FURTHER READING

Boynton, G. R. and Kim C. L. (eds) (1975) *Legislative Systems in Developing Countries*, Durham, NC: Duke University Press.

Fenno, R. F. (1966) *The Power of the Purse: Appropriations Politics in Congress*, Boston: Little, Brown & Co.

Fiorina, M. (1977) *Congress: Keystone of the Washington Establishment*, New Haven: Yale University Press.

Kim, C. L., Barkan, J., Turan, I. and Jewell, M. (1984) *The Legislative Connection: The Politics of Representation in Kenya, Korea, and Turkey*, Durham, NC: Duke University Press.

Loewenberg, G. L. and Patterson, S. C. (1979) *Comparing Legislatures*, Boston: Little, Brown & Co.

Loewenberg, G. Patterson, S. C. and Jewell, M. E. (eds) *Handbook of Legislative Research*, Cambridge, Mass.: Harvard University Press.

Matthews, D. R. (1960) *US Senators and Their World*, Chapel Hill: University of North Carolina Press.

Mayhew, D. R. (1974) *Congress: The Electoral Connection*, New Haven: Yale University Press.

Musolf, L. D. and Smith, J. (eds) *Legislature in Development*, Durham, NC: Duke University Press.

Polsby, N. (1968) 'The institutionalization of the US House of Representatives', *American Political Science Review* 62: 144–68.

Rae, D. W. (1971) *The Consequences of Electoral Laws*, New Haven: Yale University Press.

Wahlke, J. C., Eulau, H., Buchanan, W. and Ferguson, L. C. (1962) *The Legislative System*, New York: John Wiley.

19

COURTS

JOHN SCHMIDHAUSER

A court is a judicial institution created to decide legal disputes authoritatively. Modern courts are usually independent of other branches of government, but in historical perspective many of the attributes associated with judicial independence, legal professional competence and objectivity were absent or considerably modified during the many centuries of judicial institutional development which preceded the emergence of courts in the variety of contemporary legal systems of the world. Martin Shapiro has correctly observed that analysts of the attributes of courts frequently employ some sort of a model of an ideal judicial system (Shapiro 1981: 1). Of these, Max Weber's conceptual model is seminal. In accordance with the major elements of his ideal model, a court will be staffed by specially trained judges whose professional integrity and independence is ensured by fundamental constitutional safeguards. Such courts are integral parts of bureaucratic systems designed to ensure predictability and rationality. Historians such as Charles Ogilvie have traced the origins of one of the major European families of law to monarchical influence (Ogilvie 1958). Thus law common to the realm in England was not only judgemade law; it was the monarch's law. In contrast, Weber classified courts in relation to three basic types of governing regimes – traditional, charismatic and 'legal' or constitutional. In Weber's view, courts within each of these categories would be organized in accordance with the nature of the governing regime. Law in a traditional regime would originate in custom, be administered in courts staffed by judges chosen ascriptively, and render decisions in accordance with custom. In a charismatic regime, law would originate in the will of a charismatic leader and decisions would conform to the particularistic approach of such a leader. Conversely, in a constitutional regime, law would originate objectively on the basis of impartial constitutional or statutory standards, in courts staffed by judges chosen on merit after extensive professional training, and decisions would be rendered objectively upon the basis of universally applied rules and fair procedures (Trubek 1972: 735).

In reality, courts, judges and entire legal and judicial systems do not conform perfectly to such conceptual models either contemporaneously or historically. Modern courts and judicial systems often vary in accordance with legal cultural attributes rather than symmetrical conceptual models. The basic differences in court organization, judicial training, internal institutional procedures and professional organization among major families of law illustrate major cultural variations which do not conform to Weber's model. Similarly, the wide historic variations in the scope of executive authority over courts and in the presence or absence of legal professionals in courts in Western Europe modifies notions about centralized control (Dawson 1960: 35–117).

The key attributes of courts vary among the major families of law in a number of important respects. Two such families originated in Western Europe and subsequently became influential in other countries when introduced as part of the conquests and colonial expansions of Spain, Portugal, France, Great Britain, the Netherlands and, to a lesser extent, other European nations. The common law system originated in Great Britain, while the civil law family was developed on the basis of vestiges of Roman law in portions of Western Europe. Civil law's emphasis upon codification received its greatest fulfilment early in the nineteenth century from Napoleon Bonaparte (Abraham 1986: 267). Conventional analyses of the common law and civil law traditions generally emphasize certain fundamental differences between them with respect to the nature of courts, the role of judges, the significance of *stare decisis* or the rule that precedents are controlling, judicial independence, the role of lawyers, and the very sources of law itself (Zweigert and Kotz 1977).

In civil law systems, the source of law is the law-making authority, not the judges themselves. Conversely, in common law systems it is the judges operating independently. Thus in parliamentary civil law systems, law is the expression of legislative will. In an absolute monarchy, it is the expression of the monarch's will. The development of legal concepts in civil law, more often than not, reflected the significant influence of the law faculties of major universities: legal treatises were often very influential in medieval times. The advent of rigorous codification of the civil law in the Napoleonic era was expected to diminish the influence of legal scholars, but the role of law faculties in analysis of the modern codes and in commentaries on legislative reform of elements of the civil law is still important in most civil law nations, including France itself. In contrast, while scholarly commentary in common law nations is widespread, traditionally the main thrust of legal change or calculated continuity in most common law nations is still judge-determined or, in modern times, legislatively enacted and judicially interpreted. Historically, the universities in Great Britain had a far smaller role in legal commentary and virtually no role in training lawyers. The latter function was pre-empted by the Inns of Court for barristers and by provincial training centres for solicitors. Barristers were the only lawyers qualified to take part in the adversary process before higher British judges and also the only lawyers eligible for selection as judges of the higher courts (Abel and Lewis 1988: 1, 39).

The organization, procedures and composition of courts generally comprise attributes directly related to the characteristics of the major family of law from which a judicial system is derived. To illustrate the relationship of judicial system and historic family of law, some of the key attributes of the court systems of Great Britain and France, archetypes of the common law and civil law systems are described both in their nation of origin and in selected colonial and post-colonial settings. Court organization may mirror not only certain basic characteristics of the family of law, but of the fundamental political organization and historical experience of each nation as well. Thus the hierarchy of courts in Great Britain embodies organizational principles which reflect centuries of monarchical efforts at national unification, while the court system of Canada incorporates most elements of its colonial British heritage modified in certain limited aspects by its national commitment to federalism. Bora Laskin, a Chief Justice of the Supreme Court of Canada, suggested that there are five general court organizational models widely employed in modern judicial systems. One is the English model under a unitary system in which a national appellate court of general jurisdiction functions in a manner similar to a British criminal or civil Court of Appeal or, ultimately for domestic British cases, the House of Lords, 'not limited to any class of cases' (Laskin 1975: 47). A second model, of which the Supreme Court of the United States provides an example, is a higher appellate court in a federal system in which there are explicit constitutional or statutory jurisdictional powers and limitations like those in Article III, section 2, of the Constitution of the United States. With this model a major jurisdictional responsibility involves cases or controversies between a government of an entire nation and governments of its political subdivisions such as the American states, Canadian provinces, or Swiss cantons. But, in addition, a court such as the Supreme Court of the United States has some designated original jurisdiction and broad appellate jurisdiction over all matters of constitutional import. Laskin cites a third model, based on British Commonwealth experience, in which a higher appellate court is 'purely federal', dealing only with constitutionally or statutorily designated issues but excluding other constitutional issues which could be dealt with by direct appeal to the Judicial Committee of the British Privy Council (ibid.: 47). The fourth model consists of 'a purely constitutional court', presumably with no jurisdiction embracing statutory interpretation. Laskin's fifth model is adapted from France's Court of Cassation, with one chamber devoted to issues of federalism and a second to other constitutional issues (ibid.: 47–8).

Laskin's emphasis upon distinctions between unitary and federal systems as a means of classifying courts underscores that courts were frequently created and maintained to fulfil purposes more complex than the ideal of impartial dispute resolution. For example, the difficult task of choosing a final arbiter in American federal–state relations necessitated a series of compromises by the delegates to the Philadelphia Convention of 1787 which resulted in the creation of a Supreme Court designated as final arbiter after executive (Alexander Hamilton's recommendation) and legislative ('the Congressional negative' recommended by several Federalists) supremacy were rejected by anti-Federalist delegates. 'Judicial power' was defined in a manner to provide an enduring compromise between nationalist-oriented Federalists and states-rights-oriented anti-Federalists. Many of the former supported the concept of a Supreme Court as final arbiter, but feared it would be too weak to restrain states rights influence. Many of the latter also supported the Supreme Court but harboured misgivings as to whether a nationalistic Supreme Court would ultimately erode the rights of the states. The classic conflict of views between Alexander Hamilton in *Federalist* no. 80 (Cabot Lodge 1904: 494–5) and Robert Yates in his 'Letters of Brutus', especially numbers 11, 12 and 15 (Corwin 1938: 231–3, 237–43, 251–2), set the stage for decades of debate over the role of the American Supreme Court in federal–state relations and in governmental affairs in general (Corwin 1938).

Bora Laskin quite appropriately emphasized federalism as a key organizing principle for some higher appellate courts. From this perspective many of the characteristics of the courts chosen for the delicate task of maintaining a constitutional or statutory federal division of powers and responsibilities include jurisdictional power sufficient to maintain a constitutionally ordained delineation of the superior role of a national government in designated subject matter areas such as the provision of the Supremacy Clause of the Constitution of the United States stating that 'This Constitution, and the Laws of the United States which shall be made in Pursuance thereof; and all Treaties made, or which shall be made, under the Authority of the United States, shall be the supreme Law of the Land' (Article VI, section 2, 1789). Or conversely, the jurisdiction of an appellate court may reflect a broad empire-unifying role such as that fulfilled for centuries by the Judicial Committee of Great Britain's Privy Council. Similarly, the composition of courts linked to federalism sometimes incorporates fundamental accommodations designed to protect or to reassure ethnic, linguistic populations, such as the requirement that three of the members of Canada's nine-member Supreme Court be members of the French-speaking minority (Snell and Vaughan 1985: 12), or Switzerland's informal but consistently recognized policy of including members of each of the three major linguistic groups in the nation – German, French and Italian – on the Federal Court.

For many nations federalism is not an important organizing principle. Instead, courts are organized and operated in accordance with prevailing political, economic and social power. Nowhere is this more evident than in the long-term legal cultural relationship of colonial nations and their former colonies. Conversely, the organization of courts in nations which remained free of external domination is determined largely by internal domestic experiences, often of long historic duration. Sweden provides a good example. In a lecture at the University of Lund in Sweden, Nils Stjernquist (1989), Professor Emeritus of Political Science and former *Rector Magnificus* of the University of Lund, analysed the historic and contemporary reasons why judicial review in Sweden is limited and, when asserted by Swedish justices and judges, utilized with great restraint. First, federalism is not a factor in Swedish political development. Sweden was and is a unitary system. Second, the role of Swedish courts is shaped by centuries of earlier Swedish monarchical absolutism under which the monarch was supreme in two major categories of law – as monarch in council, the origin of modern Swedish administrative law, and as monarch in court, the origin of the modern Swedish judicial system. After the fundamental constitutional changes of the nineteenth century, the Swedish monarch no longer had a significant role in either category of law, but the basic distinction between administrative and judicial decision making has been maintained in the modern Swedish legal system. To some extent, Swedish administrative and judicial decision makers generally continue to view themselves as enforcers of governmental administrative, statutory and constitutional authority. There has been a gradual and increasing emphasis upon individual rights. But the historic balance generally was toward governmental authority. In the context of such a tradition extending over several centuries, it is hardly surprising that most Swedish judges and administrative decision makers are strongly oriented towards restraint. Such restraint, more often than not, takes the form of deference to the Riksdagen, the Parliament of Sweden, the successor in ultimate legal authority to the absolute monarch of earlier centuries (Stjernquist 1989).

The ideal conception of a court or a system of courts embodies the notion of impartiality, but the relationship of litigants in many courts and legal controversies is sometimes determined by power rather than legal objectivity. Historically, military conquest and its immediate and long-term consequences have provided the most dramatic examples of judicial and legal bias and partiality. Modern analysts of courts such as Alan Christelow (1985) and Hans S. Pawlisch (1985) documented and critically evaluated the uses of law and courts as instruments of cultural imperialism. Pawlisch carefully examined the relationship of Western European legal development of thirteenth-century canon law doctrines of warfare and conquest to its applications by Spain, Portugal, France, the Netherlands and Great Britain in conquests of the fifteenth, sixteenth , seventeenth, eighteenth and nineteenth centuries in which non-Western legal cultures were destroyed or seriously limited. He then examined the particular application of such legal doctrines by the British in their conquest of the Irish in Tudor and Cromwellian periods (Pawlisch 1985). Christelow documents French legal imperialism in colonial Algeria in which law was used as an instrument of subjugation, of maintaining civil order, as a subtle means of religious and racial discrimination, and as a mode of property redistribution from the indigenous Muslim Arabic population to the nine-teenth- and early twentieth-century Christian settlers from France (Christelow 1985). Similarly, courts which have been granted transnational jurisdiction have, on occasion, been charged with partiality to the legal and economic interests of the most powerful nations. In the post-Second World War era, jurists from Third World nations have not only challenged the law imposed by colonial nations such as Portugal (Isaacman and Isaacman 1982) but have also criticized the alleged Eurocentric, pro-colonial bias of international law (McWhinney 1987).

Whether a nation experienced long colonial domination or not is a key question in the determination of the organization and structure of courts, family of law, mode of training of judges and lawyers and supporting court personnel, and scope of judicial power or jurisdictional characteristics. For the relatively few nations largely free of external legal imperialism there are several major issues influencing the development of these judicial attributes. Chief among these are:

1 whether the nation is organized as a federal or unitary system as suggested by Laskin;
2 the characteristics of the internal structure of overall government organiz-ation;
3 the historical factors unique to each nation;
4 the relationship of the judiciary to democracy;
5 the relationship of judicial power to either parliamentary supremacy, or to excessive executive authority such as monarchical absolutism or military dictatorship; and
6 the special role of higher appellate courts in those nations in which judicial review, the power to determine the constitutionality of the enactments of legislature or actions of chief executives, is exercised.

The characteristic basic to all common law nations, that judges make law rather than apply a monarchically ordained (historic) or legislatively enacted (modern) code has, of course, been gradually modified in reality by the nine-teenth- and twentieth-century growth of statutory law in these common law nations. Virtually all former British colonies, including Australia, Canada, India, Israel, New Zealand, Pakistan and the United States, utilize some variation of the common law. In some of these common law nations in which there has emerged a written constitution whose provisions are designated as superior to those of ordinary legislative enactments, judges and higher appellate justices have exercised judicial power considerably greater than in most common law nations. The United States is the most important example, especially since Chief Justice John Marshall rendered his pivotal decision defining and justifying the doctrine of judicial review in *Marbury* v. *Madison* (1803: 137). It has been suggested that Canada, after the adoption of its constitutional Charter of Rights and Freedom in 1982, will increase its judicial review activities (McWhinney 1982).

Judicial review, the power of judges to declare unconstitutional the enactments of legislatures and actions of chief executives and their subordinates and administrators, is the very highest exercise of judicial authority. Courts possessing such power thus play a much broader role in national governmental affairs than those which do not. Indeed, in a number of historic periods of considerable judicial activism in the United States such as the early New Deal era of the 1930s, the American Supreme Court was characterized as exercising judicial supremacy. By contrast, the British courts, including those at the apex of British judicial hierarchy, defer to the supremacy of Parliament. Within the common law family of law, judicial review is generally found in those nations which are federal rather than unitary, notably Australia, Burma, Canada, India and Pakistan. Historically, nations with courts organized in accordance with the civil law family of law rarely incorporated judicial review as part of the judiciary's power (see below). Perhaps the major pre-1940 exception was Switzerland, a civil law nation, which utilized judicial review in its Federal Court to assess cantonal legislation.

After the Second World War, several civil law nations, whether organized as federal or unitary systems, adopted some form of judicial review. Japan, a unitary system, and West Germany, a federal system, made the change under American influence during the post-war military occupation. Austria and Italy also responded with limited forms of judicial review in the aftermath of the war. France also made a post-war change toward limited review. All the later three are unitary systems. Japan's Supreme Court comprises fifteen members including a Chief Justice. Except for occasional *en blanc* sessions, the court meets regularly in three panels of five judges each. In accordance with centuries of tradition and practice in continental European civil law systems from which Japan's system was derived in the Mejii era (French to some extent, but primarily German civil law of the era of the Imperial German Empire), Japanese judges and justices (with a few exceptions among the latter) are trained separately from attorneys as career judges. Compulsory retirement of members of the Japanese Supreme Court at the age of seventy has resulted in an inadvertent limitation on the influence of Japanese Chief Justices. Because elevation to Chief Justice is determined by seniority of service on the Court, Japanese justices generally reach that office late in their careers, often near compulsory retirement age. Thus, long tenure in that post, similar to the more than three decades experienced by American Chief Justices John Marshall and Roger B. Taney, is largely unattainable for Japanese justices. Indeed, their average tenure between 1947 and 1980 was approximately four years (Hayakawa and Schmidhauser 1987: 219).

France is the only nation in this group that adopted limited judicial review which was not subject to Allied military occupation at the conclusion of the Second World War. Its voluntary adoption of judicial review was very guarded and did not apply to courts within the regular administrative and judicial court systems of the nation. The framers of the Constitution of the Fourth Republic created a Constitutional Committee chaired by the President of the Republic and composed of the Presidents of the National Assembly and Council of the Republic plus seven members chosen by the Assembly and thereby the Council. Its role was to ensure that suggested legislation of questionable constitutionality did not become law without a constitutional amendment. This committee could not act unless requested to do so by the President of the Council of the Republic and an absolute majority of the Council. When the de Gaulle Constitution of 1958 was adopted, a Constitutional Council was created, composed of all ex-presidents of France plus nine notable individuals, three of whom are chosen by the presidents of the Republic, of the Senate, and of the National Assembly. This Council, each member usually a lawyer, may declare unconstitutional ordinary and organic laws, treaties and protocols. Despite the scope of the powers, the ability to challenge is denied to individual citizens and most groups. Access to it is limited and complicated (Abraham 1986: 310–12).

West Germany created a Federal Constitutional Court (Bundesverfassungsgericht) in 1951. It consists of sixteen judges chosen by the two houses of the legislature (the Bundestag and the Bundesrat). It meets in two chambers (Senates) and has proved considerably more assertive than its originators anticipated in major decisions such as its 1966 Political Party Finance decision and its 1975 Abortion decision (20 BVerFGe 56–59, 119, 134 and 39 BVerFGe 1–95). Austria's Constitutional Court (Verfassungsgerichtshof) was reinstated in 1945 (it had been established in 1920 and eliminated by the Nazis). It has fourteen members appointed by the president of the Republic based in part upon legislative recommendations. Since the 1970s Austria's Constitutional Court has also become more assertive, developing along the same lines as that of West Germany. Italy's Corte Constituzionale was authorized in 1948 but actually functioned as a court from 1956. This fifteen-member Constitutional Court is, indeed, the ultimate interpreter of the Italian Constitution of 1948. Thus, it is technically superior to Italy's regular higher judicial and administrative courts – the Court of Cassation, the Council of State, and the Court of Accounts. In fact, the Constitutional Court has been characterized as a very restrained tribunal albeit composed for the most part of mature individuals with extensive careers as experienced judges, attorneys, or law professors.

Despite the great attention often given to courts which exercise judicial review, the seemingly more prosaic regular judicial and administrative courts typical of the nations comprising the major families of law are basically the prototypes within the common law, civil law, religious (most importantly Islamic), and socialist families. Furthermore, the regular court systems of major colonial powers often served as models for court systems imposed upon regions or subject nations. Several broad features distinguished these systems. France, as one of the most influential of the civil law nations, imposed its legal system throughout the world, particularly during the nineteenth and early twentieth centuries, first through Napoleon Bonaparte's codification of French civil law, its dissemination in the wake of his continental military successes, and, after his final defeat, the general acceptance of versions of his code in many areas of Western Europe that had rejected his military regime. After Napoleon Bonaparte, France as a major colonial power spread its code and major portions of its court organization, its mode of legal training, and legal professional organization throughout the world. Because France at the height of its colonial influence generally incorporated its colonies as part of metropolitan France, its impact upon law in its colonies was intensive and enduring. One of the main features of French court organization is the distinction between regular judiciaries and administrative tribunals, a distinction generally not present in the English and American judicial systems. At the apex of the regular French judicial system is the Court of Cassation, a supreme court of appeal. This court does not have original jurisdiction, nor does it retry cases appealed to it. It does determine, however, the accuracy of decisions rendered by a lower court and, in the event that inaccuracy is found, remands the case to a court of similar jurisdiction and rank for retrial. If after a second appeal inaccuracy is again found, the Court of Cassation will render a determinative final decision. Below the Court of Cassation are the Courts of Appeal with civil and criminal jurisdiction plus jurisdiction for appeals from a variety of special courts including juvenile and rent tribunals. Civil appeals arise from Courts of Instance (original jurisdiction) to Courts of Major Instance (original and appellate jurisdiction). On the criminal side, Police Courts deal with minor transgressions, correctional tribunals have jurisdiction over lesser criminal offences, and the Courts of Assize deal with major criminal cases.

France's administrative tribunals consist of one level of Regional Councils of Administrative Tribunals and, at the centre of this system, the Council of State established initially by Napoleon Bonaparte in 1797. This Council has seven divisions, only one of which, the Litigation Section, is concerned with Administrative Law. The others deal with a range of administrative and legislative drafting and advisory opinions on executive and legislative matters. The Council, staffed by career civil servants, a large proportion of whom are graduates of the prestigious National School of Administration, has a role in France not replicated by any institution in the United States or Great Britain. Furthermore, just as French administrative judges are products of an exceptionally fine and intensive specialized education system, so too are regular French judges who are trained as civil servants and career jurists in a manner distinguished from the regular education of lawyers.

In the modern era of the twentieth century it was generally assumed that the courts and judges within the major common law and civil law legal systems had achieved a high level of independence from political control and a similarly high level of professional competence and ethical integrity. But the particular political circumstances within each nation were often determinative, rather than the historic traditions of each family of law. Thus, civil law nations like Germany in the 1930s or a number of Latin American nations lost judicial independence and professionalism to dictators like Adolf Hitler or to military juntas (Kirschheimer 1961; Becker 1970). Similarly, Italy lost both its judicial independence and a large measure of its judicial integrity during the fascist years of Benito Mussolini when judges were often politically controlled by the state and corrupted by private monetary inducements (Calamandri 1956). The example cited most often of the erosion of judicial independence in the twentieth century is Soviet Russia. The civil law system of its predecessor, the Tsarist absolute monarchy, was hardly a model of judicial independence, and a major feature of Tsarist absolutism and judicial control, the Procurer General, was adapted to Soviet needs by the early 1920s (Berman 1963).

In sum, modern courts often mirror the social conditions and political realities of their nations. Yet, in many jurisdictions throughout the world, judicial objectivity and independence is closer to achievement than in earlier eras.

REFERENCES

Abel, R. L. and Lewis, P. S. C. (eds) (1988) *Lawyers in Society, vol 1: The Common Law World*, Berkeley: University of California Press.

Abraham, H. J. (1986) *The Judicial Process: An Introductory Analysis of the Courts of the United States, England and France*, 5th edn, New York: Oxford University Press.

Becker, T. L. (1970) *Political Trials*, Indianapolis: Bobbs-Merrill.

Berman, H. J. (1963) *Justice in Russia: An Interpretation of Soviet Law*, New York: Random House.

Cabot Lodge, H. (ed.) (1904) *The Federalist*, New York: G. P. Putnam's Sons.

Calamandri, P. (1956) *Procedure and Democracy*, New York: New York University Press.

Christelow, A. (1985) *Muslim Law Courts and the French Colonial State in Algeria*, Princeton: Princeton University Press.

Corwin, E. S. (1938) *Court Over Constitution*, Princeton: Princeton University Press.

David, R. and Brierley, J. (1985) *Major Legal Systems in the World Today: An Introduction to the Comparative Study of Law*, 3rd edn, London: Stevens & Sons.

Dawson, J. (1960) *A History of Lay Judges*, Cambridge, Mass.: Harvard University Press.

Hayakawa, T. and Schmidhauser, J. R. (1987) 'Comparative analysis of the internal procedures and customs of the Supreme Courts of Japan and the United States', in J. R. Schmidhauser (ed.) *Comparative Judicial Systems: Challenging Frontiers in Conceptual and Empirical Analysis*, London: Butterworth.

Isaacman, B. and Isaacman, A. (1982) 'A socialist legal system in the making: Mozambique before and after independence', in R. L. Abel (ed.) *The Politics of Informal Justice*, vol. 2, New York: Academic Press.

Kirchheimer, O. (1961) *Political Justice: The Use of Legal Procedure for Political Ends*, Princeton: Princeton University Press.

Laskin, B. (1975) 'The role and functions of final appellate courts: the Supreme Court of Canada', *53 Canadian Bar Review*, in F. L. Morton (1984) *Law, Politics and the Judicial Process in Canada*, Calgary: University of Calgary Press.

McWhinney, E. (1982) *Canada and the Constitution, 1979–1982: Patriation and the Charter of Rights*, Toronto: University of Toronto Press.

—— (1987) *The International Court of Justice and the Western Tradition of International Law*, Dordrecht: Martinus Nijhoff.

Maine, H. (1963) *Ancient Law*, London: John Murray; Boston: Beacon Press.

Marbury v. *Madison* (1803) 1 Cranch 137 (1803).

Merryman, J. H. and Clark, D. S. (1978) *Comparative Law: Western European and Latin American Legal Systems*, Indianapolis: Bobbs-Merrill.

Merryman, J. H. D., Clark, S. and Friedman, L. M. (1979) *Law and Social Change in Mediterranean Europe and Latin America: A Handbook of Legal and Social Indicators for Comparative Study*, Stanford: Stanford University Press.

Ogilvie, C. (1958) *The King's Government and the Common Law 1471–1641*, Oxford: Basil Blackwell.

Pawlisch, H. S. (1985) *Sir John Davies and the Conquest of Ireland: A Study in Legal Imperialism*, Cambridge: Cambridge University Press.

Shapiro, M. (1981) *Courts: A Comparative and Political Analysis*, Chicago: University of Chicago Press.

Snell, J. G. and Vaughan, F. (1985) *The Supreme Court of Canada*, Toronto: University of Toronto Press.

Stjernquist, N. (1989) 'Judicial review in Sweden', unpublished lecture, Lund: University of Lund.

Trubek, D. M. (1972) Max Weber on Law and the Rise of Capitalism, *Law Review* no. 3, pp. 729–42, Wisconsin: University of Wisconsin.

Zweigert, K. and Kotz, H. (1977) *An Introduction to Comparative Law*, vol. I, Amsterdam: North-Holland.

20

BUREAUCRACIES

FERREL HEADY

Bureaucracies are large-scale organizations that are common in both the public and private sectors of contemporary society.

ORIGINS

The word 'bureaucracy' was coined fairly recently, but it is derived from much older Latin and Greek sources. Fritz Morstein Marx (1957: 17–18) states that the first half of the word can be traced to *burrus*, meaning in Latin a dark and sombre colour, and that in Old French *la bure* was a related word referring to a certain kind of cloth covering for tables, especially those used by public officials. The word *bureau* was first applied to the covered table, then to the surrounding room or office. Eventually, the word *bureaucratie* was created by combining *bureau* with a Greek suffix referring to type of rule. This usage is credited to an eighteenth-century French minister of commerce, Vincent de Gournay, who presumably intended the word to be a way of describing government as rule by officialdom. Soon it took the form *Bürokratie* in German, and later appeared in many other languages.

MEANINGS

This evolution explains the pejorative connotation commonly and popularly given to 'bureaucracy' when it is used as a way of expressing disapproval of the actions of government officials or objection to the procedures required in large organizations that are alleged to be cumbersome and inefficient. The term 'bureaucracy' also has, however, a less negative and more neutral meaning in the social sciences, referring to organizational arrangements of a distinctive type characteristically found in modern societies. Bureaucratic organizations, in this sense, are those that have attributes identified in the writings of the German social scientist Max Weber (1864–1920) and his successors. Bureaucracies of Weber's 'ideal-type' model are marked by traits such as hierarchy, specialization, professional competence, separation of the office and the incumbent, full-time occupational commitment, fixed monetary salaries and written regulations specifying internal relationships and procedures to be followed in bureaucratic operations (Weber 1922; Bendix 1960; Hall 1962).

Ambiguity of meaning in the use of 'bureaucracy' and 'bureaucracies' is unavoidable. The stress here is put on the identification of attributes that distinguish between bureaucratic and other types of organizations, with neither positive nor negative implications as to organizational outcomes. This is the Weberian meaning, as opposed to Harold Laski's use of the term as applying 'to a system of government the control of which is so completely in the hands of officials that their power jeopardizes the liberties of ordinary citizens' (Laski 1930: 70). Even Weber, while emphasizing the superior capabilities of bureaucracies over earlier organizational types, expressed concern late in his career because of the 'overtowering' power position of fully developed bureaucracies. More recently, Henry Jacoby (1973) has argued that bureaucracies are necessary but dangerous, with a strong potential for the usurpation of political power. His interpretation is that modern all-encompassing bureaucratic organizations are the culmination of a long process of centralization and accumulation of power begun long ago, when historical civilizations found it necessary to create and then to rely on the prototypes of present-day bureaucracies. The resulting paradox for our time is that bureaucracy is necessary and indeed inevitable but is at the same time dangerous and potentially usurpative. Contemporary societies simultaneously demand, depend on, and deplore the apparatus of bureaucracy. This outlook is basically pessimistic as to future prospects.

Another manifestation of this negative orientation is the tendency by Merton (1952: 361–71) and others (Morstein Marx 1957: 25–8; Crozier 1964: 4–5) to highlight as typical behaviour in bureaucracies traits that are 'dysfunctional', pathological, or self-defeating, tending to frustrate the realization of organizational goals. Red tape, buck passing, rigidity and inflexibility, over-secretiveness, excessive impersonality, unwillingness to delegate, and reluctance to exercise discretion are all identified as behavioural orientations typical of the 'trained incapacity' of bureaucrats. Undoubtedly, such behaviour occurs frequently within bureaucracies, but so does a range of other kinds of behaviour with more positive implications for attainment of organizational objectives. Some students of bureaucracies, including Friedrich (1963: 471) as a prime example, stress traits such as objectivity, precision, consistency and discretion, describing them as 'desirable habit or behaviour patterns' which are usually followed by members of bureaucratic organizations (Friedrich 1968: 44–5).

In contrast to these differences in describing dominant bureaucratic behavioural traits, there is considerable agreement as to the basic structural characteristics of bureaucratic organizations. A compact formulation is that of

Victor Thompson (1961: 3–4), who says that such an organization is composed of a highly elaborated hierarchy of authority superimposed upon a highly elaborated division of labour. Friedrich (1963: 468–70) asserts that the pivotal structural characteristics can be reduced to these three:

1 hierarchy;
2 differentiation or specialization; and
3 qualification or competence.

Bureaucracies with such structural characteristics are prevalent in what Robert Presthus (1978) calls today's 'organizational society'. No contemporary nation-state, for instance, can be viable without a public bureaucracy as one of its major political institutions (Heady 1991: 75; Riggs 1970: 388). Hence an understanding of the distinctive internal features of different nation-state public bureaucracies and of the relationships between these bureaucracies and other institutions in the political system is crucial both to the analysis of particular polities and to comparisons among them. One aspect of such study needs to be consideration of the negative possibilities in bureaucratic operations already mentioned, including the self-defeating proclivities of patterns of bureaucratic behaviour that undermine achievement of policy goals, and the dangers of encroachment by public bureaucracies on the appropriate roles of other political institutions.

STRUCTURAL VARIATIONS

Patterns of differentiation among national public bureaucracies as to their organizational features have received much attention, and there is considerable consensus about appropriate categories. Among the more developed countries, three such basic groupings emerge (Bendix 1968; Heady 1991; Rowat 1988). One group consists of the democracies on the European continent in an arc from Scandinavia through western and southern Europe, plus perhaps other examples geographically widely scattered such as Ireland, Israel, and Japan. A second group includes Great Britain, the United States and other former British colonies such as Canada, Australia and New Zealand. The third group consists of the Soviet Union and other nations in Eastern Europe included in the Soviet bloc since the Second World War.

Despite significant individual differences, the public bureaucracies in each of these groups share some basic similarities. Members of the first group, typified by Germany and France (with historical roots in Prussia and the French *ancien régime*), are sometimes referred to as 'classic' systems, conforming most closely to Weber's 'ideal-type' bureaucracy. The present public service can usually be traced to an earlier royal service that was itself highly professionalized. Members of the bureaucracy are recruited on a career basis according to educational attainment; mobility upward within the bureaucracy from one level to another is relatively limited; higher-ranking bureaucrats are intimately involved in the policy process, are allowed to engage in political activity, often have opportunities for second careers in either the public or private sectors, and generally enjoy high prestige in the society.

Countries in the second group have in common a 'civic culture' with widespread citizen participation in governmental affairs. A public service based on selection by competence or merit is relatively recent, with civil service reform having occurred after the middle of the nineteenth century in both Great Britain and the United States and even later elsewhere. Although educational background is increasingly important, entry points into the bureaucracy are more varied and internal mobility is greater. Higher-level bureaucrats are also heavily involved in policy making, but in a manner that varies from country to country. They are often subjected to severe restrictions as to partisan political activity, and the career paths of politicians and career bureaucrats are generally distinct and separate. Public service careers, especially in the more egalitarian former British colonies, do not rank as high in societal prestige as in the 'classic' systems.

The communist bloc countries have been in the past the most highly bureaucratized, both in the apparatus of the dominant party and of the state. A 'public' bureaucratic career of some type has been the only choice for most individuals, because of the enormous range of party and state activity. Educational and professional qualifications have gradually gained over loyalty considerations as factors in bureaucratic selection and promotion, so that the backgrounds and career paths of higher bureaucrats in these countries differ less markedly now than in the past from their counterparts elsewhere. The dramatic and unforeseen changes taking place in these systems as the decade of the 1990s begins makes prediction hazardous, but the trend seems to be toward greater similarity, rather than increasing divergence, between the communist bloc (including what was the USSR and countries of Eastern Europe) and other developed nations with regard to the societal role of bureaucratic organizations.

The public bureaucracies of developing countries in the Third World are usually lumped together as a fourth major category, but with wide variations among them in their degree of competence, and in the educational backgrounds, career prospects, degree of participation in the making of public policy and societal power status of members of the bureaucracy. Generalizations are difficult to make, beyond noting the impact of inherited colonial public service patterns, the general lack of security in bureaucratic careers, the importance of the public sector in societal decision making generally, and the frequent ascendency of military bureaucrats over both civil bureaucrats and politicians.

BEHAVIOURAL VARIATIONS

In contrast to organizational or structural distinctions, the identification and classification of distinctive national patterns of bureaucratic behaviour is as yet at an early stage of sophistication. Clearly cultural factors are basic to such efforts. Some useful analyses of specific cases have been made by knowledgeable scholars who are themselves products of the culture described. A notable example is the examination by Crozier (1964) of behavioural traits in the French bureaucracy. He traces these traits to more general French cultural characteristics, stressing the qualities of rationality, impersonality and absoluteness. He views France as essentially a 'stalemate society', with the bureaucratic system providing a means of reconciling two deep-seated but contradictory attitudes. One is an urge to avoid as much as possible direct face-to-face authority relationships, and the other is a prevailing view of authority in terms of universalism and absolutism. The bureaucratic system combines an absolutist conception of authority with the elimination of most direct dependence relationships, hence solving the basic French dilemma about authority as indispensable but hard to endure. At the same time, the system suffers from deficiencies in co-ordination, in the decentralization of decision making, and in adjusting to change.

More systematic comparative studies are dependent on advances in cultural analysis at a variety of relevant levels – societal, political, administrative and organizational. Some progress is being made at each of these levels. Hofstede (1980) has identified four value dimensions as accounting for a major proportion of cultural differences among societies. These are:

1 individualism–collectivism;
2 uncertainty avoidance, relating to attitudes toward risk-taking and ambiguity;
3 power distance, concerned with attitudes towards patterns of power distribution; and
4 masculinity–femininity, having to do with the extent that dominant values are 'masculine' in terms of assertiveness, advancement and acquisition of material goods.

Hofstede, after analysing data from forty countries showing various combinations of these value dimensions, identified eight country clusters with distinctive patterns in their value systems differentially affecting behaviour in these social groupings.

Almond and Verba (1963) undertook pioneering work in exploring the concept of political culture for differentiating among national polities. Building on their foundation, Nachmias and Rosenbloom (1978) have proposed a model for the more restricted concept of bureaucratic culture as a means of studying orientations toward the public bureaucracy as a sub-unit of political systems.

Retaining the cognitive, affective and evaluative cultural orientation sub-types suggested by Almond and Verba, they concentrated on two dimensions – orientations of citizens or the general public toward the public bureaucracy, and orientations of the bureaucrats themselves toward the bureaucracy. In addition, they were interested in assessing the congruence of these two sets of dimensions.

More recently, Schein (1985) and others (Frost *et al.* 1985) have used the concept of organizational culture to focus on specific organizations, mostly in the private sector. Organizational culture is defined by Schein as:

> a pattern of basic assumptions – invented, discovered, or developed by a given group as it learns to cope with its problems of external adaptation and internal integration – that has worked well enough to be considered valid and, therefore, to be taught to new members as the correct way to perceive, think, and feel in relation to those problems.
>
> (Schein 1985: 9)

Clearly this definition recognizes that organizational culture is significantly influenced by cultural characteristics at more inclusive levels in the society.

Among these studies, the bureaucratic culture model appears to offer most promise for systematically profiling the characteristics of different national bureaucratic systems. However, it has been applied only to Israel, and any application on a multinational basis would require a massive effort of data accumulation and analysis.

More has been accomplished in the comparative treatment in a variety of settings of the relationships between public bureaucracies and other political institutions. An assumption commonly made is that political modernization or development requires a balance between the public bureaucracy and institutions (such as chief executive officials, legislatures, political parties, courts and interest groups) in the 'constitutive' system (Riggs 1973: 28–9), so that the public bureaucracy is subjected to effective external controls from these other political institutions, and thus plays an instrumental role in the operation of the political system rather than usurping political power and taking over as the dominant political elite group.

Two factors have received most attention in the analysis of various patterns of relationships between public bureaucracies and the 'constitutive' political institutions. The first is the role of the 'state' or the degree of 'stateness' in the polity, and the second is the nature of the existing political regime.

A recent trend in comparative political studies has been a renewed interest in political institutions and a lessened interest in political functions. This 'neo-institutionalism' has emphasized the importance of the 'state' as distinct from both 'society' and 'government', and has advanced the notion of degree of 'stateness' (referring to the relative scope and extent of governmental power and authority) as a tool for making cross-societal comparisons (Nettl 1968). Metin Heper and a group of associates (Heper 1987) have undertaken to distinguish four ideal types of polity based on their degree of 'stateness', and to identify six types of bureaucracy corresponding to these polity types. 'Personalist' and 'ideological' polities rank high in 'stateness'; 'liberal' and 'praetorian' polities rank low. A one-to-one relationship between polity type and bureaucracy type is suggested in three instances: 'personalist' with a 'personal servant' bureaucracy, 'liberal' with a Weberian 'legal-rational' bureaucracy, and 'praetorian' with a 'spoils system' bureaucracy. The 'ideological' polity can produce any one of three types of bureaucracy, depending on whether the high degree of 'stateness' is linked with a ruler ('machine model' bureaucracy), the bureaucracy itself ('Bonapartist' or '*Rechtsstaat*' bureaucracy), or a dominant party ('party-controlled' bureaucracy). The application of this framework for analysis by Heper and his associates includes case examples that are both historical (ancient Rome, Prussia, nineteenth-century Russia) and contemporary. The authors do not directly address the issue of balance between the bureaucracy and other institutions, but the implication is that the 'Bonapartist' or '*Rechtsstaat*' bureaucracy in the 'ideological' polity would present the most unbalanced situation in favour of the bureaucracy, followed by the 'spoils system' bureaucracy in a 'praetorian' polity. The other linkages of polity and bureaucracy indicate that sufficient effective external control over the bureaucracy is provided by a ruler, a party, or some other source or combination of sources. The contemporary case studies (dealing with the United States, Great Britain, France, Germany, Turkey and Indonesia) seem to fit this assessment. At any rate, presumably some degree of 'stateness' can be detected in any polity, with consequences for bureaucratic behavioural characteristics and the role of the bureaucracy in the operation of the political system.

Another variable always present and likely to be highly significant for characterizing and comparing public bureaucracies is the type of political regime existent in the polity (Heady 1991: 87–8). Western democracies (whether unitary or federal, parliamentary or presidential, two-party or multi-party) are balanced in the sense that their public bureaucracies, although participating in major decisions as to public policy, are ultimately answerable to and controlled by various extra-bureaucratic political institutions (Dogan 1975: Aberbach *et al.* 1981). Distinctive national features do exist that affect bureaucratic behaviour enough to justify description and analysis on a case-by-case basis, but in their fundamental characteristics they are basically similar political regimes. European one-party communist bloc political regimes, exemplified in the past by the Soviet Union, also are balanced in this same sense, but the source of control over the official state bureaucracy has been concentrated in the dominant party, and this is likely to continue even though *perestroika* reforms open up the political arena somewhat to other parties or political groupings, leading to additional channels for maintaining bureaucratic accountability.

Third World developing countries are numerous enough and diverse enough to require groupings into broad categories of political regimes for comparative purposes. Numerous classification schemes have been proposed (Heady 1991: 289–96), with variations mainly in terminology rather than in essentials.

Some Third World democratic regimes with competitive party systems closely resemble Western democracies, but their legitimacy and stability are more subject to challenge, and they are often short-lived. Evidence indicates that vulnerability may be greater for countries that have adopted the presidential model of democracy rather than the parliamentary one. Only a few of these countries have had a lengthy record of open competition among two or more parties and of peaceful political transition after free elections. Costa Rica is a leading example. Many Third World countries have moved to single-party systems (usually communist or oriented towards some variety of Marxism-Leninism, as in China, Cuba, and numerous countries in Africa and the Middle East), with political competition from outside the party either prohibited or severely restricted. In other instances (as in India, Malaysia and Mexico), party competition is allowed, but a dominant single party has been in power either continuously or for most of the time, in some cases since independence. The presumption in these regimes is that the dominant party can be replaced peaceably after an electoral defeat. This possibility has now been demonstrated twice in India, and may be tested in Mexico during coming years. All of these Third World nations have what can be described as 'party-prominent' political regimes, with the public bureaucracies (including the military segments) playing secondary political roles.

Much more common in the Third World are 'bureaucratic-prominent' regimes, with military and/or civil bureaucrats wielding political power either directly or behind the scenes. Even in the declining group of traditional regimes with monarchical or religious leaders (such as Morocco, Saudi Arabia or Iran), a loyal and minimally competent bureaucracy is crucial for regime survival. The most prevalent Third World regime type is a personalist or collegial bureaucratic elite with one or a group of professional bureaucrats (usually military professionals) clearly dominating the political system. Examples are numerous among developing nations in every geographical region of the world. When not so openly in control, high-ranking military bureaucrats are often crucially influential behind the scenes, or are in a position to intervene to replace a civilian government in nations with a political record of pendulum-like swings between bureaucratic elite and civilian competitive regimes (Turkey, Nigeria and Argentina are representative cases from different regions). The overall picture is thus one of imbalance rather than balance in the relationship between public bureaucracies and the other political institutions that are generally considered to have a more legitimate claim to the exercise of ultimate political power.

CONTROLS OVER PUBLIC BUREAUCRACIES

The acknowledged tendency in most countries for the public bureaucracy to assume increasing importance in the formulation and implementation of public policy at the expense of executive officials and legislators, and the undeniable fact of political dominance by professional bureaucrats in numerous Third World countries have together activated various efforts to curb the excesses of bureaucracies or even to replace them with other forms of organization.

Attempted reforms by chief executives have included the creation or strengthening of managerial units with budgetary and personnel controls over administrative agencies, the expansion in numbers of political appointees in the upper leadership levels of agencies, and greater involvement in the placement of high-ranking career bureaucrats. Legislatures and legislative committees have often greatly expanded their staff capabilities in an attempt to match the expertise of bureaucratic professionals in a variety of programme areas, and have tried to strengthen their capacity to conduct investigations of administrative actions and to carry out corrective measures. Numerous countries have initiated programmes of 'equal opportunity' or 'affirmative action' to increase the proportions in the public bureaucracy of previously under-represented groups such as women and ethnic minorities. 'Sunshine' laws have allowed greater access to the proceedings of public bodies and to public documents. In the United States and other countries, courts have experienced a rapid growth in administrative law cases, and have begun to intervene more frequently to overturn or alter administrative decisions. As a remedial instrument for citizens, the Scandinavian institution of *ombudsman* has been widely imitated elsewhere to protect the public against administrative abuses or inadequacies (Rowat 1985).

This is a sampling of the measures designed to bring public bureaucracies under better control without drastic changes in their characteristics or the role they play in modern societies. Evaluations as to the results are mixed. The usual attitude is one of continuing concern, as expressed by R. E. Wraith that:

> the growing impact of government and governmental agencies on everyday life has brought a more than corresponding increase in public administration which, both by its ubiquity and its sheer size, appears to 'feed on itself' and which could grow to a point when it became virtually beyond political control.
>
> (Wraith 1982: 139)

However, Donald C. Rowat has recently concluded that the net effects of these reform efforts are likely to be that 'the influence of senior officials will more nearly represent the interests of society', that 'the bureaucracy will be supervised and controlled more closely', and that bureaucratic influence will be reduced by 'increasing the political input into policy-making' (Rowat 1988: 457).

ALTERNATIVES TO BUREAUCRACIES

Some critics of bureaucracies propose to go further, either by restricting the bureaucracies' scope of operation, or by replacing them with other organizational forms. Ramos (1981) and other advocates of 'social systems delimitation' and a 'new science of organizations' recognize a continuing need for bureaucracies with their hierarchical and coercive attributes for dealing with market-centred activities, but urge the recognition and encouragement of other institutional arrangements in which members of the organization are peers or are subject to minimal formal controls, contending that such non-bureaucratic organizational forms are more appropriate for 'social settings suited for personal actualization, convivial relationships, and community activities of citizens' (Ramos 1981: 135). The functioning of bureaucracies would thus be sanctioned but limited as compared to the present.

A more drastic reorientation is called for by proponents of substitute and presumedly more suitable organizational forms to take the place of contemporary bureaucracies (Bennis 1973; Thayer 1973). Much as Weber claimed earlier that bureaucracies were most efficient for meeting the needs of a society recognizing the legitimacy of a 'legal-rational' pattern of authority, the argument is that societal needs now are for a predominant type of organization that is post-bureaucratic, even though its exact characteristics remain to be clarified.

Organizational evolution is likely and probably desirable, but whatever its timing and shape, bureaucracies are likely to remain the most prevalent form of organization for the foreseeable future. Hence attention must continue to be focused on how to maximize the positive while minimizing the negative influences of bureaucracies as they operate in contemporary society.

REFERENCES

Aberbach, J. D., Putnam, R. D. and Rockman, B. A. (1981) *Bureaucrats and Politicians in Western Democracies*, Cambridge, Mass.: Harvard University Press.

Almond, G. A. and Verba, S. (1963) *The Civic Culture*, Princeton: Princeton University Press.

Bendix, R. (1960) *Max Weber: An Intellectual Portrait*, Garden City, NY: Doubleday.

——(1968) 'Bureaucracy', in *International Encyclopedia of the Social Sciences*, vol. 2, New York: Macmillan Free Press.

Bennis, W. G. (1973) *Beyond Bureaucracy*, New York: McGraw-Hill.

Crozier, M. (1964) *The Bureaucratic Phenomenon*, Chicago: University of Chicago Press.

Dogan, M. (ed.) (1975) *The Mandarins of Western Europe: The Political Role of Top Civil Servants*, New York: John Wiley.

Friedrich, C. J. (1963) *Man and His Government*, New York: McGraw-Hill.

——(1968) *Constitutional Government and Democracy*, 4th edn, Boston: Blaisdell Publishing Company.

Frost, P. J., Moore, L. F., Louis, M. R., Lundberg, C. C. and Martin, J. (1985) *Organizational Culture*, Beverly Hills: Sage Publications.

Hall, R. H. (1962) 'Intraorganizational stuctural variation: application of the bureaucratic model', *Administrative Science Quarterly* 7 (3): 295–308.

Heady, F. (1991) *Public Administration: A Comparative Perspective*, 4th edn, New York: Marcel Dekker.

Heper, M. (ed.) (1987) *The State and Public Bureaucracies: A Comparative Perspective*, New York: Greenwood Press.

Hofstede, G. (1980) *Culture's Consequences: International Differences in Work-Related Values*, Beverly Hills: Sage Publications.

Jacoby, H. (1973) *The Bureaucratization of the World*, Berkeley: University of California Press.

Laski, H. J. (1930) 'Bureaucracy', in *Encyclopaedia of the Social Sciences*, vol. 3, New York: Macmillan.

Merton, R. (1952) *Reader in Bureaucracy*, New York: Free Press of Glencoe.

Morstein Marx, F. (1957) *The Administrative State: An Introduction to Bureaucracy*, Chicago: University of Chicago Press.

Nachmias, D. and Rosenbloom, D. H. (1978) *Bureaucratic Culture*, London: Croom Helm.

Nettl, J. P. (1968) 'The state as a conceptual variable', *World Politics* 20: 559–92.

Presthus, R. (1978) *The Organizational Society*, rev. edn, New York: St Martin's Press.

Ramos, A. G. (1981) *The New Science of Organizations*, Toronto: University of Toronto Press.

Riggs, F. W. (ed.) (1970) *Frontiers of Development Administration*, Durham, NC: Duke University Press.

——(1973) *Prismatic Society Revisited*, Morristown, NJ: General Learning Press.

Rowat, D. C. (ed.) (1985) *The Ombudsman Plan*, rev. 2nd edn, Lanham, Md: University Press of America.

——(ed.) (1988) *Public Administration in Developed Democracies*, New York: Marcel Dekker.

Schein, E. H. (1985) *Organizational Culture and Leadership: A Dynamic View*, San Francisco: Jossey-Bass.

Thayer, F. C. (1973) *An End to Hierarchy! An End to Competition!*, New York: Franklin Watts.

Thompson, V. A. (1961) *Modern Organization*, New York: Knopf.

Weber, M. (1922) 'Bureaucracy', in H. H. Gerth and C. W. Mills (ed.) and trans, New York: Oxford University Press, 1956 *From Max Weber: Essays in Sociology*.

Wraith, R. E. (ed.) (1982) *Proceedings, XVIIIth International Congress of Administrative Sciences, Madrid 1980*, Brussels: International Institute of Administrative Sciences.

FURTHER READING

Aberbach, J. D., Putnam, R. D. and Rockman, B. A. (1981) *Bureaucrats and Politicians in Western Democracies*, Cambridge, Mass.: Harvard University Press.

Almond, G. A. and Verba, S. (1963) *The Civic Culture*, Princeton: Princeton University Press.

Bennis, W. G. (1973) *Beyond Bureaucracy*, New York: McGraw-Hill.

Crozier, M. (1964) *The Bureaucratic Phenomenon*, Chicago: University of Chicago Press.

Dogan, M. (ed.) (1975) *The Mandarins of Western Europe: The Political Role of Top Civil Servants*, New York: John Wiley.

Heady, F. (1959) 'Bureaucratic theory and comparative administration', *Administrative Science Quarterly* 3: 509–25.

——(1991) 'A focus for comparison', chap. 2 in F. Heady *Public Administration: A Comparative Perspective*, 4th edn, New York: Marcel Dekker.

Heper, M. (ed.) (1987) *The State and Public Bureaucracies: A Comparative Perspective*, New York: Greenwood Press.

Heper, M., Kim C. L. and Pai S.-T. (1980) 'The role of bureaucracy and regime types', *Administration and Society* 12: 137–57.

Jacoby, H. (1973) *The Bureaucratization of the World*, Berkeley: University of California Press.

Merton, R. (1952) *Reader in Bureaucracy*, New York: Free Press of Glencoe.

Morstein Marx, F. (1957) *The Administrative State: An Introduction to Bureaucracy*, Chicago: University of Chicago Press.

Nachmias, D. and Rosenbloom, D. H. (1978) *Bureaucratic Culture*, London: Croom Helm.

Peters, B. G. (1984) *The Politics of Bureaucracy*, 2nd edn, New York: Longman.

——(1988) *Comparing Public Bureaucracies*, Tuscaloosa: University of Alabama Press.

Presthus, R. (1981) *The Organizational Society*, rev. edn, New York: St Martin's Press.

Ramos, A. G. (1981) *The New Science of Organizations*, Toronto: University of Toronto Press.

Rowat, D. C. (ed.) (1988) *Public Administration in Developed Democracies*, New York: Marcel Dekker.

21

INTERGOVERNMENTAL RELATIONS: UNITARY SYSTEMS

R.A.W. RHODES

Amongst the earliest proponents of intergovernmental relations (IGR) was Anderson, who defined it as 'an important body of activities or interactions occurring between governmental units of all types and levels within ... the federal system' (Anderson 1960: 3). This general definition has been elaborated by Wright (1974: 1–16) who identifies five distinct characteristics. First, IGR recognizes the multiplicity of relationships between all types of government. Second, it emphasizes the interactions between individuals, especially public officials. Third, these relationships are continuous, day-to-day and informal. Fourth, IGR insists on the important role played by all public officials, be they politicians or administrators. Finally, it emphasizes the political nature of relationships and focuses on substantive policies, especially financial issues such as who raises what amount and who spends it for whose benefit with what results (see also Wright 1978). In summary, Wright claims that:

> The term IGR alerts one to the multiple, behavioural, continuous and dynamic exchanges occurring between various officials in the political system. It may be compared to a different, novel and visual filter or concept that can be laid on the American political landscape.
>
> (Wright 1974: 4)

For unitary states it is perhaps more common to talk of central–local relations. The 'visual filter' of IGR is even more novel, therefore, when it is applied to unitary systems.

FORMS OF DECENTRALIZATION

The terminology of IGR is as profuse as it is confusing. Figure 1 attempts to illustrate the profusion without the confusion. Decentralization is one of the more emotive terms in politics, almost rivalling democracy and equality in the heat it can generate. Not only is decentralization 'good' but centralization is quite definitely 'bad' (Fesler 1965). It is not necessary to take sides in such normative disputes. The multifarious forms of decentralization can be described and classified. Such a dispassionate approach requires a degree of care in the use of words.

Decentralization refers to the distribution of power to lower levels in a territorial hierarchy, whether the hierarchy is one of governments within a state or offices within a large-scale organization (Smith 1985: 1). Or more briefly, it refers to the real division of powers (Maass 1959). So defined, the term encompasses both political and bureaucratic decentralization, federal and unitary states, and multiple decentralization or decentralization between levels of government and within each type of government. Figure 1 does not purport to classify the different types of decentralized systems in the world. It has the more modest aim of identifying the forms which decentralization can take.

Deconcentration, sometimes referred to as field administration, involves 'the redistribution of administrative responsibilities ... within the central government' (Rondinelli and Cheema 1983a: 18). A broad distinction can be drawn between prefectoral and functional systems. In the integrated prefectoral system, a representative of the centre – or prefect – located in the regions supervises both local governments and other field officers of the centre. They are the superior officers in the field, embodying 'the authority of all ministries as well as the government generally and ... the main channel of communication between technical field officials and the capital' (Smith 1967: 45). Classic examples are the French departmental prefects and the collectors/district commissioners in India (Maddick 1970). In the unintegrated prefectoral system the prefect is only one of a number of channels of communication with the centre and the prefect is not superior to, and does not co-ordinate, other field officers. In addition, they only supervise local governments and are not their chief executives. Examples of the unintegrated system include the Italian prefect (Fried 1963) and the district officer in Nigeria (Smith 1967). In the functional system, field officers belong to distinct functional hierarchies. The administration of the several policy areas is separate. There is no general, regional co-ordinator. Co-ordination occurs at the centre. This system of multifarious functional territories is exemplified by Britain.

Delegation refers to 'the delegation of decision-making and management authority for specific functions to organizations that are not under the direct control of central government ministries' (Rondinelli and Cheema 1983a: 20).

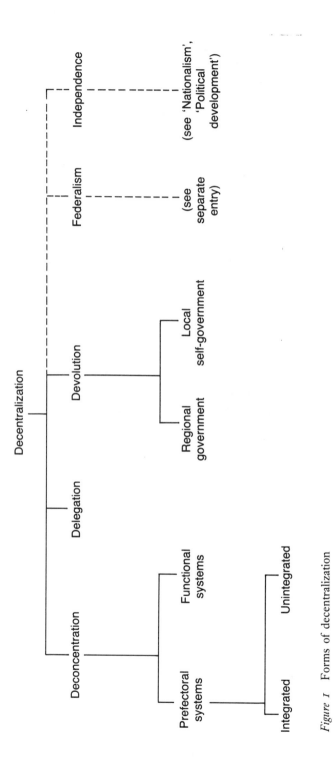

Figure 1 Forms of decentralization

Source: diagrammatic conversion and modification of text in Rondinelli and Cheema 1983a: 18–25; Smith 1985: chapter 1; Smith and Stanyer 1976: chapter 3.

Such organizations are referred to variously as parastatal organizations, non-departmental public bodies and quangos (quasi-autonomous non-governmental organizations). They include public corporations and regional development agencies. This category does not cover the transfer of functions to the private sector or voluntary bodies. Such transfers are normally referred to as privatization or debureaucratization. Privatization is not a form of delegation (nor of decentralization) because the relevant agencies are no longer part of the government's territorial hierarchy. However, privatization can have marked effects on that hierarchy and these effects will be considered below.

Devolution refers to the exercise of political authority by lay, primarily elected, institutions within areas defined by community characteristics (Smith 1985: 11). Thus, 'local units are autonomous, independent and clearly perceived as separate levels of government over which central authorities exercise little or no *direct* control' (Rondinelli and Cheema 1983a: 22). The *locus classicus* of devolution is said to be British local government. Up to this point, the discussion has focused on the decentralization of bureaucratic authority, on service-defined areas. With devolution, the discussion turns to the decentralization of political authority either to local or regional government. As the term 'regional government' is used to refer to the reform of local government, it is not possible to draw a hard and fast distinction between these two levels of government (Rhodes 1974). The distinction is necessary because there have been significant developments in regional government since the early 1980s.

Federalism is defined separately in this encyclopedia (see chapter 22) so the comment here will be brief. Federal states are normally seen as more decentralized than unitary states with devolution to local governments. However, two notes of caution are in order. First, the formal division of powers in a federal constitution can differ greatly from the practice of federalism. The federal government can exercise considerable influence and control over the individual states. Second, the degree of devolution within a unitary state can be considerable, as in the case of Northern Ireland between 1920 and 1973. In other words, it is unwise to assume, as Figure 1 implies, that there is a continuum from deconcentration to federalism. It is much more important to question whether or not 'there is anything about a federal constitution which is important for the way in which intergovernmental relations are conducted' (Smith 1985: 15).

In this essay, the term IGR covers all forms of decentralization. The identification of variations in IGR between federal and unitary systems is not seen as a matter of stipulative definition but as a matter of investigation and the theoretical standpoint of the investigator will have a marked effect on the findings.

THEORETICAL APPROACHES

There is a profusion of theoretical approaches in the study of IGR including the public/development administration, 'new right', centre–periphery, 'radical' and intergovernmental approaches (Rhodes 1988: 15–45; see also Dunleavy 1984: 56–65; and Bulpitt 1983: chapter 1).

The *public/development administration* approach focuses on the institutions, procedures and decision-making processes of government. It is concerned with description rather than theory, with practical problems rather than analysis and explanation. Its main preoccupations are the adverse consequences of centralization and the promotion of decentralization, especially local self-government (see Bulpitt 1983: 19–34) in both developed (Jones and Stewart 1983) and developing countries (Maddick 1963; Wallis 1989). The public administration approach is the source of the classic distinction in the study of IGR between the agency and the partnership models. In the agent model, local authorities implement national policies under the supervision of central departments. In the partnership model, local authorities and central departments are co-equal and local authorities have considerable discretion in designing and implementing their own policies. It is argued that in recent experience local government is ceasing to be a partner and is becoming an agent because of its dependence on central grants and increased central controls (for a more detailed summary see Rhodes 1981: chapter 2).

The *'new right'* approach has an economic, political and bureaucratic component. The economic component stresses reductions in the level of public expenditure and the centrality of markets and competition in a healthy economy. The politics component has at its heart the link between markets and freedom. The call is for a minimalist state with its functions limited to the protection of private property and external defence. The bureaucratic component criticizes the over-supply of services by bureaucrats acting from self-interest and calls for the substitution of private for public provision or, failing that, the use of private sector management methods to improve efficiency. In the context of decentralization and IGR, this approach stresses the reduced scope for local government, the transfer of services to the private sector and making services both more responsive to consumers and more efficient. The most visible policy of this approach in both developed and developing countries has been privatization.

The *centre–periphery relations* approach is concerned with the relationship between central political institutions and peripheral or territorial political interests and organizations. For example, Hechter (1975: 17–22, 39–45) argues that in Britain an economically advanced centre colonized – i.e. dominated and exploited – less advanced areas, for example Scotland (see also Bulpitt 1983; Tilly 1975). In the guise of the concept of 'political penetration', this thesis has been applied to centre–periphery relations in developing countries. For example, Coleman defines political penetration as 'an heuristic concept' concerned with the ways in which 'the political-administrative-juridical centre of a new state (1) establishes an effective and authoritative central presence throughout its geographical and sectoral peripheries, and (2) acquires a capacity for the extraction and mobilization of resources to implement its policies and pursue its goals . . .' (Coleman 1977: 3). (See also LaPalombara 1971; Cliffe *et al.* 1977; Staniland 1970.)

The *radical* approach has neo-Marxist and neo-Weberian variants (see for example Dunleavy and O'Leary 1987: chapter 5), but at a minimum this approach rejects explanations couched in terms of the behaviour of individual actors, explores the relationship between IGR and social classes, explores 'crises' to identify the social roots of administrative problems, and employs functional explanation (see Dunleavy 1982). For example, Saunders summarizes his 'dual-state thesis' as follows:

> local government in Britain is typically concerned with the provision of social consumption through competitive modes of political mediation and organized around the principle of citizenship rights and social need. Central and regional levels of government, on the other hand, are typically the agencies through which social investment and fiscal policies are developed within a relatively exclusive corporate sector of politics organized around the principle of private property rights and the need to maintain private sector profitability.
>
> (Saunders 1982: 61)

In a similar vein, Smith has argued that, in developing countries, centralization is not a function of the greater technical and administrative competence of the centre but of 'the configuration of political forces emerging in a new state as new relations of production develop with the support of state intervention' (Smith 1985: 194).

The *intergovernmental* approach is that variant of neo-pluralist theory which seeks to explain the changing patterns of interaction and behaviour in IGR. In discussions of IGR, neo-pluralism explores the impact of professional influence, the logic of technical rationality, the privileged position of a select number of interest groups, and the complex interdependencies within decentralized governmental structures. These themes have been developed for a number of advanced industrial liberal democracies. Thus, Hanf argues that the characteristic problem of such countries is that:

> the problem solving capacity of governments is disaggregated into a collection of sub-systems with limited tasks, competences and resources. . . . At the same time governments are more and more confronted with tasks where both the problems and their solution tend to cut across the boundaries of separate authorities and functional jurisdiction. . . .
>
> A major task confronting political systems in any advanced industrial country

is therefore that of securing co-ordinated policy actions through networks of separate but interdependent organizations.

(Hanf 1978: 1–2)

The limits to rational policy making, the factorizing and professionalization of policy systems, the interdependence of governmental organizations and the emergence of policy from network interaction are said to be recurrent features of advanced industrial society. Oligopoly has replaced the free market competition between groups said to characterize pluralism. (For a more detailed summary and citations see Dunleavy and O'Leary 1987: chapter 6; and for an extended illustration of the approach see Kaufman *et al.* 1986.)

This brief account of the several approaches currently employed in the study of IGR does not provide an adequate summary of each theory, nor does it provide a critique (see Rhodes 1988: 16–45 and citations). However, it does draw attention to a key feature of the field: it is multi-theoretic. Each theory differs in its unit of analysis, level of analysis and criteria of evaluation. As Allison has observed, these approaches are 'much more than *simple* angles of vision or approaches. Each conceptual framework consists of a cluster of assumptions and categories that influence what the analyst finds puzzling, how it formulates his question, where he looks for evidence, and what he produces as an answer' (Allison 1971: 245). Although he was analysing the Cuban missile crisis, Allison's general argument is equally applicable to the study of IGR. In an ideal world, any account of IGR 'should draw on *several* or all of the theories relevant to the empirical questions examined, using them as sources of competing hypotheses and interpretations' (Dunleavy 1980: 131). The following description of trends in IGR in developed and developing countries is rooted in the intergovernmental approach.

DEVELOPED COUNTRIES

Page and Goldsmith (1987a: 3–11) argue that the position of local government in the modern state can be evaluated along three dimensions: functions, discretion and access. In other words, local government systems vary in the range of services allocated to them (functions), in their ability to take decisions about the type, level and financing of services (discretion), and in the nature of their contacts with central actors (access).

After comparing central–local relations in seven unitary states, Page and Goldsmith (1987b: 156–62) conclude that there is a distinction between North European and South European states. In North European states, a category which comprises Norway, Denmark, Sweden and Britain, local authorities have more functions and there is a clearer division of labour between centre and locality. Local government in France, Italy and Spain, by contrast, spends a much smaller proportion of total public expenditure. No clear distinctions are possible for discretion in service delivery. In practice, discretion varies from service to service, not between countries. There are differences in the forms of control. In North European states the preferred method is statutory regulation: local government does as it pleases within the law. In South European states, the preferred method is administrative regulation or detailed state approval of local actions. Patterns of access are also distinctive in North European states. Local authorities in these countries have large national interest groups to conduct central–local negotiations whereas in South European states the pattern is one of local elites with direct access to central elites, as well as indirect interest group representation. As a consequence local government in South European states is better able to influence central policy making.

Why should this consistent difference between North and South European states exist? Page and Goldsmith (1987b: 163–8) identify a variety of possible explanations. For example, they suggest that the experience of a Napoleonic state could explain the preference for administrative regulation in the South European states' system of central–local relations. In North European states social-democratic regimes committed to the development of welfare state services used local government to deliver those services. The fate of clientelism in central–local relations was sealed: it was swamped by the demand for public services and the growth in scale, and professionalism, of local government. Of the possible explanations, Page and Goldsmith lay particular emphasis on 'the conditions under which local politics maintains or loses its importance to national politics' (ibid.: 167). Thus, in South European states, local government has 'a firm pillar of effective support at the national level for the expression of the needs of localities' and it has not been supplanted by professional-bureaucratic service delivery networks. However, this focus on differences should not be allowed to obscure recent developments. The impact of the squeeze in resources (see below, pp. 324–5) has led the centre in North European states to exercise more detailed control whereas in response to the same fiscal pressure the centre in South European states has decentralized functions to the regions. This convergence is not explained by any of the foregoing factors but by 'the centre's need to manage and control its local territories' (ibid.: 168).

The bulk of the literature on comparative local government provides case studies of particular local government systems, too many of which pay little or no attention to IGR. (The exceptions include Ashford 1982; Rhodes and Wright 1987b; and Tarrow 1977; and for a review of the literature see Rhodes 1980.) The advantage of Page and Goldsmith's (1987a, 1987b) account is that it not only is *comparative* but also provides descriptions of IGR in individual countries. It avoids long and tedious descriptions of structures, functions and finance. It also demolishes some of the more prominent shibboleths in the study of IGR: for example, the claim that financial dependence on the centre is a key factor determining the degree of local discretion. Above all, it avoids cross-national comparisons of the degree of centralization/autonomy of local government. Such terminology is unhelpful: for example, British local government has more functions but French local government has more access to and influence on the centre – so which system is more centralized? However, rather than comparing systems of IGR, it is possible to compare problems and/or trends within systems of IGR. Four such trends have characterized the last two decades: reorganization, the resource squeeze, political decentralization and differentiation.

The reorganization of local government has been a mini-industry in Western Europe (see Dente and Kjellberg 1988; Kalk 1971; Gunlicks 1981; Leemans 1970; Rowat 1980). Dente (1988: 178) identifies four different types of reorganization: structural reform or changes affecting the number of local units; organizational reforms; financial reforms; and functional and procedural reforms. Structural reform has taken three forms: the amalgamation of municipalities (as, for example, in Britain and Sweden); the creation of regional tiers of government (as in France, Italy, Belgium and Spain); and the introduction of participatory local service delivery agencies (as in Norway and Spain). Organizational reform refers to changes in the internal structure of local government, usually designed to increase efficiency and rationality of decision making (for example, corporate planning in Britain, personnel reform in Italy). Financial reforms in response to resource squeeze are discussed below. Functional and procedural reforms is a miscellaneous category covering, for example, the reduction in prefectoral control in France and Italy and the introduction of new, function specific, planning systems in the UK.

There was almost a 'conventional wisdom' on the need for structural reform: 'functionalism' or effective service delivery. In other words, local government units were deemed to be too small in area with too few financial resources and experts to maximize economies of scale. The consequence of reform has been a reduction in the number of local units, an increase in their size, a reallocation of functions away from the locality and a decrease in the opportunities for citizen participation (Rhodes 1980: 574–6). However, and as important, the reformers did not have it all their own way. As Dente concludes, 'the weight of local tradition, and notably the importance of the local political systems, with their clientelistic practices and their personal links between the politicians and the electorate' enabled reform to be either resisted or turned to local advantage (Dente 1988: 185).

'Resource squeeze' refers to the gap between local taxes and grants and local expenditure – it is a measure of the elasticity of local taxes and grants (Newton 1980: 12–13). In other words, in an era of inflation, has the growth of local income kept pace with the growth in local expenditure? Newton (ibid.:

18) demonstrates that the picture is varied. Denmark and Sweden had few problems, whereas the situation of local authorities in Britain was worsening, and the finances of Italian local authorities had reached crisis proportions. Sharpe (1981: 24) concludes that the only common local financial problem is the disparity between the responsibilities and powers of local authorities: a disparity exacerbated by inflation because local authority taxes were not progressive. However defined, the response of the centre to resource squeeze involved increases in the provision of resources by the centre, the consolidation of grant systems, and increases in central control of local expenditure. Moreover, as central governments were also under financial pressure, they offloaded functions to local and regional units, further exacerbating the disparity between functional responsibilities and financial powers (as, for example, in the Netherlands). The response of local authorities included cuts in local services, the transfer of services to the private sector, and raising revenue through charges and borrowing (see Newton 1980: chapter 9).

Structural and financial reforms seem to illustrate the steady centralization of advanced industrial society. However, there are contradictory trends. Sharpe (1979a: 19) argues that the 1970s saw the political decentralization of Western democracies and he itemizes the spread of neighbourhood councils and the resurgence of ethnic nationalism. In a similar vein, Tarrow argues:

> as the migration of functional conflicts to the summit of the political system erodes the effectiveness of national parliaments, citizens turn more and more not to 'functional' representation but to the territorial institutions around them, reinforcing the territorial dimension in representation just as it is being displaced in policy making and administration.
>
> (Tarrow 1978a: 3)

Moreover, centralization and differentiation went hand in hand. Rhodes and Wright (1987: 7–12) argue for a focus on policy networks rather than local authorities. Central government is non-executant: that is, it is dependent on other agencies for the delivery of services. These agencies include, but are not restricted to, local authorities: the centre works with and through a plethora of institutional tools, referred to by Beer (1978) as 'professional-bureaucratic complexes'. The resulting network of organizations will be function-specific or limited to the particular policy sector or sub-sector. In other words, individual policy sectors are disaggregated (or fragmented vertically between the centre and other agencies) and differentiated (or fragmented horizontally between central agencies). There is no unitary central actor in advanced industrial society but the co-existence of differentiation and centralization:

> Divergent interests within a centre, coupled with the professionalisation of functional policy systems, create multiple centres and erode horizontal co-ordination. . . . [W]e live in an era of 'centreless' societies. Each policy system may be centralised, however, at least in the sense of its centre repeatedly intervening.
>
> (Rhodes and Wright 1987a: 8)

(See also Luhmann 1982: xv, 353–5; Hanf and Scharpf 1978; and Kaufman *et al.* 1986.) IGR in developed countries displays contradictory tendencies between, on the one hand, structural and financial centralization and, on the other hand, political decentralization and differentiation. No easy conclusion about the onset of an era of centralization is defensible. Instead, there is an era of organizational complexity in which IGR can no longer focus on central–local government relations but must concern itself with the full range of organizations: with the professional-bureaucratic complexes or policy networks.

DEVELOPING COUNTRIES

The role and fate of local government, and the pattern of IGR, in developing countries cannot be isolated from the larger topic of political and economic development. Indeed, with independence from colonial rule, local government inherited a heavy burden of expectations. The 'classic model' is summarized as follows by Mawhood:

> A local body should exist which was constitutionally separate from government, and was responsible for a significant range of local services.
> It should have its own treasury, a separate budget and accounts, and its own taxes to produce a substantial part of its revenue.
> It should have its own qualified staff, with hire-and-fire powers over them. . . .
> Decision making on policy and internal procedure was to be in the hands of a majority-elected council.
> Finally, the central government administrators were to be external advisors and inspectors, having no role within the local authority.
>
> (Mawhood 1987: 12)

This model, and decentralization in general, was fashionable in developing countries in the 1960s (see for example Maddick 1963, 1971). There were a number of reasons for this popularity. (The following list is paraphrased from Rondinelli and Cheema 1983a: 14–16; and Smith 1985: 186–8.) First, it was seen as a way of surmounting the limitations of national planning by getting closer to problems, cutting through red-tape and meeting local needs. Second, it improved central 'penetration' of rural areas, thereby spreading knowledge of, and mobilizing support for, the plan and bypassing obstructive local elites. Third, it encouraged the involvement of various religious, ethnic and tribal groups, thereby promoting national unity. Fourth, it increased the speed and flexibility of decision making, encouraging experimentation and reducing central control and direction. Fifth, it increased the efficiency of the centre by freeing top management from routine tasks and reducing the diseconomies of scale caused by congestion at the centre. Sixth, it increased the administrative capacity of the localities and regions and improved the co-ordination of service delivery. Finally, it institutionalized participation, provided opportunities for a range of interests to acquire a 'stake' in maintaining the system, trained citizens for democracy and politicians for government and thereby promoted political maturity and democratic stability.

Theory and practice diverged markedly and rapidly. Thus, Dele Olowu concludes:

> African local governments operate effectively as extensions of state bureaucracy, and the rule in most countries is for the central government to appoint the councils or committees of the local government together with their chief executives. It is therefore doubtful whether the term 'local government' is an appropriate term for describing what in effect are local administration systems.
>
> (Olowu 1987: 5–6)

Cheema and Rondinelli (1983: 297) talk of central 'schizophrenia' about the transfer of power and responsibilities to local agencies. They also show that in Asia, as in Africa, local governments act as 'bureaucratic instruments of the center' (ibid.: 298). Smith (1985: 188) concludes that experience 'has almost everywhere fallen far short of expectations' and Mawhood (1983a: 7) talks of the 'chaotic inefficiency of decentralized government' (see also Wallis 1989: 125; Subramaniam 1980: 590). In brief, elected bodies were replaced by central nominees, important functions were not devolved; there was a high level of central control; and local governments had inadequate powers and finance. Even field administration has generated waste and duplication and suffered from the inadequate delegation of authority (Smith 1985: 188–91). There are two rays of light at the end of this gloomy tunnel. First, Cheema and Rondinelli (1983: 298) argue that there have been incremental improvements in access for people living in neglected rural areas; in the capacity of local political leaders and bureaucrats to lobby the centre for resources; and in the administrative and technical capacity of local and regional agencies. (On attempts to improve access see Schaffer 1985.) They also note the emergence of a local-regional level of development planning. Second, in the 1980s, there was a revival of interest in the classic model (Mawhood 1987: 19). The key question becomes, therefore, what conditions foster local government and build a sustainable relationship between central and local government?

There are markedly different interpretations of the constraints on decentralization and IGR. The interventions of the centre can be seen as a response to poor local standards and the need to control scarce resources. The centre is said to be technically and administratively more competent, monopolizing an urban, educated, economically powerful elite and leaving only a restricted pool of talent in local government where morale is often low and discipline is poor (Wallis 1989: 132). More important, local government faced stiff competition from traditional ruling authorities (for example, village chiefs, sultans), from established castes and classes of landowners defending their sectional interests, and from a modern governing elite striving to control national resources (Mawhood 1987: 17). Historical factors also played an important role. Subramaniam makes the point trenchantly: 'both in Africa and Asia, British rule first created its own pattern of administrative centralization and consequently unleashed a rival tendency towards centralization on the part of educated Africans and Asians' (Subramanian 1980: 583). The major difference in Francophone Africa is that 'centralist tendencies were not conceived as retaliatory safeguards *against* a centralizing colonial administration but rather as necessary replications of French centralism itself' (ibid.: 587). As Rondinelli and Cheema point out, effective local government has also been frustrated by a lack of 'both the resources and the authorities to raise sufficient revenues to carry out the tasks transferred from the centre (Rondinelli and Cheema 1983a: 30). All of these constraints were further exacerbated by technological and economic factors. Thus the new technology of communication and information collection, central planning and the 'compulsive control of resources' to promote economic development and 'the enveloping fear' of international capital and markets all facilitated centralization (Subramaniam 1980: 589). However, the key factors working in favour of recentralization were political. As Wallis (1989: 126) emphasizes, the low legitimacy of regimes, for whatever reason, led them to counter their political insecurities by concentrating power at the centre. Similarly Smith (1985: 193–7) argues that centralization is a product of the coalitions between state bureaucrats (with their control of scarce resources) and class interests (with their control of land, property or means of production).

There is clearly a battery of constraints on the development of local government and the attendant system of IGR. Rondinelli and Cheema (1983a: 27–30) identify four sets of factors shaping the implementation of decentralization policies: environmental conditions, interorganizational relationships, resources, and the characteristics of implementing agencies. To translate, briefly, the effective implementation of decentralization policies requires:

1 an understanding of a nation's political structure, its dominant ideology, policy-making processes and local power structures;
2 the interaction and co-ordination of a large number of organizations at many levels of government which depends, in turn, on *inter alia*, clear objectives, standardized budgeting, accurate communication and effective linkages;
3 sufficient financial, administrative and technical support along with control over such resources and national political support; and
4 agencies with the appropriate technical, managerial and political skills and, *inter alia*, the capacity to co-ordinate and control sub-unit decisions.

Mawhood's (1987: 20–21) list of 'tentative propositions' about the conditions supporting the classic model of decentralizatiron is briefer but no less intimidating. Thus local government flourishes where party competition is restrained;

the national government is stable; there is good public security; citizens have been socialized to the modern system of government; resources are scarce and the centre cannot meet people's expectations and, in consequence, has to seek local support and resources; and traditional authority has an important place in the system. In short, decentralization requires political strength and economic weakness, an inherently unstable combination.

IGR in developing countries approximates the command or agency model of relationship: the centre proposes and the locality disposes. Local government has been undermined and replaced by local administration. However, even systems of field administration have complex sets of organizational relationships and there is nothing automatic about the transmission of central plans into action on the ground: for example, local bureaucrats often have a high degree of discretion and the status hierarchy of a bureaucracy impairs accurate reporting.

If the history of IGR has been bleak, the future is hardly rosy. The conditions supporting effective decentralization are exacting and, as Wallis observes, 'autonomy looks very much an unattainable idea in view of the political and economic considerations prevailing in most countries' (Wallis 1989: 134). None the less, he continues, 'Scope for a limited form of the "bottom-up" approach probably exists'. Just as central governments in developed countries off-loaded functions to cope with resource squeeze, so grass-roots involvement has been part of the response in developing countries to probably even more intractable financial and economic problems. Thus, Mawhood (1987: 21) concludes that local government as the agent of social and economic change has taken the back seat to a more traditional role of providing orderly, rational administration and value for money in services. The romantic view of local self-government has taken a dreadful hammering in developing countries.

TRENDS

The year 2000 will arrive in only a few years. The resurgence of local autonomy, like miracles, will take a little longer. IGR seems to be characterized, for the near future at least, by centralization, control and declining accountability. Such a bleak scenario, however, requires some qualification.

Commentators agree that there is a clear trend towards greater centralization in both developed and developing countries. However, at the same time, central government becomes more fragmented: centralization and differentiation coexist. It is claimed that the 1980s witnessed an ideological challenge to the role of government. Its boundaries were rolled back. The rejection of central planning and the return of markets can be interpreted as an exercise in decentralization. Privatization is an oft-cited and widespread example of this process (Vickers and Wright 1988; Cook and Kirkpatrick 1988). However, privatization is an ambiguous example. It substitutes indirect control through regulation for direct control by ownership. It changes the form of government intervention but it does not abolish either intervention or the monopoly position of the industry, nor does it necessarily resolve the problem of the industry's relationship with government (Heald 1985). However, it does change the policy network, introducing new actors and relationships, and giving a fresh twist to long-standing problems of control and accountability. Above all it illustrates that governments increasingly resort to a variety of instruments for pursuing their policies. Functions are not allocated to general purpose governments (such as local government) but to special purpose authorities. Institutional 'adhocracy' is the order of the day, a process which generates conflicts between agencies competing for 'turf' and between central government and local authorities which resent being bypassed. Government has not been rolled back but splintered and politicized, a process which can only frustrate the attempt to control through centralization.

Such fragmentation not only thwarts control and fuels policy slippage (or deviation from central expectations) but it also increases governmental complexity. Elgin and Bushnell identify the following consequences arising from complexity:

  1 Diminishing relative capacity of a given individual to comprehend the overall system.
  2 Diminishing level of public participation in decision-making.
  3 Declining public access to decision-makers.
  4 Growing participation of experts in decision-making.
  5 Disproportionate growth in costs of co-ordination and control. . . .

  9 Increasing levels of unexpected and counter-intuitive consequences of policy action. . . .

15 Declining overall performance of the system.
16 Growing deterioration of the overall system unlikely to be perceived by most participants in that system.

(Elgin and Bushnell 1977: 37)

In turn, complexity undermines both control and accountability.

The reaction to centralization and control will be political decentralization. As Sharpe argues:

> the decentralist tendencies in the politics of the West are, paradoxically, also a product of the centralization of society and the state machine. That is to say, they are a *reaction* to centralization and not a mere epiphenomenon of it.

(Sharpe 1979a: 20)

Similarly, in developing countries, Wallis argues that 'there is optimism in the air' with experiments to foster effective village councils, in, for example, Kenya and Sri Lanka (Wallis 1989: 141). The crucial point is that political decentralization is a challenge to institutional centralization. It should not be equated with the revival of local government for the latter can be bastions of reaction and conservatism (Fesler 1965: 543). Rather, it can be a challenge to the vested interests entrenched in local government. The micro-politics of the city and the rise of ethnic-nationalism may have receded in the 1980s but they did not disappear. They will be the second element in the politicization of IGR in the 1990s.

This wave of politicization will highlight the inadequacies of conventional mechanisms of parliamentary accountability. In governmental systems with a high degree of differentiation, accountability cannot be defined in institutional terms but must encompass the policy networks, their relationships and the policies. The system of accountability must be designed to fit policies; to assess their effectiveness, not their procedural correctness. The search for new forms of local accountability will intensify.

IGR is on the threshold of an era of turbulence. The 1980s saw old patterns of relationship disrupted but no agreement on what should take their place. The resulting proliferation of institutional forms and increase in complexity does not augur well for any improvement in either functional effectiveness or political accountability.

REFERENCES

Allison, G. (1971) *Essence of Decision*, Boston: Little, Brown & Co.

Anderson, W. (1960) *Intergovernmental Relations in Review*, Minneapolis: University of Minnesota Press.

Ashford, D. (1982) *British Dogmatism and French Pragmatism*, London: Allen & Unwin.

Beer, S. H. (1978) 'Federalism, nationalism and democracy in America', *American Political Science Review* 72: 9–21.

Bulpitt, J. (1983) *Territory and Power in the United Kingdom*, Manchester: Manchester University Press.

Cheema, C. S. and Rondinelli, D. A. (1983) 'Decentralization and development: conclusions and directions', in D. A. Rondinelli and G. S. Cheema (eds) *Decentralization and Development*, London: Sage Publications.

Cliffe, L., Coleman, J. S. and Doornbus, M. R. (eds) (1977) *Government and Rural Development in East Africa: Essays on Political Penetration*, The Hague: Martinus Nijhoff.

Coleman, J. S. (1977) 'The concept of political penetration', in L. Cliffe, J.S. Coleman, and M.R. Doornbus (eds) *Government and Rural Development in East Africa: Essays on Political Penetration*, The Hague: Martinus Nijhoff.

Cook. P. and Kirkpatrick, C. (eds) (1988) *Privatisation in Less Developed Countries*, Brighton: Wheatsheaf.

Crozier, M. and Thoenig, J. C. (1976) 'The regulation of complex organised systems', *Administration Science Quarterly* 21: 546–70.

Dente, B. (1988) 'Local government reform and legitimacy', in B. Dente and F. Kjellberg (eds) *The Dynamics of Institutional Change*, London: Sage Publications.

Dente, B. and Kjellberg, F. (eds) (1988) *The Dynamics of Institutional Change*, London: Sage Publications.

Dunleavy, P. (1980) 'Social and political theory and the issues in central–local relations', in G. W. Jones (ed.) *New Approaches to the Study of Central–Local Government Relationships*, Farnborough: Gower/SSRC.

——(1982) 'Is there a radical approach to public administration?', *Public Administration* 60: 215–33.

——(1984) 'The limits to local government', in M. Boddy and C. Fudge (eds) *Local Socialism?*, London: Methuen.

Dunleavy, P. and O'Leary, B. (1987) *Theories of the State*, London: Macmillan.

Elgin, D. S. and Bushnell, R. A. (1977) 'The limits to complexity: are bureaucracies becoming unmanageable?', *The Futurist* (December): 337–49.

Fesler, J. W. (1949) *Area and Adminstration*, Birmingham, Ala.: University of Alabama Press.

——(1965) 'Approaches to the understanding of decentralization', *Journal of Politics* 27: 536–66.

Fried, R. C. (1963) *The Italian Prefects*, New Haven: Yale University Press.

Gunlicks, A. B. (ed.) (1981) *Local Government Reform and Reorganization*, Port Washington, NY: Kennikat Press.

Hanf, K. (1978) 'Introduction', in K. Hanf and F. W. Scharpf (eds) *Interorganizational Policy Making*, London: Sage Publications.

Hanf, K. and Scharpf, F. W. (eds) (1978) *Interorganizational Policy Making*, London: Sage Publications.

Heald, D. (1985) 'Will the privatization of public enterprises solve the problems of control?', *Public Administration* 65: 7–22.

Hechter, M. (1975) *Internal Colonialism*, London: Routledge & Kegan Paul.

Jones, G. W. and Stewart, J. D. (1983) *The Case for Local Government*, London: Allen & Unwin.

Kalk, F. (ed.) (1971) *Regional Planning and Regional Government in Europe*, The Hague: International Union of Local Authorities.

Kaufman, F. X., Majone, G., Ostrom, V. (eds) with the assistance of Wirth, W. (1986) *Guidance, Control and Evaluation in the Public Sector*, Berlin: Walter de Gruyter.

LaPalombara, J. (1971) 'Penetration: a crisis of governmental capacity', in L. Binder, *et al.* (eds) *Crises and Sequences in Political Development*, Princeton: Princeton University Press.

Leemans, A. F. (1970) *Changing Patterns of Local Government*, The Hague: International Union of Local Authorities.

Luhmann, N. (1982) *The Differentiation of Society*, New York: Columbia University Press.

Maass, A. (ed.) (1959) *Area and Power*, Glencoe, Ill.: Free Press.

Maddick, H. (1963) *Democracy, Decentralization and Development*, London: Asia Publishing House.

——(1970) *Panchayati Raj: A Study of Rural Local Government*, London: Longman.

——(1971) 'The contribution of local government', in IULA (eds) *Local Government as Promoter of Economic and Social Development*, The Hague: International Union of Local Authorities.

Mawhood, P. (1983a) 'Decentralization: the concept and the practice', in P. Mawhood (ed.) *Local Government in the Third World*, Chicester: John Wiley.

_____(ed.) (1983b) *Local Government in the Third World*, Chichester: John Wiley.

_____(1987) 'Decentralization and the Third World in the 1980s', *Planning and Administration* 14: 11–22.

Newton, K. (1980) *Balancing the Books*, London: Sage Publications.

Olowu, D. (1987) 'African local government since independence', *Planning and Administration* 14 (1): 5–7.

Page, E. C. and Goldsmith, M. J. (1987a) 'Centre and locality: functions, access and discretion', in E. C. Page and M. J. Goldsmith (eds) *Central and Local Government Relations*, London: Sage Publications.

_____(1987b) 'Centre and locality: explaining cross national variations', in E. C. Page and M. J. Goldsmith (eds) *Central and Local Government Relations*, London: Sage Publications.

_____(eds) (1987c) *Central and Local Government Relations*, London: Sage Publications.

Rhodes, R. A. W. (1974) 'Regional policy and a "Europe of regions" ', *Regional Studies* 8: 105–14.

_____(1980) 'Developed countries', in D. C. Rowat (ed.) *International Handbook on Local Government Reorganization*, London: Aldwych Press.

_____(1981) *Control and Power in Central–Local Government Relations*, Farnborough: Gower.

_____(1988) *Beyond Westminster and Whitehall*, London: Unwin Hyman.

Rhodes, R. A. W. and Wright, V. (1987a) 'Introduction', in R. A. W. Rhodes and V. Wright (eds) *Tensions in the Territorial Politics of Western Europe*, London: Frank Cass.

_____(eds) (1987b) *Tensions in the Territorial Politics of Western Europe*, London: Frank Cass.

Rondinelli, D. A. and Cheema, G. S. (1983a) 'Implementing decentralization policies: an introduction', in D. A. Rondinelli and G. S. Cheema (eds) *Decentralization and Development*, London: Sage Publications.

_____(eds) (1983b) *Decentralization and Development*, London: Sage Publications.

Rowat, D. C. (ed.) (1980) *International Handbook on Local Government Reorganization*, London: Aldwych Press.

Saunders, P. (1982) 'Why study central–local relations?', *Local Government Studies* 8 (2): 55–66.

Schaffer, B. (ed.) (1985) 'Access', special issue of *Development and Change* 6 (2).

Sharpe, L. J. (1979a) 'Decentralist trends in Western democracies: a first appraisal', in L. J. Sharpe (ed.) *Decentralist Trends in Western Democracies*, London: Sage Publications.

_____(ed.) (1979b) *Decentralist Trends in Western Democracies*, London: Sage Publications.

_____(ed.) (1981) *The Local Fiscal Crisis in Western Europe*, London: Sage Publications.

_____(1981) 'Is there a fiscal crisis in Western European local government? a first appraisal', in L. J. Sharpe (ed.) *The Local Fiscal Crisis in Western Europe*, London: Sage Publications.

Smith, B. C. (1967) *Field Administration*, London: Routledge & Kegan Paul.

_____(1985) *Decentralization*, London: Allen & Unwin.

Smith, B. C. and Stanyer, J. (1976) *Administering Britain*, Glasgow: Fontana.

Staniland, M. (1970) 'The rhetoric of centre–periphery relations', *Journal of Modern African Studies* 8: 617–36.

Subramaniam, V. (1980) 'Developing countries', in D. C. Rowat (ed.) *International Handbook on Local Government Reorganization*, London: Aldwych Press.

Tarrow, S. (1977) *Between Centre and Periphery*, New Haven: Yale University Press.

——(1978) 'Introduction', in S. Tarrow, P. J. Katzenstein and L. Grazianne (eds) *Territorial Politics in Industrial Nations*, London: Praeger.

Tarrow S., Katzenstein, P. J. and Grazianne, L. (eds) (1978) *Territorial Politics in Industrial Nations*, London: Praeger.

Tilly, C. (ed.) (1975) *The Formation of National States in Western Europe*, Princeton: Princeton University Press.

Vickers, J. and Wright, V. (eds) (1988) *The Politics of Privatization in Western Europe*, London: Frank Cass.

Wallis, M. (1989) *Bureaucracy: Its Role in Third World Development*, London: Macmillan.

Wright, D. S. (1974) 'Intergovernmental relations: an analytical overview', *Annals of the American Academy of Political and Social Science* 416 (November): 1–16.

——(1978) *Understanding Intergovernmental Relations*, North Scituate, Mass.: Duxbury Press.

FURTHER READING

There are no authoritative surveys of IGR, although Smith (1985) provides the best general account of decentralization. Consequently, this guide to further reading has three sections: theory, developed countries and developing countries.

Theory

The post-war classics on decentralization are Fesler (1949, 1965) and Maass (1959). Most theoretical contributors on IGR are country-specific and cover federal systems. None the less the following deserve attention: Beer (1978), USA; Crozier and Thoenig (1976), France, Kaufman *et al.* (1986), primarily the Federal Republic of Germany; Rhodes (1988), UK; and Wright (1978), USA. The collection edited by Hanf and Scharpf (1978) is noteworthy for Scharpf's theoretical essay and his analysis of the Federal Republic of Germany. There is a paucity of material on unitary states, although Tilly (1975) provides several excellent essays on the origins of unitary states in Western Europe.

Developed countries

There are several useful collections of essays, although the essays on individual countries tend to be better than the comparative analyses. The best collections are Hanf and Scharpf (1978); Page and Goldsmith (1987c); Rhodes and Wright (1987b); and Tarrow *et al.* (1978). On the comparative study of local government reorganization see Dente and Kjellberg (1988); Gunlicks (1981); and Rowat (1980). Sharpe (1979b, 1981) provides studies of political decentralization and resource squeeze, respectively. More restricted in scope but still comparative are Ashford (1982) and Tarrow (1977). Any listing on IGR in individual countries would be prohibitively long.

Developing countries

An introductory survey is provided by Smith (1985), who also provides an extensive bibliography. More briefly, see Wallis (1989). Useful collections of essays are Mawhood (1983b), which focuses on Africa; Rondinelli and Cheema (1983b), which encompasses Asia; and Rowat (1980), which focuses on reorganization. On local government in the immediate post-colonial era see Maddick (1963). On developments in the 1980s see Mawhood (1987). Again a listing on individual countries would be prohibitively long.

22

INTERGOVERNMENTAL RELATIONS: FEDERAL SYSTEMS

GRANT HARMAN

Federal political systems are based on political and social theories about federalism, a concept whose origins go back to the ancient world and biblical times. Federal systems have existed in various forms from the loose linking together by treaty of sovereign states for specific military or economic purposes in the Hellenic world. But their popularity increased greatly following final agreement on the United States constitution in 1787, the use of federal ideas as a guide for the Swiss, Canadian and Australian federations, and immediately after the Second World War in various experiments of nation building, particular in Europe, Asia, Africa, the Middle East and the Caribbean.

In essence, federalism provides an organizational mechanism to achieve a degree of political unity within a population whose characteristics demonstrate diversity and variety. Under this arrangement, separate regional political units (often referred to as states or provinces) are combined for limited, specified purposes under an overarching administration, but in such a way that the government of each separate regional unit maintains its integrity and substantial autonomy. This is achieved by distributing powers and responsibilities in such a manner to protect the existence and authority of both levels of government. Both levels of government can pass laws, levy taxes and relate directly to the people. Usually there is an explicit constitutional demarcation of powers and functions between central and regional governments, and generally there are specified mechanisms and procedures for resolving conflicts and disputes between central and regional governments, and also between two or more regional governments.

In all types of societies where federal systems have been established, such systems demand some degree of co-operation between central and regional governments. However, in modern societies with federal systems and a much higher degree of interdependence between all levels of government (including local government), intergovernmental relations are of crucial importance. Hence political scientists today are interested not only in theories of federalism and their application in constitutions and legislation, but also with how federal systems actually work in practice. Of particular importance is how central and regional levels of government relate to one another, how powers and responsibilities are shared, how conflict and disputes are resolved, and to what extent central and regional governmental bodies can work together effectively in the national interest in tackling problems.

CONCEPTUAL PROBLEMS

Discussions of federal systems and of intergovernmental relations within such systems are often plagued with problems of definition. This is particularly so in the case of the terms 'federalism', 'federal' and 'federation'.

In its broadest sense, the word federalism refers to the linking of people and institutions by mutual consent for a specified purpose, without the sacrifice of their individual identities. The term federal was coined by Bible-centred federal theologians of seventeenth-century Britain and New England to refer to a system of holy and enduring covenants between God and human beings, which lay at the foundations of their world view (Elazar 1968: 353–4). The word federal was derived from the Latin word *foedus*, meaning covenant. This conception of federal was taken up by nineteenth-century social theorists and used in the development of various ideas of social contract. As a political device, however, federalism can be viewed more narrowly as a form of organization in which power is dispersed as a means of safeguarding individual and local liberties. In federal political systems, political organizations generally take on a distinctive character. This applies to the interest groups and political parties as well as to the formal institutions of government (see, for example, Truman 1951).

Federalism also has been conceptualized as a means to achieve different political and social purposes. Two particular purposes stand out. First, federalism has been seen by many as a means to unite people already linked together by bonds of nationality. In such cases, the political units brought together are seen as a part of a national whole. Essentially, this is the American view of federalism, which today has become the generally accepted one. An alternative view is that federalism is a means to unify diverse peoples for important but limited purposes, without disrupting their primary ties to their existing governments. Within this latter arrangement, the federal government is much more limited in scope and powers and the particular structure is often referred to as a confederation. However, a degree of confusion remains because the terms federation and confederation are often used interchangeably. Today the confederation idea has also been used for such supra-national political

337

organizations as the European Economic Community (EEC) and the National Atlantic Treaty Organisation (NATO).

Federal systems differ from other related forms of political organization. True federal systems are different in conception from dual or multiple monarchies, where union between political units exists only through the sovereign and the exercise of his or her executive power. The dual monarchy of England and Scotland was finally eliminated through legislative union of the two nations in 1707. Such legislative unions are closely similar to federal systems, except that the terms of the union allow retention of particular non-centralizing elements. Thus, in the United Kingdom, within the framework of cabinet government, Scotland has a national ministry of its own with a separate administrative structure. Federal systems also are different from decentralized unitary states, in which local administration is usually limited in nature and subject to supervision and overall control by central authorities. In such polities local autonomy can be reduced by the central government. Many of the governments of South America which purport to be federal have in practice combined devolution of power to regional governments with an overriding authority exercised by the central governments (Watts 1966).

The word federal generally has been used loosely in political discussions. As a rule, the adjective federal has been applied to constitutions and to forms of government, although some writers (Laski 1941; Livingston 1956) have talked of federal societies and others of federal ideologies (King 1982). Livingston sees federal government as 'a device by which the federal qualities of the society are articulated and presented.... If [the diversities] are grouped territorially, i.e. geographically, then the result may be a society that is federal. If they are not grouped territorially, then the society cannot be said to be federal' (Livingston 1956: 2).

Federalism and federal systems need to be distinguished from 'intergovernmental relations' in such systems. Federalism is more than the relationships between governmental units in a federal system, since it involves principles about those relationships as well as the actual distribution of power. Federalism also is concerned with how federal principles influence political arrangements generally, including political party and electoral systems.

ESSENTIAL CHARACTERISTICS OF FEDERAL SYSTEMS

Federal systems differ considerably in terms of their formal constitutions and division of powers, how they operate, and which federal principles they emphasize. Nevertheless, political theorists and researchers involved in empirical studies have found it useful to try to specify those characteristics which are essential to a truly federal system.

Watts (1966: 10–11) thus emphasized the notion of dual sovereignty, with central and regional governments acting side by side, each separate and virtually independent of the other in its own sphere. Each relates directly to the people. There must be an explicit constitutional demarcation of powers and functions for government at each level; each must be independent within its own sphere. Generally, although not necessarily, the division of authority must be specified in a written constitution, and an independent judiciary must be created to interpret the supreme constitution and to act as a guardian of the constitutional division of powers.

Two decades earlier, K. C. Wheare (1946), whose writings had a major influence on the post-Second World War experiments with new federal systems in Asia, Africa, the Middle East and the Caribbean, especially in the British Commonwealth, discussed at some length what federal government is. He saw the division of powers between central and regional government as a central element. But the central government is not subordinate to regional governments, as it was with the post-revolutionary association of American colonies, but rather each level within its sphere is independent and autonomous. 'By the federal principle', he wrote, 'I mean the method of dividing powers so that the general and regional governments are each, within a sphere, co-ordinate and independent' (Wheare 1946: 11). This condition seems unnecessarily rigid and at variance with practice, for in many federal systems, including that of the United States and Australia, federal laws and treaties according to the constitution override those of state governments.

About a decade after Wheare, A. W. Macmahon listed the essential attributes of federalism as follows:

(a) a federal system distributes power between a common and constituent governments under an arrangement that cannot be changed by the ordinary process of central legislation . . . (b) the matters entrusted to the constituent units . . . must be substantial and not merely trivial; (c) [the] central organs are to some extent directly in contact with individuals, both to draw authority from them through elections and also for the purpose of exacting taxes and compliance with regulations . . . (d) the member states have considerable leeway in devising and changing their forms of government and their procedures . . . (e) A further essential is the equality of the constituent states, absolute as to legal status but at best relative as to such matters as size, population and wealth.

(Macmahon 1955: 4–5)

More recently, Daniel J. Elazar, a leading American scholar of federalism, defined the essential elements of federalism as a written constitution (the federal relationships must be established through a perpetual covenant of union embodied in a constitution which specifies the terms by which power is divided), non-centralization (the authority for state and federal governments to exercise powers cannot be withdrawn without mutual consent), a real division of power (the area of authority of the constituent units is territorially based), direct contact with the people (thus providing a powerful mechanism to maintain the union) and mechanisms to maintain non-centralization (such as permanent boundaries of constituent units, and effective ways of combining units of different size), and the federal principle (such as both the central governments and state governments having a substantially complete set of governing institutions). According to Elazar, viewed theoretically,

> these patterns of behavior and the arguments advanced to justify them serve to reaffirm the fundamental principles that (1) the strength of a federal polity does not stem from the power of the national government but from the authority vested in the nation as a whole; (2) both the national government and the governments of the constituent polities are possessed of delegated powers only; and (3) all governments are limited by the common national constitution.
>
> (Elazar 1968: 361)

FEDERALISM AND FEDERAL SYSTEMS

Generations before the invention of the term federal, political systems and political organizations were developed embodying elements of federal principles. In the ancient Greek world, federal arrangements were first articulated in religious, tribal and city–state alliances. The classic example was the Achaean League (251–146 BC), which was an alliance or super polis to provide military protection. The League attracted the attention of scholars in the nineteenth century as being the first federal polity. About the same time, the Israelite political system provides an example of a union of constituent polities, based on a sense of common nationality. Several of the great ancient empires, notably under Persian, Hellenic and Roman control, structured their political arrangements under the principle of cultural home rule, which was an example of a measure of contractual devolution of political power.

In medieval times, elements of federalism were seen in feudalism and in the leagues of self-protection established by the commercial towns of central Europe. Later quasi-federal arrangements developed in Spain and Italy under a system of multiple monarchy. In the sixteenth and seventeenth centuries, biblical scholars of the Reformation began to apply federal principles to state-building; such ideas provided an organizational basis for the federation of the United Provinces in the Netherlands in the late sixteenth century, while the Swiss created a loose confederation of cantons.

The first modern formulations of federal ideas were associated with the rise of the nation-state in the sixteenth and seventeenth centuries (Forsyth 1981). In this situation, federalism provided an attractive means of dealing with problems of national unity. The potential of federalism was seen in the early seventeenth century by Johannes Althusius, who, in analysing the Dutch and Swiss constitutions, saw federalism as a vehicle to achieve national unity. He was the first to connect federalism with popular sovereignty and to distinguish between leagues, multiple monarchies and confederations. But it was not until immediately following the American revolution that the ideas of British and continental thinkers combined with biblical thinking to create the first modern federal system – that of the United States in 1787. This development and its success has had a major influence on ideas about federalism internationally since then.

The founders of the United States had distinct advantages over others who had experimented earlier with federal ideas. Theirs was a post-feudal society with a relatively short history. Once established, the United States was a relatively isolated nation, with only minor external pressures until the twentieth century. Moreover, Americans were concerned above all else with the practical aspects of making federalism work. The creation of a theoretical framework for the American experiment took place in the debates over ratification of the constitution and in the formulations in *The Federalist*. The end result was a compromise between those who wished the federal government to be supreme and those who wished for the states to have the leading role. In essence, the model adopted was

> that the business of State is 'divided' between two popularly elected governments, a national government embracing the whole territory of the nation and a regional government for each of the lesser territories; that each government will possess the basic facilities to make, manage, and enforce its laws 'like any ordinary government'; that subject to the provisions of the constitution, each government is 'free' to act 'independently' of, or in concert with, the other, as it chooses; that jurisdictional disputes between the national government and the governments of the lesser territories will be settled by judicial arbitration; that the principle of national supremacy will prevail where two valid actions, national and regional, are in conflict; that the instruments of national government, but not necessarily the lesser territories, are set forth in a written constitution; that the national legislature is a bicameral system in which one house, the 'first branch', is composed according to the size of the population in each territory, while each territory has equal representation in the 'second branch'; lastly that the constitution is fundamental law, changeable only by a special plebiscitary process.
>
> (Davis 1978: 121–2)

The United States constitution and the experiment which followed had a major influence in federal thinking for the next two centuries. It provided key ideas for other federal experiments that followed, notably the federal constitutions for Canada and Australia. It also provided the popular archetype to which scholars continued to turn. Writing immediately after the Second World War, Wheare asserted that 'since the United States is universally regarded as an example of federal government, it justifies us in describing the principle, which distinguishes it so markedly and so significantly, as the *federal* principle' (Wheare 1946: 11). Similarly, in 1969 Geoffrey Sawer commented:

'Federal Government, as that expression is now usually understood, was devised by the Founders of the Constitution of the United States of America in 1787–8' (Sawer 1969: 1).

Prior to the Second World War, apart from Canada, Switzerland and Australia, a number of new nations were influenced by federal principles. For example, in Latin America, Argentina, Brazil and Mexico adopted federal structures, while federal principles were included in the constitutions of a number of other countries including Colombia and Venezuela. There were also European experiments, such as with the Weimar constitution in Germany, while federal principles were used in the United Kingdom to accommodate the Irish. But the big push towards federal systems was a post-Second World War phenomenon, as a part of post-war reconstruction in Europe and the decolonization movement in Asia, Africa, the Middle East and the Caribbean. Britain was the most prolific creator of post-colonial federations. Some of these post-war federal attempts soon collapsed, such as the attempt to build an All-Indian federation (1947); others lasted for a period before other arrangements took their place, such as Rhodesia and Nyasaland (1953). But many federal systems established by Britain remain to this day; examples include Malaysia, Nigeria, India and Pakistan.

The lasting popularity of the federal form of government has surprised many. Scholars such as Harold Laski fifty years ago had concluded that federalism was obsolete, and outmoded for the modern world. Writing in 1939, he declared: 'I infer in a word that the epoch of federalism is over' (Watts 1966: 5). But, especially in the process of building new nations in North America and Australia, and in decolonization, federalism provided a convenient model for creating political systems of reasonably large size, for achieving some degree of transcending unity in geographic areas of ethnic diversity, and as means of power sharing between major ethnic groups. In such situations, where the forces for integration and for separation have been at odds with each other, the federal solution proved a popular formula. But over the last two decades, enthusiasm for federalism has waned somewhat, especially in Africa, particularly as a number of new nations in the developing world have been plagued with economic problems. On the other hand, in modern federal systems such as the United States, Canada and Australia, the federal form of government appears remarkably durable and also adaptable to the changing requirements of modern industrial societies. Such political systems face problems of organizational complexity and in the multiplicity of power relationships; however, according to two Canadian scholars, in such systems 'there is greater opportunity for, and likelihood of, the devolution of power to lower and more manageable levels' (Bakvis and Chandler 1987: 3).

INTERGOVERNMENTAL RELATIONS

One current major concern of political scientists and other scholars interested in federalism is how well and how efficiently modern political systems actually operate, and how central and regional governments, as well as local government bodies, attempt to work together to solve shared problems. In modern federal systems, such as the United States, Canada and Australia, a particularly complex set of machinery and relationships have developed and there is ongoing debate about how well these structures cope with the current needs of citizens and the functions of government. From time to time, federal governments and intergovernment commissions suggest major structural reform, or other ways of rationalization or achieving greater efficiency and simplicity, but substantial changes have proved difficult to achieve. There is ongoing concern, too, about the strong tendency of federal government bodies and initiatives to dominate in their relations with state and local government.

Within such federal systems, central and regional governments were able to operate in their very early years with a large measure of independence. Each had separate agreed areas of responsibility, and the main policy areas for a considerable time remained largely the sole responsibility of government at one level or another. This situation, however, did not last long, though it is a matter of debate about how much shared responsibility actually operated in the early years of these systems. Elazar, for example, with respect to the American system, argues passionately that American federalism was always marked by co-operation between governments at different levels and that 'virtually all the activities of government in the nineteenth century were shared activities, involving federal, state and local government in their planning, financing and execution' (Elazar 1969: 84). But this argument needs to be seen in the context of his defence of the role of the states in the American system, and his belief that effective federalism means a real partnership and balance of power between central and regional levels of government.

Whatever the merits of the debates about the precise nature of federal arrangements in their formative stages, it is clear that today in such federal systems as the United States, Canada and Australia a highly complex set of machinery and of linkages in intergovernmental relations has developed. O'Toole (1985) sees the distinguishing features as complexity and interdependence – complexity in the sense that the intergovernmental network is large and highly differentiated, and interdependence in the sense that intergovernmental relations exhibit an amalgamated pluralism, with power and responsibility being shared among the branches and layers of government even within a single policy domain. This situation developed in response to various external pressures, such as major wars and international incidents, recessions and depressions, but also to internal problems related to areas such as social welfare, crime, education, transport and the needs of cities. In addition, there have been special problems such as racial segregation in the United States and ethnic and cultural diversity in Canada. The extent of the current network of interrelating units of government is vast: in the United States it includes approximately 80,000 separate governmental units, comprising federal, state, county, municipal and special-district jurisdictions. Their powers and responsibilities overlap and there is a considerable degree of competition in providing services to the public (O'Toole 1985: 2).

In each of these modern federal systems, complex additional political structures have been developed to enable governments at various levels to communicate and bargain, to resolve differences, and to undertake joint activities. In Australia, for instance, these structures include Premiers' Conferences, the Loan Council, and a range of separate ministerial councils covering a wide range of policy domains from agriculture and education to regulation of companies and transport. Accompanying these political structures bringing heads of government and ministers together are various administrative structures which provide for regular meetings of officials and for joint activities. Take, for example, the case of education in Australia which, at the time the federal constitution was drawn up at the beginning of the twentieth century, was to be exclusively a state matter. The Federal Government, however, gradually became involved in the education sector to the extent that today it contributes the total operating and capital funds for all public higher education (even though most institutions are legally state government institutions, responsible to a state minister) and a substantial amount of the costs of technical and further education and of both government and non-government schools. Federal and state education ministers meet regularly in the Australian Education Council, which has its own separate secretariat (located in Melbourne, a state capital) and officers, while the Council is supported by a large number of permanent and *ad hoc* committees and working groups, made up of federal and state officials (Harman and Smart 1983). Sometimes it is agreed that particular initiatives will be undertaken by either federal or state governments, but in other cases, such as with the new Curriculum Corporation, federal and state governments combine to work through a new public company structure, legally owned by the ministers.

Fiscal relations are of great concern in federal systems, especially on matters such as how income is raised through taxation and charges and by whom, and how such resources are shared and distributed. Federal governments use a number of different strategies to allocate resources to regional and local governments and to the public. These include intergovernmental transfers by block grants, and by tied or special purposes grants, shared funding between governments on an agreed formula, and direct allocations to individuals and groups (Grewal *et al.* 1980). Various mechanisms operate to try to make the resource base of each regional unit more equitable; for example, in Australia for many years a proportion of federal taxation revenue has been allocated to the less well-off states, through the Commonwealth Grants Commission established in 1933 (May 1971).

THE STUDY OF FEDERALISM

With the development of political science as a discipline in the late nineteenth and early twentieth centuries, the study of federalism shifted from being concerned with normative theory to empirical research. Such scholars as Bryce and Dicey studied federalism as part of an interest in political systems. Yet, with a few exceptions, the study of federalism was generally neglected for many years.

Renewed interest in federalism developed in the late 1930s and 1940s, stimulated by problems in intergovernmental relations within the United States and by a period of very active nation building which followed the Second World War. Beginning in the 1930s, a new generation of political scientists began to raise questions about the particular characteristics of federal systems and how federal structures influenced the development and operation of other components of political systems, such as interest groups and political parties. By the 1960s, federalism was attracting the attention of students of comparative politics and the politics of developing countries, as well as scholars interested in public administration.

Since the 1970s the main thrust internationally has been from students of intergovernmental relations, attempting to understand better the dynamics of interaction between government at different levels in complex federal systems such as the United States, Canada and Australia. This work has attracted the interest of economists and students of public finance as well as political scientists and students of public administration, and has been given considerable stimulus by the work of various commissions and committees of inquiry appointed by governments to consider ways of modifying existing arrangements.

Over the past two decades, students of federalism have concentrated attention on a variety of specialized problems. Three deserve mention here. The first concerns the reasons for establishing federations, or why people who achieve a federal union actually come together. On the face of it, one would speculate that people join together to form a federation for a variety of reasons, and that it would be unlikely that any common set of factors operated. However, there has been considerable debate on these questions and two different hypotheses will be considered here, outlined in two important books – W. H. Riker's *Federalism: Origins, Operation and Significance* (Riker 1964) and R. L. Watts's *New Federations: Experiments in the Commonwealth* (Watts 1966). Riker's study is in the quasi-scientific style of the 'behavioural movement' attempting to develop testable generalizations, while Watt's work is in the tradition of the historically oriented comparative study of Wheare, concerned with the search for significant patterns.

Riker's argument is that federalism is 'a bargain between prospective national leaders and officials of constituent governments for the purpose of aggregating territory, the better to lay taxes and raise armies'. The parties are predisposed to favour such a bargain by the existence of two circumstances, which he names as the expansion condition and the military condition. The expansion condition refers to the politicians who offer the bargain desiring to expand their territorial control to meet an external military or diplomatic threat, or to prepare for military or diplomatic aggression or aggrandizement, but who, for various reasons, are unable to use force. The military condition refers to the politicians who accept the bargain giving up some independence for the sake of union, and doing so because of some military-diplomatic threat or opportunity. Riker examines numerous examples of the establishment of federations and concludes that 'the hypothesis is confirmed that the military and the expansion conditions are necessary to the occurrence of federalism' (Riker 1964). Watts examines six new federal experiments (India, Pakistan, Malaya and Malaysia, Nigeria, Rhodesia and Nyasaland, and the West Indies) and identifies a number of social factors and motives which operated, with each being potentially either unifying or separating. He concludes that, while dominant motives varied in each case,

> two features stand out in common to them all. First, there was a geographical distribution, at least to some degree, of the diversities within each of these societies, with the results that demands for political autonomy were made on a regional basis. Secondly, in each of the recent federations, as in the older ones, there existed at one and the same time powerful desires to be united for certain purposes, because of a community of outlook or the expectation of common benefits of union, and deep rooted desires to be organized under autonomous regional governments for others, because of contrasting ways of life or the desire to protect divergent interests. The result in each was a tension between the conflicting demands for territorial integration and for Balkanization.
>
> (Watts 1966: 93)

Neither of these hypotheses have been found totally satisfactory. Davis (1978) comments that, irrespective of these two approaches, what is common to all cases of the establishment of federal systems is a discussion of what kind of political structure is to result, and a process of hammering out an agreement to accommodate different interests.

A second debate among scholars relates to how federal systems change over time, and the operation of conflicting trends towards integration and decentralization. An international comparative study undertaken by the Comparative Federalism Research Committee of the International Political Science Association (Brown-John 1988) concludes that most federal systems appear to be centralizing legislative powers, while in a small number of cases the opposite trend operates. Other recent studies have observed the same phenomenon. What factors promote integration and decentralization? Will the trend towards integration lead to the eventual modification of federal systems in favour of unitary structures, and will the trend towards decentralization lead to eventual disintegration? Debate on these topics has not been conclusive. Davis, for example, rejects the notion that the answer lies either in the factors of institutional ability or political predisposition alone, and sees a centralizing trend being dominant in federal systems in all complex societies. In such societies, he argues, to talk of independent action by either federal or regional governments is meaningless 'when two governments, whether from love or necessity, become so wedded to each other in the common bed of nationalized politics that neither can turn, talk, or breathe without immediately affecting the other (Davis 1978: 148). In such situations, there is a strong tendency for central governments to take a commanding role, especially in terms of fiscal relations. The precise way that fiscal resources are divided between different levels of government in turn affects critically the political and administrative relations between the central government and the states.

Livingston takes a different approach. His argument, in summary, is that the legal/formal or jurisprudential approach to understanding federalism is only one approach. An alternative is to concentrate on the social configuration of society – the types of interests which compose it, their diversity, their geographic distribution, etc. The degree that social diversity is distributed on a territorial basis determines the federal qualities of the society. He explains:

> Every society, every nation if you will, is more or less closely integrated in accordance with its own peculiar historical, cultural, economic, political and other determinants. Each is composed of elements that feel themselves to be different from the other elements in varying degrees. . . . Furthermore, these diversities may be distributed among the members of a society in such a fashion that certain attitudes are found in particular territorial areas, or they may be scattered widely throughout the whole of the society. If they are grouped territorially, that is geographically, then the result may be a society that is federal. If they are not grouped territorially, then the society cannot be said to be federal.
>
> (Livingston 1967: 37)

Thus the answer to integration or decentralization lies, as does understanding the dynamics of a federal system, with understanding the federal qualities of a society.

A somewhat similar theoretical approach comes from Friedrich, who sees federation essentially as a process. His argument is that in the process of federalizing

> an emergent federal order may be operating in the direction of both integration and differentiation; federalizing being *either* the process by which a number of separate political units . . . enter into and develop arrangements for working out solutions together . . . *or* the reverse process through which a hitherto unitary political community, as it becomes differentiated into a number of separate and distinct political subcommunities, achieves a new order in which the differentiated communities become capable of working out separately and on their own decisions and policies on problems they no longer have in common. Federalism refers to this process, as it does to the structures and patterns this process creates.
>
> (Friedrich 1968: 176–7)

Friedrich's work, like Livingston's approach, is full of ambiguity and difficulties. It is difficult, for example, to recognize which processes are federal and which are not. Further, he does not provide any real indication of the link between the process and structure. However, he leads us to expect that federal systems generally are not static but changing in response to various pressures.

Other scholars have approached the problem of change in federal systems, and of integrating and decentralizing trends, from other perspectives. Brown-John (1988) argues that recently in federal systems there is less use of constitutional amendments to achieve change, and more use of agreements between governments, often negotiated by public officials. This facilitates changing relations. Earlier another Canadian scholar, Donald V. Smiley (1980), drew attention to the importance of executive elite interaction as one of the particular characteristics of Canadian federalism.

Finally, especially in the United States, there has been a lively debate about intergovernmental relations and how best to conceptualize the structure of a modern federal system and the complex linkages between different levels of government and between different agencies. Grodzins emphasizes the importance of government at three levels in the United States, and, while the structure is chaotic, it works. He sees the American federal system as a structure of sharing and integration, and uses the metaphor of a marble cake:

> the American system of government as it operates is not a layer cake at all. It is not three layers of government, separated by a sticky substance or anything else. Operationally, it is a marble cake, or what the British call a rainbow cake. No important activity of government in the United States is the exclusive province of one of the levels, not even what may be regarded as the most national functions, such as foreign relations, not even the most local of functions, such as police protection or park maintenance.
>
> (Grodzins 1966: 18)

Elazar, who was a research student of Grodzins, takes a similar view, emphasizing the importance of partnership and shared responsibility. But in their work there is a certain ambiguity about the precise extent of powers at different levels, and what happens when there is a major conflict and the partners disagree.

FEDERALISM: THEORY AND EXPERIENCE

Federalism is a set of political principles and values deeply rooted in Western history, but it was not until the nineteenth century that it was successfully applied as a basis for structuring modern political systems. Since then numerous attempts have been made to establish polities based on federal principles. While some attempts have not survived in the longer term, many federal political systems have proved most durable and adaptable. In such systems – for example, the United States, Canada and Australia – there is a reasonably strong popular commitment to federal principles and arrangements.

Despite theories about federalism being a transition stage to unitary government, no truly federal system has evolved into a unitary one. On the contrary, federalism as a principle has worked well to combine diverse interests into one polity and at the same time produce some of the most stable and long-lasting political systems.

Elazar (1968: 365) argues that federalism does not suit all political cultures, but that it appears to fit particularly well with Anglo-American societies, with their strong commitment to constitutionalism and a distinct preference for non-centralization. This proposition is open to debate, but certainly the successful operation of a federal system requires a particular kind of political environment, conducive to popular democratic government and with strong traditions of political co-operation and self-restraint that minimize the need for coercion. Apart from this, federal systems appear to work best in societies with sufficient overriding shared interests to provide continuing reason for federal combination and an willingness to rely on a large measure of voluntary co-operation.

On the other hand, federal systems are not without their problems and intergovernmental relations invariably involve frustrations, tensions, conflicts and a certain degree of managerial inefficiency. In most modern federal systems, there are ongoing discussions about ways in which to improve or change the existing division of constitutional powers, and to overcome perceived problems. Still, defenders of federal systems argue that despite the costs involved, federalism provides net advantages, especially compared with alternatives such as micro-nationalism among small neighbouring countries. Within federal systems there are ongoing debates about whether federalism is a force of conservatism, or whether federal structures facilitate social and political change. Such debates vary over time even in one society, and significantly in some federal systems left-wing parties favour more central power while in others the reverse is true. However, federalism does allow simultaneous electoral success for different parties at central and state levels.

In the short-term future, existing federal systems seem likely to continue along existing lines, with even greater interest in reviewing and improving problems in intergovernmental relations. Whether federal principles will be used in any rearrangement of political systems as a result of major current changes in Eastern Europe is difficult to know, but possibly federal principles will be adopted increasingly as a convenient means of linking sovereign states for limited economic purposes (Norrie *et al.* 1986).

In terms of scholarship, there is probably more uncertainty about federalism than ever, despite the significant contributions of scholars over the past two or three decades. There are so many different perspectives, so many approaches. But it seems reasonable to expect that in the future there will be less interest in defining federalism and in discussing the extent to which different polities exhibit federal characteristics and more interest in the changing nature of federal systems, in their adaptability to meet new needs, and in the complexities of intergovernmental relations in modern federal systems.

REFERENCES

Bakvis, H. and Chandler, W. M. (eds) (1987) *Federalism and the Role of the State*, Toronto: University of Toronto Press.

Brown-John, C. L. (ed.) (1988) *Centralizing and Decentralizing Trends in Federal States*, Lanham: University Press of America.

Davis, S. R. (1978) *The Federal Principle*, Berkeley: University of California Press.

Elazar, D. J. (1968) 'Federalism', in D. S. Sils (ed.) *International Encyclopedia of the Social Sciences*, New York: Macmillan/Free Press.

——(1984) *American Federalism: A View from the States*, 3rd edn, Cambridge: Harper & Row.

——(ed.) (1969) *Cooperation and Conflict*, Ithaca, Ill.: Peacock.

Forsyth, M. (1981) *Unions of States: The Theory and Practice of Confederation*, Leicester: Leicester University Press.

Friedrich, C. J. (1968) *Trends of Federalism in Theory and Practice*, New York: Praeger.

Grewal, B. S., Brennan, G. and Mathews, R. L. (eds) (1980) *The Economics of Federalism*, Canberra: Australian National University Press.

Grodzins, M. (1966) *The American System: A New View of Government*, Chicago: Rand McNally.

Harman, G. and Smart, D. (eds) (1983) *Federal Intervention in Australian Education: Past, Present and Future*, Melbourne: Georgian House.

King, P. (1982) *Federalism and Federation*, London: Croom Helm.

Laski, H. J. (1941) *A Grammar of Politics*, 4th edn, London: Allen & Unwin.

Livingston, W. S. (1956) *Federalism and Constitutional Change*, Oxford: Clarendon Press.

——(1967) 'A note on the nature of federalism', in A. Wildavsky (ed.) *American Federalism in Perspective*, Boston: Little, Brown & Co.

Macmahon, A. W. (ed.) (1955) *Federalism, Mature and Emergent*, New York: Doubleday.

May, R. J. (1971) *Financing the Small States in Australian Federalism*, Melbourne: Oxford University Press.

Norrie, K., Simeon, R. and Krasnick, M. (1986) *Federalism and the Economic Union in Canada*, Toronto: University of Toronto Press.

O'Toole, L. J. (ed.) (1985) *American Intergovernmental Relations: Foundations, Perspectives, and Issues*, Washington, DC: CQ Press.

Riker, W. H. (1964) *Federalism: Origins, Operation and Significance*, Boston: Little, Brown & Co.

Sawer, G. (1969) *Modern Federalism*, London: C. A. Watts.

Smiley, D. V. (1980) *Canada in Question*, Toronto: McGraw-Hill.

Truman, D. B. (1951) *The Governmental Process: Political Interests and Public Opinion*, New York: Knopf.

Watts, R. L. (1966) *New Federations: Experiments in the Commonwealth*, Oxford: Clarendon Press.

Wheare, K. C. (1946) *Federal Government*, London: Oxford University Press.

PART VI

POLITICAL FORCES AND POLITICAL PROCESSES

23

PERSONALITY AND POLITICS

FRED I. GREENSTEIN

The personalities of political actors impinge on political affairs in countless ways, often with great consequences. Political life regularly generates such contrary-to-fact conditionals as 'If Kennedy had lived, such-and-such would or would not have happened'. Counterfactual propositions are not directly testable, but many of them are so compelling that even the most cautious historian would find them persuasive. Most historians would agree, for example, that if the assassin's bullet aimed at President elect Franklin D. Roosevelt in February 1933 had found its mark, there would have been no New Deal, or if the Politburo had chosen another Leonid Brezhnev, Konstantin Chernenko or Yuri Andropov rather than Mikhail Gorbachev as General Secretary of the Communist Party of the Soviet Union in 1985, the epochal changes of the late 1980s and early 1990s would not have occurred, at least not at the same time and in the same way.

The seemingly self-evident effects of many changes in leadership, including changes of a much lesser order in lesser entities than the national governments of the United States and the Soviet Union, along with the innumerable other events in the political world that are difficult to account for without taking cognizance of the actors' personal peculiarities, lead the bulk of non-academic observers of politics, including journalists, to take it for granted that personality is an important determinant of political behaviour. Yet political scientists typically do not make personality and politics a principal focus of investigation. They tend instead to focus on impersonal determinants of political events and outcomes, even those in which the participants themselves believe personality to have been significant. Or, if they do treat individual action as important, they posit rationality, defining away personal characteristics and presuming that the behaviour of actors can be deduced from the logic of their situations (compare Simon 1985).

Personality and politics as a field of academic study is controversial and poses formidable methodological challenges, but many of the controversies can be turned to constructive intellectual purposes and important phenomena demand study, even if they pose methodological difficulties. There is controversy among scholars even about such a seemingly simple matter as the definition of the terms 'personality' and 'politics', and there are more fundamental disagreements about the extent to which personality can, in principle, be expected to influence political behaviour. Reservations have been expressed about the utility of studying the personalities of political actors on the grounds that:

1 political actors are randomly distributed in roles and therefore their personalities 'cancel out';
2 political action is determined more by the actors' political environments than by their own characteristics;
3 the particular stratum of the psyche many political scientists equate with *personality*, psychodynamics and the ego defences, does not have much of a political impact;
4 the social characteristics of political actors are more important than their psychological characteristics; and
5 individuals are typically unable to have much effect on political outcomes.

On analysis, each of these reservations or disagreements proves to have interesting substantive ramifications for the study of personality and politics.

DEFINITIONAL QUESTIONS

Narrowly construed, the term *politics* in *personality and politics* refers to the politics most often studied by political scientists – that of civil government and of the extra-governmental processes that more or less directly impinge upon government, such as political parties and interest groups. Broadly construed, it refers to politics in all of its manifestations, whether in government or any other institution, including many that are rarely studied by political scientists – for example, the family, school and workplace. By this broader construction, the common denominator is the various referents of *politics*, including the exercise of influence and authority and the diverse arts of interpersonal manoeuvre such as bargaining and persuasion connoted by the word 'politicking', none of which are monopolized by government.

Personality also admits of narrow and broad definitions. In the narrow usage typical of political science, it excludes political attitudes and opinions and often other kinds of political subjective states as well (for example, the ideational content associated with political skill) and applies only to non-political personal differences, or even to the subset of psychopathological differences that are the preoccupation of clinical psychology. In psychology, on the other hand, the term has a much broader definition – in the phrase of the personality theorist Henry Murray (1968), it 'is the most comprehensive term we have in psychology'. Thus, in their influential study of *Opinions and Personality*, the psychologists M. Brewster Smith, Jerome Bruner and Robert White (1956: 1) use an expression one would not expect from political scientists, describing opinions as 'an integral part of personality'.

Although usage is a matter of convention and both the narrow and the broad definitions encompass phenomena worthy of study, this seemingly semantic controversy has a significant bearing on what scholars study. As Lasswell (1930: 42–4) argued long ago, there are distinct advantages to adopting the broader definition. A perspective that transcends governmental politics encourages the study of comparable phenomena, some of which may happen to be part of the formal institutions of governance and some of which may not. Browning and Jacobs (1964), for example, compared the needs for power, achievement and affiliation (friendship) of business people and public officials in highly diverse positions that imposed sharply divergent demands. They found that the public officials were by no means all cut from the same psychological cloth, but that there were important similarities between certain of the public officials and business people. The underlying principle appears to be that personality tends to be consistent with the specific demands of roles, whether because of preselection of the role incumbents or because of in-role socialization.

THE DISTRIBUTION OF INDIVIDUALS IN ROLES

If the first of the reservations sometimes expressed about the value of studying personality and politics – the claim that individuals are randomly distributed in political roles and therefore their impact is somehow neutralized – is empirically sound, that is by no means a reason not to study personality and politics. If one visualizes political processes as analogous to intricately wired computers, political actors can be viewed as key junctures in the wiring, such as circuit breakers, for example. If anything it would be *more*, not less, urgent to know the performance characteristics of the circuit breakers if their operating properties were random, with some capable of tripping at inappropriate times, losing valuable information, and others failing to trip, exposing the system to the danger of meltdown.

In the real political world, events sometimes do more or less randomly assign individuals with unanticipated personal styles and proclivities to political roles, often with significant consequences. This was the case of two of the national leaders referred to in the opening of this chapter: neither Franklin Roosevelt's nor Mikhail Gorbachev's contemporaries anticipated the innovative leadership they displayed in office. As the Browning and Jacobs (1964) study suggests, however, people do not appear to be randomly distributed in political roles, though the patterns of their distribution appear to be complex and elusive. Ascertaining them and examining their political consequences is an important part of the intellectual agenda for the study of personality and politics.

PERSONALITY AND ENVIRONMENT

The second reservation about the study of personality and politics – that environment has more impact than personality on behaviour – and the other three reservations need to be considered in the context of a general clarification of the types of variables that in principle can affect personality and politics and their possible interconnections. An important example of such a clarification is M. Brewster Smith's well-known 'map for the study of personality and politics' (Brewster Smith 1968). (See also Stone and Schaffner's (1988: 33) depiction of 'political life space'.) The representation that I will employ (Greenstein 1975) is introduced in segments in Figures 1 and 2 and set forth in its entirety in Figure 3.

The most fundamental distinction in the map is the rudimentary one that, as Kurt Lewin put it, 'behaviour or any kind of mental event . . . depends on the state of the person and at the same time on the environment (Lewin 1936: 11–12). Figure 1 shows the links between the two broad classes of behavioural antecedent Lewin refers to and behaviour itself, using the terminology of Lasswell and Kaplan (1950: 4–6), who ground an entire conceptual framework for the analysis of politics on the equation that human response (R) is a function of the respondent's environment (E) and predispositions (P): E→P→R. Here again, terminology is a matter of convenience. Instead of *predispositions*, it would have been possible to use many other of the eighty terms Donald Campbell (1963) enumerates in his account of the logic of studying 'acquired behavioural dispositions'. Such terms as *situation*, *context* and *stimulus* are common alternative labels for all or part of the environment of human action.

The E→P→R formula provides a convenient way of visualizing the fallacy in the claim that behaviour is so much a function of environments that individuals' predispositions need not be studied (reservation two). In fact, environments

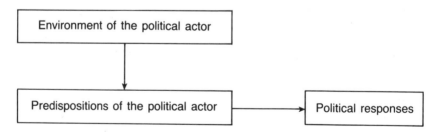

Figure 1   Basic antecedents of political behaviour: E→P→R

are always mediated by the individuals on whom they act; environments cannot shape behaviour directly, and much politically important action is not reactive to immediate stimuli. Indeed, the capacity to be *proactive* (Murray 1968) and transcend existing perceptions of what the environment dictates is at the core of effective leadership. But the debate about whether environments determine political behaviour is a reminder of the endless interplay of individuals and the political contexts in which they find or place themselves.

Some contexts are indeed associated with the kind of behaviour that leads social determinists to be sceptical about the need to study personality. Informed of the impending collapse of a building, everyone – irrespective of temperament and personality type – will seek to leave it. Other contexts illustrate Gordon Allport's aphorism that 'the same heat that hardens the egg, melts the butter' (Allport 1937: 325). Still others are virtual ink blots, leading individuals with varying characteristics to project their inner dispositions onto them.

The connection between personality and context is so integral that this relationship has become the basis of an important approach to personality theory known as interactionism (Magnusson and Endler 1977; Pervin and Lewis 1978; Endler 1981). By systematically analysing personality and politics in interactional terms, the analyst is sensitized to the kinds of contingent relationships that make the links between personality and politics elusive.

A good example of a contingent relationship in which the impact of personality is mediated by the environment is to be found in the work of Katz and Benjamin (1960) on the effects of authoritarianism in biracial work groups in the north and the south of the USA. Katz and Benjamin compared white undergraduates in the two regions who scored low and high on one of the various authoritarian personality measures to see how they comported themselves in interracial problem-solving groups. They found that in the south authoritarianism (which previous studies showed to be associated with racial prejudice) was associated with attempts of white students to dominate their black counterparts, but that in the north the authoritarians were more likely than the non-authoritarians to be *deferential* to blacks. The investigators' conclusion was that the socio-political environment of the southern authoritarians enabled them to give direct vent to their impulses, but that the liberal environment of the northern university led students with similar proclivities to go out of their way to avoid conflict with the prevailing norms.

The relative effect of environment and personality on political behaviour varies. Ambiguous environments – for example, new situations and political roles that are only sketchily defined by formal rules (Budner 1962; Greenstein 1969: 50–7) – provide great latitude for actors' personalities to shape their behaviour. Structured environments – for example, bureaucratized settings and contexts in which there are well-developed and widely known and accepted norms – tend to constrain behaviour. The environment also is likely to account for much of the variance in political behaviour when strong sanctions are attached to certain possible courses of action.

The dramatic reduction of political repression in the Soviet Union and Eastern Europe in the late 1980s led to an outpouring of political action. Just as the absence of authoritarian rule leads individuals in the aggregate to express their personal political proclivities, its presence magnifies the effects of leaders, assuming that the authoritarian system is one in which the individual or individuals at the top have more or less absolute power (Tucker 1965). The striking capacity of leaders' personalities to shape events in an authoritarian system was evident in the leeway Gorbachev appears to have had at the time of the initiation of *glasnost* and *perestroika*, if not later when the forces of pluralism began to bedevil him.

Just as environments vary in the extent to which they foster the expression of individual variability, so also do predispositions themselves. There is an extensive literature on the tendency of people to subordinate themselves to groups and consciously or unconsciously suppress their own views when they are in the company of others. Some individuals, however, are remarkably resistant to such inhibitions while others have compliant tendencies (Asch 1956; Allen 1975; Janis 1982). The intensity of psychological predispositions promotes their expression. Most people suppress their impulses to challenge the regimes of authoritarian systems, but those with passionate convictions and strong character-based needs for self-expression or rebellion are more likely to oppose such regimes. (In doing so, they alter the environment, providing social support for their more compliant peers to join them.)

PSYCHOPATHOLOGICAL AND OTHER POLITICAL MOTIVATION

One of the ways in which humans vary is in the extent to which they manifest emotional disturbance and ego defensiveness. Equating all of personality with the psychological stratum that traditionally concerns clinical psychologists, some students of politics voice the third of the reservations about the study of personality and politics, arguing that the links between psychopathology and politics are rare and unimportant. A specific exploration of the general question of whether ego-defence motivation is common in politics can be found in the extensive empirical literature on the student political protest movements of the 1960s. Some research findings appeared to indicate that protest was rooted in 'healthy' character traits, such as an inner strength to stand by one's convictions and the cognitive capacity to cut through propaganda, whereas other reports suggested the possible influence of the kinds of neurotic needs that might, for example, arise from repressed resentment of parents or other authority figures from everyday life.

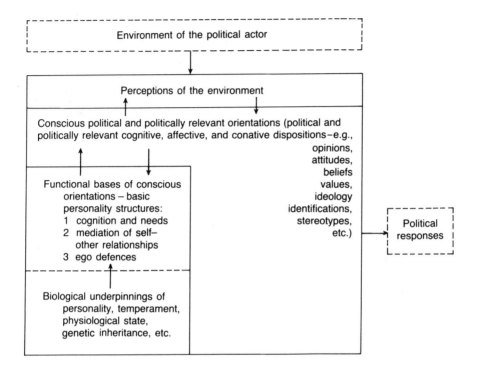

Figure 2   Predispositions of the politcal actor

In order to consider the general issue of the role of psychopathology in politics and the specific issue of the roots of protest, it is necessary to elaborate the E→P→R formula. Figure 2 expands the personality panel in Figure 1. The panel is constructed so as to suggest, in a metaphor common in personality theory (Hall and Lindzey 1970), 'levels' of psychic functioning. The level closest to the surface and most directly 'in touch' with the environment is the perceptual. Perceptions can be thought of as a cognitive screen that shapes and structures environmental stimuli, sometimes distorting them, sometimes reflecting them with considerable verisimilitude. In the 1970s and 1980s there was a burgeoning of inquiry into political perception and cognitive psychology more generally (Lau and Sears 1986; Jervis 1976; Jervis *et al.* 1985; Vertzberger 1990). Also at the surface, in the sense that they are conscious or accessible to consciousness, are political orientations such as attitudes, beliefs and convictions. Psychologists commonly conceive of dispositions at this level as composites of the more basic processes of cognition (thought), affect (emotion) and conation (proclivities toward action).

The sub-panel of Figure 2 labelled 'functional bases of conscious orientations' and, more or less synonymously, 'basic personality structures', represents the level of psychic activity that political scientists often have in mind when they speak of personality. Different personality theorists emphasize the importance of different underlying personality structures, but most of them distinguish (in varied terminology) three broad classes of inner processes – those bearing on thought and perception, on emotions and their management (including feelings of which the individual may have little conscious understanding) and on the relation of the self to significant others. The terms used for these processes in Figure 2 are cognition, ego defence and mediation of self–other relations. Figure 2 also includes a sub-panel identifying the genetic and acquired physical states that contribute to personality and diffuse into political behaviour (Masters 1989; Park 1986).

Both the broad question of whether psychopathology manifests itself in political behaviour and the narrow question of what motivates political rebels can be illuminated by reference to Figure 2. One way of thinking about political attitudes and behaviour is in terms of the functions they serve for the personality (Smith *et al.* 1956; Pratkanis *et al.* 1989) – hence the use of the phrase 'functional bases of conscious orientations'. What might on the surface seem to be the same belief or class of action, may serve different functions in the motivational economies of different people. For one individual a certain view – for example, a positive or negative racial stereotype – may result from the available information in the environment, mainly serving needs for cognitive closure. For another, it might be rooted in a need to take cues from (or be different from) significant others. For a third, it might serve the ego-defensive function of venting unacknowledged aggressive impulses. (More often than not, a political behaviour is likely to be fuelled by more than one motivation, but with varying mixes from individual to individual.)

The incidence of psychopathological and other motivational bases of political orientations needs to be established by empirical inquiry. Just as some environmental contexts leave room for the play of personality in general, some are especially conducive to the expression of ego defences. These include stimuli that appeal to the powerful emotional impulses that people are socialized to deny, but that remain potent beneath the surface. For example, there is an especially steamy quality to political contention over issues like abortion and pornography that bear on sexuality. Nationalistic issues such as flag burning and matters of religious doctrine also channel political passions (Davies 1980), for reasons that have not been adequately explained. Extreme forms of behaviour are also likely (though not certain) to have a pathological basis, as in the behaviour of American presidential assassins such as Ronald Reagan's would-be killer, John Hinckley, Jr (Clarke 1990).

The circumstances under which psychopathology and its lesser variants find their way into politics are of great interest, as are those under which the other motivational bases of political behaviour come into play. Depending upon the basic personality systems to which a given aspect of political performance is linked, differences can be expected in the conditions under which it will be aroused and changed, as well as in the detailed way it will manifest itself. Opinions and actions based in cognitive needs will be responsive to new information. Those based on social needs will respond to changes in the behaviour and signals provided by significant others. Those based on ego defences may be intractable, or only subject to change by extensive efforts to bring about self-insight, or by certain manipulative strategies such as suggestion by authority figures (Katz 1960).

The functional approach to the study of political orientations provides a useful framework for determining whether and under what circumstances political protest has motivational sources in ego-defensive needs. There is much evidence bearing on this issue, at least as it applies to student protest. A remarkable number of empirical studies were done of student protest activity of the late 1960s and early 1970s in the United States and elsewhere, no doubt because that activity occurred in contexts where numerous social scientists were available to conduct research. A huge literature ensued, abounding in seemingly contradictory findings, many of which, however, appear to fit into a quite plausible larger pattern, once one takes account of the diversity of the institutions in which protest was studied and of the particular periods in the cycle of late 1960s and early 1970s student protest in which the various studies were conducted.

The earliest student protests of the 1960s occurred in colleges and universities with meritocratic admissions policies and upper middle-class student bodies. The first studies of this period, those by Flacks (1967) of University of Chicago students, suggested that student protest was largely a cognitive manifestation – the response of able students to the perceived iniquities of their political environment. Later analyses of data collected in the same period on similar populations (students at the University of California, Berkeley) suggested a more complex pattern in which some of the activists did seem to have the cognitive strengths and preoccupations that Flacks had argued were the mark of *all* of them, but others appeared to be channeling ego-defensive needs (based in troubled parent–child relations) into their protest behaviour. The students who the later analysts concluded had ego-defensive motivations and those who they concluded were acting out of cognitive needs showed different patterns of protest behaviour, the first directing their activity only on the issues of national and international politics, the second taking part in local reform activities (Block *et al.* 1969).

The psychological correlates of student activism changed over time in the United States, as activism developed from the actions of a few students in the 'elite' universities to a widespread form of behaviour, which at the time of the Nixon administration's incursion into Cambodia and the killing of student protesters at Kent State University manifested itself in the bulk of American college and university campuses. Studies conducted at that time found little in the way of variation in the characteristics of protesters (Dunlap 1970; Peterson and Bilorusky 1971).

PERSONALITY, HISTORICAL CONTEXT AND SOCIAL BACKGROUND

Variation according to historical context and change over time are so important in determining how personality becomes linked with politics that the map around which this article is organized needs to be expanded, as it is in Figure 3, which encompasses the time dimension and differentiates the immediate and remote features of the political environment. Figure 3 suggests that the fourth reservation about the utility of studying personality and politics – the claim that social backgrounds are more important than psychological characteristics – is grounded in a confusion which can be readily dissolved. The social backgrounds of political actors (panel 2 of Figure 3) influence their actions, but only as mediated by the individual's developing predispositions (panel 3) and the different levels of personality they shape (panels 4, 5 and 6). Thus, to take a final example from the literature on student protest in the 1960s, it was fallacious (as Block *et al.* 1969, pointed out at the time) for Lipset (1968) to argue that because so many student activists were young, middle-class Jews, personality was not an important determinant of activism. To the extent that Jewish background was connected with activism, it had to be part of a causal sequence in which developmental experiences specific to Jews contributed to their psychological orientations. The latter, not Jewish background *per se*, would have been the mediator of behaviour.

The study of how ethnicity, class and other of the so-called background characteristics affect political behaviour is important and highly relevant to (but no substitute for) the study of personality and politics. To the extent that a characteristic becomes part of an actor's personal make-up, it is no longer 'background' – it is an element in the psyche. But evidence of whether background experience distinguishes members of one social group from those of others is grist for political psychologists. Lipset may have been correct in sensing that Jewish political activists of the 1960s had some distinctive qualities that were important for their behaviour, but the observation that many student

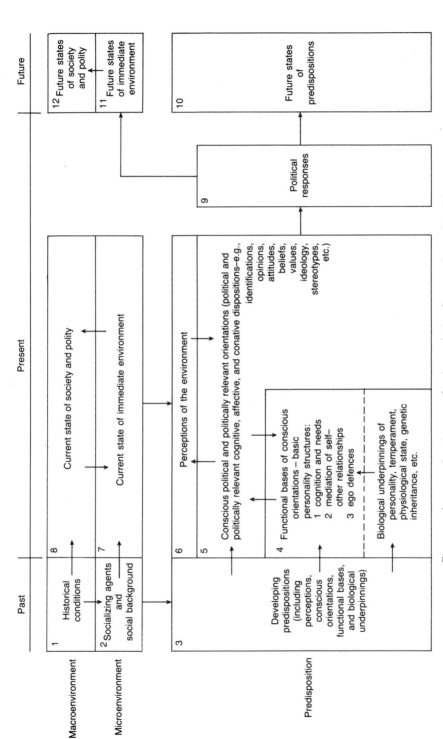

Figure 3 A comprehensive map for the analysis of personality and politics

protesters were Jewish not only fails to prove this, it also forecloses systematic inquiry.

An appropriate programme of inquiry into Lipset's claim would entail specifying the precise psychological dynamics that ostensibly make Jewish protesters distinctive and comparing Jewish and non-Jewish protesters with comparable non-protesters in order to determine whether the imputed patterns existed. If they did, one would want to know whether they resulted from particular developmental histories, whether they had predictable consequences for political behaviour, and why some Jews protested and some did not. Whether a distinctly Jewish psychology of political protest exists is an empirical question, and is part of a broader set of questions that can be asked about how group membership affects personality and political behaviour.

THE IMPACT OF PERSONALITY ON EVENTS

The last of the reservations about the study of personality and politics derives from the view that individuals are not likely to have much impact on events. Such a premise underlies many theories of history. In the nineteenth century the question of whether historical actors have an impact on events was the basis of a fruitless grand controversy, with such social determinists as Herbert Spencer denying the efficacy of historical actors and such 'Great Man' theorists as Thomas Carlyle proclaiming their overriding importance (Kellerman 1986: 3–57). Contemporary leadership theorists typically describe themselves as interactionists, emphasizing the interdependence of leaders and their environments and the contingent nature of the leader's impact on larger events (Burns 1978; Tucker 1981).

The debate about whether actors can shape events is about the causal chain from personality (panels 4–6 of Figure 3), through political response (panel 9), to future states of the immediate and more remote political and social environment (panels 11 and 12). Claims that particular actors did or did not have an impact on events usually prove to be claims about actor dispensability and action dispensability (Greenstein 1969: 40–6) – that is, about whether the actions of the individuals in question were necessary for the outcome to have occurred or whether the actions were ones that any similarly placed actors would have taken. The second issue is one I have already explored under the heading of personality and environment, but the first requires clarification.

The capacity of actors to shape events is a variable, not a constant. The sources of variation parallel the determinants of success in the game of pool. The number of balls a player will be able to sink is in part a function of the location of the balls on the table. The parallel in politics is the malleability of the political environment (Burke and Greenstein 1989: 24). The second determinant of success in the pool room is the position of the cue ball. This is analogous to the actor's position in the relevant political context. Roosevelt and Gorbachev could not have had an impact from lower-level administrative positions. The third class of variable has the same labels in the games of pool and politics – skill, self-confidence and the other personal requisites of effective performance.

KINDS OF PERSONALITY AND POLITICS ANALYSIS

Every human being is in certain ways like all other human beings, in certain ways more like some human beings than others, and in certain ways unique (Kluckhohn and Murray 1953). Each of these resemblances is reflected in a different kind of personality-and-politics analysis. The universality of human qualities is explored in writings that seek in some broad way to make the connection stated in the title of Graham Wallas's *Human Nature and Politics* (Wallas 1908). Sigmund Freud's *Civilization and its Discontents* (Freud 1930), Fromm's *Escape from Freedom* (Fromm 1941), Norman O. Brown's *Life Against Death* (Brown 1959) and Herbert Marcuse's *Eros and Civilization* (Marcuse 1966) are notable contributions to this tradition. At their best such works provide fascinating and provocative perspectives on the human condition. Many of them are rich in insights that suggest testable hypotheses.

Because they seek to explain the variable phenomena of political behaviour with a constant, such efforts are not themselves subject to confirmation or disconfirmation. In contrast, it *is* possible to conduct systematic, replicable inquiries into political actors' unique qualities (single-case analysis) and the qualities that make them more like some individuals than others (typological analysis). The ways in which individual and typical political psychology affects the performance of political processes and institutions (aggregation) can also be studied systematically.

Single-case personality analysis is more important in the field of personality and politics than it has come to be in personality psychology generally, because students of politics are concerned with the performance of specific leaders and their impact on events. There have been noteworthy personality-and-politics studies of leaders as diverse in time, culture and the circumstances of their leadership as Martin Luther (Erikson 1958), Louis XII (Marvick 1986), Woodrow Wilson (George and George 1956), Kemal Ataturk (Volkan and Itzkowitz 1984) and Josef Stalin (Tucker 1973), as well as many others. There also have been valuable single-case psychological analyses of figures whose political importance derives from their impact on leaders – for example, George and George's analysis of the influence of Colonel Edward House on Woodrow Wilson (George and George 1956) and Kull's of US defence policy advisers (Kull 1988). In addition, there is a tradition in the field of personality and politics of single case analyses of 'faces in the crowd' – people who are without policy influence but who illustrate in depth the psychological process that can only be examined more superficially in surveys (Riesman and Glazer 1952; Smith *et al.* 1956; Lane 1962).

Typological study of political and other actors is of potentially great importance: if political actors fall into types with known characteristics and propensities, the laborious task of analysing them *de novo* can be obviated, and uncertainty is reduced about how they will perform in particular circumstances. The notion of a psychological *type* can be stretched to include all efforts to categorize and compare the psychology of political actors, even straightforward classifications of the members of a population in terms of whether they are high or low on some trait such as ego strength, self-esteem, or tolerance of ambiguity. The more full-blown political psychology typologies parallel diagnostic categories in medicine, including psychiatry. They identify syndromes – patterns of observable characteristics that reflect identifiable underlying conditions, result from distinctive developmental histories and have predictable consequences.

Of the many studies that employ the first, simpler kind of psychological categorization, the studies by Herbert McClosky and his students are particularly valuable because of their theoretical and methodological sophistication and the importance of the issues they address (McClosky 1967; Di Palma and McClosky 1970; Sniderman 1974; McClosky and Zaller 1984). Political personality typologies of the second, more comprehensive variety go back at least to Plato's account in the eighth and ninth book of *The Republic* of the aristocrat, the democrat, the timocrat and the tyrant – political types that Plato believed were shaped in an intergenerational dialectic of rebellion of sons against their fathers' perceived shortcomings. (For a gloss on Plato's account see Lasswell 1960.) Latter-day typologies that have generated important bodies of literature are the authoritarian, dogmatic and Machiavellian personality classifications (Adorno *et al.* 1950; Rokeach 1960; Christie and Geis 1970). Within political science the best-known personality typology is James David Barber's classification of the character structures of American presidents (Barber 1985).

Single-case and typological studies alike make inferences about the inner quality of human beings (panels 4, 5 and 6 of Figure 3) from outer manifestations – their past and present environments (panels 1, 2, 7 and 8) and the pattern over time of their political responses (panel 9). They then use those inferred constructs to account for the very same kind of phenomena from which they were inferred – responses in situational contexts. The danger of circularity is obvious, but tautology can be avoided by reconstructing personality from some response patterns and using the reconstruction to explain others.

The failure of some investigators to take such pains contributes to the controversial status of the personality-and-politics literature, as does the prevalence of certain other practices. Some biographers, for example, impose diagnostic labels on their subject, rather than presenting a systematic account of the subject's behaviour in disparate circumstances (George 1971). Some typological analysts categorize their subjects without providing the detailed criteria and justifications for doing so. Some analysts of individuals as well as of types have engaged in the fallacy of observing a pattern of behaviour and simply attributing it to a particular developmental pattern, without documenting causality, and perhaps even without providing evidence that the pattern existed. Finally, some analysts commit what might be called the psychologizing and clinical fallacies: they explain behaviour in terms of personality without considering possible situational determinants, or conclude that it is driven by psychopathology without considering other psychological determinants, such as cognition. Both fallacies are evident in the body of literature attributing the high scores of poor blacks and other minorities on the paranoia scale of the Minnesota Multiphasic Personality Inventory (MMPI) to emotional disturbance. The scores appear actually to have reflected cognitively based responses to the vicissitudes of the ghetto environment (Gynther 1972; Newhill 1990).

It is not surprising that some personality-and-politics studies are marked by methodological shortcomings. Certain of the inferences mapped in Figure 3 pose intrinsic difficulties. Claims about the determinants of personality characteristics (that is, of the connections between panels 1 and 2 and panels 3–6) are unlikely to be conclusive. Characterizations of personality structures themselves are never wholly persuasive, if only because of the absence of uniformly accepted personality theories with agreed-upon terminologies. Fortunately, the variables depicted in Figure 3 that *can* be characterized with great confidence are those closest to and therefore most predictive of behaviour: the environments in which political action occurs (panels 7 and 8) and the patterns that action manifests over time (panels, 9, 10, etc.). Those patterns are themselves variables, and they can be treated as indicators of an important further dimension of personality and politics – *political style*.

Two examples of political biographies that provide impressively comprehensive accounts of the precise patterns of their subjects' behaviour are Walter's study of the Australian Prime Minister Gough Whitlam (Walter 1980) and Landis's of Senator Joseph McCarthy (Landis 1987). Richard Christie's studies of the types of people who manifest the Machiavellian syndrome (Christie and Geis 1970) – the characterological proclivity to manipulate others – provide a model of careful measurement and theoretically sophisticated analysis in which contingent relationships are carefully explored. People who score high on tests of Machiavellianism do not differ in their behaviour from non-Machiavellians in all contexts, only in contexts in which their manipulative impulses can be effective – for example, in situations that permit improvisation and in situations requiring face-to-face interaction.

Personality is likely to interest most political scientists only if it has aggregate consequences for political institutions, processes and outcomes. The literature on the aggregate effects of personality on politics is varied because the processes of aggregation are varied. Broadly speaking, political psychology affects the performance of political systems and processes through the activities of members of the public and the deliberations and decision making of leaders. The impact of mass publics on politics, except through elections and severe perturbations of public opinion, is partial and often elusive. The political impact of leaders and others in the active political stratum is, on the other hand, more generally direct, readily evident, and potentially momentous in its repercussions.

The first efforts to understand the psychology of mass populations go back to the accounts by writers in the ancient world such as Tacitus of the character of the members of remote tribes and nations. Such disquisitions are an antecedent of the vexed post-Second World War national character literature in which often ill-documented ethnographic reports and cultural artifacts such as child-rearing manuals, films and popular fiction were used to draw sweeping conclusions about modal national character traits. That literature came to be known to students of politics mainly because of its methodological shortcomings, but it anticipated later, more systematic studies of political culture (Inkeles and Levinson 1967; Inkeles 1983).

By the 1950s, there was broad scholarly consensus that it was inappropriate simply to attribute psychological characteristics to mass populations on the basis of anecdotal or indirect evidence. Direct assessment of publics through survey research became the dominant mode of studying mass populations. Studies like those of McClosky and his associates (McClosky 1967; McClosky and Zaller 1984) provided survey data on basic personality processes such as ego-defences and cognitive styles and how they affect political opinion. But basic personality processes have not been persuasively linked to the aspect of mass behaviour that most clearly and observably has an impact on political institutions and processes – electoral choice. Most members of the general public appear to be too weakly involved in electoral politics for their voting choices to tap deeper psychological roots, and many of those who are involved appear to take their cues from party identifications formed in their early years and from short-run situational stimuli.

If what is commonly thought of as personality is not linked to electoral choice, attitudinal political psychology most definitely is. The literature on electoral choice (Niemi and Weisberg 1984) is too vast to begin to review here, but the research of Kelley (1983) is of particular interest in that it is explicitly aggregative; it reveals the precise distributions of attitudes and beliefs about issues and candidates that were associated with post-Second World War American election outcomes. So is the research of Converse and Pierce (1986), who have convincingly linked certain attributes of the French political system to the distinctive ways members of that nation's electorate orient themselves to political parties.

In contrast to the ambiguous links between mass publics and political outcomes other than in elections, the connections between political decision makers and political outcomes are direct and palpable. Nevertheless, many historical reconstructions of political decision making are insufficiently specific about which actors in what precise contexts took which actions with what consequences. Sometimes the historical record does not contain the appropriate data. Often, however, the difficulty lies not with the record but with the way in which it has been analysed.

The questions the analyst needs to ask of the historical record are suggested by the analytic distinctions of *actor* and *action dispensability*: Were the actions a decision maker took those that any individual placed in a comparable context would have taken? That is, were they imposed by the actor's situation? Did those actions make a difference? That is, would the outcome have been the same if they were not taken? Questions of actor dispensability call for examination of the contexts in which the decision makers act. Questions of action dispensability call for reconstructions of the determinants of particular outcomes and assessment of the part particular actors played in them.

A good example of a reconstruction that addresses both questions is the analysis by George and George (1956) of Woodrow Wilson's role in the crisis over ratification of the Versailles Treaty. The intense, uncompromising qualities of Wilson the man, at least in certain kinds of conflicts, are an essential part of any account of the ratification fight. There is abundant evidence that the political context did not impose a course of action on Wilson that would have kept him from achieving his goal of ratification. All that was required was that he accept certain nominal compromises that his supporters urged upon him, pointing out that they had no practical significance. Moreover, Wilson's actions are necessary to explain the outcome. Wilson's supporters were lined up for a favourable ratification vote, but were unprepared to act unless he authorized them to accept mild qualifying language. This he refused to do.

The explanatory logic of propositions about whether an individual's actions and characteristics were consequential in some episode is that of counterfactual reasoning. This is the only available alternative in analyses of single events to the quantitative analysis that would be called for if data existed on large numbers of comparable episodes. Counter-factual reasoning is not falsifiable, but it can be systematic. To be so it must be explicit and addressed to bounded questions – not conundrums about remote contingencies. 'Was Lyndon Johnson's action necessary for the 1965 American escalation in Vietnam to have occurred?' is an example of a question that is susceptible to investigation (Burke and Greenstein 1989). 'If Cleopatra's nose had been an inch longer, how would world history have been changed?' is an example of one that is not.

Personality and political psychology more generally affect political processes not only through the actions taken by leaders more or less on their own, but also through group processes such as the collective suspension of reality testing manifested in what Irving Janis (1982) has characterized as groupthink. Groupthink occurs in highly cohesive decision-making groups. The members of such groups sometimes become so committed to their colleagues they more or less unconsciously suspend their own critical faculties in order to preserve group harmony. Janis, who is scrupulous about setting forth the criteria for establishing whether a group has engaged in groupthink, analyses a number of historical episodes (the most striking example being the Bay of Pigs) in which a defective decision-making process appears to have led able policy makers to make decisions on the basis of flawed assumptions and defective information. To the extent that groupthink is a purely collective phenomenon, emerging from group interaction, it is a manifestation of social psychology rather than personality psychology. But, as Janis suggests, personality probably contributes to groupthink in that some personalities are more likely than others to suspend their critical capacities in group settings.

CONCLUDING REMARKS

Political institutions and processes operate through human agency. It would be remarkable if they were *not* influenced by the properties that distinguish one individual from another. In examining that influence, this article has emphasized the logic of inquiry. It does not constitute a comprehensive review of the literature. For a variety of useful reviews and compendia, readers should consult Greenstein and Lerner (1971), Knutson (1973), Stone (1981), Herman (1986) and Simonton (1990).

To the extent that this article brings out possible pitfalls in studies of personality and politics, its message to cautious scholars may seem to be: find pastures that can be more easily cultivated. Even daring scholars might conclude that the prospects for the systematic study of personality and politics are too remote to justify the investment of scholarly time and effort. Nothing in this article is meant to support such conclusions. In a parable on the shortcomings of scientific opportunism, Kaplan (1964: 11, 16–17) relates the story of a drunkard who lost his keys in a dark alley and is found searching for them under a street lamp, declaring, 'It's lighter here'. The drunkard's search is a poor model. If the connections between the personalities of political actors and their political behaviour are obscure, all the more reason to illuminate them.

BIBLIOGRAPHY

Adorno, T. W., Frenkel-Brunswick, E., Levinson, D. J. and Sanford, R. N. (1950) *The Authoritarian Personality*, New York: Harper.

Allen, V. L. (1975) 'Social support for nonconformity', *Advances in Social Psychology* 8: 1–43.

Allport, G. W. (1937) *Personality: A Psychlogical Interpretation*, New York: Holt.

Asch, S. E. (1956) 'Studies of independence and conformity: "A minority of one versus a unanimous majority" ', *Psychological Monographs* 70: 9.

Barber, J. D. (1985) *The Presidential Character: Predicting Performance in the White House*, 3rd edn, Englewood Cliffs, NJ: Prentice-Hall.

Block, J. H., Haan, N. and Smith, M. B. (1969) 'Socialization correlates of student activism', *Journal of Social Issues* 25: 143–77.

Brown, N. O. (1959) *Life Against Death*, Middletown, Conn.: Wesleyan University Press.

Browning, R. P. and Jacobs, H. (1964) 'Power motivation and the political personality', *Public Opinion Quarterly* 24: 75–90.

Budner, S. (1962) 'Intolerance of ambiguity as a personality variable', *Journal of Personality* 30: 22–50.

Burke, J. P. and Greenstein, F. I. (1989) *How Presidents Test Reality: Decisions on Vietnam, 1954 and 1965*, New York: Russell Sage Foundation.

Burns, J. M. (1978) *Leadership*, New York: Harper & Row.

Campbell, D. T. (1963) 'Social attitudes and other acquired behavioral dispositions', in S. Koch (ed.) *Psychology: A Study of a Science*, vol. 6, New York: McGraw-Hill.

Christie, R. and Geis, F. L., (1970) *Studies in Machiavellianism*, New York: Academic Press.

Clarke, J. W. (1990) *On Being Mad or Merely Angry: John W. Hinckley Jr and Other Dangerous People*, Princeton: Princeton University Press.

Converse, P. E. and Pierce, R. (1986) *Political Representation in France*, Cambridge, Mass.: Harvard University Press.

Davies, A. F. (1980) *Skills, Outlooks and Passions: A Psychoanalytic Contribution to the Study of Politics*, Cambridge: Cambridge University Press.

Di Palma, G. and McClosky, H. (1970) 'Personality and conformity: the learning of political attitudes', *American Political Science Review* 64: 1054–73.

Dunlap, R. (1970) 'Radical and conservative student activists: a comparison of family backgrounds', *Pacific Sociological Review* 13: 171–81.

Endler, N. S. (1981) 'Persons, situations, and their interactions', in A. I. Rabin, J. Aronoff, A. M. Barclay and R. A. Zucker (eds) *Further Explorations in Personality*, New York: John Wiley.

Erikson, E. H. (1958) *Young Man Luther: A Study in Psychoanalysis and History*, New York: Norton.

Flacks, R. (1967) 'The liberated generation: an exploration of the roots of student protest', *Journal of Social Issues* 25: 52–75.

Freud, S. (1930) 'Civilization and its Discontents', in Stratchey, J., *The Standard Edition of the Complete Psychological Works of Sigmund Freud*, vol. 17, London: Hogarth Press.

Fromm, E. (1941) *Escape from Freedom*, New York: Rinehart.

George, A. L. (1971) 'Some uses of dynamic psychology in political biography: case materials on Woodrow Wilson', in F. I. Greenstein and M. Lerner (eds) *A Source Book for the Study of Personality and Politics*, Chicago: Markham.

George, A. L. and George, J. L. (1956) *Woodrow Wilson and Colonel House: A Personality Study*, New York: John Day (reprinted by Dover, 1964).

Greenstein, F. I. (1969) *Personality and Politics: Problems of Evidence, Inference and Conceptualization*, Chicago: Markham (current edn: Princeton University Press, 1987).

——(1975) 'Personality and politics', in F. I. Greenstein and N. W. Polsby (eds) *The Handbook of Political Science: Micropolitical Theory*, vol. 2, Reading, Mass.: Addison-Wesley.

Greenstein, F. I. and Lerner, M. (1971) *A Source Book for the Study of Personality and Politics*, Chicago: Markham.

Gynther, M. (1972) 'White norms and Black MMPIs: a prescription for discrimination', *Psychological Bulletin* 78: 386–402.

Hall, C. S. and Lindzey, G. (eds) (1970) *Theories of Personality*, 2nd edn, New York: John Wiley.

Herman, M. G. (ed.) (1986) *Political Psychology*, San Francisco: Jossey-Bass.

Inkeles, I. (1983) *Exploring Individual Modernity*, New York: Columbia University Press.

Inkeles, I. and Levinson, D. J. (1969) 'National character: the study of modal personality', in G. Lindzey and E. Aronson (eds.) *The Handbook of Social Psychology*, vol. 4, 2nd edn, Reading, Mass.: Addison-Wesley.

Janis, I. L. (1982) *Groupthink: Psychological Studies of Policy Decisions and Fiascos*, 2nd edn, Boston: Houghton Mifflin.

Jervis, R. (1976) *Perception and Misperception in International Politics*, Princeton: Princeton University Press.

Jervis, R., Lebow R. N. and Stein, J. (1985) *Psychology and Deterrence*, Baltimore: Johns Hopkins University Press.

Kaplan, A. (1964) *The Conduct of Inquiry: Methodology for Behavioral Sciences*, San Francisco: Chandler.

Katz, D. (1960) 'The functional approach to the study of attitudes', *Public Opinion Quarterly* 24: 163–204.

Katz, I. and Benjamin, L. (1960) 'The effects of authoritarianism on biracial work groups', *Journal of Abnormal and Social Psychology* 61: 448–56.

Kellerman, B. (ed.) (1986) *Political Leadership: A Source Book*, Pittsburgh: University of Pittsburgh Press.

Kelley, S. K., Jr (1983) *Interpreting Elections*, Princeton: Princeton University Press.

Kluckhohn, C. and Murray, H. A. (1953) 'Personality formation: the determinants', in C. Kluckhohn and H. A. Murray (eds) *Personality in Nature, Society and Culture*, 2nd edn, New York: Knopf.

Knutson, J. N. (1973) *Handbook of Political Psychology*, San Francisco: Jossey-Bass.

Kull, S. (1988) *Minds at War: Nuclear Reality and the Inner Conflict of Defense Policymakers*, New York: Basic Books.

Landis, M. (1987) *Joseph McCarthy: The Politics of Chaos*, Cranbury, NJ: Associated Universities Presses.

Lane, R. E. (1962) *Political Ideology: Why the Common Man Believes What He Does*, New York: Free Press of Glencoe.

Lasswell, H. D. (1930) *Psychopathology and Politics*, Chicago: University of Chicago Press.

____(1960) 'Political character and constitution', *Psychoanalysis and Psychoanalytic Review* 46: 1–18.

Lasswell, H. D. and Kaplan, A. (1950) *Power and Society: A Framework for Political Inquiry*, New Haven: Yale University Press.

Lau, R. R. and Sears, D. O. (eds) (1986) *Political Cognition*, Hillsdale, NJ: Lawrence Erlbaum Associates.

Lewin, K. (1936) *Principles of Topological Psychology*, New York: McGraw-Hill.

Lipset, S. M. (1968) 'The activists: a profile', in D. Bell and I. Kristol (eds) *Confrontation: The Student Rebellion and the Universities*, New York: Basic Books.

McClosky, H. (1967) 'Personality and attitude correlates of foreign policy orientations', in J. N. Rosenau (ed.) *Domestic Sources of Foreign Policy*, New York: Free Press of Glencoe.

McClosky, H. and Zaller, J. (1984) *The American Ethos: Public Attitudes Toward Capitalism and Democracy*, Cambridge, Mass.: Harvard University Press.

Magnusson, D. and Endler, N. S. (eds) (1977) *Personality at the Crossroads: Current Issues in Interactional Psychology*, Hillsdale, NJ: Lawrence Erlbaum Associates.

Marcuse, H. (1966) *Eros and Civilization*, rev. edn, Boston: Beacon.

Marvick, E. W. (1986) *Louis XII: The Making of a King*, New Haven: Yale University Press.

Masters, R. D. (1989) *The Nature of Politics*, New Haven: Yale University Press.

Murray, H. A. (1968) 'Personality: contemporary viewpoints: components of an evolving personological system', *International Encyclopedia of the Social Sciences*, vol. 12, New York: Macmillan.

Newhill, C. E. (1990) 'The role of culture in the development of paranoid symptomatology', *American Journal of Orthopsychiatry* 60: 176–85.

Niemi, R. and Weisberg, H. E. (1984) *Controversies in Voting Behavior*, 2nd edn, Washington, DC: Congressional Quarterly Press.

Park, B. E. (1986) *The Impact of Illness on World Leaders*, Philadelphia: University of Pennsylvania Press.

Pervin, L. A. and Lewis, M. (eds) (1978) *Perspectives on Interactional Psychology*, New York: Plenum.

Peterson, R. E. and Bilorusky, J. A. (1971) *May 1970: The Campus Aftermath of Cambodia and Kent State*, New York: Carnegie Foundation for the Advancement of Teaching.

Pratkanis, A. R., Breckler, S. J. and Greenwald, A. G. (eds) (1989) *Attitude Structure and Function*, Hillsdale, NJ: Lawrence Erlbaum Associates.

Riesman, D. and Glazer, N. (1952) *Faces in the Crowd: Individual Studies of Character and Politics*, New Haven: Yale University Press.

Rokeach, M. (1960) *The Open and the Closed Mind: Investigations into the Nature of Belief Systems and Personality Systems*, New York: Basic Books.

Simon, H. A. (1985) 'Human nature in politics: the dialogue of psychology with political science', *American Political Science Review* 79: 292–304.

Simonton, D. K. (1990) 'Personality and politics', in L. A. Pervin (ed.) *Handbook of Personality: Theory and Research*, New York: Guilford.

Smith, M. B. (1968) 'A map for the study of personality and politics', *Journal of Social Issues* 24: 15–28.

Smith, M. B., Bruner, J. S. and White, R. W. (1956) *Opinions and Personality*, New York: John Wiley.

Sniderman, P. M. (1974) *Personality and Democratic Politics*, Berkeley: University of California Press.

Stone, W. F. (1981) 'Political psychology: a Whig history', in S. L. Long (ed.) *The Handbook of Political Behavior*, vol. 1, New York: Plenum.

Stone, W. F. and Schaffner, P. E. (1988) *The Psychology of Politics*, 2nd edn, New York: Springer Verlag.

Tucker, R. C. (1965) 'The dictator and totalitarianism', *World Politics* 17: 555–83.

——(1973) *Stalin as Revolutionary, 1879–1929: A Short Study in History and Personality*, New York: Norton.

——(1981) *Politics as Leadership*, Columbia, Mo.: University of Missouri Press.

Vertzberger, Y. Y. I. (1990) *The World in their Minds: Information Processing, Cognition, and Perception in Foreign Policy Decisionmaking*, Stanford: Stanford University Press.

Volkan, V. D. and Itzkowitz, N. (1984) *The Immortal Ataturk: A Psychobiography*, Chicago: University of Chicago Press.

Wallas, G. (1908) *Human Nature and Politics*, 3rd edn, New York: Crofts, 1921.

Walter, J. (1980) *The Leader: A Political Biography of Gough Whitlam*, St Lucia, Queensland: University of Queensland Press.

24

INTEREST GROUPS

HARMON ZEIGLER

Interest groups are formal organizations that seek to influence public policy in democratic polities. That is all they are, and to be more precise is to become more inaccurate. Other definitions, using phrases such as 'shared attitudes', 'cohesion' or even 'representation', can be shown to be wrong.

Interest groups are indigenous to open societies. However, their methods of organization, their claims upon their members' loyalties, their techniques of asserting their demands, and their success in achieving their goals vary with the political culture in which they operate. The two modes of political culture most used for the understanding of interest groups are pluralism and corporatism.

PLURALISM

Interest groups are the linchpin of pluralist theory. For pluralists they are transformed from unavoidable evils in the mind of Madison (1961) to agents of connection. At the very core of pluralist theory is belief that individuals can best convey their needs and desires to the government through concerted group activity. In a large, complex society one stands little chance of being heard – much less of affecting the governmental decision-making process. But, so the argument runs, when many people who share a particular concern coalesce, their collective opinion speaks with more authority than the sum of their individual voices. Thus pluralists view interest groups as channels through which people realize the democratic ideal of legitimate and satisfying interaction with government:

> Voluntary associations are the prime means by which the function of mediating between the state and the individual is performed. Through them the individual is able to relate . . . effectively and meaningfully to the political system.
> (Almond and Verba 1965: 245)

Dahl argues that autonomous organizations are 'necessary to the functioning of the democratic process itself, to minimizing government coercion, to political liberty, and to human well-being' (Dahl 1982: 1). This is very different from Madison, who praised the potential of the new American government to 'break and control the violence of faction' and to control the 'mischiefs' of factions (Madison 1961: 77–8).

PROBLEMS OF PLURALISM

Critics of pluralism assert that the very organizations said to provide a linkage between rulers and ruled are themselves undemocratic. One such critic suggests that 'the voluntary associations or organizations that the early theorists of pluralism relied upon to sustain the individual against a unified omnipotent government have themselves become oligarchically governed hierarchies' (Kariel 1961: 74). But this criticism is facile, and even distorts the position of the pluralists. Indeed, pluralism never claimed that mass participation was necessary or even possible. 'Competing elites', a phrase often used by pluralists, encompasses the notion of the undemocratic organization serving a legitimate representative function.

Equality of political resources

According to the pluralist canon, people join groups because they expect that it is to their political advantage to do so. Pluralism thus assumes that people are rational self-maximizers, just as does the abstract social contract (between people and government) of Hobbes and Locke. Tacitly, they presume that organizations are easily formed in response to individual demands (Marsh 1976: 258). Organization breeds counter-organization. Although critics (Newton 1976) allege that the 'organization equals counter-organization' contention implies political equality, leading pluralists deny this to be the case. Truman (1951) did not explicitly address inequality, but Dahl (1982) did. Conceding that a 'regrettably imprecise' sentence ('I defined the "normal" American political process as one in which there is a high probability that an active and legitimate group in the population can make itself heard effectively in the process of decision') in *A Preface to Democratic Theory* (Dahl 1956: 145) led the opponents of pluralism to argue that he believed in political equality, Dahl rejects the proposition (equality of resources) as 'absurd' (Dahl 1982: 207). Jack Walker proved just how absurd such notions are (Walker 1983: 398) by documenting how extraordinarily difficult and expensive the creation of organizations can be: it takes time, money, 'boldness', and generally an 'angel' or two.

Yet, even with Dahl's disclaimer, and the even stronger repudiation by his co-pluralist, Charles Lindblom (1977), the problem of equality continues to vex pluralists. As Manley explains:

> Unless power is de-centralized among many groups, pluralism is falsified, and some form of elite theory or class analysis better fits the empirical facts ... it is hard to see how pluralism can dispense with the notion of some sort of balance, some sorts of rough parity of countervailing power.
>
> (Manley 1983: 378)

Thus, pluralists must either accept an 'absurd' premise or abandon their theory.

The decision to participate

More serious is the assertion that people's reasons for joining a group are not, as pluralists assume, political. Pluralism accepted, without really giving alternative possibilities much thought, the idea that people joined groups to achieve public policy aspirations. Therefore 'interest groups are associations of individuals who share a desire for a contested political good' (Zeigler and Peak 1972: 2).

Pluralists attribute more political interest to potential group members than is justified by the evidence. Besides, the mere existence of a joint interest in a collective good (shared attitudes) is not a sufficient condition for rational people to unite in organized group activity – or for an individual to join an existing group – unless the 'potential' group is very small. Such a person will realize that if others organize, the value added to the group by their membership will be insignificant. Also, since the good in question is collective (since policy choices ratified by public bodies are collective), people will benefit from an organized group's acquisition of the good regardless of whether they participated in the process by which it was obtained (Olson 1965: 61). Since group membership is never without a price for the individual, no rational person will incur the costs of organizational participation unless the anticipated payoff resulting from such participation is appreciably higher than the probable payoff resulting from non-participation, and that the payoff exceeds the costs of group membership.

These arguments are in keeping with what we know about people's interest in politics. For most people, joining a group is a 'marginal act' not easily controlled by organizational incentives (Salisbury 1969: 19). While there is an active strata of those who are politically active and aware, most people are more interested in their everyday life than politics; when the two coalesce, political activity may occur only to cease when the intersection recedes (Zeigler 1988: 64; Rothenberg 1988: 1144).

The everyday life versus political commitment dilemma is addressed by the distinction between collective good and selective good mentioned briefly above

(p. 379). The former are goods that cannot be distributed selectively – to some people but not to others. The latter are benefits derived from membership in an organization and thus can be denied to non-members. Members of the American Association of Retired People (AARP) cannot deny to non-members the benefits of universal health insurance, for which the organization lobbied. But they *can* deny to non-members reduced rates on pharmaceuticals, travel and insurance, which the AARP makes available, through mass purchasing arrangements, to its members. Thus, 'rational' retired persons (or rather people aged 50 or more) would not join for benefits that they could enjoy without membership (they can be 'free riders').

The implications for pluralism of personal motives in joining an organization are substantial. How can organizations be the link between members and government if people join to obtain selective benefits? If people join the AARP to get discounts on prescription medicine, can they be regarded as a political constituency when 'their' lobbyist testifies on a complex social security problem? If their lobbyist took a position contrary to that of a majority of members, would they instruct the lobbyist to stop? If he or she did not, would they resign from the organization?

> We can see that a group's formal membership is not a valid indicator of its political support. . . . Formal membership indicates that the group is successful at selling selective incentives, not that it is politically popular. Indeed, since selective benefits have nothing whatever to do with the group's goals, there is no guarantee that any dues-payers even agree with those goals. What could be farther from pluralist preconceptions?
>
> (Moe 1980: 30)

Recent research has undermined some of these suppositions. In many organizations, selective benefits are the primary reason for joining, but in others there is a genuine political commitment. Doctors may join the American Medical Association to receive selective benefits, but women join the National Association of Women because they wish to support its programmes (Moe 1980; Zeigler 1988; Rothenburg 1988).

Additionally, the original arguments against the pluralists were developed by American economists using American examples (not, in Olson's case (Olson 1965), data) of individual choice. Since the United States is more individualist in mass and elite attitudes, less corporatist in governance, and more fragmented politically than most other industrial democracies, one naturally wonders if other cultures produce such self-maximizing, rational individuals. Although the evidence is far from comprehensive, there is ample reason to assume that other political cultures are inhabited by interest groups whose members are 'irrational' according to the norms of economic maximization. In the United Kingdom, not a good example of corporatism or collectivism, Marsh found that while the small businesses who joined the Confederation of Business did so for services, that is, selective benefits, large firms did not (Marsh 1976: 262; see also King 1985). In West Germany anti-nuclear protestors joined groups both because they believed themselves to be in imminent danger and because they enjoyed protesting (Opp 1986: 106). And, as we have noted, in the United States, individual motivations vary with the nature of the organiz- ation and with the nature of the decision. The decision to *renew* membership may be dissimilar from the decision to *join* an organization, as it is apprised by more knowledge (Zeigler 1988; Rothenberger 1988). Generally, selective benefits become more important as membership is renewed, giving lobbyists more freedom; yet, since new members know less than veteran members about an organization's policy aspirations, they too are a weak source of constraint.

Perhaps the most significant aspect of the intense exploration of individual motives for joining and renewing membership is that the notion of the econ- omic person is too simple: people join for a myriad of reasons. Some organiza- tions – citizens' groups for example – attract people who are genuinely con- cerned with political reform. Others – trade associations for example – attract those with a more personalized vision.

THE TWO MODES OF PLURALISM

Pluralism describes a political routine characterized by a roughly equal distri- bution of opportunities to acquire political resources, although not by the actual distribution of these resources. However, another understanding of the term, especially among European political scientists, is a system of multiple, competing interest groups that, through bargaining and compromise, contrib- ute to the shape of public policy. This view enunciates a political process in which interest groups organize, attempt to influence, survive, or disappear, largely without the participation or encouragement of governmental bureauc- racies.

Decisions are a result of elite bargaining and compromise. Elite competititon helps to safeguard individual non-participants from governmental abuse, since no set of interests is likely to be in the ascendant indefinitely. Thus a particular interest will win in some years, lose in others, and win on some issues, lose on others. Pluralism, then, is – besides being a process with at least the pretensions of balanced power – a loosely structured 'free market' system, with groups coming and going without negative or positive sanctions from the government. Although, depending upon the criteria employed, the United States, the United Kingdom, France, Canada, Ireland and Italy have all been called pluralist, only the United States has consistently and consensually been so regarded (Wilson 1985: 33).

While business associations clearly enjoy a privileged position (Lindblom 1977; Schlozman and Tierney 1986), the privilege is more a matter of money and prestige than of 'official' sanction or regulation. The very phrase 'pressure group' implies that American interest groups do not have the ease of access afforded by quasi-governmental status and therefore must 'lobby':

> [Pressure groups] suggests a distance and a separation of function between business organizations and government that would not make sense in many countries.... [I]t remains more common to think of business organizations in [the United Kingdom and the United States] as outside pressure groups than as groups incorporated into the framework of government. This tendency is strongest in the USA.
>
> (Wilson 1985: 128)

(See also Cox 1988: 198–222.) What is true of business associations is even more certain for the less privileged groups: labour, consumers, civil rights organizations and the like. With freedom to organize but no guaranteed access, pressure groups gain their advantage by creating obligations and cashing in on them. Since the ill-fated reforms of the 1970s in the USA, the number of such groups – and their attendant political action committees – has increased exponentially.

With the free commerce in interest groups came doubts about the efficacy of interest groups for democracy. Having caused pluralist theorists to reassess the *representative* function of organizations, Olson also caused them to reassess their political consequences. He argued that 'distributional coalitions' – interest groups – doing what they do best, that is defending their interests, constrain the polity's ability to make difficult choices. Interest groups, unless they are subordinated to a more encompassing view, ensure economic decline (Olson 1982). Olson alleges that two examples of economic decline – the United States and the United Kingdom – establish his point. Of the United Kingdom, Olson offers the classic description of a pluralist group pattern:

> The number and power of its trade unions need no description. The vulnerability and power of its professional associations is also striking.... [L]obbying is not as blatant as in the United States but it is pervasive and often involves discreet efforts to influence civil servants as well as ministers and other politicians.
>
> (Olson 1982: 77–8)

Clearly Olson's idea of pluralism is related not to the *distribution* of power but rather to its use: interest groups are not encompassing, therefore they pursue their (special) interest to the detriment of the polity.

As Olson simplified individual motivation, so he glossed over major *institutional* differences between governments, pluralist in *group* structure or not. Again, the United Kingdom and the United States provide an instructive example. A presidential, federal government with deteriorating party discipline is, in Rose's apt words, no government (Rose 1988: 71). Echoing Theodore Lowi's lament (Lowi 1967, 1969), Rose asserts that the president cannot 'override the preferences of subgovernments [interest groups] in the name of broader national interests' (Rose 1988: 71). Therefore, 'there is no government there' (ibid.). Parliamentary democracies, especially unitary ones such as the United Kingdom, do indeed have a government. They also have interest groups, quite powerful ones in the case of the United Kingdom, but 'the cabinet has the collective authority to hold subgovernments [interest groups] in check' (Rose 1988: 71).

Thus the notion that interest groups destroy collective purpose seems flawed. Such a notion also exaggerates the divorce between interest groups and government in the world's most 'pluralist democracy'. As Walker (1983: 399) and Ware (1989: 110–11) have shown, organizations are often sponsored by the American national government. Additionally, the 'iron triangles' – tight policy networks with Congressional subcommittees at the hub – provide preferential access, albeit to groups that give them money. Nevertheless, fragmented sectors of the American government, including bureaucracies, are tightly aligned with interest groups. The point is that parliamentary governments can co-ordinate and subordinate the behaviour of interest groups, whereas pure presidential ones cannot. The American economic decline can therefore be blamed – partially – upon narrow distributional coalitions. Paul Kennedy, like Olson, blames interest groups that 'by definition' sabotage the public good (Kennedy 1987: 524).

Beyond the American example one is hard pressed to illustrate the premise that interest groups are incompatible with broad images of the public good. In the United Kingdom, the Thatcher government took on the unions and substantially reduced their institutionally assured access (Kreiger 1986: 36–58). Other countries – Sweden, Japan, Switzerland, Norway, Germany – have enjoyed vibrant economies while simultaneously encouraging vibrant organizational activity. It is not interest groups which enhance or impede a polity's ability to enunciate and achieve its goals, but the degree of co-ordination imposed or encouraged by the government, and the ability or failure of governments to weaken divisive groups (Richardson and Jordan 1985). In the United Kingdom, the economic decline lamented by Olson has been abated (Riddell 1989: 168–84). As Richardson and Jordan conclude: 'Whether governments utilize the capacity of groups skillfully or turn the opportunities into opposition is the test of successful governance' (Richardson and Jordan 1985: 291). Since Rose has insisted that as a pluralist, presidential system the United States lacks governance, it obviously cannot meet this challenge. A more structured pluralist, parliamentary system, the United Kingdom, does better. Corporatist regimes are said to be best at managing interest groups because they incorporate them directly and deliberately into the governing process.

CORPORATISM

Corporatist schemes are meticulously co-ordinated. In these countries:

> Important aspects of public policy are made after consultations approximating negotiations between government and 'monopolistic' interest groups with the exclusive right to represent employers and unions. Government generally plays an active role in shaping economic development through plans for the economy as a whole or individual sectors.... [T]he economic interests speaking for employers or unions should have a high degree of *influence* ... in shaping government policy. Governments turn as easily to the leaders of employers organizations or the unions and perhaps more frequently than they turn to legislators or parties for advice, permission and approval in undertaking major policy changes.
>
> (Wilson 1985: 12)

The government tailors and sculpts interest group operation. There are, however, degrees of co-ordination. Some systems – Switzerland, Japan, Austria, Norway and Sweden – are corporatist on a polity-wide basis. Others – Germany and possibly France (Keeler 1987) – are corporatist in some economic sectors more than others.

Problems with corporatism

The earlier, simplistic views of corporatism (Schmitter 1974) were obtuse and resistant to operationalization. More systematic studies (Keeler 1987: 11) have developed a manageable understanding of the phenomenon. Keeler outlines the dynamics of strongly pluralist and corporatist arrangements and invites us to array governments along a continuum. His scheme is depicted in Table 1.

Keeler and others (Zeigler 1988: 114) interested in empirically testable measures of the degree of corporatism suggest a *continuum* rather than an absolute classification. Keeler's continuum includes the following range of possibility.

Strong pluralism	Structured pluralism	Weak corporatism	Moderate corporatism	Strong corporatism

Countries can vary in corporatism by economic sector, as Keeler shows in relation to France. France was typically regarded as among the more pluralist of European political systems (Wilson 1985: 907–9). Between 1958 and 1981, France moved from strong pluralism to structured pluralism in the labour sector, from structured pluralism to moderate corporatism in the business sector, and from structured pluralism to strong corporatism in the agricultural sector (Keeler 1987: 19). West Germany's corporatist arrangements 'expanded

Table 1

	Strong	Strong corporatism
Role of the state in shaping the pattern of interest intermediation	The state plays no active role, serving as a broker *vis-à-vis* competing interest groups.	The state plays a very important role as an architect of political order, acting so as to bolster an official client group.
Nature of group–state interaction in the public policy-making process	Groups attempt to influence policy by lobbying decision makers. No groups are *formally* incorporated into the policy process.	The *official* clients benefit greatly from biased influence, structured access and devolved power. *Non-official* groups lobby (see strong pluralism).
Nature of intra-group (elite–member) relations	Group leaders respond (imperfectly) to member demands. Groups 'defend' their members against the state.	Elites unresponsive to member demands; leaders enjoy 'immunity' through state protection. Group acts as 'transmission belt' between members and the state, mobilizing members in support of policy and disciplining dissidents.
Nature of inter-group relations	Groups compete for membership and influence without state interference. Members join and remain in an organization because of the attractiveness of incentives.	The *official* client group enjoys an enormous competitive advantage, as the state provides it with resources or even makes membership compulsory. *Non-official* groups receive no such resources and may even be repressed.

and later contracted in response to changing economic and political conditions' (Hancock 1989: 131). Thus, while France became more corporatist, West Germany became less so (Katzenstein 1985: 368).

General patterns do allow an imperfect placement on the continuum. Just as the United States, even with the 'micro-corporatism' of the iron triangles, is conceded the most pluralist of the industrial democracies, Austria, Switzerland and Japan are rarely challenged as among the most corporatist. True, van

Wolferen argues that to regard Japan as corporatist is to 'render the theory almost meaningless' (Wolferen 1989: 81). And unquestionably Austria's labour-dominated corporatist arrangement differs from Switzerland's business driven one (Katzenstein 1984). Nevertheless, no two countries are identical. Without doubt the United Kingdom's pluralism is very different from that of the United States. Few would argue with the following classification:

System	Examples
Strong pluralism	United States
Structured pluralism	United Kingdom
Weak corporatism	France
Moderate corporatism	Germany
Strong corporatism	Austria, Switzerland, Japan

THE CORPORATIST POLITICS OF EXCLUSION

Generally, corporatist governments recognize 'peak' associations – those organizations that represent a large population of smaller organizations. For example, a peak labour organization would include the building trades, truck drivers, electricians, and so on. A business peak association would include computer manufacturers, textile manufacturers, and the like. The component organizations do not engage in political activities in defiance of, or even in augmentation of, the peak association.

As the primary interest of corporatist decision making is economic – wages or incomes policies, international trade balances, deficits, and so on – only those groups directly related to such policies are invited to participate. As Keeler (1987: 19) observes, others must resort to the traditional lobbying techniques of the pluralist political processes. Yet, pluralist systems also exclude, albeit with less certainty. This is especially true when some groups can claim a monopoly on expertise, as for example in educational policy making (Kogan 1975).

At any rate, corporatism is more 'officially' exclusive in granting the representative franchise. As an example, an informal collaboration between unions and business in Austria was institutionalized in 1957 as the Joint Commission on Prices and Wages. Labour representation to the Commission is from the Austrian Federation of Trade Unions and from the Chambers of Labour. The Federal Chamber of Business and the Conference of Presidents of Chambers of Agriculture represent business. The Austrian government merely provides the structure for interest-group bargaining and ratifies the decisions reached by the participating interest groups (Katzenstein 1985: 142–4).

In the European corporatist governments, labour's governmental role is generally (except in Switzerland) firmly set, and it has no need to show its muscle. Indeed, Marxist critics of corporatism allege that its fundamental goal is to de-radicalize labour unions. By entering into these agreements, labour groups are said to act contrary to the intentions that guided their origins; that is, they co-operate in the preservation of a stable rather than an inflationary economy by not pursuing excessive wage demands. Panitch believes that unions in corporatist arrangements are instruments of oppression. He is especially anxious to have proponents of corporatism lay bare their ideological bias, which he believes to be intensely anti-egalitarian, and calls our attention to the incompatibility of corporatism (which assumes the existence of co-operation between labour and capital) and Marxism (which assumes their perpetual antagonism). Unions must be able to assure business and government that their members will comply with the terms of the 'social contract' (Panitch 1977: 61–90).

In classical Marxist thought the state is an instrument of oppression, initially at the bidding of the ruling capitalist class, and – in its transitional phase – of the proletariat. In corporatism, the state is not *necessarily* oppressive. On the contrary the state is liberating, in the tradition of Rousseau and the collectivist romantics. Corporatism is therefore compatible with authoritarian or even totalitarian regimes, but need not be so. Fascist governments can be corporatist as can democratic ones.

The fundamental idea of corporatism is that geographical representation is inadequate and that functional representation should replace or augment it. Governments create and sanction occupational associations of farmers, electricians, computer programmers and so on. In some forms of corporatism these organizations have been given authority for policy implementation; in others they are legitimately influential in policy formation. In Japan, Austria and Switzerland, for example, the distinction between public and private is uncertain. Austrian labour unions and Japanese manufacturers are as much a part of the governing process as are legislators and bureaucrats.

In Austria, for example, a decision to strike cannot be made by an individual union acting unilaterally, but only after a protracted and complex set of negotiations between peak associations. The unions eschew the ideologically loaded subject of inequality in exchange for maximum influence 'at the very highest levels in the arenas of economic and social policy most critical to Austria's strategy in the world economy; labour as a force for conservatism is of course not unique to Austria' (Katzenstein 1985: 247).

In Switzerland, labour is equally conservative. Unions are weak, more akin to Japanese examples than those in left-corporatist governments like Sweden or Austria. The unions are non-monopolistic, much more so than is the case for business, and are rent by internal divisions (Katzenstein 1985: 101). Since 1937, the unions and employers' associations have operated 'peace treaties', which amount to no-strike deals that also outlaw lock-outs and boycotts. These peace agreements rarely go beyond the local level. The federal government stays out, and the national unions and employers' associations have rights for binding arbitration. They have 'Swiss' power, probably more than do unions in Japan. Here again, the constitution provides for 'generally binding' agreements; unions may collect dues from non-members and bargains struck by the unions and employers bind all workers. The agreements are thus public law. Unions and business groups unite to maintain the (somewhat) discriminatory treatment of foreign workers (25 per cent of the work force), without which the unemployment rate would be far higher than it is. Labour's ostensible ally, the Social Democrats, committed themselves to various (unsuccessful) referenda to improve the status of foreign labourers. This cosy pact means there are almost no strikes.

Corporatism's politics of exclusion are not therefore in the traditional rhetoric of Marxism, although these politics co-opt workers who might otherwise be attracted to Marxism. Labour and business are *the* incorporated groups, not the various single-issue, citizens' and protest groups that scatter themselves across the landscapes of democracies. Corporatism embraces only those organizations that the economic division of labour creates; some students of corporatist societies virtually define corporatism in terms of the bargain struck with organized labour. It is primarily the labour movement that extracts concessions from the government or wins concessions by allying with other interest groups. Corporatism is an alliance between *economic* interest groups.

CORPORATISM AND DEMOCRACY

Corporatism creates major incentives by granting quasi-official status to economic interest groups, and by connecting these peak associations directly to the appropriate government bureaucracies. The justification for corporatism is precisely its ability to remove policy from those without the expertise to comprehend complexity, parliaments or legislatures, and to transfer it to bureaucracies (those with a specialized expertise). Corporatism is designed to make policy immune from ideological passion, from partisan preference, or shifting public opinion. The adoption of corporatist mechanisms and processes was a conscious effort to ensure continuity in economic policy: 'What permitted stability ... was a shift in the focal point of decision making. Fragmented parliamentary majorities yielded to ministerial bureaucracies, or sometimes directly to party councils, where interest group representatives could more easily work out social burdens and rewards' (Meier 1975: 593).

CONCLUSION

Neither pluralist nor corporatist systems are superior in representing the view of members of voluntary associations. Whereas the reliance upon selective benefits is less crucial when membership is almost compulsory and access assured, no evidence or theory suggests that the functional representation of corporatism is more likely to be 'accurate' than is the 'accidental', *laissez-faire* mode of pluralist representation. As Keeler (1987: 19) suggests, in pluralist systems elite response to members' demands is imperfect, whereas in corporatist systems elites can afford insulation.

Is either more likely to balance narrow interests against a large public good? Here the answer is less ambiguous. Corporatism can deliver more. As Wilson puts it:

> [Corporatist] systems have aroused the interest and envy of other states for some years now. Their success in securing above-average incomes and economic growth with lower than average inflation has fueled both admiration and envy.... [Corporatist] systems have provided their inhabitants with 30 years of high employment, low inflation, and considerable economic growth.
>
> (Wilson 1985: 110, 113)

Of the United States, said by Rose to be so fragmented that it lacks a government in the true sense of the word, there is reason to assume that:

> America's economy has been slowly unraveling. The economic decline has been marked by growing unemployment, mounting business failures, and falling productivity.... America's politics have been in chronic disarray. The political decline has been marked by the triumph of narrow interest groups.
>
> (Reich 1983: 3)

Corporatism is more fiscally sound, providing stable growth without massive debt (Zeigler 1988: 99–100).

If interest groups – subordinated by corporatism or at least structured and balanced by unitary, parliamentary governments – are beneficial, and if they – inhibited by the impotence of strong pluralism – contribute to economic stagnation and decline, is this not a paradox for pluralism? For, as the linchpins of pluralism, interest groups are hastening its death. In an internationally interdependent economy, governments that can govern will prevail over those that surrender to narrow coalitions.

However, one can hardly attribute the rise and decline of economies solely to the relations between interest groups and the state. British economic decline since the 1870s is attributable as much to the accidents of empire as to narrow distributional coalitions. As the British empire and the industrial revolution developed simultaneously, the British relied more on their colonies for commercial and industrial development than did other, less imperialist countries. British firms continued to sell to semi-industrial colonies while other countries were competing in the more developed European market and were producing more technologically sophisticated products. The seeds of decline were sown by empire rather than modes of interest group intermediation (Hall 1987: 9–12). France has become more corporatist and has prospered; Germany has become less corporatist and has prospered even more. Nations need an institutional articulation of a public interest.

REFERENCES

Almond, G. and Verba, S. (1965) *The Civic Culture: Political Attitudes and Democracy in Five Nations*, Boston: Little, Brown & Co.

Cox, A. (1988) 'The failure of corporatist state forms and policies in postwar Britain', in A. Cox and N. O'Sullivan (eds) *The Corporate State*, Aldershot: Edward Elgar.

Dahl, R. A. (1956) *A Preface to Democratic Theory*, Chicago: University of Chicago Press.

——(1982) *Dilemmas of Pluralist Democracy*, New Haven: Yale University Press.

Hall, P. (1987) 'Decline and fall', *New Society* (January): 9–12.

Hancock, M. D. (1989) *West Germany: The Politics of Democratic Corporatism*, Chatham, NJ: Chatham House.

Kariel, H. (1961) *The Decline of American Pluralism*, Stanford: Stanford University Press.

Katzenstein, P. (1984) *Corporatism and Change: Austria, Switzerland and the Politics of Industry*, Ithaca, NY: Cornell University Press.

——(1985) *Small States in World Markets*, Ithaca, NY: Cornell University Press.

Keeler, J. (1987) *The Politics of Neocorporatism in France*, New York: Oxford University Press.

Kennedy, P. (1987) *The Rise and Fall of the Great Powers*, New York: Random House.

King, R. (1985) 'The organization, structure and political function of selected chambers of commerce', in A. G. Jordan and J. J. Richardson (eds) (1987) *Government and Pressure Groups in Britain*, Oxford: Clarendon Press.

Kogan, M. (1975) *Educational Policy-Making*, London: Allen & Unwin.

Kreiger, J. (1986) *Reagan, Thatcher, and the Politics of Decline*, New York: Oxford University Press.

Lindblom, C. (1977) *Politics and Markets*, New York: Basic Books.

Lowi, T. (1967) 'The public philosophy: interest group liberalism', *American Political Science Review* 61: 5–24.

——(1969) *The End of Liberalism: Ideology, Policy, and the Crisis of Public Authority*, New York: Norton.

Madison, J. (1961) 'Federalist no. 10', in C. Rossiter (ed.) *The Federalist Papers*, New York: New American Library.

Manley, J. (1983) 'Neopluralism: a class analysis of pluralism I and pluralism II', *American Political Science Review* 77: 368–84.

Marsh (1976) 'On joining interest groups: an empirical consideration of the works of Mancur Olson, Jr', *British Journal of Political Science* 6: 257–71.

Meier, C. S. (1975) *Transforming Bourgeois Europe*, Princeton: Princeton University Press.

Moe, T. (1980) *The Organization of Interests*, Chicago: University of Chicago Press.

Newton, K. (1976) *Second City Politics*, Oxford: Clarendon Press.

Olson, M. (1965) *The Logic of Collective Action: Public Goods and the Theory of Groups*, Cambridge, Mass.: Harvard University Press.

——(1982) *The Rise and Decline of Nations*, New Haven: Yale University Press.

Opp, K. D. (1986) 'Soft incentives and collective action', *British Journal of Political Science* 16: 87–112.

Panitch, L. (1977) 'The development of corporatism in liberal democracies', *Comparative Political Studies* 10: 61–90.

Reich, R. (1983) *The Next American Frontier*, New York: Times Books.

Richardson, J. J. and Jordan A. G. (1985) *Government Under Pressure: The Policy Process in a Post Parliamentary Democracy*, Oxford: Basil Blackwell.

Riddell, P. (1989) *The Thatcher Decade*, Oxford: Basil Blackwell.

Rose, R. (1988) *The Postmodern Presidency*, Chatham, NJ: Chatham House.

Rothenberg, L. (1988) 'Organizational maintenance and the retention decision in groups', *American Political Science Review* 82: 1130–52.

Salisbury, R. (1969) 'An exchange theory of interest groups', *Midwest Journal of Political Science* 12: 1–32.

Schlozman, K. and Tierney, J. E. (1986) *Organized Interests and American Democracy*, New York: Harper & Row.

Schmitter, P. C. (1974) 'Still the century of corporatism?', *Review of Politics* 85: 85–131.

Truman, D. (1951) *The Governmental Process*, New York: Knopf.

Walker, J. (1983) 'The origins and maintenance of interest groups in America, *American Political Science Review* 7: 390–406.

Ware, A. (1989) *Between Profit and State: Intermediate Organizations in Britain and the United States*, Princeton: Princeton University Press.

Wilson, G. (1985) *Business and Politics*, Chatham, NJ: Chatham House.

Wolferen, K. van (1989) *The Enigma of Japanese Power*, New York: Knopf.

Zeigler, H. (1988) *Pluralism, Corporatism, and Confucianism*, Philadelphia: Temple University Press.

Zeigler, H. and Peak, G. W. (1972) *Interest Groups in American Society*, 2nd edn, Englewood Cliffs, NJ: Prentice-Hall.

FURTHER READING

Dahl, R. A. (1982) *Dilemmas of Pluralist Democracy*, New Haven: Yale University Press.

Katzenstein, P. (1984) *Corporatism and Change: Austria, Switzerland and the Politics of Industry*, Ithaca: Cornell University Press.

——(1985) *Small States in World Markets*, Ithaca, NY: Cornell University Press.

Keeler, J. (1987) *The Politics of Neocorporatism in France*, New York: Oxford University Press.

Moe, T. (1980) *The Organization of Interests*, Chicago: University of Chicago Press.

Olson, M. (1965) *The Logic of Collective Action: Public Goods and the Theory of Groups*, Cambridge, Mass.: Harvard University Press.

——(1982) *The Rise and Decline of Nations*, New Haven: Yale University Press.

Richardson, J. J. and Jordan, A. G. (1985) *Government Under Pressure: The Policy Process in a Post Parliamentary Democracy*, Oxford: Basil Blackwell.

Schlozman, K. and Tierney, J. E. (1986) *Organized Interests and American Democracy*, New York: Harper & Row.

Wilson, G. (1985) *Business and Politics*, Chatham, NJ: Chatham House.

Zeigler, H. (1988) *Pluralism, Corporatism, and Confucianism*, Philadelphia: Temple University Press.

25

POLITICAL PARTIES

JOSEPH LAPALOMBARA AND JEFFREY ANDERSON

Political parties are about power. In democracies, they represent the principal instrument through which segments of the population compete to secure control of elective institutions, and through them to exercise predominant influence over public policies. Everywhere, including in dictatorial regimes, rulers try to legitimize their domination via this same instrument. In recognition of the basic power role of political parties, V. O. Key once remarked that they 'provide a good deal of the propulsion of the formal constitutional system' (Key 1964: 154).

It is not simply that parties are central to elections and to policy making, or that they make and break governments, administer patronage, and take decisions that deeply affect a nation's welfare. Under their aegis, mass publics are mobilized for good and evil, revolutions are fomented, dissidents are arrested, tortured and killed, and ideologies are turned into moral imperatives. Not only democracies, then, but political systems of every conceivable variety seem unable to function without the presence of one or more parties. The recent scramble to form political parties across Eastern Europe, in anticipation of the first free elections held in these countries in a half century or more, provided a most vivid confirmation of the continuing and universal relevance of parties.

The omnipresence of parties suggests that they perform important functions independent of the level of economic development or of the type of regime. In other words, the British Conservative Party, the Communist Party of the Soviet Union and El Salvador's ARENA party all carry out comparable tasks as 'organizational instrumentalities' (LaPalombara 1974: 515). Among other things, each organizes public opinion, transmits demands from society to its governors and vice versa, recruits political leaders, and engages in oversight of the implementation of public policies.

Admittedly, some would deny the comparability of democratic and totalitarian parties (Friedrich and Brzezinski 1966). Neumann, a noted scholar of

393

parties, virtually rules out comparisons altogether, arguing that 'a party's character can be spelled out only in time and space' (Neumann 1956: 396). Our premiss is that we can indeed compare political parties and make certain generalizations about them. In order to clarify what these human organizations have in common, and how such characteristics have evolved and changed, we require a working definition of the political party itself.

A DEFINITION

Political parties are not quarks. That is, they are visible and easily recognized in the wild. Despite these tangible qualities, the scholarly literature has yet to reach consensus on a definition of party. One long-standing disagreement centres on the glue that binds together a party: public interest or private gain. Edmund Burke is perhaps the first and certainly the most eloquent spokesperson for public interest. 'Party is a body of men united, for promoting by their joint endeavors the national interest, upon some particular principle upon which they are all agreed' (Burke 1839: 425–6). Joseph Schumpeter, the best-known antagonist of the public interest school, counters with the following definition of party, full of the grit of power and political gain:

> A party is a group whose members propose to act in concert in the competitive struggle for power . . . . Party and machine politicians are simply the response to the fact that the electoral mass is incapable of action other than in a stampede, and they constitute an attempt to regulate political competition exactly similar to the corresponding practice of a trade association.
>
> (Schumpeter 1976: 283)

E. E. Schattschneider, an early political scientist who minced no words about the power-centred nature of politics, promotes this narrowly instrumental view of parties in even more forceful terms (Schattschneider 1942: 35). For him, the essence of party is the urge to gain and keep power.

Such conceptual disunity should not surprise us. Parties occupy the main intersections of the political process – conflict regulation, integration, public opinion formation, policy formulation. They are therefore complex, multi-faceted aspects of the political system. As nothing more than a working definition, we offer the following: a party is any political group, in possession of an official label and of a formal organization that links centre and locality, that presents at elections, and is capable of placing through elections (free or non-free), candidates for public office.

There are numerous advantages to this formulation, an amalgam of LaPalombara and Weiner (1966) and Sartori (1976). By stressing both free and non-free elections, it preserves comparability across regime-type. Moreover, unlike the Burkean and Schumpeterian definitions, it addresses several broader considerations (Sartori 1976: 58–64). First, the definition delimits parties from other actors that are or have been involved in the rough and tumble of politics: court factions, parliamentary clubs, mass movements, interest groups, bureaucracies, church organizations and the military. As the only organizations to operate formally in the electoral arena (Panebianco 1988: 6; Schlesinger 1965: 767), political parties are distinctive. Second, the definition is minimal. That is, it contains only those elements necessary for delimitation, and it leaves all other properties as hypotheses subject to empirical verification. Too often, parties are defined in functional terms, which makes it almost impossible to disprove that the putative functions are in fact carried out by parties (King 1969: 116). Finally, our working definition avoids any identification of parties with party systems, a common confusion that often leads to the conclusion that parties found in dictatorial settings are aberrations.

THE ORIGINS OF POLITICAL PARTIES

The arguments of Madison and Tocqueville – namely, that parties emerge wherever there exist salient differences of interest among the public (Madison 1961: 77–84; Tocqueville 1969: 174) – are clearly incomplete. The presence of conflicting interests is a necessary but not sufficient condition for the emergence of parties. Were this otherwise, parties would surely number among the oldest forms of social organization. Instead, parties are a phenomenon of the last 150 years, the creatures of modernity.

There are three distinct explanations of the recent origins of parties (LaPalombara and Weiner 1966: 8–21):

1 institutional theories that stress the transformation of parliaments;
2 historical theories that emphasize systemic crises tied to the nation-building process; and
3 theories of modernization and political development.

While each successive approach seeks to embed political parties in progressively more inclusive theories of social and political change, they all acknowledge a common determining factor in the appearance of parties: social mobilization, or the entry of the masses onto the political stage. Once politics could no longer be confined to a small circle of aristocratic elites, parties emerged as the instruments to link the centre of political power with the masses. In this parties proved consistently indispensable, whether the transformation of politics was induced by competition among elites or by mass pressures from below.

Parties and the evolution of parliaments

Institutional theories, informed primarily by the Western experience, locate the origins of political parties in the gradual extension of suffrage and the resulting transfiguration of parliamentary bodies. Scholars credit Duverger with the seminal contribution, though Weber is often mentioned in the same breath (Duverger 1954: xxiii–xxxvii; Weber 1946: 102–7). Duverger suggests three stages in the development of parties: the birth of parliamentary groups, the formation of local electoral committees, and the creation of permanent links between the two. The expansion of the electorate and the responses of elites in and outside the parliamentary arena drive the process.

Under a restricted suffrage, politics is very much an elite intramural affair. Factions and other loose associations of notables form within assemblies, but these are often ephemeral groupings. Even where they endure, they display little continuity of purpose, and no institutionalized connections to the extra-parliamentary environment. Disrupting this cosy state of affairs, the initial expansion of the suffrage prompts and indeed compels like-minded notables to create local electoral machinery to woo the new electors, and to organize them as reliable supporters. Disraeli's efforts on behalf of the Conservative Party in mid-nineteenth-century Britain represents perhaps the classic example of this dynamic. As the electorate expands still further, and party notables begin to face competition from emergent parties outside of parliament (see below), they seek to improve the integration of the national and local levels, both vertically and horizontally. The result is a modern mass political party. Whatever the specific circumstances of its origins, the party emerges to deal with the incorporation of unprecedented numbers of persons into the political process.

The preceding describes the genesis of political parties created by the legislators themselves. Classic examples include the British Conservative and Liberal Parties, the Democratic and Republican Parties in the United States, the National Liberal Party of Wilhelmine Germany, and the Liberals of nineteenth-century Italy. Duverger distinguishes these 'internally created' parties from those that originate outside the established representative insti-tutions, and that typically present ideological and electoral challenges to the ruling elites. Externally created parties also derive their sustenance from an expanded electorate, yet they seek to enter the corridors of power to pursue the interests of previously excluded groups, or even to transform the political system itself. The vehicle is again a mass political party. Typical examples in the European context are socialist parties, communist parties, christian democratic parties, as well as parties of agrarian defence.

Although Duverger's analysis retains a certain plausibility where the Western experience is concerned, its limited reach is all too apparent. The theory is space-bound; it does not connect with the experience of colonial regimes or developing nations, where parliamentary assemblies – centre ring for Duverger – were either non-existent or excluded the indigenous population, and yet political parties emerged nevertheless. The theory is also time-bound, in that it does not illuminate the process by which new parties form in places where universal suffrage has been the norm for many decades. The recent emergence of ecological and environmental parties in Western democracies is a prime example. To correct these deficiencies, scholars have offered more complex theories to explain the origins of parties.

Parties and the nation-state

As political elites cope with the economic, social, political, military and administrative problems that typically accompany the nation-building process, they create institutions that endure long after earlier moments of crisis, despair and euphoria have passed. The rise of parties accompanies certain types of crises, in particular those relating to national integration, the nation's legitimacy, and demands for increased participation. More importantly perhaps, the content and sequencing of these crises will determine the pattern of evolution that parties will follow. In Europe and in developing countries in the past, in Eastern Europe at the present, and in China in the future, we can and will discern how intimately related are legitimacy, integration and participation, on the one side, and the nature of political parties on the other.

According to proponents of this approach, legitimacy crises explain the emergence of some of the earliest examples of political parties, both on the European continent and in the developing countries. Duverger's internal parties formed at a time when the legitimacy of existing representative institutions was placed in doubt. In the post-colonial era, which saw an effervescence of new nations, political parties emerged from nationalist movements that questioned the legitimacy not just of representative institutions, but of the existing state as a whole. The rise of fascist and communist parties in the twentieth century also reflected legitimacy crises in liberal democracies. Ironically, these crises were engendered to some degree by the malfunctioning and negative repercussions of party pluralism (Sartori 1976: 39).

Participation demands prove to be even more closely linked to the formation of political parties. The timing, as well as the nature, of elite responses to them will tend to influence not only the parties' organizational forms and political behaviour but their ideologies as well. The incorporation of new social groups into the political system typically requires extended suffrage. As nations develop along this particular participatory dimension, the creation of political parties is the natural outcome. As a rule then, almost all externally created parties are formed either along with system-expanding crises of electoral participation, or with more or less sweeping attacks on the inadequacies of the extant system.

Parties and modernization

A broader formulation is that mass parties are the product of societal modernization. New social groups seek more direct access to the political process as the results of 'increases in the flow of information, the expansion of internal markets, a growth in technology, the expansion of transportation networks, and, above all, increases in spatial and social mobility' (LaPalombara and Weiner 1966: 20). Other factors associated with modernization, like secularization of values, the emergence of voluntaristic collective action and improvements in the means of communication, also facilitate the emergence of the political party as the prime form of political organization.

Samuel Huntington goes so far as to argue that the political party – not public bureaucracy, not parliament, not election – is *the* distinctive institution in the modern polity (Huntington 1968: 89). Modern society is everywhere mass society and, as such, requires an institution (the party) to organize the inclusion and integration of mass publics into the system. Others pursue a less deterministic line, but nevertheless associate the emergence of political parties with the effects of industrialization. In this vein, Daalder states, 'the modern political party . . . can be described with little exaggeration as the child of the Industrial Revolution' (Daalder 1966: 52). As Marx anticipated, the concentration of workers in industrial urban centres carried political consequences. He did not fully appreciate, however, that the political party would emerge to mobilize these masses not for revolution but rather for quite routine and indeed productive and system-reinforcing forms of electoral participation. Yet whatever the aims of power-seeking elites they have found the political party of extraordinary instrumental utility.

Industrialization also generates substantial costs for traditional social groups like artisans, small shopkeepers and farmers. In self-defence, therefore, industrial society spurs the creation of political parties whose purpose it is to defend these threatened groups. The agrarian parties of Scandinavia, as well as the fascist parties elsewhere in Europe, are examples of such reactions to modernization. Later in the modernization process, negative externalities of industrial activity – like the threat to the environment – lead to another wave of party formation, as with the so-called Greens and other ecology-sensitive parties.

Modernization theory also has its shortcomings. Most obvious among these is that we have not yet clearly delineated alternative paths to modernity or nation building. For this reason, there is little that can be said with assurance as to when, in what circumstances and with what probable consequences particular kinds of political parties will in fact materialize. With this caveat in mind, we turn to some additional observations regarding these important institutions.

Party origins: so what?

One might well suppose that a party's origins would affect its organizational structure, internal dynamics, functions and ideological principles. Duverger offers an unalloyed statement to this effect: 'It is the whole life of the party which bears the mark of its origins' (Duverger 1954: xxxv). According to him, internally created parties are less ideologically coherent and disciplined, less centralized, open to greater influence by their parliamentary wings, and more likely to place supreme emphasis on the parliamentary arena of political conflict than are other parties.

Similar, though not as deterministic in tone, are propositions that derive from those who associate the advent of parties with modernization or national development. For example, parties that are associated with crises of legitimacy of older orders, or that are involved in the dismantling of the latter, will rely on ideology as a means of cementing relationships among party members, motivating them and others to action, and establishing the legitimacy of the new order. Such parties also develop hierarchical and secretive organizational structures to protect themselves against penetration by opponents. The 'vanguard party' outlined by Lenin is the classic example (Lenin 1969). Emphasis on mass membership, self-conscious attention to ideology, and political activism are presumably characteristics of parties that have their origins in demands for expanded participation. Only the modernization school seems to be reluctant to ascribe political party characteristics to the circumstances that surround their birth.

These arguments or propositions are neither wholly implausible nor incorrect. For example, Duverger's distinctions between elite-based parties and mass-based parties are reasonable and interesting (Ware 1987: 6). As formulated, however, they are static and therefore ill-equipped to help us understand changes in the structure, ideology and functions of parties that may have occurred since their birth. Preconditions and context will certainly leave their imprint. But it stands to reason that these will eventually fade and that, in any case, parties that persist in time do so because they manage to adapt – that is, to change – as they encounter modifications in their respective environments. The graveyards of history are strewn with political parties that failed to respond to such challenges.

Two attempts to grapple with these shortcomings are worthy of mention. Von Beyme, pursuing the line of inquiry begun by Duverger, ascribes the often complex relationship between a party's parliamentary and extra-parliamentary wings neither to the parties themselves nor to their origins, but rather to other aspects of the political system (Von Beyme 1983). His work amplifies the arguments of scholars like Mckenzie who assert that the organization and behaviour of political parties tend to adapt to structural and configurative dimensions of the systems in which they operate (Mckenzie 1963). He cites as particularly important the type and institutional position of the governmental executive, the role of interest groups, and the professionalization of politicians. Unlike Duverger, Von Beyme does not see the two party wings locked into a zero-sum relationship. He suggests instead that twentieth-century developments of the kind mentioned have simultaneously strengthened both groups (Von Beyme 1983: 392).

A striking and promising recent application of organizational theory to political parties (Panebianco 1988) takes as its starting point the work of Michels, who proposed the Iron Law of Oligarchy for political parties (Michels 1962). Panebianco suggests a three-phase model of party development, namely, genesis, institutionalization and maturity. Over time, a party's internal hierarchy, its objectives, and even its principles are determined by the changes in the needs and power positions of party elites and rank-and-file members (Panebianco 1988: 18). His work is an intriguing answer to those who lament the lack of theories that address the internal workings of parties (Daalder 1983: 22).

PARTY FUNCTIONS

Theories of course can be hopelessly abstract, and nowhere is this more apparent than in the many efforts to delineate the functions of political parties. More often than not, these functions are simply imposed on the parties, by theoretical or logical fiat, and without regard to empirical verification as to what parties do in practice. Yet as Sartori reminds us, 'What parties are – that is, what their functions, placement, and weight in the political system are – has not been designed by a theory but has been determined by a concurrence of events' (Sartori 1976: 18). With this admonition in mind, we can ask what specific functions parties have carried out, whether these vary (in space or time), and which are shared with other actors in the political system. If we can specify party functions, we may also ask how well and in what circumstances they perform them.

Leadership recruitment

Wherever they exist, parties are a critical aspect of the structure of political opportunity (Schlesinger 1966). They serve the interests of ambitious men and women. They help to cull from society individuals who assume positions to which considerable power and authority attach. In the system within which political elites operate, parties are powerful 'gatekeepers' (Putnam 1976: 49–61). Given our definition of the political party, it would be a real puzzle were this not the case.

Recruitment is far from a simple matter; to understand its nuances requires more detail than is typically provided in the literature. Analysis in depth is required of such things as 'the motives that lead individuals to seek or accept political roles or inhibit them from doing so; the "catchment pools" from which the political classes are drawn . . . ; the criteria by which they are selected; and the characteristics and aims of those selecting them' (King 1969: 129). Another critical question is the extent to which the political parties monopolize the recruitment of persons to key political positions. Were parties to share this responsibility widely with other organizations (like interest groups) or actually fall into their shadow, they would lose a principal *raison d'être* (Daalder 1966: 75; Katz 1980: 4).

It goes without saying that, in pluralist democracies, parties do share this particular function with other organizations, including the military, the public bureaucracy, the court, the academic community, trade unions, business enterprises and a wide variety of other interest groups. All of them represent competing channels through which individuals enter the leadership stratum of a given society. In practice, then, the weight of parties in the selection of lawmakers and bureaucrats, and in some places judges as well, will vary. The United States, even in the era of Jacksonian Democracy, would be at one extreme. At the other, we might place Austria during the heyday of the *Proporz*, when the two leading parties monopolized access to elite positions in the polity.

Even where parties are strong, however, it is useful to think about them in part as 'an abstraction – a label under which a number of organized groups compete for a share of the elective offices to be filled' (LaPalombara 1974: 546). In many developing countries, weak party organizations take a back seat to the military or the civil bureaucracy in the recruitment of the political elite. Only in established one-party states of the fascist or communist type is political recruitment performed on a virtually exclusive basis by parties. These dictatorial parties by definition seek to negate pluralism. Even there, however, party monopoly of recruitment may have its negative side, encouraging the creation of a narrowly based, conservative, and even reactionary leadership stratum. Lenin understood this danger, as did Mao, whose 'mass line' campaigns were explicitly designed to loosen the party bureaucracy's hold on recruitment.

Formation of governments: the ruling function

According to Katz, the key function of the party is 'to rule and to take responsibility for ruling' (Katz 1987: 4). This is the truly distinctive function of the party, one which sets it apart from other organizations. In short, it intends to capture control of the political system under its own name, exclusively if possible or, failing that, in coalition with another party or parties. Bagehot remarked upon the close connection between party and government in his pathbreaking nineteenth-century treatise on the English constitution (Bagehot 1963: 158). The modern literature also highlights this critical aspect of the political party (Schattschneider 1942: ix; Neumann 1956: 400). Daalder identifies the spectacular collapse of the Weimar Republic in 1933 and its horrible aftermath as the principal source of the discipline's overwhelming concern with effective party control of the apparatus of government (Daalder 1983: 6).

The notion of 'grasp' is one way of conceptualizing a party's capacity to form governments, to rule, and to be responsible for rulership itself (King 1969: 132). We know that the capacity varies – from country to country, within the same country, and, indeed within the same political party over time. This last type of variation signals why parties, as opposed to party systems, should be studied in their own right, as complex organizations that may be well or poorly endowed with leadership, well or poorly managed, and so on. Panebianco's recent study provides important evidence that these capacities are strongly influenced by the circumstances that surround not the birth but, rather, the institutionalization of each political party, and by the type of party, i.e. 'mass bureaucratic' or 'electoral professional', that emerges (Panebianco 1988: part II and chapter 14).

Examples of extensive party grasp would be Austria during the period of the Red–Black coalition (1945–66), the *Parteienstaat* in the Federal Republic of Germany, and the established one-party government in the pre-Gorbachev Soviet Union. One source of a party's capacity to penetrate a system is its ability to dominate the elite recruitment process. Presumably, the greater the number and diversity of positions a party is able to fill with its people – the military, the judiciary, the public economic sector, the bureaucracy – the more likely it is to forge an effective and purposeful government.

Extensive grasp may facilitate the formation of government, but it does not automatically produce effective rulership. One reason for this is, again, to be sought within the party itself. Parties are not necessarily coherent organizations, and even more rarely are they the monoliths that we sometimes imagine. Thus, the Italian Christian Democrats and the Japanese Liberal Democrats are both dominant, hegemonic parties whose grasp in the sense just described is extensive. But both are also faction-ridden; they encompass fluid and shifting internal coalitions of 'notables', each of which represents a somewhat autonomous power base (LaPalombara 1987; Calder 1988; Zuckerman 1979). Even the Soviet Communist Party, despite its domination of the instruments of government, faces formidable internal obstacles to its effective rulership; witness the ability of lower-level party functionaries to thwart Gorbachev's economic reform programme.

In thinking about parties, rather than impute to them certain 'functions' of the kind we review here, we should ask what it is they actually do or achieve. Where the formation of government and rulership are concerned, we must ask not only what are the capacities of individual parties to do these things; we must also probe to establish whether these represent the mission of the parties, that is, the *intentions* of those who control them (Katz 1987: 7–11). Theories of democracies and of one-party governments suggest that parties exist to provide political direction to the institutions of government. In practice, however, parties often cede the field to the bureaucracy, the military or interest groups. The typical result is policy drift, or a segmentation of political authority exercised by narrow coalitions of interest that colonize the governmental apparatus. Moreover, if rulership or 'party government' implies the formulation of coherent, distinctive and purposive public policies, the empirical evidence suggests that the impact of political parties remains at best contingent. The position of a given country in the world economy, or the strength of its labour unions, strongly conditions and limits party performance (Hibbs 1977; Cameron 1984).

Political identity and the vote

Parties are also described as instruments that structure a person's political identity and that channel the popular vote (Schattschneider 1942: 52; Key 1964: 314). This particular function, unlike the others so far discussed, requires an electoral market in which more than one party competes for political currency, that is, for the citizen's vote. To encourage loyal customers who will stay with the party over the longer course, parties utilize techniques that range from official labels and symbols to party platforms and complex ideologies, from propaganda and educational programmes to a vast apparatus of auxiliary party organizations. For many parties, election day is simply a recurring opportunity to display how well their efforts to instil a particular political party identity in the voter have proceeded. This matter is so obviously vital to the survival of the party that it is given the highest priority, even by parties in dictatorships that face no electoral opposition at all. George Orwell chillingly captures the extremes to which these parties will go in pursuit of this goal (Orwell 1949).

Parties of course will also seek to shape public opinion in the broader sense that encompasses the identification of public issues, the assignment of valence to them, and the specification of policies designed to deal with them. In one-party systems, the party line will be handed down from on high and disseminated by the party faithful. The phenomenon of 'agitprop' under Stalin and of the 'mass line' under Mao are good examples of this approach. In more open and democratic systems, not only do party lines compete with each other for the voter's support, but other voluntaristic organizations, as well as the mass media, compete with the parties to register the same effect.

It is self-evident that the grasp of the party – that is, how far and deeply it can actually penetrate a society – will bear directly on its capacity to structure political identities and to attract voters at the polls. The relationship, however, is not linear; absolute monopoly control by the party of the instruments of communication and of political socialization does not translate into equal success in the moulding of citizen identity and voter support. Recent events in Eastern Europe and the Soviet Union attest that, even after decades of such control, the party may actually fail.

In fact, not even in so-called totalitarian systems does the single party ever really monopolize all of the institutions and channels of communication that mould public opinion. Schools, churches, village markets, the factory, the halls and labyrinths of the bureaucracy, the military and even the units of the party itself become places where information is exchanged – and where subversive thoughts are born, matured and disseminated. Furthermore, advances in literacy and the untrammelled transmission of sound and visual images across space make it unlikely that one party can successfully impose an Orwellian Newthink or Newspeak on a national population.

Therefore, on this matter of moulding and reinforcing the citizen's political identity and structuring his or her vote, the party not only competes with other institutions but must also seek to achieve this particular purpose indirectly, through the mediating influence of these self-same institutions. This is quintessentially and increasingly the case in pluralistic democratic societies where, in an era that some call 'post-modern', the individual citizen does a lot of independent shopping around before selecting a party to support at the polls. And as for strong and long-enduring party identification, the cards now seem permanently stacked against any party that seeks to achieve this degree of knee-jerk allegiance. Indeed, the advent of the electronic revolution, and the political salience of the media, have raised in some minds the thought – not entirely reassuring for any democratic society – that the political party itself may go the way of the dinosaur.

Mobilization and integration

This leads us to ask whether parties may be of particular salience where mass mobilization and/or the integration of national political systems are concerned. The mobilization of masses of people has typically been associated with single party systems in both developed and developing nations (Friedrich and Brzezinski 1966: 47). This is obviously too narrow a view. As complex organizations driven by persons with great ambitions to exercise power and influence, parties tend to be opportunistic everywhere. Thus if they are unable to have their way through the regular and orderly procedures of governmental institutions, they may easily shift to mass mobilization techniques. In the West, left-wing parties have not hesitated to use their affiliated trade unions or youth organizations to bring hundreds of thousands of persons into the streets and squares. Similarly, right-wing political parties use forms of mass mobilization as one of the weapons in their political arsenal. Indeed, as the suffrage is extended to include earlier non-participants, the process (with the party situated typically at the very centre) whereby these persons are incorporated is itself described as 'social mobilization' and 'political development' (Huntington 1968: 32 ff., 132–7; LaPalombara and Weiner 1966: 400–7).

In recent years, parties like the Greens in Germany and the Radicals in Italy have deliberately combined both parliamentary and extra-parliamentary forms of political intervention and opposition. Furthermore, events of the late 1960s in the West showed that the line between 'normal' political participation and forms of mobilization ranging from mass demonstrations to riots and acts of terrorism can be very thin indeed. Historically, political parties have served as models for every conceivable type of political intervention, including mobilization.

Parties may not be the only organizations in society that lean in this direction, but they are certainly those from which we *normally* expect such efforts to emanate. Indeed, one way to gauge the stability of any democratic system is to weigh the relative frequency of modes of political intervention engaged in or promoted by its political parties, as opposed to other organizations whose main purpose is *not* that of linking the citizenry to governmental institutions or to the policy-making process (Lawson 1980; Barnes and Kasse 1979).

It is also true, of course, that mass mobilization can occur outside party channels and is often associated with mass movements. When this occurs, it implies a challenge to existing political institutions and authority, and may actually represent a direct assault on the political system *in toto*. The 1926 General Strike in Britain, student revolts of the late 1960s followed by waves of terrorism in some countries, the rise of Solidarity in Poland after 1980, the Chinese June 4 Movement and the awesome display of people power in the Eastern Bloc during 1989 and after are prime examples. Where such movements occur, one finds existing parties, including previously dictatorial single parties, scrambling to catch up with these outbursts of collective action and new manifestations of the public mood.

Where parties do succeed in becoming and remaining the main linkage between citizen-voters and ruling office holders, they clearly contribute to the integration of the overall political system. Psychological and social affinities to the party, at least where the latter are not clearly of the anti-system variety (Sartori 1976: 132–4), serve as an integrative mechanism that brings the individual more meaningfully into a political regime, thus indirectly benefiting the latter as well (Kirchheimer 1966: 188–9).

Political parties that lead successful revolutions, as well as nationalist movements that overthrow colonial rule and then assume party form, may also be described as aiding the effective integration of new regimes. The earliest example of both of these phenomena is the United States (Lipset 1963). Parties in established liberal democracies perform an integrative function too. For example, the British Conservative Party, with its intimate ties to the Church of England, the Royal Family and other symbols of British nationality, accomplishes similar ends. Indeed, even in the case of allegedly anti-system parties, like the communist parties of Western Europe, active involvement in the normal and constitutional types of political mobilization and participation have the effect of reinforcing the legitimacy as well as the integration of the same systems these parties presumably would like to overthrow.

In some cases, the principal beneficiaries of integration are the party itself and a social order yet to be realized. Neumann speaks of parties of 'social integration', typically on the left and engaged in 'permanent revolution', that seek to envelop the individual in an all-encompassing ideology and a self-contained network of social, political and economic relationships (Neumann 1956: 404). These integrative efforts often, but not always, challenge the principles and values of the existing political order.

National integration is one of those important but elusive concepts for which precise empirical indicators are hard to specify. This being so, it is even more difficult to show whether parties are any more effective than other organizations or institutions in bringing about minimum or higher levels of integration (King 1969: 124–6). Indeed, far from winning much praise on this particular score, parties are often condemned as the principal reason why so many modern societies seem to wallow in deep-seated crises – evidenced by citizen apathy, mass alienation and antisocial behaviour. As important as that particular allegation may be, it addresses the political party *system* and not the political parties that are our prime concern in this essay.

POLITICAL PARTIES: FACING THE FUTURE

Bagehot, writing in 1867, predicted that parties would change the face of British parliamentary politics, substituting an unstable and even dangerous form of 'Constituency Government' for the more virtuous 'Parliamentary Government' (Bagehot 1963: 161). His gloomy assessment has been echoed by others writing in this century. The recurring message has been that mass-based, disciplined parties are not necessarily healthy for democracy (Ostrogorski 1902; Beer 1966). Schattschneider attributes the 'plebiscitary presidency' in the United States to political parties, which 'took over an eighteenth-century constitution and made it function to satisfy the needs of modern democracy in ways not anticipated by the authors' (Schattschneider 1942: 2).

Whether sanguine or discouraging, the prognoses of early students of parties generally agree upon one unassailable fact: parties, the product of expanded suffrage, quickly transcended election-oriented tasks and arrogated to themselves responsibilities and authority belonging to other, more formal, institutions. As complex and effective instrumentalities, parties triumphed over older and less specialized organizational competitors. In doing so, these newer, complex and ubiquitous organizations managed to transform the struggle for power itself, and in ways that the framers of older regimes and constitutions neither anticipated nor intended. As the key instrumentality designed to give substance to the concepts of participation and representation (Huntington 1968; Schumpeter 1976), or to provide linkage between the electorate and the formulation and execution of public policy (Lawson 1980: 3–24), the advent of parties represents a quantum change in the nature of the polity.

Nevertheless, in less than two centuries, we find claims that these same organizations are now of dubious relevance as components of modern political systems. If they are not on the verge of extinction, so one argument goes, they risk losing the centrality they once enjoyed. In less developed countries, they have tended to give away to military or other forms of dictatorship that do not tolerate party organizations – at least not those they are unable to control. In developed countries, the claim is that technological advances in communication and information-processing have undercut their role as the principal links between governors and governed. In addition, new social movements, particularly among the young and the emerging professional middle classes, have emerged apart from and even in open hostility toward parties.

There is more. In advanced industrial society, a growing *lumpenproletariat* – unskilled, illiterate, and increasingly isolated – is said to be impervious to direction from parties. The complexities of a vast, interdependent and volatile world economy are said to privilege organized capital and labour at the expense of parties in the policy-making process. Indeed, the brave new world of neo-corporatism is said to make impotent bystanders of parliaments as well as parties (Berger 1981; Schmitter and Lehmbruch 1979). In this framework, it is easy to conclude that parties are indeed institutional has-beens, whose time has come and gone.

In fact, almost all such formulations are at best only half-truths. One reason, as a seasoned observer points out, is that parties are typically victims of the inflated expectations of those who theorize about them (King 1969). As scholars looked more closely at reality, earlier notions, sometimes raised to the status of myth, as to what parties are all about had to be recast. These second looks have produced much more reasonable statements as to what these institutions really mean, what it is they might or might not, can or cannot, do in one setting or another.

Of course, literacy, the electronics revolution and the advent of new modes and norms of collective behaviour will have an impact on the parties too. Of course, parties are not today what they were even as recently as a generation ago. Nevertheless, rumours of their atrophy or demise are greatly exaggerated. On the contrary, they remain the only organizations that operate on the electoral and governmental scenes in the sense we have described. Until this changes, parties will rightly continue to occupy the attention of journalists and politicians, citizens and academic researchers.

The sophisticated treatment of parties as organizations (Panebianco 1988) marks a refreshing return to earlier modes of studying these institutions. For decades now, research has centred on parties as seen from the vantage point of the individual citizen and voter, or alternatively, as the components of the party system itself. Thus, in certain respects, the newer trend brings us full circle, back to the focus suggested by writers like Michels (1962), Ostrogorski (1902), and Duverger (1954). Equipped with new analytical techniques and better data than were available to them, we can explore questions of our own as to, for example, the relationship between parties and the particular configuration that a variety of political systems now in transition might eventually assume.

On that score, recent developments in Eastern Europe seemingly conspire to make this a most promising time to return to the study of parties as organizations. In almost all of these countries, communist parties, once the monopolizers of power, were compelled to adapt to electoral competition. New parties literally emerged by the dozen, alongside trade union movements like Solidarity in Poland or intellectual circles like Civic Forum in Czechoslovakia. If, as some scholars have claimed, the unions, the bureaucrats and the plant managers are the 'natural' components of corporatist systems of policy making, we must seek to explain why there has been such a veritable explosion of political parties in these countries.

In all of these countries, one encounters unlimited opportunities to observe parties that are born anew or that seek to reconstitute themselves from a past that only a handful of persons can remember as part of an earlier and different experience. It may very well be, as some claim, that the establishment of the market is a necessary condition for the eventual emergence of democracy. Be that as it may, it seems apparent that, long before the economic market is established or reemerges, all of these countries will have had to deal with the critical issue of the *political* market, and of the degree and kind of competition that can take place within it without causing additional and unwanted upheaval.

Whatever the outcome of the transitions currently under way, we can predict with confidence that the political party as a complex organization will play a major role, and perhaps *the* central role, in these processes. Not only is this prospect intellectually exciting in its own right, but it will also provide the opportunity to test a wide range of extant propositions about the nature of political development, and the precise role of the political party in settings where degrees of tolerance of organized efforts to win control of the machinery of government, and/or to oppose those who succeed in this undertaking, now vary quite markedly.

In dealing with the political party, it is essential to avoid all forms of sociological reductionism of the kind that notoriously suggest that the form, meaning and function of political institutions are the abject dependent expressions of much deeper societal determinants. The more accurate reality, as Panebianco (1988: 275–6) has reminded us, is that the political party was and remains prominent among the *political* institutions that shape the configuration and plot the direction of social institutions, as well as the destinies of humankind. They richly deserve to be studied in this vein, and in their own right.

REFERENCES

Bagehot, W. (1963) *The English Constitution* (1867), Ithaca, NY: Cornell University Press.

Barnes, S. H. and Kasse, M. (eds) (1979) *Political Action: Mass Participation in Five Western Democracies*, Beverly Hills: Sage Publications.

Beer, S. (1966) *British Politics in the Collectivist Age*, New York: Knopf.

Berger, S. (ed.) (1981) *Organizing Interests in Western Europe*, New York: Cambridge University Press.

Burke, E. (1839) 'Thoughts on the cause of the present discontents' (1770), in *The Works of Edmund Burke*, vol. 1, Boston: Little, Brown & Co.

Calder, K. (1988) *Crisis and Compensation*, Princeton: Princeton University Press.

Cameron, D. (1984) 'Social democracy, corporatism, labor quiescence, and the representation of economic interest in advanced capitalist society', in J. Goldthorpe (ed.) *Order and Conflict in Contemporary Captialism*, Oxford: Clarendon Press.

Castles, F. and Wildenmann, W. (eds) (1986) *Visions and Realities of Party Government*, Berlin: de Gruyter.

Daalder, H. (1966) 'Parties, elites, and political developments in Western Europe', in J. LaPalombara and M. Weiner (eds) *Political Parties and Political Development*, Princeton: Princeton University Press.

——(1983) 'The comparative study of European parties and party systems: an overview', in H. Daadler and P. Mair (eds) *Western European Party Systems: Continuity and Change*, Beverly Hills: Sage Publications.

Duverger, M. (1954) *Political Parties*, New York: John Wiley.

Friedrich, C. and Brzezinski, Z. (1966) *Totalitarian Dictatorship and Autocracy*, New York: Praeger.

Hibbs, D. (1977) 'Political parties and macroeconomic policy', *American Political Science Review* 71: 1467–87.

Huntington, S. (1968) *Political Order in Changing Societies*, New Haven: Yale University Press.

Katz, R. S. (1980) *A Theory of Parties and Electoral Systems*, Baltimore: Johns Hopkins University Press.

——(ed.) (1987) *Party Government: European and American Experiences*, Berlin: de Gruyter.

Key, V. O. (1964) *Politics, Parties, and Pressure Groups*, New York: Thomas Y. Crowell.

King, A. (1969) 'Political parties in Western democracies: some skeptical reflections', *Polity* 2: 112–41.

Kirchheimer, O. (1966) 'The transformation of the Western European party systems', in J. LaPalombara and M. Weiner (eds) *Political Parties and Political Development*, Princeton: Princeton University Press.

LaPalombara, J. (1974) *Politics within Nations*, Englewood Cliffs, NJ: Prentice-Hall.

——(1987) *Democracy Italian Style*, New Haven: Yale University Press.

LaPalombara, J. and Weiner, M. (1966) 'The origin and development of political parties', in J. LaPalombara and M. Weiner (eds) *Political Parties and Political Development*, Princeton: Princeton University Press.

Lawson, K. (ed.) (1980) *Political Parties and Linkage: A Comparative Perspective*, New Haven: Yale University Press.

Lenin, V. I. (1969) *What is to be Done?* (1902), New York: International Publishers.

Lipset, S. M. (1963) *The First New Nation*, New York: Basic Books.

Mckenzie, R. (1963) *British Political Parties*, New York: Praeger.

Madison, J. (1961) 'No. 10.', A. Hamilton, J. Madison and J. Jay (eds) in *The Federalist Papers*, New York: New American Library.

Michels, R. (1962) *Political Parties: A Sociological Study of the Oligarchical Tendencies of Modern Democracy*, New York: Free Press; translation of (1911) *Zur Sociologie des Parteiwesens in der Modernen Demokratie*, Leipzig: Klinghardt.

Neumann, S. (1956) 'Toward a comparative study of political parties', in S. Neumann (ed.) *Modern Political Parties*, Chicago: University of Chicago.

Orwell, G. (1949) *Nineteen Eighty-Four*, New York: Harcourt Brace.

Ostrogorski, M. (1902) *Democracy and the Organization of Political Parties*, 2 vols, London: Macmillan.

Panebianco, A. (1988) *Political Parties: Organization and Power*, New York: Cambridge University Press.

Putnam, R. D. (1976) *The Comparative Study of Political Elites*, Englewood Cliffs, NJ: Prentice-Hall.

Sartori, G. (1976) *Parties and Party Systems*, New York: Cambridge University Press.

Schattschneider, E. E. (1942) *Party Government*, New York: Farrar & Rinehart.

Schlesinger, J. A. (1965) 'Political party organization', in J. March (ed.) *Handbook of Organizations*, Chicago: Rand McNally.

——(1966) *Ambition and Politics: Political Careers in the United States*, Chicago: Rand McNally.

Schmitter, P. and Lehmbruch, G. (eds) (1979) *Trends Toward Corporatist Intermediation*, Beverly Hills: Sage Publications.

Schumpeter, J. (1976) *Capitalism, Socialism, and Democracy* (1942), New York: Harper & Row.

Tocqueville, A. de (1969) *Democracy in America*, Garden City, NY: Anchor Books.

Von Beyme, K. (1983) 'Governments, parliaments, and the structure of power in political parties', in H. Daadler and P. Mair (eds) *Western European Party Systems: Continuity and Change*, Beverly Hills: Sage Publications.

Ware, A. (1987) 'Introduction: parties under electoral competition', in A. Ware (ed.) *Political Parties: Electoral Change and Structural Response*, Oxford: Basil Blackwell.

Weber, M. (1946) 'Politics as a vocation', in H. Gerth and C. W. Mills (eds) *From Max Weber: Essays in Sociology*, New York: Oxford University Press.

Zuckerman, A. (1979) *The Politics of Faction: Christian Democracy in Italy*, New Haven: Yale University Press.

FURTHER READING

Baerwald, H. (1986) *Party Politics in Japan*, Boston: Allen & Unwin.

Barnes, S. (1967) *Party Democracy: Politics in a Socialist Federation*, New Haven: Yale University Press.

Blondel, J. (1978) *Political Parties: A Genuine Case for Discontent?*, London: Wildwood House.

Budge, I. Crewe, I. and Farlie, D., (eds) (1976) *Party Identification and Beyond*, New York: John Wiley.

Butler, D. and Stokes, D. (1969) *Political Change in Britain*, New York: St. Martin's Press.

Castles, F. (1979) *The Social Democratic Image of Society*, London: Routledge & Kegan Paul.

——(ed.) (1982) *The Impact of Parties: Politics and Policies in Democratic Capitalist States*, Beverly Hills: Sage Publications.

Chambers, W. N. (1963) *Political Parties in a New Nation: The American Experience 1776–1809*, New York: Oxford University Press.

Coleman, J. S. and Rosberg, C. G. (1964) *Political Parties and National Integration in Tropical Africa*, New Haven: Yale University Press.

Dahl, R. (ed.) (1966) *Political Oppositions in Western Democracies*, New Haven: Yale University Press.

Downs, A. (1957) *An Economic Theory of Democracy*, New York: Harper & Row.

Epstein, L. (1975) 'Political parties', in F. Greenstein and N. Polsby (eds) *Handbook of Political Science*, vol. IV, Reading, Mass.: Addison-Wesley.

Esping-Anderson, G. (1985) *Politics against Markets: The Social Democratic Road to Power*, Princeton: Princeton University Press.

Irving, R. E. M. (1979) *The Christian Democratic Parties of Western Europe*, London: Allen & Unwin.

Jowitt, K. (1978) *The Leninist Response to National Dependency*, Berkeley: Institute of International Studies, University of California at Berkeley.

Lipset, S. and Rokkan, S. (eds) (1967) *Party Systems and Voter Alignments*, New York: Free Press.

Maisel, L. and Cooper, J. (eds) (1978) *Political Parties: Development and Decay*, Beverly Hills: Sage Publications.

Paterson, W. E. and Thomas, A. H. (eds) (1977) *Social Democratic Parties in Western Europe*, London: Croom Helm.

Pizzorno, A. (1981) 'Interests and parties in pluralism', in S. Berger (ed.) *Organizing Interests in Western Europe*, New York: Cambridge University Press.

Powell, G. B. (1982) *Contemporary Democracies*, Cambridge, Mass.: Harvard University Press.

Rokkan, S. (1966) *Citizens, Elections, Parties*, Oslo: Universitetsforlaget.

Rose, R. (1969) *The Problem of Party Government*, Harmondsworth: Penguin.

——(1980) *Do Parties Make a Difference?*, New York: Chatham House.

Schapiro, L. (1971) *The Communist Party of the Soviet Union*, New York: Random House.

Weiner, M. (1967) *Party Building in a New Nation: The Indian National Congress*, Chicago: University of Chicago Press.

26

CAMPAIGNS AND ELECTIONS

DAVID DENVER

National governments are freely elected in only a minority of the world's states. Although elections in some countries of the communist bloc have recently assumed a significance undreamt of before the late 1980s, it remains the case according to Harrop and Miller (1987: 7) that in a world of over 160 states there are only about thirty in which there is a real chance of the government being replaced through the ballot box. More precisely, the journal *Electoral Studies* keeps track of national election results in just thirty-seven countries which have a population of more than a million and 'which have an established record of competitive multi-party elections'.

None the less, the study of elections and voting behaviour has generated an enormous literature. The subject attracts the interest of sociologists, geographers, economists and psychologists, among others, and is one of the major sub-fields of political science. In part, this wide interest is explained by the fact that elections are a central element in theories of democracy. Different versions of democratic theory vary in the precise importance they attach to elections, and they assign them various functions, but all agree that the open, competitive election of the national government is a fundamental and distinguishing characteristic of states that would normally be described as democratic. It is via elections that citizens participate directly in the political process and are able to hold governments accountable.

Interest in elections extends well beyond academic social scientists, however. National elections are major events in the life of a nation. They are accompanied by greatly increased discussion of, and interest in, politics on the part of the population as a whole, by intense political activity and by massive coverage in the mass media.

Election campaigns are a familiar and integral part of free elections. For as long as there have been elections there have been campaigns during which candidates and their supporters seek to persuade the electorate to vote for them. In most democracies today there is a formally defined campaign period

– usually prescribed by a combination of law and custom (see Penniman 1981: 110–5) – during which various rules which regulate campaigning come into force. Although election campaigns and the electoral process itself can be separated conceptually, the two are so inextricably linked that in common usage any reference to 'the election' is usually intended to include the period of 'hot' campaigning which precedes actual voting.

The literature dealing with election campaigns and campaigning is diverse and extensive. It includes survey studies of voters of the kind pioneered in the 1940 American presidential election (Lazarsfeld *et al.* 1968) as well as descriptive/analytical accounts of single national elections. Examples of the latter include the series of 'Nuffield Studies' of British elections (see, for example, Butler and Kavanagh 1988), the 'Making of the President' series by Theodore H. White (see White 1982) and the 'At The Polls' series produced by the American Enterprise Institute, which has covered elections in a variety of countries from (alphabetically) Australia to Venezuela. There are numerous studies of the development of campaigning (see Salmore and Salmore 1985) and the role of the mass media in campaigns (see Patterson and McClure 1976). Other works have focused on campaigning techniques (Leuthold 1968) and local campaigning (Kavanagh 1970). There have been, however, relatively few comparative studies which get beyond the somewhat arid listing of points of similarity and difference between states in terms of their campaign laws (for a notable exception, however, see Butler *et al.* 1981).

Part of the reason for the relative absence of comparative studies is the sheer diversity in campaigning in different countries. Variations in the nature of the political system (federal versus unitary systems, for example, or presidential versus parliamentary systems) and in the electoral system (proportional versus plurality) make for wide variations in campaign styles. Variations in geography can also be important (Dutch party leaders do not need private jets as American presidential candidates do). Differences in political culture or tradition make for differences in electorates' receptiveness to or aversion from particular campaign styles.

Campaigning styles and techniques have also changed dramatically over time. Factors such as an increase in the size of the electorate due to extensions of the suffrage and simple population growth, the rise of mass circulation newspapers and the introduction of various campaign laws have prompted major changes in campaigning. In this essay, however, four factors which have had a marked impact upon election campaigning in more recent years are considered. The four are the growth of television, the use of public opinion polls, the development of computer technology and the cost of campaigns. In all four cases the effects of these developments are clearest in the United States, but they are evident too in other modern democracies and it seems likely that campaigning in the latter will, in some respects at least, develop in a similar way.

TELEVISION

There is no doubt that the growth of television has revolutionized election campaigning in modern societies. Its importance derives mainly from the fact that television reaches a mass audience and that it is by far the most important source of political information for voters. British party leaders can now talk to more people in a few minutes that did Gladstone and Disraeli together throughout their entire careers. Writing of the United States, Hunt observes: 'Any modern presidential campaign is dominated by the awesome importance of television' (Hunt 1987: 57). The more prosaic view of an anonymous American gubernatorial candidate is quoted by Salmore and Salmore: 'If you're not on television, you don't exist' (Salmore and Salmore 1985: 145).

It is not simply the size of the television audience that gives the medium its importance in campaigns, however. Television reaches the mass of voters whose interest in an election is largely passive and fleeting – those who would rarely follow a campaign in newspaper reports or attend a campaign meeting – to a greater extent than the printed media. In addition, in most democratic societies television coverage of domestic politics in news broadcasts, campaign reports and so on is required to be neutral or even-handed. This kind of coverage is generally regarded by voters as being more trustworthy and reliable than the political reporting in the (often avowedly partisan) press.

The enormous potential of television to influence voters has been recognized (and perhaps even feared) by politicians in most states, and various rules, regulations and conventions have grown up which control coverage of elections (see Smith 1981). In some countries (most obviously the United States), paid advertising by candidates and parties is allowed, but in most it is prohibited. In many of the latter, parties are granted free air time in which to put their case (as in party election broadcasts in Britain). As indicated above, almost all countries have a rule requiring balanced coverage.

Despite restrictions of this kind, the impact of television upon campaigning style has been enormous. To a great extent parties can control the format and content of their advertising spots or the free slots provided for their campaign broadcasts. They take great pains to ensure that these are used to the fullest effect. The art, or science, of 'spot' political advertising is most developed in the United States (see Diamond and Bates 1984), where parties and candidates are advertised in the same way as commercial products like coffee or beer. As with commercial adverts, election adverts have developed from relatively crude pitches in the 1950s to highly sophisticated, professionally produced, meticu-lously planned minor masterpieces of the art today. In countries where there is no paid advertising, party election broadcasts have likewise become more professional. In Britain, for example, 'talking heads' – party leaders speaking directly to camera – are now less common than they used to be. In the 1987 general election a Labour broadcast

> opened with a warplane streaking across the sky, switching to a seagull soaring effortlessly, backed by the muted strains of the party's theme from Brahms's first symphony. Distant figures, soon revealed as Neil and Glenys Kinnock, walked hand in hand across a sunny headland with Neil Kinnock voicing over his belief that the strong should help the weak.
>
> (Harrison 1988: 153–4)

Examples like this could be multiplied.

Parties have less control over how they and their campaigns are reported in news bulletins, current affairs programmes, election reports and so on. In the United States coverage of this kind is referred to as 'free time', for obvious reasons. The special importance of this sort of coverage (and the effects that it has on campaigning) arises from the fact that voters are suspicious, on the whole, of broadcasts and adverts which are partisan in origin and content. They expect news reporters and commentators, on the other hand, to be impartial and consequently may be more open to their influence. Campaigners make great efforts, therefore, to secure the best possible coverage in this kind of political television. Projecting a 'good image' on television has become the key to successful campaigning.

Campaign events and plans are made primarily to fit in with the schedules and requirements of television. It used to be, for example, that in British elections party leaders would address large meetings at which opponents would barrack and heckle. Today they address audiences composed of only their own supporters and rather than speaking to the live audience – who are occasionally glimpsed glassy-eyed with incomprehension – they speak to the audience which will see clips from the speech on television. Speeches are carefully planned to include 'sound bites' – brief quotable patches – which begin and end with applause to make the task of the videotape editor easier. Politicians also used to meet electors personally, 'pressing the flesh' in the street. They still do this, although usually surrounded by security men and 'minders', but only so that they can be *seen* doing it by the television audience. 'Pseudo-events' are organized – visits to schools, factories, individual families and so on – whose sole purpose is to provide 'photo-opportunities' for the media. Contact between candidates/party leaders and the voters is now mediated through television.

Television, particularly in relatively short news broadcasts, deals more easily with images and personalities than with political issues, which are often complex and detailed. This has led to a style of campaign reporting that is more candidate-oriented (including detailed probing of private lives). This process has gone furthest in presidential systems like the United States and France, but American congressional elections are also now more candidate-oriented than before and in parliamentary systems party leaders are projected in almost the same way as presidential candidates.

Ever since the famous Kennedy–Nixon television debates in the 1960 presidential election, when Nixon's 'five o'clock shadow' and general physical appearance apparently told against him (see White 1964: 279–95), campaign managers have paid detailed attention to how politicians look and sound on the small screen. After Mrs Thatcher became Conservative leader, she had her teeth capped, her hair restyled and her make-up improved, and she undertook exercises which lowered the pitch of her voice by 'almost half the average difference in pitch between male and females voices' (Atkinson 1984: 113). Later in her prime ministership she began to engage in 'power dressing'.

Similar attention is paid to the background against which politicians are viewed on television, to ensure that these too convey the 'right' images. Thus, in the 1984 presidential election, President Reagan made a major campaign speech near the Statue of Liberty which figured prominently in clips broadcast later on television news. British parties employ professionals to ensure that their leaders are appropriately lit for television, that the colours and symbols used as backdrops convey the desired messages to the viewers, and so on.

In sum, modern campaigns are media campaigns. The distinction between election campaigns and television coverage of campaigns has become non-existent and, as a consequence, parties and candidates are now thoroughly packaged for television (see McGinniss 1969; Jamieson 1984).

In parliamentary systems, the growth of television has increased the importance of the national campaign at the expense of local electioneering. Party activists in local constituencies or electoral districts still canvass voters, put up posters, deliver leaflets and mount 'get out the vote' operations on election day. Candidates address local meetings and go for 'walkabouts'. But for most voters 'the campaign' is the national campaign which they see reported on television. In the United States, the same is true for presidential elections but 'local' campaigns for the Senate and House of Representatives, as well as for state and local offices, are also commonly dominated by television (although the importance of television is affected by the match between electoral areas and the areas covered by television stations).

The need to adapt to television-dominated campaigns has had two important consequences in terms of campaign management. First, it has greatly increased the cost of campaigning (see pp. 422–4). Second, parties and candidates have increasingly turned to media experts, advertising agencies, specialist advisers and so on for guidance. The British Conservative Party, for example, used the advertising firm of Saatchi and Saatchi in the general elections of 1979, 1983 and 1987, and the role of the firm went well beyond devising advertisements.

At the 1986 Conservative conference the firm 'devised the conference theme, suggested some of the contents of ministers' speeches and coordinated the publicity' (Butler and Kavanagh 1988: 35). Labour has less money and has relied largely on volunteer help from individuals in the advertising and media industries.

The trend towards the professionalization of campaigns has gone furthest in the United States, where, according to Senator Proxmire, 'a candidate's most important decision is not necessarily his stand on the issues but his choice of media advisor' (quoted in Luntz 1988: 72). In all modern societies, however, the pressure upon politicians to use television effectively forces them to employ or obtain the help of professional media specialists.

The extent to which television campaign coverage affects voters' decisions, and hence the outcomes of elections, is a matter of considerable debate. Most research on the question concludes, however, that television has little *direct* effect on party choice other than to reinforce voters' previously-held opinions (see, for example, Blumler and McQuail 1967; Patterson and McClure 1976). It should be stressed, however, that these sorts of studies have usually been undertaken in situations in which all parties have access to television and use it with roughly equal effectiveness. Where coverage is disproportionate or a candidate comes across particularly badly (or well) then aggregate effects are clearly discernible. In the New Hampshire primary election of 1972, for example, Edmund Muskie was seen on television weeping over newspaper attacks on his wife, and his candidacy for the presidency never recovered. Labour's humiliation at the hands of Mrs Thatcher in the 1983 general election was due in part to the fact that the Labour leader, Michael Foot, appeared badly dressed, rambling and quaintly old-fashioned in television coverage; Neil Kinnock's popularity in the polls shot up overnight after the screening of the election broadcast referred to above (p. 416). Studies of media effects on elections also tend to concentrate upon short-term changes in voting intentions during campaigns. The influence of television may be more long term, slow and indirect.

There is general agreement, however, that television is now the major campaign agenda setter. Parties or candidates no longer determine what the election is 'about': it is television producers and commentators who decide which campaign issues will be discussed and which events reported. Interviewers pursue topics with party leaders which the interviewers, not the politicians, think are important. In the United States, a more specific form of agenda setting occurs during presidential primary elections. In reporting results, commentators regularly make assessments, based on expectations that they themselves have helped to create, of how well or badly the various candidates have performed. These assessments tend to be accepted by the electorate and can help or hinder candidates' future progress, even though the election results themselves may bear different interpretations. In the 1972 primary election mentioned above, for example, Muskie was widely reported as having 'lost' despite the fact that he obtained 46.4 per cent of the vote compared wth 37.2 per cent for his closest rival (Kessel 1984: 8). In this way television can define not just 'what' an election is about but also 'who' it is about.

One final clear effect of television in elections is a change in the kind of politician who is successful. Modern party leaders simply must be good on television. Old campaigning skills, such as 'glad-handing' or the ability to electrify a large audience with passionate speeches like William Jennings Bryan did, are largely irrelevant. More important is a friendly, conversational manner such as that displayed by Ronald Reagan. It is difficult to imagine the crusty and diffident Clement Attlee, who was a highly effective post-war Labour prime minister, ever being a successful party leader in the age of television.

OPINION POLLS

Public opinion polls are a familiar feature of modern election campaigns. In Britain the number of nationwide polls published during the formal campaign period more than doubled, from twenty-five to fifty-four, between the elections of 1970 and 1987 (Denver 1989: 105). A similar growth in political polling has occurred in other democracies (Kavanagh 1981). Public polls usually concentrate on reporting the current voting intentions of the electorate, although they also often detail voters' opinions on campaign issues, assessments of party leaders or candidates, and so on.

Even more remarkable, however, has been the growth of private polling. In parliamentary systems, major parties now usually hire polling firms to provide them with regular information, while in the United States, all serious aspirants to the presidency since the 1960s have included a massive polling operation as a routine element in their campaigns. Numerous candidates for Congress and state and local offices also frequently employ pollsters to provide a polling package. This normally includes a 'bench-mark' poll, undertaken well before the election, to gather basic information about the relevant electorate, a series of 'trend' polls in the run up to the election and a series of daily 'tracking' polls during the final stages of the campaign (see Salmore and Salmore 1985: 119–24).

The purpose of such private polls – which are much more detailed than public polls – is to provide reliable information to candidates and parties so that they can campaign more effectively. Slogans, symbols and themes are tested before being adopted; the popularity of various policy positions is gauged, and some consequently emphasized at the expense of others; the impact of campaign broadcasts and advertisements is assessed. Polls tell campaign managers which voters where are most or least receptive to their messages, and enable them to target their campaign effort more precisely. Private polls do not, of course, *entirely* determine campaign strategy. Politicians do have other sources of information, programmatic parties are disinclined to alter policies no matter what the polls say, and poll results are frequently open to differing interpretations. Moreover, the bare facts provided by polls do not speak for themselves. How a party should respond to them is a political rather than technical decision. It is clear, however, that politicians rely increasingly on polls and that poll results influence campaign strategies.

Concern about the potential impact of public polls upon voters, and in particular about the possibility of poll results being manipulated to serve partisan ends, has led some European countries such as France, Spain and Germany to impose restrictions on the publication of polls during campaigns. Calls are regularly made for similar restrictions to be imposed elsewhere. Those who favour banning campaign polls argue that they tend to trivialize elections, reducing them to 'horse-races' and deflecting the attention of voters from the serious issues at stake (Whiteley 1986). Opponents suggest that it is better to have polls produced by reputable companies with no political axe to grind rather than have selective leaking of private polls, rumours and deliberate disinformation campaigns which would flourish if the publication of polls were prohibited. In addition, it is argued, there is no justification in a democracy for denying to voters reliable information about the level of support for the parties, which they may wish to take into account before deciding how to vote.

The results of opinion research now affect heavily the ways in which campaigns are conducted. They influence the contents of election manifestos, which issues leading politicians talk about and which ones they avoid, the content and style of campaign advertisements and party broadcasts, the schedule of meetings and visits arranged for party leaders and candidates, and which politicians the parties seek to keep before the public and which ones they try to keep off television.

Scientific polling is a specialized business and the increased use of polls is another factor which has led to the professionalization of campaign organization. Politicians have learned to listen to polling experts and are less inclined to trust their hunches, regard constituents' letters as reliable indicators of public opinion or talk to their local station master (as Stanley Baldwin, three times Prime Minister of Britain between 1923 and 1937, claimed to do). But polling does not come cheaply and it has also been an important element in driving up the cost of campaigns.

While polls clearly play an important part in campaigns, the extent to which they influence voters is debatable. Commentators have described public opinion polls as having a 'bandwagon' effect (voters switch to the party which the polls suggest is in the lead) or a 'boomerang' effect (voters switch to the apparent underdog). But there is no evidence that either of these effects occurs consistently on a significant scale. In addition, polls themselves reveal that few voters admit to being influenced by seeing campaign polls (Crewe 1986). On the other hand, a 'good' poll showing (usually defined as such and highlighted by the media) can catapult a relatively obscure presidential candidate into serious contention. In this and other similar cases, however, it is difficult to assess whether polls are merely faithfully reflecting a genuine trend among voters or give added impetus to minor movements in opinion.

The influence of polls on election outcomes is usually indirect. Their results can affect the morale of party workers. It is well established, for example, that on Thursday 4 June 1987 (which came to be known as 'Wobbly Thursday'), the British Conservative Party's campaign organization was afflicted by a severe crisis of confidence when a couple of polls appeared to indicate some slippage in Conservative support (Butler and Kavanagh 1988: 107–11). More generally, candidates or parties which make sophisticated use of private polls are likely to mount more effective campaigns and in certain situations this may give them an electoral edge.

COMPUTERIZATION

Political parties have sometimes been slow to recognize the implications of technological change for campaigning. British parties, for example, have not made much use of the simple fact that most homes now have telephones. In the United States, in contrast, 'telephone banks' are commonly used to allow campaign workers and candidates to talk directly to voters. Some parties have also been slow to react to the realities of the television age or to exploit the opportunities presented by scientific opinion polling. The use of computer technology by British parties is relatively recent. It was not until 1981 that the Social Democratic Party (SDP) became the first British party to maintain a computerized list of party members (and to allow the payment of subscriptions by credit card). But computer use has become more common in British elections. In the 1987 general election, many local party organizations made use of micro-computers and both major parties had direct computer links between headquarters and their local organizations (Butler and Kavanagh 1988: 214). In part, the increased use of computers at local level in Britain has been prompted by the fact that computerized electoral registers are now common.

In the United States, however, campaign organizers were quick to recognize the importance of the way in which television evangelists made use of computers in their campaigns and they are now extensively used in every facet of political campaigning. Modern American election campaigns are complex and massive operations. They generate masses of information about voters, the media, opposing parties and candidates, issues, and so on. Campaign staff have to co-ordinate complicated travel schedules, press conferences, television appearances, party rallies and visits for leading campaign figures and to ensure effective linkages between campaign headquarters and the localities. To store and process all the data accumulated in a campaign and to assist planning and co-ordination, powerful computing facilities are essential.

In fund raising, for example, computers are used to store detailed records of potential and past contributors, mailing lists and so on, which can be accessed in seconds. More importantly, computerized addressing and mailing of letters enables thousands of appeals for support to be sent in a fraction of the time it would take volunteers to do by hand. Computer mailing also extends to personalized letters in which particular appeals can be targeted to different groups of voters. During the campaign itself, whereas television enables candidates to broadcast their appeals to the electorate, the computer, with its direct mailing facility, enables them to 'narrowcast' specialized messages to targeted groups (see Chartrand 1976). Computer–voter contact is more common than face-to-face candidate–voter contact. In addition, computer analysis of polls, census returns, voting histories and alternative strategic scenarios are used to help determine campaign themes, activities, strategy and tactics. The records held by the computer are the modern equivalent of the detailed knowledge of the voters in a local district which local politicians and party workers previously carried around in their heads.

The use of computer technology, no doubt, has made for more efficient campaigning. It is also a further source of the professionalization of campaign management – computers require experts to run them – and of increased campaign expenditure. But their use probably has little effect on election results. In the past, the more rapid 'modernization' of campaign techniques by the Republican Party and right-wing political action committees in the United States may have played a part in defeating Democratic candidates (see Sabato 1981), but when all campaigns use modern technology there is no comparative advantage to any one party or candidate. New campaigning techniques quickly become routine and commonplace, and when adopted by all candidates any effect is cancelled out. The main effect of computers has been to make campaigning itself more specialized, detailed and complex.

CAMPAIGN FINANCE

All three of the factors affecting campaigning discussed so far have contributed to a rapid escalation in the costs of campaigning. Modern elections are very expensive, especially in the United States where television advertising has to be paid for. In the 1984 American presidential election, candidates spent about $200 million compared with $91 million in 1968, and in 1988 $37 million had been paid in matching funds (see below) to presidential candidates by 8 February – before the first primary election that year. Total spending in House and Senate campaigns rose from $66.4 million in 1972 to $450 million in 1988 (Nelson 1989: 122, 124). In Britain in 1987, the three major parties spent £15 million centrally (compared with £7.6 million in 1983) and a further £7.5 million in local constituencies (Butler and Kavanagh 1988: 235). In many other democracies the pattern of rapidly increasing costs is the same (see Paltiel 1981: 141–2). The ability to raise large sums of money has become a necessity for serious campaigning almost everywhere.

Most states have laws which regulate campaign finance. Among modern democracies, only Switzerland relies on custom and public opinion to control campaign finance. Britain, however, is also unusual in having no limitations upon, and no statutory reporting of, central campaign expenditure by the parties while maintaining tight control over the spending of individual candidates in the constituencies. The intention of such laws is not simply to limit overall expenditures, however. They are intended also to limit any possible electoral advantage that may accrue to wealthy candidates and parties and to prevent wealthy campaign contributors having undue influence over elected politicians. The main methods used to control campaign finance are statutory reporting of income and expenditure, limitations upon contributions and expenditures, and public financing of campaigns (see Paltiel 1981).

The United States is the clearest and most comprehensively documented example of a state in which campaign finance laws have recently been reformed with important consequences for the conduct of campaigns. In 1974 the US Congress passed a Federal Election Campaign Act which, according to Malbin, 'probably represented the most sweeping set of campaign finance law changes ever adopted in the United States, if not in the world' (Malbin 1984: 7). Despite subsequent amendment, owing to decisions of the Supreme Court as well as legislative and administrative action, the Act remains the basis of current campaign finance regulation. The rules are detailed and complex, but four main provisions are worth noting. First, the amount which any individual (other than a candidate) may contribute to a campaign is severely limited ($1,000 in 1988): candidates can no longer turn to 'fat cats' for large donations but must seek many small donations. Second, the amount that interest groups can contribute through their political action committees (PACs) *directly* to a campaign is also limited ($5,000 in 1988), but there is no limit on their 'uncoordinated' spending, that is spending incurred in campaigning independently on behalf of or against a candidate. Third, federal funding (matching the amount raised by candidates themselves) is available to presidential candidates (in primary elections as well as the 'run-off' election). Those who accept matching funds (and all have to date) also have to accept a limit on their total expenditure. Finally, political parties are limited in the amount that they can directly contribute to the campaigns of individual candidates.

These provisions have had a major impact on campaign politics. Raising large sums of money from small contributors is a major operation and any serious campaign now has to include a professional fund raising and accountancy organization. More campaign time has to be devoted to simply raising money, and candidates have to begin their campaign effort earlier in order to build up a 'war chest'. This has tended to advantage incumbent Senators and Representatives since they are in a better position to raise money than challengers are (Salmore and Salmore 1985: 68–70).

Another consequence of the changed finance laws has been a proliferation of PACs. In 1972 there were 113 registered PACs, but by 1986 there were 4,157. In the same period, contributions made by PACs to congressional candidates rose from $8.5 million to $130.3 million (Sabato 1987: 157). Since PACs obviously expect some return for their money there has been considerable disquiet over their role in campaign funding.

The reformed campaign laws have also hastened the decline in the importance of American political parties. Not only are they limited in the amount of financial support that they can offer candidates, but it is the *candidates* and not parties which qualify for federal funding. More and more the organization of campaigns is candidate-centred, with candidates having personal machines, and the old style of voter mobilization by party activists has become less common.

It is difficult to isolate any consistent effect of campaign spending upon election outcomes. In some places, in some circumstances, massive spending may bring dividends but there are numerous examples of big spenders being defeated by poorer opponents. While it is probably the case, especially in the United States, that substantial campaign spending is now a necessary condition of electoral success, it is far from a sufficient condition.

CONCLUSION

A number of themes have emerged in this review of election campaigns. First, campaigning techniques and styles have changed rapidly in response to developments such as the growth of political television, the explosion of information technology, and changes in campaign laws. Second, campaign organization has become much more professionalized and institutionalized than ever before. Agranoff gives 'a selected list of the various specialists that are now employed in campaigns' (Agranoff 1976: 25). The list contains thirty-four specialists including advance person, fund raiser, management scientist, market researcher, TV-time buyer, speech coach and (gratifyingly) political scientist. Campaigning is now an industry with specialist firms and 'campaign consultant' is a recognized profession. Third, campaigns have increasingly focused on candidates and personalities rather than on parties and issues. Campaign organization, at least in the United States, is less party-dominated and more candidate-centred. Fourth, in almost all democracies developments of this kind have led to huge increases in the costs of campaigning. Fund raising has become a vital campaign task and worries about campaign finance have led to reforms, or calls for reform, of campaign finance laws in many cases.

Despite all of this, it is not obvious that campaigns make a great deal of difference to election results. In the past, political scientists viewed campaigns as having very little effect on voters' decisions, since these were usually the products of long-term social processes. Voters generally had a 'standing decision' about which party to support, and the function of campaigns was mainly to reinforce this and to mobilize supporters. In a number of democracies, however, long-term attachments to parties have weakened and voters have become more responsive to short-term forces (Crewe and Denver 1985). In these circumstances campaigns are potentially more likely to have an effect. Examples of apparently decisive campaigns can be found. Harrop and Miller 1987: 228) cite the cases of the West German election of 1972 and the Canadian election of 1974. Particular apparent campaign effects – such as surges or declines in minor party support – may be discerned in specific elections.

In general, however, election outcomes are determined by a complex set of interactions between long-term and short-term factors, and the 'hot' campaign – which is in any case becoming more difficult to define, as in many countries campaigning is now almost continuous – is only one of these. When all election contestants campaign with roughly equal effectiveness – and this is ensured by professionalization – the effect of the campaign on election outcomes is likely to be slight. It remains important to be effective, of course, as any candidate or party which did not campaign seriously and well would soon discover.

REFERENCES

Agranoff, R. (ed.) (1976) *The New Style in Election Campaigns*, 2nd edn, Boston: Holbrook Press.
Atkinson, M. (1984) *Our Masters' Voices*, London: Methuen.
Blumler, J. G. and McQuail, D. (1967) *Television in Politics*, London: Faber & Faber.
Butler, D. and Kavanagh, D. (1988) *The British General Election of 1987*, Basingstoke: Macmillan.
Butler, D., Penniman, H. R. and Ranney, A. (eds) (1981) *Democracy at the Polls*, Washington, DC: American Enterprise Institute.
Chartrand, R. L. (1976) 'Information technology and the political campaigner', in R.

Agranoff (ed.) *The New Style in Election Campaigns*, 2nd edn, Boston: Holbrook Press.

Crewe, I. (1986) 'Saturation polling, the media and the 1983 election', in I. Crewe and M. Harrop (eds) *Political Communications: The General Election Campaign of 1983*, Cambridge: Cambridge University Press.

Crewe, I. and Denver, D. (eds) (1985) *Electoral Change in Western Democracies*, London: Croom Helm.

Denver, D. (1989) *Elections and Voting Behaviour in Britain*, Hemel Hempstead: Philip Allan.

Diamond, E. and Bates, S. (1984) *The Spot: The Rise of Political Advertising on Television*, Cambridge, Mass.: MIT Press.

Harrison, M. (1988) 'Broadcasting', in D. Butler and D. Kavanagh (eds) *The British General Election of 1987*, Basingstoke: Macmillan.

Harrop, M. and Miller, W. L. (1987) *Elections and Voters*, Basingstoke: Macmillan.

Hunt, A. R. (1987) 'The media and presidential campaigns', in A. J. Reichley (ed.) *Elections American Style*, Washington, DC: Brookings Institution.

Jamieson, K. H. (1984) *Packaging The Presidency*, Oxford: Oxford University Press.

Kavanagh, D. (1970) *Constituency Electioneering in Britain*, London: Longman.

——(1981) 'Public opinion polls', in D. Butler, H. R. Penniman and A. Ranney (eds) *Democracy at the Polls*, Washington, DC: American Enterprise Institute.

Kessel, J. H. (1984) *Presidential Campaign Politics*, 2nd edn, Homewood, Ill.: Dorsey Press.

Lazarsfeld, P., Berelson, B. and Gaudet, H. (1968) *The People's Choice*, 3rd edn, New York: Columbia University Press.

Leuthold, D. A. (1968) *Electioneering in a Democracy*, New York: John Wiley.

Luntz, F. (1988) *Candidates, Consultants and Campaigns*, Oxford: Basil Blackwell.

McGinniss, J. (1969) *The Selling of the President 1968*, New York: Trident Press.

Malbin, M. J. (ed.) (1984) *Money and Politics in the United States*, Chatham, NJ: Chatham House.

Nelson, M. (ed.) (1989) *Elections '88*, Washington, DC: Congressional Quarterly.

Paltiel, K. Z. (1981) 'Campaign finance: contrasting practices and reforms', in D. Butler, H. R. Penniman and A. Ranney (eds) *Democracy at the Polls*, Washington, DC: American Enterprise Institute.

Patterson, T. E. and McClure, R. D. (1976) *The Unseeing Eye*, New York: Putnam Books.

Penniman, H. R. (1981) 'Campaign styles and methods', in D. Butler, H. R. Penniman and A. Ranney (eds) *Democracy at the Polls*, Washington, DC: American Enterprise Institute.

Sabato, L. J. (1981) *The Rise of Political Consultants: New Ways of Winning Elections*, New York: Basic Books.

——(1987) 'Real and imagined corruption in campaign financing', in A. J. Reichley (ed.) *Elections American Style*, Washington, DC: Brookings Institution.

Salmore, S. A. and Salmore, B. G. (1985) *Candidates, Parties, and Campaigns*, Washington, DC: CQ Press.

Smith, A. (1981) 'Mass communication', in D. Butler, H. R. Penniman and A. Ranney (eds) *Democracy at the Polls*, Washington, DC: American Enterprise Institute.

White, T. H. (1964) *The Making of the President 1960*, New York: Atheneum Publishers.

——(1982) *America in Search of Itself*, New York: Warner Books.

Whiteley, P. (1986) 'The accuracy and influence of the polls in the 1983 general election', in I. Crewe and M. Harrop (eds) *Political Communications: The General Election Campaign of 1983*, Cambridge: Cambridge University Press.

FURTHER READING

Agranoff, R. (ed.) (1976) *The New Style in Election Campaigns*, 2nd edn, Boston: Holbrook Press.

Alexander, H. E. (1984) *Financing Politics*, Washington, DC: CQ Press.

Butler, D. (1989) *British General Elections since 1945*, Oxford: Basil Blackwell.

Butler, D. and Kavanagh, D. (1988) *The British General Election of 1987*, Basingstoke: Macmillan.

Butler, D., Penniman, H. R. and Ranney, A. (eds) (1981) *Democracy at the Polls*, Washington, DC: American Enterprise Institute.

Crewe, I. and Harrop, M. (eds) (1989) *Political Communications: The General Election Campaign of 1987*, Cambridge: Cambridge University Press.

Diamond, E. and Bates, S. (1984) *The Spot: The Rise of Political Advertising on Television*, Cambridge, Mass.: MIT Press.

Harrop, M. and Miller, W. L. (1987) *Elections and Voters*, Basingstoke: Macmillan.

Hess, S. (1988) *The Presidential Campaign*, 3rd edn, Washington, DC: Brookings Institution.

Jamieson, K. H. (1984) *Packaging The Presidency*, Oxford: Oxford University Press.

Kessel, J. H. (1984) *Presidential Campaign Politics*, 2nd edn, Homewood, Ill.: Dorsey Press.

Luntz, F. (1988) *Candidates, Consultants and Campaigns*, Oxford: Basil Blackwell.

Malbin, M. J. (ed.) (1984) *Money and Politics in the United States*, Chatham, NJ: Chatham House.

Patterson, T. E. and McClure, R. D. (1976) *The Unseeing Eye*, New York: Putnam Books.

Pomper, G. (ed.) (1989) *The Election of 1988: Reports and Interpretations*, Chatham, NJ: Chatham House.

Sabato, L. J. (1981) *The Rise of Political Consultants: New Ways of Winning Elections*, New York: Basic Books.

Salmore, S. A. and Salmore, B. G. (1985) *Candidates, Parties, and Campaigns*, Washington, DC: CQ Press.

Ware, A. (1987) *Political Parties: Electoral Change and Structural Response*, Oxford: Basil Blackwell.

Witcover, J. (1977) *Marathon: The Pursuit of the Presidency*, New York: Viking Books.

White, T. H. (1982) *America in Search of Itself*, New York: Warner Books.

27

POLITICAL PARTICIPATION AND VOTING BEHAVIOUR

W. L. MILLER

There is no such thing as a free choice in politics. People's preferences are influenced and conditioned by the social and political context in which they live. Moreover, their political *actions* are distinct from their *preferences*. Political behaviour depends upon the interaction between personal preferences and the political context, since institutional incentives and constraints affect the translation of preferences into action.

Some aspects of institutional/contextual influences are easily observable: voters, for example, cannot choose a party that does not put forward a candidate in their constituency. Many constraints and incentives are a lot less deterministic and less visible. Constraints may be psychological as well as legal.

Verba, Nie and Kim have argued that there is a universal tendency for citizens with higher levels of 'socio-economic resources' to be more willing to participate in politics (Verba *et al.* 1978: 63–79). By socio-economic resources they mean, primarily, education and income. These resources provide the skills, the stimulation and the capability to participate in many kinds of political activity. However, the influence of these personal resources is likely to vary with the particular type of activity, and with the particular institutional context.

We can distinguish three 'modes' or kinds of political participation:

1 voting;
2 electoral campaigning;
3 non-partisan lobbying – particularly on local community affairs, or even particularized contacts with officials to achieve some personal benefit or ventilate some personal grievance.

These three kinds of political participation differ in terms of the degree of institutional conflict implied, and the amount of individual initiative and effort required. Activities that involve the most individual effort and the least institutional conflict should be the least affected by institutional incentives and constraints. Conversely, those that involve the most institutional conflict and the least individual effort should be the most susceptible to institutional influence. The act of voting requires very little effort by the individual and involves a great deal of institutional – in this case, party – conflict. So the natural propensity for individuals with high levels of income and education to participate more than others should be least evident in the case of voting. Parties will be both willing and able to mobilize relatively apathetic citizens into such an important (for the parties) but easy (for the citizen) form of political activity.

In general the evidence confirms this theory (Table 1). Within a wide range of countries there is a uniformly high correlation between citizens' socio-economic resources and their psychological involvement with politics – that is their interest in politics and their inclination to discuss political questions. But there is a much lower and more variable correlation between citizens' socio-economic resources and their actual, physical participation. The correlation with voting is particularly low overall, though it ranges from almost nothing at all in some countries to a modest 0.24 in the USA (Verba et al. 1978: 75). This suggests that powerful institutional forces generally work to prevent the natural pattern of psychological involvement being reflected in actual participation.

Table 1 Correlation between socio-economic resources and various indicators of political participation

Psychological Participation	
Correlation with political interest	0.37
Correlation with political discussion	0.36
Physical Participation	
Correlation with lobbying	0.23
Correlation with electoral campaigning	0.18
Correlation with voting turnout	0.08

Source: Average figures calculated by author from figures given in Verba *et al.* (1978: 75) for Austria, India, Japan, The Netherlands, Nigeria, USA, Yugoslavia.

There is, of course, no guarantee that institutional incentives and constraints will reduce the influence of personal socio-economic resources on political participation. They may amplify the effects of personal resources. It all depends upon whether institutions mobilize citizens with few personal resources and/or exclude citizens with high levels of personal resources or, alternatively, whether they exclude the poor and/or mobilize the rich.

In extreme cases, institutional incentives and constraints may be constitutional. Voting may be legally compulsory – in which case most (but not all) citizens are likely to vote at least in national elections. Conversely, particular groups may be legally excluded from the franchise – like conscientious objectors after the First World War in Britain for example, or women in Spain before 1977. Such requirements and restrictions have rather obvious consequences for participation. Less obviously, some citizens may be discouraged from participation because they cannot legally form a party to represent their interests, or because politics in their country is dominated by a set of parties, none of which represents their interests and values. Conversely, citizens can be mobilized into active participation not just by legal pressure but also through psychological identification with a party which does represent their interests and values. This match or mismatch between citizens and parties has a much less obvious and mechanical effect upon participation than legal requirements or exclusions, but it none the less exerts a significant influence.

Socialist, social democrat and trade-union based parties are committed to mobilizing the relatively poor. Wherever they are strong they are likely to ensure that the poor turn out to vote even though they are relatively uninterested in politics. Less obviously, some religious-based parties in Europe and in Japan appeal to religious groups that just happen to be poor. (Rural peasant communities tend to be both poor and religious.) So these religious-based parties also tend to mobilize the poor and offset the personal factors influencing participation. But where, as in the United States, politics is not dominated by class conflict, where socialist parties are virtually non-existent, and where there are no religious parties with a strong link to a relatively poor religious or ethnic group, then there is much more scope for purely personal factors to influence political participation. So, in America especially, the rich and well-educated are not just more interested in politics, they actually participate much more than the poor and ignorant do.

Amongst the three kinds of participation studied by Verba *et al.* (1978), lobbying provides the greatest contrast with voting. Voting involves the most institutional (i.e. party) conflict, lobbying the least. Voting requires the least personal initiative, lobbying the most. So we should expect that the citizens with the highest levels of education and income would be prepared to lobby most actively and that this tendency would be relatively *un*affected by institutional incentives or constraints. That seems to be the case. The correlation between socio-economic resources and lobbying activity is moderately high – much higher than for voting, though still lower than for political interest and discussion (see Table 1).

The three kinds of participation discussed by Verba *et al.* have been christened 'conventional' or 'elite-directed' to distinguish them from other 'unconventional', 'protest' or 'elite-challenging' modes of participation such as demonstrations, strikes, damage to property and violence against people (Inglehart 1977: 299). Perhaps surprisingly, citizens tend to see at least some of these options as supplements rather than alternatives to voting, campaigning and lobbying. Few citizens express support for outright violence against people or

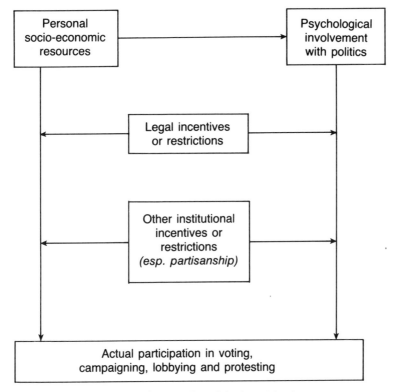

Figure 1 A general model of participation

property. So most of the empirical findings refer to protest activity that goes no further than demonstrations and occupying (not damaging) buildings: this has been described as 'democratic direct action' because it is in fact as much a part of conventional democratic activity as the three modes discussed by Verba *et al.*, and should not be confused with terrorist activity or 'violent direct action' (Miller *et al.* 1982).

There is a moderately sized *positive* correlation between support for such (peaceful) protest activity and 'conventional' participation such as voting and electoral campaigning. Across Austria, Britain, Germany, the Netherlands and the USA this correlation averages 0.24 (Marsh and Kaase 1979: 93). There are some differences in the patterns of elite-directed and elite-challenging participation. The young are much more inclined than the old to support demonstrations and occupations, while they are less inclined than the old to turn out and vote. However, the highly educated and strong partisans are more likely than others to engage in all kinds of political activity/protest activity as well as electoral activity (Dalton 1988: 51–69).

In summary therefore, the rich and well-educated are almost always more interested in politics than the poor; they *do not* usually participate much more than the poor in easy activities like voting (except in the USA) because working-class or religious parties mobilize the poor in order to compete in elections. But the rich and well-educated *do* play a much larger part than the poor in electoral campaigning and even more so in lobbying. They also play a larger part in (peaceful) political protests.

There is a great irony here. Western democracies provide responsible government but they do not, in general, provide representative government – at least not socially representative. Elected bodies are notoriously unrepresentative in the social sense. The American Congress is a congress of lawyers, the German parliament is a parliament of civil servants, and British local government councils are councils of the self-employed and the retired. Even at much lower levels of participation than holding elective office, political activists are socially unrepresentative and are drawn disproportionately from those who are adding the advantage of political influence to the advantages of income and education. Young elites may challenge old elites, but even protest action fails to compensate for the unrepresentative nature of political activists.

What are the likely effects of increasing levels of education and income? They are likely to have least effect upon voter turn-out which may well be 'saturated'. Party competition has proved sufficient to mobilize even the relatively ill-equipped and apathetic into this minimal form of political activity. On the other hand, rising levels of education and affluence should have most effect on those forms of activity which depend most on citizens' own personal resources: that suggests further growth in campaigning – perhaps single-issue and pressure-group campaigning as much as party campaigning, further growth in lobbying activities and more willingness to challenge established, incumbent elites through protest activity.

Voting choice, like participation, is not just a matter of personal preferences. Obviously voters are more likely to vote for a party they like than one they dislike, but their likes and dislikes are influenced and conditioned by a variety of outside forces – in particular by their social and family background and by the way the parties are portrayed in the media. And irrespective of their likes and dislikes, voters cannot vote for a party that does not put forward a candidate in their constituency. Even when their preferred party does contest the election, voters may be reluctant to vote for it if they feel it has no chance of winning in their local constituency and/or if they feel it has no chance of winning a majority or even holding the balance of power in parliament. At other times – especially at by-elections – voters who want to protest about specific government policies without throwing the government out of office may switch their votes to a new or extremist party precisely because they are sure that it cannot win power. So it makes little sense to discuss voting without paying attention to the situation of the voter and the circumstances of the election.

Various models have been proposed to explain why people vote the way they do. Figure 2 summarizes and synthesizes these models into a single, comprehensive, general model of voting. Apart from voting itself, the general model contains six elements:

1 **The social context.** This includes not only the voter's own class, age, sex, religion, region, etc., but also the social characteristics and political attitudes of the voter's family, neighbours, workmates and friends.
2 **Party identification.** This has been a key concept in the most popular models of voting behaviour. It means the voter's sense of attachment to or 'identification' with a political party – the extent to which the voter is a party

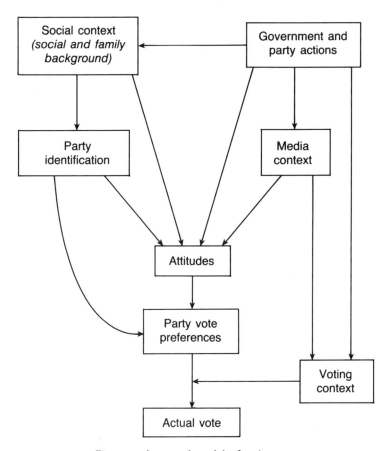

Figure 2   A general model of voting

'supporter' rather than a dispassionate observer of the party battle. Party identification has two aspects: *direction* (which party) and *strength*. Mere preferences give an indication of the direction of party choice but the concept of party identification is particularly important because it draws attention to the difference between those who have a deep preference and those who have only a shallow, lightly held preference.

3 **Attitudes.** The term 'attitudes', in the wide sense in which it is used in the general model, includes attitudes towards issues, performance, personalities, values and ideology. For example: the *issue* of defence policy; the *performance* of the government in managing the economy; the *personality* of the president or prime minister; the *values* of egalitarianism; the *ideology* of socialism.

4 **The election context.** This includes the voter's assessment of the point or purpose of the election and the range of credible options available. If voters feel the election is unimportant or pointless they may ignore it and abstain. If it is a by-election they may feel it is a suitable and safe opportunity for a protest. If it is a local government election they may feel it is appropriate to express a view on domestic affairs but not on defence policy. Their choice *must* be limited by the range of available candidates; it *may* also be limited still further by the (smaller) range of credible candidates.

5 **The media context.** This includes all the news, commentary, and advertising that reaches the voter through channels of mass communication rather than by word of mouth. The most pervasive medium is now usually television, though a minority of voters may get more information from the 'highbrow' press.

6 **Government and party actions.** Party activity provides much of the input to the mass media. It makes news. Of course, the media make their own selections from the available news and sometimes create or even concoct the news, but to a large extent the media are just that – media through which politicians conduct a public debate and communicate with the voters. However, it is important to stress the unique role of government. The governing party is not just the 'first among equals'. While opposition parties argue, governments act. Oppositions propose policies and criticize policies, but governments implement policies. So there is far more action, and more important action, by governments than by other parties.

The literature on voting behaviour is littered with the names of more limited and specific voting models which stress particular aspects of this general model. Though the exigencies of academic debate may obscure the fact, differences between these more limited models are not essentially differences of principle so much as differences of focus and emphasis. Of course, differences of emphasis are not unimportant: the difference between an ostrich and an eagle is also a difference of emphasis rather than principle. The real question is not which model of voting is *correct* but which is *relevant* to an understanding of voting behaviour in a particular time and place. Across the range of recent experience in contemporary democracies, none of the elements shown in the general model can be dismissed as irrelevant.

Since there is so much in the general model, however, we can use partial models as a way to focus attention on different parts of the general model in turn. Amongst widely discussed partial models are the *sociological* model, the *party identification* model, the *rational choice* model, the *dominant ideology* model and the *election context* model.

THE SOCIOLOGICAL MODEL

The basic claim of the sociological model is that each social group votes for the party that serves its interests. Individuals as individuals – that is, as independent decision makers – do not exist. What voters claim to be their own, personal political attitudes simply reflect the interests of the group to which they belong. Some social theorists qualify the stark, elegant simplicity of this model by introducing the question of what might induce a social group to mistake its real interests, but that is tantamount to an admission that the sociological model is incomplete and that a more general model is required.

The sociological model focuses on only two elements from the general model: social context and voting choice. All other elements are ignored. Party identification and political attitudes have no real independent existence, they merely reflect social backgrounds and do not significantly qualify the simple causal link from social context to voting choice. It is an elegantly parsimonious model if it fits the facts, or even if it approximates the facts. It is a sufficient explanation of voting behaviour in a society that is highly polarized along class, religious or ethnic lines. In Northern Ireland for example, the amount of cross-sectarian voting – Catholics voting Unionist or Protestants voting Republican – is negligible. However, it is not much help in explaining why some voters in Northern Ireland vote for 'non-sectarian' parties that are neither intransigently Unionist nor Republican. And it offers even less help in explaining how Protestants choose between the various Unionist parties, or how Catholics choose between different Republican parties.

The sociological model could also explain highly polarized class voting which characterized so much of European, Commonwealth and American politics in the past (Alford 1964). However, sequences of survey studies show a very sharp decline in class polarization in the USA during the 1950s, followed by a similar decline in Germany in the 1960s and in Britain in the 1970s and 1980s (Dalton 1988: 157). In the USA, middle-class and working-class voters split their votes more evenly between the Republicans and the Democrats. In Britain, class depolarization had another dimension: not only did the two classes split their votes more evenly between Labour and Conservative, but many voters in both classes switched to the self-proclaimed 'classless' alternative – the Liberals and their successors, the Alliance and the Liberal Democrats. The class version of the sociological model is clearly declining in relevance – though not yet irrelevant.

There is little evidence of a similar decline in sectarian and religious (i.e. the religious versus the irreligious) polarization. Regional polarization has been increasing at British elections for three decades now. And long suppressed but well-remembered ethnic tensions within the emerging democracies of Eastern Europe point to the possibility of increasing social polarization – though not on class lines.

THE PARTY IDENTIFICATION MODEL

The party identification model (sometimes called the *socialization* model, or *expressive* model) stresses the importance of enduring partisan commitment. Its basic claims are that:

1 substantial numbers of voters self-consciously identify with a party and regard themselves as party supporters; they inherit their partisanship from their parents or are 'socialized' into it by their acquaintances as they grow up;
2 their party identification is a relatively stable and enduring part of their political outlook – certainly more stable than their attitudes to particular issues and political personalities;
3 their party identification has a significant influence upon their attitudes towards issues, personalities and government performance;
4 their party identification also affects their voting choice directly, i.e. it partially outweighs their attitudes as well as influencing them.

Although party identification may be *relatively* stable and enduring, there is no suggestion that it is immutable. This model can be used to explain, and possibly even predict, periods of electoral stability or volatility. If party identification is widespread and strong, then relatively few voters will be swayed by current events, their voting choice will largely reflect their party identification and will be stable because party identification itself is stable. Conversely, if few voters identify with parties or if they only weakly identify with parties, then their votes are 'up for grabs' – they can be swayed quickly and easily by events, election campaigns, advertising, temporary economic booms or set-backs, scandals and the like (Crewe and Denver 1985).

During the late 1960s and the 1970s, the number of voters with a strong sense of party identification declined sharply in Britain and America – from, it should be said, rather high starting levels. In the 1980s partisanship began to increase again in the USA, though it continued to decline in Britain. This erosion of partisanship was accompanied by increasing voter volatility and a rise in split-ticket voting (where two or more votes had to be cast for different offices at the same time).

It has become clear that the strength of party identification is not nearly so stable and durable as its direction. It is a big step to switch from being a Labour supporter to being a Conservative supporter, but a much smaller step to switch from being a strong to a weak supporter or vice versa. An electoral cycle is clearly visible with the strength of partisanship declining between elections and rising again at election time. Such cyclical fluctuations are superimposed on longer-term trends and serve to remind us that trends can be reversed.

Even though the strength of partisanship has declined, it remains a significant influence upon both attitudes and behaviour. For example, British panel surveys show that, by manipulating the economy as an election approaches, the government is able to increase the economic optimism of uncommitted voters more easily than that of its own supporters (who already feel loyally optimistic) or of opposition party supporters (who remain stubbornly pessimistic) (Miller *et al.* 1990: 100–1).

THE RATIONAL CHOICE MODEL

The rational choice model focuses attention on the link between attitudes and voting. It ignores the question of where the voters derive their attitudes from and confines attention to the fit between voters' attitudes and their voting choice. A variety of even more specific names are used for rational choice models, depending upon the particular attitudes that best predict voting choice. So the model may be called an *issue voting* model, a *values* model, a *prospective* model (if votes reflect attitudes towards future party policy), a *retrospective* model (if votes reflect attitudes towards the government's past record), an *economic* model (if votes reflect attitudes to the government's economic performance record in particular), an *egocentric* model (if votes reflect reactions to the voter's own personal economic experience), a *sociotropic* model (if votes reflect reactions to the voter's assessment of national economic performance), or a *leadership* model, a *personality* model or a *candidate* model (if votes reflect attitudes towards party leaders or presidential candidates). Though these are important differences, all these models are merely variants of the same *rational choice* model.

The basic claim of the rational choice model is that voters make up their own minds about issues, performance and personalities, and then vote for the party that comes closest to delivering the policies and performance they want. The model fails some simple tests in spectacular fashion, though that may be

437

the fault of the tests rather than the model. If voters voted for the party they said had the best policy on the issue they themselves said was most important then Labour would have tied with the Conservatives in 1983 and beaten the Conservatives in 1987 instead of losing both elections by a landslide (Heath *et al.* 1985: 98; Crewe 1987: 7). But the rational choice model is not restricted to policy attitudes. Though analyses suggest a great deal of variation from place to place, from time to time, and across subgroups of voters, the general pattern of findings suggests that economic performance is more influential than policy preferences, that retrospective evaluations are more influential than prospective, that attitudes towards the government are more influential than attitudes towards the opposition, and that sociotropic evaluations are more influential than egocentric. Clearly the nature of the parties, their leaders and their programmes affect the relative weights of these different influences. As long as two parties maintain a bipartisan foreign policy they may be judged solely on economic performance, but if they become bitterly divided over foreign policy that issue may suddenly become more influential.

We might usefully contrast extreme and over-drawn caricatures of the party identification and rational choice models. In their purest, most extreme, and therefore most unrealistic forms the party identification model suggests that partisanship determines political attitudes while the rational choice model suggests that political attitudes determine party choice. Which is correct? Reality is not so clear-cut as these caricatures. Empirical studies suggest that they are *both* correct: pre-existing partisan loyalty helps to form political attitudes towards issues, performance and leaders – but it does not completely determine those attitudes; and both old party loyalties and current political attitudes influence voting choice in a particular election.

We can be more precise than that. Panel studies suggest that for relatively uncommitted voters – that is, voters who may have party preferences but deny being party supporters – political attitudes have more influence on party choice than vice versa; conversely, among those who do claim to be party supporters, party choice has more influence on political attitudes than vice versa (Miller *et al.* 1990: 124–6). In crude and very approximate terms, the *party identification* model explains the attitudes and behaviour of *party supporters*, while the *rational choice* model explains the behaviour of the *rest of the electorate*. In the 1980s about half the British electorate claimed to be party 'supporters', while nearly all the rest declared a party preference yet denied being party supporters.

THE DOMINANT IDEOLOGY MODEL

The notion of a dominant ideology has been used by Marxist scholars to explain why the simple sociological model (in their case, a simple class-interest model) does not fit the facts. Here, I shall use it in a looser sense and focus

438

upon government rather than the elusive concept of ideology. Incumbent governments hold the levers of power; so they are administratively dominant. Governments are also intrinsically much more news-worthy than oppositions; so they can be politically dominant without having to resort to administrative devices to control public debate or media reporting.

Government can influence the voters in three ways. First it can act to influence political attitudes directly – for example, by cutting unemployment or negotiating an arms-reduction treaty. Second, it can act to influence the media and thus indirectly influence political attitudes – for example, by changing the way in which the unemployment rate is calculated in order to bring about an apparent, but not real, reduction in unemployment or by attending an international summit conference which provides good television pictures even though nothing of substance occurs. Third, it can use its power to change society – for example, by privatizing industries, houses, the health service or the school system, or by curbing trade union power and membership. By these means, government can change even the social context. In electoral contests, governments are not only players, they also set the rules – even in mature, liberal, Western democracies.

Once again we have to ask the questions avoided by rational choice theorists: *Why* do voters have the attitudes they do? *Where* do they get their attitudes from? For example, there is general agreement that perceptions of economic prosperity were the key to the British government's re-election for a third term in 1987, yet we cannot ignore the fact that the voters had been extremely pessimistic about the state of the economy a year previously and only became optimistic a few months before the election. This pattern is not unique to Britain nor to the 1980s.

As the election approached, the government put great pressure on the BBC to give it favourable coverage, the Prime Minister went on a series of very glamorous foreign visits, taxes were cut and public spending increased at the same time, rising inflation was tolerated, unemployment reduced and a consumer boom encouraged. No wonder the voters began to feel more optimistic. But if government was the cause of their new optimism then their behaviour fits a dominant ideology model rather than a rational choice model; personal political attitudes can be as illusory in such circumstances as in the highly polarized world of the sociological model.

THE ELECTION CONTEXT MODEL

Academics have paid remarkably little attention to voters' perceptions of the electoral context, though they loom large in popular journalists' accounts of electoral behaviour which are full of such terms as 'tactical voting', 'protest voting', 'party credibility', 'momentum', or 'by-election atmosphere'.

Voters clearly do not regard all elections as equally important and the turn-out rates reflect that. At Congressional elections in the 'off-years' (when there is no presidential contest), only two-thirds as many Americans vote as in a presidential contest. In Britain, elections to the European Parliament or to local government councils attract only half as many voters as at UK parliamentary elections. When elections are held simultaneously, large numbers of voters (though more in the USA than elsewhere) 'split their ticket' and vote for different parties in the different contests. When elections do not take place simultaneously, many voters still distinguish quite consciously between their votes in different contests. Some voters in by-elections and local elections explicitly state that they would vote differently in a parliamentary general election. Voters who claim that their local government vote is cast on the basis of local issues and/or local candidates are particularly likely to deviate from their normal parliamentary preference (Miller 1988: 167).

In any election, voters take account of the 'tactical' situation – that is which parties have local credibility, and which are strong enough to win or at least be the main challenger to the incumbent party. The local tactical situation varies from time to time as the parties' national strength varies. It also varies from place to place according to local traditions. Less obviously it varies according to the office for which the election is being held. Local government wards are small, parliamentary constituencies much larger, and European parliament constituencies very much larger still. So the same voter may face a different tactical situation in different contests. A party may have a very good chance of victory within the local government ward yet have no chance of even coming second in the larger Euro-constituency.

In general, the larger the constituency the more local variations will be 'averaged out'. So local government contests are the most likely to take place in safe constituencies (i.e. wards) while European Parliament contests are the most likely to take place in marginal constituencies. Generally weak parties that have carefully built up pockets of support (the Liberals, for example) will have a credibility advantage in small local government wards. Even weaker parties which have no local pockets of support, scant funds and very few competent candidates (the Greens, for example) may have a better chance of winning votes in a European election where there are a few large constituencies than in a local government election where there are many small wards.

The issues also vary according to the nature of the election context. Central–local government relations have a higher profile in local elections, defence issues a higher profile in national parliamentary elections, environmental issues and consumer protection a higher profile in European parliament elections.

Questions about the election context are inevitably highly specific and detailed. None of these details may be of general importance. What is of general importance is that there always is an electoral context – whatever the content of that context – and that the electoral context has a significant influence on the way voters translate their preferences into votes. Voters' preferences are not usually so strong or so uniquely tied to one single party that they will vote only for their most preferred party. During the 1980s, panel surveys showed that at least half the British electorate switched preferences between two or more of the three main parties and, at any one time, a similar number indicated that they only *marginally* preferred their first-preference party to their second. Consequently it is not surprising that the degree of volatility was high nor that voters' choices were influenced by tactical considerations as well as by party loyalties and political attitudes.

REFERENCES

Alford, R. (1964) *Party and Society*, London: John Murray.

Crewe, I. (1987) 'Why Mrs Thatcher was returned with a landslide', *Social Studies Review* 3: 2–9.

Crewe, I. and Denver, D. (eds) (1985) *Electoral Change in Western Democracies*, London: Croom Helm.

Dalton, R. J. (1988) *Citizen Politics in Western Democracies*, Chatham, NJ: Chatham House.

Heath, A., Jowell, R. and Curtice, J. (1985) *How Britain Votes*, Oxford: Pergamon.

Inglehart, R. (1977) *The Silent Revolution*, Princeton: Princeton University Press.

Marsh, A. and Kaase, M. (1979) 'Measuring political action', in S. Barnes and M. Kaase (eds) *Political Action*, Beverly Hills: Sage Publications.

Miller, W. L. (1988) *Irrelevant Elections? The Quality of Local Democracy in Britain*, Oxford: Oxford University Press.

Miller, W. L., Brand, J., Jordan, M., Balsom, D., Madgewick, P. and Mechelen, D. van (1982) *Democratic or Violent Protest?* Strathclyde Studies in Public Policy, no. 107, Glasgow: University of Strathclyde, Centre for the Study of Public Policy.

Miller, W. L., Clarke, H. D., Harrop, M., LeDuc, L. and Whiteley, P. F. (1990) *How Voters Change*, Oxford: Oxford University Press.

Verba, S., Nie, N. H. and Kim, J. (1978) *Participation and Political Equality*, New York: Cambridge University Press.

FURTHER READING

Barnes, S. and Kaase, M. (eds) (1979) *Political Action*, Beverly Hills: Sage Publications.

Berelson, B., Lazarsfeld, P. and McPhee, W. (1954) *Voting*, Chicago: University of Chicago Press.

Budge, I., Crewe, I. and Farlie, D. (eds) (1976) *Party Identification and Beyond*, London: John Wiley.

Butler, D. (1989) *British General Elections since 1945*, Oxford: Basil Blackwell.

Butler, D. and Stokes, D. (1974) *Political Change in Britain*, London: Macmillan.

Butler D., Penniman, H. R. and Ranney, A. (eds) (1981) *Democracy at the Polls*, Washington, DC: American Enterprise Institute.

Campbell, A., Converse, P., Miller, W. E. and Stokes, D. (1960) *The American Voter*, New York: John Wiley.

Crewe, I. and Denver, D. (eds) (1985) *Electoral Change in Western Democracies*, London: Croom Helm.

Dalton R., Flanagan, S. and Beck, P. (1984) *Electoral Change in Advanced Industrial Societies*, Princeton: Princeton University Press.

Dalton, R. J. (1988) *Citizen Politics in Western Democracies*, Chatham, NJ: Chatham House.

Dunleavy, P. and Husbands, C. T. (1985) *British Democracy at the Crossroads*, London: Allen & Unwin.

Harrop, M. and Miller W. L. (1987) *Elections and Voting: A Comparative Introduction*, London: Macmillan.

Heath, A., Jowell, R. and Curtice, J. (1985) *How Britain Votes*, Oxford: Pergamon.

Inglehart, R. (1977) *The Silent Revolution*, Princeton: Princeton University Press.

Miller, W. L. (1988) *Irrelevant Elections? The Quality of Local Democracy in Britain*, Oxford: Oxford University Press.

Miller, W. L., Clarke, H. D., Harrop, M., LeDuc, L. and Whiteley, P. F. (1990) *How Voters Change*, Oxford: Oxford University Press.

Norris, P. (1990) *The Volatile Electorate*, Oxford: Oxford University Press.

Powell, G. B. (1982) *Contemporary Democracies: Participation, Stability and Violence*, Cambridge, Mass.: Harvard University Press.

Sarlvik, B. and Crewe, I. (1983) *Decade of Dealignment*, Cambridge: Cambridge University Press.

Verba S., Nie, N. H. and Kim, J. (1978) *Participation and Political Equality*, New York: Cambridge University Press.

28

POLITICAL
SOCIALIZATION

STANLEY RENSHON

Over thirty years ago, Herbert Hyman (1959) used the term political socialization in the title of his study on the psychology of political behaviour. He did
so to call attention to the fact that political orientations could be productively
analysed as learned behaviour, a view which, though obvious now, represented
a new departure at the time. In doing so, he laid the groundwork for an
interdisciplinary field combining psychological theories of learning with political theories of regularity and change (Turiel 1989: 48).

That foundation also corresponded with a paradigmatic change in one of
the field's three major disciplinary sources: political science (Dahl 1961). The
behavioural paradigm in political science emphasized four major points in
studying political process: the importance of the individual in the functioning of
political institutions and processes; the importance of interdisciplinary political
theory; the use of systematic measurement strategies; and the development of
generalizable theories regarding political behaviour and its causes. The result
of these congruent trends in political socialization and political science was an
outpouring of theory and research.

The field of political socialization was attractive to political scientists for two
reasons. First, it attempted to link socialization processes to the development
of politically relevant views and activities, and second, it attempted to link the
development of individual citizens with the functioning of the larger political
system. Much of the early research in the area was generated by the attempt
to document these links, as well as to establish the nature of the mechanisms
that shaped the process.

Several questions now arise from these efforts. A first set of questions
concerns whether political socialization has successfully demonstrated the validity of its premises. In over three decades of study, has the field accumulated
empirically supported theory which links the development of individuals with
their political functioning and to that of the larger political system?

A second and related set of questions concerns the state of political socialization, its prospects and the various prescriptions which are offered for ensuring its future. There is a sense in which the pace of research and publication in the field has slowed (Cook 1989; Merelman 1989; Allen 1989; Turiel 1989). It is further assumed by some that this slowing represents an intellectual hiatus. This has led some critics to suggest that the field, 'has not fulfilled its promise' (Rosenberg 1985: 715). On the other hand, Dennis writes that, 'While the science of political socialization is far from the idea of a cumulative, fully codified body of knowledge, we have made considerable strides towards being able to give a systematic account of these processes and of their products since the late fifties' (Dennis 1985: vii).

Both these views reflect assumptions about what political socialization was supposed to accomplish. In the absence of agreement on this issue, diagnoses and prescriptions alike are likely to lead in varied directions. We begin our discussion therefore with an examination of several rationales that have been put forward as the basis of study in the field.

THE RATIONALE FOR STUDYING POLITICAL SOCIALIZATION

There are several plausible rationales for studying political socialization. The first and most general is based on the fact that socialization is a central part of every society's social process. According to Allen, 'it is a phenomenon taking place continually in every organized society' (Allen 1989: 4). Part of this process concerns learning about authority and rule-making institutions. In this formulation therefore, political socialization can lay claim to legitimacy on the basis of centrality, universality, and the fact that the general content of socialization has, or would appear to have, political implications.

A second rationale stems from a 'concern with the proper development of offspring – with their acquisition of needed skills, the curbing of aggressive tendencies, the directing of their feet to paths of righteousness' (Clausen 1968: 20). In this formulation, the importance of socialization and the nature of its impact is assumed, and study is directed at the best method(s) of bringing about desired ends. Theories of socialization found in Plato's *Republic*, Machiavelli's *The Prince*, and Rousseau's *Social Contract*, to name three of many, are reflective of this rationale.

Finally, a third and somewhat more direct theoretical and political rationale for political socialization rests on its posited effects on the continuity, change and persistence of political systems (Easton and Dennis 1969). In this view, early political socialization, especially in relation to authorities and the public's understanding of citizenship roles, provides leaders and policy makers with a cushion of 'diffuse support'. This cushion represents the range of policy latitude available to elites in pursuit of (their understanding of) the national interest, and allows them to occasionally take unpopular but necessary steps.

None of these has provided an unambiguous rationale for the field. The first rationale, for example, falters on the grounds of generality. It fails to differentiate sufficiently between the process of socialization and its outcomes. Research to be examined in this essay strongly supports the view that there is no one political socialization process, but rather a variety of processes at work.

The second rationale, which stems from a concern with attempting to socialize citizens into the 'good citizen' role, raises the basic question of whose views of that role should be paramount. Dowse (1978: 409), among others, questions the wisdom of this approach as the basis for political socialization, however laudable it may appear. He points out that political alienation, for example, may be a perfectly rational response to real powerlessness. In such cases he argues, political education cannot reverse the effects of structural disadvantage, and may in fact end up reinforcing them.

The third rationale proposes a specific link between political socialization and the operation of the political systems. However, this linkage, while intuitively plausible, has proved difficult to establish. Part of the problem is the measurement of outcomes such as 'stability', 'change', 'continuity', etc., but this is only part of the problem. Because the best evidence for the systemic effects would come from the kinds of large-scale research efforts that have been comparatively rare in the social sciences, the logic of support has rested on the accumulation of inferences from small-scale studies.

Imperfect as they have proved, each rationale provides some justification for taking the concern of political socialization seriously. It is true, after all, that infants are not born with politically relevant adult characters, beliefs and skills. A logical corollary therefore must be that these characteristics develop over time. It is this fundamental insight, the 'developmental hypothesis', which forms the basis of Lasswell's early observation that political analysis must try to 'discover what developmental experiences are significant for the political traits and interests of the mature' (Lasswell 1930: 8), and which functions as a continuing rationale for the field.

POLITICAL SOCIALIZATION AS AN INTERDISCIPLINARY FIELD: PROBLEMS AND PROSPECTS

The study of political socialization rests primarily on three major disciplinary foundations, political science, psychology and sociology, along with a somewhat smaller major contribution from anthropology (but see Almond and Verba 1963 and Pye 1968 for the linkage between political socialization and political culture). Of the three, political science has been concerned for the shortest time with three central concepts of the field: socialization, learning and development. As a result, political socialization has borrowed many models, theories and concepts from the other two core disciplines, psychology and sociology.

There are advantages to borrowing from other disciplines. Concepts and theories not yet developed in the interdisciplinary field can be borrowed when needed. In the case of political socialization, borrowing was not only attractive but also necessary. Concepts such as learning, maturation, development, identification, etc., were central to the processes being researched in the field, but had little history of theoretical development within political science. More importantly, without theory to guide research linking these processes with political socialization, the field could not seriously address questions relevant to its premises.

However, while borrowing may be necessary it is not without costs. There is, for example, the problem of paradigmatic compatibility. It is one matter for researchers to deal with a discipline's major paradigm, but quite another when there are three or more paradigms involved. Consider in this respect some aspects of the basic paradigms of sociology and psychology. Wrong (1961) pointed out some time ago that sociology tended to view individuals as products of social forces, while downplaying the role of individual agency. Psychology on the other hand, has a long history of concern with individuals, whether with the psychology of individual differences or, more recently, with life histories. These two views of psycho-social process are not necessarily irreconcilable, but they do not automatically point researchers in the same direction. For example, in discussing the different views of sociology and psychology, Rosenberg argues that:

> The distinguishing characteristic of systematic sociology is a focus on the collective dimension of human activity. A central assumption is that social reality constitutes a domain which exists between and beyond individuals ... which is understood to determine individual-level phenomena. ... [T]he sociological conception of political activity renders any consideration of individual-level phenomenon inappropriate and uninteresting.
>
> (Rosenberg 1985: 716–17)

The problem of paradigmatic compatibility is made somewhat more complicated by the fact that at least one of political socialization's core disciplines, psychology, has several paradigms rather than just one which is dominant. Cognitive psychology is certainly prominent within psychology (Gardner 1987), but the behaviouralist, developmental and psychoanalytic paradigms continue to maintain a strong disciplinary presence. As a result, problems of theoretical and paradigmatic integration are more complex.

Paradigmatic integration is one of several issues that using interdisciplinary theory raises. These issues make interdisciplinary research more demanding and difficult in some respects than traditional disciplinary research. Greenstein recognized one reason for this in his early analysis of the 'personality and politics' literature. In that analysis, Greenstein noted that when researchers in the field of personality and politics look to psychology to borrow meanings of such terms as 'personality' they find that:

> Rather than finding a psychological science on which to draw for insight, [they find] congeries of more or less competing models and frames of reference, with imperfect agreement on the nature of man's inner dispositions, on the appropriate terms for characterizing them, and on the methodologies for observation.
>
> (Greenstein 1967: 12–13)

Greenstein's point was that the term 'personality' had different meanings which were tied to theoretical views. Trait theorists, psychoanalytic theorists, developmental theorists, and so on, defined and researched personality in very different ways. Therefore one could not simply adapt a definition of personality and apply it without being aware of the controversies surrounding the concept in its home discipline.

Political socialization has shared this need/knowledge dilemma. On one hand, political socialization theorists needed to examine other disciplines for knowledge about processes central to the field's premises. On the other hand, detailed knowledge of, for example, development or psychoanalytic theory is no small undertaking, since each of these theories has its own historical development and theoretical controversies.

Clearly there is a balance to be struck here. Yet it appears difficult, particularly in the early stages of interdisciplinary research and field development, to integrate fully a borrowed theory's range and complexity into research designs. One result is that the full range of a theory's possible contributions are not adequately explored. For example, by the 1960s psychoanalytic theory had developed rich and diverse models of psychological functioning that went well beyond unconscious impulse and childhood. Yet early political socialization theorists made use of only a limited aspect of the theory ('fear of authority' as the basis for political identification).

This continues to be a problem for interdisciplinary work and for political socialization. Turiel (1989: 49) notes, for example, that, although the use of developmental theories to explain political socialization has become more sophisticated, they are still narrowly applied. What most researchers using development models have done, for instance, is directly apply Piaget's model of stages to political thinking. This has been productive, but in Turiel's view it does not exhaust the range of potential applications of these developmental theories. Turiel proposes expanding the application of Piaget's model to include the epistemological analyses of the definitions and classifications of the substantive domains of politics.

However, even being more fully conversant with the range of a discipline's major theories and applications may no longer be sufficient in interdisciplinary research. As an interdisciplinary field like political socialization develops, it may become necessary to be more fully conversant with a range of theories and applications *within* a discipline, as well as with theoretical applications across disciplines. Consider, for example, the question of whether social learning or developmental theory provides a better model to explain political learning. Being conversant with, and even empirically testing, one model does not necessarily resolve all the researcher's problems.

Moore (1989; see also Moore *et al.* 1985) argues that some aspects of political learning conform to social learning theory, an argument he bases on assessments of increased exposure to political stimuli. But as Turiel points out in this connection, 'both social learning and cognitive developmental approaches expect greater exposure to influence learning, but by different processes (Turiel 1989: 47). In other words, the empirical findings linking exposure with political learning do not necessarily resolve the question of which theory more fully accounts for the data.

These examples suggest that the conduct of interdisciplinary research raises difficult, complex theoretical issues. In the sections that follow, we will examine some of these with a view towards laying out, even if not fully resolving, the two sets of questions raised at the beginning of this essay. We begin with an overview of the field, its framework of definitions and early studies.

POLITICAL SOCIALIZATION: EARLY DEFINITIONS AND FRAMEWORKS

Political socialization attracted social scientists because it promised a pay-off in explaining the functioning of political institutions and processes. The framework which most clearly articulated that rationale was systems theory (Easton 1965). The political theory of political socialization derived from that framework (Easton and Dennis 1969; Hess and Torney 1969) provided researchers with an agenda as well as a rationale.

Since political systems were stable and persisted because institutions socialized citizens into providing political authorities with diffuse support, one major item on the research agenda was to see how particular agents (the word itself reflects a view of institutions as surrogates for political authorities) inculcated the relevant 'norms'. Thus a number of studies examined various agents to analyse how they shaped political development. (For an early summary of such research see Renshon (1977), which includes chapters on: the comparative analysis of agents (Beck 1977); the family (Davies 1977); schools (Patrick 1977); peers (Silbiger 1977); media (Chaffe 1977), and so on.)

Since political authorities could hardly afford to wait until adulthood to generate diffuse support, research was also oriented towards finding the origins of adult support in childhood. The number of studies examining the political orientations of children, and later 'youth', led one researcher (Greenstein 1970) to include the study of children as one basic definition of the field. These twin related pillars, the moulding of citizens to norms (in reality those of the political regime and particular political authorities) and the focus on children, were the basis of much of the research undertaken in the field.

The understanding of 'socialization' as a conservative process has a long intellectual history. Clausen (1968: 21) notes that as early as 1828 the term appeared in the *Oxford English Dictionary* with the meaning 'to render social, to make fit for living in society'. Early definitions in the field followed this lead and stressed the child's accommodation to the adult world, particularly the normative values of the society. Hyman's view that 'humans must learn their political behaviour early and well and persist in it' (Hyman 1959: 17) was echoed in many theories. Sigel's observation that 'political socialization refers to the learning process by which the political norms and behaviours acceptable to an ongoing political system are transmitted from generation to generation' (Sigel 1961: 1) was one of several influential views of the process that took this position.

This view has persisted, although not unchallenged, to the present. For example, Allen, in introducing a recent symposium on 'Children's political socialization and cognition' in *Human Development* (Allen 1989: 2), defines the process as 'an individual's adaptation to the political environment'. Less emphasis has generally been given to the ways in which individuals selectively accept, develop and shape political orientations. Similarly, insufficient attention has been given to the ways in which individuals may influence and shape the very social and political systems that supposedly socialize them to regime support.

From the beginning there has been dissatisfaction with the view that individuals are generally passive accommodators to institutional norms. Reservations about this view were expressed quite early in the field's development (Connell and Goot 1972–3) and continued to be expressed periodically (Sears 1975; Renshon 1977). Criticisms of this view took several forms.

Connell and Goot (1972–3) argued that the forced-choice format of the research methodology imposed a structure on the children's answers which tended to suppress the expression of their full range of understandings. He pointed out that Greenstein and Tarrow's study of children using semi-projective and open-ended questions (Greenstein and Tarrow 1970) had revealed that children know more about 'political realities' than they could express in a typical forced-choice format. Sears (1975: 95) pointed out that socialization models tended to overlook the child's idiosyncratic growth, while Renshon's analysis of the basic assumptions behind models of political learning (Renshon 1977: 22–40) detailed exactly why this criticism was well taken.

The most telling argument by far against the conformity to social norms model, however, was the rise of student activism in the 1960s and 1970s by the very same cohorts who had provided researchers with evidence of early support for political authorities. Clearly something had changed. Early research (for example, Greenstein 1965; Hess and Torney 1969) had found that children, especially those in the political and economic mainstream, had a 'positivity bias' in favour of authority. While there was some controversy about whether these findings were an artefact of method (see the discussions in Sullivan and Minns 1976; Greenstein 1976; and Maddox and Handberg 1979), the general consensus was that these findings tended to support the view of the socialization process as developing 'diffuse support', although there were some research caveats to these general findings.

Research on children who were not integrated into the economic and political mainstream, for example American children in economically depressed Southern rural areas (Jaros *et al.* 1968), found that they were substantially less supportive of the political authorities and more alienated from the political and social system. In some cases, economic or political marginality did not lead to wholesale alienation from the political system. Greenberg (1970), for example, found that, while black children were less likely to support political leaders and some governmental institutions than were a comparative sample of white children, they were still generally supportive of the Supreme Court, a finding which the authors plausibly argue reflected the court's long involvement in civil rights. This study is not only important because it examined black children, but in addition because it showed that even among children learning could be selective.

A similar dynamic was uncovered in studies of children's responses to the Watergate crisis. Atherton (1975), for example, found that children's positive evaluations of political leaders and institutions were negatively influenced by the Watergate scandals. This finding was supported by Meadow's two-wave panel study, which uncovered a decline in children's support for the President (Meadow 1982) as more damaging evidence became public. These findings should have made the unexpected activism of the 1960s and 1970s less mysterious, since it suggested that even children could and did respond to changes in the political environment.

In retrospect, it seems clear that students of political socialization erred in focusing primarily on explaining political stability and continuity. This was a plausible and understandable focus given the politics of that period, but socialization theory paid a price for its failure to place that particular period in American politics within a larger historical context. Had that been done, stability (although not necessarily continuity) might have been seen as less of a rule and more the product of a particular set of historical and political circumstances, which themselves were in need of analysis.

As noted, the focus on childhood was dictated in part by the theory of the origins of diffuse support, but this is not the only reason. The focus on childhood was probably influenced as much by the lack of alternative models of development after childhood as it was by the theoretical requirements of systems theory. Although Erikson's eight-stage theory of psychological development, extending from childhood through adulthood, had been published in 1950, its implications for political socialization were not appreciated or integrated for many years. The same could be said of other models of development in adulthood (Levinson 1978; Gilligan 1982). In the first major review of the topic of 'adult political socialization', Sigel wrote that 'there does not exist as yet a theory of adult political socialization' (Sigel 1977: 261). Twelve years later, the first major book on adult political socialization has been published with its editor, Sigel, noting:

> Attention to political socialization over the entire life span – especially attention to adult development – broadly defined – is still the exception rather than the rule. While we do have much information about how adults at a given moment act or react . . . we lack systematic knowledge of whether such behaviour is a carry-over from values learned during childhood or whether it has arisen in response to changed social or personal circumstances not anticipated in childhood.

(Sigel 1989: x)

The absence of alternative theories and the implications of the political theory of political socialization led research to focus on childhood. The numerous studies of this period of political development uncovered basic and previously unknown information about the process, but ran into several difficulties. At first, large numbers of studies concentrated on uncovering the dynamics of children's attitudes towards authority (in keeping with the theory of diffuse support). However, questions were soon raised about whether children had attitudes at all. Vaillancourt (1973) found so much variability in children's responses over time that she questioned whether political attitudes were the appropriate level of childhood socialization analysis. Others had doubts too. Knutson (1974) suggested that rather than attitudes, 'pre-political ideologies' might be the appropriate unit of childhood analysis, while Renshon (1974) argued that analysis of children's 'basic beliefs' about the nature of the social and political world might prove productive.

But there was a more basic problem to be addressed. Meadow's panel study (Meadow 1982) suggested that even when one could reliably measure political attitudes in children there was evidence that these attitudes could change and develop. These changes were not related to the failure to develop and consolidate attitudes, as Vaillancourt had suggested was true for her younger panel sample, but rather because there was a dynamic relationship between the child's views and his/her understanding of and reaction to external political events.

The importance of this finding is that it underscores the fact that the *political* theory of political socialization put forward as the most important rationale for the field had paradoxically failed to take into account the importance of actual political events. These research findings further suggested that in addition to trying to find models which linked childhood learning with adult political activity, one would need to account, independent of that objective, for changes and development in childhood itself. This is still an area in need of exploration.

POLITICAL SOCIALIZATION: CONTROVERSY AND DEVELOPMENT

The general question of impact

At the core of the political socialization debate are questions about the impact of the process. Somewhat paradoxically, the same research has both established the existence for the political socialization process, and begun to uncover the extent and nature of its impact. Yet many more questions are raised about the latter than the former.

One must, at the beginning, distinguish between potential and actual impact. The fact that some children's books, for example, may contain 'anti-authority' messages (Cook 1983) does not in and of itself confer importance. Children may not read such books, or, if they do, they may remain unaffected by them. Thus the question of impact can only be answered by establishing some relational connection. Establishing this connection has frequently been approached through the analysis of correspondence, that is the extent to which various relational permutations (for example, parent–child, person–institution, etc.) correspond.

One can conceive of at least three possible levels of impact. The first, an individual level, would look for the impact of socialization on the development of a person's individual orientations. The second, the group/institutional level, would look to small aggregates of individuals to see how particular clusters of individuals developed politically. This level might also seek to tie such group development to the operation of specific contexts or aspects of institutional functioning. Lastly, we can examine the functioning of the polity itself for evidence of socialization effects.

As noted above (p. 443), the promise of political socialization for many political scientists was to be found in its ability to document a set of causal relationships between political socialization and systematic functioning. This has proved difficult to accomplish. Aside from difficulties in terminology, definition and operationalization of the main terms involved (for example, 'stability', 'persistence', etc.), the fundamental dilemma of linking the field's accomplishment to this particular requirement has been the daunting level-of-analysis problem. This problem is not unique to political socialization theory, but it is more central to its premises. The question, briefly put, is how can studies, most of which are done at the individual level of analysis, be aggregated to account for systemic effects?

Even when we examine some of the nationally representative samples that have been very influential and informative in political socialization, questions of systemic effects are not unambiguous. Himmelweit, for example, in discussing the Jennings and Niemi panel study points out that stability at the aggregate level may occur either 'because people's views haven't changed or because people's views have changed but in different ways with the result that changes at the aggregate level cancel each other out' (Himmelweit 1983: 247). And of course, the empirical determination of stability and change in a sample is not necessarily synonymous with the use of these terms to characterize the operation of political systems.

Problems in this area have proved difficult given that a majority of studies in the field are neither nationally representative nor designed as panel studies. Inference in these cases therefore becomes tricky. Do we simply sum up the results of the survey or other research findings and generalize them across the whole system? Is there some kind of step level, or critical mass function, which will accelerate the effects we uncover? Is the impact of the various dynamics uncovered interactive? And what is to be done with issues of individual and collective change over time, and in response to changes in circumstance? Simply to state these questions underscores the enormous complexity of the problems involved. That these problems have not been solved by political socialization is not surprising. Other areas of social science inquiry have fared no better.

One by-product of the attempt to forge aggregate linkages has been that less attention has been paid to making individual or 'mid-range' (Merton 1968) linkages. These are effects that might be felt at the institutional level, without necessarily having dramatic effects on the overall functioning of the system. For example, a rise in the level of sceptical reactions to political leaders after political experiences like Watergate might lead to an emphasis on 'honesty' and 'integrity' as campaign themes. This, in turn, might even result in somewhat more actual political behaviour of this kind. However, it is probably too much to require of socialization theory that in order to prove its worth all or most political leaders must become dramatically more honest in response to more sceptical socialization. Would the effect of greater honesty be less of an impact than a step-level change in the behaviour of all political office-holders? Of course. Is there no discernible or important socialization effect in this example because the latter has not occurred? I think not.

Finally, in addition to the aggregate and institutional level of political socialization effects, there is the impact of socialization on individuals. Of course, discussions of impact at both the societal and institutional level assume individual-level impact. But it is at this level of analysis that research documenting the effects of political socialization is the most substantial and convincing.

Research demonstrating individual-level effects has actually proceeded along two tracks. The first is simply the basic documentation of the fact that children do have a wide range of political orientations. This fact, first demonstrated in the early studies of Greenstein (1960), Hess and Easton (1960) and others, is now taken for granted, but its implications are important and worth pausing a moment to consider. If children as young as four and five have the beginnings of political understandings (however much they may evolve) and if these understandings are not innate, then a strong logical case has been made for the reality of political learning. This is important because whatever debates there are in the field, and there are many (who learns what, how, when, under what circumstances and to what degree), there is empirical evidence that there is something to explain.

The empirical demonstration that political learning exists, as important as it is, is but a first step. The next steps are to gain an appreciation of the areas affected by the process as well as to understand the nature of the process itself. In the first of these two areas, especially, the empirical demonstration of effects in a variety of areas and contexts has been significant. For example, there is by now a large body of evidence to support the proposition that parents do have an impact on the political views of their children (Jennings and Niemi 1968; Cundy 1982), an indication of impact being a correlation between the political orientations of different family members when these orientations are independently sampled. But these are not the only kinds of studies that have documented individual-level impact. Chapman (1987), studying a sample of women candidates for political office in Scotland, found that having been part of a women's group was the strongest and best predictor of these candidates' political orientations. Using a causal model she concludes that 'there is no doubt that the effect we are measuring is that of experience on consciousness, and not the other way around' (Chapman 1987: 323).

Finally, Zaslavsky and an unnamed (for reasons of personal safety) colleague (Zaslavsky and Z. 1980) studied Soviet workers' support for their country's invasion of Czechoslovakia. They found that workers in 'closed enterprises' (industries that produce something deemed strategically important by the government) were much more likely to support the invasion than those who worked in relatively 'open' industries. Related to workers in 'closed' industries were party membership, past military service, higher pay and special status. They interpreted their findings in terms of 'embeddedness' in the regime, a concept which is consonant with the cumulative effects model of socialization that we will discuss later (see page 459).

Overall, these and numerous other empirical studies have documented the

existence of socialization effects. However, these effects have been more effectively documented at the individual and group/institutional levels. Documented
effects at the social level remain largely inferential.

Specification: the maturing of political socialization models

It may well be one hallmark of social science fields that in the beginning they
put forward rather global and relatively undifferentiated theories and models.
These may take the form of general if–then propositions, inference from
smaller studies to larger effects, or simply a set of models which purport to
describe general processes but which in hindsight and on the basis of accumulated research experience are shown to be much more complex and differentiated than originally thought.

Specification, then, is a process by which these original formulations of a
field are modified on the basis of research findings. To the sceptical, such a
process looks as if the original formulations have been found wanting (they
have), and that therefore the whole enterprise is suspect. A different view is
put forward here. Specification of process to take account of context, individual
and developmental differences, and so on, represents a maturing of social/
political theory, not its demise. We will illustrate this process in political
socialization theory in this section by looking more closely at the question of
impact and the models which have been developed to account for it. We begin
with an examination of the question of the persistence of socialization effects
over time.

The necessity to develop models of persistence stem from the logical
requirements imposed by systems theory and the fact that politics is most
frequently the province of adults. Some have put the matter forcefully. Dowse
argues, for example, that political socialization research 'makes sense *only* if
the child is father to the man' (Dowse 1978: 403). Still, it is true that, while
children's political learning may be of interest in and of itself, it becomes more
important for research and analysis if it can be shown to influence or shape
adult political behaviour (not necessarily the operation of the political system)
in some ways. Therefore, the effects of socialization must be found not only
to originate early in the life cycle, but to persist in some form over it.

These requirements are the basis of two of the most well-known models of
impact in the literature: the primacy principle (Searing *et al.* 1976) and the
structuring principle (Searing *et al.* 1973). Taken together, these principles
suggest: (a) that crucial political learning takes place in childhood; (b) that this
early learning is a filter (structures) through which subsequent political learning
passes; and (c) that these crucial behaviours, acquired in childhood, persist
into adulthood to influence adult political behaviour. These are basic principles

which Searing and his colleagues note 'everyone subscribes to . . . in varying degrees' (Searing *et al.* 1973: 415).

As noted, political socialization research has found pervasive evidence that assumption (a) is correct. Children do begin to develop political attitudes, political information and policy opinions, identifications with political parties, pre-political ideologies, basic beliefs, and so on. But whether and to what degree these orientations structure subsequent learning and persist through time are other matters.

The fate of these two principles suggest the ways that failures to substantiate early, generally formulated theoretical assumptions can lead to developments in theory specification. Consider in this regard one empirical test of the structuring principle. Searing and his colleagues tested the structuring hypothesis with cohort data by seeing whether political attitudes acquired in childhood could predict later political opinions. They did not. From this they conclude 'that the primacy principle is surely overstated' (Searing *et al.* 1976: 94). In this they are no doubt correct. But on the other hand does 'approval of police officers', or 'approval of conservatives' constitute the basic orientations discussed in the literature? And is there some compelling reason why approval of police officers should be correlated with an individual's position on admission of China into the United Nations (Searing *et al.* 1973: 423)?

The emphasis on attitudes is one that political scientists find particularly comfortable and has been the basis for much early work in political socialization. Even Hess and Torney (1969), who argue that the main product of early socialization is a generalized attachment to the political system, state their case in terms of attitudes. But why should we expect attitudes to be the key element of what is learned in childhood? It makes much more intuitive sense, and appears to fit better with the findings of political learning, to suggest that more global beliefs (Knutson's 'pre-political ideologies' (1974) or Renshon's 'basic beliefs' (1974) for example) would be the building blocks of subsequent political orientations. And if 'ideology', with its implications of a coherent, interrelated system of beliefs, appears too cognitively and developmentally advanced, one could begin to use the concept of 'schema', to address questions raised by the primacy and structuring principles (Peterson and Somit 1981–2: 325–6).

In some respects, however, the concept of structuring does not go directly to the heart of the question at the core of political socialization's research premises, that of persistence itself. If what is learned during childhood does not persist to shape adult politics, a basic premiss of the field has proved untenable. Yet, for a concept so central to the field's rationale and development, early models of persistence were surprisingly general in their formulation.

Early political learning was simply expected to persist relatively unchanged through adulthood. In this form the theory is relatively undifferentiated. It does not specify exactly which orientations learned in childhood are expected to persist and which are not. Nor does it go very far in distinguishing the many possible meanings of persistence: it is possible that orientations may persist in most important respects, but not remain static. Sears, for example, suggests such a possibility in his review of some data on the transmission of racism from fathers to sons. He cites evidence that suggests that 'a latent racism had been passed on and retained over the years, but was manifested in different forms' (Sears 1990: 84).

In retrospect, the model of 'unchanging persistence' was a theoretically naïve expectation, and the fact that it has not fully held up should come as no great surprise. One source of this expectation can be traced to a selective reading of psychoanalytic theory. In that theory, unconscious childhood conflicts were theorized to persist relatively unchanged into adulthood, resulting in wide ranges of adult behaviour.

The only problem with borrowing this formulation is that unconscious conflicts are not a suitable model of political orientations. Most of the latter, unlike the former, are conscious, relatively unconflicted, and clearly responsive to changes in individual development and situational dynamics. The 'repetition compulsion' familiar to psychoanalysts hardly describes the evolution of the child's political world in which cognitive development, modelling and learning from experience (to name just three mechanisms of political learning and change) are the rule, not the exception.

Not unexpectedly, findings that political learning and development take place throughout the life cycle have forced the refinement of this theory. Connell (1971) interviewed 119 children aged from five to sixteen in Australia and found that between ages five and seven is a period of 'intuitive thinking' about politics, with children moving somewhat freely between political fact and fantasy. Between seven and nine a stage of primitive realism develops, between nine and twelve the children actually begin to construct their political world; and between twelve and sixteen they become able to engage in abstract political thought. Based on these findings, Connell argues that the political world of the young child is too much in a process of development to expect that it will 'persist' through adulthood.

Moore and his colleagues (Moore *et al.* 1985) reported the results of a longitudinal study of American children. They began their study with children in kindergarten and then reinterviewed them every year up until the fourth grade and reported their results. The authors demonstrated clearly that children do develop their political views over time. Indeed, they found evidence of a clear cognitive progression of children's political understanding, as suggested by Piaget's general model. Yet they did not find evidence for some of that theory's general hypotheses regarding children's thinking, namely that they are unable to think abstractly before about the fourth grade.

In Britain, Himmelweit *et al.* (1981) reported the results of an extended panel study begun with a group of men in 1951 when they were 13–14 years old, and then reinterviewed again in 1962, 1964, 1966, 1970 and 1974. That study was centred around voting, but also collected enormous amounts of data about a variety of political and social views. They found 'many of the attitudes to be remarkably stable over the eight-year period', but surprisingly this did not extend to the act of voting. Of interest to us here is that only 31 per cent of the sample voted the same way on all six occasions (Himmelweit 1983: 241). Himmelweit's model of socialization and voting preference gives more weight to situational determinants of such choice, a view in keeping with political learning as having an important situationally specific dimension.

Finally, Jennings and Marcus (1984) analysed the results of a three-wave panel study conducted in the years 1965, 1973 and 1982 and focused on party identification and electoral choice. They found much more variability in the younger cohorts compared to their parents, yet, in the years between 1973 and 1982 partisan stability among the younger group increased dramatically. Jennings and Marcus put forward 'a political experience' model in which as a person gathers political experience his/her political orientations tend to crystallize.

These and other studies have all documented what appears to be a fundamental fact of the socialization process, variability *within* and *across* stages of development. This leads to a view of the political socialization process as 'development in progress'. The rule at each stage of development and for each set of orientations seems to be 'incompleteness', rather than completion. No agency, or set of agencies, has been documented in the USA or any other country (including authoritarian regimes) to fully form or shape political orientations.

These findings raise a more general issue concerning the need to develop models which explain change and development, and not just correspondence. It is therefore one sign of theoretical development in political socialization that continuing questions about undifferentiated theories of impact have prompted a whole new generation of models. Sears (1990), for example, recently discussed three new models of persistence, which he compares with the traditional mode which asserts that 'the residues of early socialization are relatively immune to change in latter years'. One new model is the *life-long openness* model, which asserts that 'age is irrelevant for attitude change'; a second model, the *life-cycle* view, suggests that 'persons are particularly susceptible to adapting particular dispositions at certain life stages'; and a third model, the *impressionable years* model, suggest that 'any dispositions are unusually vulnerable in late adolescence and early adulthood given strong enough pressure to change' (ibid.: 77).

The importance of these models may ultimately be not in their mutually exclusive accuracy, but in their attempts to come to grips with the problems of persistence and change in the political socialization process. Even these 'second generation' models contain some ambiguities, which suggest the need for further specification. Sapiro, for example, in reviewing these models, finds some ambiguity in the use of the term 'life-cycle' (Sapiro 1990: 4). She points out that this term may have two different (but not necessarily unrelated) meanings, with different implications for studies of persistence and change: one would imply that change is a natural consequence of ageing itself; the other that it is a consequence of socially constructed 'expected' life events. A question that arises given this differentiation is what specific kinds of orientations are expected to change in each model.

Other models of persistence and impact have been put forward. One of the best of these is the 'cumulative effects' model put forward by Langton (1984). Langton reanalysed the Almond–Verba five-nation study and also presented data of his own from a random sample of interviews with 494 workers in the central Andes in Peru. His strategy was to assess the impact of family, school and jobs, not to see which contributes most to socialization but to see what effects continuity and discontinuity of experience had on the development of particular political orientations like political efficacy.

Not surprisingly perhaps, he found that similar experiences in home, school and work tended to have a cumulative effect. That is, growing up in a non-repressive family, and then attending a school which encouraged participation, and then going into a job in which independence was valued tended to result in individuals having the highest levels of political confidence. When respondents were reared in a repressive home (associated with low political efficacy), but then went on to a school setting which encouraged efficacy, their efficacy scores increased by 17 points. However, when this same group was then subjected to a repressive work environment, their efficacy scores plunged 35 points.

New models alone, however, while crucial to the field's continuing development, will not fully address the needs of political socialization theory and research by themselves. There must be new data too. This is said with the knowledge that the behavioural movement in political science has been criticized for its emphasis on data collection, measurement and statistical analysis. This movement has also been criticized for being ahistorical, non-contextual, and too concerned with drawing generalized 'laws' from data and subjects which do not support that pursuit.

Many of these concerns, especially as evidenced in the early years of the behavioural movement, have some validity. On the other hand, a concern with the representativeness and generalizability of results, asking questions in a systematic way, and a concern with uncovering and explaining patterns of behaviour would seem to be no drawback for the development of the field of political socialization. This would appear to be as true for case studies as it is for more traditional survey designs.

459

Just what well-designed studies can do to refine the theories of the field can be seen in the landmark University of Michigan socialization studies conducted by Jennings and his colleagues (Jennings and Niemi 1968). They drew a representative sample of high school seniors and one or another of the adolescents' parents who completed an interview schedule in 1965. Eight years later 81 per cent of the students and 76 per cent of the parents who were originally interviewed were re-interviewed. That study and the analyses drawn from it are a prime example of the way in which second generation research studies facilitate the specification of relationships originally framed in a general, relatively undifferentiated way. Consider, for example, the effects of the family on the transmission of political orientations. The family has long been regarded as the most important agency for transmitting political orientations (Hyman 1959: 69) by many theorists in the area, but the Jennings and Niemi (1968) study was able to test not only *if*, but *when* it was the case.

Jennings and Niemi analysed parent–child correspondence in several areas including party identification, four political issues, and the sense of political cynicism. Briefly, the strongest correspondence they found was in the area of party identification ($\tau - b = 0.47$), although there were some indications of a decline in such identifications. On the policy issues, Jennings and Niemi found only moderate overlap in parent–child views, and they did not find much overlap on feelings towards certain political groups in the country (for example, labour unions, negroes, big business, etc.). Finally, on the political cynicism measure, the parent sample was much more cynical than the high school senior sample.

Next, Jennings and Niemi (1968) examined the impact of several factors that might influence the transmission process. They examined the effects of parent–student sex combinations (mother–daughter, father–son, etc.), feelings of closeness among family members, power and authority relationships in the family, and the level of family politicization. Most of these factors had only modest effects on the degree of correspondence, but the level of family politic-ization did affect the degree of correspondence in the cases of party identifi-cation and political cynicism (Jennings and Niemi 1968: 182).

Jennings and Niemi sum up their findings by observing that 'any model of socialization which rests on assumptions of pervasive currents of parent-to-child value transmissions of the types examined here, is in serious need of modification' (Jennings and Niemi 1968: 183) And that is precisely the point. The Jennings–Niemi study is a good representative example of the ways in which theories can be specified for particular factors within a given context.

It is important to keep in mind that Jennings and Niemi did not examine the kinds of basic orientations and consensual attachments to the political system (support of the regime, political institutions, etc.) that others like Hess and Torney (1969) had argued were the foundation of the family's influence. Nor did they examine the more basic political/psychological/philosophical frameworks (for example, 'pre-political ideologies', 'basic beliefs', etc.) that others have suggested are an important area of family impact. Their study assumed that these attachments were in place (Jennings and Niemi 1968: 172).

Even leaving aside these matters, did the Jennings and Niemi study negate the role of the family in the political socialization process? Not really; it specified it. Does the fact that the family appears to have a more limited role in the transmission of some political orientations than previously thought call into question the existence or impact of socialization processes? No, but it does point researchers toward other factors and time frames needed to specify further what gets acquired when.

Carefully drawn studies can not only be used to specify theoretical relation-ships but can also help in making comparative assessments of different theoretical approaches to the same phenomenon. A longitudinal study by Moore *et al.* (1985), begun with children in kindergarten and extending four years, was designed to assess the explanatory power of social learning and cognitive development theories. They found that although social learning theory could explain knowledge acquisition (recognition of political symbols, understanding policy issues, etc.), a capacity to move from concrete to abstract thinking was also involved. Thus the findings here seem to support the idea of theoretical complimentarity, at least as far as mechanisms of early childhood political learning are concerned.

Another exemplar of this possibility is the Jennings and Niemi study described above (p. 460). In addition to the parent–child interviews (panels) conducted in 1965 and 1973, they also collected data from a sample of all senior classes in 97 schools in both 1965 and 1973. This data set therefore consists of three panels (i.e. the parent's panel, the youth panel, and the 1965 and 1973 senior classes), which combine both cross-sectional and longitudinal designs. With this vast array of data, Jennings and Niemi (1981) were able to distinguish empirically between life-cycle effects (youth panel converges with parent panel, youth cohorts remain the same), life-cycle effects mixed with generational effects (youth panel converges with parent panel, youth cohorts diverge), and period effects (generations begin the same move congruently over time).

In reporting the results of the parent–child panel study described above, Jennings and Niemi also used the data specifically to address the persistence question. They found substantially more persistence in the adult panels than in the youth panels in both political and non-political domains. Yet overall they found that political orientations were far from stable for both groups, although there were differences in specific areas. This led them to favour the life-long openness model.

In sum, the hallmark of young fields and disciplines is unspecified theory, while field maturity is reflected in part by studies that can address comparative theoretical questions. There is an important relationship between theory and data: not only can data be used to test theory, but data can function to generate theory. Incompatible, anomalous findings are an important aspect of the search for sounder theory.

Political socialization: prescriptions and possibilities

This essay began with two general questions. First, has political socialization theory demonstrated the validity of its premises? Second, what is the status of the field's development and what are its prospects for the future? Let us turn briefly to summarize each before making some observations on future directions in the field.

The question of whether the field has demonstrated the validity of its premises rests, as noted, on a view of what these premises are. Two general positions have been advanced on this matter. One locates the importance of the field in demonstrating linkages between political learning and systemic functioning. The other, not unrelated position locates the importance of political socialization in its impact on the individual's political development.

It seems clear that the three decades of research in the area have conclusively demonstrated the validity of the fundamental political socialization axiom, namely the 'developmental hypothesis'. That is, there is political learning over time to be explained, and there is little doubt that theories of socialization impact have helped to explain them. There are now numerous studies tracing the development of a range of political orientations, attitudes, beliefs, feelings, values, policy positions, and so forth, most of which have tried to ascertain which factors are instrumental in shaping them. That there is not full agreement about the latter should not obscure the gains in understanding derived from the former.

The attempt to link political socialization with systemic functioning has proved more difficult for reasons already discussed. This linkage makes intuitive sense, and is probably accurate in the general sense, but the size and complexity of the political systems for which it is proposed are simply too large and complex for anything but inference. Having said this, it must be noted that there is more direct evidence and correspondingly less inference involved in seeing the effects of political learning on the functioning of particular aspects of the political system. The combination of period effects (Watergate, Vietnam, etc.) and life-cycle effects on political cynicism found in the Jennings and Niemi (1981) study, and the relationships of those sets of variables to political participation, suggest one way in which theories of political socialization can be plausibly linked to one aspect of systemic functioning. This is a more modest linkage than 'system persistence' or 'system continuity', but perhaps a more realistic one.

Questions about the current state of political socialization are subject to different interpretations. While there is evidence of a decline in the amount of published research, this does not, I think, reflect a decline of interest and intellectual vitality. On the contrary, the decline in published research may well reflect the field's success, not its failure.

There are several reasons to advance this view. First, many of the basic models and concepts of the field (for example, learning, development, etc.) have been incorporated into cognate research fields such as political behaviour (Sapiro 1990) and comparative political analysis (Arian 1989). Sapiro provides an illustration of this phenomenon in noting the dearth of political socialization and development studies which focus specifically on adults. She observes, however, that one can, 'develop a considerable bibliography of studies of partisanship, political behaviour and public opinion [which] considers "life-cycle" explanations for change or the impact of specifically adult experiences and settings on people's orientations and behaviour' (Sapiro 1990: 15). In other words, a measure of a field's development may be not only the number of studies published within a field but the degree of conceptual transfer of its ideas and theories to other arenas. This is a dimension which critics of the political socialization field have failed to consider.

Second, many of the concepts and models of political socialization have also been integrated into the mainstream of the various 'foundation disciplines', particularly political science. This can be seen by reading through the *American Political Science Review* and other major disciplinary journals, but it can be seen in its most dramatic form by noting the presidential address to the American Political Science Association in 1981 by Charles Lindblom, whose research and publications have not been in the field. In that address he noted that the question of political learning and political socialization was 'as important a question for political science as can be examined' (Lindblom 1982: 17). This is not a reflection on a field whose intellectual importance is in decline.

Additionally, political socialization continues to generate a steady stream of articles and books which are clearly and directly in the 'political socialization' domain. This is worth noting because it is one sign of the field's maturity that this domain has expanded over the past thirty years. Since the number of publications is only an indirect indicator of field vitality and development, it is worth commenting briefly on some of the new developments that these publications represent.

First, there has been a dramatic shift away from a focus on childhood to a concern with political socialization through the life cycle. This has been spurred by anomalous findings and also by the integration of 'newer' theories of adult development into political socialization research. This, in turn, has opened up new vistas of analysis.

One indication of this is the development of new and more refined models of impact, and its counterpart persistence. Political socialization now has a competing set of models in each of these important areas rather than the few relatively undifferentiated ones that characterized the early stages of the field's development. That these more differentiated theories have generated their own controversies may also be read as a sign of intellectual ferment (one possible reflection of vitality) rather than a lack of erudition.

The range of adult experience is much wider than those of most children. Thus, in addition to the familiar litany of childhood agents (for example, family, school, peers, media, etc.), there are whole new contexts to explore, such as the work environment (Lafferty 1989), military service (Lovell and Stiehm 1989), careers in politics (Renshon 1989, 1990) and international political administration (Peck 1979), experiences connected with movement politics (Morris *et al.* 1989), and immigration and acculturation (Lamare 1982).

The integration of theories of adult development into political socialization research has also been partially responsible for new efforts to collect data relevant to these theories. We have already noted the Himmelweit *et al.* (1981) and Jennings and Niemi (1968, 1981) studies, but there are others too. Whalen and Flacks (1989), Braungart and Braungart (1990a, b), Bermanzohn (1990), and Fendrich and Turner (1989) have all re-interviewed selected groups of political activists to chart the course of their political lives from early radicalism through adulthood.

In examining the developments of the last several decades, a word is also in order about the developing sophistication of the research designs and data analysis. I do not mean by this more and better statistical technique, but rather research which incorporates several different data gathering modalities, and which is designed to assess the comparative value of different socialization theories. As an example of the first, the Moore *et al.* panel study (1985) used a combination of open-ended and closed questions and gathered all the data in face-to-face interviews, thus bypassing the problems associated with the administration of closed-ended survey instruments to large groups of individuals. As an example of the second point, the Jennings and Niemi (1968, 1974, 1981) studies were designed to allow comparisons of different models of persistence and change.

Finally, in assessing the development of the field one must also note the introduction and examination of other models of psychological development and functioning. Social developmental models associated with Piaget, Kohlberg and others have received more attention over the past decade, and several recent books have directly addressed the contribution of these theories to political socialization (Rosenberg 1985; Rosenberg *et al.* 1988).

A somewhat newer development on the theoretical horizon is the application of other cognitive theories, most particularly those associated with schema analysis (Torney-Purta 1990) to political socialization theory. Schema analysis is addressed as much to the issue of how political understanding gets organized in individuals' minds as it is to the particular content involved (although the latter is important also). Schemata may be thought of as mental filing systems which are organized in both socially conventional and idiosyncratic ways.

Torney-Purta (1990: 113) notes that a major question at this point is how useful schemata will prove in helping to understand important aspects of political life. The structure of schemata may tell us something about how individuals organize their political world, and by what rules political experiences through the life cycle are assigned to different intra-psychic categories. This, in turn, may help to explain variations in response to similar political experiences. These would seem to be useful additions to knowledge about the political socialization process. Moreover, if schema theory does prove useful, questions of acquisition and development over the life cycle will come to the fore.

The develement and application of new models of individual functioning in political socialization theory, coupled with the refinement of the more 'traditional' models of the past, underscore an important point about the relationship of models to the phenomenon that the field of political socialization studies. One can argue that the increase in the number of new and old competing models in the field reflects either a state of robust intellectual vigour or a failure to fully test and discard those theories which do not pull their own explanatory weight.

Some recent criticisms of the field have appeared to adopt the second view. Cook (1985) argues that the decline (as he sees it) of political socialization is directly related to the 'misunderstood psychological theories'. While his critique of the 'invariant persistence' model is well taken, his suggestion that the field re-orient itself on the basis of Vygotsky's model of cognitive development is not likely to prove of decisive help. Rosenberg's call to reorient the field by fully developing a psychological approach, which he defines as a person's subjective understanding of the political world, runs the risk of equating and confounding socialization with perception (Rosenberg 1985: 725).

The problem with these calls for reorientation is not that political socialization would fail to benefit from further model development. Rather the problem is that given the complexity and diversity of the processes the field covers, no one model is likely to be decisive. Do children learn according to principles of social learning theory? Yes. Do children go through, in some form, the developmental stages that Piaget and others described? Yes. Is affectively charged political experience important in shaping political orientations both in childhood and adulthood? Yes. However, if the answers to all these, and similar questions that could be raised, is affirmative, then the road to further progress in the field will not lie in finding a single master theory of the process.

One of political socialization's needs is to develop *integrative* models. To give one example, individual-level theories of cognitive functions are presented as if affect and cognition are unrelated in actual practice. Given that feelings about leaders, for example, have come to be the single best predictors of voting choices, this would appear to be a serious omission indeed. So too, integration must also be maintained between sociologically oriented and psychologically oriented theories. Politics does not take place solely in the psyche, nor do many external political 'realities' go uninterpreted.

The question of political socialization's larger impact (for example, beyond individuals) remains an open and important question. Strategies of aggregated inference to make the case at the societal level have not proved productive. Perhaps an alternative may be found in the attempt to trace such aggregated impacts at a more local level, or in more clearly circumscribed institutional contexts.

Finally, a word about new areas of research for the field. We have already noted that adult development theories have opened up new areas for analysis, and these need not be repeated. However, the concern with *how* people think politically, as well as what they think, represents a promising avenue for development.

REFERENCES

Allen, G. (1989) 'Introduction' (Special topic: Children's political socialization and cognition), *Human Development* 32: 1–4.

Almond, G. and Verba, S. (1963) *The Civic Culture*, Princeton: Princeton University Press.

Arian, A. (1989) 'A people apart: coping with national security problems in Israel', *Journal of Conflict Resolution* 33: 605–31.

Atherton, F. C. (1975) 'Watergate and children's attitudes towards political authority revisited', *Political Science Quarterly* 90: 477–96.

Beck, P. A. (1977) 'The role of agents in political socialization', in S. A. Renshon (ed.) *Handbook of Political Socialization: Theory and Research*, New York: Free Press.

Bermanzohn, S. (1990) 'Survivors of the Greensboro massacre; ten years later', paper presented to the International Society for Political Psychology, Washington, DC.

Braungart, M. M. and Braungart, R. G. (1990a) 'The life course development of left- and right-wing youth activist leaders from the 1960s', *Political Psychology* 11: 243–82.

———(1990b) 'Studying political youth: a reply to Flacks', *Political Psychology* 11: 293–308.

Chaffe, S. H. (1977) 'Mass media in political socialization', in S. A. Renshon (ed.) *Handbook of Political Socialization: Theory and Research*, New York: Free Press.

Chapman, J. (1987) 'Political socialization and out-group politicization: an empirical study of consciousness-raising', *British Journal of Political Science* 17: 15–40.

Clausen, J. (ed.) (1968) *Socialization and Society*, Boston: Little, Brown & Co.

Cook, T. E. (1983) 'Another perspective on political authority in children's literature: the fallible leader in L. Frank Baum and Dr Seuss', *Western Political Quarterly* 36: 326–36.

——(1985) 'The bear market in political socialization and the costs of misunderstood theories', *American Political Science Review* 79: 1079–93.

——(1989) 'The psychological theory of political socialization and the political theory of child development: the dangers of normal science', *Human Behavior* 32: 24–34.

Connell, R. W. (1971) *The Child's Construction of Politics*, Carlton: Melbourne University Press.

Connell, R. W. and Goot, M. (1972–3) 'Science and ideology in American political socialization research', *Berkeley Journal of Sociology* 27: 323–33.

Crosby, T. L. (1984) 'Gladstone's decade of crisis: biography and the life course approach', *Journal of Political and Military Sociology* 12: 9–22.

Cummings, S. and Taebel, D. (1978–9) 'The economic socialization of children: a neo-Marxist analysis', *Social Problems* 26: 198–210.

Cundy, D. (1982) 'Parents and peers: dimensions of political influence', *Social Science Journal* 19: 13–23.

Dahl, R. (1961) 'The behavioral approach in political science: epitaph for a monument to a successful protest', *American Political Science Review* 55: 69–81.

Davies, J. C. (1977) 'Political socialization: from womb to childhood', in S. A. Renshon (ed.) *Handbook of Political Socialization: Theory and Research*, New York: Free Press.

Dennis, J. (1985) 'Foreword', in S. W. Moore, J. Lare and K. A. Wagner, *The Child's Political World: A Longitudinal Perspective*, New York: Praeger.

Dowse, R. (1978) 'Some doubts concerning the study of political socialization', *Political Studies* 26: 403–10.

Easton, D. (1965) *A Systems Analysis of Political Life*, New York: John Wiley.

Easton, D. and Dennis, J. (1969) *Children in the Political System*, New York: McGraw-Hill.

Erikson, E. E. (1950) *Childhood and Society*, New York: Norton.

Fendrich, J. M. and Turner, R. W. (1989) 'The transition from student politics to adult politics', *Social Forces* 67: 1049–57.

Gardner, H. (1987) *The Mind's New Science: The History of the Cognitive Revolution*, New York: Basic Books.

Gilligan, C. (1982) *In a Different Voice: Psychological Theory and Women's Development*, Cambridge, Mass.: Harvard University Press.

Greenberg, E. S. (1970) 'Children and government: a comparison across racial lines', *Midwest Journal of Political Science* 14: 249–79

Greenstein, F. I. (1960) 'The benevolent leader: children's images of political authority', *American Political Science Review* 54: 934–43.

——(1965) *Children and Politics*, New Haven: Yale University Press.

——(1967) *Personality and Politics*, New York: Markham.

——(1970) 'A note on the ambiguity of "political socialization": definitions, criticisms, and strategies of inquiry', *Journal of Politics* 32: 969–78.

——(1976) 'Item wording and other interaction effects on the measurement of political orientations', *American Journal of Political Science* 20: 773–9.

Greenstein, F. I. and Tarrow, S. (1970) *Political Orientations of Children: The Use of a Semi-projective Technique in Three Nations*, Sage Comparative Politics Series 1, pp. 479–558, Beverly Hills: Sage Publications.

Hess, R. D. and Easton, D. (1960) 'The child's changing image of the president', *Public Opinion Quarterly* 24: 632–44.

Hess, R. D. and Torney, J. (1969) *The Development of Political Attitudes in Children*, Chicago: Aldine.

Himmelweit, H. T. (1983) 'Political socialization', *International Social Science Journal* 35: 237–56.

Himmelweit, H. T., Humpreys, P., Jaeger, M. and Katz, M. (1981) *How Voters Decide*, London: Academic Press.

Hyman, H. (1959) *Political Socialization*, Glencoe, Ill.: Free Press.

Jaros, D., Hirsch, H. and Felron, F. J. (1968) 'The malevolent leader: political socialization in an American sub-culture', *American Political Science Review* 62: 564–75.

Jennings, M. K. and Niemi, R. G. (1968) 'The transmission of political values from parents to child', *American Political Science Review* 62: 169–84.

————(1981) *Generations and Politics*, Princeton: Princeton University Press.

————(1984) 'Partisan orientations over the long haul: results from a three-wave political socialization panel study', *American Political Science Review* 78: 1000–18.

Knutson, J. N. (1974) 'Pre-political ideologies: the basis for political learning', in R. Niemi (ed.) *The Politics of Future Citizens*, San Francisco: Jossey-Bass.

Lafferty, W. M. (1989) 'Work as a source of political learning among wage-laborers and lower level employees', in R. S. Sigel (ed.) *Political Learning in Adulthood*, Chicago: University of Chicago Press.

Langton, K. (1984) 'Persistence and change in political confidence over the life-span: embedding life-cycle socialization in context', *British Journal of Political Science* 14: 461–81.

Lasswell, H. D. (1930) *Psychopathology and Politics*, Chicago: University of Chicago Press.

Levinson, D. (1978) *The Seasons of a Man's Life*, New York: Knopf.

Lindblom, C. (1982) 'Another state of mind' (APSA presidential address, 1981), *American Political Science Review* 76: 9–21.

Lovell, J. P. and Stiehm, J. H. (1989) 'Military service and political socialization', in R. S. Sigel (ed.) *Political Learning in Adulthood*, Chicago: University of Chicago Press.

Maddox, W. S. and Handberg, R. (1979) 'Presidential effect and chauvinism among children', *American Journal of Political Science* 23: 426–33.

Meadow, R. G. (1982) 'Information and maturation in children's evaluation of government leadership during Watergate', *Western Political Quarterly* 35: 539–51.

Merelman, R. (1972) 'The adolescence of political socialization', *Sociology of Education* 45: 134–66.

————(1986) 'Revitalizing political socialization', in M. G. Hermann (ed.) *Political Psychology*, San Francisco: Jossey-Bass.

————(1989) 'Commentary' (Special topic: Children's political socialization and cognition), *Human Development* 32: 35–44.

Merton, R. K. (1968) *Social Theory and Social Structure*, New York: Free Press.

Moore, S. (1989) 'The need for a unified theory of political learning: lessons from a longitudinal project', *Human Development* 32: 5–13.

Moore, S., Lare, J. and Wagner, K. A. (1985) *The Child's Political World: A Longitudinal Perspective*, New York: Praeger.

Morris, A. D., Hatchett, S. J. and Brown, R. E. (1989) 'The civil rights movement and black political socialization', in R. S. Sigel (ed.) *Political Learning in Adulthood*, Chicago: University of Chicago Press.

Patrick, J. (1977) 'Political socialization and political education in schools', in S. A. Renshon (ed.) *Handbook of Political Socialization: Theory and Research*, New York: Free Press.

Piaget, J. (1965) *The Moral Development of the Child*, New York: Free Press.

Peck, R. (1979) 'Socialization of permanent representatives in the United Nations: some evidence', *International Organization* 33: 365–90.

Peterson, S. A. and Somit, A. (1981–2) 'Cognitive development and childhood political socialization: questions about the primacy principle', *American Behavioral Scientist* 25: 313–34.

Pye, L. (1968) *The Spirit of Chinese Politics*, Cambridge, Mass.: MIT Press.

Renshon, S. A. (1974) *Psychological Needs and Political Behavior: A Theory of Personality and Political Efficacy*, New York: Free Press.

——(1977) 'Assumptive frameworks in political socialization theory', in S. A. Renshon (ed.) *Handbook of Political Socialization: Theory and Research*, New York: Free Press.

——(1989) 'Psychological perspectives on theories of adult development and the political socialization of leaders', in R. S. Sigel (ed.) *Political Learning in Adulthood*, Chicago: University of Chicago Press.

——(1990) 'Educating political leaders in a democracy', in O. Ichilov (ed.) *Political Socialization, Citizenship Education and Democracy*, New York: Teachers College Press.

Rosenberg, S. W. (1985) 'Sociology, psychology and the study of political behavior: the case of research on political socialization', *Journal of Politics* 47: 715–31.

——(1988) *Reason, Ideology and Politics*, Princeton: Princeton University Press.

Rosenberg, S. W., Ward, D. and Chilton, S. (1988) *Political Reasoning and Cognition: A Piagetian View*, Durham, NC: Duke University Press.

Sapiro, V. (1990) 'What do we know about political socialization during adulthood?', paper prepared for delivery at the Annual Scientific Meeting of the International Society for Political Psychology, Washington, DC, July 11–14.

Searing, D. D., Schwartz, J. J. and Lind, A. B. (1973) 'The structuring principle: political socialization and belief systems', *American Political Science Review* 67: 415–32.

Searing, D. D., Wright, G. and Rabinowitz, G. (1976) 'The primacy principle: attitude change and political socialization', *British Journal of Political Science* 6: 83–113.

Sears, D. O. (1975) 'Political socialization', in F. I. Greenstein and N. Polsby (eds) *Handbook of Political Science*, vol. 4, Reading, Mass.: Addison-Wesley.

——(1990) 'Whither political socialization research: the question of persistence', in O. Ichilov (ed.) *Political Socialization, Citizenship Education and Democracy*, New York: Teachers College Press.

Sigel, R. (1965) 'Assumptions about the learning of political values', *Annals of the American Academy of Social and Political Science* 361: 1–9.

——(1977) 'Perspectives on adult political socialization: areas of research', in S. A. Renshon (ed.) *Handbook of Political Socialization: Theory and Research*, New York: Free Press.

——(ed.) (1989) *Political Learning in Adulthood: A Sourcebook of Theory and Research*, Chicago: University of Chicago Press.

Silbiger, S. (1977) 'Peers and political socialization', in S. A. Renshon (ed.) *Handbook of Political Socialization: Theory and Research*, New York: Free Press.

Sullivan, J. L. and Minns, D. R. (1976) 'The benevolent leader revisited: substantive finding or methodological artifact?', *American Journal of Political Science* 20: 673–772.

Torney-Purta, J. (1990) 'From attitudes and knowledge to schemata: expanding the outcomes of political socialization research', in O. Ichilov (ed.) *Political Socialization, Citizenship Education and Democracy*, New York: Teachers College Press.

Turiel, E. (1989) 'Commentary' (Special topic: Children's political socialization and cognition), *Human Development* 32: 45–64.

Vaillancourt, P. M. (1973) 'Stability of children's survey's responses', *Public Opinion Quarterly* 37: 373–87.

Whalen, J. and Flacks, R. (1989) *Beyond the Barricades: The Sixties Generation Grows Up*, Philadelphia: Temple University Press.

Wrong, D. (1961) 'The oversocialized concept of man in modern society', *American Sociological Review* 26: 183–93.

Zaslavsky, V. and Z. (1980) 'Adult political socialization in the USSR: a study of attitudes of Society workers to the invasion of Czechoslovakia', *Sociology* 15: 407–23.

FURTHER READING

Bilu, Y. (1989) 'The other as nightmare: the Israeli–Arab encounter as reflected in children's dreams in Israel and the West Bank', *Political Psychology* 10: 365–90.

Braungart, R. G. and Braungart, M. M. (1984) 'Life course and generational politics', special issue of *Journal of Political and Military Sociology* 12: 1–207.

Flacks, R. (1990) 'Social basis of activist identity: comment on Braungart article', *Political Psychology* 11: 283–92.

Ichilov, O. (ed.) (1990) *Political Socialization, Citizenship Education and Democracy*, New York: Teacher's College Press.

Kearney, R. N. (1984) 'The mentor in the commencement of a political career: the case of Subhas Chandra Bose and C. R. Das', *Journal of Political and Military Sociology* 12: 37–48.

Lamare, J. W. (1982) 'The political integration of Mexican-American children: a generational analysis', *International Migration Review* 16: 169–88.

Shernick, S. K. (1984) 'Politics and opportunity in the post-revolutionary generation: the cases of Nazi Germany, Stalinist USSR and Maoist China', *Journal of Political and Military Sociology* 12: 113–36.

Sidanius, J. and Lau, R. R. (1989) 'Political sophistication and political deviance: a matter of context', *Political Psychology* 10: 85–110.

Wagner, J. (1990) 'Rational constraint in mass beliefs systems: the role of developmental moral stages in the structure of political beliefs', *Political Psychology* 11: 147–76.

29

POLITICAL COMMUNICATION

DENIS MCQUAIL

Political institutions, from the most primitive to the most complex, cannot exist without communication, which is essential to the symbolic representation of authority and to competition for, and exercise of, power. The conduct of modern, democratic politics also depends on participation by citizens, for which extensive means of public communication are indispensable. Although all these fundamental matters cannot be fully dealt with here, we should be aware of the broad extent of the territory indicated by the term 'political communication'. There is also a historical dimension to the topic and particular importance attaches to the rise of the newspaper press.

This essay provides a brief overview of the most important issues relating to political communication, including: the centrality of the print media to the emergence of democratic politics; the relation of mass media to mass politics and propaganda; the influence of mass media on election campaigns and on the formation of public opinion; political communication as a means of 'tolerant repression'; and contemporary media policy issues (in effect, the politics of public communication). Finally, it will consider future trends both in research in this field and in political communication itself.

HISTORY

The newspaper was the chief instrument of political communication, as we now use the term, from the eighteenth until the mid-twentieth century. During this period, it served (however variably) as: a reporter of political events and the proceedings of political assemblies; a platform for the expression of political opinion; an instrument for party political organization and mobilization and for forging ideology; a weapon in inter-party conflict; a critic of and 'watchdog' on governmental actions; and an instrument of government for information and influence. These remain the essential political functions of the mass media to the present day.

The close interconnection between politics and the press largely accounts for the privileged position granted to the newspaper press in many constitutions and for the access often guaranteed to political parties and government in most public broadcasting systems. Representative of the protection given to the press (largely identifying freedom to publish with freedom of speech and assembly) are the First Amendment to the US Constitution which states that 'Congress shall make no law . . . abridging the freedom of the Press', or the (still valid) Article of the 1848 Dutch Constitution which states that 'no prior permission is required for publishing thoughts or views by way of the press, aside from everyone's responsibility before the law'.

The print media played a critical role during the Age of Enlightenment and in the subsequent popular revolutions in America (1776), France (1789), Central Europe (1848) and Russia (1917) in disseminating new ideas and providing organized political groups with the tools for gaining and holding onto power. Because of this historical legacy, political communication has generally been associated with the expression and diffusion of ideas (thus, ideologies) and also with conflicts: between rival contenders for office; between parties and ideologies; between government and opposition and government and people.

THE RISE OF MODERN COMMUNICATIONS MEDIA

While political communication is as old as politics, it was the organized use of the modern mass media for political ends, especially in the conduct of election campaigns, which first led to the development of systematic inquiry into political communication and has given the topic its main contemporary identification. However, political communication is more than just political campaigning. In the terms used by Seymour-Ure (1974), it has a *horizontal* as well as a *vertical* dimension. The former refers to communication between equals, whether these are members of the same political elite, or citizens who interact and assemble together. Vertical communication takes place between government (or parties) and people (in principle in either direction). The early emphasis on campaigns focused attention on the 'top-down' flow on the vertical dimension (from government or party to citizens and followers). This, however, led to the neglect of communication within elites and of interpersonal, informal communication. We should also take note of the flow of communication 'upwards', to the political 'top', in the form of voting 'feedback', opinion poll results, or other forms of intelligence gathering by politicians and governments.

Political communication thus refers to all processes of information (including facts, opinions, beliefs, etc.) transmission, exchange and search engaged in by participants in the course of institutionalized political activities. We can most usefully confine our attention to those activities which belong to the 'public sphere' of political life, a reference both to the content of open political debate and the 'arenas' where such debates occur. Such arenas comprise institutionally guaranteed social space, as much as locations set aside for political debate.

In practice, political communication covers the following:

1 activities directed towards the formation, mobilization and deployment of parties and similar political movements;
2 all forms of organized campaign designed to gain political support for a party, cause, policy or government, by influencing opinion and behaviour (and the course of elections);
3 many processes involving the expression, measurement, dissemination and also 'management' of public opinion (this includes informal, interpersonal discussion;
4 the activities of established mass media in reporting or commenting on political events;
5 processes of public information and debate related to political policies;
6 informal political socialization and the formation and maintenance of political consciousness.

MASS MEDIA AND MASS POLITICS

The study of political communication during the twentieth century, beyond the story of the rise of the political newspaper press, has been shaped by a trend towards 'mass politics', based on universal suffrage within large-scale bureaucratically organized societies (Mills 1955). This trend placed a premium on the capacity of political leaders to manage the direction of individual choice of large numbers of citizens, with whom ties are inevitably remote or superficial. Against this background, the central issues have concerned: the role and influence of a more commercialized mass press, especially in affecting the balance of power between an established 'bourgeois' government and any socialist or radical challenge; the question of 'propaganda' – the organized and massive use of all forms of modern communication by power holders to gain popular support; and the development of the scientifically, or professionally, planned election campaign using new means and techniques of communication and opinion measurement.

MASS MEDIA AND POLITICAL PARTIES

The first of these issues called for particular attention to changes in the relationships between press and political parties and to questions of ownership and monopoly of the means of communication. As Seymour-Ure (1974) points out, there are three main bases for a (political) relationship between a newspaper and a party:

1 organizational correspondence – the paper belongs to the party, and is designed to serve the ends of the party;

2 support for the goals of a party – a newspaper can decide to choose editorially to support a party and consistently advocate its policies; and

3 correspondence between readership and support for a given party – for reasons other than those named, a newspaper may happen to draw its readers from a class or social sector which predominately leans in a particular political direction, without a conscious political choice being made.

In the case of the organizational link, each of the other conditions is also likely to be met, but the three variables provide a key to examining the relationship of press to party from total symbiosis to complete independence.

The first condition (a newspaper actively supports the goals of a party) was a common feature of early newspapers in the United States and it was equally common in continental Europe, at least until the Second World War. It has greatly declined as a result of general trends towards: less ideological and more pragmatic forms of politics; more commercialization of the press (favouring neutrality or political balance in the interests of extending market coverage); the decline in competition and choice (monopoly papers tend to be less openly party-aligned); and increased professionalization of journalism, which has also favoured the objective and informative over the advocatory or propagandist role of the press. Press partisanship has also been under pressure from the rise of the more balanced, objective journalism practised (often as a matter of public policy) in broadcasting.

The question of concentration of ownership remains an issue, although for somewhat altered reasons. The original fear was that a large capitalist press concern (or several such) would throw its weight explicitly behind a political party of the right and use its dominance of circulation to influence opinion directly. Because of the trends affecting the press and because of changes in the modern corporation towards a diversified concern, often with multinational interests, it is now less common to find newspaper proprietors engaging actively in party politics. The rise of alternative channels of communication offered by radio and television has also diminished the fear of capitalist press monopoly. The present concern is more about general loss of diversity and about the 'depoliticization' and 'commercialization' of the press and broadcasting, leading to a reduction in the informative as well as propagandist potential of the press and the impoverishment of democratic life. Recent liberalization of broadcasting increases the chance of 'cross-media' ownership by large conglomerates. The trends described have also been said to favour a very consensual, 'mainstream' version of politics, to the detriment of marginal or radical voices and of forces for conflict and change.

474

PROPAGANDA

The modern study of political communication virtually began with the study of propaganda, especially as a response to the uses made of new means of communications (press and film) during and after the First World War to promote patriotism and other ideologies amongst national mass publics. The early equation of political communication with propaganda was reinforced by the example of the Soviet Union and Nazi Germany, both of which used their monopoly of control of mass media (now including radio) for their own different projects of social transformation.

Not surprisingly, the term 'propaganda' acquired a negative connotation. It was used to indicate a form of persuasive communication with the following features: the communication is for the purposes of the sender, rather than for the receiver, or for mutual benefit; it involves a high degree of control and management by the source; the purpose and sometimes the identity of the source is often concealed. In general, propaganda is strongly 'manipulative', one-directional and coercive (Jowett and O'Donnell 1987). In a modified and somewhat less pejorative meaning, the term propaganda still refers to direct communications from political parties by way of mass media designed to persuade or mobilize support.

Confidence in the irresistible power of mass media persuasion suffered at the hands of early empirical communication research in the 1940s and 1950s, which showed that individuals were able to resist persuasive messages the more these conflicted with existing opinion and the more such opinion was anchored in strong personal convictions or by the norms of the social group or reference group to which a person belonged. The concept of a 'two-step flow' of communication was proposed to refer to a typical process by which political messages often need to pass the test of a small minority of 'influentials' or 'opinion leaders', whose endorsement would help in achieving planned effects (Lazarsfeld et al. 1944).

ELECTION CAMPAIGN RESEARCH

The systematic study of election communication was itself made possible by advances in the techniques for measuring attitudes and opinion and methods of multivariate statistical analysis. However, such methods favoured inquiry into short-term effects on individuals and led to a neglect of other kinds of effect – on institutions and on long-term political change.

Despite the cautionary findings of empirical research on campaign effectiveness (it was very difficult to prove any direct effects of significance), political communication came, in the post-war period and especially after the rise of television, to be largely identified in many countries with the conduct of

475

intensive and expensive multi-media campaigns by parties and candidates in the run-up to elections. These campaigns were often modelled on commercial advertising and increasingly adopted the thinking and the methods appropriate to marketing products, seeking to establish and then 'sell' the 'images' of parties and leaders. Neither objections in principle to these strategies nor uncertainty about their efficacy were able to prevent this trend.

Several factors worked together to encourage increased reliance on mass media campaigns. One was the rise of television, which not only offered a convenient and efficient way of instantly reaching large numbers, but also soon became the only effective way, as party organizations and party-related press systems declined and as access to broadcasting became an institutionalized right in many political systems. Television also enjoyed an enormous reputation as a manipulative device, far in excess of any evidence, though its popularity was undeniable. Belief in the power of television had self-fulfilling consequences, since parties and politicians could not afford *not* to do their best by way of television, whatever its real efficacy. These consequences went beyond a direct use of the medium to address the public, leading to the detailed planning of campaign news and political events so as to maximize the chance of gaining attention and minimize unfavourable publicity. The term 'pseudo-event' was coined to refer to this artificial 'manufacture' of news.

Research into political communication campaigns has reminded us of the multiple uses and functions of the campaign for citizens as well as for politicians and parties. The media, also, have a strong self-interest in politics, since it is a major source of news events and the typical election campaign yields large amounts of news which helps to attract viewers, sell newspapers, and earn advertising revenue. For citizens, election campaigns offer several possible benefits: information with which to 'keep up' with events; a basis for making choices; reinforcement of beliefs; and an arcane form of spectator sport (Blumler and McQuail 1968). Politicians can choose between the roles of party standard-bearer, competitor for votes, informant and public performer.

POLITICAL EFFECTS OF TELEVISION

The rise of television as the most favoured medium of political communication (although it often follows the lead of the newspaper press and is much less politically free), in conjunction with other social changes, has had a number of wider, unintended results (although the causal connections can never be fully established). It has probably contributed to a greater centralization of politics, a decline in mass grassroots organization, a decrease in sharp partisan and ideological divisions (because television favours the political 'middle ground'), an increase in the use and influence of opinion polling to guide campaign planning and to monitor its success, and an increase in voter volatility as attachments are weaker and voting more swayed by current concerns and single issues.

It also seems to be the case that the relative power of those who control the 'gates' of the media in general has increased *vis-à-vis* that of politicians, as the centrality of mass media to political communication has increased. In the short term, politicians need access to the media more than the media need politicians, and the political role of media decision makers has increased and become more sensitive. Even governments and office holders are dependent on media attention, although their own power to control events and to claim access gives them a countervailing advantage.

One of the early expectations from television – that it would give a differential advantage to charismatic leaders or open the way to manipulation by way of personality and image making – has received little support from research or experience. Having a reputation as an attractive and effective television performer has gained in significance as a criterion for political advancement, but it has not replaced other, more crucial political qualities. There is no evidence of an increase in personal demagogy or emotional appeals. Nor is there much support for the view that television can invent and 'sell' qualities for which there is no basis in the reality of candidate or party. There is, all the same, a widespread belief that an effect of television has been in the direction of 'presidential style' politics. It may also be significant that national (and international) politics is still thought of in terms of individual personalities in an era of increased systematization and bureaucratization.

'MEDIA LOGIC' VERSUS 'PARTY LOGIC'

A corollary of the steadily increasing role of mass media in political affairs is the relatively greater weight attached to what has been referred to as 'media logic' (Altheide 1985), by contrast with 'political logic'. The term refers, most broadly, to the adoption of strategies of political action by contenders for office, which are influenced by considerations of getting favourable media attention, especially in news or other 'objective' formats. In more detail, it refers to paying close attention to the form, rather than substance, to presentation and packaging, rather than issues and policies. 'Media logic' may be followed by politicians or by the media themselves. It has been noted, for instance, that television coverage of modern election campaigns is inclined differentially to attend to personalities and human interest features, to the 'horse race' aspects of elections rather than the democratic choices at stake (Graber 1980).

Television, by comparison with older forms, has also been associated with a decline in the quality of political reasoning, with 'spot' advertising taking over from the argued case or the rhetorical appeal. There appears to be no way to consciously 'repoliticize' elections, except when and where history takes a hand and forces issues to the forefront. On the other hand, television itself has developed new formats which provide much solid political information, often in new forms, in addition to the efforts of party persuaders and their interventions in news. These forms include debates between party leaders, in-depth reporting and, most significant perhaps, the extension of television coverage to the continuing proceedings in parliaments and similar places otherwise largely closed to public view. It would be hard to sustain the view that television has in itself been a cause of a 'decline of politics'.

The salience of the mass media as the main gate and channel for reaching the mass public has led to the increasing use of strategies for gaining media attention by way of public demonstrations or dramatic actions, which the media tend to report because of their dramatic or intrinsic interest. The type of political act, whose primary objective is often to gain publicity, also extends to some acts of violence and terrorism – hijacking, hostage-taking and bombings, which often have communicative as well as military objectives.

POLITICAL INFORMATION VERSUS POLITICAL PERSUASION

Campaigns typically have multiple (and sometimes inconsistent) objectives: to inform about policy and proposal; to establish and modify party and leader 'images'; to identify a party with certain issues; to attract converts and waverers; to mobilize supporters. Despite the emphasis on persuasion and image making, the clearest evidence from research has been of informational learning. Two main features of campaign learning have been singled out by researchers. One of these has become known under the heading of 'agenda-setting'. This refers to the process whereby the volume of attention given to an issue in mass media (whether or not by design) tends to shape the public perception of what are the most salient issues of the moment. This perception, in turn, can be influential in the formation of opinion and of party or candidate preference (party stands on salient issues can influence the direction of voting). The logic is plausible, and it can be demonstrated that trends in attention to issues do follow the relative weight of media attention. However, because of the complexity of real-life politics and the limitations of research methods, the decisive source of the pattern of issue salience which emerges in a given case has never been clearly established. Is it the voting public (to whose concerns appeals are usually oriented)? Or the media (who also want to anticipate public concerns)? Or the politicians (who follow opinion as much as they lead it)?

A second concept that relates to political learning is that of the 'knowledge gap'. This refers to structured inequalities in knowledge (not only about politics) in a whole population, as a result of a differential growth in knowledge on the part of those who are rich in information resources (education, motiv-

478

ation, the means of being generally informed). The early development of democratic politics was accompanied by a necessary diffusion of basic political knowledge throughout a citizen body, newly enfranchised, aided by the mass newspaper press. The possibility has been canvassed that this process of levelling up (closing of the knowledge gap) has been halted or reversed as a result of several forces, but especially: the relative decline of the informational and political newspaper press in the face of the ever more popular and entertainment-oriented television medium and of the popular entertainment press; the increasing complexity of political information; and the decline in political participation (for instance low voting rates in US presidential elections) and in partisanship generally (for whatever reasons), leading to a detachment from the substance of politics. A minority of the population remains intensely involved and well informed, while a growing minority ceases to participate or to be easily reachable by mass political communication. In the light of such research evidence, there has been an increased interest in how well television news (now a principal source of political information) is understood and recalled by the mass audience (Robinson and Levy 1986). However, circumstances are continually changing, making assessment on such matters uncertain, particularly as television news becomes more oriented to entertainment, in response to sharper competition for the mass audience. Those developments in the range of formats available for political communication, noted above (pp. 473–7), are also relevant for assessment.

POLITICAL COMMUNICATION AS AN INTERACTIVE PROCESS

Research into the persuasive potential of political campaigns, although often inconclusive, has also established a number of generalizations about the probabilities and the conditions for the achievement of intended effects. Opinion and information changes are more likely to occur on 'distant' and newly emerging issues than on matters on which attitudes have already been informed. Monopoly control of the source or simply consonance and repetition of messages may also achieve results in a predictable direction. It is easier to reinforce existing support than to recruit new supporters by conversion. The status, attractiveness and credibility of the communicator do matter. Effects are easier to achieve in relation to separate facts and opinions than on deeper attitudes, outlooks, or world view. In general much more depends on the receivers – their dispositions, motivation, prior attitudes and knowledge – than on the message itself or the status of the source. As noted above, opinions are anchored in immediate social relationships, which to some degree 'protect' individuals from media influence.

An important development in political communication research was a closer attention to the motives of the audience, the possible uses and satisfactions of political communication and to the interactive nature of the process. Early models of persuasive communication, of the kind borrowed from advertising, identified the receiver as a passive target rather than as an active participant. This assumption was mistaken and especially misleading when applied to politics. It has become clear that actual and potential audiences for political communication vary considerably and have diverse motives and expectations, including the wish to be informed, re-activated, entertained, excited and advised (Blumler and McQuail 1968). Reception is also often accompanied by informal response and discussion. Audiences vary not only in the strength of motivation to engage in politics but also in their attitudes to politics itself, a minority being very negative to the whole process and resentful of 'propaganda'. Anticipating and taking account of such potential variations is largely beyond the ability of even the most astute and best-equipped campaigners, if only because the message can never be sufficiently controlled and diversified to reach the many possible target groups.

PUBLIC OPINION AND THE 'SPIRAL OF SILENCE'

As noted above, much also depends on the social and group context of reception. In this connection, an interesting theory of opinion formation has been advanced to account for the apparent growth of a dominant political consensus, largely as a result of the working of mass media. It was named the 'spiral of silence' theory by its originator (Noelle-Neumann 1984). Its main foundation is the idea that most people have a psychological need to avoid the isolation and discomfort of disagreement. Thus, under conditions where certain views seem, because of the unanimity and frequency of their public repetition (especially by way of mass media), to represent what the great majority think, or ought to think, then those who hold different views remain silent, whatever the actual strength and extent of such dissident opinion. The more they remain silent, the more the impression of dominance increases, and the fewer are those prepared to speak out, hence the 'spiralling' effect referred to. Under conditions where media are monopolistically controlled, this seems a plausible theory, although it should not have much application in normal, open democratic political life with a diversity of political sources.

There has been a continuing debate since the 1950s about how 'powerful' the mass media are in politics, as in other areas of social life. The continuation of uncertainty on the matter stems in part from the intrinsic methodological difficulties of delivering clear empirical evidence of powerful effects, especially those which involve long-term changes.

POLITICAL LINGUISTICS

The study of political communication is represented by traditions other than that of research into campaigns and public opinion. An alternative route has been by way of the study of language and rhetoric, which has concentrated on the uses of political symbols, and on the texts and documents of politics, rather than on the effects of these messages (Edelman 1977). One of the routes does, however, also lie in the study of political propaganda which was concerned with the manipulation of language as well as people. George Orwell's *Animal Farm* is an early, imaginative reflection on the devices by which language was misused and distorted to reverse the truth. All political movements and ideologies have sought, consciously or not, to establish usages of words and symbols that suit their own purposes. As one student of political language has remarked, 'Politics is largely a word game' (Graber 1981: 195).

Graber (1976) has made an inventory of the different 'functions' of political language, under five headings. Under the heading 'informational', she includes the giving of facts and also the invoking of connotations by the use of code words in such phrases as 'welfare state' or 'founding fathers'. Words and phrases in politics can carry inferences and symbolic meanings which help the purpose of the communicator. A second heading is that of 'agenda-setting', a process noted above (p. 478), in which a communicator tries to become identified with an issue. A third function of political language is that of 'interpretation and linkage', which refers to the construction and structuring of wider patterns of meaning and association. The two other categories are 'projection to past and future' (tradition and continuity) and 'action stimulation' (the 'mobilizing' and 'activating' function of language). Words (and pictures) can thus do many different things in politics – invoke associations, provide symbolic rewards, structure the context of debate, be a substitute for action as well as a means of action, and address themselves to numerous different receivers. This is a brief discussion of a complex field of enquiry which also includes the study of 'rhetoric' – or the art of speaking well, in the sense of effectively or persuasively.

CRITICAL THEORY

The study of political language has also been central in another tradition of political communication research, represented by critical or neo-Marxist theory and research. A left-critical version of the theory of mass society has viewed the mass media in general as (witting or unwitting) instruments of 'tolerant repression', spreading a conformist, consumerist ideology, culture and consciousness, which has stifled the growth of organized political opposition, especially amongst the working classes (Mills 1955: Marcuse 1964). This form of political theory has several variants, but in the stronger neo-Marxist versions the mass media have been seen either as willing propaganda tools in the interests of the ruling class, which usually owns or controls them, or as an 'ideological state apparatus' (Louis Althusser's term) which serves to maintain control. The concept of 'hegemony' was also coined by the Italian communist, Gramsci, to refer to the exercise of dominance over ideas exercised by a ruling class, using all means of communication available to it.

Some empirical evidence for such views has been provided (and not only by the critical theorists themselves) by the extensive analysis of the content of mass media, especially of news. The news media, whether in private or public hands, have appeared, more often than not, to carry the message of the reigning social consensus and to support the established political and social order by various means: by giving legitimacy and attention to established authority; by silence about problems and alternative solutions; by directing attention to scapegoats; by labelling opponents as extremists who challenge established order and, with it, the democratic system. While such theories have many critics, it is quite plausible to suppose that the broad tendency of established mass media is likely to be in support of the established political system and of the dominant consensus, especially since the mass media are integrated into the same system.

This tradition of critical theory and research has had several beneficial effects. It has helped draw attention to the underlying historical processes of political change, rather than concentrate on short-term campaigns viewed from the point of view of political persuaders. It has obliged us to pay attention to the wider context of political communication and the alternative perspectives and meanings that are embodied in communication practices and rituals. We are reminded that messages are not necessarily received ('decoded') as they are sent. In particular, it has forced a recognition of the fact that the mass media cannot simply be regarded as neutral transmitters of political values, culture and information, as if guided by some unseen, benevolent hand. The media are also, and always have been, instruments of politics.

MEDIA POLICY

The general political significance attributed to the mass media is evident from the universality of systems of regulations and the continuing active debates about media policy, however much governments in liberal democracies are supposed to keep their distance from the media and to guarantee independence of the press. Media policies take a wide variety of forms, varying especially along a dimension of degree of state control. Previous Soviet and Eastern European regimes placed all media under state supervision. In Western Europe, regulatory frameworks have been legally established to maintain strong, although democratic, supervision of radio and television, often by way of public monopolies. Even where these arrangements are being adapted in order to increase market freedom, policies have remained in force to guarantee some forms of public service. The most relevant political aims of regulation have usually been to secure diversity of expression and fair access to channels, to provide the means for governments and social institutions to reach citizens with information, and to protect national cultural and economic interests. These aims also often underlie policies of support for newspapers which are, otherwise, outside the public sector (Picard 1985). The growing economic significance of communication technology in national and global markets has added a new dimension to the politics of communication.

TRENDS IN RESEARCH

There have been a number of significant developments in political communication research since its early days, when it was largely a matter of studying propaganda, political campaigning and political socialization. First, there has been a move to recognize that political communication is not just one-way 'transportation' of information and beliefs, but a matter of interaction and transaction between sender and receiver. Second, there has gradually been less emphasis on the 'attitude' as object of influence or the key to understanding behaviour. Instead, there has been more attention to political 'cognitions' of several kinds – awareness of issues, formation of images based on information, connotations and associations. Third, there has been a trend to more 'holistic' investigations, looking at 'critical events' in the political life of a society which are played out over time and involve several different kinds of participant and not just the communicators and receivers (Chaffee 1977).

There has also been more appreciation of the 'ritual' aspects of public communication, such as election campaigns, which are not just rational means to some persuasive end, but symbolic expressions and celebrations of political beliefs and values. The ubiquity of political messages has also been more generally recognized. Initially, political communication was looked for almost exclusively in party or national propaganda. There has been a gradual recognition (by politicians themselves, as well as researchers) that one should look more to the *news* (especially on television) for potential political effects, because of its wide reach, high credibility and apparent impact. A further trend has been to look as well at fiction and drama (especially film and television) for the less overt, but no less potent, political messages of the day which reach the less politically involved.

THE FUTURE OF POLITICAL COMMUNICATION

Currently changing conditions of public communication seem to call for yet further revision of ideas. The trends of the time (not least because of the economic-industrial imperatives noted) are towards a multiplication of channels of all kinds, more choice for the 'consumer', less regulation and control, more commercialization of media systems. These changes offer more opportunities to individuals to find the information and ideas they like, but they may offer less benefit to established political sources (parties and politicians), who may find it harder to gain access to their chosen targets. Politics has to compete, in the same 'audience market', with more popular communication goods. The result may be a less well-informed political mass, and a widening gap between the active, involved and resourced minority and the majority detached from political institutions. On the other hand, the sheer amount of political communication shows every sign of increasing.

The international dimension of political communication should also be firmly on the agenda of political communication research. In recent times, international politics has increasingly come to be played out on the public stage of television and other media, especially on issues of 'terrorism', of peace, war and disarmament and in relation to changes taking place in the Soviet Union and Eastern Europe, as well as in the affairs of the European Community. Global power relations are closely reflected in differential ownership of, and access to, the means of international communication. These trends are unlikely to be a passing phase, since they result from the globalization of many political issues and the larger economic significance of communication. These developments have increased the political and public salience of issues concerning the development, ownership, control and regulation of media technologies and systems.

The future of political communication and the issues for research are closely linked to wider trends in society. It has been argued that we are entering a new type of society – the Information Society – in which information of all kinds becomes the key economic resource and where information work is the central economic activity. If so, we will be more concerned than before with the politics of communication and information, rather than with political communication as such. Access to information goods will form an increasing part of welfare and thus provide a more salient political issue. Meanwhile, the most pressing concerns (as for some time past) are likely to remain the maintenance of widespread and informed involvement in political life. This will require continued attention to securing favourable conditions of access for political communicators and 'rights to communicate', in the widest sense, for citizens.

REFERENCES

Altheide, D. L. (1985) *Media Power*, Newbury Park, Calif.: Sage Publications.

Blumler, J. G. and McQuail, D. (1968) *Television and Politics: Its Uses and Influence*, London: Faber & Faber.

Chaffee, S. (ed.) (1977) *Political Communication*, Beverly Hills: Sage Publications.

Edelman, M. (1977) *Political Language: Words that Succeed and Policies that Fail*, New York: Academic Press, 1977.

Graber, D. A. (1976) *Verbal Behaviour and Politics*, Urbana, Ill.: University of Illinois Press.

——(1980) *Mass Media and American Politics*, Washington, DC: Congressional Quarterly Press.

——(1981) 'Political language', in D. Nimmo and K. Sanders (eds) *Handbook of Political Communication*, Beverly Hills: Sage Publications.

Jowett, G. S. and O'Donnell, V. (1987) *Propaganda and Persuasion*, Newbury Park, Calif.: Sage Publications.

Lazarsfeld, P. F., Berelson, B. and Gaudet, H. (1944) *The People's Choice*, New York: Columbia University Press.

Marcuse, M. (1964) *One Dimensional Man*, London: Sphere Books.

Mills, C. W. (1955) *The Power Elite*, New York: Oxford University Press.

Noelle-Neumann, E. (1984) *The Spiral of Silence*, Chicago: University of Chicago Press.

Picard, R. (1985) *The Press and the Decline of Democracy*, Westport, Conn.: Greenwood Press.

Robinson, J. and Levy, M. (1986) *The Main Source*, Beverly Hills: Sage Publications.

Seymour-Ure, C. (1974) *The Political Impact of Mass Media*, London: Constable.

FURTHER READING

Ferguson, M. (ed) (1990) *Public Communication: The New Imperatives*, London: Sage Publications.

Glasgow Media Research Group (1980) *More Bad News*, London: Routledge.

Gouldner, A. (1976) *The Dialectic of Ideology and Technology*, London: Macmillan.

Kraus, S. and Davis, D. (1976) *The Effects of Mass Communication on Political Behavior*, University Park, Pa., and London: Pennsylvania University Press

Lang, K. and Lang, G. E. (1968) *Politics and Television*, Chicago: Quadrangle Books.

Murdock, G. and Golding, P. (eds) (1986) *Communicating Politics*, Leicester: Leicester University Press.

Nimmo, D. D. and Sanders, K. (eds) (1981) *Handbook of Political Communication*, Beverly Hills: Sage Publications.

Paletz, D. and Entman, R. (1981) *Media, Power, Politics*, New York: Free Press.

30

RECRUITMENT OF ELITES

JOHN NAGLE

ELITE THEORY AND DEMOCRATIC THEORY

The study of elite recruitment has had a long and chequered history. In part this derives from its association with modern elite theory as developed since the middle of the nineteenth century. Any theory of political elites immediately touches on a critical point in every system of government, namely the question: who rules? The focus on elites has often tended towards either justification of processes which select certain people for leadership, or challenge to the legitimacy of those same processes. The history of elite analysis is complicated by the fact that elite theory has largely been associated with Gaetano Mosca, Vilfredo Pareto and Robert Michels. In their works on elite recruitment and elite circulation these authors sought to justify the authority of rulers and to question the basis for democratic government as it was developing in Europe towards the end of the nineteenth century (Nye 1977). In their view, all societies are sharply divided into rulers and masses. Ruling elites are recruited in a self-perpetuating manner from the higher strata of society, are autonomous in their exercise of power, and control the masses through superior political skills and organization. While professing scientific grounding, their works were in fact driven by a political agenda which opposed the rise of the universal franchise, and which feared that extension of voting rights to the masses, to ordinary workers and peasants, would threaten the just authority of political leaders, and, worse still, would also open the door to socialism. Michels, a German disciple of Mosca and in his early years a syndicalist, later accepted a professorship at the University of Turin and ended his career as a scholarly supporter of Mussolini and Italian fascism. Pareto also judged fascism as a positive development in Italy. Mosca, a political liberal, none the less opposed the extension of voting rights to ordinary workers and peasants, which in his view would be lowering standards and dangerously flirting with the possibility of socialism through manipulation of the proletariat. While Sereno (1968: 29) has argued that Mosca expressed opposition to Mussolini's fascism, Nye (1977: 20) points out that Mosca, like many other liberals of his time, was more fearful of the left, and thus accepted the fascist regime as necessary although not measuring up to preferred bourgeois standards. Mosca's commitment to liberalism, as was the case with many German, Italian and French liberals of the time, did not preclude opposition to parliamentary democracy with universal adult voting rights. Indeed, in the inter-war years, many liberal intellectuals turned their backs on embattled democratic parties and parliaments, and became supporters, perhaps reluctantly, of anti-democratic movements and governments. Common to these elite theorists is their opposition to the further evolution of parliament beyond middle-class participation, their distrust of ordinary workers and peasants as potential voters and citizens, and their abiding fear of socialism in any form. This orientation was part of the more general disdain, characteristic of both liberal and conservative intellectual thought, for notions of popular sovereignty. While this antipathy pre-dated the First World War and the Great Depression, it also linked the crisis of democracy with the need for a stronger, and more aggressively anti-socialist, political authority. This was, of course, a period in which parliamentary leaders, especially in Italy and Weimar Germany, but also in France and Great Britain, were often seen as failures, both in military and in economic affairs. The Weimar democracy was from the start saddled with the acceptance of the Versailles Treaty, and was later associated with the Great Depression. The Italian parliamentary system was blamed for Italy's humiliations both during and at the end of the First World War and was seen as riddled with corruption and political intrigue. It is this association of elite theory and the leading elite theorists with the fascist challenge to parliamentary democracy as the dominant political system-type of Western Europe which stigmatized this field and which has generated an ongoing conflict on the purposes of elite studies. On the left, there is suspicion that contemporary elite theorists have an unspoken agenda of minimizing or even thwarting popular democracy and effective citizen participation. On the right, there is the tendency to see critics of elite theory as proponents of social upheaval or as unscientific political activists. Much of this conflict has little to do with the theoretical potential of elite research, but has a close relationship with the actual political history of the field and its practitioners.

With the rise of fascism and bolshevism in Europe in the inter-war period, some scholars committed to the values of liberalism *and* democracy began to search for ways to combine the insights of elite theory with the basic requirements of democratic theory. Joseph Schumpeter (1942) was one of the leading pioneers in attempting to create a more realistic, or empirical, theory of democracy which could utilize the lessons of elite theory without abandoning political democracy as either impossible or ineffectual. Schumpeter's work borrows from elite theory the notion that even in a democracy elites must rule;

the question is how to structure the selection of political leadership according to democratic procedures that result in an effective and stable governing elite. A main problem for Schumpeter is the avoidance of mass movements led by anti-system elites (fascists or communists) in societies which are increasingly 'mass societies'. The concept of 'mass society' in the development of realist democratic theory is heavily influenced by the notions of elite theory, in which the popular masses are seen as basically unreliable supports for democratic values, and in critical situations prone to anti-system mobilization by extremist movements of the right or left. Kornhauser (1959), Riesman et al., (1950), and Adorno et al. (1950) stress the authoritarianism of the working and lower middle classes, the mass dependence on leaders, and the manipulability of mass psychology for political upheaval. A realistic democratic theory must depend on 'responsible' political elites to constrain popular choice to system-supportive competition among contending leadership groupings. There must be an overarching elite consensus on upholding the democratic framework which implies a self-imposed limitation on mobilizing popular masses for political gain, and filtering out popular demagogues who threaten to utilize mass 'prejudices' in the political process. As classic elite theory argued, elites must uphold the proper standards and must insulate elite recruitment from mass influences. Only in this way can democratic elites survive crisis points and ensure their own survival as leaders of democratic systems. A 'realistic' theory of democracy must revise the classic ideals of citizen participation in political decision making by limiting the roles of ordinary citizens and expanding the roles to be played by elites (Burnham 1941: 202; Schumpeter 1942: 263). By borrowing from elite theory, the 'realists' hoped to rescue democratic theory from itself and from its own too lofty ideals which did not correspond to empirical reality. Elite theorists, especially Mosca (Pareto and Michels somewhat less so), were rehabilitated from 'misconceptions' about their anti-democratic intentions; therefore those, such as Harold Lasswell et al. (1952), who borrowed from their assumptions and theories should not be seen as compromising democratic theory (Shils 1982: 13–14; Eulau 1976: 18–19). Sometimes with sadness (Friedrich 1950), often with more enthusiasm for modern functional elites (Keller 1963), the realists gave up on the ethical and educative goals of democracy, and abandoned the notion of meaningful citizen participation as the critical means to such goals. Dahl's 'polyarchy' (Dahl 1956), perhaps the most popular version of realist democratic theory, requires a certain level of apathy for the health of the system, and the classic Civic Culture study (Almond and Verba 1963: 474–9) treats non-participation by large numbers of citizens as a positive feature, avoiding system overload on demands and permitting elites more leeway. Lipset (1964: lxiii) utilizes Ostrogorski's pioneering work on elite control in British and American party machines in the nineteenth century to argue that party oligarchies contribute positively to the operations of mass democracy. While there was some scholarly resistance to this realist revision of democratic theory (Nye 1977: 40–2), the emphasis on stability and effectiveness predominated in the theory of democratic elites for a generation after the turmoil of the depression and two world wars.

With the rise of 'new social movements' representing values of participation, civil rights, peace, environment and feminism, a challenge was mounted against the realist, or 'elitist' theory of democracy (Kariel 1970). The challengers argued that realist theory had incorporated so many assumptions from elite theory that it had become a fearful opponent to the further evolution of democratic societies. Realist democratic theory had reduced democracy to democratic elitism, with regular elections to choose among competing establishment elites, and precious little role for citizen initiative and the incorporation of new issues on the political agenda through institutional procedures. Realist democratic theory had narrowed democracy down to the expectations of elite theory, with democracy as Mosca's 'political formula' of elite consensus. Bachrach and Baratz (1962) pointed to the ability of established elites to agree not to compete on key issues, to keep certain choices off the political agenda, and to ignore problems that elites felt were too difficult or too divisive to allow for public debate and choice. Walker (1966) argued that democratic elites, even in a multi-party system with regular elections, had found ways to sanitize or formalize democracy, while becoming increasingly suspicious of and hostile to independent citizen participation in politics. In West Germany, an undoubted success in reconstructing parliamentary democracy in the first postwar decades, younger generations of citizens in particular were becoming alienated from the consensus politics of the major party elites (Narr 1977; Mayer-Tasch 1985). Unless democracy went beyond formalities to encourage and then accept greater citizen participation, it would atrophy and lose its moral/ethical advantage over non-democratic systems.

This challenge highlighted anew the difficult relationship between elite theory and democratic theory. The realists had correctly recognized the importance of elite theory as a basic caution to democratic theory; in attempting to construct a permanent framework of elite consensus in which to isolate some core of democratic practice, they had surrendered much of its dynamic idealism and legitimacy (Bottomore 1964: 148–9). It appears that in any given organization, as Michels argued, there is a trend towards elite rule and rank-and-file marginalization, and this includes the organization of realist democratic systems. However, Michels, Mosca and Pareto downplay the recurrence of popular demands for meaningful accountability arising in reaction to elitist control, which is just as much a part of political history as is the emergence and circulation of elites. The 'participatory democracy' theorists have rightly noted these trends, yet they often attempt to construct systems in which 'co-option' of new leaderships into establishment politics will be blocked, 'bureaucratiz-ation' and 'professionalization' of the 'new politics' will be somehow avoided. The Greens in Germany, and many of the new 'green' or 'alternative' parties and citizen coalitions in Europe and North America, attempt to build formal rules and structures (rotation in office, no re-election, modest compensation for office-holders, policy making by party base mandate, open and endless debate on policy) to maintain control of leaders by the rank and file (Hase 1984). Yet it seems likely that the emerging leaders in these 'new social movements' will in various ways structure their own behaviour and careers to undermine the goals of effective control of leaders by ordinary members. Hence the ongoing struggle between the Realos (realists) and the Fundis (fundamentalists) within the German Greens.

The dialectic of democracy and elitism generates an ongoing search for new modes of participation, new practices of citizen expression, giving rise to new forms of elite control and manipulation. Whether this democratization/elitism dialectic is merely cyclical or results in higher-level syntheses is debatable. The long-term expansion of literacy, mobility and satisfaction of basic needs might seem to strengthen the belief that higher levels of leader–citizen inter-action emerge as more citizens demand political voice, yet the increasing complexity and anonymity of productive relations also make informed and effective citizen input more problematic as well (Burnheim 1985). The study of elites itself is not at question; it is the classic theory of elites which is at odds with democratic theory and with the historical process of democratization.

APPROACHES AND FINDINGS IN RECRUITMENT RESEARCH: WHO RULES?

Putnam, in his comprehensive review of comparative elite analysis, finds that political elites are always recruited disproportionately from higher-status back-grounds and privileged families (Putnam 1976: 22), that non-elected adminis-trative elites are even more exclusive, and that economic elites are the most privileged. In virtually every system, particularly over time, a process of 'aggluti-nation' orients the selection processes to screen out most, though never all, lower status citizens. Putnam then poses a question to this type of analysis: 'agglutination: so what?' (ibid.: 41–4). Putnam mentions research implications for elite self-interest, elite socialization, the social seismology of power struc-tures and elite integration, but all are subsidiary to the issue of elite legitimacy. Elite recruitment is a fundamental function of every political system, perhaps the one which most visibly touches the critical issue of system legitimacy.

Researchers have studied political elite recruitment from two qualitatively different approaches: processes and outcomes. A research focus on both formal and informal processes of leadership training and promotion will pick up on the pluralism of aspirants, the competition for both elected and appointive offices, the uncertainty of outcomes, the responsiveness to actual or anticipated constituent demands, and the unplanned or chance aspects of elite recruitment. Studies of political ambition and career-building (Schlesinger 1966: 195–8; Herzog 1975: 225–7), for example, draw attention to the inexact course for a political career and the openness of the recruitment filtering process from the perspective of the individual. Studies of internal gatekeepers or selectorates (Putnam 1976: 52–65) within elite hierarchies reveal the roles of skills and credentials which are most valued at different times among possible contenders for office. A degree from Oxford or Cambridge in the United Kingdom, from the École National d'Administration in France, from the National Autonomous University in Mexico City, or from a Soviet polytechnical institute has been an important filtering device, but still leaves degrees of openness and competition for elite advancement.

Studies which focus on the composition of elites, on the background characteristics of elite groupings relative to the general population, on common ties among elites, on elite groupings rather than individual leaders, draw attention to pervasive and systemic inequalities. These studies tend to illustrate that beyond the indeterminacy at the individual level, and regardless of process or institutional setting, in either formal or informal ways, the social hierarchy has a great deal of power to reproduce itself in elite recruitment outcomes (Matthews 1954; Miliband 1969; Jaeggi 1969). Social revolutions, such as in the Soviet Union, Yugoslavia and China, have initially opened up elite recruitment to younger workers and some peasants and have eroded former privileges, but over time the new social order develops its own status hierarchy (Nagle 1977: 65–7, 89–92; Barton *et al.* 1973: 25, 125).

Institutional, reputational and decision-making definitions have been used to identify political elites for research, and there has been debate, most notably in studies of community power structures, over whether the method significantly affects the findings (Parry 1969: 114–19; Putnam 1976: 15–19; Marger 1987: 184–9). No one approach will serve to answer all questions, and each leaves something to be desired. Method choice can make a greater difference at the local level, where informal power structures may diverge more from formal institutions. This may, however, also apply at the national level for many developing nations, where formal institutions are weak and penetrated by strong outside elites. Here research context and purpose must be used to avoid misleading definitions, and multi-approach techniques can check for divergencies. Most elite studies have been one-time snapshots of a single political elite; individual studies of this type, though often interesting as case studies, have been less useful to generalization and theory building than comparative and longitudinal or time-series studies. Cross-national aggregate analyses of elite characteristics (Quandt 1970: 179–84) need to be reinforced by individual-level analysis and by seminal-case longitudinal research (Nagle 1977: 5–13). In general, issues of research methods are no longer so central to the field.

If the basic approaches to research on elite recruitment are now less controversial, the characterization of research results is anything but straightforward, and evinces the most divergent evaluations. Elite recruitment studies have been used to characterize regimes through examinations of three key questions: 'How open is elite recruitment?'; 'How unified is the resulting elite?'; 'Is some transformation taking place?' One of the key assumptions of much elite recruitment analysis, and one of its sources of recurring interest, is that the political regime may be typed according to its system of elite recruitment, both processes and results.

Marger (1987: 141–63) notes that analyses of elites in the United States have led to judgements that the United States is dominated either by a ruling class, or by a 'power elite', or by multiple, pluralist, competing elites. Marger concludes that the United States:

> seems closest to a power elite since (1) elite differences do not represent basic disagreements on essential issues of the political economy; (2) the corporate elite may not decide all issues, but it is able to set the agenda and boundaries of political debate; (3) the necessary overlapping of government and corporation gives rise to a natural elite cohesiveness, though not a conspiring group.
>
> (Marger 1987: 163)

While elite recruitment is not entirely closed to the lower strata, and indeed there will always be some penetration of lower-class individuals into top positions, '[t]he outstanding fact of elite recruitment in the United States and other Western industrial societies is that leaders are chosen overwhelmingly from socially dominant groups, and have been for many generations' (Marger 1987: 180). On the other hand, Keller (1963: 273) has argued that all modern societies give rise to a pluralism of 'strategic elites', each with specialized functions and limited to a particular sphere of social activity. These elites, Keller finds, have relative autonomy and independence, are functionally vital to the society, but cannot dominate the entire system. The trend is towards recruitment on individual merit rather than social inheritance, and the pluralism of strategic elites provides a defence against dictatorship and abuse of power. From a Marxist perspective, Miliband (1969) and Domhoff (1967, 1971) have characterized the United States as a ruling class system, in which the state is dominated by the class which owns and controls the productive assets of the society. The economic power of the capitalist class is sufficient to manipulate the state, and to use it broadly to safeguard its overall interests. Domhoff and Miliband show that elite posts are held by wealthy capitalists far beyond their proportion in the society, and that most other leading positions go to those managers, lawyers, and other professionals closely tied to the ruling class.

In an epoch when so much is made of democracy, equality, social mobility, classlessness and the rest, it has remained a basic fact of life in advanced capitalist countries that the vast majority of men and women in these countries have been governed, represented, administered, judged, and commanded in war by people drawn from other, economically and socially superior and relatively distant classes.

(Miliband 1969: 66–7)

The debate over the origins and nature of the Soviet system has been closely related to the evaluation of the Leninist party's concept and practice of elite recruitment. This debate has its roots in Lenin's organizational thesis of his 'party of a new type' presented in *What is to be Done?* (Lenin 1902). From Marxist perspectives, Martov, Trotsky and Luxemburg presented characterizations of the future Soviet regime based primarily on Lenin's new 'bolshevik' culture of revolutionary leadership (Tucker 1987: 12–71), pinpointing principally the tensions between socialist democracy and the vanguardist elitism of Lenin's centralist organizational innovations. The evolution of the Leninist culture into Stalinist dictatorship provoked further Marxist recharacterizations of the regime by Trotsky (1957) and then by Djilas (1957). For Marxist analysts the key problem has been to evaluate the ruling elite's control over the means of production, and then to identify the class nature of that ruling elite according to Marxist categories of exploitation of surplus value, inheritability of elite privilege and class consciousness. A central feature in all these critiques is the evaluation of the processes and results of elite recruitment for the overall judgement of the Soviet system. This debate emphasizes once again the theoretical tension between elitism and democracy, in this case within the socialist ideological tradition.

In the early post-war years, much scholarship on elite recruitment focused on totalitarian elites of both communist and fascist varieties, the better to combat the threat to democracy. Lasswell and Lerner argued that:

until recently the spokesmen of liberal capitalism were riding the tide of success, confident that the business revolution was carrying all before it. The sobering impact of recent events has done more than to undermine faith in business, science and technology. It has brought about a revival of man's distrust in himself.

(Lasswell and Lerner 1965: 29–30)

Lasswell and Lerner's rather apocalyptic essay mirrored the uncertainties which the communist revolutions in Russia and China, and fascist victories in Germany, Italy and Japan, had provoked, justifying increased attention to those characteristics which distinguish communist and fascist elites both from the general population and from established elites.

493

The closely-held communist *nomenklatura* system of party appointments to full-time functions in party, government and other organizations has been a clear example of a consciously self-recruited political class. It has been closely watched to discern changes in the nature of the Soviet system. In the post-Stalin years, Fleron (1969) and Fischer (1968) noted trends towards recruitment of managerial-technical specialists into top party positions, replacing those with lower educational attainment and with lesser professional experience. This trend towards co-optation of managerial-technical elites into top party positions seemed to foreshadow a declining ideological orientation and a growing regard for those skills needed to administer an increasingly urban and industrial Soviet economy. However, this trend declined in the 1970s, and the implication that the elites of the party apparatus would soon give way to functional elites of the scientific-technological revolution was shelved.

Much attention has been given to the question of elite succession in the Soviet system, especially the succession of elite generations. Scholars have identified elite age cohorts whose formative experiences in politics and in the party, it is argued, make their perspective broadly similar (Nagle 1977: 187–94). The earliest generation of 'revolutionary theorists', who formed the small cadre party and its Leninist revolutionary ideology, gave way to the 'revolution managers' who joined the party during the revolution and civil war and rose within the expanding party apparatus. This nascent apparatus elite formed the backbone for Stalin's consolidation of power, but was composed of men with poor educational backgrounds. In the era of the purges of the 1930s, Stalin promoted a very young 'managerial modernizer' cohort, from proletarian-peasant backgrounds but with some higher technical qualifications, to oversee the industrial revolution of the first Five-Year Plans (Unger 1969; Nagle 1975). The managerial modernizer generation, which included Brezhnev, Kosygin, Suslov, Andropov, Chernenko, Ustinov and Gromyko, had an extraordinarily long run of dominance in the Soviet system. The members of this elite cohort, whose careers were launched during Stalin's purges and whose lives at the same time were threatened by Stalin's tyranny, were able, after 1953, to make the Soviet system safe for themselves. Some (Rush 1965) predicted that the Soviet system required a single dictator at the top, with the power to purge incumbents, and predicted that one contender would eliminate all rivals. Yet a collective leadership avoided a return to Stalinist purge mechanisms for elite rejuvenation, and this generational bloc was able to prevent younger aspirants from dislodging them (Hough 1967, 1972, 1981). Only the advent of Gorbachev in the latter 1980s ended this 'petrification' and brought a new pluralism of generational representation into the Soviet Central Committee.

A contentious theme of elite research on communist systems has been control by a single, unified elite versus a trend towards a 'pluralism' of elites.

With the rise of specialist elites, some researchers began to describe the Soviet system in terms of interest-group politics (Lodge 1969) with some influence by sub-elites over policy-making decisions. This trend towards more visible interest-group activity, both inside and outside the party, has produced recharacterizations of the Soviet and East German regimes as 'consultative authoritarian', or of the Yugoslav regime as 'democratizing and pluralistic authoritarian' (Skilling 1971: 222–8; Ludz 1972) rather than totalitarian.

In the early post-war Hoover Institute studies on fascist elites, Lerner (1951) introduced the concept of 'marginality' to describe the Nazi elite; Lerner defined marginality as deviation from the common attributes of the larger society, and it was this outsider mentality which linked various Nazi sub-elites such as propagandists, administrators, police and military. For Lerner, the Nazi elite was a group of social misfits, disproportionately from 'plebeian' or lower middle-class origins, an anti-modernist counter-elite which once in power would revolutionize ruling elites. Kater (1983: 182–9) has shown how influential this early study has been in judgements on the Nazi elite and moreover the Nazi regime. Yet later research by Kater (1983), Fischer (1979) and Nagle (1983), as well as Knight's (1952) earlier but often overlooked work, have demonstrated that the Nazi elite was neither so marginal to Weimar society, nor revolutionary, nor clearly divorced from established elites. Kater judges that between the Nazi elite and the establishment, 'there were too many elements of accommodation, of fusion, or absorption. In social composition alone, the pattern of mutual interactions and interlockings between the two groups was nearer to collusion than to collision' (Kater 1983: 232–233). Nagle has shown that the Nazi Reichstag faction, in comparison to the other parties, represented not a plebeian counter-elite but a broad coalition including modern professionals, new middle-class elements, big business, military and working-class representatives (Nagle 1983: 88). After the Nazis gained power in 1933, it was in fact the older middle-class elements, mainly smallholders, which declined in importance while newer white-collar employees and professionals in engineering, medicine and teaching continued to increase. More recent research has argued that the NSDAP (National Socialist German Workers' Party) was a pragmatic and modern catch-all party (Hamilton 1982; Childers 1983) with specific appeals to very diverse elements of the German electorate. This catch-all strategy was as volatile and unstable as it was successful, and showed signs in late 1932 of decline; ultimately anti-democratic coalition-building projects led by established conservative elites including Papen and Hugenberg (Kühnl 1985) were needed in January 1933 to bring the Nazis to power and to destroy the Weimar Republic. New research has intensified the debate over responsibility of established industrial, military and party elites for the triumph of Nazism and over the nature of their collaboration with the Nazi regime (Turner 1985; Abraham 1986).

The agenda for elite recruitment research in the developing nations has been less well-defined and less productive. Much of the research has been focused on Latin American which has a longer period of independence and, at the end of the Second World War, was more highly developed than other regions. An important focus has been the relation between elite recruitment and the prospects for democratic development (Smith 1974; Burns and Skidmore 1979). The Lipset and Solari (1967) volume presented analyses of various elites as non-revolutionary modernizing forces in the era of the US-sponsored Alliance for Progress. But even here, weak governments and parties, penetrated by stronger social and economic elites, made the initial search for a democratic political elite problematic. Scott (1967: 117–19) concentrates on the transition from a unified ruling class of traditional elites of landowners, military and church to a system led by middle-class modernizing elites from business and the professions. But these modern elites are still too weak to dominate or to lead, and often have themselves become dependent on traditional and external elites to maintain their own interests from periodic popular discontent and desperation. This 'crisis of elites' (Scott 1967: 140) may then lead to challenges from revolutionary elites. A strong state system has emerged in only a few states, notably in Mexico, where political elite recruitment could be studied within the framework of the Partido Revolucionario Institucional (PRI). The PRI has been able to reduce the role of the military, church and landowners to provide for relatively smooth generational succession (Nagle 1977: 81–7), and to develop a clear political elite recruitment system (Smith 1979). Camp (1980) has outlined the roles of education, political skills and personal ties within the PRI recruitment system, evolving in the 1980s into more strained relations between financial-managerial *tecnicos* and party apparatus *politicos*.

The rise of military-dominated regimes in Latin America in the 1960s and 1970s gave rise to the characterization of many regimes as 'corporatist' (Wiarda 1978), representing a modernizing 'new authoritarianism' (Collier 1979). This new corporatism is an alliance among major established elites but aimed now at modernization rather than maintaining traditional economic structures. This perspective, developed primarily with reference to Latin American experiences, has also been extended to regimes in Korea, Taiwan, Singapore, Thailand and Indonesia, where economic successes have been greater and more durable. Though overly elastic, corporatism as a concept reflected the dimming prospects of democratic party and parliamentary elites as leading forces in the modernization process, and elevated the military (Stepan 1978) as a potent anti-communist state elite.

In many newly independent nations, attention has been drawn to the rise and expansion of the state elite. Nafziger describes the new statist bourgeoisie in Africa as a ruling class which uses taxes, government spending, indigenization, currency exchange rates and control of public employment to both accumulate personal wealth and maintain power, at the cost of slowing growth and increasing inequality (Nafziger 1988: 108–9). Even in 'socialist' states like Tanzania, Nafziger finds that access to superior education for the children of elites is the mechanism to transmit high status (ibid.: 138–9). But the attempt at a state-led economic development project has failed, and has created mainly a parasitic and corrupt ruling elite, clinging to power and fearful of mass participation.

FUTURE RESEARCH IN ELITE RECRUITMENT

The potential for elite studies is closely related to major political transformations observable in different systems. After a post-war era of growing state power (Migdal 1988) in liberal welfare democracy, in Leninist one-party communism, in Latin American corporatism, and in the great variety of newly independent Third World states, there is a perception that state size and responsibility has outrun either leadership capacity or legitimacy, or both, resulting in new challenges to basic processes of elite recruitment. This trend is associated with the rise of social movements and new elites outside the mainstream or establishment institutions of leadership recruitment. A time for special attention to research on anti-statist counter-elites may have arrived.

In the liberal democracies, the 'new social movements' have blossomed suddenly into new 'green' and 'alternative' parties in most of Europe. Eldersveld in 1981 still judged the established party's recruitment of new leaders in Germany as 'dynamic, open to social renewal, vote-maximizing, and providing incentives for activists to join and to work and to move upward in the organization' (Eldersveld 1982: 88). Future research needs to address questions of how emerging patterns of elite recruitment through alternative/green movements will affect citizen–elite relations, how the new leaders will be able to affect the political agenda, and how established party recruitment will respond over the longer run to the alternative/green challenge, especially in recruitment opportunities for women (Nagle 1989: 148–55). One may note the erosion of the post-war elite consensus, and a variety of attempts to rework the political landscape with new party formations, including, on the far right, the National Front in France, the Republicans in Germany, and the National Front in Britain. The 1990s may well be a more severe test of the political centre. Research may also focus on whether the welfare state democracies are 'governable' (Crozier et al. 1975) in the sense of permitting elites to perform their roles effectively; Shils (1982) worries that in modern Western society 'collectivistic liberalism' has emasculated political leadership, destroyed any semblance of a political class in Mosca's sense, and made it nearly impossible to govern effectively.

497

The communist party monopoly on political elite recruitment and the *nomen-klatura* system of recruitment within the party was swept away in Eastern Europe in the revolutions of 1989–90, and is being dismantled in the wake of the failed August 1991 coup in the Soviet Union. In Eastern Europe, communist parties have been removed from power, and have been replaced by a variety of democratic, nationalist, populist and in a few cases 'reform socialist' parties and movements. In this 'post-communist' era, elite analysis has an opportunity to describe and clarify the new inter-elite struggle between liberal democratic, reform socialist and nationalist leaderships to shape the new emerging polity. Solidarity, once the uniting opposition and then suddenly in 1989 the governing party in Poland, is beginning to splinter into more liberal democratic and national-populist parties. In Bulgaria, the Communist Party (now renamed Socialist Party) was able to win in multi-party elections in 1990 after deposing the old Zhivkov leadership, but now is strongly challenged by a diverse umbrella of opposition elites. In Czechoslovakia, the liberal intellectuals of Civic Forum who led the 'velvet revolution' of 1989 also won the first free multi-party elections, but are confronted with both an unreformed communist party in opposition and new forces of Slovak nationalism. In Yugoslavia, multi-party elections in some republics (Slovenia and Croatia), and the rise of ethnic nationalist elites in virtually all republics and Kosovo have put the survival of Yugoslavia, not just the role of Yugoslav communist elites, in question. The rise of new elites from the urban professional middle class displacing older elites from worker backgrounds marked the revolutions of 1989–90, but the modern intelligentsia may not retain its new-found leadership role. In a period of extraordinary fluidity, a wide variety of outcomes may emerge from this new elite competition to give substance to 'post-communism'.

In the Soviet Union, the democratization process, beginning with Gorbachev's elite-initiated reforms and later accelerated through mass-based popular movements, undermined the legitimacy and power of the party apparatus over the nomination and selection processes for political office. In the 1989 elections to the Congress of People's Deputies, nominations were initiated at the grassroots level, competing candidates from a wide range of issue and ideological orientations were presented to voters, and apparatus candidates were soundly defeated in many contests. Even in districts where the apparatus was able to impose a single candidate (party boss Solovev in Leningrad, for example), the voters were able to defeat him, forcing a second round of multi-candidate elections. Newly elected members of the Congress of People's Deputies, in nationally televised debates, broke with the pattern of docile rubber-stamp parliaments and criticized nearly every aspect of the Soviet system, including such previous taboo areas as the KGB, the military, Lenin and Gorbachev himself. The Supreme Soviet selected from the Congress membership, the first sitting parliament in Soviet history, likewise surprised observers by rejecting numerous nominees for ministerial posts, developing legislative initiatives on its own, and developing a pattern of factional voting and pointed debate. The growth of unofficial local political clubs and broader movements of environmentalists, peace activists, ethnic popular fronts, reactionary groups such as Pamyat, and religious and labour activists, now offers a rich and realistic agenda for elite recruitment research, which will help answer questions about the character of a future Soviet system. Finally, ethnic nationalist movements in 1990 gained control of most Soviet republic-level parliaments in local elections and were able to set the agenda of those parliaments, which announced their 'sovereignty' or 'independence' from the central Soviet government. The building of new inter-ethnic elite relations, and the intra-ethnic elite conflicts between more radical and more moderate nationalists, may well determine the future constitutional system of the component Soviet republics, whether federal, confederal, or independent state.

The June 1989 crackdown by the Deng regime in China against the democracy movement reminds us that renewed repression is yet possible in the short term, and regime dissidents may well have to await the passing of the octagenarian elite to renew their challenge to the party monopoly. The transformation of communist systems in the 1990s will be closely related to the nature and outcomes of these challenges, and will define the character of a new political system.

In most developing nations, the failure of ruling elites, civilian and military, democratic and authoritarian, to fashion and to lead a development project which provides for the general welfare has given rise to new leadership aspirants, but not to any single pattern of elite transformation. Putnam's comprehensive synthesis of findings on political elites contains some evaluations of elite transformation trends in Western democracies and the communist systems (Putnam 1976: 205–14), but no section on trends in Third World nations. The 'crisis of elites' which commonly characterized Latin American systems in the 1960s can now be extended to most of the Third World. In a few cases, as with the New People's Army in the Philippines, the FMLN (Farabundo Martí National Liberation Front) in El Salvador, or Sendero Luminoso in Peru, revolutionary leadership poses a serious alternative to the entire array of existing elites. A small number of basically nationalist elites, including the Palestine Liberation Organization, the African National Congress in South Africa, and the Eritrean People's Liberation Front in Eritrea, also represent strong challenges to currently dominant political elites, but do not clearly threaten the existing economic and social elites. Integralist Muslim religious leaderships, following the Islamic revolution in Iran, now pose a serious threat to existing political and social elites in the Middle East, in South-West Asia and across northern Africa. Growing labour movements in Korea, Brazil and South Africa also show signs of producing more influential leaders, though not revolutionary challengers for state power. In Mexico, India, Taiwan and South Korea, new and viable opposition parties may be developing from the shadow of hegemonic one-party or military-led regimes. Can any of these challenges develop the broad social integration and value consensus which existing elite recruitment has failed to provide?

Finally, future elite research must begin to treat non-national elite recruitment, and to investigate interaction of non-national and national elite recruitment, in a systematic way. The emergence of a more unified European Community is one obvious case. The study of international finance elites from the International Monetary Fund and World Bank should be integrated into research agendas on political elite recruitment for Mexico, Brazil, Argentina or the Philippines. Religious leadership recruitment from papal appointments of bishops and cardinals, new leaders arising from transnational Islamic fundamentalism, and multinational corporate elites may be systematically treated, regardless of formal citizenship.

REFERENCES

Abraham, D. (1986) *The Collapse of the Weimer Republic: Political Economy and Crisis*, 2nd edn, New York: Holmes & Meier.

Adorno, T. W., Frenkel-Brunswick, E., Levinson, D. and Sanford, R. N. (1950) *The Authoritarian Personality*, New York: Harper & Row.

Almond, G. and Verba, S. (1963) *The Civic Culture*, Boston: Little, Brown & Co.

Bachrach, P. (1967) *The Theory of Democratic Elitism*, Boston: Little, Brown & Co.

Bachrach, P. and Baratz, M. (1962) 'Two faces of power', *American Political Science Review* 56: 947–52.

Barton, A., Denitch, B. and Kadushin C. (1973) *Opinion-making Elites in Yugoslavia*, New York: Praeger.

Bottomore, T. B. (1964) *Elites and Society*, London: Penguin.

Burnham, J. (1941) *The Managerial Revolution*, New York: John Day.

Burnheim, J. (1985) *Is Democracy Possible?*, Berkeley: University of California Press.

Burns, E. B. and Skidmore T. E. (1979) *Elites, Masses and Modernization in Latin America 1850–1930*, Austin: Univeristy of Texas Press.

Camp, R. A. (1980) *Mexico's Leaders, Their Education and Recruitment*, Tucson, Ariz.: University of Arizona Press.

Childers, T. (1983) *The Nazi Voter*, Chapel Hill, NC: University of North Carolina Press.

Collier, D. (1979) *The New Authoritarianism in Latin America*, Princeton: Princeton University Press.

Crozier, M., Huntington S. and Watanuki J. (1975) *The Crisis of Democracy: Report on the Governability of Democracies to the Trilateral Commission*, New York: New York University Press.

Dahl, R. (1956) *A Preface to Democratic Theory*, Chicago: University of Chicago Press.

——(1961) *Who Governs: Democracy and Power in an American City*, New Haven: Yale University Press.

Djilas, M. (1957) *The New Class*, New York: Praeger.

Domhoff, G. W. (1967) *Who Rules America?* Englewood Cliffs, NJ: Prentice-Hall.

——(1971) *The Higher Circles*, New York: Vintage.

Eldersveld, S. (1982) 'Changes in elite composition and the survival of party systems: the German case', in M. Czudnowski (ed.) *Does Who Governs Matter?*, De Kalb, Ill.: Northern Illionois University Press.

Eulau, H. (1976) 'Elite analysis and democratic theory: the contribution of Harold D. Lasswell', in H. Eulau and M. Czudnowski (eds) *Elite Recruitment in Democratic Politics*, New York: John Wiley.

Fischer, F. (1979) *Bündnis der Eliten*, Dusseldorf: Droste.

Fischer, G. (1968) *The Soviet System and Modern Society*, New York: Atherton.

Fleron, F. J. (1969) 'Towards a reconceptualization of political change in the Soviet Union: the political leadership system', in F. J. Fleron (ed.) *Communist Studies and the Social Sciences*, Chicago: Rand McNally.

Friedrich, C. (1950) *The New Belief in the Common Man*, Boston: Little, Brown & Co.

Hamilton, R. (1982) *Who Voted for Hitler?*, Princeton: Princeton University Press.

Hase, F. (1984) 'Die Grünen im Rechtsstaat: Basis – repräsentative und pluralistische Demokratie', in T. Kluge (ed.) *Grüne Politik*, Frankfurt: Fischer.

Herzog, D. (1975) *Politische Karrieren: Selektion und Professionalisierung politischer Führungsgruppen*, Opladen: Westdeutscher Verlag.

Hough, J. (1967) 'The Soviet elite', *Problems of Communism* 16: (1, 2): 28–35, 18–25.

——(1972) 'The Soviet System: petrification or pluralism?', *Problems of Communism* 21(2): 25–45.

——(1981) *Soviet Leadership in Transition*, Washington, DC: Brookings Institution.

Jaeggi, U. (1969) *Macht und Herrschaft in der Bundesrepublik*, Frankfurt am Main: Fischer.

Kariel, H. (ed.) (1970) *Frontiers of Democratic Theory*, New York: Random House.

Kater, M. H. (1983) *The Nazi Party: A Social Profile of Members and Leaders 1919–1945*, Cambridge, Mass.: Harvard University Press.

Keller, S. (1963) *Beyond the Ruling Class: Strategic Elites in Modern Society*, New York: Random House.

Knight, M. (1952) *The German Executive*, Stanford: Hoover Institute.

Kühnl, R. (1985) *Die Weimarer Republik*, Hamburg: Rowohlt.

Kornhauser, W. (1959) *The Politics of Mass Society*, New York: Free Press.

Lasswell, H. D. and Lerner, D. (1965) *World Revolutionary Elites*, Cambridge, Mass.: MIT Press.

Lasswell, H. D., Lerner, D. and Rothwell, C. E. (1952) *The Comparative Study of Elites*, Stanford: Stanford University Press.

Lenin, V. I. (1902) *What is to be Done?*

Lerner, D. (1951) *The Nazi Elite*, Stanford: Stanford University Press.

Lipset, S. M. (ed.) (1964) *Democracy and the Organization of Political Parties*, vol. 1, Chicago: Quadrangle.

Lipset, S. M. and Solari, A. (eds) (1967) *Elites in Latin America*, New York: Oxford University Press.

Lodge, M. (1969) *Soviet Elite Attitudes since Stalin*, Columbus, Ohio: Bobbs-Merrill.

Ludz, P. C. (1972) *The Changing Party Elite in East Germany*, Cambridge, Mass.: MIT Press.

Marger, M. N. (1987) *Elites and Masses: An Introduction to Political Sociology*, Blemont, Calif.: Wadsworth.

Matthews, D. (1954) *The Social Background of Political Decision-Makers*, New York: Random House.

Mayer-Tasch, P. C. (1985) *Die Bürgerinitiativbewegung*, Hamburg: Rowohlt.

Migdal, J. (1988) *Strong Societies and Weak States: State–Society Relations and State Capabilities in the Third World*, Princeton: Princeton University Press.

Miliband, R. (1969) *The State in Capitalist Society*, New York: Basic Books.

Nafziger, E. W. (1988) *Inequality in Africa: Political Elites, Proletariat, Peasants and the Poor*, Cambridge: Cambridge University Press.

Nagle, J. D. (1975) 'A new look at the Soviet elite: a generational model of the Soviet system', *Journal of Political and Military Sociology* 3: 1–13.

——(1977) *System and Succession: The Social Bases of Political Elite Recruitment*, Austin: University of Texas Press.

——(1983) 'Composition and evolution of the Nazi elite', in M. Dobkowski and I. Walliman (eds) *Towards the Holocaust: The Social and Economic Collapse of the Weimar Republic*, Westport, Conn.: Greenwood Press.

——(1989) 'The West German Greens: an evolving response to political conflict', in L. Kreisberg, T. Northrup and S. Thorson (eds) *Intractable Conflicts and their Transformations*, Syracuse, NY: Syracuse University Press.

Narr, W.-D. (1977) 'Parteienstaat in der BRD – ein Koloss auf tönernden Füssen, aber mit stählernen Zähnen', in W.-D. Narr (ed.) *Auf dem Weg zum Einparteienstaat*, Opladen: Westdeutscher Verlag.

Nye, R. A. (1977) *The Anti-Democratic Sources of Elite Theory: Pareto, Mosca, Michels*, London: Sage Publications.

Parry, G. (1969) *Political Elites*, New York: Praeger.

Putnam, R. D. (1976) *The Comparative Study of Political Elites*, Englewood Cliffs, NJ: Prentice-Hall.

Quandt, W. (1970) *The Comparative Study of Political Elites*, Beverly Hills, Calif.: Sage Publications.

Riesman, D. and Glazer, N. and Denney, R. (1950) *The Lonely Crowd*, Garden City, NY: Doubleday.

Rush, M. (1965) *Political Succession in the USSR*, New York: Columbia University Press.

Schlesinger, J. A. (1966) *Ambition and Politics: Political Careers in the United States*, Chicago: Rand McNally.

Schumpeter, J. (1942) *Capitalism, Socialism and Democracy*, New York: Harper & Brothers.

Scott, R. E. (1967) 'Political elites and modernization: the crisis of transition', in S. M. Lipset and A. Solari (eds) *Elites in Latin America*, New York: Oxford University Press.

Sereno, R. (1968) *The Rulers*, New York: Harper.

Shils, E. (1982) 'The political class in the age of mass society: collectivistic liberalism and social democracy', in M. Czudnowski (ed.) *Does Who Governs Matter?*, De Kalb, Ill.: Northern Illinois University Press.

Skilling, H. G. (1971) 'Groups in Soviet politics: some hypotheses', in H. G. Skilling and F. Griffiths (eds) *Interest Groups in Soviet Politics*, Princeton: Princeton University Press.

Smith, P. H. (1974) *Argentina and the Failure of Democracy: Conflict Among Political Elites 1904–1955*, Madison: University of Wisconsin Press.

——(1979) *Labyrinths of Power: Political Recruitment in Twentieth-Century Mexico*, Princeton: Princeton University Press. .

Stepan, A. (1978) *The State and Society: Peru in Comparative Perspective*, Princeton: Princeton University Press.

Trotsky, L. (1957) *The Revolution Betrayed* (1939), London: Plough Press.

Tucker, R. C. (1987) *Political Culture and Leadership in Soviet Russia*, New York: Norton.

Turner, H. (1985) *German Big Business and the Rise of Hitler*, New York: Oxford University Press.

Unger, A. L. (1969) 'Stalin's renewal of the leading stratum: a note on the Great Purge', *Soviet Studies* 20: 321–30.

Von Beyme, K. (1982) 'Elite input and policy output: the case of Germany', in M. Czudnowski (ed.) *Does Who Governs Matter?*, De Kalb, Ill.: Northern Illinois University Press.

Walker, J. (1966) 'A critique of the elitist theory of democracy', *American Political Science Review* 60: 285–95.

Wiarda, H. (1978) 'Corporatism rediscovered: right, center, and left variants in the new literature', *Polity* 10: 416–28.

FURTHER READING

Bachrach, P. (1967) *The Theory of Democratic Elitism*, Boston: Little, Brown & Co.

Bottomore, T. B. (1964) *Elites and Society*, London: Penguin.

Keller, S. (1963) *Beyond the Ruling Class: Strategic Elites in Modern Society*, New York: Random House.

Lane, D. (1988) *Elites and Political Power in the USSR*, Brookfield, Vt: Gower.

Marger, M. N. (1987) *Elites and Masses: An Introduction to Political Sociology*, Blemont, Calif.: Wadsworth.

Michels, R. (1962) *Political Parties: A Sociological Study of the Oligarchical Tendencies of Modern Democracy*, New York: Free Press.

Mills, C. W. (1956) *The Power Elite*, New York: Oxford University Press.

Mosca, G. (1939) *The Ruling Class*, ed. and rev. A. Livingston, New York: McGraw-Hill.

Nagle, J. D. (1977) *System and Succession: The Social Bases of Political Elite Recruitment*, Austin: University of Texas Press.

Nye, R. A. (1977) *The Anti-Democratic Sources of Elite Theory: Pareto, Mosca, Michels*, London: Sage Publications.

Pareto, V. (1966) *Vilfredo Pareto: Sociological Writings*, New York: Praeger.

Parry, G. (1969) *Political Elites*, New York: Praeger.

Putnam, R. D. (1976) *The Comparative Study of Political Elites*, Englewood Cliffs, NJ: Prentice-Hall.

Sereno, R. (1968) *The Rulers*, New York: Harper.

PART VII

CENTRIPETAL AND CENTRIFUGAL FORCES IN THE NATION-STATE

31

POLITICAL CULTURES

MICHAEL THOMPSON, RICHARD ELLIS AND
AARON WILDAVSKY

Political culture entered the lexicon of political science in the late 1950s and early 1960s. Intimately linked with the so-called 'behavioural revolution', the term signalled a move away from the study of formal institutions to the informal behaviour which breathed life into them. Political culture was heralded as a concept capable of unifying the discipline. By relating the behaviour of individuals to the system of which the individual was a part, it promised to 'bridge the "micro-macro" gap in political theory' (Almond and Powell 1966: 51–2; see also Almond and Verba 1963: 32–6; and Pye 1965: 9). In recent decades, however, the concept of political culture has fallen out of academic fashion amidst criticisms that it is tautological, that it is unable to explain change, that it ignores power relations, and that its definition is fuzzy.

We have no intention of bombarding the reader with the myriad definitions of political culture that have been tried and discarded only to reappear without agreement among scholars. One study counted no less than 164 definitions of the term 'culture' (Kroeber and Kluckhohn 1952). Among students of political culture, the most widely accepted definition views culture as composed of values, beliefs, norms and assumptions, i.e. mental products (see for example Pye 1968: 218). This 'mental' definition of culture has the virtue of clearly separating the behaviour to be explained from the values and beliefs that are doing the explaining. On the other hand, a definition of culture that separates the mental from the social has the unfortunate tendency of encouraging a view of culture as a mysterious and unexplained prime mover.

This disembodied view of political culture leads to it being treated as a residual variable, an explanation of last resort dragged in to fill the void when more conventional explanations fail. A recent study appearing in a pre-eminent political science journal typifies this usage of culture. The authors show that standard demographic variables (income, education, religion, race, age, gender) cannot explain intrastate variation in party and ideological identification, and then attribute this unexplained variance to political culture (Erikson *et al.*

1987). Invoking political culture in this way is no better than saying 'I don't know'.

The most common criticism levied against the political culture literature is that it takes values as a given. Culture, critics insist, is a consequence, not (or at least not only) a cause, of institutional structures. Typical is Barry's argument (Barry 1970) that a democratic political culture is a learned response to living under democratic institutions rather than, as he claims Almond and Verba (1963) argue in their influential work on *The Civic Culture*, a pre-rational commitment exerting a causal force upon those institutions. Similarly, Pizzorno (1966) criticizes Banfield's classic study of *The Moral Basis of a Backward Society* (Banfield 1958) for explaining the absence of collective action in southern Italy as a product of an irrational 'ethos' rather than as a rational response to their 'marginalized' position in the economic and political structure.

To deny that political culture is shaped by institutional structure, critics continue, makes the concept of culture deeply mysterious and unfathomable. As Hall points out, 'unless cultural theories can account for the origins of . . . attitudes by reference to the institutions that generate and reproduce them, they do little more than summon up a *deus ex machina* that is itself unexplainable' (Hall 1986: 34). We agree that political culture must not be treated as an uncaused cause purportedly explaining why people behave as they do yet incapable of itself being explained. To do so is to posit a world in which values are disembodied, unattached to human subjects. The continued adherence of people to certain doctrines and habits must be explained. One way to do this, we believe, is to conceive of culture not only as mental products (ideas, values, beliefs), as is commonly done, or as patterns of social relations, but as values justifying relationships indissolubly bound together.

Political culture is transmitted from generation to generation, but it is not transmitted unchanged, nor is it transmitted without question. Cultural transmission is not a game of pass-the-parcel. Political culture is a lively and responsive thing that is continually being negotiated by individuals. A plausible theory of political culture must not turn the individual into an automaton passively receiving and internalizing societal norms.

A first step in this direction is to allow for the importance of adult, rather than only childhood, experience in shaping individual orientations. Experience with institutions counts. Throughout the course of their lives, human beings use their reasoning powers in order to scrutinize their social relationships and to compare the performance of these relationships with alternative arrangements. For example, a quarter century of dictatorships in Burma has led the Burmese towards a favourable view of capitalism and democracy.

A second step in avoiding cultural determinism is to allow for competing political cultures within a society. Political cultures are like scientific theories in that they may predict outcomes that prove false, create blind spots that lead to disaster, or generate expectations that go unfulfilled. When one culture falters, others are available to fill in the vacuum. Justifications or beliefs that once seemed powerful gradually (or perhaps even suddenly) seem to lose their hold. Witness, for instance, the significant increase in cynicism about government in the United States in the decades since publication of Almond and Verba's *The Civic Culture* (Almond and Verba 1963). To stay as we were requires vast energy. Conceived as ways of life that are continually being negotiated, tested and probed by individuals, there is no reason why theories of political culture cannot make sense of change, long considered as the Achilles heel of cultural theories.

POLITICAL CULTURE AND NATIONAL CHARACTER

A notion of political culture has existed as long as people have speculated about observable differences among countries or groups. Herodotus, Plato, Aristotle, Machiavelli, Montesquieu and Tocqueville are among the more prominent political philosophers who have tried to account for differences in government in terms of variations in a people's mores and temperament (Almond 1980: 1–6). While these classic works in political theory provide the deep intellectual background for the concept of political culture, a more immediate impetus was provided by the anthropological studies of 'national character' pioneered by Ruth Benedict (1934, 1946), Margaret Mead (1942, 1953), and Geoffrey Gorer (1948, 1955).

This anthropological literature focused upon the unique configuration of values, beliefs and practices that constituted a nation's culture. Russian culture was different from Japanese culture was different from Chinese culture was different from French culture was different from American culture and so on. Comparison seemed beyond hope. Anyone who sought to draw parallels between one national culture and another (or, even more grandly, to formulate a universal generalization about human behaviour) was liable to have those whose stock-in-trade is the deep-seated particularities of a society immediately step in with their anthropologist's veto: 'Not in my tribe'.

If the concept of culture was to be of utility to political scientists, some classification of cultures was necessary. Perhaps the most influential was the typology of parochial, subject and participatory orientations presented by Almond and Verba (1963), who addressed themselves to one of the great questions of post-war social science: why, in the period between the First and Second World Wars, did democracy survive in Britain and the United States while collapsing on the European continent? A stable democratic policy, Almond and Verba suggest, requires a balanced political culture (the civic culture) that combines both a participatory and subject (or deferential) orientation to politics. Were everyone to participate in every decision, they argue,

the political system would be overloaded and governing would become impossible; were everyone to defer to their superiors, democracy would cease to be
responsive to citizen needs and thus give way to authoritarianism.

The classificatory scheme advanced in *The Civic Culture* (Almond and Verba
1963) enabled scholars to make cross-national comparisons among what had
hitherto been regarded as unique national cultures. The categories could be
applied to advanced industrial nations as well as non-Western, technologically
primitive societies. Yet the book's research design – explaining divergent
institutional outcomes in different countries – meant that the analytic focus
largely remained, as in past anthropological works on national character, at
the levels of the nation-state. Differences between, rather than within, nations
have remained the central focus of inquiry of most research on political culture.
Conflict within nations is left largely unexplained.

The tendency to attach political culture to nations persists despite strong
evidence suggesting that variations in political attitudes and values within
countries are often greater than those between countries. Introducing a recent
book of essays on European democracies, Dogan, for instance, finds that:

> There is not a British civic culture nor a German, French or Italian one. The
> differences among countries are differences in degree, not of kind, differences
> of a few percentage points. The differences within nations appear greater than
> the differences among nations. There are more similarities in the beliefs of a
> French and German social democrat than between a French socialist and a
> French conservative or between a German social democrat and a German Christ-
> ian democrat.
>
> (Dogan 1988: 2–3)

Even Almond and Verba's own evidence suggests that differences within each
country are at least as striking as the variation between countries.

GRID-GROUP THEORY

Perhaps the most ambitious effort to order the cultural variation within societies
is the grid-group theory formulated by Douglas (1970, 1982). Beneath the
luxuriant diversity of human customs and languages, Douglas argues, the basic
convictions about life are reducible to only four cultural biases: egalitarianism,
fatalism, hierarchy and individualism. Unlike other attempts at constructing
typologies of political culture, Douglas's categories are derived from underlying
dimensions.

The variability of an individual's involvement in social life, Douglas argues,
can be adequately captured by two dimensions of sociality: *group* and *grid*. The
'group' dimension, explains Douglas, taps the extent to which 'the individual's
life is absorbed in and sustained by group membership'. A low group 'score'
would be given to an individual who 'spends the morning in one group, the

evening in another, appears on Sundays in a third, gets his livelihood in a fourth' (Douglas 1982: 202). In contrast, a person who joined with others in 'common residence, shared work, shared resources and recreation' would be assigned a high group rating (ibid.: 191). The further one moves along the group dimension, the tighter the control over admission into the group and the higher the boundaries separating members from non-members.

Although the term 'grid', as used here, may be unfamiliar to social scientists, the concept it denotes is not. In *Suicide*, Durkheim presented much the same idea in his discussion of social 'regulation' (Durkheim 1951: chapter 5). A highly regulated (or high grid) social context is signified by 'an explicit set of institutionalized classifications that keeps individuals apart and regulates their interactions' (Douglas 1982: 203). In such a setting, 'male does not compete in female spheres, and sons do not define their relations with fathers' (ibid.: 192). As one moves down the grid, individuals are increasingly expected to negotiate their own relationships with others.

Strong group boundaries coupled with minimal prescriptions produce social relations that are *egalitarian*. However, because egalitarian groups lack (as a consequence of their low grid position) internal role differentiation, relations between group members are ambiguous. And since no individual is granted the authority to exercise control over another by virtue of his/her position, internal conflicts are difficult to resolve. Individuals can exercise control over one another only by claiming to speak in the name of the group, hence the frequent resort to expulsion in resolving intragroup differences. Because adherents are bound by group decisions but no one has the right to tell others what to do, consensus is the preferred method of internal decision making. Only active participation, each one counting as one but no more than one, can confer legitimacy on decisions.

When an individual's social environment is characterized by strong group boundaries and binding prescriptions, the resulting social relations are *hierarchical*. Individuals in this social context are subject both to the control of other members in the group and the demands of socially imposed roles. In contrast to egalitarianism, which has few means short of expulsion for controlling its members, hierarchy 'has an armoury of different solutions to internal conflicts, including upgrading, shifting sideways, downgrading, resegregating, redefining' (Douglas 1982: 206). The exercise of authority (and inequality more generally) is justified on the grounds that different roles for different people enable people to live together more harmoniously than alternative arrangements do.

Individuals who are bound neither by group incorporation nor prescribed roles inhabit an *individualistic* social context. In such an environment all boundaries are provisional and subject to negotiation. Although the individualist is, by definition, relatively free from control by others, that does not mean that he/she is not engaged in exerting control over others. On the contrary, the individualist's success is often measured by the size of the following commanded.

A person who finds himself/herself subject to binding prescriptions and is excluded from group membership exemplifies the *fatalistic* way of life. The fatalist is controlled from without. As in the case of the hierarchist, the sphere of individual autonomy is restricted. The fatalist may have little choice about how he/she spends his/her time, with whom he/she associates, what he/she wears or eats, where he/she lives and works. Unlike the hierarchist, however, the fatalist is excluded from membership in the group responsible for making the decisions that rule his/her life.

The categories generated by the grid and group dimensions possess the dual advantage of holding on to the best in previous research, thus cumulating findings, while opening up relatively unexplored, but important, avenues of cultural expression. Any theory of viable ways of life must be able to account for the two modes of organizing – hierarchy and markets – that dominate social science theories. Lindblom (1977) and Williamson (1975) are only two of the many scholars who have based entire bodies of theory on this fundamental distinction. Sensing that there may be more than markets and hierarchy, some organizational theorists occasionally mention 'clans' (Ouchi 1980) or 'clubs' (Williamson 1975), but these types do not come from the same matrix, built out of the same dimensions, as markets and hierarchies. A contribution of Douglas's grid-group typology is to derive the egalitarian and fatalist political cultures from dimensions that can also produce the more familiar categories of individualism and hierarchy.

Unlike conventional conceptions of political culture that focus on how patterns of belief and behaviour are passed on but neglect to explain why particular patterns are the way they are, Douglas's theory, by bringing social relationships and values together, offers an explanation of why members of some social groups find certain ideas plausible, while adherents of other groups do not. Political cultures, from this Durkheimian perspective, not only transmit but also form categories of thought. Rather than simply showing that different people, faced with the same situation, desire different things and confer a different meaning upon the situation, Douglas asks the crucial question: given that different people in the same sort of situation want different things, why do they want the different things they want?

STOLEN RHETORIC AND CULTURAL TRAITORS

Douglas's theory identifies which social contexts prevent the sharing of which values. The question thus arises of whether it is possible for adherents of culture A to use the rhetoric of culture B to support the positions of culture

A. In answering this question, it is important to distinguish between rhetoric that binds and rhetoric that leaves people free to do whatever they please. Peace and brotherhood do not bind; espousing competition, equality of condition, fixed statuses, fatalistic resignation, or renunciation of all desires does bind. For Soviet leaders to have proclaimed equality of condition as the guiding norm of their society, for instance, would have threatened the legitimacy of their rule. Consequently they both preached and practiced inequality, reserving equality for some distant future (Wildavsky 1983).

To use the core values of one's opponents in order to undermine those opponents and broaden one's own appeal is a path fraught with danger. Witness, for instance, anti-abortionists who attempt to discomfort their pro-choice opponents and appeal to those on the fence by referring to 'the equal rights of the foetus'. By insisting on the equal rights of all, anti-abortionists abandon (and hence undermine) their hierarchical commitments to the community's right to make distinctions among its members, and its duty to regulate the morality of its members. If it is illegitimate to make distinctions between a foetus and a child, then perhaps egalitarians are justified in denying that it is illegitimate to discriminate between humans and animals, men and women, old and young.

The perils of stealing rhetoric are further evidenced by the experiences of the American Whig party. Repeated failures in national presidential elections led many hierarchical Whigs to adopt the anti-authority rhetoric of the more successful Jacksonian party. Aping Jacksonian rhetoric did help the Whigs become more electorally competitive, but at the same time capitulation to Democratic rhetoric and categories of thought meant that they subverted their own preferred way of life. Within a decade the Whig party disintegrated, and the hierarchical belief system it institutionalized receded from the American political scene. In winning the electoral battle the Whigs lost the cultural war (Ellis and Wildavsky 1989: 116–20).

Look at stolen rhetoric in reverse. If it were possible for adherents of each way of life to steal at will the more successful rhetoric of their rivals, we would today have much less variation than is apparent in the world today. Every individual or group would come to sound much like every other. Such a world would be not only homogeneous but unpredictable, for there would be little constraint on individual belief systems. Yet all of us know of people, whether we number them among our personal acquaintances or hear about them as public figures, whose actions and speech are so predictable that we can say what is on their mind and in their speech before they have an opportunity to reveal themselves. We can do this because values and beliefs come in packages.

If it is not easy to steal rhetoric and to use it effectively, is it still possible for individuals to adopt a position at variance with their current cultural bias without going over to one of the other ways of life? Our view is that to take a position not in accord with one's way of life on an occasional issue does not make a cultural traitor. Were an individual to move beyond occasional disagreement into a pattern of disagreements, however, his/her cultural allegiance would be suspect. Were an individualist to feel, for instance, that there ought to be more protection against environmental oil spills and less logging of old stands in the forests, that person could probably still maintain an individualistic identity. But if that person went on to join the anti-nuclear movement, became upset about the release of genetically engineered organisms into the environment, saw water and air pollution as major threats to human health, and so on, it would become increasingly difficult to maintain his/her original cultural identity.

The reasons for this are both social and cognitive. Joining several environmental and safety groups, for instance, would put our individualist in contact with many people who held similar views on deforestation but who also held anti-individualist views on system blame, on poverty, on social programmes, on foreign policy, and a panoply of other issues. Anyone who has sat in a room for some time with people who differ not only on one or two issues but on a wide spectrum of issues knows that this is difficult to bear. Caught between rival ways of life, the would-be cultural traitor will feel pressured either to move back to whence he/she came or to become something quite different.

The other constraint on individuals stems from the interconnected character of belief systems. For an individualist to accept the proposition that the forest industry must be regulated is to make an exception to a preference for untrammelled self-regulation. If the exceptions multiply, however, the rule itself at some point begins to be thrown into question. To suggest, moreover, that the unfettered cutting of trees is bad is to acquiesce, even if unintentionally, in the egalitarian view that nature is essentially fragile and to call into question the individualist conception of nature as resilient. And if one comes to believe that the least little upset is sufficient to lead Mother Nature to wreak vengeance on the human species, it becomes difficult to justify to oneself and to others the decentralized system of trial and error upon which the individualist life of self-regulation depends. The interdependence of beliefs thus makes it difficult to reject a part without unravelling the whole.

WHAT IS POLITICAL IN POLITICAL CULTURE?

What, the reader might wonder, distinguishes culture from political culture? To what does the 'political' in political culture refer? Defining political culture as patterns of orientation to political action or objects sidesteps the question of what is to count as political. Some insist that all action is political. So, for instance, Leslie Gottlieb of the Council on Economic Priorities declares, 'shopping is political. Buying a product means casting an economic vote for that company' (quoted in Bizjak 1989). If 'political' denotes power relations, then there is nothing that is not political, from child-rearing to marriage to attending school. If culture is by definition political, then the term 'political' is superfluous. To avoid this redundancy, students of political culture have attempted to define political culture as orientations towards government (as opposed to, say, the economy, religion, or the family). This conception includes attitudes about what government does (or should do) together with what people outside government try to get it to do.

As these competing definitions of the 'political' attest, the boundary between political and non-political is not graven in stone, inherent in the nature of things. Definitions of what is political are themselves culturally biased. When one person accuses another of 'politicizing' a subject, the disagreement is about how far the governmental writ should run. Constructing the boundary between political and non-political is thus part and parcel of the struggle between competing ways of life. Thus rather than join in a debate about what is 'really' political, we prefer to show how different culturally biased definitions of the political support different ways of life.

Egalitarians desire to reduce the distinction between the political and non-political. Defining the family or firm as non-political or private, egalitarians believe, is a way of concealing and hence perpetuating unequal power relations. Egalitarians view the public sphere, in which all can actively participate and give their consent to collective decisions, as the realm in which the good life can best be realized.

Because individualism seeks to substitute self-regulation for authority, its adherents are continually accusing others of politicizing issues. Their interest is in defining politics as narrowly as possible so as to maximize that behaviour which is considered private, and thus beyond the reach of governmental regulation. Hence their reluctance to admit the egalitarian charge that private resources dominate public decision making, for this admission would imply capitulation.

If egalitarians see the political sphere as that realm in which human beings most fully realize their potential, the fatalist regards the political with nothing but fear and dread. The more power is exercised, the more they expect to suffer. Fatalists respond to their plight by trying to get as far out of harm's way as possible. Unlike the individualist, however, the fatalist does not discriminate sharply between the private and public spheres. Whether called public or private, the blows come without apparent pattern or meaning. The task of fatalists then becomes personal or at most familial survival, and they cope as best they can without trying to distinguish the source of their difficulties.

Hierarchists, for the same reasons that they approve of putting people and products in their properly ordered place, approve differentiating the public and private spheres. They frequently harbour an expansive view of state functions, hence their conflict with individualists, but they insist, contra the egalitarians, that politics is not for everyone, but rather reserved for a qualified few. Where hierarchists draw the line between the public and private will vary, but that boundary is likely to be well-defined.

Running through these four ways of life shows that the type of behaviour or institution that is deemed political, or whether a boundary is even drawn at all, is itself a product of political culture. This suggests that the study of political culture (as distinct from culture generally) should pay special attention to the ways in which the boundary between the political and non-political is socially negotiated. It also means, more importantly, that political scientists must give up the notion that the distinction between politics and other spheres (whether economic, social or whatever) is 'out there' in the world, ready-made to be picked up and used. If, moreover, the boundaries between the political and non-political are socially constructed, then the study of political culture must assume a central place in the discipline.

POLITICAL CULTURE: AN EXPLANATORY PANACEA?

Is political culture an explanatory panacea, a universal nostrum, good for all problems, like some quack medicine? Surely, there must be subjects not amenable to cultural analysis. Suppose, for instance, a wall of water rushes towards us; presumably we would not need to resort to culture to tell us to get out of the way – self-preservation would be sufficient. Or would it? Even in this most extreme instance, where all involved are likely to agree on the danger, culture can have a critical role in explaining behaviour. A cultural theory may tell us why some individuals adopt an attitude of 'each for himself and the devil take the hindmost', while others advocate 'women and children first' or 'follow the leader', while still others decide that 'it's no use, I'll stay here'.

What is culturally rational may conflict with (and even lose out to) individual self-interest. Consider, for instance, the business firm that seeks governmental subsidies, thereby enriching itself at the expense of weakening competitive individualism. The NIMBY ('not in my backyard') syndrome for the location of potentially dangerous facilities might be another example of self-interest overriding cultural bias. But, lest we concede too much, we hasten to add that determining what is in one's interests is often an exceedingly difficult task. Deciding whether a nuclear facility endangers one's safety, for instance, depends on one's perception of risk, which in turn is a function of one's political culture (Douglas and Wildavsky 1982; Dake and Wildavsky 1990). A cultural approach does not try to deny the operation of self-interest as a motivation, but it does insist on asking how individuals come to believe where those interests lie.

THE FUTURE OF POLITICAL CULTURE

Political culture is currently undergoing something of a renaissance (see Inglehart 1988; Eckstein 1988; Schwarz and Thompson 1990; Thompson *et al.* 1990). In large part, this is due to a dissatisfaction with the limits of rational choice approaches to human behaviour. Rational choice explanations are fine as far as they go. Our objection is not to explaining human behaviour in terms of individual efforts to realize objectives, but instead with the assumption that the objectives themselves require no explanation. Instead of a social science that begins at the end – assuming preferences and interests – a cultural approach makes why people want what they want into the central subject of inquiry (Wildavsky 1987).

If this renewed interest in political culture is to be worthwhile, future research must give sustained attention to the way in which institutions are related to values. People do not experience values apart from those who share them, or engage in social relations without justifying their behaviour to others. What is needed is not further wrangling over how to define culture but rather the construction of theories that will enable us to join institutional relationships and modes of perception, social relations and values. It is because Douglas's grid-group analysis does exactly this that we find her theory so promising.

REFERENCES

Almond, G. A. (1980) 'The Intellectual History of the Civic Culture Concept', in G. A. Almond and S. Verba (eds) *The Civic Culture Revisited*, Boston: Little, Brown & Co.

Almond, G. A. and Powell, G. B. (1966) *Comparative Politics: A Developmental Approach*, Boston: Little, Brown & Co.

Almond, G. A. and Verba, S. (1963) *The Civic Culture: Political Attitudes and Democracy in Five Nations*, Princeton: Princeton University Press.

Banfield, E. C. (1958) *The Moral Basis of a Backward Society*, New York: Free Press.

Barry, B. (1970) *Sociologists, Economists and Democracy*, London: Collier-Macmillan.

Benedict, R. (1934) *Patterns of Culture*, Boston: Houghton Mifflin.

——(1946) *The Chrysanthemum and the Sword: Patterns of Japanese Culture*, Boston: Houghton Mifflin.

Bizjak, T. (1989) 'New dictums of the "politically correct"', *San Francisco Chronicle*, 17 March, p. 8.

Dake, K. and Wildavsky, A. (1990) 'Comparing rival theories of risk-reception: who fears what and why?', *Daedalus* 119(4): 41–60.

Dogan, M. (ed.) (1988) *Comparing Pluralist Democracies: Strains on Legitimacy*, Boulder, Colo.: Westview Press.

Douglas, M. (1970) *Natural Symbols: Explorations in Cosmology*, London: Barrie & Rockliff.

——(1982) 'Cultural bias', in *In The Active Voice*, London: Routledge & Kegan Paul.

Douglas, M. and Wildavsky, A. (1982) *Risk and Culture*, Berkeley: University of California Press.

Durkheim, E. (1951) *Suicide: A Study in Sociology*, Glencoe, Ill.: Free Press.

Eckstein, H. (1988) 'A culturalist theory of political change', *American Political Science Review* 82: 789–804.

Ellis, R. and Wildavsky, A. (1989) *Dilemmas of Presidential Leadership: From Washington Through Lincoln*, New Brunswick: Transaction Publishers.

Erikson, R. S., McIver, J. P. and Wright, G. C., Jr (1987) 'State political culture and public opinion', *American Political Science Review* 81: 797–814.

Gorer, G. (1948) *The American People: A Study in National Character*, New York: Norton.

——(1955) *Exploring English Character*, New York: Criterion.

Hall, P. (1986) *Governing the Economy: The Politics of State Intervention in Britain and France*, New York: Oxford University Press.

Inglehart, R. (1988) 'The renaissance of political culture', *American Political Science Review* 82: 1203–30.

Kroeber, A. L. and Kluckhohn, C. (1952) *Culture: A Critical Review of Concepts and Definitions*, Cambridge, Mass.: Harvard University Press.

Lindblom, C. (1977) *Politics and Markets: The World's Political-Economic Systems*, New York: Basic Books.

Mead, M. (1942) *And Keep Your Powder Dry: An Anthropologist Looks at America*, New York: Morrow.

——(1953) 'National character', in A. L. Kroeber (ed.) *Anthropology Today: An Encyclopedic Inventory*, Chicago: University of Chicago Press.

Ouchi, W. G. (1980) 'Markets, bureaucracies, and clans', *Administrative Science Quarterly* 25: 129–41.

Pizzorno, A. (1966) 'Amoral familism and historical marginality', *International Review of Community Development* 15 and 16: 55–66.

Pye, L. W. (1965) 'Introduction: political culture and political development', in L. W. Pye and S. Verba (eds) *Political Culture and Political Development*, Princeton, NJ: Princeton University Press.

——(1968) 'Political culture', in D. L. Sills (ed.) *International Encyclopedia of the Social Sciences*, New York: Macmillan/Free Press.

Schwarz, M. and Thompson, M. (1990) *Divided We Stand: Redefining Politics, Technology and Social Choice*, Hemel Hempstead: Harvester-Wheatsheaf.

Thompson, M., Ellis, R. and Wildavsky, A. (1990) *Cultural Theory*, Boulder, Colo.: Westview Press.

Wildavsky, A. (1983) 'The soviet system', in A. Wildavsky (ed.) *Beyond Containment: Alternative American Policies Toward the Soviet Union*, San Francisco: Institute for Contemporary Studies.

——(1987) 'Choosing preferences by constructing institutions: a cultural theory of preference formation', *American Political Science Review* 81: 3–21.

Williamson, O. (1975) *Markets and Hierarchies, Analysis and Antitrust Implications: A Study in the Economics of Internal Organization*, New York: Free Press.

FURTHER READING

Almond, G. A. (1956) 'Comparative political systems', *Journal of Politics* 18: 391–409.

Brown, A. (ed.) (1984) *Political Cultures and Communist Studies*, Armonk, NY: M. E. Sharpe.

Brown, A. and Gray, J. (eds.) (1977) *Political Culture and Political Change in Communist States*, New York: Holmes & Meier.

Chilton, S. (1988) 'Defining political culture', *Western Political Quarterly* 41: 419–46.

Dittmer, L. (1977) 'Political culture and political symbolism', *World Politics* 29: 552–82.

——(1982) 'The comparative analysis of political culture', *Amerikastudien* 27: 19–41.

Douglas, M. (ed.) (1982) *Essays in the Sociology of Perception*, London: Routledge & Kegan Paul.

——(1986) *How Institutions Think*, Utica, NY: Syracuse University Press.

Douglas, M. and Isherwood, B. (1979) *The World of Goods: Towards an Anthropology of Consumption*, London: Allen Lane.

Douglas, M. and Wildavsky, A. (1982) *Risk and Culture*, Berkeley: University of California Press.

Elazar, D. J. (1966) *American Federalism: A View from the States*, New York: Thomas Y. Crowell.

——(1970) *Cities of the Prairie: The Metropolitan Frontier and American Politics*, New York: Basic Books.

Elkins, D. J. and Simeon, R. (1979) 'A cause in search of its effect, or what does political culture explain?', *Comparative Politics* 11: 127–45.

Geertz, C. (1973) *The Interpretation of Cultures*, New York: Basic Books.

Gross, J. and Rayner, S. (1986) *Measuring Culture*, New York: Columbia University Press.

Jowitt, K. (1974) 'An organizational approach to the study of political culture in Marxist-Leninist systems', *American Political Science Review* 68: 1171–91.

Keesing, R. M. (1974) 'Theories of culture', *Annual Review of Anthropology* 3: 73–97.

Kluckholm, C. (1945) 'The concept of culture', in R. Linton (ed.) *The Science of Man in the World Crisis*, New York: Columbia University Press.

Lehman, E. 'On the concept of political culture: a theoretical reassessment', *Social Forces* 50: 361–70.

Mars, G. (1982) *Cheats at Work: An Anthropology of Workplace Crime*, London: Allen & Unwin.

Parsons, T. (1951) *The Social System*, New York: Free Press.

Pateman, C. (1971) 'Political culture, political structure and political change', *British Journal of Political Science* 1: 291–305.

Putnam, R. D. (1971) 'Studying elite political culture: the case of ideology', *American Political Science Review* 65: 651–81.

Putnam, R. D., Leonardi, R., Nanetti, R. Y. and Pavoncello, F. (1983) 'Explaining institutional success: the case of Italian regional government', *American Political Science Review* 77: 55–74.

Putnam, R. D., Leonardi, R. and Nanetti, R. Y. (1988) 'Institutional performance and political culture: some puzzles about the power of the past', *Governance* 1: 221–42.

Pye, L. W. (1988) *The Mandarin and the Cadre: China's Political Cultures*, Ann Arbor: University of Michigan Press.

Schwartz, M. and Thompson, M. (1990) *Divided We Stand: Redefining Politics, Technology and Social Choice*, Hemel Hempstead: Harvester-Wheatsheaf.

Thompson, M. (1979) *Rubbish Theory: The Creation and Destruction of Value*, Oxford: Oxford University Press.

Wildavsky, A. (1988) 'A cultural theory of Budgeting', *International Journal of Public Administration* 11: 651–77.

——(1989) 'Frames of reference come from cultures: a predictive theory', in M. Freilich (ed.) *The Relevance of Culture*, New York: Bergin & Garney, pp. 58–74.

Wildavsky, A. and Polisar, D. (1989) 'From individual to system blame: analysis of historical change in the law of torts', *Journal of Policy History* 1: 129–55.

32

RELIGION AND POLITICS

ROBIN LOVIN

Religion gives individuals their most comprehensive ideas about reality and the meaning of events. Scriptures and oral traditions narrate the origins of the world and prescribe appropriate actions and attitudes in response to the cosmic order (Eliade 1969: 80–7). Theologies and philosophies offer reasoned elaborations of the mythic premises, providing speculative systems that link contemporary events to the primal order and practical assurances that adherence to religious norms is not in vain. Ritual re-enactments and collective reflection secure a shared conviction that reality is as the religion has described it, and provide legitimacy for activities and attitudes seen to be in conformity to its requirements (Geertz 1973: 90).

Politics is among the most important of these activities explained and legitimated by religion. In a great variety of historical and cultural settings, political order has been linked to a religious cosmogony, and political leadership has thus acquired a sacred status. The story of the sun goddess Amaterasu, for example, links the creation of the Japanese archipelago and the founding of the imperial dynasty, while the Chinese emperors derived their power from a 'mandate of heaven'. The Hebrew scriptures make no distinction between sacred and civil law, and obligations in the community rest on a covenant between God and the people. Meso-American mythology links the authority of the Aztec rulers to their role in the sacrifices that sustained the world order.

One might almost say that the primary relation of religion and politics is that religion legitimates the political order by linking it to a cosmic order of sacred origin. Yet differentiation and conflict between religious and political powers are equally familiar. Christianity spread through the Roman world in defiance of the imperial authorities, and European peasants in the era of the Reformation used religious change to demand a new order in politics and society. Today Islamic fundamentalists and Hindu traditionalists resist the modernization plans of secular authorities, while Japanese politicians debate the place of traditional Shinto rites in state ceremonies.

The historical relationships between religion and politics include differentiation, and even conflict, as well as legitimation. The purpose of this chapter is to review some of the theoretical frameworks in which these changing relationships have been understood. We will consider both functionalist and secularization theories, which offer differing accounts of a general history of religion's political role, and then turn to a typology that suggests a more pluralistic approach to the connections between religion and politics.

FUNCTIONALISM

The widespread tendency of political systems to draw on the legitimating power of religion has led some theorists to propose a functionalist account of religion's social role. Religions are identified by their power to inspire the attitudes and commitments that the political order requires, and any substantial transformation of the political order necessarily overthrows the religious regime as well. A new political order requires a new religion, and every political system will eventually generate a religious affirmation of its basic beliefs and requirements.

Explicit functionalist accounts of religion appear early in the modern era. Hobbes understood a 'Christian commonwealth' as one in which the sovereign controls religious ritual and doctrine with the same absolute authority that determines civil law. Here, the marks of a true prophet are the doing of miracles and 'not teaching any other Religion than that which is already established' (Hobbes 1968: 412). Rousseau provided for a 'civil religion' (*la religion civile*) in his theoretical elaboration of a society that would provide for both individual freedom and social solidarity (Rousseau 1973: 268–77), while Auguste Comte drew up plans for what he called 'positivism', a humanistic religion complete with nine 'social sacraments' (Comte 1891: 90).

The functional religion that early modern thinkers provided as part of their programme of religious and political reform appeared to some later social theorists as an inevitable feature of any stable social system. For Emile Durkheim, Catholicism had in an earlier age served the social purposes that Rousseau and Comte anticipated for civil religion and positivism (Durkheim 1965: 475). Historical changes may diminish the authority of a particular religion, or sweep it aside completely, but they cannot eliminate the need for a centre of devotion and enthusiasm that sustains moral unity in a people. Talcott Parsons draws on Durkheim's understanding of religion in his theoretical delineation of the role of religion in social systems (Parsons 1952: 368). Robert Bellah utilizes the concept of a 'civil religion' existing alongside and independent of organized religious traditions to explain the elements of religious aspiration and commitment that have historically characterized politics in the United States (Bellah 1967).

From this perspective, the politically relevant religion is just whatever system of beliefs provides this unifying, inspiring, and, for Bellah, self-critical and self-correcting function (Bellah 1975: 162). Alternative beliefs, even if they are more clearly related to a religious tradition, will either be rendered politically quiescent by the prevailing civil faith, or they will form communities of retreat and withdrawal for those who do not participate in political life. Thus, for example, churches in the United States typically draw sharp distinctions between an acceptable moral and religious witness on public questions and the unacceptable mingling of religion and partisan politics. In the post-war era in Eastern Europe, many churches explicitly accepted the 'leading role' of the Communist Party in political matters. A functional theorist might argue that in those cases, examination of traditional Christian groups would shed little light on the enduring relationships between religion and politics. To accomplish that, one would need to look at the civil religion or the Marxist ideology that had replaced the political functions of earlier forms of Christianity.

DIFFERENTIATION

Functionalist theories help to explain the symbolic significance of founding events to political ideologies by highlighting the analogies between these social forces and traditional religions. The Durkheimian effort to identify a unifying and inspiring function that would characterize all religion fails, however, to capture a differentiation between religion and politics that has developed in many historically important religions. Focusing attention on the beliefs and aspirations that bind a people together may obscure the political significance of religious systems that no longer sustain or have not yet achieved this central unifying role.

In addition to providing a 'civil religion' in the sense of Rousseau or Durkheim, religion may be used to legitimate the cultural hegemony of one group at the expense of others. Reformed Protestantism is sometimes used in this way in South Africa today, and Protestantism was used during the nineteenth century in the United States to legitimate the dominance of elites of British, German and Dutch over immigrants of Jewish and Roman Catholic background. A displaced religious tradition may sustain the aspirations of those who hope for a political restoration of the old order, keeping alive with religious hope movements whose realistic political chances have long since died. Hence Tsarist *emigrés* sought to gain control of Russian Orthodox churches outside the Soviet Union, and there have long been connections between French monarchists and Roman Catholic traditionalism. Religious traditions introduced into new areas can be vehicles of cultural and political transformation, as for example when Christian missions hastened modernization in parts of

Asia. Religion can also be a conservative force, resisting the efforts of political leaders who would exchange traditional ways for modern systems of production and economic development.

Most importantly, a religion which begins in close association with a particular people and a particular system of rule can assert itself as an independent centre of authority, leading to a differentiation within the society between moral or religious authority on the one hand, and political power on the other. Buddhism and Christianity, for example, both spread widely in their early centuries. Buddhism tended to cultivate support by the conversion of local rulers, while Christianity grew among the urban poor and middle classes. Both religions counselled obedience to political authorities, but each also established distinctive, highly organized structures of religious authority which resisted coercion and exercised their own influences on the rulers. The *Sangha*, the order of Buddhist monks, provided counsellors to the princes of India and South-East Asia and generated an important literature on the ideals of Buddhist rulership (Tambiah 1976: 32–3). Christian bishops framed a network of local leadership that rivalled the organization of the Roman Empire.

The separation of religion and government is not inevitable, but once in place it tends to persist, even when subsequent developments once again produce close links between religious and political powers. Despite the tendency of modern observers to describe European Christianity of the Middle Ages or the Puritan communities of colonial New England as 'theocracies', it is doubtful whether Western Christianity has ever produced a genuine theocracy, in which all decisions are taken by a single authority applying a sacred law. Differentiated roles for religious and political leaders and a measure of respect for contextual political prudence have been important elements of both theory and practice, even where religious and political leaders shared the closest allegiance to the common faith.

Once religious and political authorities have become clearly differentiated, even their co-operation is marked by an inherent tension, and the possibility of religious delegitimation or political coercion is always present. The inescapable possibility of conflict between religion and politics colours even those moments when the two sources of authority enjoy the closest harmony and agreement.

SECULARIZATION

As an alternative to a single social function that defines religion's political role, other theorists have sought to identify a general pattern of historical development that links the fate of all religions in a variety of cultural contexts.

Here, too, the roots of the argument lie early in modern social thought. Hume hypothesized that monotheism developed from a polytheism based in primitive humanity's vulnerability to the forces of nature (Hume 1927:

269–73). In the nineteenth century, James Frazer and Edward Tylor argued for the development of a rational, scientific world view out of the failures of primitive magic and superstition (Evans-Pritchard 1965: 24–9). For these observers, the history, and perhaps the eventual disappearance, of religion was conditioned by the development of rationality.

Early in the twentieth century, Max Weber (1958, 1964) traced this development of rationality and its impact on religion in social terms. Weber's views grew initially out of his study of the emergence of modern European capitalism and its relationship to the ethics of Protestant Christianity, but this later gave rise to a general theory of history and of religion.

In developed industrial society, religion has a far less important role than in the pre-modern world of Protestant piety. The disciplines which once depended on faith are now imposed by the bureaucratic and economic structures on which we all depend for a livelihood, structures which create, in Weber's grim image, an 'iron cage' in which we are all confined, and where we shall remain 'until the last ton of fossilized coal is burnt' (Weber 1958: 181). Religion in such a society undergoes a process of secularization. A rationalized, historically developed form of religion triumphs, at least in the sense that its ethics are incorporated into the *saeculum*, the order of the world itself; but the beliefs, institutions and authorities of such a religion become irrelevant. They lose their power to shape events or to mitigate the demands of economic rationality.

Later developments of secularization theory moderate Weber's tendency towards economic determinism, but they continue to stress the demands of rationality on all ways of thinking. Ideas can be used only to the extent that they shed their pre-rational, affective orientation towards the world and make sense in terms of this modern understanding. Religious traditions may enhance our understanding of human aims and our appreciation of human dignity, but they can make these contributions only if they give up their historical particularities and the mythic presentations of their truth for the formulation of a rational morality (Horkheimer 1972: 129–31; Habermas 1984: 43–74).

Secularization theories call attention to important changes in the place of religion in modern society as contrasted to earlier ages and traditional cultures. The differentiation of artistic, economic and educational organizations from religious institutions reduces the importance of specific religious texts and symbols in intellectual and creative life, and religious leadership, like all leadership, becomes more specialized and professionalized. The prestige and authority once concentrated in religious institutions as centres of education and culture are now distributed among schools, museums, theatres and publishers, and the religious ceremonies that once provided generally shared opportunities for recreation and inspiration now serve the specifically religious needs of a limited number of worshippers.

THE PERSISTENCE OF RELIGION

There is a tendency, for research purposes, to measure secularization in terms of the decline of religious observance (Acquaviva 1979) or the changing status of clergy (Martin 1978: 278–308). These may mark important social changes, but they do not directly reveal the fate of religious beliefs. For purposes of political analysis, the persistence of religious ideas as an opposition to forces of modernization, or as social ideals in a liberal democracy, may be as important as a falling away from traditional practices or the loss of clerical authority. Secularization theory should not be used in a way that uncritically interprets all measurable religious changes as signs of religious decline. When it is, the persistence of religious ideas will be missed.

This is particularly true where changes in religious practice have been enforced, subtly or openly, by economic or political powers that do not enjoy the loyalty of the religious communities. Sabbath observances, conscientious objection to military service, and the rejection of state-sponsored education are among the many overt expressions of religious beliefs which may be temporarily repressed by economic penalties or state persecution, only to emerge at a later date in demands for political reform and constitutionally protected religious rights. An assessment of the political importance of religion based on a measurement of participation during the period of repression would miss the potentially explosive power of the religious ideas to fuel revolt against persecuting authorities, or to demand political adjustments of educational, cultural and social welfare programmes to make them more acceptable to the religious population.

The vigilant, worldwide efforts of the Seventh-Day Adventists, linking their apocalyptic theology to campaigns for religious freedom and human rights, is one instance of the political significance of religious ideas in secular contexts. The emergence of fundamentalist movements in religions as diverse as American Protestantism and Shi'ite Islam provides an even further-reaching example of the persistence of religion in the face of social and cultural changes that appeared at one point to mark the triumph of modernity and Western rationalism (Marty 1988).

In addition to movements which seek to maintain religious beliefs and make them politically effective in the face of powerful or widespread opposition, the religious beliefs of private individuals may shape their political choices even where the political realm is overtly 'secular', for instance, free of publicly recognized religious symbols and norms. In those contexts, diversity of religious and moral beliefs, expanded options created by material wealth, and emphasis on individual freedom may encourage the development of procedural democracy, in which outcomes are supposed to be determined by rationally self-interested individuals making the case for their goals by offering publicly accessible reasons. Those reasons alone, however, may not provide criteria for decisions about such important public questions as abortion, criminal justice and welfare rights. In such cases, private citizens and even judges and political leaders may have to rely on religious convictions to arrive at answers to the problems (Greenawalt 1988: 12). A political analysis which considers only secular, public rationales without attempting to relate them to the religious convictions of the participants thus may miss important determinants of the outcomes.

Even more important, religious ideas are politically relevant in liberal democracies because they contribute to a broader social discussion of human aims and purposes. If the political choices of a procedural democracy are made by particular interests seeking limited policy objectives, the range of political possibilities is set by ideas debated more widely and over a longer period of time. Political choices may differ sharply over proposals to fight poverty with a negative income tax, or with 'workfare' programmes, yet the parties may share the belief that 'the justice of a community is measured by its treatment of the powerless in society' (National Conference of Catholic Bishops 1986: 21). Religious thought may be divided or indecisive regarding the policy options, and yet be crucial to the development of the values that shape and limit the policy choices.

DIFFERENTIATION AND PERSISTENCE: A TYPOLOGY

Both civil religion and secularization tell us much about religion and politics in modern states influenced historically by Western Christianity. Any single explanatory model will, however, appear radically incomplete when used as a tool for understanding the interactions of religion and politics on a larger, global scale. Reliance on them will lead both political leadership and political scientists to overlook significant groups and individuals who, for the moment at least, neither provide functional support for the political order nor yield to the requirements of modern, rationalized social and economic life.

The principal reason why the relations between religion and society and the political impact of religion cannot be reduced to a single model is the persistence of religious ideas themselves. Formed in a religious context, ideas about personal morality, obligations to family and associates, the acquisition and use of wealth, and the legitimacy and limits of power have remarkable tenacity in the face of changing ideas about productive rationality or political expedience. Confronted with material circumstances or political opposition, the leaders and communities who are the bearers of these ideas may adapt and modify them to fit the new conditions, or they may resist and create alternative forms of community and loyalty that will allow them to maintain traditional values. Either way, political possibilities will be altered by the specific norms that are given importance in the new social context, or by the presence of groups that challenge the functional social consensus.

The political implications of religious ideas thus require a number of models for the interaction. This theoretical pluralism can be represented in a typology. This has been well understood by historians, theologians and sociologists who have tried to understand the social thought of Christianity across the centuries (Troeltsch 1976) or to interpret the complexity of denominational Christianity in the United States (Niebuhr 1965; Roof and McKinney 1987). Ernst Troeltsch saw the history of Christian social teaching as the development of two basically different ideas about the relationship of Christian truth to social life, ideas he identified as 'church' and 'sect'. To those forms, present from the beginning, he also added a distinctly modern 'mystical' type, which fails to take the institutionalized forms characteristic of church and sect (Troeltsch 1976: 729–802). H. Richard Neibuhr adapted this typology for constructive theological purposes, expanding Troeltsch's three types to a more differentiated five (Niebuhr 1956).

The need now, however, is for a typology that can be used for comparative purposes beyond the boundaries of Western Christianity. While Christianity provides us with important lessons in religion's adaptation to modernity, an account that draws the possibilities from Christianity alone will leave much out. The following typology is therefore offered as a scheme for organizing understandings of the relationships between religion and politics which may have some validity for other traditions and nations, as well as modern Western Christianity. It suggests five principal forms which that relationship may take, though as with all such schemes, the types may be found in many variations, and the boundaries between different types may in practice be difficult to determine.

Sacralizing religions maintain an unproblematic relationship of legitimation and support for the political order. Indeed, religious and political authority will not be sharply differentiated. These religions may have existed in some form from the very beginnings of an ethnic or national history, and continue to provide a distinctive sense of identity for a people as a whole. Traditional forms of Hinduism and Shinto, despite extensive changes through history, thus relate to the politics of India and Japan. In other cases, religious changes in historical times have taken place with such completeness that the events also represent a new political foundation. The expansion of Islam after 633 CE provides an example, as does, perhaps, the conversion of the Slavic peoples to Byzantine Christianity after c.860. In most of these cases, religious identity becomes a feature of ethnic or national identity, and the ruler assumes certain sacred characteristics.

Differentiated religions acknowledge important distinctions between religion and other spheres of social life, such as government, economics, family life and education. While religious norms and values may permeate the whole society, differentiated religions place limits on the extent of religious authority and specifically religious law and accord a relative autonomy to each of the spheres. Concepts of natural law or moral consensus may allow for co-operation with members of other religious groups on issues of justice and social welfare, without requiring religious unanimity. Indeed, where the differentiations between religion, law and morality are well-developed and long-standing, it may be difficult to determine whether a specific normative position is or is not based on religious convictions. Western Christianity, particularly in modern liberal democracies, provides the clearest examples of differentiated religion. Buddhism, however, has often taken differentiated forms as it has moved into new contexts and, as with Christianity, its capacity for differentiation and its relationship to a variety of political systems partly accounts for its success as a missionary religion. Despite the close connections that have sometimes prevailed between church and state, or between the *Sangha* and the king, it is possible for at least some adherents of these religions to speak of a 'Christian society' or a 'Buddhist society' in terms of its treatment of the poor and its limitations on the use of coercive force, and without a necessary connection to a particular form of political organization.

Sectarian religions maintain religious norms and values in the face of hostility or indifference from civil powers, or in dissent from the religious ideas of a dominant religious authority. Religious conceptions of the proper ordering of human life can adapt to a wide variety of circumstances, as differentiated religions demonstrate, but the religious ideas are not infinitely flexible. At some point, religious communities and leaders will see themselves in insurmountable opposition to the prevailing political or religious system, and they may at that point seek to preserve the possibility of religious life as an alternative community. Characteristically, sectarian religions withdraw from politics, eschewing both the burdens and the benefits of citizenship and striving to maintain economic self-sufficiency. While the religious community may itself remain politically inactive, preferring even persecution to a political defence of its interests, sectarian religions none the less pose unavoidable questions for political life about how far the claims and obligations of citizenship extend and what the limits of conscientious dissent from societal norms will be. Sectarian religions usually take the form of small communal communities, typified by the Essene communities of early Judaism, some Christian monastic orders, and the Anabaptist communities of the Reformation era. For some Christian theologians, however, a sectarian rejection of the values of an individualist, consumption-oriented society marks an appropriate contemporary Christian stance (Yoder 1984). Similar movements can be found among contemporary followers of ascetic 'forest saints' in South-East Asian Buddhism (Tambiah 1984).

Fundamentalist religions arise when norms of identity and conduct characteristic of a sacralizing religion are in conflict with their social context. Typically, the new context overtakes the religious community by imposition from outside, or draws traditional believers into a new industrialized or urban environment by economic incentives. In fundamentalist religions, the difficulties the new context pose for traditional patterns inspire a systematization of belief and ethics and coercive enforcement of the newly formulated requirements on members of the religious community, as well as attempts to make the standards normative for society as a whole. Contemporary Islamic fundamentalism is the paradigm for the political realization of these demands, but some Protestant fundamentalists in the United States have made similar proposals. Hindu traditionalists also reject modern and foreign innovations, and the collapse of Marxist politics in Eastern Europe may create possibilities for the emergence of an Eastern Orthodox fundamentalism in traditionally Orthodox countries.

Individualist religions exist primarily in modern liberal societies that place a high value on individual freedom and may encompass many different religious traditions in the same state. Individualist religions thus reflect Troeltsch's observation that an individualistic 'mystical' type is the characteristically modern form of religious social organization, distinguished precisely by the fact that it does not create large, permanent religious institutions. While sectarian religions find the religious and moral neutrality of the modern secular state inimical to their religious life, individualist religions see it as a sphere of freedom in which persons can follow their own religious consciousness without seeking to impose it on others or making it conform to authoritative doctrines and practices. From the standpoint of more closely defined religious traditions, individualist religions often appear eclectic, even idiosyncratic (Luckmann 1970). Because individualist religions usually accept the differentiation of religious beliefs from systems of law, government, and even from the basic norms of social morality, their political activity and impact is generally limited to support for norms of individual choice and religious freedom.

In each of these types – sacralizing, differentiated, sectarian, fundamentalist, or individualist – religion provides the comprehensive explanations and orientations that enable people to understand their place in the political order as part of the ultimate reality in which they live and act. Because religious traditions hold definite ideas about that reality and are not merely social functions, the forms they can take and the politics they can support are limited, and specific traditions may become closely identified with a particular religious form. Because major traditions endure through history and take root in a variety of cultures, however, they will assume nearly every one of the characteristic types at one time or another.

Understanding the political dimension of a religious tradition begins by comprehending the affinities between its basic orientation toward life and the world and the types of relationships to politics outlined here, and identifying the ways of relating to social order and political power that are most congenial to the conception of ultimate order and power that this particular tradition holds. Estimating the political impact of religious belief, by contrast, requires attentiveness to the new or unusual types of relationships to politics that a religious tradition may take on in changing economic and cultural circumstances. In the last few centuries in the industrialized countries of the West, those circumstances have largely favoured Protestant Christianity and other traditions which have historically tended toward the differentiated type of religion. Other traditions, notably Judaism, that found themselves in those circumstances have developed previously uncharacteristic differentiated types. Social theory, which emerged simultaneously with these developments, has charted them well, but has also lent a certain sense of inevitability to the rise of differentiated and individualist types of religion. As our attention widens to include more of the world's religious traditions, and as the material circumstances that marked the rise of modern industrialism shift dramatically, our understanding of religion must also expand to include other religious types and to anticipate their impact on politics.

REFERENCES

Acquaviva, S. S. (1979) *The Decline of the Sacred in Industrial Society*, New York: Harper & Row.

Bellah, R. N. (1967) 'Civil religion in America', *Daedalus* 96 (Winter): 1–21.

——(1975) *The Broken Covenant*, New York: Seabury Press.

Comte, A. (1891) *The Catechism of Positive Religion*, London: Kegan Paul.

Durkheim, E. (1965) *The Elementary Forms of the Religious Life*, New York: Free Press.

Eliade, M. (1969) *The Quest: History and Meaning in Religion*, Chicago: University of Chicago Press.

Evans-Pritchard, E. E. (1965) *Theories of Primitive Religion*, Oxford: Oxford University Press.

Geertz, C. (1973) 'Religion as a cultural system', in C. Geertz (ed.) *The Interpretation of Cultures*, New York: Basic Books.

Greenawalt, K. (1988) *Religious Convictions and Political Choice*, New York: Oxford University Press.

Habermas, J. (1984) *Theory of Communicative Action*, vol. 1, trans. T. McCarthy, Boston: Beacon Press.

Hobbes, T. (1968) *Leviathan*, edited and with an introduction by C. B. Macpherson, Baltimore, Md.: Penguin.

Horkheimer, M. (1972) *Critical Theory*, trans. M. J. O'Connell, New York: Continuum.

Hume, D. (1927) 'The natural history of religion', in C. W. Hendel (ed.) *Hume: Selections*, New York: Charles Scribner's Sons.

Luckmann, T. (1970) *The Invisible Religion: The Problem of Religion in Modern Society*, London: Macmillan.

Martin, D. (1978) *A General Theory of Secularization*, New York: Harper & Row.

Marty, M. E. (1988) 'Fundamentalism as a social phenomenon', *The American Academy of Arts and Sciences Bulletin* 42 (November): 15–29.

National Conference of Catholic Bishops (1986) *Economic Justice For All: Pastoral Letter on Catholic Social Teaching and the US Economy*, Washington, DC: United States Catholic Conference.

Niebuhr, H. R. (1956) *Christ and Culture*, New York: Harper & Row.

——(1965) *The Social Sources of Denominationalism*, Cleveland: World Publishing.

Parsons, T. (1952) *The Social System*, London: Tavistock Publications.

Roof, W. C. and McKinney, W. (1987) *American Mainline Religion*, New Brunswick: Rutgers University Press.

Rousseau, J.-J. (1973) *The Social Contract and Discourses*, rev. edn, London: J. M. Dent & Sons.

Tambiah, S. J. (1976) *World Conqueror and World Renouncer*, Cambridge: Cambridge University Press.

——(1984) *The Buddhist Saints of the Forest and the Cult of Amulets*, Cambridge: Cambridge University Press.

Troeltsch, E. (1976) *The Social Teaching of the Christian Churches*, trans. O. Wyon, 2 vols, Chicago: University of Chicago Press.

Weber, M. (1958) *The Protestant Ethic and the Spirit of Capitalism*, trans. T. Parsons, New York: Charles Scribner's Sons.

——(1964) *The Sociology of Religion*, trans. E. Rischoff, Boston: Beacon Press.

Yoder, J. H. (1984) *The Priestly Kingdom: Social Ethics as Gospel*, Notre Dame, Ind.: University of Notre Dame Press.

FURTHER READING

Barth, K. (1960) *Community, State, and Church: Three Essays*, Garden City, NY: Doubleday.

Bellah, R. N. (1965) *Religion and Progress in Modern Asia*, New York: Free Press.

——(1967) 'Civil religion in America', *Daedalus* 96 (Winter): 1–21.

Fingarette, H. (1972) *Confucius: The Secular as Sacred*, New York: Harper & Row.

Gutiérrez, G. (1973) *A Theology of Liberation: History, Politics and Salvation*, Maryknoll, NY: Orbis.

Hauerwas, S. (1985) *Against the Nations: War and Survival in a Liberal Society*, Minneapolis: Winston Press.

Lewis, B. (1988) *The Political Language of Islam*, Chicago: University of Chicago Press.

Locke, J. (1983) *A Letter Concerning Toleration*, ed. H. Tully, Indianapolis: Hackett Publishing.

McBrien, R. P. (1987) *Caesar's Coin*, New York: Macmillan.

Mendenhall, G. E. (1954) 'Law and covenant in Israel and the ancient Near East', *Biblical Archaeologist* 17 (May): 26–46; (September): 49–76.

Niebuhr, H. R. (1956) *Christ and Culture*, New York: Harper & Row.

Niebuhr, R. (1960) *The Children of Light and the Children of Darkness*, New York: Charles Scribner's Sons.

Tambiah, S. J. (1976) *World Conqueror and World Renouncer*, Cambridge: Cambridge University Press.

Tinder, G. (1989) *The Political Meaning of Christianity*, Baton Rouge: Louisiana State University Press.

Troeltsch, E. (1976) *The Social Teaching of the Christian Churches*, 2 vols, trans. O. Wyan, Chicago: University of Chicago Press.

Walzer, M. (1987) *Exodus and Revolution*, New York: Basic Books.

Watt, W. M. (1968) *Islamic Political Thought: The Basic Concepts*, Edinburgh: Edinburgh University Press.

Yoder, J. H. (1984) *The Priestly Kingdom: Social Ethics as Gospel*, Notre Dame, Ind.: University of Notre Dame Press.

33

RACE AND POLITICS

SHAMIT SAGGAR

When the writer and sometime Pan African activist, W. E. B. DuBois, wrote that 'the problem of the twentieth century is the problem of the colour line', it would be fair to say that he did not have the emerging research priorities of political science in mind. Throughout the course of the century, the relationship between race and politics has always tended to occupy a fairly esoteric status within the established political science literature. Whilst it would be misleading to claim that race has been ignored by the discipline, it is certainly the case that the interest of scholars in race-related issues has been led by other areas of concern. Racial conflict and related policy issues have not occupied a major strand within academic writing; however, the research that there has been in this field has been primarily focused on major – and more familiar – questions of political science and political philosophy such as democracy, representation and power. An illustration of this conditional interest can be seen in Myrdal's 1944 study of race relations in the United States, *An American Dilemma*, which clearly sought to address itself to the application of democracy in the first democratic nation (Myrdal 1944). Indeed, the more one examines the literature in this field, the more one is struck by the extent of scholars' interest in the subject matter for broader purposes.

Notwithstanding the latent motives underscoring academic research in this field, it is important to note that *specifically* political analyses of race and racism remain relatively sparse and underdeveloped compared with other disciplines of social enquiry. Chief amongst this larger and better developed literature has been the contribution of sociology and, to a lesser degree, social psychology and social anthropology (see for example Park 1950; Cox 1948; Barth 1969; Hechter *et al.* 1982; Weinreich 1986). However, these neighbouring and sometimes overlapping traditions are not part of our remit, which is, among other things, to explore the contribution of political studies of race and racism. A cursory glance at writing in this field will reveal a preponderance of research on, *inter alia*, non-white electoral participation, state immigration policy, public policy governing minority–majority relations, race and class, and autonomous black political thought and activity. The greatest attention has tended to fall on the former two areas, whilst the emphasis of recent theoretical – and arguably more interesting and challenging – debates has been centred around the latter areas.

Before proceeding any further, it is important to signal that an essay such as this must be selective in its approach and coverage. It hardly needs to be said that this survey cannot hope to be comprehensive and that certain themes and debates are therefore given greater attention than others. The purpose is to draw together and discuss several central themes found in the literature, and to evaluate the broad trends in the volume of research which has grown rapidly in recent years. The interests of researchers, however, have tended to be patchy and clustered around several major topics and approaches.

The main body of this discussion comprises seven parts. First, a number of preliminary points are considered that serve to shape the nature of our survey of the literature. Second, an overview is presented of some of the substantial findings of research on race and politics. Third, the dominant institutional and behavioural framework of research in this field is examined. Fourth, attention is given to the largely neglected debate on race and political power. Fifth, the discussion turns to the contribution of Marxism and state theory. Sixth, the commonly overlooked work of students of comparative race politics is explored. Finally, the article concludes with a brief discussion of trends and priorities in the future agenda of research on race and politics.

MAPS AND COMPASSES

It is worth pausing to consider some of the foundations on which race has been a politically interesting subject of study. We cannot merely assume that the literature represents a uniform and consistent approach to race issues in political affairs. It does not. Moreover, a number of theoretical, conceptual and empirical approaches have characterized the study of race and politics.

First, explicit racial conflict has frequently been presented as a factor guiding research interest. Illustrations can be found in the writing on the US civil rights movement, non-white immigration to western Europe, and South African race relations (see for example Preston et al. 1982; Miles 1982; and Wolpe 1970; respectively). Whilst much of this material has proved to be illuminating, the theoretical basis for it has varied considerably. One such dominant theoretical approach has been the Parsonian functionalist tradition which purports an often unwieldy and rather deterministic societal-level explanation for racial conflict and its underlying causes. The specifically race-related aspects of racial conflict appear to hold little interest, and the overall thrust of this approach is weakened as a consequence.

535

Second, much of the research has been governed by the familiar reductionist themes and principles of academic scholarship. Much sociological writing for instance, notably within the Marxist and Weberian traditions, seeks to account for and explain the relationship between race and politics in terms of detached and unbending theoretical criteria. Consequently it is rarely found embracing a multiplicity of explanatory approaches (see for example the Centre for Contemporary Cultural Studies 1982; Rex 1981). The result is that research is peculiarly handicapped by the lack of multi-theoretical approaches. Political scientists have been afflicted by such theoretical narrowness no less than their sociologist counterparts.

This leads to a third factor involved in this field of study: unlike the volumes of sociology or social policy literature, the political analysis of race and racism remains comparatively atheoretical. By this it is not meant that political scientists have been entirely unconcerned about theoretical questions to do with race, but rather that their efforts have tended to be fairly empirically-led and less noticeably bogged down in sectarian disputes of theory (so often a hallmark of the volume of sociological writing in this field). The problems encountered in the political analysis of race have undoubtedly been confounded by the relative absence of deep theoretical foundations. Political science research has consequently tended to become highly empirical in purpose and content, and rests heavily upon the much stronger theoretical foundations of sociological race research. For example, Katznelson's comparison of the experiences of racial politics in Britain and the United States, *Black Men, White Cities* (Katznelson 1976), although heavily theoretical in its scope and aims, appears to take its cue from a number of essentially non-political science debates. In noting the dearth of comparative studies of race and politics, Katznelson correctly emphasizes the obvious, yet often absent, centrality of politics to studies of race:

> By themselves, the physical facts of race are of little or no analytical interest. Racial-physical characteristics assume meaning only when they become criteria of stratification. Thus studies of race inescapably put politics – which, fundamentally, is about organized inequality – at the core of their concern.
>
> (Katznelson 1976: 14)

Fourth, the study of racial tensions and conflicts has a number of obvious implications for political stability. Banton cites the example of Enoch Powell's critical contribution to debates in British politics on the question of nationhood in a multiracial society (Banton 1986: 51–2). Claims about the supposed racial and ethnic building-blocks of the modern nation-state and worries about political stability were clearly at the core of Powell's message. Sensing an underlying concern for the viability of British nationhood in a rapidly transformed multiracial society, Powell argued that:

536

Our response has been to attempt to force upon ourselves a non-identity and to assert that we have no unique distinguishing characteristics. . . . A nation which deliberately denies its continuity with its past and its rootedness in its homeland is on the way to repudiate its own existence.

(quoted in Banton 1986: 52)

Finally, political scientists, in common with social scientists at large, have turned their attentions to race with at least one eye on the need to formulate universal truths. In a number of cases they have failed to do so and the result has been a preponderance of over-generalizations about the link between race and politics. A further associated fault has been the extent of unrefined approaches to, and claims made about, racial and ethnic minority political action. To be sure, at the basic yet critical level of nomenclature, writers concerned with describing non-white political behaviour (all too) frequently speak of 'the black community' or 'black politics' and similar terms. The difficulty with doing so is that these overarching terms may deny the tremendous degree of internal diversity within such minority populations. In Britain, for instance, a strong debate has been generated on this theme, with several commentators at pains to stress the deep running yet historically smothered distinctions which exist between not merely Afro-Caribbean and South Asian-origin groups but also between sub-groups within these larger groups (see for example Banton 1977; Smith 1989; Robinson 1986). The argument is largely one concerned with preserving and resurrecting the notion of ethnicity in both practical and analytical terms. It is claimed that the distinction and precision of ethnic identity lies at the heart of the experience – and therefore politics – of these minority groups. Although it is indeed the case that the bulk of the literature stands collectively guilty of such myopia, we should none the less be cautious in our abandonment of the traditional race categories and relationships of social science enquiry. For one thing, the persistence of racially exclusionary policies, practices and routines, both by public agencies as well as by private groups and individuals, suggests that the emphasis should continue to rest with established racial umbrella categories, albeit at the risk of over-generalization (Blumer and Duster 1980; Husbands 1983; Smith 1989). Further, social science students of race should guard against the temptation of allowing their research strategies and priorities to be guided solely by the dictums of so-called grassroots action research. As Mason notes in relation to one example of such a research strategy (Ben-Tovim et al. 1986), 'what may result . . . is not so much research in the service of the oppressed as manipulation of researchers by minority interest groups or the rule of the mob' (Mason 1986: 14).

RACIAL CONFLICT AND POLITICAL PROCESSES

Many of the substantive studies of the race–politics nexus have tended to concentrate on a number of behavioural questions. These have included, for example, the relationship between racial groups and levels and forms of political participation, single issue interest group activity, and group mobilization towards areas of political protest and/or violence. Starting from this perspective, it is possible to see the different ways in which race has shaped not merely formal political processes but also a wide range of underlying social tensions including, *inter alia*, differential public service delivery and competition for scarce resources in urban political environments. Of course, the question that much of this research leads to is the extent to which race plays either a determining or consequential role. Or put another way, do black people in the United States or South Africa differ from their white counterparts in terms of the level and type of public service consumption or political participation as a result of their racial background or because of other factors such as economic or educational status? In terms of the research that has been carried out on this broad question, it seems that, whilst a certain amount of correlation between race and political behaviour has been established, the task of demonstrating causal explanation has proved more difficult.

Arguably the significance of race as a concept stems from its potential as an exclusionary variable. Thus its capacity to give focus to shared values and backgrounds cannot be underestimated, since, unlike other similar variables, it usually operates in an unambiguous, dichotomous manner. Social class, ethnic group, regional origin, generational cohort and other familiar variables of political analysis differ from race in that they exhibit various degrees of internal overlap and conceptual imprecision. In contrast, the political impact of race, whilst regularly burdened by theoretical and empirical confusion with that of collective ethnic group action, has been analysed in rather clearer and more tangible terms. To take the well-documented example of residential segregation between black and white communities in the United States, researchers have encountered *relatively* few methodological difficulties in assigning individual behaviour to forms of group cohesion. The difficulty that arises is being able to account for political action based on such cohesion, particularly in the absence of external constraints fuelling racially specific shared interests such as legally sanctioned force (as in South Africa since the early 1960s) or technical obstacles to electoral participation (as in parts of the United States until the mid-1960s). It is not sufficient to suppose that discrimination alone will result in collective political action on the basis of race. The processes behind such action, if it is to occur, are commonly more complex and involve a wide range of social interaction between, and political integration of, different racial groups (Verba and Nie 1972: 149–73).

538

The voting behaviour of black minority groups in advanced industrial states appears to confirm this point. Crewe (1983), Studlar (1983), Williams (1982) and St Angelo and Puryear (1982) have all pointed to variance in black voting patterns in Britain and the United States. They show that black voters do *not* respond uniformly to their shared experiences as subjects of discrimination. Williams (1982: 78–99), for example, notes that regional concentrations of black voters in the United States in 1980 produced great variance in (though only limited correlation with) the successful election to office of black candidates: southern states comprising more than 50 per cent of the nation's black population returned over 60 per cent of all black elected officials, whilst in the north-east the comparable figures were one in ten yielding one in twenty. However, what is equally important is the generally high level of similar voting patterns among minority racial groups. Using survey data from the late 1970s, Crewe (1983: 272) reports that the British Labour Party held the support of 44 per cent of white voters compared with 95 per cent and 92 per cent of West Indian and Asian voters respectively.

Of course, racial differences are not only significant in terms of their impact on formal political participation, but are also closely intertwined with the distribution of power. Indeed, in several polities that have been characterized by overt legal discrimination on racial grounds, underlying power relations have served to exclude certain groups from key social and economic resources. In doing so, the skewed picture of control and influence below the level of formal participation served to reflect what was already apparent at the level of mass party politics. Moreover, as Wilson reminds us, the power relationship between racial groups is invariably uneven: 'Differential power is a marked feature of racial-group interaction in complex societies; the greater the power discrepancy between subordinate and dominant racial groups, the greater the extent and scope of racial domination' (Wilson 1973: 18). But why should domination necessarily extend beyond the political realm? The response to this question must point to sociological and historical understanding of power as a multi-faceted concept which goes further than the use of coercive force in the face of interest confrontation. Economic and cultural dependency, for example, are both key forms through which domination has occurred 'and facilitated the emergence of still another, more sophisticated form of control: psychosocial dominance' (Baker 1983: 80). This historical process was exemplified by the South African and Rhodesian cases, but it is important to note that, despite great emphasis placed on coercive and structural dominance, it has perhaps been the psychosocial that has had the most enduring consequences (Baker 1983: 81). The counterforces of black African nationalism have been conspicuous by their diluted impact in both these societies compared with numerous other post-colonial African states. Moreover, as many writers have commented, white hegemony in terms of cultural awareness and discussion of inter-race power relations has transcended the nominal southern African divide, and is manifest in several diverse multi-racial societies. For example, the adoption of European-based parliamentary systems by a number of black African states following post-war struggles for independence has inevitably shaped political development in ways that have sometimes been in conflict with local circumstances. The relative inability of these states to reform their political infrastructures – beyond that associated with large-scale political violence – is perhaps further testimony to the persisting dominance of European-based philosophical assumptions concerning representation and individual rights. Moreover, as Smith (1986: 223–25) notes, considerable problems of political instability have occurred in many black African states owing to their diverse plural compositions and structures; in a number of cases such as Nigeria, Sierra Leone, Uganda, Ethiopia and Chad this mismatch has been closely linked to the colonial legacies of past European-imposed constitutional-legal settlements (Davidson 1983). Elsewhere, a succession of civil rights leaders in the United States have observed, and created issues over, the lexicon of race in political debate. In the 1960s radical black leaders in the United States fashioned a new rejectionist philosophy of anger leading to positive mobilization of black communities. Central to their analysis was opposition to perceived white-dominated cultural categories that had historically viewed black thought and contributions as marginal to mainstream society. In this context a campaign was launched for black self-awareness in which it was declared, 'I am a man – I am somebody', a cry echoed during the 1980s by the Revd Jesse Jackson's call for the term 'Afro-American' to displace 'black' as the collective reference for the black minority he (partly) aimed to lead.

Some of the sharpest and most interesting political conflicts based on race have been the product of inequalities in public service provision. The policy process, whilst rather neglected as a focus of empirical investigation outside the United States (see also 'Race and political power', p. 543), serves as a useful arena of study for those interested in questions ranging from the formation of policy agendas through to evaluation of programme outcomes. Studlar and Layton-Henry's (1990) recent work in relation to the former in the British context has highlighted the comparatively limited resources of non-white citizens to affect the agenda of race policy. Rather, the agenda has been highly crisis-led, *ad hoc* in treatment of specific race-related issues, and atomized in the formation of clearly identifiable policy networks or communities. Saggar (1991a) has argued that the origin of many of these problems can be traced back to the liberal settlement in British race relations which served to constrain public policy debate away from overt discussion of racial inequality and instead placed a premium upon the attainment of short-term racial harmony.

Policy-oriented research in the United States has been fairly substantial.

But even here it seems, researchers are aware of the problems associated with examining modes and scales of participation in isolation from wider political analyses of power and influence. In their major study of political participation in the United States, Verba and Nie (1972: 172–73) concluded that sharp black–white disparities were apparent, particularly in the area of the establishment and maintenance of direct contact(s) with government officials. However, the blocking of black citizens from a key channel of influence occurred in the context of generally poor and ineffective black participation; but the race factor itself, they argued, appeared to provide a major, often underutilized factor around which group consciousness could be 'a great resource for political involvement' (ibid.).

Sharp disparities in black–white experience in employment, education and housing in the United States have been confirmed by empirical evidence. Freedman (1983) has shown that black members of the labour market suffered widespread discrimination in applying for vacancies as well as in attaining similar status and remuneration to their white counterparts once in work. For example, whilst the period 1964–79 shows there to have been a one-third improvement in the representation of black male graduate managers, they still remained under-represented in relation to their white counterparts by a factor of one-quarter. Despite continuing significant levels of labour market discrimination against black workers, the scale of reduction in discrimination achieved since the 1964 Civil Rights Act has impressed some commentators. One such commentator, William Wilson, has viewed this process as part of an irreversible absorption of black Americans into the mainstream class structure. In *The Declining Significance of Race* he argues that:

> Race relations in America have undergone fundamental changes in recent years, so much so that now the life chances of individual blacks have more to do with their economic class position than their day-to-day encounters with whites.
>
> (Wilson 1978: 1)

This important thesis has been generally greeted with controversy in the debate on black–white relations in the United States. For one thing, it appeared to challenge the established view that saw black political participation in purely or largely racial terms. Moreover, it provided the groundwork for a neo-conservative attack on existing perceptions of racism hindering the socio-economic progress of black Americans. Wilson's alternative explanation for lower black performance in economic competition with white Americans claimed that such differential attainment was broadly in line with differences in educational and other skills associated with the promotion of individual life chances. Certainly Wilson has not stood alone in advancing such a neo-conservative perspective and was joined by the publication of David Kirp's *Doing Good by Doing Little* (1979) and *Just Schools* (1982). In these books Kirp contended that both British and US educational policy makers (Kirp 1979 and 1982 respectively) ought to return to so-called 'colourblind' approaches to publicly funded school programmes. He emphasized in particular three factors working against the use of racially determined public education programmes in the United States: first, since their high water mark in the early 1970s, there had been a general decline in the public's faith in government intervention to ensure integration; second, the period had also witnessed a secular fall-off in public perceptions of government having a strong role to play in many aspects of society; and third, and most crucial of all, the black constituency itself reported increased disillusionment with the prospects for, and necessity of, an integrated system of public education (Kirp 1982: 100–1).

INSTITUTIONAL AND BEHAVIOURAL CONCERNS

In common with the major trends in political science since the 1950s, specialist studies of race and politics have tended to follow mainly institutional and behavioural frameworks of enquiry. That is to say, the rise of racially plural societies – most notably in European and north American countries – have had a number of important consequences for the operation of different political systems. These consequences, commonly impacting on areas such as party competition, labour migration and civil rights policies, have captured the attention of researchers and have been at the forefront of research in this field (see for example Welch and Secret 1981; Layton-Henry and Rich 1986; Welch and Studlar 1985; Pinderhughes 1987). Institutional and behavioural approaches have thus dominated investigations of the race–politics nexus and, to that extent, the literature does not present us with any new or particularly novel questions for the understanding of this topic.

This guiding framework includes a number of specific areas of study involving the political impact of race. An example of one such area has been that of state immigration policy, which has resulted in a veritable trove of research on the Western European experience in particular (Rogers 1985; Freeman 1979; Castles et al. 1984). The policies of various national governments to fill domestic labour shortages through foreign recruitment in the 1950s and 1960s came to have an increasingly politicized dimension by the 1970s and 1980s. The popular-cum-electoral politicization of these policies came about not least because of the non-European origin of much of the labour force involved in this process, and the negative anti-immigrant backlash it provoked in many receiving countries. A number of writers have emphasized the economically related aspects of such immigration policies and their eventual reversal during the 1970s and 1980s. Writing on the West German case, Katzenstein has argued that the appearance of the immigration issue in domestic politics compelled 'policy-makers to confront the social consequences of decisions made largely for economic reasons' (Katzenstein 1987: 213). Elsewhere the electoral spoils of explicit anti-immigrant platforms have been seen most vividly in France, where, as Schain (1987) reminds us, the Communist party now competes openly with the far-right National Front for anti-immigrant votes.

Writers have not limited themselves to state immigration policy in a narrow sense but have also extended their interest to matters concerning the processes underlying and resulting from the politicization of immigration. Interest has grown, for example, in areas such as the political rights of immigrant labour (Layton-Henry 1989), the experience of racism and racially exclusionary public policies (Castles et al. 1984), and the anti-immigrant backlash of the right (Husbands 1989). However, the thrust of this literature has emerged from within the conventional lines that have shaped the discipline and, in general, has not attempted to challenge or reach beyond them. The interpretations of political scientists and commentators were thus able to note and dispense with the politics of race with comparative ease. Underlying conflicts and issues of power relations involving race have been largely neglected for the same reason that such broader critical approaches to political analysis were themselves overlooked and relegated to the fringes of the discipline for so long. For example, writers on British politics such as Dearlove and Saunders (1984) have argued that preoccupations with narrow views of politics will preclude fuller understanding not only of British politics as a whole but also of key interlocking aspects of the broader picture (such as divisions of race, gender, and so on). The political analysis of race has usually taken as its frame of reference an unsatisfactorily narrow view of politics and, in doing so, has merely replicated the dominant scholastic frameworks of the discipline, but on a smaller scale.

RACE AND POLITICAL POWER

In recent years some researchers have begun to broaden their theoretical and conceptual starting points for the understanding of race and politics. At least part of this process can be attributed to underlying shifts of emphasis within the discipline away from the strong institutional and behavioural preoccupations of the past. The political analysis of social divisions and inequalities has been one area of renewed interest, reflecting the major reappraisals within the discipline that occurred during the 1970s. Undoubtedly, the most voluminous and significant research in the field of race and politics has emanated from the United States in the half-century since the 1930s. But even here the chief locomotive of interest has been questions pertaining to US democracy and, in the last thirty years, the location of power in the mosaic of social, political and economic relationships which are to be found in US cities (Myrdal 1944; Glazer and Moynihan 1963; Greenstone and Peterson 1973).

Borrowing heavily from the findings of studies of social policy, a handful of political scientists have turned to examine the political causes and consequences of racial inequality stemming from discrimination and disadvantage. For example, Glazer and Young (1983) present a timely comparative exposition of the public policy considerations in the old (Britain) and new (United States) worlds. One of the more interesting conclusions of this comparison is the extent to which policy content and substance are shaped by underlying dominant philosophies and belief systems. The predisposition found in the United States towards the practice of making groups the principal subjects of public policy (in contrast to Britain where policy discussion remains stalled at the definition of policy subjects as geographic areas) is held to be one of the most significant factors explaining the differences in experience of race policy. Furthermore, Glazer notes that the US political system contains many more separate points at which policy can be created and carried out than in Britain; the result, he reports, is that US policy makers possess something of a head start in the development of issues of racial and ethnic pluralism in the policy process (Glazer 1983: 1–7).

The transatlantic contrasts do not stop there. Indeed, they have been an important source of comparison for researchers interested in the underlying influence of political culture on policy choices and dilemmas involving race (Young 1983; Banton 1984). Debates have taken place at several levels, ranging from the theoretical discussion of liberal democratic power structures to empirically based policy studies. For example, Gordon observes the constraining influence – and indeed clash – of value systems between 'the principles of equal treatment and individual meritocracy [and] principles that call upon group compensation for undeniable past injuries' (Gordon 1981: 181). The evolving pluralist tradition within the discipline has been a dominant and attractive paradigmatic starting point for writers such as Glazer who have somewhat over-celebrated the capacity of

> Anglo-Saxon political tradition . . . to accept a remarkable degree of pluralism, not only in culture and society, but also in politics. It offers hope that we may yet manage to contain these problems of ethnic and racial diversity and to become richer societies as a result.
>
> (Glazer 1983: 6)

The restatement of the liberal, pluralist ideal of a multiracial society that this view embodied is, of course, a familiar feature of the literature not merely on race and politics but also on the distribution of political power. The inclusion of wider questions to do with power structures and relations underpinning pluralist views of the politics of race have generally been overlooked, although students of power in US cities have been keen to redress this imbalance (see for example Bachrach and Baratz 1970: 3–16). In seeking to explore behind the political structures inherent in cosy pluralist orthodoxies, they cite the following important remarks of Schattschneider:

> All forms of political organization have a bias in favour of the exploitation of some kinds of conflict and the suppression of others because *organization is the mobilization of bias*. Some issues are organized into politics while other are organized out.
>
> (Schattschneider 1960: 71)

The pluralist interpretation contains important conceptions of the context and framework shaping public policy. These involve conceptualization of the relationship between race and politics at a very general level and issues of race in the policy process more precisely (Banton 1985: Saggar 1991a). There are at least four major problems associated with the pluralist approach to these questions. To begin with, as Bachrach and Baratz (1970) are at pains to point out, the unchallenged and comprehensive inclusion of race issues into urban politics and policy process cannot be taken for granted. Indeed, on the basis of their evidence from a medium-sized US city, the opposite seems to be the case. Urban politics may be conducted within a guiding framework which, put simply, leaves out race. This may be done through a combination of two processes. Policy makers may refuse to give explicit legitimacy to issues of race and ethnicity or, as is more usually the case, they may routinely absorb and effectively deflect such issues into the otherwise common 'colour-blind' approach of public agencies (Saggar 1991a). Another related difficulty emerges from the concept of non-decision making in urban politics. The maintenance of 'colour-blindness' constitutes a major mobilization of bias away from open recognition of the legitimacy of race issues and conflicts. In failing to give such recognition, urban policy makers can be said to be engaging in the 'suppression or thwarting of a latent or manifest challenge to [their] values or interests' (Bachrach and Baratz 1970: 44). Of course, the validity of this view remains to be empirically tested and it may be that the evidence suggests that non-decision making has given way to a new phase of highly active decision making which serves to incorporate formally the race dimension into the policy process. But, even here, a third problem can be identified whereby forms of co-option and participatory democracy, as Selznick put it, 'gives the opposition the illusion of a voice without the voice itself and so stifles opposition without having to alter policy in the least' (quoted in Coleman 1957: 17). Finally, recent research reveals that race-related policy debate has been focused towards questions of direct discriminatory behaviour at the expense of subtler questions to do with the indirect discriminatory impact of the routines, procedures and established norms of public policy. The primary factor responsible for this narrow conceptualization of race in the policy process, argues Saggar (1991a), has been the 'liberal policy framework' of British race relations estab-

545

lished in the 1960s. Racial harmony presided as the chief policy goal of this framework, something which Hill and Issacharoff (1971: 284) remind us is by no means the same thing as – and may be detrimental to – racial equality. Writing about London local politics, Saggar reports that policy discussion remained restricted to comparatively 'safe' issues and ensured that:

> direct [race] conflicts often failed to see the light of day and many issues were labelled 'off limits' even before they were discussed. It [was] often easiest to disarm rivals or challengers by claiming that they [did] not support the legitimate 'ground-rules' of the existing policy framework.

(Saggar 1991b: 26)

These interpretations suggest that the explanatory emphasis should turn to focus more sharply on the factors that develop and sustain competing value systems – or the mobilization of bias as this variable is more commonly known. The routine and successful influence of such systems in politics and policy processes is, after all, an area that has gained greater exposure in the discipline in recent years. In short, these and other studies in the same vein represent an abandonment of the narrow institutional and behavioural concerns of political scientists interested in race. Recent studies of the policy process in particular have given the discipline a model for deeper and broader exploration of the relationship between race and politics. At least one result of this change has been to dissuade researchers from even further attention being placed on narrowly conceived and somewhat familiar questions about formal participatory politics. A greater degree of intellectual pluralism can now be observed in the literature which, like other aspects of the discipline, is less interested in how the system is said or supposed to work and more interested in how the system actually does work (Dearlove 1982; Dearlove and Saunders 1984).

MARXISM AND STATE THEORY

One of the central themes of cross-national social and political research on race has been the debate about the relationship between race and class formation. The links between working-class support for racist political movements and ideologies – notably in industrial liberal democracies – has been a major source of interest for researchers (Castles et al. 1984; Castles and Kosack 1985; Omi and Winant 1986). In at least one sense there is little that is new about the broad focus of this research, concerned, as it is, with the complex interrelationship between class and race politics as well as the underlying role played by the state. For example, Cox's Caste, Class and Race sought to explore the divisive impact of race on the construction of working-class politics, arguing that racial inequalities constituted a special category of class-based inequality (Cox 1948). As the fairly exclusive community of neo-Marxist writers in this field are only too aware, the model originally laid down by Cox has served as a major catalyst of further research and debate (Miles 1980, 1984; Phizacklea and Miles 1980; the Centre for Contemporary Cultural Studies 1982; Banton 1986). Indeed, to the non-Marxist, non-North American scholar, Cox's arguments still seem to hold an inordinate degree of significance within contemporary debates about race and class relations. Thus, much of the recent writing on race and politics in liberal democracies from a neo-Marxist perspective represents a familiar return to questions first raised almost half a century ago.

That said, there is most certainly a great deal that is new and incisive in recent contributions to this debate to warrant further discussion. In keeping with the general thrust of Cox's work (1948), more recent work has retained an essentially sociological approach to the debate. Consequently, the first and possibly most significant development worthy of comment is to note the relative *absence* of theoretical political analyses of the relationship between race and class relations. Of course there are a handful of exceptions to this general pattern, with Phizacklea and Miles's (1980) work on the British situation being a case in point. Additionally, segments of neo-Marxist writing have served to advance political science understanding of the role of race in wider class-based political processes. In particular, the analysis of the state in the context of mature industrial capitalism has been at the forefront of this literature. The attention given to the role of racial divisions and conflicts within this analysis has grown markedly (see for example Hall 1980; Jessop 1982; Coates 1984).

Such state-centred modes and levels of explanation must, by definition, add to the contribution of political-sociology research. However, the conventional approach taken by political science has, as noted previously, tended to adopt the behavioural and institutional aspects of race as its starting point. The study of what some writers have termed 'state racism' (i.e. the racialization of the role and activities of the state in both political and public policy terms) has been a relatively new addition to the literature (Hammar 1985; Miles 1990). The main impetus behind much of this work, however, has been the broader and longer-standing theoretical interest of political-sociologists in the state in capitalist societies (Jessop 1982). The extension of this debate into the area of race and racism is to be welcomed for its contribution to the *political* analysis of race. However, one of the problems with this literature seems to be its confinement within traditional Marxist points of debate to do with the state's role in facilitating exploitation (Nikolinakos 1973). It does not require too great an intellectual leap to realize that an exclusive concern with capitalist exploitation might be missing the mark. As Yinger correctly observes, 'this leads one to wonder why ethnic and racial inequalities have persisted in Communist states' (Yinger 1983: 33).

The point being made is that, whilst the contribution of the largely Marxist literature on the state is clearly a step towards the fuller understanding of race and politics, it is disturbing that most of this work lies outside the main

547

institutional and behavioural focus of the discipline. Political scientists have only come to examine variables of race on the road to wider exploration of familiar political-sociology themes and debates. Even then, the overwhelming bulk of the work has been addressed to a debate internal to Marxist thought on the state. The specific contribution of political science to the political analysis of race has therefore been relegated to a somewhat tangential, almost proxy status. This characteristic of the literature may be less disturbing if allowance is made for the inter-disciplinary nature of much recent research. Even so, the tendency towards the 'piggy-back' phenomenon, so common in our survey, remains a serious weakness in the theoretical understanding of the relationship between race and politics.

COMPARATIVE RACE POLITICS

As already mentioned, comparisons between the experience of the politics of race in Western European countries and with the US case have been familiar features of research activity. But what of race and politics beyond this narrowly and hemispherically defined context? In one obvious sense it is worrying that consideration of what must surely be an important topic is so sharply compartmentalized – and even segregated – from the other themes of this essay. This is undesirable for a number of reasons, not least because of the opportunities it misses for comparison across the developed and developing world. Furthermore, it still remains an open question as to whether the guiding themes of research have been shaped by the priorities and developments within a modern discipline that has emerged from, and to this day heavily concentrated upon, the study of Western industrial democracies. The debates surveyed earlier concerning participation, power and class – to name just three – have of course been closely rooted to Western political-sociology, but this does not mean that their relevance or input ends there. It has been suggested that the broad brush approach of research in the developed world may be left conceptually and theoretically wanting in the context of studies of the developing world. Smith, for example, criticizes the tendency of most (Western) academics to jumble up what are considered to be distinct analytical categories:

> To understand [racial and ethnic] relations . . . it is essential to distinguish them clearly as objects of study, and not to conflate them, as is now the dominant fashion among white 'experts' on race and ethnic relations, who treat inter-racial and inter-ethnic relations as one and the same for purposes of documentation, analysis and comparison.
>
> (Smith 1986: 191)

However, in another sense the choice of and demarcation between the themes of this essay can be defended as a fair reflection of the literature in this field. The leading debates within many developing nations about race have been the subject of a body of literature largely separate from that discussed previously (Kuper and Smith 1969; Davidson 1983). For instance, there is an absence of studies of racialized state immigration policies, a topic that has preoccupied many researchers in Western Europe in recent years.

Furthermore, the theme of race in urban politics has largely emerged in the context of the development of the discipline in developed countries such as the United States. It is hard to spot a similar debate in studies of developing countries that compares with the works of Bachrach and Baratz (1970) and Key (1949). This literature in fact largely developed as part of a debate within the political science of industrial democracies concerning the distribution of power in these societies. The broader contextual setting of urban politics, however, may enable scholars to pursue similar questions about the location of power in developing countries. It would seem that, despite the seeming distinctiveness of much of this literature, there are clear and urgent comparisons to be made across the developed and developing world about the impact of race upon the conceptual understanding of political power. Indeed, these types of questions have been the mainstay of cross-national comparative work within the discipline in the developed world and there is little reason to suggest that they are any less relevant in African or Asian contexts (Kurian 1982; Taylor and Hudson 1983). Moreover, such comparative work is commonplace in the area of race and political behaviour, uncovering, for example, interesting distinctions between the experience of black African-Americans in the United States and lower caste Harijans in India (Verba et al. 1971). Finally, parallel bodies of literature exist on long-standing Marxist questions concerning race and class structures, making it much easier to draw together research findings both from the developed and developing world. The location of the South African case in all of this undoubtedly presents difficulties of classification, but the work of Wolpe (1987) has highlighted the complex interrelationship between race and class factors in that country.

FUTURE RESEARCH AGENDAS

The future research agenda of race and politics is likely to move beyond the traditional, strait-jacketed institutional and behavioural focus as illustrated by the recent growth of policy studies devoted to the so-called 'race dimension' in matters of mass public service delivery. These studies have served to shift the emphasis towards new areas of research and have concomitantly promoted the development of more theoretical analysis. Interest has moved to examining the impact of race in the policy process and, building on the impressive developments in the discipline in this field, a theoretical debate has begun on the problems of establishing coherent and sustainable race policy. Factors that mobilize bias against, and deny full legitimacy to, race issues in public policy making have been of particular interest. In this respect, the discipline has played an important part in developing the theoretical literature on race and political power. The theoretical understanding of the relationship between race and politics can only benefit from this development rooted in the policy studies branch of the discipline.

Questions relating to political stability have previously played a significant part in research on race and politics and are likely to continue to do so. Racial and ethnic conflicts have never been far from the core of studies of nation building, particularly in post-colonial Asian and African states. But the issue of stability has been of considerable relevance in various Western industrial states where the political consequences of labour migration have produced new tensions and conflicts. With recent developments across Europe highlighting the long-term, underlying distinctiveness of these immigrant communities, it is likely that the attention of researchers will return to basic questions about social integration, cultural pluralism and political stability.

Finally, in whatever way the research agenda of race and politics evolves, future work is likely to be increasingly underscored by the conceptual heterogeneity of race. The political impact of race, as successive scholars have found, is not a single and easily identifiable phenomenon. Instead, the politics of race has many facets, which suggests that explanation will be aided by a multi-theoretical, multi-disciplinary strategy. Unfortunately, so much of the existing research has tended to box itself into one narrowly defined approach or another. The result has been that the many complex facets of the phenomena have not been fully appreciated or explored. The political analysis of race is therefore a little like the old story of the proverbial elephant: it is not always possible to describe it clearly or effectively, but its positive identification is rarely in doubt.

REFERENCES

Bachrach, P. and Baratz, M. (1970) *Power and Poverty: Theory and Practice*, New York: Oxford University Press.

Baker, D. (1983) *Race, Ethnicity and Power: A Comparative Study*, London: Routledge & Kegan Paul.

Banton, M. (1977) *The Idea of Race*, London: Tavistock.

——(1984) 'Transatlantic perspectives on public policy concerning racial disadvantage', *New Community* 11: 280–7.

——(1985) *Promoting Racial Harmony*, Cambridge: Cambridge University Press.

——(1986) 'Epistemological assumptions in the study of racial differentiation', in J. Rex and D. Mason (eds) *Theories of Race and Ethnic Relations*, Cambridge: Cambridge University Press.

Barth, F. (ed.) (1969) *Ethnic Groups and Boundaries*, Bergen: Universitetsforlaget.

Ben-Tovim, G., Gabriel, J., Law, I. and Stredder, K. (1986) 'A political analysis of local struggles for racial equality', in J. Rex and D. Mason (eds) *Theories of Race and Ethnic Relations*, Cambridge: Cambridge University Press.

Blumer, H. and Duster, T. (1980) 'Theories of race and social action', in *Sociological Theories: Race and Colonialism*, Paris: UNESCO.

Castles, S. and Kosack, G. (1985) *Immigrant Workers and Class Structure in Western Europe*, London: Oxford University Press.

Castles, S., Booth, H. and Wallace, T. (1984) *Here for Good: Western Europe's New Ethnic Minorities*, London: Pluto Press.

The Centre for Contemporary Cultural Studies (1982) *The Empire Strikes Back: Race and Racism in 70s Britain*, London: Hutchinson.

Coates, D. (1984) *The Context of British Politics*, London: Hutchinson.

Coleman, J. (1957), *Community Conflict*, New York.

Cox, O. (1948) *Caste, Class and Race*, New York: Monthly Review Press.

Crewe, I. (1983) 'Representation and the ethnic minorities in Britain', in N. Glazer and K. Young (eds) *Ethnic Pluralism and Public Policy: Achieving Equality in the United States and Britain*, London: Heinemann.

Davidson, B. (ed.) (1983) *Africa South of the Sahara*, London: Europa Publications.

Dearlove, J. (1982) 'The political science of British politics', *Parliamentary Affairs* 35 (4): 436–54.

Dearlove, J. and Saunders, P. (1984) *Introduction to British Politics*, Oxford: Polity Press.

Freeman, G. (1979) *Immigrant Labour and Racial Conflict in Industrial Societies: The French and British Experience, 1945–75*, Princeton, NJ: Princeton University Press.

Glazer, N. (1983) 'Introduction', in N. Glazer and K. Young (eds) *Ethnic Pluralism and Public Policy: Achieving Equality in the United States and Britain*, London: Heinemann.

Glazer, N. and Moynihan, D. (1963) *Beyond the Melting Pot*, Cambridge, Mass.: MIT Press.

Glazer, N. and Young, K. (eds) (1983) *Ethnic Pluralism and Public Policy: Achieving Equality in the United States and Britain*, London: Heinemann.

Gordon, M. (1981) 'Models of pluralism: the new American dilemma', *Annals of the American Academy of Political and Social Science* 45: 178–88.

Greenstone, J. and Peterson, P. (1973) *Race and Authority in Urban Politics: Community Participation and the War on Poverty*, New York: Russell Sage Foundation.

Hall, S. (1980) 'Race, articulation and societies structured in dominance', in UNESCO (ed.) *Sociological Theories: Race and Colonialism*, Paris: UNESCO.

Hammar, T. (ed.) (1985) *European Immigration Policy*, Cambridge: Cambridge University Press.

Hechter, M., Friedman, D. and Appelbaum, M. (1982) 'A theory of ethnic collective action', *International Migration Review* 16: 412–34.

Hill, M. and Issacharoff, R. (1971) *Community Action and Race Relations*, London: Oxford University Press.

Husbands, C. (1983) *Racial Exclusionism and the City*, London: Allen & Unwin.

——(1989) *Race and the Right in Contemporary Politics*, London: Pinter.

Jessop, R. (1982) *The Capitalist State*, Oxford: Martin Robertson.

Katzenstein, P. (1987) *Policy and Politics in West Germany: The Growth of a Semi-Sovereign State*, Philadelphia: Temple University Press.

Katznelson, I. (1976) *Black Men, White Cities: Race, Politics, and Migration in the United States, 1900–30, and Britain, 1948–68*, Chicago: University of Chicago Press.

Kirp, D. (1979) *Doing Good by Doing Little*, London: University of California Press.

——(1982) *Just Schools: The Idea of Racial Equality in American Education*, Berkeley: University of California Press.

Key, V. (1949) *Southern Politics in State and Nation*, New York: Random House.

Kuper, L. and Smith, M. (eds) (1969) *Pluralism in Africa*, Berkeley: University of California Press.

Kurian, G. (ed.) (1982) *Encyclopaedia of the Third World*, 3 vols, New York: Facts on File Inc.

Layton-Henry, Z. (ed.) (1989) *The Political Rights of Migrant Workers in Western Europe*, London: Sage Publications.

Layton-Henry, Z. and Rich, P. (eds) (1986) *Race, Government and Politics in Britain*, London: Macmillan.

Mason, D. (1986) 'Introduction: controversies and continuities in race and ethnic relations theory', in J. Rex and D. Mason (eds) *Theories of Race and Ethnic Relations*, Cambridge: Cambridge University Press.

Miles, R. (1980) 'Class, race and ethnicity: a critique of Cox's theory', *Ethnic and Racial Studies* 3: 169–87.

——(1982) *Racism and Migrant Labour: A Critical Text*, London: Routledge & Kegan Paul.

——(1984) 'Marxism Versus the Sociology of "Race Relations"?', *Ethnic and Racial Studies* 7: 217–37.

——(1990) 'The racialization of British politics', *Political Studies* 38: 277–85.

Myrdal, G. (1944) *An American Dilemma*, New York: Harper Brothers.

Nikolinakos, M. (1973) 'Notes towards an economic theory of racism', *Race* 14: 365–81.

Omi, M. and Winant, H. (1986) *Racial Formation in the United States*, London: Routledge.

Park, R. (ed.) (1950) *Race and Culture*, New York: Free Press.

Phizacklea, A. and Miles, R. (1980) *Labour and Racism*, London: Routledge & Kegan Paul.

Pinderhughes, D. (1987) *Race and Ethnicity in Chicago Politics*, Chicago and Urbana: University of Illinois Press.

Preston, M., Henderson, L. J., Jr., and Puryear, P. (eds) (1982) *The New Black Politics: The Search for Political Power*, New York: Longman.

Rex, J. (1981) 'A working paradigm for race relations research', *Ethnic and Racial Studies* 4: 1–25.

Rex, J. and Mason, D. (eds) (1986) *Theories of Race and Ethnic Relations*, Cambridge: Cambridge University Press.

Robinson, V. (1986) *Transients, Settlers and Refugees. Asians in Britain*, Oxford: Clarendon Press.

Rogers, R. (ed.) (1985) *Guests Coming to Stay: The Effects of European Migration on Sending and Receiving Countries*, Boulder: Westview Press.

Saggar, S. (1991a) *Race and Public Policy: A Study of Local Politics and Government*, Aldershot: Avebury.

——(1991b) 'The changing agenda of race issues in local government', *Political Studies* 39: 100–21.

St Angelo, D. and Puryear, P. (1982) 'Fear, apathy and other dimensions of black voting', in M. Preston, L. J. Henderson Jr. and P. Puryear. (eds) *The New Black Politics: The Search for Political Power*, New York: Longman.

Schain, M. (1987) 'The National Front in France and the construction of political legitimacy', *West European Politics* 10: 229–52.

Schattschneider, E. (1960) *The Semi-Sovereign People*, New York.

Smith, M. G. (1986) 'Pluralism, race and ethnicity in selected African countries', in J. Rex and D. Mason (eds) *Theories of Race and Ethnic Relations*, Cambridge: Cambridge University Press.

Smith, S. (1989) *The Politics of 'Race' and Residence*, Cambridge: Polity Press.

Studlar, D. (1983) 'The ethnic vote, 1983: problems of analysis and interpretation', *New Community* 11: 92–100.

Studlar, D. and Layton-Henry, Z. (1990) 'Non-white minority access to the political agenda in Britain', *Policy Studies Review* 9 (2): 273–93.

Taylor, C. L. and Hudson, M. (1976) *World Handbook of Social and Political Indicators*, New Haven: Yale University Press.

Taylor, C. and Jodice, D. (1983) *World Handbook of Political and Social Indicators*, 2 vols, New Haven; Yale University Press.

Verba, S., Bashiruddhin, A. and Bhatt, A. (1971) *Caste, Race and Politics: A Comparative Study of India and the United States*, Beverly Hills: Sage Publications.

Verba, S. and Nie, N. (1972) *Participation in America: Political Democracy and Social Equality*, New York: Harper & Row.

Weinreich, P. (1986) 'The operationalisation of identity theory in racial and ethnic relations', in J. Rex and D. Mason (eds) *Theories of Race and Ethnic Relations*, Cambridge: Cambridge University Press.

Welch, S. and Secret, P. (1981) 'Sex, race and political participation', *Western Political Quarterly* 34: 5–16.

Welch, S. and Studlar, D. (1985) 'The impact of race on political behaviour in Britain', *British Journal of Political Science* 15: 528–40.

Williams, E. (1982) 'Black political progress in the 1970s: the electoral arena', in M. Preston, L. J. Henderson Jr. and P. Puryear (eds) *The New Black Politics: The Search for Political Power*, New York: Longman.

Wilson, W. J. (1978) *The Declining Significance of Race: Blacks and Changing American Institutions*, Chicago: Chicago University Press.

Wolpe, H. (1970) 'Race and industrialism in South Africa', in S. Zubaida (ed.) *Race and Racialism*, London: Tavistock.

——(1987) *Race, Class and the Apartheid State*, London: James Currey.

Yinger, J. M. (1986) 'Intersecting Strands in the Theorisation of Race and Ethnic Relations', in J. Rex and D. Mason (eds) *Theories of Race and Ethnic Relations*, Cambridge: Cambridge University Press.

Young, K. (1983) 'Ethnic pluralism and the policy agenda in Britain', in N. Glazer and K. Young (eds) *Ethnic Pluralism and Public Policy: Achieving Equality in the United States and Britain*, London: Heinemann.

FURTHER READING

Bachrach, P. and Baratz, M. (1970) *Power and Poverty: Theory and Practice*, New York: Oxford University Press.

Banton, M. (1987) 'The beginning and the end of the race issue in British politics', *Policy and Politics* 15: 39–47.

Barth, F. (ed.) (1969) *Ethnic Groups and Boundaries*, Bergen: Universitetsforlaget.

Castles, S. and Kosack, G. (1985) *Immigrant Workers and Class Structure in Western Europe*, London: Oxford University Press.

Freeman, G. (1979) *Immigrant Labour and Racial Conflict in Industrial Societies: The French and British Experience, 1945–75*, Princeton, NJ: Princeton University Press.

Glazer, N. and Young, K. (eds) (1983) *Ethnic Pluralism and Public Policy: Achieving Equality in the United States and Britain*, London: Heinemann.

Hammar, T. (ed.) (1985) *European Immigration Policy*, Cambridge: Cambridge University Press.

Hill, M. and Issacharoff, R. (1971) *Community Action and Race Relations*, London: Oxford University Press.

Katznelson, I. (1976) *Black Men, White Cities: Race, Politics, and Migration in the United States, 1900–30, and Britain, 1948–68*, Chicago: University of Chicago Press.

Kirp, D. (1979) *Doing Good by Doing Little*, London: University of California Press.

Kuper, L. and Smith, M. (ed.) (1969) *Pluralism in Africa*, Berkeley: University of California Press.

Layton-Henry, Z. (ed.) (1989) *The Political Rights of Migrant Workers in Western Europe*, London: Sage Publications.

Myrdal, G. (1944) *An American Dilemma*, Harper Brothers: New York.

Omi, M. and Winant, H. (1983) 'By the rivers of Babylon: race in the United States', *Socialist Review* 71: 31–65 and 72: 35–69.

Phizacklea, A. and Miles, R. (1980) *Labour and Racism*, London: Routledge & Kegan Paul.

Rex, J. and Mason, D. (ed.) (1986) *Theories of Race and Ethnic Relations*, Cambridge: Cambridge University Press.

Rex, J. and Moore, R. (1967) *Race, Community and Conflict*, London: Oxford University Press.

Saggar, S. (1991) *Race and Public Policy: A Study of Local Politics and Government*, Aldershot: Avebury.

UNESCO (1980) *Sociological Theories: Race and Colonialism*, Paris: UNESCO.

Wilson, W. (1980) *The Declining Significance of Race*, Chicago: University of Chicago Press.

Wolpe, H. (1987) *Race, Class and the Apartheid State*, London: James Currey.

34

CLASS AND POLITICS

BARRY HINDESS

The idea that classes and the relations between them are fundamental aspects of political life has played an important part in the formation of the modern world. Two of the most influential political movements of the last hundred years, communism and European social democracy, have been based on some version of this idea and it is impossible to understand contemporary politics without taking their impact into account. Nevertheless, the precise significance of class in the modern world remains a matter of considerable dispute, and it does so for two distinct but related reasons. First, there is disagreement as to the nature of the concept of class and of the place it should play in a general understanding of society. Second, a number of recent developments have brought into question the understanding of society as a matter of classes and the relations between them on which the earlier successes of these movements appear to have been based: notably, the political weaknesses of European social democracy, the internal collapse of some communist regimes and the growing political tensions within others. The question of the role of class in contemporary politics is also, inescapably, a question of the role of ideas of class both in political analysis and in the practical conduct of politics.

On the conceptual issue we can distinguish two broad approaches. Both accounts of the relevance of class have been influential in Western social democratic and labour movement politics.

The first approach treats class simply as a category of persons (usually identified by reference to occupational characteristics) that may or may not prove useful for the purposes of distributional analysis. Here class is used as one of a number of variables (such as sex, age, ethnicity, union membership, or housing tenure) that may be related to the social distribution of income, health, attitudes and voting behaviour. In this view class may be regarded as relevant to politics either because it relates to the distribution of political attitudes and voting behaviour or because it relates to education, life expectancy, and other aspects of the life chances of the population that are thought to be important on normative grounds. There are competing views as to how the categories of class themselves should be identified, giving rise to competing accounts of the political significance of class.

At the other extreme is a treatment of classes both as categories of persons and as major social forces that are characteristic of certain types of society, and of modern capitalist societies in particular. In this view classes and the most significant relations between them arise out of basic structural features of society and they inevitably have major social and political consequences. This approach to class has been influential in the politics of communist parties throughout the world and on the left wing of labour and social democratic movements. While there are considerable disagreements as to the precise conceptualization of class, there is nevertheless a common insistence on the importance of classes and class relations for the understanding of politics in capitalist societies. Marxism provides the best-known example of this type of approach, but there are also influential non-Marxist versions.

While the distinction between these two approaches is not always as clear-cut as the above remarks suggest, it is nevertheless important to recognize that one does not necessarily imply the other. In Marxist political analysis, class struggle would be regarded as an important part of politics in capitalist society even if class differences did not show up in the pattern of voting behaviour. On the other hand, the fact that the class variable has significant distributional implications in Britain and other capitalist societies does not establish that classes must themselves be regarded as social forces. Differences between the south of England and the north-west also have significant distributional implications but no one would regard those regions as social forces in the way that classes have often been seen.

This essay considers the idea of class as a social category that may be related to the distribution of political attitudes and behaviour, before moving on to consider the idea of classes as social forces. The latter has had greater significance in the modern period and will be given correspondingly greater attention here. On both accounts the practical political implications of class may vary over time and from one society to another but there are important differences in the way these changes are evaluated. In one, changes in the significance of class are an empirical matter, the consequences, as the case may be, of changes in the occupational structure, the character of party competition or other features of the society in question. In the other, changes in the apparent significance of class are either relatively superficial, masking a deeper underlying continuity, or else they represent a major change in the character of the society in question. All of these responses can be found in attempts to make sense of the changing fortunes of class-based political movements. These are examined in the third section of this essay.

CLASS AND POLITICAL BEHAVIOUR

In the period between the end of the Second World War and the late 1950s, it seemed clear to most commentators on British politics that the division between the working class (that is, manual workers and their families) and the rest of the population was the single most important influence on voting behaviour. Electoral politics were strongly polarized between the Labour and Conservative Parties, with only about a quarter of the electorate abstaining or voting for minor parties. Roughly two-thirds of working-class voters supported the Labour Party and the evidence of opinion polls suggested that most of them did so because they regarded it as being in some sense the party of the working class. Labour, it seemed, was the natural political home of the working class, and only the deviant, Conservative-voting minority posed a particular problem of explanation. The middle and upper classes were overwhelmingly Conservative, with only a deviant minority supporting Labour.

The class polarization of British politics was widely regarded as providing the clearest example amongst the larger Western democracies of the influence of class on political behaviour (Alford 1963; Rokkan 1970). In the United States, the absence of a major socialist party was seen as resulting in a somewhat weaker relationship between class and political behaviour. Elsewhere in Europe the class polarization of political behaviour was complicated by the influence of religious parties, significant regional and cultural differences, and divisions within the organized labour movement.

By the end of the 1950s, however, there were indications that this picture of the class character of British politics might be too simplistic. Some commentators had already noted signs of the slow but steady erosion of Labour's support that continued, with minor variations, into the 1980s (Abrams *et al.* 1959; Crosland 1960). Some years later a major study of political attitudes and voting behaviour found a marked weakening in the class alignment of electoral politics throughout the 1960s. It also suggested that the image of politics as a matter of conflicting class interests was most widely accepted amongst those who entered the electorate during and immediately after the Second World War. 'But such an image was accepted less frequently among Labour's working class supporters who entered the electorate more recently' (Butler and Stokes 1974: 200–1). Subsequent studies found both that party allegiances within the electorate were becoming weaker and that the relationship between class and party affiliation was declining. By the time of the 1983 general election it was possible to argue that housing tenure had replaced class membership as the single most important social characteristic influencing voting (Rose and McAllister 1986: 79). Surveys conducted at the time of the 1987 election indicated that Labour secured 34 per cent of the votes of the skilled working class, compared with over 40 per cent for the Conservatives

(*Guardian*, 15 June 1987). Rather than continue to vote on class lines, it seemed to many commentators that important sections of the working class were making a more pragmatic, hard-headed assessment of where their interests lay and that many of them were therefore voting Conservative.

The class polarization of British politics in the 1950s had been seen as reflecting an influence of class on political behaviour that was characteristic of the larger Western democracies. The erosion of that polarization was seen as part of a broader international development. This thesis is most forcefully expressed in the course of Peter Jenkins's reflections on the so-called Thatcher revolution:

> everywhere in the industrialised democratic world the old manual working class was in decline, trade union membership was falling, old class loyalties were crumbling. . . . In southern Europe socialist parties might still have a role to play as agents of belated democratisation; democratic socialism survived in the small neutralist countries of Scandinavia; but across the whole swathe of northern Europe the mode of politics which had dominated the post-war period was in decline.
>
> (Jenkins 1989: 335)

In other words, European social democracy was on the way out, the Labour party in Britain was a victim of this trend, and Mrs Thatcher had helped it on its way.

However, it would be misleading to close the discussion of class and political behaviour at this point. It has been suggested that the declining significance of class in British politics is more apparent than real. The argument is that the traditional working class/middle class dichotomy provides too simple a model of class structure, and that a more refined model (with an intermediate class including many who would otherwise be regarded as skilled workers) is required to take account of the impact of significant changes in the occupational structure since the 1950s. This more refined model, it is claimed, would show that the relevance of class to politics is not declining (Heath *et al.* 1985; Marshall *et al.* 1989). The relevance of class, then, would appear to depend on how classes are to be identified. Against that view Rose and McAllister insist that however classes are identified 'most British voters do not have their vote determined by occupational class' (Rose and McAllister 1985: 50).

This more refined model of class nevertheless shares with the traditional view the idea of a natural affinity between classes and political parties such that a relative change in the size of one invariably leads to a corresponding shift in the political fortunes of the other. That idea is difficult to square with the comparative success of social democratic and labour parties in parts of northern Europe and in Australasia. This shows that these parties may have greater sources of potential support than the pessimistic sociological determinism of that approach appears to suggest. The example of Sweden in particular, as we shall see in the third part of this essay (pp. 564–5), has been used to argue that the relationship between class and politics may well depend on the conduct of parties themselves.

CLASSES AS SOCIAL FORCES

This idea of classes as constituting one set of social categories amongst others is in marked contrast with the idea of classes as major social forces generated by the fundamental structure of society. In the one case, class is a feature of social structure that may or may not have an impact on how people vote, and therefore on the behaviour of parties. In the other, the relationship of classes to politics is an essential feature of classes themselves. There are many different versions of this view, but perhaps the best-known formulation can be found in the opening section of *The Communist Manifesto*, first published in 1848:

> The history of all hitherto existing society is the history of class struggles. Freeman and slave, patrician and plebeian, lord and serf.... [I]n a word, oppressor and oppressed, stood inconstant opposition to one another, carried on an uninterrupted, now hidden, now open fight, a fight that each time ended, either in a revolutionary re-constitution of society at large, or in the common ruin of the contending classes.
>
> (Marx and Engels 1848: 35–6)

In this view of classes, their political significance is not primarily a matter of electoral behaviour. Class membership may be closely related to voting behaviour or it may not – but in either case politics has to be seen as really a matter of class struggle. In Marx's view, classes are the main contending forces in society. Classes, and the relations between them, are the key to the understanding of politics and, in particular, to the identification of the forces promoting or resisting progressive social change. Class struggle may be open or it may be hidden, but it will make its presence felt for as long as classes themselves exist.

The treatment of classes as social forces is most commonly associated with Marxist thought, but Marx insisted that he was not the discoverer of 'the existence of classes in modern society or [of] the struggle between them' (Marx 1852). Much contemporary non-Marxist political analysis has also been concerned with the identification of classes and the relations between them because of their supposed significance as social forces. For example, in his discussion of the implications of social mobility for the prospects of egalitarian social change in Britain, Goldthorpe takes care to distance himself from Marxism. Nevertheless, to 'this extent at least we would agree with Marx: that if class society is to be ended – or even radically modified – this can only be through conflict between classes in one form or another' (Goldthorpe 1980: 29; see also Dahrendorf 1959; Parkin 1979). What matters for these non-

Marxist authors is not so much the existence of class divisions in Marx's sense, but rather the formation of classes as social collectivities capable of a significant degree of collective action. Social mobility is important in Goldthorpe's argument, for example, because of its effects on the development of class identification and the ties of solidarity required for the formation of classes as collective actors.

There is no space to consider the differences between the various Marxist and non-Marxist forms of class analysis here. For present purposes it is more important to concentrate on what they share: namely, an insistence on the importance of classes and class relations for the understanding of capitalist societies. Any treatment of classes as social forces involves some combination of two elements. One is a notion of classes as collective actors. The other is a conception of class interests as objectively given to individuals by virtue of their class location, and therefore as providing a basis for action in common. Both are problematic. The suggestion that classes play a fundamental role in politics involves the further claim that crucial features of political life can be understood in terms of the actions or the interests of classes themselves. We consider each of these issues in turn.

The problem with the idea that classes can be regarded as collective actors is simply that even the most limited concept of actor involves some means of taking decisions and of acting on them. Human individuals are actors in that sense, and so are capitalist enterprises, political parties, trade unions and state agencies. There are other collectivities, such as classes and societies, that have no identifiable means of taking decisions – although it is not difficult to find those who claim to take decisions and to act on their behalf. Actors' decisions play an important part in the explanation of their actions – and that is the most important reason for restricting the concept of actor to things that are able to take decisions and act on them. To suggest, for example, that the current crisis of the British welfare state could be explained as the actions of a *class* is to construct a fantastic allegory in which the factions, parties and other organizations involved and their often confused and conflicting objectives are reduced to the actions of a single actor. Such allegories appear to simplify our understanding of the state of affairs in question while thoroughly obscuring the question of what can or should be done about it.

What of the attempt to understand classes as social forces in terms of structurally determined class interests? These interests are supposed to be determined by the structure of relations between classes, and the parties, unions and other agencies of political life are then to be seen as their more or less adequate representations. Two features of this concept of interests are particularly significant.

One is that it appears to provide an explanatory link between the behaviour of individuals and their position in the structure of society: interests provide us with reasons for action, and are determined by our position as members of a particular class, gender or community. Marxist class analysis suggests, for example, that the working class has an objective interest in the overthrow of capitalism in favour of a socialist society. The difficulty here, of course, is that the vast majority of those who are thought to have an objective interest in socialism rarely acknowledge those interests as their own. Far from providing an effective explanatory link between the structure of capitalist society and political behaviour, the idea of structurally determined class interests generates a host of explanatory problems. A considerable part of Marxist political analysis has been devoted to considering why the working classes in the capitalist West have not pursued their objective interests in socialism.

The other significant feature of this concept of interests is that it seems to allow us to combine a variety of discrete relationships and conflicts into a larger whole. In Britain, for example, the 1984–5 miners' strike, industrial action by transport workers, and the defence of the National Health Service against cuts could all be regarded as instances of a wider struggle between one class and another on the grounds that the same set of class interests was ultimately at stake in each of these conflicts. The use of class interests as a means of bringing together a variety of distinct relationships and conflicts suggests that the participants in each case be regarded as standing in for the classes whose interests are supposed to be at stake. It brings us back, in other words, to the allegory of classes as collective actors.

This brings us to the third issue, the question of reductionism. No serious advocate of class analysis, Marxist or non-Marxist, maintains that the analysis of class relations tells us all we might want to know about the political forces at work in the modern world. The allegory of classes as collective actors is nevertheless intended to provide us with a key to the understanding of political life. This is the point of the passage from *The Communist Manifesto* quoted earlier (p. 559).

Goldthorpe's study of social mobility in modern Britain provides a clear non-Marxist example of this device. We have seen that he regards class conflict as necessary to bring about significant social change. He therefore proceeds to examine the implications of social mobility for the patterns of 'shared beliefs, attitudes and sentiments that are required for concerted class action' (Goldthorpe 1980: 265) – as if those implications could be identified quite independently of the actions of political parties, the media, or state agencies. What is involved here is a failure to take seriously the consequences of movements, organizations and their actions, both for political forces and the conditions under which they operate, and for the formation of the political interests and concerns which bring them into conflict. Political attitudes, beliefs and behaviour may then be treated as if they reflect other social conditions, in this case the strength and consciousness of the contending classes. The implication is that these other conditions are in some sense more real than the political phenomena that reflect them.

This example brings out a general feature of the idea that classes provide the key to an understanding of political life. This type of approach claims to bring together two distinct but related levels of analysis. At one level are the factions, parties, ideologies and the like that constitute the political life of society. At the other level is the allegory of classes as collective actors, the key to our understanding of the mundane. Unfortunately, there is at most a gestural connection between these two levels. The class analysis of politics, in other words, combines an insistence on the irreducibility of political phenomena with the explanatory promise of reductionism. How the trick is done, of course, remains obscure.

PROSPECTS FOR LABOUR AND SOCIAL DEMOCRATIC POLITICS

Both communism and European social democracy have been based on some version of the idea that classes and class relations are fundamental aspects of the political life of modern societies. Supporters of both movements have been disappointed in their expectations. It is beyond the scope of this essay to consider the fate of communist regimes, but what of the responses of the labour and social democratic parties of the capitalist West?

Social democratic attempts to come to terms with the failures of their expectations can be divided into two broad clusters. On the one side there is the 'revisionist' response that class in either of the above senses has become less relevant to politics in the modern world and that labour and social democratic parties must therefore broaden their appeal if they are to succeed – that is, they must modernize and revise their doctrines and objectives to take account of the effects of social and economic change. The opposite view is that the political salience of class is, to a considerable extent, a consequence of the policies pursued by social democratic parties themselves and by the broader labour movement. The declining salience of class in Britain and many other Western democracies would then be, at least in part, a consequence of the failure of their labour or social democratic parties to pursue an appropriate form of class politics.

The revisionist response operates at two levels. One involves the general claim that classes are becoming less relevant as a consequence of economic development, at least in the democratic societies of the modern West. Towards the end of the nineteenth century, the German socialist Edward Bernstein argued that capitalist economic development had brought about a situation in which 'the ideological, and especially the ethical factors, [had] greater space for independent activity than was formerly the case' (Bernstein 1961: 15). The revisionist argument here assumes a hierarchy of human needs: once material needs have been satisfied then people will turn their attention to non-material values. The appeal to class interests may have been important in the earlier stages of capitalist development, but it must now be replaced by a politics organized around the ethical appeal of socialist values.

A closely related argument about the effects of economic growth was set out in Crosland's *The Future of Socialism* (1956) and his Fabian pamphlet *Can Labour Win?* (1960). At one time class was the main determinant of voting behaviour, but with rising living standards 'we may find . . . as material pressures ease and the problem of subsistence fades away, people become more sensitive to moral and political issues' (Crosland 1960: 22). More recently, the literature on what are often called 'new' social movements has given a new twist to the old revisionist argument by suggesting that conflict between classes has been displaced by feminist, environmentalist and other 'new' forms of politics in the more advanced societies of the modern world (Cohen 1985; Inglehart 1979).

This general argument in favour of developing a non-class political appeal is often supplemented by a second, more pragmatic level of revisionist argument. Bernstein used German census material to argue that the peasantry and the middle classes were far from disappearing, as orthodox Marxism appeared to suggest, and that the working class was far from being an overwhelming majority of the population. The implication, at least for the foreseeable future, was that there would always be a substantial part of the electorate, neither capitalist nor working class, whose votes could significantly affect the chances of achieving any major socialist objective. The social democratic party needed therefore to dilute its sectional appeal to the interests of a single class if it was to have any hope of winning power.

Similarly, Crosland's *Can Labour Win?* (published in 1960, following the Labour Party's third successive post-war election defeat) maintains that long-term social changes have eroded the significance of class differences in British politics, with the result, first, that a growing proportion of the electorate no longer votes on the basis of class identification and, second, that Labour's working-class image is a wasting electoral asset. Crosland argued that economic development was producing changes in the occupational structure. The relative size of the manual working class fell throughout the 1950s (by about 0.5 per cent a year) and it has continued to do so. Assuming a straightforward association between class position and voting behaviour, such a fall in the relative size of the working class entails a corresponding fall in Labour's class-based support. In Crosland's argument, Labour's difficulty is compounded by the gradual breakdown of that association as a result of increasing affluence, social and geographical mobility and the breakup of old working-class communities. In the more prosperous sections of the working class, people had 'acquired a middle class income and pattern of consumption, and sometimes a middle class psychology' (Crosland 1960: 12). This inexorable erosion of class as a basis for Labour's electoral support means that the party has to concentrate on other determinants of electoral behaviour, particularly on its image and performance in office.

The revisionist argument, then, is that the analysis of politics in class terms has become less informative as other, non-class forms of politics have come to the fore. Here the contrast between a past in which socialist politics could be conducted in class terms, and a present and future in which it cannot, serves as a rhetorical device. It is a means of arguing against the analysis of politics in class terms without directly confronting the conceptual weaknesses of class analysis.

In fact, the revisionist account of the implications of economic change is open to challenge on a number of points. First, many of those recruited into the expanding middle-class occupations came from working-class backgrounds. It is far from clear that they would be repelled by Labour's class identification. As for the affluent-worker explanation of political change, its advocates have been remarkably unclear as to the processes that are supposed to connect increasing prosperity with Conservative voting. Academic critics have shown that what might seem to be the most plausible mechanisms have little empirical foundation (Goldthorpe *et al.* 1968).

More seriously, the revisionist argument reproduces many of the problems noted above with regard to the analysis of classes as social forces. In particular, it treats the political concerns and orientations of the electorate as if they were formed independently of the political activities of parties and other political agencies, and ultimately as if they were a function of changes in the economy. The anti-revisionist case attempts to incorporate this point into its class analysis of society. It advances the argument that while politics is ultimately a matter of class struggle, the apparent significance of class in the political life of a capitalist society will itself depend on the strength of the working class in that society. Where the working class is strong it will be in a position both to force an accommodation on the ruling capitalist class and to insist on the class content of the political disputes in which it is engaged. Where it is weak, the class content of politics will be less apparent.

Many authors take Sweden as an exemplary case in point. Esping-Anderson and Korpi (1984) argue that classes develop parties, unions and other organizations in order to further their collective interests and that they will attempt to shape public institutions in their favour. In the area of social policy, for example, they suggest that the primary concerns of the working-class parties have been to reduce workers' dependence on market forces by developing a system of basic citizenship rights and maintaining full employment:

'Among the Western nations since 1973, it is only the three with the most powerful labour movement – Sweden, Norway and Austria – which have utilized macro-economic, wage or labour-market policies in order to hold unemployment at relatively low levels.

(Esping-Anderson and Korpi 1984: 205)

Whether the working class can impose such an arrangement will depend on the relative strengths of the different classes. Its aim then, must be both to defend its material interests and to promote social conditions that foster its organizational strength. It therefore favours universalistic forms of social security provision on the grounds that they promote solidarity within the population rather than the pursuit of sectional interests. The capitalist class, on the other hand, has an interest in limiting the political and economic strength of the working class. It therefore favours decentralized wage bargaining and forms of social policy that promote sectional divisions – for example, by separating manual workers from other employees and fostering the growth of private pensions and insurance schemes.

Where working-class politics are relatively unsuccessful, the class itself will be divided and class solidarity will have limited political appeal. Working-class parties will then be vulnerable to the revisionist temptation, that is, to seek electoral support on non-class grounds – thereby further reducing the appeal of class politics. In the British context, for example, Minkin and Seyd (1977) have suggested that the declining salience of class is partly a result of the Labour Party's all too successful attempts to manipulate its image and electoral appeal in line with the recommendations of *Can Labour Win?* (Crosland 1960).

Nevertheless, it is far from clear that the comparative success of Swedish social democracy compared with the British labour movement need be interpreted as reflecting the relative strengths in these countries of different classes, considered as collective actors engaged in conflict. At most, the argument shows that *conceptions* of class interests may well be significant elements of political life. The strongest point in the anti-revisionist case is its insistence that the relative strength of class-based forms of politics in, say, Britain and Sweden, cannot be explained without reference to the outcomes of past conflicts within and between parties and other organizations.

In other words, class politics do not simply reflect changes in the occupational structure or economic growth, as the revisionist case suggests. What this last point shows is that the role of ideas in political life (in this case, ideas about the political significance of class) is never a simple reflection of social structure conditions.

CONCLUSIONS

Judgements about the political significance of class must depend first on whether or not classes are regarded as social forces. If they are so regarded, then the judgements then depend on whether classes are regarded as characteristic of capitalist (and possibly other) societies, as Marxism and much non-Marxist class analysis suggests, or as forces that have been superseded by non-class forms of political life, as the revisionist and 'new social movement' literature suggests. If classes are not regarded as political forces, then the significance of class is a matter either of the distribution of voting behaviour in the population or of the significance of class and related patterns of inequality in the political ideas of the major political parties. Since ideas of class are widely disputed and the role of such ideas in political life is not a simple reflection of social conditions there is little prospect of these questions being settled in the foreseeable future.

REFERENCES

Abrams, M., Hinden, R. and Rose, R. (1959) *Must Labour Lose?*, Harmondsworth: Penguin.

Alford, R. (1963) *Party and Society*, Chicago: Rand McNally.

Bernstein, E. (1961) *Evolutionary Socialism*, New York: Schocken.

Butler, D. and Stokes, D. (1974) *Political Change in Britain*, 2nd edn, London: Macmillan.

Cohen, J. (ed.) (1985) *Social Movements*, winter issue of *Social Research*, vol. 5.

Crosland, C. A. R. (1956) *The Future of Socialism*, London: Cape.

——(1960) *Can Labour Win?*, Fabian Tract no. 324, London: Fabian Society.

Dahrendorf, R. (1959) *Class and Class Conflict in Industrial Society*, London: Routledge & Kegan Paul.

Esping-Anderson, G. and Korpi, W. (1984) 'Social policy as class politics in post-war capitalism', in J. Goldthorpe (ed.) *Order and Conflict in Contemporary Capitalism*, Oxford: Clarendon Press.

Goldthorpe, J. H. (1980) *Social Mobility and Class Structure in Modern Britain*, Oxford: Clarendon Press.

Goldthorpe, J. H., Lockwood, D., Bechofer, F. and Platt, J. (1968) *The Affluent Worker*, Cambridge: Cambridge University Press.

Heath, A., Jowell, R. and Curtice, J. (1985) *How Britain Votes*, Oxford: Pergamon Press.

Inglehart, R. (1979) *The Silent Revolution*, Princeton: Princeton University Press.

Jenkins, P. (1989) *Mrs Thatcher's Revolution: The Ending of the Socialist Era*, 2nd edn, London: Pan.

Marshall, G., Newby, H., Rose, D. and Vogler, C. (1989) *Social Class in Modern Britain*, London: Hutchinson.

Marx, K. (1852) Letter to Weydemeyer, 5 March, in K. Marx and F. Engels, *Selected Works*, p. 679, London: Lawrence & Wishart, 1968.

Marx, K. and Engels, F. (1848) 'The Communist Manifesto', in K. Marx and F. Engels, *Selected Works*, London: Lawrence & Wishart, 1968.

Minkin, L. and Seyd, P. (1977) 'The British Labour party', in W. E. Patterson and A. H. Thomas (eds) *Social Democratic Parties in Western Europe*, London: Croom Helm.

Parkin, F. (1979) *Marxism and Class Theory: A Bourgeois Critique*, London: Tavistock.

Rokkan, S. (1970) *Citizens, Elections, Parties*, Oslo: Universitetsforlaget.

Rose, R. and McAllister, I. (1986) *Voters Begin to Choose*, London: Sage Publications.

FURTHER READING

The clearest accounts of what was once the standard view of the relation between class and political behaviour in Western democracies are Alford (1963) and Rokkan (1970). The shifting patterns of electoral support in Western Europe are surveyed in H. Daalder and P. Mair, *Western European Party Systems: Continuity and Change* (London: Sage Publications, 1983). There are numerous treatments of the apparent decline in the salience of class in British elections: see especially, M. Franklin, *The Decline of Class Voting in Britain* (Oxford: Clarendon Press, 1970), Butler and Stokes (1974), Rose and McAllister (1985) and Marshall *et al.* (1989). The last two provide useful discussions of the implications of different definitions of class for the analysis of electoral behaviour. The idea of classes as social forces has generated an enormous literature and continues to do so. Marxist and non-Marxist versions are discussed in B. Hindess, *Politics and Class Analysis* (Oxford: Blackwell, 1987). P. Calvert, *The Concept of Class* (London: Hutchinson, 1982), is a general historical survey of various uses of the concept. The claim that class politics have become less significant as a result of economic development can be found in the writings of socialist revisionism (Bernstein 1961; Crosland 1956, 1960) and, in a rather different form, in the 'new social movements' literature (Cohen 1985). Variants of a contrary argument to the effect that the apparent salience of class is itself a consequence of the political strategies pursued by social democratic parties and by their opponents can be found in A. Przeworski, *Capitalism and Social Democracy* (Cambridge: Cambridge University Press, 1985), and several contributions to J. H. Goldthorpe (ed.) *Order and Conflict in Contemporary Capitalism* (Oxford: Clarendon Press, 1984).

35

ETHNICITY AND POLITICS

T. DAVID MASON

Since the end of the Second World War, the world has witnessed the revival, intensification and stubborn persistence of ethnicity as an issue in politics, as a focal point of popular political mobilization, and as a source of domestic and interstate conflict. The political salience of ethnicity has endured not just in the former colonial territories of the Third World but also in the advanced post-industrial democracies of Western Europe and North America, as well as in the major communist nations of the Soviet Union, Yugoslavia, Eastern Europe, and the People's Republic of China. The structural conditions that give rise to ethno-regional politics, the immediate causes that catalyse ethnic conflict, and the forms that ethnically based conflict assumes differ markedly both across and within the three worlds. What is apparent, however, is that the penetration of 'modernity' into all regions of the world has *not* led to the 'withering away' of ethnicity as a source of political conflict; indeed, its salience appears to have increased as a consequence of the diffusion of modernity.

What is perhaps most striking about the study of ethnic politics is that, with a few exceptions, the resurgence of ethnicity as a political force has been all but ignored in the mainstream academic literature on social change and political development. Walker Connor (1972: 319–20) once noted that, among a sample of ten works that would now be regarded as among the classics of the development literature, none of them contained a section, a chapter, or a major subheading on ethnicity. Six of the ten contained not a single reference to ethnic groups, ethnicity, or minorities in their indexes, and the remaining four made only passing references to the subject in an occasional isolated passage. Thus, while there is a theoretically rigorous and empirically rich body of research on the dimensions and dynamics of ethnic politics, this literature has not been fully recognized by the mainstream scholarship on comparative social change and political development.

To some extent, the relegation of ethnicity to the theoretical periphery of contemporary social science is attributable to the paradigmatic competition between modernization and Marxist schools of social development. Both have depicted ethnic identification as a primordial sentiment whose relevance would diminish with the expansion and penetration of the modern industrial society. Contrary to the expectations of both schools, however, we have witnessed a resurgence of ethnic politics at a point in time when the penetration of the global political economy and the diffusion of the modern culture into all corners of the globe had led mainstream comparative analysts to anticipate the imminent demise of ethnicity as an issue nexus for politics within nations. The frustration of these expectations is summarized by Walker Connor:

> The preponderant number of states are multiethnic. Ethnic consciousness has been definitely increasing, not decreasing, in recent years. No particular classification of multiethnic states has proven immune to the fissiparous impact of ethnicity: authoritarian and democratic; federative and unitary; Asian, African, American, and European states have all been afflicted. Form of government and geography have clearly not been determinative. Nor has the level of economic development. But the accompaniments of economic development – increased social mobilization and communication – appear to have increased ethnic tensions and to be conducive to separatist demands. Despite all this, leading theoreticians of 'nation-building' have tended to ignore or slight the problems associated with ethnicity.
>
> (Connor 1972: 332)

Thus, we are presented with the questions that will serve as the focus of this essay. Why has ethnicity remained such a powerful focus of political identification in the contemporary global community? Why has the diffusion of global political culture, economic institutions and modernization processes not led to the anticipated decline in the salience of ethnicity in politics and perhaps even intensified its political relevance? What are the different forms that ethnic political mobilization assumes, and what structural, cultural and individual factors account for differences in the probability, form and issue focus of ethnic collective action?

This essay presents an overview of some of the more compelling themes in recent research on ethnic politics. By describing the theoretical principles upon which this body of research is grounded, this essay can perhaps illustrate the extent to which this research is in fact integrated theoretically into the broader paradigmatic terrain of collective political action. In this manner, we can perhaps highlight the relevance of research on ethnicity and politics to the evolution, refinement and elaboration of the major research traditions dealing with social change and political development.

DIMENSIONS OF ETHNICITY AND ETHNIC CONFLICT

When one realizes that ethnic heterogeneity is the norm among the nations of the contemporary global community, it should not be surprising that ethnicity has remained such a powerful factor in the domestic politics of so many nations. Nearly twenty years ago, Walter Connor (1972: 320) pointed out that, of the 132 nation-states in existence at that time, only twelve (9.1 per cent) were essentially ethnically homogeneous, while twenty-five (18.9 per cent) had one ethnic group that accounted for more than 90 per cent of the population and another twenty-five had one group that accounted for between 75 and 90 per cent of the population. However, in thirty-one nations (23.5 per cent) the largest ethnic group comprised only 50 to 74 per cent of the population, and in another thirty-nine (29.5 per cent) the largest single ethnic group accounted for less than half of the population. In fifty-three states (40.2 per cent) the population was divided among more than *five* significant groups. In view of what Connor termed 'the remarkable lack of coincidence . . . between ethnic and political borders', it should not be surprising to find that ethnicity remains a focal point of political organization and competition throughout the world.

The evidence on the extent of ethnic violence testifies to the intensity with which ethnic issues are prosecuted in the political arena. In a study of conflicts in Africa occurring between 1946 and 1976, Istvan Kende categorized 120 conflicts into three types: internal anti-regime, internal tribal, and border wars (Kende 1978: 231-2). He found that 85 per cent of these conflicts were of the two internal types, which were not only the most frequent (102 out of 120 conflicts) but also the most persistent (97.7 per cent of the total number of 'nation-years' of war). In the last ten years covered by his study (1967-76), there was an increase in the proportion of all war that was internal, and internal tribal war with foreign intervention was found to be the form most rapidly increasing in frequency. All of the internal tribal and most of the internal anti-regime wars had an ethnic component to them.

For instance, Horowitz (1985: 10-12) points out that the independence movement in Guinea-Bissau was confined largely to the Balante with little support from the Fula. In Mozambique the Makone provided most of the soldiers for the war against Portugal while the Shangana provided most of the movement's political leadership. The three rebel armies in Portuguese Angola were ethnically based, and Jonas Savimbi's UNITA (National Union for the Total Independence of Angola) has continued to wage war against the post-independence government of Angola from its ethnic base among the Ovambo of the south of the country. Across the border in Namibia, Sam Nujoma's SWAPO (South-West Africa People's Organization) is largely a movement of the Ovambo. In Zimbabwe, Robert Mugabe's support was from the Shona majority while Joshua Nkomo's army drew on the Ndebele minority.

What Kende's study indicates is that, once the dismantling of colonial sovereignty was virtually completed, civil conflict did not disappear in the Third World. Instead, indigenous ethnic and tribal hostilities supplanted colonial domination as the predominant issue driving the continuing diffusion of revolution throughout the Third World. Many of the newly independent nations became subject to conflict involving the efforts of ethnically and regionally based groupings to gain regional independence, or the efforts of revolutionaries from the subordinate ethnic group to seize control of the government from a superordinate group. In both forms of civil strife, ethnicity has provided a powerful and perhaps critical basis for popular mobilization. Hence, we have witnessed secessionist warfare in Burma, Bangladesh, the Sudan, Nigeria, Morocco, Iraq, Ethiopia and the Philippines, ethnically based civil wars in Lebanon, Zaire, Angola and Afghanistan, interstate war between Ethiopia and Somalia over the Ogaden region, between India and Pakistan over Kashmir, ethnic riots in India, Sri Lanka, Malaysia, Zaire and Guyana, attacks by an army of one ethnic group against civilians from another ethnic group in Uganda and Zimbabwe, and the expulsion of Asians from Uganda, and of Beninese from the Ivory Coast and Gabon (Horowitz 1985: 3; see also Small and Singer 1982: 59–60, and 80 for a listing of conflicts).

Ethnic conflict has by no means been confined to the former colonial territories of the Third World. Basque separatism in Spain, South Tyrolean discontent with Italian rule, resurgent Scottish and Welsh nationalism in the United Kingdom, the chronic violence of Northern Ireland, Franco-Canadian separatist sentiments in Quebec, the Walloon–Flemish rivalry in Belgium, continued racial conflict in the United States and the emergence of similar strife in Great Britain all attest to the durability of ethnic loyalties as a source of conflict in the major post-industrial democracies of Western Europe and North America (see Connor 1972: 327; Ragin 1979; Hechter 1974; Birch 1978; Tiryakian and Rogowski 1985).

Nor has the adoption of Marxist-Leninist ideology in Eastern Europe immunized those nations against ethnically based internal conflict. The Lithuanian declaration of independence from the Soviet Union and the persistence of similar sentiments within the other two Baltic republics of Latvia and Estonia, the bloody interethnic conflicts between Armenians and Azerbaijanis in the disputed region of Nagorno-Karabakh, and the rumblings of separatist sentiments among the peoples of the other southern republics of the Soviet Union reveal the extent to which ethnically based nationalist sentiments have endured in the Soviet Union despite more than a generation of officially sanctioned socialization promoting the notion that such sentiments are revisionist in nature. The escalation of Slovenian and Croatian separatist sentiments into interethnic warfare in Yugoslavia, recent persecution of Hungarian minorities in Romania, the suspicion with which ethnic Germans are regarded by Poles in the territory returned to Poland at the end of the Second World War, and the failure of the People's Republic of China to eradicate independence sentiment among Tibetans likewise attest to the pervasiveness of ethnic loyalties and identity among the peoples of the putatively proletarian states of Eastern Europe and Asia.

This raises the question of why ethnicity has persisted and even intensified amid the rapid diffusion of 'modernization' (however one wishes to conceive it) and its many correlates, such as industrialization, urbanization and the penetration of modern communications and modern values into every corner of the globe. Indeed, it is this paradigmatic anomaly, common to both the Marxist and modernization schools of development, that has served as the starting point for much of the contemporary theoretical work on ethnicity and politics. In the next section, we explore some of these arguments.

MODERNIZATION AND THE PERSISTENCE OF ETHNIC POLITICS

The proposition that the multi-dimensional process of modernization should lead to a withering away of ethnicity as a source of group identity is by no means new to the social sciences. As far back as the middle of the nineteenth century, social theorists believed that with the evolution of industrial society economic interests would supersede ethnicity as the focus of people's social identity and participation in politics. Ethnicity was regarded as a set of 'residual loyalties from an earlier phase of social development' that inevitably would be displaced by economic rationality as the motivational basis of people's behaviour (Birch 1978: 325). More recently, authors such as Parsons and Smelser (1956), Lipset and Rokkan (1967) and Butler and Stokes (1969) have argued that 'extensions in the scope and centrality of the market would lead to the erosion of ethnic attachments' because ethnic identities have no direct relevance to the transactions of the market-place and, therefore, should lose their social meaning (Leifer 1981: 24–5). The expanded spatial mobility of labour, capital, and goods and services should likewise discourage the geographic concentration of any ethnic group and thereby facilitate its assimilation into a more universal social order (Hechter and Levi 1979: 266).

Yet, as we have seen above, the diffusion of modernization throughout the world has not resulted in the diminution of ethnicity as a political force. How, then, do we account for this? Ethno-regional movements could have been anticipated in some of the multi-ethnic nation-states of Asia and Africa in the aftermath of independence from colonial rule. In Africa, nation-state boundaries were drawn with little or no regard for the ethnic boundaries among indigenous peoples. In many cases an explicit component of the colonial power's 'divide and rule' strategy was to preserve intact the cultural autonomy of the various ethnic groups. Upon achieving independence, the institutions of the newly formed state posed no immediate threat to this patchwork of ethnically distinct social subsystems left over from the colonial era. However, as the central state increased its capacity to regulate society and extended its authority into the ethno-regional enclaves, the isolation that had allowed ethnically distinct subsystems to retain their autonomy under colonial rule gradually dissolved. All too often, the resultant challenges faced by ethnic groups evoked in them an almost xenophobic 'reactive ethnicity' characterized by the resistance of previously autonomous ethnic enclaves to the potentially corrosive and exploitive penetration of the modern state's institutions and authority (Connor 1972: 329; Hechter and Levi 1979: 263; Nielsen 1985: 134).

The persistence of ethnic conflict in the advanced industrial societies of Western Europe and North America is less readily explained by modernization theory or Marxism. Indeed, both schools postulate the displacement of 'primordial' identities such as ethnicity by more universal modern identities such as class and other identities based on shared economic interest (Rogowski and Wasserspring 1971: 9). The continued reality of ethnicity as a force in advanced societies poses an anomaly of paradigmatic import for both Marxists and modernization theorists alike. Rogowski and Wasserspring (1971: 9–10) have argued that, contrary to modernization theory, greater interaction does not increase the 'cognitive problem' of placing people by particularistic criteria; indeed, it may serve to crowd out *all but* ascriptive criteria. Amid the cognitive overload that inevitably accompanies the transition from tradition to modernity, race and ethnicity often become more salient as determinants of people's behaviour because they are identification mechanisms that have a low cost of information. The increasing complexity of modern society, and the accompanying difficulty of distinguishing potential allies from potential rivals in the competitions that characterize it, reinforce the tendency toward ethnic solidarity because it is easier to distinguish allies from rivals on the basis of ethnicity than on the less obvious (and hence more costly to determine) criteria of occupation, class, political preferences, or other non-ascriptive criteria.

A major structural consequence of these tendencies is that ethnic solidarity and the ethnic identification are reinforced because the benefits of modernization are not equally (or at least equitably) distributed across ethnic groups (Brass 1976; Melson and Wolpe 1970; Bates 1974; for an alternative view see Horowitz 1985: 103). The questions of why ethnicity has remained a salient criterion for the distribution of the rewards and costs of modernization, and what consequences flow from this tendency, have come to serve as the central foci of much of the theoretical literature on contemporary ethnic politics. We turn now to these works.

ETHNICITY AND POLITICS: THEORETICAL APPROACHES

The realization that modernization theory and Marxism's depictions of ethnicity were at best incomplete in their failure to account for the persistence of ethnicity has led to a number of theoretical efforts to resolve this paradigmatic blind spot. An important initial step was to define ethnicity in terms that allow its integration as a concept into existing theoretical frameworks on social change, political development and collective action. Rogowski's (1974: 71) definition of a 'stigma' as any identifying characteristic that has a low cost of detection and a high cost of conversion has proven to be theoretically rich in that it provides us with access to the conceptual tools with which to explore the extent to which ethnicity and other ascriptive characteristics affect individual political behaviour and participation in collective action. By this definition, for instance, race and gender are relatively powerful stigmas in that one's race or gender can be determined rather easily by others and can be altered only at great expense, if at all; by contrast, language and accent are less powerful stigmatic bases for group solidarity because they are less readily detected and more easily altered.

From this perspective, it becomes possible to conceive of ways in which modernization or any other form of social change could reinforce ethnic identity and interethnic conflict. First, modernization creates benefits and costs, both public and private in nature. These benefits must be allocated among different constituencies in society. Ethnicity is one way in which constituencies can be distinguished from each other in that it is relatively easy to allocate benefits and costs differentially according to ethnic criteria. In this manner, the opportunity structure and the changes in it that are generated by modernization may be biased in favour of one ethnic group over another.

The differential distribution of the benefits of modernization may occur for a number of reasons. Largely serendipitous environmental factors may advantage one ethnic group over another when, for instance, one group happens to occupy territory in which rare minerals are located or the soil and climate are more appropriate for a particularly valued cash crop. In other cases, geography affords one group earlier and more frequent contact with the outside world and thereby gives that group a developmental 'head start' over other ethnic enclaves that are more isolated from global contacts. Some cultural groups may be more predisposed than others to take advantage of the new opportunities presented by the advent of modernization and to compete for the benefits of modernization (Melson and Wolpe 1970: 1115–16; see also Bates 1974: 464–6). In some cases this cultural predisposition may be a function of the niche occupied by that group in the pre-modern 'cultural division of labour'. For instance, an ethnic group that traditionally was denied access to land and therefore became concentrated in commercial activity as merchants may find

574

itself favourably positioned to take advantage of the changes in the indigenous economy and social structure brought on by its integration into the global economy.

If the benefits of modernization are distributed according to ethnic criteria, then the structural relationship between different ethnic groups becomes significant for explaining ethnic differences in the distribution of social costs and benefits, the extent to which these differences lead to ethnic conflict and what form that conflict will assume. The fundamental distinction between forms of ethnic differentiation is between vertical and horizontal differentiation, or between 'ranked' and 'unranked' systems. In a vertically integrated or 'ranked' system of interethnic relations, stratification is synonymous with ethnicity in the sense that the social structure is characterized by one ethnic group being subordinate to the other. Because ethnicity and class coincide, mobility is restricted by ascriptive criteria (Horowitz 1971: 232; 1985: 23–5). Generally, the different ethnic groups are intermixed geographically so that interaction between members of the different ethnic groups is a routine feature of everyday social life. However, the relations between groups are governed by clearly recognized norms of superordinate and subordinate status. Behavioural norms governing intergroup relations in ranked systems typically have ritualized modes of expressing the subordinate group's deference and the superordinate group's dominance and interactions approximate the etiquette of a caste system (Horowitz 1985: 26).

Despite the rigidity of ranked systems, relations between superordinate and subordinate ethnic group are usually characterized by some measure of social cohesion and shared expectations in addition to the coercion and conflict that preserve the status quo. The dominant modality of interactions between members of the subordinate and superordinate groups is that of a clientelist exchange: members of the subordinate group seek protection from their patrons in the superordinate group in exchange for providing those patrons with services, loyalty, deference and goods (Horowitz 1985: 26; for patron–client politics, see Powell 1970; Scott 1972). To challenge the system is to jeopardize one's security against threats to bare survival and, as Scott (1976) and Popkin (1979) have argued (though from different perspectives), such an extreme risk is not undertaken lightly. Thus, we witness the persistence of ethnically ranked social structures in many Third World nations despite the rather obvious inequities that characterize them.

However, such structures are subject to erosion by what Horowitz (1971: 236) terms the 'diffusion of universalistic norms' that accompanies modernization. The exchange relationship between ethnic groups breaks down as a result of changes in the local political economy induced by the nation's increasing integration into the global political economy. This process alters the local markets for land, labour and capital in such a way that elites in the superordinate group find it profitable to divert resources away from production for local consumption and towards production for world markets. Under such circumstances, the cost of insuring their clients against the risks of subsistence crisis begins to appear less attractive compared to the returns they could accrue from diverting those resources into additional production for global markets. Consequently, they begin displacing clients from land and reducing their labour costs. When, as a consequence, members of the subordinate group lose their protection against the threat of subsistence crisis, the rationale for continued deference to the superordinate group erodes, and the masses of the subordinate group are subject to mobilization for collective action.

The alternative to ranked systems is the 'unranked' or horizontally integrated system. Here, each ethnic group has its own stratification system internal to the group and distinct from all other groups. Different ethnic groups co-exist as parallel social hierarchies, with each group organized effectively as an incipient whole society. Indeed, in many cases they were formerly constituted as more or less autonomous whole societies (Horowitz 1985: 24). In unranked systems, relations among members of different ethnic groups are far less predictable. There is often a lack of mediating national authority to establish a high level of reciprocity premised on equality in interactions between members of different groups (ibid.: 28). In this respect relations between groups take on the character of international relations (Horowitz 1971: 234).

Horowitz (1985: 35) argues that unranked systems have more ability to survive the changes and dislocations that accompany modernization and development because, within each ethnic group, there are opportunities for upward mobility, and the exploitation of these opportunities does not necessarily lead to interethnic conflict. When interethnic conflict does occur in an unranked system, it usually aims not at social transformation but at the exclusion from power of one group by another and the desire to revert to some ethnically homogeneous *status quo ante* (Horowitz 1971: 235). For this reason, violent interethnic conflict in an unranked system is more likely to take the form of a separatist revolt than a social revolution.

The implications of this distinction between ranked and unranked systems has been elaborated theoretically in the analytical juxtaposition of Michael Hechter's 'internal colonialism' model of interethnic relations with the emerging 'ethnic competition' model of such relations. Internal colonialism explores the social and behavioural implications of ranked structures of interethnic relations while the competition model can be seen as an elaboration of the social and political implications of unranked structures of ethnic relations.

Central to Hechter's internal colonialism model is the concept of a 'cultural division of labour' (CDL). This refers to a pattern of structural discrimination such that 'individuals are assigned to specific types of occupations and other social roles on the basis of observable cultural traits or markers' (Hechter

1974: 1154). From this perspective, the structure of relations between subordinate and superordinate ethnic groups corresponds to the sort of exploitation that characterizes relations between peripheral and core nations in neo-colonial patterns of international relations (hence the term 'internal colonialism'). Ethnic boundaries coincide with lines of structural differentiation, and as a consequence ethnic solidarity is intensified (Nielsen 1985: 133). Where the stratification system links ethnic identity and economic status, it confers a meaning to ethnic identity that persists so long as this linkage between status and ascriptive stigmas remains. Ethnic solidarity is reinforced as a reaction of a culturally distinct periphery against exploitation by the centre. Hence, a number of scholars have referred to this consequence of CDL as 'reactive ethnicity', whereby ethnic solidarity is reinforced by the perceived exploitation of the subordinate group by the superordinate (Nielsen 1985: 133). Under these circumstances, ethnic differences do not disappear and indeed may form the basis for collective action by members of the peripheral communities against the core community because ethnic identity cannot be detached from one's economic and political interests within the system (Leifer 1981: 26; Birch 1978: 326–7).

Whereas the 'internal colonialism' argument and other reactive ethnicity variants predict that ethnic resurgence is more likely when there is a cultural division of labour, there has emerged an alternative 'ethnic competition' model that predicts that ethnic resurgence is more likely where the cultural division of labour has broken down and group inequalities have diminished (Nagel and Olzak 1982: 130–7). In an unranked system, competitive ethnicity emerges as members of different groups find themselves competing for the same resources (Nielsen 1985: 134). As culturally heterogeneous societies become industrialized, the extension of the market economy throughout the nation along with the increasing bureaucratization of society and other correlates of modernity should enhance the precedence of universalistic criteria that cut across the traditional ethnically based systems of ascribed status. The assignment of individuals to occupations and the distribution of societal rewards in general will increasingly be made on the basis of rational and achievement-based criteria that transcend ethnic boundaries.

However, this does not render ethnic distinctions irrelevant. The benefits of modernization are highly desired but relatively scarce. Consequently, members of different ethnic groups increasingly find themselves in a position to compete against each other for the same occupations and rewards. As these changes progress, they tend to reinforce rather than erode ethnic solidarity (Nielsen 1985: 133–4; see also Hannan 1979; Nielsen 1980; Ragin 1979; Olzak 1983). Extension of the rational labour market renders the types of interests motivating members of an ethnic group more nearly homogeneous and thereby makes the ethnic group more salient as an organizational channel for collective action (Nielsen 1985: 142). Therefore, ethnic groups persist because of their capacity to extract goods and services from the modern sector and thereby satisfy the demands of their members for the benefits of modernity (Bates 1974: 471).

The capacity of ethnic groups to extract resources from the modern sector depends upon their capacity to impose sanctions on those of their membership who do not act to advance the status of the group, especially elites who do not use their elite status to enhance their standing within their own ethnic group. Many modernized members of an ethnic group convert their success in the modern sector into status in the traditional sector of the ethnic group, often by using the income they have received from the modern sector to cultivate clientelist support networks among those members of their own ethnic group (Bates 1974: 472–4). If they decline to do so, they may be subject to sanctions by the membership of their own ethnic group. The likelihood of this occurring would depend on how easily they can be identified as members, how readily their non-support can be detected, and how capable the existing regime is in imposing its will on a discontented ethnic group. Hence, ethnicity becomes salient in the competition over the benefits of modernization for both elites and non-elites.

Bates (1974: 465–6) has argued that in many African nations the rise of ethnic competition is a direct legacy of colonial administration. By delineating administrative boundaries along tribal lines, colonial powers made it in the interests of their subjects to organize along ethnic lines so as to gain control over the administrative machinery with which the modernization process was managed. Local administration controlled such things as access to markets and market stalls, the regulation of crop production and animal husbandry, the construction of roads for the export of produce, and, in many cases, access to land. Local councils often acted to bias the distribution of and access to these resources in favour of the local ethnic group. Because control over the distribution of the benefits of modernity was vested in the local administration whose jurisdiction corresponded with ethnic boundaries, it was natural for local communities to coalesce into politically cohesive ethnic groupings and to utilize this solidarity to restrict the degree to which local or national administration could compel the sharing of the benefits of modernity with members of other ethnic groups (Bates 1974: 464–7).

Ranked and unranked systems create two rather distinct bases for ethnic competition and conflict. However, conflict of interests does not necessarily lead to collective action. Cultural divisions of labour and competitive ethnicity are far more pervasive than ethnic conflict. Theories of ethnic conflict must address the question of how mobilization along ethnic lines is achieved. With ethnicity as the basis of shared interests, what are the obstacles to collective action in pursuit of those interests and what role does ethnicity play in overcoming those obstacles to collective action?

ETHNIC CONFLICT

The research discussed above describes the ways in which scholars have depicted ethnicity as a source of shared interests that could become the basis for collective action. However, shared interests do not automatically lead to collective action. Hechter *et al.* (1982: 414) note the relative rarity of ethnic collective action and attribute this to the obstacles to such action posed by the disjunction between individual interest and collective action. Ethnic divisions, as we have seen, are rather common features among the members of the contemporary nation-state system, and ethnic groups typically co-exist in some structural arrangement characterized by the differential distribution of societal benefits on the basis of ethnicity. If such discrimination were sufficient to induce ethnic conflict, then such conflict would be far more pervasive and persistent than it is in fact. Indeed, what is striking is the relative rarity of ethnic collective action in a global system in which ethnic stratification is anything but rare.

Rational choice theory offers an explanation for why such conflict is so rare: despite the presence of shared interests defined along ethnic lines, it is still not rational for individuals to participate in ethnic collective action to advance those interests (or redress their grievances) unless the free rider problem, as elaborated by Mancur Olson (1965) can be overcome. According to Olson, individuals have an incentive to withhold their support for or participation in group action aimed at the production of collective benefits because, should the action succeed, they will be able to partake of the collective benefits anyway and, assuming the group is large enough, their own particular contribution will not substantially affect the probability that the collective action will produce the desired public benefits. Free rider tendencies can be overcome by the provision of 'selective incentives', which are private benefits (or punishments) that are available only to those who participate (or do not participate) in the collective action. Beyond selective incentives, anything that decreases the cost of participation or increases the impact of one's own contribution on the production of collective benefits will make an individual more inclined to participate. In particular, free rider tendencies can be diminished by the presence of a leadership whose organizational skills give people the assurance that their contributions will make a difference and will not be in vain (Frohlich *et al.* 1971). Hence, the central issue of specifically ethnic conflict is how ethnicity facilitates the task of overcoming free rider tendencies (Rogowski 1985: 88–9).

Accordingly, rational choice theory suggests that 'the position of an ethnic

579

group in the stratification system has no direct bearing either on any member's decision to participate or on the group's propensity to engage in collective action' (Hechter *et al.* 1982: 420). Instead, 'the role of stratification in collective action is indirect; it operates principally through its effects on group solidarity (that is, the member's compliance with the group's normative obligations) and organization' (ibid.: 421).

According to Rogowski and Wasserspring (1971: 20–1), the necessary and sufficient conditions under which it will be rational for an individual to engage in ethnically based collective action are:

1 the individual must be a member of a stigmatized group;
2 he/she must perceive some group-specific collective good as desirable;
3 ethnic collective action must offer a 'cheaper' way of obtaining the good than does conversion out of the group;
4 the individual must believe that his/her own contribution will make at least some difference in determining whether or not the desired good is produced.

For the individual to conclude that ethnic collective action is a cost-effective way of producing the collective benefits and that his/her contribution will make some difference in whether or not the benefits are provided, there must emerge from among the aggrieved ethnic group a leadership that is capable of organizing collective action and persuading potential contributors that their contributions will make a difference.

Rogowski (1985) argues that the tendency toward ethnically based collective action will differ depending upon whether the structure of interethnic relations is characterized by a cultural division of labour (i.e. a ranked system) or, alternatively, a 'pillarized' structure of parallel (i.e. unranked) ethnic communities. In the former, upward social mobility effectively requires assimilation into the culture of the superordinate ethnic group (ibid.: 92). The ease with which they can be assimilated will be a function of the willingness of the superordinate group to accept them and the ability of the upwardly mobile to avoid negative sanctions from the subordinate group for assimilating. This, in turn, will often depend upon the strength of the stigma that distinguishes the subordinate from the superordinate group. Ethnicity, as a stigma that is relatively easy to detect and costly to alter, renders the detection and punishment of defectors relatively easy and therefore makes upwardly mobile members of a subordinate ethnic group more inclined to pursue the mobilization of their own ethnic compatriots rather than to seek assimilation into the superordinate group.

If the superordinate group resists assimilation of upwardly mobile members of the subordinate group, then eventually the subordinate group will have its own cadre of skilled leaders. Having been denied access to leadership positions in the society because of their ethnic heritage, these leaders have a powerful incentive to organize the subordinate group for collective action aimed at altering permanently the cultural division of labour in such a way as to create opportunities for themselves to assume leadership positions. For example, the independence movement in India was led by British-educated Indians who, despite their qualifications, were denied acceptance into British society or advancement beyond middle levels of the British colonial administration. In these circumstances, free rider tendencies are overcome, first for the elite of the subordinate group by the promise of the selective incentives of leadership positions in the new social order that will result from collective action, and for the masses of the subordinate group by the organizational activities of these aspiring elites. The creation of an organization increases non-elites' estimate of the likelihood that their contributions, no matter how small, will be aggregated with those of others in such a way as to produce the collective benefits. In short, the creation of an organization enhances their willingness to participate in collective action by giving them greater confidence that their contributions will not be in vain (Frohlich *et al.* 1971). Following Rogowski (1985), then, the role of ethnicity in collective action is that it simplifies the identification of potential allies in the collective action and the detection and sanctioning of those members who attempt to free ride and/or assimilate into the status system of the rival ethnic group.

In Hechter and Levi's (1979: 266) resource mobilization formulation of ethnic conflict, any group will engage in collective action only if it has the capacity to do so, and this will depend upon the tolerance of dissident cultural and political organization by the central state; an infrastructure of pre-existent voluntary associations; and the availability of sufficient resources to sustain organized activity (see also Tilly 1978; McCarthy and Zald 1977). In an ethnically divided society, whether ranked or unranked, traditional communal organizations typically will be ethnically based: because social benefits are distributed along ethnic lines, shared needs and grievances will likewise correspond to ethnic divisions as will the communal organizations that emerge to address those needs.

We can expect the state to be more tolerant of such organizations when they are ethnically based because to attempt their suppression would be to invite an ethnic backlash. Furthermore, in a ranked system, a central state controlled by the superordinate ethnic group would prefer the emergence of local communal organizations among the subordinate groups to the necessity of the state itself having to provide the same services out of its own resources. Similarly, in an unranked system, the central state will be tolerant of ethnically based communal organizations because, by definition, each ethnic group has a complete hierarchy of social strata and, consequently, will develop its own organizational infrastructure to address the needs of its members.

Indeed, for these reasons, the central state may be more tolerant of an ethnically based network of dissident political organizations in an unranked system than in a ranked one. In a ranked system, the state has a greater capacity to suppress such organizations. And in a ranked system, the constituency of such organizations would have at their disposal a smaller pool of resources to contribute to the support of opposition political organizations. Hence, ethnically based communal organizations are less likely to arise and more easily repressed in ranked than in unranked systems. In summary, because ethnicity facilitates mobilization, we would expect collective action to be more easily mobilized in ethnically divided societies than in ethnically homogeneous societies. Likewise, among those that are ethnically divided, we would expect unranked social systems to be more susceptible to ethnic collective action than ranked systems are.

This still leaves us with the question of how individual members of an ethnic group can be induced to participate in ethnic collective action generally and ethnic conflict specifically. Individuals can be induced to participate in collective action if they perceive that their participation will bring them private rewards ('selective incentives') and if they perceive that their contribution to the collective action will make some difference in the outcome (i.e. the production of the collective benefits). According to Hechter et al. (1982: 425–7), an individual's estimate of the private rewards from participation in collective action will increase when: the organization has a store of resources apart from those to be gained through collective action; the organization's monitoring capacities are extensive enough that it can identify those supporters who are deserving of selective incentives and those free riders who are deserving of negative sanctions; and the organization has a proven record of justice in distribution. Following Olson (1965), they note that both the organization's ability to monitor and the individual's perception of the efficacy of the monitoring process will be increased when membership is small.

Ethnicity can enhance the individual's willingness to contribute to collective action in several ways. First of all, ethnicity makes the identification of potential participants easier for the leadership. They can target their recruitment efforts more efficiently by not wasting time and effort on non-members of the aggrieved ethnic group. Likewise, it is easier for the leadership to detect and sanction those who attempt to free ride. In short, as Rogowski (1985) has argued, ethnicity reduces the cost of information for the leadership in its efforts to overcome free rider tendencies.

When collective action takes the form of violent conflict, the calculus of participation is complicated by the additional consideration of the risks of participation. Here, too, ethnicity can enhance the ability of leaders to overcome the tendency of group members to free ride in order to avoid the risks of participation in violent conflict. The strategy that the incumbent government adopts in dealing with ethnically based challenges to its stability and legitimacy is likewise affected by the ethnic component of the conflict. Just as ethnic divisions enhance the ability of dissident leaders to identify and sanction free riders, the government can also use ethnicity as a means of identifying its actual, potential, or imagined enemies. If the government confines its repressive actions to known participants in opposition activities, the fact that those participants are from an identifiable ethnic group facilitates the government's ability to identify and punish them. So long as government is precise in targeting its repression, it can undermine the ability of the opposition leadership to mobilize additional participants in its programme. However, if government repression escalates in scope and intensity to the point that its selection of targets for repression becomes relatively indiscriminate, then the ethnic character of the conflict can become an advantage for the opposition. When repression becomes so widespread and indiscriminate that membership in the dissident ethnic group effectively marks one as a target for repression regardless of one's participation or non-participation in opposition activities, then members of the opposition ethnic group will have an incentive to join the opposition organization if for no other reason than to seek protection from indiscriminate government repression (Mason and Krane 1989). Free rider tendencies are overcome by the calculus of fear that is induced by government repression targeted indiscriminately against members of the dissident ethnic group.

CONCLUSION

That ethnicity remains a powerful force in the contemporary political arena cannot be denied. This essay has presented an overview of the central theoretical issues defining the study of ethnic politics and the major conceptual frameworks that have evolved from the efforts of scholars to resolve these issues. While this body of work is complex and compelling in its analysis of ethnic politics, several scholars have noted that the mainstream literature on social change and political development has not accorded ethnic politics a great deal of attention. As a consequence, the rich body of literature on the various dimensions of ethnic politics has remained somewhat isolated from this mainstream. In discussing the major theoretical frameworks in the field of ethnic politics, I have tried to illustrate their grounding in existing paradigms of behavioural science, their compatibility with those paradigms, and their contributions to the elaboration of the mainstream of research traditions on social change and development. In so doing, perhaps this essay will contribute in some small way to the recognition of this body of research by the mainstream and its incorporation into its rightful place in textbooks and scholarly discourse on the general themes of development.

REFERENCES

Bates, R. (1974) 'Ethnic competition and modernization in contemporary Africa', *Comparative Political Studies* 6: 457–84.

Birch, A. H. (1978) 'Minority nationalist movements and theories of political integration', *World Politics* 30: 325–44.

Brass, P. R. (1976) 'Ethnicity and nationality formation', *Ethnicity* 3: 225–41.

Butler, D. and Stokes D. (1969) *Political Change in Britain*, New York: St Martin's Press.

Connor, W. (1972) 'Nation-building or nation destroying?', *World Politics* 24: 31–55.

Frohlich, N., Oppenheimer, J. A. and Young, O. (1971) *Political Leadership and Collective Goods*, Princeton, NJ: Princeton University Press.

Hannan, M. (1979) 'The dynamics of ethnic boundaries in modern states', in M. Hannan and J. Meyer (eds) *National Development and the World System: Educational, Economic, and Political Change 1950–1970*, Chicago: University of Chicago Press.

Hechter, M. (1974) 'The political economy of ethnic change', *American Journal of Sociology* 79: 1151–78.

Hechter, M. and Levi, M. (1979) 'The comparative analysis of ethnoregional movements', *Ethnic and Racial Studies* 2: 260–74.

Hechter, M., Friedman, D. and Appelbaum, M. (1982) 'A theory of ethnic collective action', *International Migration Review* 16: 412–34.

Horowitz, D. (1971) 'Three dimensions of ethnic politics', *World Politics* 23: 232–44.
——(1985) *Ethnic Politics*, Berkeley: University of California Press.

Kende, I. (1978) 'Wars of ten years, 1967–1976', *Journal of Peace Research* 15: 227–41.

Leifer, E. M. (1981) 'Competing models of political mobilization: the role of ethnic ties', *American Journal of Sociology* 87: 23–47.

Lipset, S. M. and Rokkan, S. (1967) *Party Systems and Voter Alignments*, New York: Free Press.

McCarthy, J. D. and Zald, M. N. (1977) 'Resource mobilization and social movements: a partial theory', *American Journal of Sociology* 82: 1212–41.

Mason, T. D. and Krane, D. A. (1989) 'The political economy of death squads', *International Studies Quarterly* 33: 175–98.

Melson, R. and Wolpe, H. (1970) 'Modernization and the politics of communalism: a theoretical perspective', *American Political Science Review* 64: 1112–30.

Nagel, J. and Olzak, S. (1982) 'Ethnic mobilization in new and old states: an extension of the competition model', *Social Problems* 30: 127–43.

Nielsen, F. (1985) 'Toward a theory of ethnic solidarity in modern societies', *American Sociological Review* 50: 133–49.

Olson, M. (1965) *The Logic of Collective Action*, Cambridge, Mass.: Harvard University Press.

Parsons, T. and Smelser, N. (1956) *Economy and Society*, New York: Free Press.

Popkin, S. L. (1979) *The Rational Peasant: The Political Economy of Rural Society in Vietnam*, Berkeley: University of California Press.

Powell, J. D. (1970) 'Peasant society and clientelist politics', *American Political Science Review* 64: 411–25.

Ragin, C. C. (1979) 'Ethnic political mobilization: the Welsh case', *American Sociological Review* 44: 619–35.

Rogowski, R. (1974) *Rational Legitimacy: A Theory of Political Support*, Princeton, NJ: Princeton University Press.

——(1985) 'Causes and varieties of nationalism: a rationalist account', in E. A. Tiryakian and R. Rogowski (eds) *New Nationalisms of the Developed West*, Winchester, Mass.: Allen & Unwin.

Rogowski, R. and Wasserspring, L. (1971) *Does Political Modernization Exist? Corporatism in Old and New Societies*, Beverly Hills Calif.: Sage Professional Papers.

Scott, J. C. (1972) 'Patron–client politics and political change in Southeast Asia', *American Political Science Review* 66: 68–90.

——(1976) *The Moral Economy of the Peasant*, New Haven: Yale University Press.

Small, M. and Singer, J. D. (1982) *Resort to Arms*, Beverly Hills, Calif.: Sage Publications.

Tilly, C. (1978) *From Mobilization to Revolution*, Reading, Mass.: Addison-Wesley.

Tiryakian, E. A. and Rogowski, R. (1985) *New Nationalisms of the Developed West*, Winchester, Mass.: Allen & Unwin.

FURTHER READING

Armstrong, J. (1982) *Nations before Nationalism*, Chapel Hill: University of North Carolina Press.

Bonacich, E. (1972) 'A theory of ethnic antagonism: the split labor market', *American Sociological Review* 37: 547–59.

Enloe, C. H. (1973) *Ethnic Conflict and Political Development*, Boston: Little, Brown & Co.

Esman, M. J. (1977) *Ethnic Conflict in the Western World*, Ithaca, NY: Cornell University Press.

Glazer, N. and Moynihan, D. P. (eds) (1975) *Ethnicity and Experience*, Cambridge, Mass.: Harvard University Press.

Gourevitch, P. A. (1979) 'The reemergence of "peripheral nationalisms": some comparative speculations on the spatial distribution of political leadership and economic growth', *Comparative Studies in Society and History* 21: 303–22.

Hall, R. L. (ed.) (1979) *Ethnic Autonomy – Comparative Dynamics: The Americas, Europe and the Developing World*, New York: Pergamon Press.

Hechter, M. (1975) *Internal Colonialism: The Celtic Fringe in British National Development*, London: Routledge & Kegan Paul.

——(1978) 'Group formation and the cultural division of labor', *American Journal of Sociology* 84: 293–318.

Horowitz, D. (1973) 'Direct, displaced, and cumulative ethnic aggression', *Comparative Politics* 6: 1–16.

——(1981) 'Patterns of ethnic separatism', *Comparative Studies in Society and History* 23: 165–95.

Jenkins, J. C. (1983) 'Resource mobilization theory and the study of social movements', *Annual Review of Sociology* 9: 527–53.

Kende, I. (1971) 'Twenty-five years of local wars', *Journal of Peace Research* 8: 5–22.

Laver, M. (1980) 'Political solutions to the collective action problems', *Political Studies* 28: 195–209.

Levi, M. and Hechter, M. (1985) 'A rational choice approach to the rise and decline of ethnoregional political parties', in E. A. Tiryakian and R. Rogowski (eds) *New Nationalisms of the Developed West*, Winchester, Mass.: Allen & Unwin.

Margolis, H. (1982) *Selfishness, Altruism, and Rationality: A Theory of Social Choice*, Cambridge: Cambridge University Press.

Milne, R. S. (1981) *Politics in Ethnically Bipolar States*, Vancouver: University of British Columbia Press.

Olzak, S. (1983) 'Contemporary ethnic mobilization', *Annual Review of Sociology* 9: 355–74.

Parenti, M. (1967) 'Ethnic politics and the persistence of ethnic identification', *American Political Science Review* 61: 717–26.

Polèse, M. (1985) 'Economic integration, national policies, and the rationality of regional separatism', in E. A. Tiryakian and R. Rogowski (eds) *New Nationalisms of the Developed West*, Winchester, Mass.: Allen & Unwin.

Ragin, C. C. (1977) 'Class, status, and "reactive ethnic cleavages": the social bases of political regionalism', *American Sociological Review* 42: 438–50.

Rothschild, J. (1981) *Ethnopolitics: A Conceptual Framework*, New York: Columbia University Press.

Young, C. (1976) *The Politics of Cultural Pluralism*, Madison: University of Wisconsin Press.

Zald, M. N. and McCarthy, J. P. (ed.) (1979) *The Dynamic of Social Movements*, Cambridge, Mass.: Winthrop.

36

LANGUAGE AND POLITICS

J. A. LAPONCE

Languages that come into contact become linked by a communication network, the density of which varies according to circumstances; but, loose or dense, communication among these languages is unavoidable. There is no example of a living language not linked by translation to at least one other living language. Bilingualism and multilingualism are thus worldwide phenomena (Mackey 1966). Humans cannot ignore humans, languages cannot ignore other languages. This seemingly trivial fact has consequences of considerable importance which have been studied by psycholinguists, sociolinguists, geographers and, more recently, by political scientists (for an overview of the field see Williams 1988).

Bilingual and multilingual political systems (henceforth *bilingual* to simplify) are markedly affected by the kind of relations – co-operative or conflictual – associated with the transfer of information from one language to another; inversely, political systems – notably the modern state – attempt, more and more frequently, to regulate language contact by means of language planning (Poole 1979). Among the 166 independent states surveyed by Laponce, 104 had linguistic minorities accounting for more than 10 per cent of their population, thirty of these states used more than one official language in the operations of their central government, and all of them were engaged in some form of language planning, if only at the school level (Laponce, 1987: 90–4).

Much confusion has resulted from the use of the single term 'bilingual' to describe a variety of phenomena ranging from the rough school-type of knowledge of a foreign language to the knowledge of different languages learned in infancy and constantly needed for communication within the family or within the surrounding community; so much confusion that, before considering the specifically political aspects of language contact, we need to distinguish various situations resulting from two languages co-existing within the mind of a given individual.

THE BILINGUAL MIND

Can one say exactly the same thing in two different languages? Does the language we use shape what we think or is it on the contrary a neutral instrument under our complete control? The so-called 'Whorf–Sapir' hypothesis (Whorf 1956; Sapir 1949), according to which language shapes thought, has fallen into disfavour among contemporary linguists who point out that any language is 'potentially' able to express what is said or written in any other language. English may not have as many words as Dene to express different types of snow but can express all these varieties by means of periphrases; Arabic is not, at present, able to describe simply and effectively the complexities of modern science but it is potentially capable of doing so; Malay still needs to develop a complex legal vocabulary before it could fully replace English in the courts of law of Malaysia. But demotic Greek created in a short time the thousands of words needed for the translation of the regulations of the European Commission into that language following the entry of Greece into the European Community.

The Whorf–Sapir hypothesis, however, is far from dead. It continues to inspire research. Take, for example, the work of Rogers, TenHouten and their colleagues who, measuring the brain activity of bilingual children reacting to either Hopi or English story telling, found that their Hopi subjects had more right brain wave activity when reacting to Hopi than to English sounds (Rogers *et al.* 1977; TenHouten 1980); the explanation, according to the authors, is that Hopi, as a language, puts one into more direct contact with nature, while English, being more analytical, puts one at a distance from what it describes (for a review of supporting and negating experiments, see Hamers and Blanc 1989: 45). Tsunoda (1978), in a controversial experiment that still needs to be duplicated, found that his Japanese–English bilingual subjects used their right brain to a greater extent when processing Japanese than when processing English sounds. According to Tsunoda, this was due to the fact that in Japanese, unlike in English, the steady vowel, a natural sound, has semantic meaning, hence blurring the distinction between the musical and the analytical.

Whether or not different languages are wired differently in the brain and whether or not the bilingual differs from the unilingual brain (Albert and Obler 1978) it remains that, even if we are capable of learning two languages in the same context and to the same degree of fluency, in fact we practically never do so. The languages we know typically form a hierarchy of both knowledge and liking and trigger different social and psychological contexts. Different languages embody different historical experiences: the longer history of the languages themselves as well as the shorter history of the speaker who will typically relate different languages to different roles and events. Mackey (1971) has shown, for example, that the associations of ideas built into French and English by means of composite words and expressions vary considerably on some of the most commonly used words (lady-killer does not convey the same meaning as its French translation '*homme à femme*'); and it is quite rare for two languages, even if learned simultaneously in infancy, not to be distinguished by remarkable specificity such as one being the language of the mother and the other that of the father or the school friends. The perfect fit of two languages – a fit measurable by such means as Osgood's Semantic Differential – is an ideal from which there are considerable variations, but an ideal that is practically never reached.

The cost of acquiring a second language – a cost measurable in terms of time, effort and frustration – and the difficulty of obtaining a perfect bilingual fit would suffice to explain that the mind tends to reject language redundancy. Rare are the individuals who, in the absence of any need to communicate with foreigners, acquire an extra language for the sole sake of having more than one. They belong to the pathological cases studied by Steyn (1972), a classic example of which is offered by Psalmanazar, who obtained an appointment at the University of Oxford in the seventeenth century to teach a language that was supposedly spoken by Formosans but was in fact a personal invention. In the absence of the need to communicate with people who speak a language other than one's own, the mind rejects language redundancy as it rejects true synonymy within a given language (Genouvrier and Peytard 1970).

Bilingualism, thought to be harmful to a child's intellectual development by most pre-Second World War educators, has subsequently been shown to have no such negative effect and in fact to facilitate what is variously called the 'Leopold effect' (Leopold 1939–49) or 'divergent thinking' – the ability to distinguish the significant from the signifier (Skutnabb-Kangas 1981).

The fact of most direct relevance to the politics of language contacts is in the finding that one can normally distinguish, even among so-called 'balanced' bilinguals (bilinguals with a seemingly equal knowledge of their two languages), a dominant language (L1) and a second or dominated language (L2). In a series of simple experiments, Dornic (1975, 1980) found that while nearly indistinguishable on simple tasks, the reaction times of bilinguals using either their L1 or their L2 increased markedly as one increased the difficulty of the problem to be resolved. Thus, in a conversation between two individuals speaking the same two languages but not having the same L1, the speaker who imposes his or her dominant language has a communication advantage over the other speaker, and the latter will often feel frustrated by his or her inability to operate at their normal level of effectiveness.

Since the knowledge of a second language is costly in terms of acquisition and maintenance time, and since the use of an L2 is less efficient than that of an L1, it follows that individuals will naturally tend to group themselves socially and geographically in such a way as to reduce the overlap among languages, unless of course they want to use more than one language to separate social functions, as in some cases of diglossia.

BILINGUALISM WITH AND BILINGUALISM WITHOUT DIGLOSSIA

Ferguson (1959) coined the term 'diglossia' to distinguish two types of bilingualism according to whether the bilingual individual uses two languages across all social roles or uses one language in some specific situations and contexts while the other language is used in other cases. These ideal types have been useful in separating two kinds of bilingualism that do not result in the same type of language contact (Fishman 1967) and hence do not call for the same types of language policies even though the object of the policies may be the same, for example to prevent conflict and reinforce inter-ethnic collaboration.

The strong correlation between social role and language use which characterizes diglossia appears most clearly when a language such as Latin, Old Slavonic or Hebrew is used as a sacred tongue while another language – English, Russian or Yiddish, for example – is used in the secular domain. The separation is not as marked, but obvious nevertheless, when the diglossic contact is between secular languages that distinguish private from public domains and are used, the one to affirm one's local ethnicity, the other to participate instrumentally if not emotionally in the communication system of a wider community.

Unlike the Francophone Swiss who uses only standard French, the German-ophone Swiss uses two forms of German, the standard literary language that links the user to the greater German community, and a local Swiss German that is learned and spoken at home as well as in public life at the local level (Swiss German is spoken in the cantonal legislatures while standard German is used in the federal parliament; see McRae 1984). In Luxemburg, nearly all citizens speak three languages: Luxemburgese in private and either French or German in public settings, with French dominating in church and government and German in the field of business. This type of diglossia is the norm in Africa and Asia where local, regional and international languages are typically associated with markedly different social roles and contexts.

Diglossic bilingualism tends to be relatively stable when the languages in contact collaborate at separating social roles that the individual wishes to keep separated (rather than conflict with each other). The more the diglossic situation is wanted by the individual concerned – as in German Switzerland, Luxembourg, Andorra or Paraguay – the more the contact between the languages concerned will be collaborative, hence stable and thereby in lesser need of intervention by the political system to either assimilate or protect one of the languages.

By contrast, instability characterizes the cases where diglossia is imposed by circumstances and is perceived as a burden by the individuals who have to know two languages – one to communicate with their parents for example, and the other to communicate with their own children, as in Brittany in the early twentieth century. In such cases diglossia fades rapidly into unilingualism (Dressler and Wodak-Leodolter 1977).

Bilingualism without diglossia is a more frequent source of individual frustrations, hence of social and political conflicts. Extending as they do to all the social roles, ready to be used in all or at least in most important social contexts, the languages are engaged in a competition for dominance.

If everyone in the community concerned preferred the same L1, then there would be no reason – internal to the group – to retain the L2. The latter would be abandoned, if not by the individuals who acquired it then at least by their children or grandchildren. This is the way most languages 'imported' into English-speaking North America keep being assimilated and would be quickly annihilated in the absence of new migrations. However, if the individuals in contact do not all have the same preferred L1, then differences between languages are very likely to become associated with differences in social and political power, differences that are likely to lead to the formation of ethno-linguistic minorities.

Asymmetrical power sharing between two language groups results in the dominant group having the power to decide how the burden of bilingualism will be borne and what language will have the greater social spread. In some rare occasions the dominant group decides to assume the cost of bilingualism. This happens when an invader, being comparatively small in number compared to the population conquered, adopts the latter's language to avoid the military and social costs of imposing its own tongue. The Roman conquerors spoke Greek in their Eastern empire and the Arabs who invaded Persia adopted Persian (MacKey 1988). In Bolivia, in the early days of Spanish colonization, the ruling group decided to learn Quechua because the natives were thought unworthy, if not incapable, of learning Castilian (Breton 1976).

More frequently the dominant group shifts the cost of bilingualism onto the ethnic minority. Flemish Belgians were and are still more likely to speak French than Walloons to speak Dutch; French Canadians are more likely to speak English than English Canadians to speak French; and in Switzerland, in the federal bureaucracy, the Francophones are more likely to use German than the Germanophones to use French (Laponce 1987).

If the minority accepts that its language be given subordinate status, or if it obtains satisfactory compensations (in Switzerland, for example, the weakness of French at the federal level is compensated by its uncontested dominance in the western cantons), the asymmetrical sharing of the bilingual burden may not be a source of tension. If, on the contrary, subordinate status is resented or if the compensations are thought to be insufficient, the language asymmetry characterizing bilingualism without diglossia will often be a major source of ethnic and political conflicts.

STUDYING AND PREDICTING LANGUAGE OUTCOMES

The language strategies of individuals and groups – whether to prefer unilingualism or bilingualism and, in the latter case, what language to select as L1 and in what circumstances – are typically the result of the interplay of relatively few factors, notably communication costs, social benefits and ethnic loyalty. The importance of these factors has led some social scientists to propose the use of simple rational-choice models and two-player games to explain bilingual outcomes (Pool 1991; Laitin 1988). These powerful models will, of course, often fail to predict the actual outcome, and if they do predict accurately will sometimes do so for the wrong reasons. Nevertheless, they are one of the more promising developments in a field much in need of theoretical constructs, and even when they fail they can still be turned to profit, if only as an invitation to identify the factors that were overlooked.

Most political analysts of language contacts and conflicts have preferred the case study approach that enables the analyst to study languages within the specificity of a complex socio-historical context. Many of these studies are based on interviews with respondents who are typically asked to indicate what language they use and in what circumstances (see notably Rubin (1968) for Paraguay; Fishman (1966) and Fishman et al. (1971) for the United States; O'Brian (1976) and Corbeil and Delude (1982) for Canada; Gendron (1973) for Quebec; and Laitin (1977) for Somalia). Relatively rare are the studies, such as those of Gumperz (1971), Bourhis (1984) or Gardner-Chloros (1985), that use non-reactive measures such as the taping of conversations to produce accurate behavioural maps of language use. The technique developed by Wiegele et al. (1985) and Schubert (1988) to measure voice stress could be (but has not yet been) applied to the study of recorded language interactions in multilingual settings to determine the level of stress associated with the use of a second language and with the shift from one language to another.

LANGUAGE COMPARED TO OTHER ETHNIC DEFINERS

Can the study of the ethno-linguistic minorities created by language contact be done by means of the general typologies and theories used for the study of minority-dominant group relations? To a very large extent it is indeed possible. One may use, among others, the typology proposed by Louis Wirth

(1945), who distinguishes assimilationist, pluralist, secessionist and militant minorities; or that suggested by Laponce (1960), who contrasts minorities according to whether they accept remaining as minorities for the sake of preserving their distinctiveness or are forced to retain their separateness by a dominant group refusing to assimilate them; or that of Schermerhorn (1970), who relates the respective attitudes of the minority and of the dominant group according to whether these attitudes are centripetal or centrifugal. One can also apply the theory of Tajfel and Turner (1979), which posits that in order to avoid self-doubt and debasement a minority must think of itself as superior to the dominant group in at least one domain of thought or activity.

The fact that asymmetrical power relationships between language groups is the norm in non-diglossic situations justifies to a large extent the fact that the study of language minorities is so often subsumed under the larger study of ethnic relations, as in the study of ethnic groups in conflict by Horowitz (1985). But that should not lead one to forget or push to the background a very specific characteristic of language minorities to which geographers and political scientists have been more sensitive than sociologists and sociolinguists: the need of a language group, particularly so of a language minority, for a territory of its own; the need for a secure spatial base covered by the same L1.

Since in most bilingual societies the members of minority groups are more likely to know the language of the dominant group than the latter to know the minority language, and since the dominant group normally has greater power over the production of spoken and written material (from TV and radio broadcasts to internal memos and contracts), the minority, as already noted, will be at a disadvantage in an unregulated system where the languages are allowed to mix and to be chosen freely for all kinds of interactions. Thus, unless it accepts a diglossic situation that would restrict the use of its language to certain domains of activity, a minority will become all the more frustrated as the communication system grows more dense.

Unlike religions or races that can adjust their survival strategies to geographical dispersion and geographical penetration by the dominant group, a language needs a degree of spatial concentration that is commensurate with the degree of development of the society concerned.

Some Indian languages of the Canadian West Coast or the jungle of Venezuela could survive for centuries even though they are spoken by very few people. But this could happen only as long as they remain isolated from the more powerful ethnic groups that surround them and as long as the types of activities required for the survival of the community are limited to primitive fruit gathering, hunting, or agriculture.

A modern industrial society that needs a university to educate its elites will need a relatively large concentration of population. With only 100,000 inhabitants, Iceland cannot operate its university fully in Icelandic (although its language is protected by isolation); with only about half a million speakers, the Swedes of Finland and the Francophones of Ontario experience similar difficulties in operating a full-scale university covering the scientific as well as the other disciplines in their own languages. Languages *qua* languages need geographical concentration and, to protect themselves against the inroads of more powerful languages, linguistic minorities need linguistic territorial homogeneity. Consequently, languages pose to political systems problems involving boundaries that non-linguistic minorities do not pose to the same extent, if they pose them at all. While non-linguistic minorities will often be satisfied with the granting of territorially transportable individual rights, linguistic minorities will typically want group rights that are territorially grounded.

THE 'WAR' AMONG LANGUAGES

Writing the history of languages as one writes the natural history of animal species led Cailleux (1953) – who had restricted his corpus to major literary languages such as Latin, Greek, Chinese, German and French – to note that languages had a positive birth rate. For any language that died, he estimated that two were born. His figures should not be taken for more than what they could possibly be: a rough indication of a general trend. For the period he had selected – the last three millennia – Cailleux's observations are probably valid beyond the limits of his selected corpus of cases. The world was then in a process of linguistic diversification. This appears no longer to be the case. A trend dating back to the origins of humanity seems to have been reversed. Languages are in a period of negative birth rate, and this is unlikely to be a passing phase. In the intensified system of communication that characterizes what Paul Valéry (1945) called the 'completed world' – *le monde fini* – the stronger languages eliminate the weaker ones, sometimes violently but more often peacefully as a result of people shifting from a language with a weaker purchasing power to a language with a greater purchasing power, whether the purchase be of economic, political, or cultural goods.

Adapting Hirschman's voice-exit model (Hirschman 1970) to our subject, we note that when the voice that a language offers is no longer heard or no longer heard adequately, exit to a better language will take place, unless there be a strong enough loyalty boundary preventing such a transfer, a loyalty that will typically be measured by the strength of one's ethno-linguistic identity.

Large markets and population mobility – from countryside to cities as well as from poorer to richer and from overpopulated to low birth-rate countries – reduce the purchasing power of small languages and weaken the ethnic identity tied to these languages. Hence the prediction that most of the existing 7,000-odd languages spoken today in the world will disappear and that relatively few will be born (7,000 is the upper estimate given by Ferguson); other estimates are lower, notably those of Muller (1964) and Burney (1966), who give a range of 2,500 to 3,500).

In the intensified 'war' among languages, what factors will favour survival and expansion? The answer varies, of course, according to whether we consider local, regional, or international contexts.

Mackey (1973) has drawn attention to six factors: the number of speakers; the geographical implantation of the same language in different areas of the world; geographical mobility of individuals; the economic achievements of the groups using the language; their ideological diffusion (whether religious or political); and their cultural power measured by indices such as book production. Tsunoda (1983) has measured the recent evolution of the languages of science to show the increased dominance of English (see also Fishman *et al.* 1975 on the spread of English as a world language). To these measures, Laponce (1987) added military and economic power, and predicted that, irrespective of the factors listed above, the languages best able to survive the worldwide competition among languages would be those that had a state as their champion, or more precisely the languages used in the central administration of an independent state. In the mid-1980s there were only sixty-five such languages, forty-eight of which were the central administrative language of only one state. The languages used in the central administration of more than five states were few. English 'had' forty-two states, French twenty-eight, Spanish twenty-one, Arabic twenty-one and Portuguese seven.

Many of the states with only one language of government have an abundance of local languages. This is the case with nearly all the states of Black Africa. Why should these local languages not survive as the many languages of the Turkish Empire survived? The prediction of the weakening and disappearance of most of them is based on the assumption that the state will modernize, hence urbanize and industrialize, and will use a state language as an instrument of mass mobilization and integration rather than use it as an instrument of segregation separating a state elite from its local constituencies (Calvet 1974).

When the state is integrative, seeking its legitimacy from the identification of the masses with their governments, and when, additionally, it is democratic, governing less by the manipulation of symbols than by means of explanations and justifications, the need to simplify the linguistic composition of the *polis* increases. In such a state the pressure towards unilingualism is great. At the time of the French Revolution of 1789, the majority of French people did not speak French; a century later most of them did so; and now, after two hundred years, French is spoken by practically all of them. Not all states of Europe have become as unified linguistically as France but they have all moved in the same direction, even Switzerland where the number of local language varieties has been markedly reduced.

The formula of the nineteenth-century school of nationalism, 'one state-one-language-one-nation' – to which 'one-religion' was sometimes added – has increasingly been simplified to a 'one-state-one-language' formula, henceforth made to apply to the multinational as well as to the one-nation state. The English-only movement of the 1980s in the United States is to be explained in part as an anti-foreign reaction, but it is also explainable by the fact that to some of its supporters the rate of Spanish immigration appears to outpace the rate of assimilation (on the relation between these two rates see Deutsch 1953). The insistence on a common language is then seen as a condition for the preservation of a peaceful and equalitarian multi-ethnic society (Schmidt 1989).

Modern states are both assimilators and protectors of languages. They destroy their weaker languages internally and protect their own dominant languages on the international scene.

THE STATE AND LANGUAGE PLANNING

State language planning takes three major forms according to whether the state attempts to affect a language's corpus, status, or usage.

Corpus planning seeks to improve the quality of the language as an instrument of communication. Such a goal was, among others, that of Richelieu when he created the French Academy in 1634, an Academy assigned the task of writing and revising a French dictionary; such was the goal of the Government of Quebec when it created the *Conseil de la langue française* which has among its functions that of improving the quality of the French used in Quebec; such was the goal of the Norwegian state when at various times in the twentieth century it created commissions of linguists whose task was to standardize the two versions of the Norwegian language.

The creation of many new words of science and technology and the need to standardize their meaning and application has created a competition against time that few languages can sustain if they want to be world languages. In an attempt to keep French at the level of English, as well as to facilitate communication between its two official languages, the Canadian federal government has created and maintains a terminology bank of French–English scientific and technological concepts that contains over a million terms in each language, the translation of which is accessible on line by computer from government departments as well as from non-governmental institutions such as universities.

Between the antiquated ways of the French Academy and the computer ways of the Canadian Secretariat of State, there are many means of intervention in corpus planning. Most effective are those forcing schools to use texts and examinations that act as references for the correct forms of speech and writing. Hence the importance, in the United States, of the debate over whether 'Black English' should be considered as a faulty variant of standard English or accepted as a legitimate form of the language (Sonntag and Pool 1987).

Status planning leads the state to giving legitimacy or dominance to specific languages. High status is typically given to a language by recognizing it as official. That is the case, for example, of English in some American states; of French and English at the federal level in Canada; of French, German and Italian in the Swiss Confederation; of Swedish and Finnish in Finland; of English and Gaelic in Ireland; of French and English in Cameroon, and of French and Dutch in Belgium. Sometimes a lower rank than official is attributed to a language by calling it 'national'. That is the case of Romanche in Switzerland, Bichlamar in Vanuatu, Guarani in Paraguay and Wanda in Rwanda.

More important, however, than any constitutional and legal recognition, is the actual practice regulating language use in schools, in parliaments, in the courts, and more generally in the providing of government information and services. The study of that practice involves considering the rules regarding speaking, writing and understanding (see Laponce 1987).

The Canadian constitution of 1867 gave French-speaking parliamentarians the right to use their language, but their right to be understood was not recognized until immediate translation was introduced in parliament, then in committees, then at cabinet meetings almost hundred years later. Gaelic is deemed to be both the national and official language of Ireland and that country's stamps rarely use any language other than Gaelic, but the discussions at cabinet meetings are entirely in English. Singapore has four official languages that appear on its banknotes – English, Mandarin, Malay and Tamil – but its laws are published solely in English. By contrast the laws of Switzerland are published in German, French and Italian; and in Belgium, as in Canada, the meetings of the cabinet accommodate two official languages by means of immediate translation. Sometimes a defendant before a court of justice is merely given the right to an interpreter; in other cases – for example in Quebec and in New Brunswick – that defendant is given the right to a trial in the official language of his or her choice.

The imposition of a national language as that of the state is often used as a means of state and nation building. In the thirteenth century Alphonso X of Spain required the use of Castilian instead of Latin in the writing of government documents, and three centuries later Francis I of France imposed French on his public servants (Lapierre 1988). But state, if not nation, building is also frequently done by avoiding the use of a native language in the conduct of government. Selecting English in India or French in Senegal as the major or sole language of government had the advantage of not offending the ethnic groups that resent the use of Hindi or Woulof.

In addition to regulating the use of language in parliaments, courts, public schools and bureaucracies, the governments of multilingual societies have occasionally regulated the use of language in what is usually considered to be the private domain. Indonesia forbids the use of Chinese on commercial signs, and Quebec forbids the use of English on billboards as well as requiring the use of French in the writing of the contracts and internal notices of firms employing more than fifty people (Leclerc 1989).

TERRITORIAL OR PERSONAL SOLUTIONS

When seeking to regulate the contact among languages in non-diglossic situations, the state has the choice of two fundamentally different solutions: *territorial* solutions of the kind used by Belgium and Switzerland; and *personal* solutions of the kind used by Estonia between the two world wars, and used also, to a lesser extent, by Finland and the Canadian federal government.

The classic example of a territorial solution is offered by Switzerland, where language boundaries separate German, Italian and French areas in such a way that unilingualism is the general rule in the operations of local government services, schools and public life. Swiss citizens are free to cross the language boundaries, but if they do they are expected to change language as would the typical immigrant to a foreign country. The political strategy guiding these stringent regulations consists of separating languages as much as possible at the regional level and restricting bilingualism or multilingualism to the central level of government; a strategy that seeks, in other words, to prevent contact in order to prevent conflict. Belgium adopted a similar system by making Flanders Flemish-speaking and Wallonia French-speaking, but it has not been able to apply fully the Swiss model because its capital, Brussels, is a predominantly Francophone city cast in Flemish territory. As an exception to the rule of territorial unilingualism the Belgian capital has been set aside as a bilingual area.

The political justification for the system of fixed language boundaries is given by the following decision of the Swiss Federal Tribunal when it rejected the claim of a businessman who had argued that a local regulation forbidding him to advertise his products in the language of his choice was in violation of the equality clause of the Federal Constitution:

> The linguistic borders of our country, once established, must be considered to be unchangeable. Safeguarding the harmonious relationship among the various segments (ethnic groups) of our country requires that each be guaranteed the integrity of the territory over which its language is spoken and over which extends its culture; and that each be given the right to prevent any encroachment.
>
> (translated from Héraud 1974: 247)

In the Swiss case, and to a lesser extent in the Belgian case, the languages are rooted territorially, and are thus given security niches of their own. The power to protect the boundaries so created is given not to individuals but to collectivities – the cantons in Switzerland and, the regions in Belgium (McRae 1975, 1984, 1986).

In marked contrast to the Swiss system, that used by the Baltic countries, notably in Estonia (Aun 1940), between the two World Wars allowed any ethnic group comprising at least 3,000 people to set up a nation-wide community with institutions of its own; institutions with the power to tax its members and to administer its own public and private schools. These nation-wide ethnic governments resembled local governments except in their not being territorially grounded and having extensive language rights, in particular that of selecting the language of instruction in the schools. That system – which had its forerunners in the Polish Jewish kahal and in the millets of the Ottoman empire (Laponce 1960) did not survive the war and has not been imitated.

Between the extremes of the Swiss and the Estonian models, Finland offers the case of partially and temporarily grounded languages. Wherever the Swedish minority accounts for at least 8 per cent of the population of a given commune (the basic unit of local government), the public services are offered in the two official languages, Swedish and Finnish; however, a bilingual district will normally become unilingual Finnish if the Swedish population is shown by the census to have declined below the required minimum. (In the Åaland Islands, however, the Swiss system of territorial unilingualism protects the Swedish minority as a result of the international treaties that regulate the status of that territory.)

The Canadian Federal Government has by and large patterned its language policies on those of Finland rather than those of either Switzerland or Belgium, responding in so doing to the wishes of its English-speaking population but also out of fear that a unilingual French Quebec might be closer to secession than if it remained bilingual. One cannot deny that possibility but, interestingly, the increase in language security of the Quebecois population through the language legislation mentioned earlier (p. 598) was correlated with a lowering of separatist fervour. This appears to confirm that the Swiss strategy of reducing contact between competing languages by juxtaposing unilingual areas rather than merging the languages within the same territory has the desired effect of lowering tensions – at least when the language cleavage is not reinforced by other non-linguistic cleavages that would make the ethnic groups concerned incompatible on too many grounds.

CONCLUSION

The rooting of political into economic analysis, especially Marxian analysis, has frequently led analysts of contemporary societies to view ethnic conflicts, and language conflicts in particular, as outdated conflicts, of a type that would disappear as the state became more modern. In fact, the general lowering of class tensions in most industrial societies after the Second World War has led to reconsideration of this forecast. Like religion, language does not lend itself easily to compromise, least of all when the conflict is over boundaries, whether internal or external. Languages and states are both territorial animals.

REFERENCES

Albert, M. and Obler, L. (1978) *The Bilingual Brain: Neurophysiological and Neurolinguistic Aspects of Bilingualism*, New York: Academic Press.

Aun, K. (1940) *On The Spirit of the Estonian Minority Laws*, Stockholm: Societies Litteraturn Estonia.

Barrett, D. B. (1982) *World Christian Encyclopedia*, Oxford: Oxford University Press.

Bourhis, R. (1984) 'Cross-cultural communication in Montreal', *International Journal of the Sociology of Language*, 46 (1): 33–47

Breton, R. (1976) *Géographie des langues*, Paris: Presses Universitaire de France.

Burney, P. (1966) *Les langues internationales*, Paris: Presses Universitaires de France.

Cailleux, A. (1953) 'L'Evolution quantitative du langage', *Societé préhistorique française* 505–14.

Calvet, J. L. (1974) *Linguistique et colonialisme, petit traité de glottophagie*, Paris: Payot.

Corbeil, I. and Delude, C. (1982) *Etudes des communautés francophones hors Québec et des communautés anglophones au Québec*, Montreal: CROP.

Deutsch, K. (1953) *Nationalism and Social Communication*, New York: John Wiley.

Dornic, S. (1975) *Human Information Processing and Bilingualism*, Stockholm: Institute of Applied Psychology.

——(1980) 'Information processing and language dominance', *International Review of Applied Psychology* 29 (1): 119–40.

Dressler, W. and Wodak-Leodolter, R. (eds) (1977) 'Language death', special issue of *International Journal of the Sociology of Language* 12 (1).

Ferguson, C. A. (1959) 'Diglossia', *Word* 15: 325–340.

——(1964) 'On linguistic information', *Language and Linguistics* 201–8.

Fishman, J. A. (1966) *Language Loyalty in the United States*, The Hague: Mouton.

——(1967) 'Bilingualism with and without diglossia, diglossia with and without bilingualism', *Journal of Social Issues* 23 (2): 29–38.

Fishman, J. A., Cooper, R., Roxana, M. A., *et al.* (1971) *Bilingualism in the Barrio*, The Hague: Mouton.

Fishman, J. A., Cooper, R. L. and Conrad, A. (1975) *The Spread of English*, Rowley, Mass.: Newbury.

Gardner-Chloros, P. (1985) 'Language selection and switching among Strasbourg shoppers', *International Journal of the Sociology of Language*.

Gendron, J. D. (1973) *Rapport de la Commission d'enquête sur la langue française au Québec*, 3 vols, Quebec: Editeur officiel.

Genouvrier, E. and Peytard, J. (1970) *Linguistique et enseignement du français*, Paris: Larousse.

Gumperz, J. J. (1971) *Language in Social Groups*, Stanford: Stanford University Press.

Hamers, J. F. and Blanc, M. (1989) *Bilinguality and Bilingualism*, Cambridge: Cambridge University Press.

Héraud, G. (1974) *L'Europe des ethnies*, 2nd edn, Paris: Presses d'Europe.

Hirschman, T. O. (1970) *Exit, Voice, and Loyalty*, Cambridge: Cambridge University Press.

Horowitz, L. (1985) *Ethnic Groups in Conflict*, Berkeley: University of California Press.

Laitin, D. (1977) *Politics, Language, and Thought: The Somali Experience*, Chicago: University of Chicago Press.

———(1988) 'Language games', *Comparative Politics* 20 (3): 289–302.

Lapierre, J. W. (1988) *Le pouvoir politique et les langues*, Paris: Presses Universitaires de France.

Laponce, J. A. (1960) *The Protection of Minorities*, Berkeley and Los Angeles: University of California Press.

———(1987) *Languages and Their Territories*, Toronto: Toronto University Press.

Leclerc, J. (1989) *La Guerre des langues dans l'affichage*, Montreal: VLB éditeurs.

Leopold, W. F. (1939–49) *Speech Development of a Bilingual Child: A Linguistic Record*, 4 vols, Evanston: Northwestern University Press.

Mackey, W. F. (1966) *Le bilinguisme phénomène mondial*, Montreal: Harvest House.

———(1971) *La distance interlinguistique*, Quebec: Presses de l'Université Laval.

———(1973) *Three Concepts for Geolinguistics*, Quebec: Presses de l'Université Laval.

———(1988) 'Geolinguistics: its scope and principles', in C. Williams (ed.) *Language in Geographic Context*, pp. 20–46, Clevedon: Multilingual Matters.

McRae, K. D. (1975) 'The principle of territoriality and the principle of personality in multilingual states', *Linguistics* 158 (4): 33–54.

———(1984) *Conflict and Compromise in Multilingual Societies: Switzerland*, Waterloo, Ont.: Wilfrid Laurier University Press.

———(1986) *Conflict and Compromise in Multilingual Societies: Belgium*, Waterloo, Ont.: Wilfrid Laurier University Press.

Muller, S. H. (1964) *The World's Living Languages*, New York: Frederick Ungar.

O'Bryan, K. G., Reitz, J. G. and Kuplowska, O. M. (1976) *Non-official Languages: A Study in Canadian Multiculturalism*, Ottawa: Department of Supply and Services.

Pool, J. (1979) 'Language Planning and Identity Planning', *International Journal of Sociology of Language* 20 (1): 5–21.

———(1991) 'The official language problem', *American Political Science Review* 85 (2): 495–514

Rogers, L., Ten Houten, W. D. and Gardiner, M. (1977) 'Hemisphere specialization of language: an EEG study of bilingual Hopi Indian children', *International Journal of Neuroscience* 8 (1): 1–6.

Rubin, J. (1968) *National Bilingualism in Paraguay*, The Hague: Mouton.

Sapir, E. (1949) Selected Writings of Edward Sapir, in D. Mandelbaum (ed.) *Language, Culture and Personality*, Berkeley: University of California Press.

Schubert, N. J. (1988) 'Politics under the microscope: observational methods in political science', *International Political Science Review* 9 (4): 305–26.

Schermerhorn, R. A. (1970) *Comparative Ethnic Relations: A Framework For Theory and Research*, New York: Random House.

Schmidt, R. J. (1989) 'Language policy and equality: a value critical analysis', paper given at the APSA annual meeting in Atlanta, 28–31 August.

Skutnabb-Kangas, T. (1981) *Bilingualism or Not: The Education of Minorities*, Clevedon: Multilingual Matters.

Sonntag, S. K. and Pool, J. (1987) 'Linguistic denial and linguistic self-denial: American ideologies of language', *Language Problems and Language Planning* 11 (1): 46–65.

Steyn, R. W. (1972) 'Medical implications of polyglottism', *Archives of General Psychiatry* 27 (2): 245–7.

Tajfel, H. and Turner, J. C. (1979) 'An integrative theory of intergroup conflict', in W. C. Austin and S. Worchel (eds) *The Social Psychology of Intergroup Relations*, Monterey, Calif.: Brooks & Cole.

TenHouten, W. D. (1980) 'Social dominance and central hemisphericity: discriminating race, socioeconomic status, and sex groups by performance on two lateralized tests', *International Journal of Neuroscience* 10 (4): 223–37.

Tsunoda, T. (1978) *The Japanese Brain*, Tokyo: Taishuukau (in Japanese).

——(1983) 'Les langues internationales dans les publications scientifiques et techniques', *Sophia Linguistica* 140–55.

Valéry, P. (1945) *Regards son le monde actuel*, Paris: Gallimard.

Whorf, B. L. (1956) *Language, Thought, and Reality: Selected Writings*, Cambridge, Mass.: MIT Press.

Wiegele, T. C., Hilton, G., Oaks, K. L. and Kisiel, S. V. (1985) *Leaders Under Stress: A Psycholinguistic Analysis of International Crises*, Durham, NC: Duke University Press.

Williams, C. (ed.) (1988) *Language in Geographic Context*, Clevedon: Multilingual Matters.

Wirth, L. (1945) 'The problem of minority groups', in R. Linton (ed.) *The Science of Man in the World Crisis*, New York: Columbia University Press.

FURTHER READING

Beer, W. R. and Jacob, J. E. (eds) (1985) *Language Policy and National Unity*, Totowa, NJ: Rowman & Allanheld.

Fishman, J. A. (ed.) (1972) *Advances in the Sociology of Language*, The Hague: Mouton.

——(ed.) (1978) *Advances in the Study of Societal Multilingualism*, The Hague: Mouton.

Fishman, J. A., Ferguson, C. A. and Das Gupta, J. (1968) *Language Problems of Developing Nations*, New York: John Wiley.

Haarmann, H. (1986) *Language in Ethnicity: A View of Basic Ecological Relations*, Amsterdam: de Gruyter.

Haugen, E. (1972) *The Ecology of Language*, Stanford: Stanford University Press.

Kloss, H. (1966) 'Types of multilingual communities: a discussion of ten variables', *Sociological Enquiry* 36: 135–45.

——(1967) 'Bilingualism and nationalism', *Journal of Social Issues* 23 (2): 39–47.

Mackey, (1982) *Bibliographie internationale sur le bilinguisme*, 2nd edn, Quebec: Presses de l'Université Laval.

Mackey, W. F. and Verdoodt, A. (eds) (1975) *The Multilingual Society*, Rowley, Mass.: Newbury House.

Rossi-Landi, F. (1975) *Linguistics and Economics*, The Hague: Mouton.

Vaillancourt, F. (1983) 'The economics of language and language planning', *Language Problems and Language Planning* 7 (2): 162–78.

Weinreich, U. (1953) *Languages in Contact: Findings and Problems*, The Hague: Mouton.

37

GENDER AND POLITICS

JONI LOVENDUSKI

Although 'the woman question' has often figured as a political issue since the middle of the nineteenth century, the question of the political significance of gender only became an issue in the study of politics in the 1970s. It arose partly in response to the women's studies movement which first emerged as part of the Women's Liberation Movement (WLM) which began in the 1960s. Prior to that the study of women and politics was not regarded as important enough to warrant any special attention. Gender was not regarded as a category of political analysis and women's political behaviour went at best undescribed or at worst misrepresented. If discussed at all, women tended to be regarded as surrogates of men and also as their inferiors. Women were widely believed to be less politically interested, active and competent than men. Such contentions were often based on prejudice, a reflection not of scientific analysis or reasoned debate, but of sexism in a male-dominated profession.

During the 1970s these prevailing views were challenged (Borque and Grossholtz 1974; Goot and Reid 1975; Jaquette 1974; Lovenduski 1981) and a wide-ranging debate was generated which continued throughout the 1980s. One product of this debate was a large and increasingly sophisticated subfield of political studies devoted to the study of gender and politics. This subfield has been constructed mainly by feminist political scientists, political theorists and political philosophers, and seeks to change the nature of the discipline. It has evolved from an initial and modest concern with mapping women's political behaviour using traditional categories of analysis – the 'add women and stir' approach – to a challenging critique of the very basis of political science. From the outset the question of why political science had so long ignored over half the population was regarded as an important issue, and it was from this initial preoccupation that the feminist critique of mainstream political science grew. That critique forms the core of the study of gender and politics and provides a major part of the dynamic of feminist political science.

But other factors are also at work here. The WLM marked an upswing that was so pronounced, first in the political mobilization of women and later in their political integration, that mainstream political scientists could not ignore it. Changes were apparent in voting behaviour, in political activism, in agenda construction, policy formulation and political organization. The point here is that the current study of gender and politics is informed both by feminist political consciousness and by women's political behaviour. This essay will describe the inputs of each of these two factors and will assess the effect of their interaction on the development of the discipline.

FEMINISM

By the end of the 1980s many Western societies had experienced more than two decades of what is sometimes referred to as the second wave of feminism. Moreover, the movement had spread and was also apparent in a variety of forms and guises in the state socialist systems of Eastern Europe and in the Third World. The WLM was thus not only a large-scale social movement, it was also a powerful political force affecting state institutions, political parties, economic organizations and attitudes. One result was that women became a political constituency recognized and courted by a range of previously complacent, gender-blind or sexist organizations.

But, as is true of men, women are not a uniform political category. There is a range of different groups of women with both common and separate interests. What is true is that although some of the differences between women parallel differences between men, as for example in class, race, religion, region or nation, other differences, notably those to do with reproduction and domestic life, are gender specific and affect most aspects of women's and men's lives in ways that are different, but politically significant. Feminism is in part a response to this, but as a political force it has not had a uniform effect on women's lives and has not been universally espoused by women.

To consider this further we must first define some terms. Feminism, to paraphrase Dahlerup (1986), is the ideology whose basic goal is to remove the discrimination against and the degradation of women and to break down the male dominance of society. Feminists are those who subscribe to this feminist ideology. The WLM is the new feminist movement which appeared in Europe and the USA in the 1960s and 1970s. Its avowed goal is the liberation of women from male oppression, a goal whose implications went well beyond mere equality. The movement was characterized by the lack of an organizational hierarchy, spontaneous activities and new kinds of political action such as consciousness-raising groups, peace camps, etc. In many countries the WLM originated in the New Left, but traditional women's organizations also generated feminist politics, particularly over such issues as equal opportunity policy, fertility control and welfare politics. In many countries the movement received its impetus from events organized by international organizations spreading versions of the feminist message (Randall 1987: 243–4). Amongst the most important capacities of the WLM was the ability to mobilize large numbers of previously politically inactive women. Although early recruits came from the student, peace and New Left movements, it soon became apparent that the WLM represented an idea whose time had come. It spread quickly and brought family and personal life to the political agenda. Traditional ideas of politics were challenged by the slogan 'the personal is political'. Activities were addressed to other women rather than, in the traditional political formula, to the state.

Philosophically, feminism draws on the three great liberatory traditions of European thought: liberalism, socialism and the social theories constructed from political readings of major psychoanalytic texts. Added to the basic corpus has been the influential post-war theoretical work of the major European post-structuralists on language and power. On the face of it feminist theory includes three distinct and contested positions normally typed liberal feminism, socialist feminism and radical feminism. Liberal and socialist feminism have both emerged from and developed in tandem with liberal and socialist thought, which they have also influenced. For example, the absorption by socialist feminists of theories of language and power parallel a similar (and related) absorption by mainstream socialists. Liberal and socialist parties devoted considerable attention to the development of equal opportunity strategy during the 1980s. Radical feminism, however, is rather different. It makes use of elements of all three liberatory traditions, and was at first clearly linked with socialist feminism. A number of divisions soon emerged. Radical feminists sought to credit women's lives and skills with central importance. In identifying women with nature they were wary of what they regarded as the somatophobia of Western traditions of reason and logic. The fundamental division has been over the issue of essentialism or difference in the meaning of gender, the feminist variant of the nature/nurture argument. Put simply, radical feminists hold that the differences between men and women are innate, whilst socialist and liberal feminists believe these differences to be socially constructed. Male power and the oppression of women are, say radical feminists, not caused by society, they are caused by men. The root innate difference is one of sexuality. Male sexuality is the site of male power. It is a compulsive sexuality innately associated with violence and aggression. The world as viewed by radical feminists is divided by gender on the basis of innate and immutable characteristics. At its most extreme the theory holds that men hate women, are frightened by them, and use sexual violence and the doctrines of heterosexism to keep women under their dominance. This is an interesting argument which is much oversimplified here but has found response from many women. Texts of radical feminist authors such as Andrea Dworkin and Mary Daly were widely read throughout the world during the 1980s (for example Dworkin 1981 and Daly 1979).

Politically the significance of the feminist nature/nurture debate lies in its organizational and strategic consequences. Taken to its logical conclusions, radical feminism means the biological, social and political separation of women and men. As a result, political activity is activity directed not at the penetration and reform of existing powerful institutions, but at the construction of alternatives. The mainstream, often called the 'malestream', of politics is consciously avoided. Such strategies have important consequences for action over specific policy areas in the short term, and in the short and long term for the nature of women's political roles. Moreover the assumption that there is an innate female nature obscures differences between women.

The emergence of the WLM in the 1960s was held to be a response to a particular social and political conjuncture. Vicky Randall (1987: 221–2) offers three related explanations here: predisposing factors, facilitating factors, and specific triggering events. Predisposing factors are the aspects of women's situation which predisposed them to recognize their oppression. These include (in the USA where the movement began) increased numbers of educated women in the population, the presence of more divorced and separated women, a tendency to smaller families, awareness and availability of new contraceptive technology, a growing experience of paid employment outside the home and a growing sense of relative deprivation. Much is made, in published personal accounts of becoming a feminist, of the role of consciousness raising. Women from a variety of social and geographical backgrounds have described their growing sense of recognition as others recounted familiar experiences of the realization of the possibility that 'things were not my fault'. Facilitating factors are the ideological and institutional developments facilitating a feminist revival. In some countries this meant the coming of age of the first full generation of women to have grown up with the complete array of citizen rights. In others it was the general introduction of civil and human rights, either for the first time or after a long period of oppression (for example, Spain, Greece and Portugal). The social movement politics of the baby boomers, as they came of age in the 1960s and organized in peace, anti-war and civil rights groups, were important in the USA and in the European and English-speaking democracies. Such activities supplied a significant group of talented women with important political skills which, as Jo Freeman (1975) recounts, were readily transferable from one social movement to another. Specific triggering events sometimes occurred within the politics of the new social movements. In the New Left a general stress on equality, liberatory goals and the unmasking of systematic oppression did not apparently extend to sex equality. The male-dominated left of the 1960s and 1970s, like its nineteenth-century predecessors, dismissed the case for women's liberation as at best irrelevant and at worst divisive. The result was that angry women began to form their own groups to discuss their situation. These groups soon established journals, devised their own political activities and were an early manifestation of the WLM.

In organizational, ideological and political terms the WLM is a new social movement. Thus when feminism does, for whatever reasons, engage the institutions of state and government, its central problem is the lack of fit between a social movement and a hierarchical political organization. Feminism, although a diverse movement, has exhibited a preference for the simplicity of direct democracy. It has been uncomfortable with the forms and practices of representative democracy which it suspects of being hierarchical, elitist, draconian and generally undemocratic. A process of feminists coming to terms with this problem occurred only during the 1980s. This was not only because of a desire on the part of some feminists to have access to the power and authority that political office brings, but also because the feminist experience highlighted a number of major political issues in which women had a particular stake. Matters such as equal pay, equal rights, access to abortion, reproductive rights, protection from violence, the rights of sexuality, the maintenance of family forms, the availability of pornography, etc. were all issues over which the state exercised some control and which had for some time been matters of public policy. This was recognized by feminists, but initially self-help, direct action and campaigns were the preferred modes of influence. It gradually became apparent, however, that other forms of activity were more effective, and feminists faced the dilemmas posed by the risks of co-option as against the dangers of powerlessness. The tensions thus posed are continuing ones, but two key trends of the 1980s were a manifestation of efforts to deal with the dilemma. These were the widespread phenomenon of feminists attempting to move into traditional organizations, and the accompanying phenomenon of those organizations adapting to feminist entry.

It is at this point that a distinction between the political roles of women and the political roles of feminists becomes important. Not all of the women who are politically active would regard themselves as feminists; indeed, many of those women engaged in the struggle for sex equality in their political party or trade union would explicitly deny that they are feminist (the 'I am not a feminist, but . . .' syndrome). It is not possible, on the evidence available, to argue that the general rise in women's political activism and the change in women's political behaviour in many countries that was apparent by the beginning of the 1980s was a direct result of the rise of feminism. But it is almost certainly the case that the phenomena are related and that the factors leading to the growth of the WLM also led to changes in women's political and social behaviour. It is likely, but not certain, that feminism as a phenomenon affected and influenced these developments. With this proviso in mind the political behaviour of women may be considered.

THE POLITICAL BEHAVIOUR OF WOMEN

Investigations of women's political behaviour prior to the 1970s reflected the concerns of the discipline as it was then constructed. The major work was Duverger's *The Political Role of Women* (Duverger 1955), which was commissioned by UNESCO and compared the political participation of women in four West European countries. This was an important study which, despite some lacunae, remains of interest today. Other work was less systematic, and it was not until the 1970s that studies of women and politics began to be reviewed in the main academic journals and to appear on student reading lists. At first interest focused on rescuing women from the invisibility to which previous generations of political scientists had assigned them. Initially, scholars used the categories determined by a discipline designed to study men to identify and describe how and where women fitted in. According to these categories, women were less politically active and engaged, and it was also revealed that often no data describing the roles of women existed. Thus an early concern of feminist political scientists was to write women in, in order to map out their political behaviour (Randall 1982; Lovenduski and Hills 1981; Jaquette 1974). This endeavour continued, but before very long scholars began to believe that important questions were not being asked and were being obscured by the conventions of political science. Questions were raised about what women's political involvement was. A need to begin researching individuals at local and community level and to build outward to the national arenas was identified. It was recognized, particularly amongst Scandinavian researchers, that only by defining politics in its widest sense would it be possible to analyse and understand the politics of gender (Hernes 1984a; Siltanen and Stanworth 1984).

The perception that women are less politically active and interested than men has some empirical basis. Immediately after their enfranchisement women were less likely to vote than were men. Amongst those who did vote, women were more likely than men to vote for parties of the right. Many of the explanations offered for this tended to essentialism and were often rather sexist (Borque and Grossholtz 1974; Siltanen and Stanworth 1984). Serious analysis showed that explanation lay with economic, educational and religious differences between men and women. As these differences declined or changed in nature so did the behaviour with which they were associated. Thus, by the 1980s, in the USA and in some northern European countries women outvoted men, and in many places a bias to the right was replaced by a preference for the parties of the left (Mueller 1988; Norris 1987). Such phenomena are termed gender gaps and occur at the level of political attitudes, interest and behaviour and are of increasing concern to political parties and others concerned with political campaigning. The idea of a woman's vote has become important, but the phenomenon of the gender gap is not well studied. Most of the research has been conducted in the USA and suggests that gender became increasingly politicized from the 1970s onwards. Gurin (1985) demonstrated the existence of shifts in gender group awareness amongst US women. Miller *et al.* (1988) devised a concept that they called gender consciousness, which taps the relationship between gender group awareness and support for policies that enhance group interest. They showed that over time gender consciousness tended to become more connected with political beliefs.

The timing of these changes suggests a relationship between the WLM and a general change in the political activism of women. This view is also supported by data about women's political representation. Council of Europe data on women's membership of European lower houses of parliament show that the first elections after the Second World War returned legislatures in which women's membership ranged from 1.5 per cent in Belgium to 7.8 per cent in Sweden. By the late 1980s the range was from 1.2 per cent in Cyprus to 34.4 per cent in Norway. The percentage increases in representation varied from a low 1.2 per cent in France to 29 per cent in Norway. The bulk of the larger increases, which were in the Nordic States and the Netherlands, took place between 1975 and 1985 (Sineau 1988). Other evidence indicates that these years were a time of rising levels of political interest, activism and organization for women (Lovenduski 1986; Haavio-Mannila *et al.* 1986).

Information about the political representation of women in formal political arenas has become more widely available, but less is known about informal activities. Hernes has written that 'women's traditional activities have been incorporated into the political system later than men's, less completely than men's, and under different political conditions from men's' (Hernes 1984b: 6). Moreover their organizational activity is less well recognized. National studies often overlook local organizations and women's memberships tend to be less likely to be counted. Nevertheless, the available data confirm that throughout Europe women are less often members of organizations than men.

But what of other participation? Marsh and Kaase (1979) have shown that young women are more predisposed to direct action than men of similar age. Women have played key roles in national liberation struggles and in the great political revolutions of modern times. Women are prominent in the resistance movements of Latin America. There is a robust and growing WLM in India (Randall 1987: 242–3). Norwegian studies have indicated that women in Norway in general participate as often as men, but in different kinds of activity. There are also data which indicate that women who are in paid employment, full or part time, participate more frequently than full-time housewives (Hernes 1984b). This suggests that where women are economically integrated they are more likely to be politically integrated, a finding that has been replicated in a number of countries.

This list is only a taste of the available information, which is, although incomplete, now rather extensive. We know that women are less likely to be present in political elites than men, and that this is true at practically all levels of the political system. We also know that the law of increasing disproportions works for gender, that the higher we ascend a power hierarchy the fewer women we will find. It also appears that liberal democratic forms are a resource for feminists who have had great difficulty organizing in the state socialist countries and under many of the autocratic regimes of the Third World. There are paradoxes, however. The United States, with perhaps the strongest instance of second wave feminism, will feature a numerical advantage of women over men in the voting electorate for the forseeable future, yet it has a relatively low legislative representation of women for a liberal democracy. We also know, however, that in some places, notably the Nordic states, women have captured increasing shares of positions of political power. It seems clear that the advanced welfare states with their liberal democratic forms and longstanding feminist traditions are, if not woman-friendly, then certainly more receptive to women than are other political systems.

DO WOMEN HAVE AN INTEREST?

An important question that this raises is the one of whether the politicization of gender – increasing representation of women – makes a difference. Often this question is addressed in terms of simple policy outputs and, on the basis of a proliferation of equal opportunity policies, it is concluded that a difference has been made. But policy which especially affects women need not be policy on 'the woman question'. In a society in which there is a gendered division of labour there is almost no area of policy in which women and men are not differently affected. For example, in London women are the main users of public transport, making public transportation a gendered issue. Women have a greater interest than men in the design of buses and trains, in the frequency of their services in the hours that they run, in the security and safety provisions they offer.

Clearly, the question of whether women make a difference is a complicated one and must be addressed on several levels. This takes us back to the issue of what women do politically, but also raises questions about whether women constitute an interest. During the 1980s both empirical and theoretical research became more concerned with these questions, which are at the heart of debates about gender, power and political science.

Empirical approaches to the issue of women's representation were constrained both by funding limitations which severely restrict work on political attitudes and grassroots participation, and by the obvious limits of having only a very small number of women who were members of political elites. The exception was Scandinavia, where research programmes tended to be well funded and where a sizeable sample of women had experience of national political office. Not surprisingly, many of the important research developments of the 1980s were Scandinavian-led.

The Danish political scientist, Drude Dahlerup, studied the changes brought about when women became a sizeable minority in a national legislature (Dahlerup 1988). She tested the notion that only when the minority of women in legislatures reaches a certain size (critical mass) will the presence of women make a difference. She hypothesized that one would expect to find six different kinds of change: in reactions to women politicians; in the performance and efficiency of the women politicians; in the political culture; in the political discourse; in policy (political decisions); and in the empowerment of women. Using public opinion data and data collected in qualitative and quantitative studies of Nordic women politicians, she found that voters have become more receptive to women politicians, that turnover rates amongst women politicians have fallen, that new forms of politics have been consciously and successfully introduced and that issues about the position of women have become part of the political discourse. Change was apparent on each of her first four items. Before addressing her last two indicators, policy change and women's empowerment, she questioned the concept of the critical mass itself. The idea of the critical mass is borrowed from physics and refers to the point at which enough fissionable material is assembled to generate a chain reaction. Transferred to political representation, it refers to the number of representatives required for the rate of representation to accelerate. Dahlerup regards the analogy as a tortured one and suggests that the concept of a critical act would be more appropriate to political analysis. A critical act is one which will change the position of the minority considerably and will lead to further changes. Most significant will be 'the willingness and ability of the minority to mobilise the resources of the organization or institution to improve the situation for themselves and the whole minority group' (Dahlerup 1988: 296). For parliamentary women these are critical acts of empowerment. In the Nordic states such critical acts have taken place. For example, women politicians began consciously to recruit other women during the 1980s, they have been instrumental in instituting party quotas for women and they have been involved in the initiation, design and implementation of equality legislation and institutions. In the Nordic case, increasing the number of women politicians made a difference.

Dahlerup's research coincided with work by other feminist political scientists which re-examined the concept of political interest in the light of insights about the relationships between gender and political power. Kathleen B. Jones and Anna G. Jonasdottir (1988) argue that the language of political theory and political science is so constructed that it excludes women, and they use the concept of political interest to make their case. Their argument is an extension of earlier critiques of political science. It affirms that if gender is to be understood in the political science canon, then basic categories of analysis must be reformulated in terms of gender. This entails effort both to analyse the political meanings of gender and to deconstruct standard political concepts (Jones and Jonasdottir 1988: chapter 1).

This is easier said than done, and what Jones and Jonasdottir achieve is a demonstration of the limitations of previous efforts to construct a feminist political science. They criticize work by Sapiro (1981, 1983), Hernes (1984a) and others for implicit support of a patriarchal hierarchy of values. Sapiro is taken to task for implying that it is women who need changing rather than affirming that it is politics that must change if it is 'to accommodate the multiplicity and vitality of women's voices' (Jones and Jonasdottir 1988: 24).

We cannot assess the gender and political interest debate unless we acknowledge that developing a gender-sensitive political science is work in progress. Contributions by Gilligan (1982), Nelson (1984), Hartsock (1982) and Harding (1986) underline the value of analysis that starts with women's experiences and perceptions. Sapiro's (1981) essay on the political interests of women was a major advance on what had gone before. Similarly, new work on gender and power will generate criticism which informs its progress. What will be central to the best of the analysis to come is a normative understanding that 'women should be able to act on the strength of being women and not mainly despite being women' (Jones and Jonasdottir 1988: 53). What feminism brings to political science is the theoretical opportunities offered by a commitment to this standpoint. What political science offers to feminism is the affirmation of the importance of politics, the knowledge that to concede the political arena is to concede the crucial sites of power.

REFERENCES

Borque, S. C. and Grossholtz, J. (1974) 'Politics an unnatural practice: political science looks at female participation', *Politics and Society* 4: 255–66.

Dahlerup, D. (1986) 'Introduction', in D. Dahlerup (ed.) *The New Women's Movement: Feminism and Political Power in Europe and the USA*, London: Sage Publications.

——(1988) 'From a small to a large minority: women in Scandinavian politics', *Scandinavian Political Studies* 4: 275–98.

Daly, M. (1979) *Gyn/Ecology*, London: The Women's Press.

Duverger, M. (1955) *The Political Role of Women*, UNESCO.

Dworkin, A. (1981) *Pornography*, London: The Women's Press.

Freeman, J. (1975) *The Politics of Women's Liberation*, New York and London: Longman.

Gilligan, C. (1982) *In A Different Voice: Psychological Theory and Women's Development*, Cambridge, Mass.: Harvard University Press.

Goot, M. and Reid, E. (1975) *Women and Voting Studies: Mindless Matrons or Sexist Scholarship?*, Beverly Hills: Sage Publications.

Gurin, P. (1985) 'Women's gender consciousness', *Public Opinion Quarterly* 49: 143–63.

Haavio-Mannila *et al.* (1986) *Unfinished Democracy: Women in Nordic Politics*, Oxford: Pergamon Press.

Harding, S. (1986) *The Science Question in Feminism*, Ithaca, NY: Cornell University Press.

Hartsock, N. (1982) *Money, Sex and Power*, New York: Longman.

Hernes, H. (1984a) 'Women and the welfare state: the transition from private to public dependence', in H. Holters (ed.) *Patriarchy in a Welfare Society*, Oslo: Universitetsforlaget.

——(1984b) 'The role of women in voluntary associations and organisations', part III of *The Situation of Women in the Political Process in Europe*, Strasbourg: Directorate of Human Rights, Council of Europe.

Jaquette, J. (1974) *Women and Politics*, New York: John Wiley.

Jones, K. B. and Jonasdottir, A. G. (1988) *The Political Interests of Gender*, London: Sage Publications.

Lovenduski, J. (1981) 'Toward the emasculation of political science', in D. Spender (ed.) *Men's Studies Modified*, Oxford: Pergammon Press.

——(1986) *Women and European Politics*, Brighton: Harvester Wheatsheaf.

Lovenduski, J. and Hills, J. (eds) (1981) *The Politics of the Second Electorate: Women and Public Participation*, London: Routledge & Kegan Paul.

Marsh, M. and Kaase, M. (1979) in Barnes, S. H. and Kaase, M. (eds) *Political Action: Mass Participation in Five Western Democracies*, Beverly Hills and London: Sage Publications.

Miller, A. H., Hildreth, A. and Simmons, G. L. (1988) 'The mobilization of gender group consciousness', in K. B. Jones and A. G. Jonasdottir (eds) *The Political Interests of Gender*, London: Sage Publications.

Mueller, C. M. (ed.) (1988) *The Politics of Gender Gap: The Social Construction of Political Influence*, Newbury Park, Calif.: Sage Publications.

Nelson, B. (1984) 'Women's poverty and women's citizenship: some political consequences of economic marginality', *Signs* 10: 209–31.

Norris, P. (1987) *Politics and Sexual Equality*, Brighton: Wheatsheaf.

Randall, V. (1982) *Women and Politics*, London: Macmillan.

——(1987) *Women and Politics: An International Perspective*, 2nd edn, Basingstoke and London: Macmillan.

Sapiro, V. (1981) 'When are interests interesting? the problems of the political representation of women', *American Political Science Review* 75: 701–16.

——(1983) *The Political Integration of Women*, Chicago: University of Illinois Press.

Sineau, M. (1988) *Ways and Means of Improving the Position of Women in Political Life*, Report to the Council of Europe, Strasbourg: Directorate of Human Rights, Council of Europe.

Siltanen, J. and Stanworth, M. (eds) (1984) 'The politics of private woman and public man', ch. 1 in *Women and the Public Sphere: A Critique of Sociology and Politics*, London: Hutchinson.

FURTHER READING

Borque, S. C. and Grossholtz, J. (1974) 'Politics an unnatural practice: political science looks at female participation', *Politics and Society* 4: 255–66.

Dahlerup, D. (1986) *The New Women's Movement: Feminism and Political Power in Europe and the USA*, London: Sage Publications.

——(1988) 'From a small to a large minority: women in Scandinavian politics', *Scandinavian Political Studies* 4: 275–98.

Daly, M. (1979) *Gyn/Ecology*, London: The Women's Press.

Duverger, M. (1955) *The Political Role of Women*, UNESCO.

Dworkin, A. (1981) *Pornography*, London: The Women's Press.

Eisenstein, H. (1984) *Contemporary Feminist Thought*, London: Unwin Paperbacks.

Elshtain, J. B. (1981) *Public Man/Private Woman*, Princeton: Princeton University Press.

Evans, J. *et al.* (1987) *Feminism and Political Theory*, London: Sage Publications.

Freeman, J. (1975) *The Politics of Women's Liberation*, New York and London: Longman.

Gilligan, C. (1982) *In A Different Voice: Psychological Theory and Women's Development*, Cambridge, Mass: Harvard University Press.

Goot, M. and Reid, E. (1975) *Women and Voting Studies: Mindless Matrons or Sexist Scholarship?*, Beverly Hills: Sage Publications.

Gurin, P. (1985) 'Women's gender consciousness', *Public Opinion Quarterly* 49: 143–63.

Haavio-Mannila *et al.* (1985) *Unfinished Democracy. Women in Nordic Politics*, Oxford: Pergamon Press.

Harding, S. (1986) *The Science Question in Feminism*, Ithaca, NY: University Press.

Hartsock, N. (1982) *Money, Sex and Power*, New York: Longman.

Hernes, H. (1984a) 'Women and the welfare state: the transition from private to public dependence', in H. Holters (ed.) *Patriarchy in a Welfare Society*, Oslo: Universitetsforlaget.

——(1984b) 'The role of women in voluntary associations and organisations', part III of *The Situation of Women in the Political Process in Europe*, Strasbourg: Directorate of Human Rights, Council of Europe.

Jaggar, A. M. (1983) *Feminist Politics and Human Nature*, Brighton: Harvester.

Jaquette, J. (1974) *Women and Politics*, New York: John Wiley.

Jones, K. B. and Jonasdottir, A. G. (1988) *The Political Interests of Gender*, London: Sage Publications.

Lovenduski, J. (1981) 'Toward the emasculation of political science', in D. Spender (ed.) *Men's Studies Modified*, Oxford: Pergamon Press.

——(1986) *Women and European Politics*, Brighton: Wheatsheaf.

Lovenduski, J. and Hills, J. (eds) (1981) *The Politics of the Second Electorate: Women and Public Participation*, London: Routledge & Kegan Paul.

Lovenduski, J. and Outshoorn, J. (1986) *The New Politics of Abortion*, London: Sage Publications.

Meehan, E. (1987) *Women's Rights at Work*, London and Basingstoke: Macmillan.

Mueller, C. M. (ed.) (1988) *The Politics of the Gender Gap: The Social Construction of Political Influence*, Newbury Park, Calif.: Sage Publications.

Nelson, B. (1984) 'Women's poverty and women's citizenship: some political consequences of economic marginality', *Signs* 10: 209–31.

Norris, P. (1987) *Politics and Sexual Equality*, Brighton: Wheatsheaf.

Randall, V. (1982) *Women and Politics*, London: Macmillan.

——(1987) *Women and Politics: An International Perspective*, 2nd edn, Basingstoke and London: Macmillan.

Sapiro, V. (1981) 'When are interests interesting? The problems of the political representation of women, *American Political Science Review* 75: 701–16.

——(1983) *The Political Integration of Women*, Chicago: University of Illinois Press.

Siltanen, J. and Stanworth, M. (eds) (1984) *Women and the Public Sphere: A Critique of Sociology and Politics*, London: Hutchinson.

38

DEVELOPMENT

RONALD H. CHILCOTE

Accounts of development do not generally incorporate a clear conception of the term itself, but instead dwell on theoretical perspectives or politics that change in response to evolving conditions within countries and between countries and the world order, whether they be characterized as advanced capitalist, command socialist, developing capitalist or socialist, or backward and underdeveloped cases. In his attention to mainstream thinking, Eckstein (1982) concluded that the past endeavour has been a 'muddle' and that we must apply more observation and lucid thought in understanding development. In his critique, David Booth affirmed that the Marxist-influenced sociology of development had reached an impasse and a general malaise in inquiry, the consequence of 'commitment to demonstrating the "necessity" of economic and social patterns, as distinct from explaining them and exploring how they may be changed' (Booth 1985: 761).

Despite this pessimism, a conceptualization is possible. *Webster's Third New International Dictionary* simplistically defines development as 'a gradual unfolding' and a 'gradual advance or growth through progressive changes'. Mittelman refers to development as 'the increasing capacity to make rational use of natural and human resources for social ends', whereas underdevelopment is 'the blockage which forestalls a rational transformation of the social structure' (Mittelman 1988: 22). Baran reminds us that, historically, development means 'a far-reaching transformation of society's economic, social, and political structure, of the dominant organization of production, distribution, and consumption' and that it 'has never been a smooth, harmonious process unfolding placidly over time and space' (Baran 1957: 3). Rodney correctly tells us that development is 'a many-sided process', implying for the individual 'increased skill and capacity, greater freedom, creativity, self-discipline, responsibility, and material well-being' (Rodney 1974: 3). He goes on to show that 'a society develops economically as its members increase jointly their capacity for dealing with the environment' (ibid.: 4). He argues that people have the capacity for improving their ability to live more satisfactorily through the exploitation of the resources of nature: 'Everywhere, man was faced with the task of survival by meeting fundamental material needs; and better tools were a consequence of the interplay between human beings and nature as part of the struggle for survival' (ibid.: 5). Chilton (1987) works towards a definition of political development by applying a Piagetian psychological theory of individual development to a symbolic conception of political culture in order to link individual and institutional change in the developmental process, and thereby identify developmental 'sequences' in the ways people relate to one another. Other efforts at defining political development are to be found in Binder (1986) and Palmer (1989), while Riggs (1981) suggests that the term cannot be conceptualized.

All these definitions suggest that development is a multi-faceted process, involving political, economic, social and cultural dimensions at the levels of individual and society as a whole. Whereas the political science approach to development during the 1950s and 1960s concentrated on the 'political' nature of development (see Almond 1970; Packenham 1964; Pye 1966), the literature increasingly recognized the relationship of political development to economic and other facets of development. Development came to be viewed as a process involving all of society so that academic attention to development evolved from single to multi-disciplinary perspectives. Eventually, with the emergence of capitalism and socialism as predominant economic systems, theories and policies of development turned toward one or the other of these alternatives. Graphically the evolution of the concept development can be delineated:

Dimensions	Process
Political	Representative and participatory democracy
Economic	Central and decentralized planning
Social	Provision of human needs
Cultural	Fostering of selflessness, collaboration, solidarity, political consciousness and social responsibility

Thus, the central concern of the political thrust of development would be with democracy in its major forms, whereas the economic emphasis on development might be concerned with planning; the social aspect with people's basic needs such as food and shelter, health care, education and employment; and the cultural level with the building of individual outreach to others.

Another way of portraying the characteristics of development is according to historical, geographical and ideological distinctions:

First World	Second World	Third World
Private capitalism	Command socialism	Human needs
Political + Economic	Economic + Social	Social + Economic

The First World of advanced capitalist societies reflects patterns of representative or formal democracy and private ownership of the means of production, usually in concert with state policy, including planning and action favouring capitalism (Sweezy 1942). The Second World of socialist societies has traditionally (until the upheavals in 1989) existed under command economies emphasizing central planning, and the provision of basic social needs, but with limited democratic space and little experimentation with representative and participatory forms of democracy (Post and Wright 1989). The Third World of less developed and underdeveloped countries has, in the case of revolutionary situations, directed the attention of the state to resolving basic human needs and implementing centralized planning, while experimenting with representative and participatory forms of democracy in the face of domination of outside capital and the pressures of the financial and corporate world. Cultural resistance and the defence of traditional values has often been a response of indigenous peoples to colonial rule. Cultural expression has also accompanied socialist and revolutionary experiences as a means for reshaping the commitment and solidarity of people. Political culture is usually associated with development as a means of characterizing the extent people participate in the civil society.

EVOLVING PERSPECTIVES

The field of development can be thought of as evolving through various historical phases since the Second World War. A first phase, predominant in the 1950s and 1960s, emphasized the idea that the Anglo-American experience in political democracy and capitalist accumulation could be diffused to the rest of the world (Rostow 1960). A second phase, conspicuous in the 1960s and 1970s, embraced views from the Third World that argued that the diffusion of capitalism and technology from the advanced industrial nations tended to promote underdevelopment and backwardness in the less developed regions of the world (Baran 1957). A third phase, evident during the 1980s, involved a reassessment of the impact of the earlier ideas on the mainstream of political science, together with a disenchantment in both capitalism and socialism, a call for a balance of resources to lessen inequality, and new policies to deal with environmental and other issues confronting the world at large (Brown *et al.* 1990). The changing theoretical and practical perspectives of development reflected changing relations between developing and developed countries as well as changes in the theoretical discourse.

At least six schools of thought are evident in the literature on development over the past half-century. A first school, based on a traditional view that growth produces development, relies on liberal democracy and capitalism (Almond and Coleman 1960). It presumes that, once the foundation of capitalist growth is established, policy makers will be able to allocate resources to meet social needs and mitigate differences in income and other inequalities among individuals in society. A second school, opposed to the view that capitalism promotes the welfare of society, embraces the perspectives of dependency and underdevelopment, advocating resistance to external influences and the building of autonomous societies, premissed either on capitalism or socialism (Frank 1966; Dos Santos 1970). A third school turns to the world system and to international political economy in its depiction of central, semi-peripheral and peripheral countries evolving through centuries of capitalist influence and dominance and cycles of economic prosperity and decline (Bollen 1983; Chase-Dunn 1977; Hopkins and Wallerstein 1977; Wallerstein 1974). A fourth school emphasizes the mode of production as a means for assessing the relations people have to their work and the possibilities of transitions from pre-capitalist social formations to capitalism and socialism (Foster-Carter 1978). A fifth school identifies trends toward the internationalization of capital and labour (Palloix 1975), the rise of multinational corporations (Baran and Sweezy 1966), and the impact of late capitalism in the less developed parts of the world since the Second World War (Mandel 1975). The sixth school incorporates old and new understandings of imperialism in its view of the world (Brewer 1980).

Many theoretical tendencies run through these schools of development, and the task of delineating and sorting them out is complex and difficult. Pye (1966) set forth ten views related to economic development, industrialization, political modernization, the nation-state, administrative and legal organization, mass mobilization, democracy, orderly change, power and social change, but his review of these tendencies settled on democracy as the essential ingredient of development. In their overview of political development, Huntington and Domínguez (1975) identified two currents as converging in a focus on political development, one emanating with the expansion of area studies and American influence into Africa, Asia, the Middle East and Latin America after the Second World War, and the other stemming from the behavioural movement in political science and its attention to empirical theory and research in the search for a systemic framework. They noted at least three directions in the literature: the system–function approach that focused on systems theory and structural functionalism in the work of Levy (1966), Almond and Powell (1966), and others; the social process approach that applied comparative quantitative analysis to the study of urbanization, industrialization and the media in the work of Lerner (1958), Deutsch (1961), Tanter (1967) and others; and the comparative history approach of Black (1966); Eisenstadt (1966), Moore (1966), and Huntington (1968). Chodak (1973) emphasized five approaches: evolutionary theories, macro-sociological theories of industrialization, psychological explanations, political and economic development, and modernization. Chilcote (1981) surveyed beyond these approaches to suggest six general themes in the literature: political development, development and nationalism, modernization, underdevelopment, dependency, and imperialism. A few years later he emphasized the latter three themes in a historical synthesis of ideas on development in the Third World, and drew a dichotomy between, on the one hand, reformist, nationalist and capitalist views (for example, Furtado 1964; Cardoso and Faletto 1979, and revolutionary and socialist views on development and underdevelopment (for example, Baran 1957; Frank 1966; Amin 1974, on the other (Chilcote 1984). Blomström and Hettne (1984) and Hettne (1983) also moved beyond the theories on Western capitalist development to analyse dependency theory and approaches to underdevelopment in the Third World. Both Blomström and Hettne (1984) and Chilcote (1984) suggested that new directions in Marxism, particularly in the modes of production analysis (Foster-Carter 1978) and in internationalization of capital theory (Palloix 1975), had carried the discourse on development beyond these interpretations. Evans and Stephens (1988) chose four areas of interest to specialists on developmental problems: the state in the process of development; the distribution of resources generated by development; the relation between industrialization and political democracy; and national development and world political economy. Finally, Park (1984) and Dube (1988) offered a reappraisal of development and modernization by focusing on their weaknesses and strengths and addressing issues of the quality of life and human needs. (Other overviews are presented in Bernstein 1973; DeKadt and Williams 1974; Foster-Carter 1985; Goulet 1968; Griffin and Gurley 1985; Griffin and James 1981; Kay 1975, 1989; Oxaal et al. 1975; Roxborough 1979; Weiner and Huntington 1987.)

   Given these diverse interpretations and overviews of the development literature, the reader can be guided to an understanding of different approaches through the rough classsification of perspectives below. One perspective emphasizes patterns of capitalist accumulation and growth in economic development and sees formal or representative democracy as politically compatible with economic progress; it is generally reflective of developmental progress in Western advanced industrial nations and its classical theoretical inspiration likely derives from Adam Smith. The other perspective emphasizes human needs, planned economies, and participatory or informal democracy alongside representative democratic practices; it is generally reflective of developmental advances in the state bureaucratic regimes professing socialism as well as in nations that have experienced revolution and advocated transitions to socialism and equality where classical theoretical inspiration tends to stem from Marx.

DEVELOPMENT APPROACHES IN ADVANCED CAPITALIST NATIONS

A synthesis of the literature on the historical development of the advanced capitalist nations reveals many prominent approaches:

Classical growth model

W. Arthur Lewis (1955), a well-known proponent of this model, applied the classical view (that development is based on per capita growth and not distribution) to the possibility of sustainable growth in static and retarded economies of the Third World (particularly in the Caribbean and Africa). Although its influence has persisted, the model was largely discredited by the failure of much of the Third World to achieve significant growth.

Stages of growth

The notion of developmental stages is old, but its thrust has been especially influential in the work of Rostow (1960), who projected a five-stage model based on economic conditions: traditional, based on lack of technology and intensive labour in agriculture; preconditions for take-off based on technological advances; take-off or self-sustaining economic growth; the drive to maturity; and mass consumption oriented to consumer goods and services. Organski's (1965) four-stage political scheme followed a similar pattern: primitive unification; industrialization; national welfare; and politics of abundance. However, stage theory is limited by its failure to account for historical conditions, particularly the relationship of underdeveloped countries with now developed countries. Frank (1971), for example, attacked the theory for assuming that underdevelopment is an original stage of traditional society rather than the consequence of European capitalist expansion.

Poles of development

The French economist, François Perroux, advocated that the activities of a new enterprise could be integrated with the economy of a region or country where a development pole could link the processing of raw materials with labour supply and productivity and be oriented to domestic producers and consumers. This approach could overcome the inequity between centres and peripheries and mitigate the negative impact of dependent relationships through central planning. Rational diffusion of capital and technology would allow for development of autonomous outlying centres which, in turn, could be integrated into a national scheme of development, ensure national control, and provide a balance between international and domestic investment. However, the idea had limited success in the Third World, where domestic capital was often overwhelmed by stronger international investors and where domestic capital itself was concentrated in only a few centres, often the capital city.

Modernization

Usually associated with capitalist development, Eisenstadt (1966) understood modernization as highly differentiated political structure and diffusion of political power and authority into all spheres of society. In his early work Apter (1965) considered modernization as a particular form of development, involving a stable social system, differentiated social structures, and social skills and knowledge adaptable to a technologically advanced world. Later he described this form of modernization as the attempt of traditional societies to replicate the institutions and values of advanced industrial societies. Parallel to this was another form of modernization that takes conflict and inequality rather than integration into account (Apter 1987). These approaches, however, tend to be general, related to stages of growth from traditional to modern forms, applicable to historical development in advanced industrial societies, and for much of the Third World reliant on ideal types rather than accurate descriptions of reality. Although the early theory was largely discredited, some observers (So 1990) believed that it had transcended its crisis of the late 1960s and assumed a fruitful line of inquiry two decades later.

Developmental nationalism or autonomous national development

Nationalism, essentially a late eighteenth- and nineteenth-century European idea, evolved with the rise of nation-states such as Germany and Italy and is referred to in the developmental literature as an ideological force that draws people together in common cause (Senghass 1985). Its cohesion may be based on identification of a single territory, a common language, symbols of nationhood and national heroes, but many types of nationalism appear according to various experiences. Radical nationalism, for example, is associated with the national liberation movements that fought for independence in the emerging national states of Africa, Asia and Latin America (Scalapino 1989). In the mainstream literature Deutsch (1953) linked the idea of nationalism to development, while in radical perspective Horace Davis (1967) showed the relevance of nationalism and the national question to Marxism and socialist societies. Thus, national consciousness can be oriented to the nature of society, realizing the goals of the nation-state, and ensuring broad involvement in shaping future direction. While the forces of nationalism may serve the cause of development, a theory of nationalism and development is not clearly discernible. Further, the pervasive impact of the international capitalist system in particular has tended to diminish the importance of the nationalist alternative.

Political democracy and order

The relationship of representative democracy to political development is a conspicuous theme in Pye (1966) and runs through the work of Almond (1970), Lipset (1959), Rustow (1970), Bollen (1979) and others. Political democracy becomes an ideal of consensus and bargaining in a give-and-take process. Apter (1971) emphasized that people make rational choices that relate to development and order and argued, like Hobbes, that development and order are interrelated, and that disorder may make development difficult to attain. Bates argued that 'while economic elites are behaving in ways that are economically irrational, they are behaving in ways that are politically rational' (Bates 1988: 244). They may make rational choices in seeking solutions to political problems, but sometimes at economic costs that retard development. Huntington (1965) elaborated on stability in the face of rapid social and economic changes, and advocated control and regulation of development through constraints on new groups entering politics, limits to exposure to mass media, and suppression of mass mobilization. These approaches lean toward institutional continuity and harmony rather than deep-rooted change.

Crises of development

Binder et al. (1971) suggested that development is the capacity of a political system to make decisions and implement policies to meet new demands and goals such as equality of opportunity, social justice and involvement while sustaining continuous change. They focused on a 'developmental syndrome' in which crises of identity, legitimacy, participation, penetration and distribution occur as the polity develops. This perspective tends to stress American political values and to skirt around a theory of structural change.

Post-liberal development

Bowles and Gintis (1986) sought space for a radical democratic synthesis and posited a post-liberal democracy on the expansion of personal rights through the affirmation of traditional political forms of representative democracy and individual liberty while ensuring the establishment of innovative and democratically accountable economic freedoms in community and work. Capitalism and democracy, they argued, are incompatible, and the welfare state does not give citizens the power to make democratic decisions in the economic sphere, and democratic theory is in disarray. Their synthesis rejected many ideas of

Marxism, in particular a view of class consciousness and direct democracy (ignoring Marx's advocacy of representative democracy in certain instances or his association of democracy with direct participatory activities). Their argument that Marxism reduces institutions to class terms leads to an emphasis on conflictual pluralism while obscuring class interests, diminishing the role of the state, and playing down the internal contradictions of capitalism which affect relations of production and often lead to class struggle. In capitalist society, development is also associated with decentralization of authority, routinization of bureaucratic tasks, competition among various interests for resources and power, consensus and bargaining, yet negative consequences appear with authoritarian regimes or the consolidating oligopolistic and monopolistic tendencies in the economy. In socialist society, rational planning and efficient management are expected to ensure economic growth and a more egalitarian distribution of resources to the people, but these goals are often undermined by mismanagement and lack of resources as well as failure to involve people in decisions affecting their production, basic needs, and material standards of living.

DEVELOPMENT APPROACHES IN SOCIALIST AND THIRD WORLD NATIONS

Capitalist development of underdevelopment

The argument that capitalism fosters underdevelopment as capital and technology diffuse from the advanced capitalist to the backward nations runs through an important literature emanating particularly from Paul Baran. Baran's *The Political Economy of Growth* (Baran 1957) was influential and popular among Third World scholars and students, particularly in Latin America. Baran identified forms of economic surplus (actual, potential and planned) in an explanation of the 'roots' and 'morphology' of backwardness. He despaired that 'the colonial and dependent countries today have no recourse to such sources of primary accumulation of capital as were available to the now advanced capitalist countries' and that 'development in the age of monopoly capitalism and imperialism faces obstacles that have little in common with those encountered two or three hundred years ago' (ibid.: 16).

Among the major regional studies that analysed this theme were André Gunder Frank's *Capitalism and Underdevelopment in Latin America* (Frank 1967), Walter Rodney's *How Europe Underdeveloped Africa* (Rodney 1974), Malcolm Caldwell's *The Wealth of Some Nations* (Caldwell 1977), and Manning Marable's *How Capitalism Underdeveloped Black America* (Marable 1983). Frank believed that national capitalism and the national bourgeoisie, unlike their counterparts in England and the United States, could not promote development in Latin America. He argued that the contradictions of capitalism had led to the expropriation of economic surplus which generated development in the metropolitan centres and underdevelopment in the peripheral satellites. Cumings (1984) has delved into this problem and elaborated on its significance for the Asian political economy. Criticism of these views relates to emphasis on commercial patterns of international trade rather than to processes and relations of production. (See also Aleshina *et al.* 1983; Bagchi 1982; Beckford 1972; Bornschier and Chase-Dunn 1985; Brenner 1976; Clarkson 1972; Frank 1966; Kay 1975, 1989; Laclau 1971; Roxborough 1979; Szentes 1971).

New dependency

Three forms of dependency appear in history: colonial dependency, evident in trade monopolies over land, mines and labour; financial–industrial dependency, accompanied by imperialism and the expansion of big capital at the end of the nineteenth century; and the new dependency, characterized by the capital of multinational corporations in industry oriented to the internal markets of underdeveloped nations after the Second World War. Dos Santos (1970) described this new form as conditioned by the relationship of dominant to dependent countries so that the expansion of the dominant country could have a positive or negative impact on the development of the dependent one. Dussel (1990) and Mohri (1979) criticized the dependency theorists for failure to root their conceptualization in the method of Marx (for other criticisms, see Brewer 1980; Caporaso 1980; Cardoso 1977; Chilcote 1974; Frank 1974; Henfrey 1981; Johnson 1981; Lehman 1979; Munck 1981).

Internal colonialism

A relationship similar to the colonial ties between nations, internal colonialism involved dominant and marginal groups within a single society. For example, according to the political sociologist González Casanova (1961), internal colonialism was represented by the monopoly of the ruling metropolis in Mexico City over the marginal Indian communities. The underdevelopment of the marginal society is the consequence of its exploitation by and dependence on the developing metropolis. (See Kahl 1976 for a critique.)

Inward directed development (desarrollismo)

Advocated by the Argentine economist, Raúl Prebisch, and the Economic Commission for Latin America (ECLA), *desarrollismo* implied autonomous or domestic capitalist development through the imposition of tariff barriers, the building of an infrastructure for the local economy, and import substitution to stimulate production. Although this view reveals differences between capitalism in the advanced industrial centre and capitalism in the backward periphery, its reformist solutions to underdevelopment are usually insufficient to overcome the dominance of international capital.

Associated dependent capitalist development

Associated dependent capitalist development is defined as a situation in the periphery in which the domestic bourgeoisie ties itself to capitalism, associates with international capital, and through mediation of the state stimulates capitalist accumulation. According to Cardoso (1973) and Evans (1979), who used Brazil as an example, the accumulation and expansion of local capital thus depend on the dynamic of international capital. Socialist critics argue that this view promotes capitalist exploitation.

Unequal development

As set forth by Amin (1974), this line of thinking sees the world as comprising developed and underdeveloped societies, some of which are capitalist and others socialist, all integrated into a commercial and financial capitalist network on a world scale. Amin (1976) analysed unequal development in terms of disarticulation of different sectors of an economy, domination from the outside, and dependence caused by large foreign industrial business.

Unequal exchange

Elaborated by Emmanuel (1972) and based on David Ricardo's thesis on comparative costs and natural advantages of countries participating in commercial exchange, the theory of unequal exchange portrays capitalist production relations as penetrating a world economy whose units are distinguished by differences in specialization in the international division of labour and by unequal wage levels. (See also Chase-Dunn and Rubinson 1978.)

Combined and uneven development

Drawn from the thinking of Trotsky, this theory argues that the most backward and the most modern forms of economic activity and exploitation are found in variable forms in different countries, but they may be linked or combined in their development, especially under the impact of imperialism. A combined and uneven social formation is evident, for example, in the period of transition from a pre-capitalist to a full capitalist economy so that elements of feudalism and capitalism might co-exist (see Lowy 1981; Mandel 1970; Novack 1966). Lenin (1956) demonstrated how Russia in the late nineteenth century evidenced this formation.

Late capitalism

Ernest Mandel (1975) provided an overview of capitalism since the Second World War, attempting to apply the laws of the capitalist mode of production to the post-war period of boom and decline. Late capitalism is a consequence of the integrated international system which necessitates the transfer of surplus from underdeveloped regions to industrialized regions, thereby delaying the development of the former. Some less developed countries have tried to minimize this tendency by nationalizing international capital (for example, Mexican petroleum in 1938 and Chilean copper during the early 1970s).

Mode of production

Development is largely determined by the level of the forces of production – the capital and technology, labour skill and efficiency attained by society. Capital accumulation and reproduction are essential for the maintenance and expansion of capitalism (Rey 1973). Crucial in promoting the forces of production, especially in the Third World, is whether capitalism itself must be strengthened *en route* to socialism or the capitalist stage skipped altogether. Amin (1976) identified pre-capitalist modes, including the communal mode, the tribute-paying mode, the feudal mode, and the slave-owning mode of production. This approach is sometimes deterministic in its reliance upon successive stages of development or limited by its reliance on predetermined modes that may not appear in some societies at particular historical periods (see Chilcote and Johnson 1983; Foster-Carter 1978; Taylor 1979).

Human needs development

Development can be understood in terms of meeting the basic needs of all people, a proposition emphasized by Dube (1988) and Kruijer (1987). Park (1984) identifies a fourfold structure of human needs: survival, belongingness, leisure and control. While it is problematic whether capitalist societies can meet such needs as health, food, shelter and employment, the politically representative character of many of them is usually viewed as a step towards development. Yet in capitalist societies large numbers of people often absent themselves from the electoral process, political participation is minimal, and grassroots political involvement may be dwarfed by electoral campaigns influenced by monied interests. Although socialist societies have generally been able to deal with basic human needs through the socialization of most means of production and planned distribution of resources, they have usually failed to establish either effective representative or participatory democracies. Thus, the welfare of all classes, groups and individuals is essential in societal development.

627

New imperialism and post-imperialism

Theories of imperialism were posited by J. A. Hobson (who utilized an under-consumption theory), Rudolf Hilferding (finance capital), and N. Bukharin and Lenin (monopoly capital). Contemporary analyses by Baran and Sweezy (1966), Brewer (1980), Fieldhouse (1967) and Girvan (1976), emphasized the advanced character of capitalism, especially in its monopoly form and its impact on colonial and less developed areas, while Palma (1978) carefully examined Lenin's thought for the roots of a theory of underdevelopment. These writers showed the negative consequences of the imperialist advance, yet some on the left, for example Warren (1980), have attempted to demonstrate that imperialism tends to destroy pre-capitalist social formations and provides for capitalist development everywhere.

In an effort to move beyond imperialist and dependency explanations of capitalist underdevelopment or associated capitalist development, Becker *et al.* (1987) argued that global institutions tend to promote the integration of diverse national interests on a new international basis by offering access to capital resources and technologies. This necessitates the location of both foreign labour and management in the dependent country as well as local participation in the ownership of the corporation. In such a situation two segments of a new social class appear: privileged nationals, or a managerial bourgeoisie, and the foreign nationals who manage the businesses of transnational organizations. This coalescing of dominant class elements across national boundaries suggests the rise of an international oligarchy. According to Becker *et al.*, a theory of post-imperialism serves as an alternative to a determinist Leninist understanding of imperialism and to dependency orthodoxy. However, international capital has dominated Third World situations, and there is little evidence to affirm that a managerial national bourgeoisie will emerge as hegemonic and other classes will decline, nor that the national bourgeoisie will favour democracy over authoritarianism.

Sub-imperialism

Dependent capitalism, according to Marini (1978), is unable to reproduce itself through the process of accumulation. However, in some dependent countries where an authoritarian military leadership takes charge, the economy can be reorganized and the working class and opposition oppressed to allow for a project of sub-imperialism. In this case the regime facilitates foreign investment and technology and increases domestic industrial capacity, but must also seek new markets, necessitating expansion into neighbouring countries. The dependent country thus becomes an intermediary between imperialist countries and other less developed countries which are vulnerable to exploitation. Criticism of this perspective focuses on its economic determinism and its implication that only a revolutionary and not a reformist course would be necessary to overcome the ensuing exploitation.

Internationalization of capital

This theory permits an analysis of the movement of capital and class struggle on an international level, particularly the foreign investments and capital accumulation by capitalist enterprises of the centre that operate in the developing countries, and the rapid growth in the internationalization of other forms of capital such as private and public export credits, bank loans and commodity exports. This theory was elaborated by Hymer (1972) and Palloix (1975), and applied to a case study in West Africa by Marcussen and Torp (1982).

Strategies and issues

A central issue for much of the world, according to Mittelman (1988), is how to attain an investable surplus while reducing global inequality in the face of international organizations, aid agencies, technological agreements, multinational corporations and banks. He argues that underdevelopment is not inevitable in the Third World, but is the consequence of three forces: capital accumulation, the state, and social classes. He delves into three general strategies of how nations could join global capitalism, retreat from the world capitalist system, and balance the bonds of dependency.

Kruijer (1987) focuses directly on the poor and the oppressed by analysing their plight in terms of the national and international wealth system of domination. He suggests a 'liberation' strategy to provide for basic needs such as education and health care, shelter and clothing, to ensure balanced development of the forces of production, orient social values in a socialist direction; emancipate women, abolish class distinctions, establish political power with the people, and end economic relationships with the wealthy powerful capitalist world. He sees the process of change as evolving through phases: from the capitalist mode of production in which the bourgeoisie is the ruling class and dominates the state; to a transitional phase in which the capitalist mode is gradually abolished and the interests of the people are represented by the state but the people have little say; to a state-socialist phase in which private enterprise has largely disappeared and the people still have little input; to a democratic socialist phase in which the power of the state is gradually reduced and decisions are increasingly vested in the people.

Dube (1988) sums up a number of policy recommendations in the direction of rethinking the goals and strategies of development: plans for economic growth must be balanced by enriching the quality of life and meeting the basic needs of all people; eliminate all poverty, not by welfarism but by a radical altering of planning and implementation policies; instil in people recognition of their rights and responsibilities through programmes of conscientization; ensure participation in a policy of affirmative action to include all deprived sectors of society; implement administrative restructuring, renovation and innovation, and remove vestiges of colonial and Western-style democratic practices that have failed in Third World countries; manage the socio-cultural environment so as to avoid counter-development; and re-examine the global context of development so as to close the bipolar gap between rich and poor worlds, find an equitable sharing of scarce resources, and improve the human condition of all peoples.

These policy issues are analysed around the notion of sustainable development in an effort to raise global consciousness about environmental degradation and the deterioration of the planet (Brown *et al.* 1990). This notion, according to the World Commission on Environment and Development, is possible when 'Humanity has the ability to make development sustainable – to ensure that it meets the needs of the present without compromising the ability of future generations to meet their own needs' (World Commission on Environment and Development 1987: 8). Goldsworthy (1988) emphasizes the politics of such policy issues, while Fuentes and Frank (1989) show the importance of popular social movements in political struggle and change. More particularly, Molyneux (1986) and Sen and Grown (1987) demonstrate how both capitalist and socialist development ignore the role of women, and Redclift (1984) draws out the strengths and weaknesses of environmental movements. Some of the issues and strategies for dealing with sustainable development can be outlined as follows:

Strategies	Issues
Capitalism versus socialism	Growth or human needs
	Private or public ownership of means of production
	Market or planned economy
	Capitalist path or non-capitalist path
	One path or multilinear paths
	Physical investment (plant and equipment) or human capital investment
	Evolution versus revolution
	Growth or distribution of resources
	Reforms or radical restructuring
Endogenous versus exogenous orientation	Self reliance or interdependence

Market or planning	Industrial or agricultural
	Industrial or environmental protection
	Development or non-development
Aid versus trade	Import substitution or export promotion
	Regional integration or open international exchange

Fagen *et al.* argue for a transformation of the model of accumulation and capitalist social formation to a socialist model. They see the need for 'social ownership of the commanding heights of the economy and a relatively comprehensive system of planning' in which production and distribution are tied to basic needs of the population; forms of privilege (income, race, gender, class, etc.) are terminated; and the popular classes participate fully in determining public policy (Fagen *et al.* 1986: 10). Their analysis is particularly concerned with uneven and underdeveloped capitalism on the periphery and revolutionary activity for socialism away from the advanced capitalist countries, but these socialist experiments on the periphery may also have relevance for capitalist and socialist development elsewhere.

TOWARDS A SYNTHESIS OF DEVELOPMENT

The search for an understanding of development entails a multiplicity of ideas and practices, a kind of dialectical interplay between theory and practice, and an interdisciplinary endeavour. Thus, the political dimension of development involves both representative and participatory democracy, preferably with down-up grassroots and collective actions rather than decisions based on top-down processes of indirect decision making. It comprises collective participation in decisions among individuals in activities extending beyond boundaries of government and political parties, including classes and groups outside and within the state. It is linked to economic and social consequences, largely dependent on the mode of production (under capitalism or socialism) and associated with the provision of basic human needs. Finally, it is a consequence of capital accumulation and distribution of its rewards in egalitarian ways.

Development, however, is unequal, uneven, and combines modes of production through history. Both progression and retrogression are possible. Sources of development relate to the economic base (largely capitalism in the contemporary world) and to state bureaucratic activity (in the capitalist and socialist countries). Development links institutions to egalitarian participation, individual and collective choice, interchange of roles (for instance, managers and workers, teachers and students, and so on), and mitigation of class divisions in society. Development involves advances in the productive forces of society (under capitalism or socialism at national and international levels) and in the drive for egalitarian participation and distribution of resources to meet basic needs and collectively raise the quality of material life of all people. Development affects individuals by eliminating vestiges of selfishness and egoism, fostering collaboration, promoting solidarity among people, raising political consciousness and social responsibility, and struggling against injustice and exploitation of person by person. The contradictions of economic and political life in the struggle for participatory and representative democracy, egalitarian distribution of resources, provision for basic needs, protection of the environment, and so on may lead to crisis and ultimately to some resolution of the issues identified above.

REFERENCES

Aleshina, I. *et al.* (1983) *Economic Development of the Newly Free Countries*, Developing Countries: Problems and Perspectives Series, no. 3, Moscow: USSR Academy of Sciences.

Almond, G. (1970) *Political Development: Essays in Heuristic Theory*, Boston: Little, Brown & Co.

Almond, G. and Coleman, J. S. (eds) (1960) *The Politics of Developing Areas*, Princeton: Princeton University Press.

Almond, G. and Powell, G. B. (1966) *Comparative Politics: A Developmental Approach*, Boston: Little, Brown & Co.

Amin, S. (1974) *Accumulation on a World Scale: A Critique of the Theory of Underdevelopment*, 2 vols, New York: Monthly Review Press.

——(1976) *Unequal development*, New York: Monthly Review Press.

Apter, D. (1965) *The Politics of Modernization*, Chicago: University of Chicago Press.

——(1971) *Choice and the Politics of Allocation: A Developmental Theory*, New Haven: Yale University Press.

——(1987) *Rethinking Development: Modernization, Dependency, and Postmodern Politics*, Newbury Park, Calif.: Sage Publications.

Bagchi, A. K. (1982) *The Political Economy of Underdevelopment*, New York: Cambridge University Press.

Baran, P. (1957) *The Political Economy of Growth*, New York: Monthly Review.

Baran, P. and Sweezy, P. (1966) *Monopoly Capital: An Essay on the American Economic and Social Order*, New York: Monthly Review Press.

Bates, R. H. (ed.) (1988) *Toward a Political Economy of Development: A Rational Choice Perspective*, Berkeley: University of California Press.

Becker, D. G., Frieden, J., Shatz, S. P. and Sklar, S. L. (1987) *Postimperialism, International Capitalism and Development in the Late Twentieth Century*, Boulder: Lynne Rienner Publishers.

Beckford, G. (1972) *Persistent Poverty, Underdevelopment in Plantation Economies of the Third World*, Oxford: Oxford University Press.

Bernstein, H. (ed.) (1973) *Underdevelopment and Development*, Baltimore: Penguin.

Binder, L. (1986) 'The natural history of development theory', *Comparative Studies in Society and History* 28 (1): 3–33.

Binder, L. *et al.* (1971) *Crises and Sequences in Political Development*, Princeton, NJ: Princeton University Press.

Black, C. E. (1966) *The Dynamics of Modernization*, New York: Harper & Row.

Blomström, M. and Hettne, B. (1984) *Development Theory in Transition. The Dependency Debate and Beyond: Third World Responses*, London: Zed Books.

Bollen, K. (1979) 'Political democracy and the timing of development', *American Sociological Review* 44: 572–87.

———(1983) 'World system position, dependency, and democracy', *American Sociological Review* 48: 468–79.

Booth, D. (1985) 'Marxism and development sociology: interpreting the impasse', *World Development* 13 (7): 761–87.

Bornschier, V. and Chase-Dunn, C. (1985) *Transnational Corporations and Underdevelopment*, New York: Praeger.

Bowles, S. and Gintis, H. (1986) *Democracy and Capitalism: Property, Community, and the Contradictions of Modern Social Thought*, New York: Basic Books.

Brenner, R. (1976) 'The origins of capitalist development: a critique of neo-Smithean Marxism', *New Left Review* 104: 24–92.

Brewer, A. (1980) *Marxist Theories of Imperialism: A Critical Survey*, London: Routledge & Kegan Paul.

Brown, L. R. *et al.* (1990) *State of the World: A Wordwatch Institute Report on Progress Toward a Sustainable Society*, New York: W. W. Norton & Co.

Caldwell, M. (1977) *The Wealth of Some Nations*, London: Zed Books.

Caporaso, J. A. (1980) 'Dependency theory: continuities and discontinuities in development studies', *International Organization* 39: 605–28.

Cardoso, F. H. (1973) 'Associated-dependent development: theoretical and practical implications', in A. Stepan (ed.) *Authoritarian Brazil: Origins, Policies, and Future*, New Haven: Yale University Press.

———(1977) 'The consumption of dependency theory in the United States', *Latin American Research Review* 10 (3): 7–24.

Cardoso, F. H. and Faletto, E. (1979) *Dependency and Development*, Berkeley: University of California Press.

Chase-Dunn, C. (1977) 'Toward a structural perspective on the world-system', *Politics and Society* 7 (4): 453–76.

Chase-Dunn, C. and Rubinson, R. (1978) 'Unequal development', *Insurgent Sociologist* 8: 78–81.

Chilcote, R. H. (1969) 'Development and nationalism in Brazil and Portuguese Africa', *Comparative Political Studies* 1: 501–25.

———(1974) 'Dependency: a critical synthesis of the literature', *Latin American Perspectives* 1: 4–29.

———(1981) *Theories of Comparative Politics: The Search for a Paradigm*, Boulder, Colo.: Westview Press.

———(1984) *Theories of Development and Underdevelopment*, Boulder, Colo.: Westview Press.

Chilcote, R. H. and Johnson, D. L. (eds) (1983) *Theories of Development: Mode of Production or Dependency?*, Beverly Hills: Sage Publications.

Chilton, S. (1987) *Defining Political Development*, Boulder, Colo.: Lynne Rienner Publishers.

Chodak. S. (1973) *Societal Development: Five Approaches with Conclusions from Comparative Analysis*, New York: Oxford University Press.

Clarkson, S. (1972) 'Marxism-Leninism as a system for comparative analysis of underdevelopment', *Political Science Review* 11: 124–37.

Cumings, B. (1984) 'The origins of development of the northeast Asian political economy: industrial sectors, product cycles, and political consequences', *International Organization* 40: 195–238.

Davis, H. B. (1967) *Nationalism and Socialism: Marxist and Labor Theories of Nationalism to 1917*, New York: Monthly Review Press.

DeKadt, E. and Williams, G. (eds) (1974) *Sociology and Development*, London: Tavistock Publications.

Deutsch, K. W. (1953) *Nationalism and Social Communication: An Inquiry into the Foundation of Nationality*, New York: MIT Press/John Wiley.

——(1961) 'Social mobilization and political development', *American Political Science Review* 55: 493–514.

Dos Santos, T. (1970) 'The structure of dependence', *American Economic Review* 60: 231–6.

Dube, S. C. (1988) *Modernization and Development: The Search for Alternative Paradigms*, London: Zed Books; Tokyo: The United Nations University.

Dussel, E. (1990) 'Marx's economic manuscripts of 1861–63 and the "concept" of dependency', *Latin American Perspectives* 17 (2): 62–101.

Eckstein, H. (1982) 'The idea of political development: from dignity to efficiency', *World Politics* 34 (4): 451–86.

Eisenstadt, S. N. (1966) *Modernization: Protest and Change*, Englewood Cliffs, NJ: Prentice-Hall.

Emmanuel, A. (1972) *Unequal Exchange: A Study of the Imperialism of Trade*, with additional comments by C. Bettelheim, New York: Monthly Review Press.

Evans, P. B. (1979) *Dependent Development: The Alliance of Multinational, State and Local Capital in Brazil*, Princeton, NJ: Princeton University Press.

Evans, P. B. and Stephens, J. D. (1988) 'Development and the world economy', in N. J. Smelsor (ed.) *Handbook of Sociology*, Newbury Park, Calif.: Sage Publications.

Fagen, R. R., Deere, C. D. and Coraggio, J. L. (eds) (1986) *Transition and Development: Problems of Third World Socialism*, New York: Monthly Review Press.

Fieldhouse, D. K. (1967) *The Theory of Capitalist Imperialism*, London: Longmans, Green & Co.

Foster-Carter, A. (1978) 'The modes of production controversy', *New Left Review* 107: 47–77.

——(1985) *The Sociology of Development*, Ormskirk: Causeway Press.

Frank, A. G. (1966) 'The development of underdevelopment', *Monthly Review* 18: 17–31.

——(1967) *Capitalism and Underdevelopment in Latin America: Historical Studies of Chile and Brazil*, New York: Monthly Review Press.

——(1971) *Sociology of Development and Underdevelopment of Sociology*, London: Pluto.

——(1974) 'Dependence is dead, long live dependence and the class struggle: a reply to critics', *Latin American Perspectives* 1: 87–106.

Fuentes, M. and Frank, A. G. (1989) 'Ten theses on social movements', *World Development* 17 (2): 179–91.

Furtado, C. (1964) *Development and Underdevelopment*, Berkeley and Los Angeles: University of California Press.

Girvan, N. (1976) *Corporate Imperialism: Conflict and Expropriation: Transnational Corporations and Economic Nationalism in the Third World*, White Plains, NY: M. E. Sharpe.

Goldsworthy, D. (1988) 'Thinking politically about development', *Development and Change* 19 (3): 505–30.

González Casanova, P. (1961) 'International colonialism and national development', in I. L. Horowitz, J. de Castro and J. Grassi (eds) *Latin American Radicalism*, New York: Vintage Books.

Goulet, D. (1968) 'Development for what?', *Comparative Political Studies* 1: 295–12.

Griffin, K. and Gurley, J. (1985) 'Radical analyses of imperialism, the Third World, and the transition to socialism: a survey article', *Journal of Economic Literature* 23: 1089–143.

Griffin, K. and James, J. (1981) *The Transition to Egalitarian Development: Economic Policies for Structural Change in the Third World*, New York: St Martin's Press.

Henfrey, C. (1981) 'Dependency, modes of production, and the class analysis of Latin America', *Latin American Perspectives* 8: 17–54.

Hettne, B. (1983) 'The development of development theory', *Acta Sociologica* 26 (3,4): 247–66.

Holt, R. T. and Turner, J. E. (1975) 'Crises and sequences in collective theory development', *American Political Science Review* 69: 979–94.

Hopkins, T. K. and Wallerstein, I. (1977) 'Patterns of development of the modern world-system', *Review* 1: 111–45.

Huntington, S. P. (1965) 'Political development and political decay', *World Politics* 17: 386–430.

——(1968) *Political Order in Changing Societies*, New Haven: Yale University Press.

Huntington, S. P. and Domínguez, J. (1975) 'Political development', in F. I. Greenstein and N. Polsby (eds) *Handbook of Political Science*, vol. 3, Reading, Mass.: Addison-Wesley.

Hymer, S. (1972) 'The internationalization of capital', *Journal of Economic Issues* 6 (1): 91–110.

Johnson, C. (1981) 'Dependency theory and processes of capitalism and socialism', *Latin American Perspectives* 8: 55–81.

Kahl, J. A. (1976) *Modernization, Exploitation, and Dependency in Latin America: Germani, González Casanova, and Cardoso*, New Brunswick, NJ: Transaction Books.

Kay, C. (1975) *Development and Underdevelopment: A Marxist Analysis*, London: Macmillan.

——(1989) *Latin American Theories of Development and Underdevelopment*, London: Routledge.

Kruijer, G. J. (1987) *Development through Liberation: Third World Problems and Solutions*, Atlantic Highlands, NJ: Humanities Press International.

Laclau, E. (1971) 'Feudalism and capitalism in Latin America', *New Left Review* 67: 19–38.

Lehman, D. (ed.) (1979) *Development Theory: Four Critical Essays*, London: Frank Cass.

Lenin, V. I. (1956) *The Development of Capitalism in Russia: The Process of the Formation of a Home Market for Large-Scale Industry*, Moscow: Foreign Languages Publishing House.

Lerner, D. (1958) *The Passing of Traditional Society: Modernizing the Middle East*, Glencoe, Ill.: Free Press.

Levy, M. J., Jr (1966) *Modernization and the Structure of Societies: A Setting for International Affairs*, Princeton, NJ: Princeton University Press.

Lewis, W. A. (1955) *The Theory of Economic Growth*, London: Allen & Unwin.

Lipset, S. M. (1959) 'Some social requisites of democracy: economic development and political legitimacy', *American Political Science Review* 53: 69–105.

Lowy, M. (1981) *The Politics of Combined and Uneven Development: The Theory of Permanent Revolution*, London: Verso.

Mandel, E. (1970) 'The laws of uneven development', *New Left Review* 59: 19–38.

——(1975) *Late Capitalism*, London: NLB.

Marable, M. (1983) *How Capitalism Underdeveloped Black America*, Boston: Southend Press.

Marcussen, H. S. and Torp, J. E. (1982) *The Internationalization of Capital: The Prospects for the Third World*, London: Zed Books.

Marini, R. M. (1978) 'World capitalist accumulation and sub-imperialism', *Two Thirds* 1: 29–39.

Mittelman J. H. (1988) *Out from Underdevelopment: Prospects for the Third World*, New York: St Martin's Press.

Mohri, K. (1979) 'Marx and "underdevelopment" ', *Monthly Review* 30: 32–42.

Molyneux (1986) 'Mobilization without emancipation? Women's interests, state, and revolution' in R. R. Fagen, C. D. Deere and J. L. Coraggio (eds) *Transition and Development: Problems of Third World Socialism*, New York: Monthly Review Press.

Moore, B. (1966) *Social Origins of Dictatorship and Democracy: Lord and Peasant in the Making of the Modern World*, Boston: Beacon Press.

Munck, R. (1981) 'Imperialism and dependency: recent debates and old deadends', *Latin American Perspectives* 8: 162–79.

Novack, G. (1966) *Uneven and Combined Development in History*, New York: Merit Publishers.

Organski, A. F. K. (1965) *The Stages of Political Development*, New York: Knopf.

Oxaal, I., Barnett, T. and Booth, D. (eds) (1975) *Beyond the Sociology of Development*, London: Routledge & Kegan Paul.

Packenham, R. A. (1964) 'Approaches to the study of political development', *World Politics* 17: 108–20.

Palma, G. (1978) 'Dependency: a formal theory of underdevelopment or a methodology for the analysis of concrete situations of underdevelopment', *World Development* 6: 881–94.

Palmer, M. (1989) *Dilemmas of Political Development: An Introduction to the Politics of the Developing Areas*, 4th edn, Itasca, Ill.: F. E. Peacock Publishers.

Palloix (1975) *L'Internalisation du capital*, Paris: François Maspero.

Park, H. S. (1984) *Human Needs and Political Development: A Dissent to Utopian Solutions*, Cambridge, Mass.: Schenkman Publishing Company.

Pateman, C. (1970) *Participatory Democratic Theory*, Cambridge: Cambridge University Press.

Post, K. (1989) *Socialism and Underdevelopment*, London: Routledge.

Post, K. and Wright, P. (1989) *Socialism and Underdevelopment*, London: Routledge.

Pye, L. (1966) *Aspects of Political Development*, Boston: Little, Brown & Co.

Redclift, M. (1984) *Development and the Environment Crisis. Red or Green Alternatives?*, London: Methuen.

Rey, P.-P. (1973) *Les alliances de classes*, Paris: François Maspero.

Riggs, F. W. (1981) 'The rise and fall of political development', in S. L. Long (ed.), *The Handbook of Political Behavior*, vol 4, New York: Plenum.

Rodney, W. (1974) *How Europe Underdeveloped Africa*, Washington, DC: Howard University Press.

Rostow, W. W. (1960) *The Stages of Econmic Growth: A Non-Communist Manifesto*, Cambridge: Cambridge University Press.

Roxborough, I. (1979) *Theories of Underdevelopment*, Atlantic Highlands, NJ: Humanities Press.

Rustow, D. A. (1970) 'Transitions to democracy: toward a dynamic model', *Comparative Politics* 2: 337–63.

Scalapino, R. A. (1989) *The Politics of Development: Pespectives on Twentieth-Century Asia*, London: Harvard University Press.

Sen, G. and Grown, C. (1987) *Development, Crises, and Alternative Visions: Third World Women's Perspectives*, New York: Monthly Review Press.

Senghaas, D. (1985) *The European Experience: A Historical Critique of Development Theory*, Dover, NH: Berg Publishers.

Skocpol, T. (1979) *States and Social Revolutions*, Cambridge, Cambridge University Press.

So, A. Y. (1990) *Social Change and Development: Modernization, Dependency, and World-System Theories*, Newbury Park, Calif.: Sage Publications.

Sweezy, P. M. (1942) *The Theory of Capitalist Development*, New York: Oxford University Press.

Szentes, T. (1971) *The Political Economy of Underdevelopment*, Budapest: Centre for Afro-Asian Research, Hungarian Academy of Sciences.

Tanter, R. (1967) 'Toward a theory of political development', *Midwest Journal of Political Science* 11: 145–72.

Taylor, J. G. (1979) *From Modernization to Modes of Production: A Critique of the Sociologies of Development and Underdevelopment*, New York: Macmillan.

Wallerstein, I. (1974) *The Modern World System*, vol. 1, New York: Academic Press.

Warren, B. (1980) *Imperialism: Pioneer of Capitalism*, ed. J. Sender, London: NLB.

Weiner, M. and Huntington, S. P. (eds) (1987) *Understanding Political Development*, Boston: Little, Brown & Co.

World Commission on Environment and Development (1987) *Our Common Future*, New York: Oxford University Press.